Data Structures and Algorithms in Java

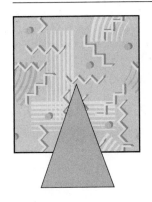

Data Structures and Algorithms in Java

Adam Drozdek

BROOKS/COLE

THOMSON LEARNING

Australia • Canada • Mexico • Singapore • Spain • United Kingdom • United States

BROOKS/COLE

THOMSON LEARNING

Sponsoring Editor: *Kallie Swanson*
Marketing Team: *Chris Kelly, Samantha Cabaluna*
Editorial Assistant: *Grace Fujimoto*
Production Coordinator: *Kelsey McGee*
Production Service: *Forbes Mill Press*
Manuscript Editor: *Frank Hubert*
Permissions Editor: *Mary Kay Hancharick*
Interior Design: *Forbes Mill Press/Robin Gold*

Cover Design: *Roy R. Neuhaus*
Cover Photo: *David Bishop*
Interior Illustration: *Audrey Miller*
Print Buyer: *Vena Dyer*
Typesetting: *Wolf Creek Press & Forbes Mill Press*
Cover Printing, Printing
 and Binding: *R.R. Donnelley/Crawfordsville*

Library of Congress Cataloging-in-Publication Data

Drozdek, Adam
  Data structures and algorithms in Java/Adam Drozdek.
        p.   cm.
  Includes references (p.) and index.
  ISBN 0 534-37668-1 (text)
        1. Java (Computer program language) 2. Data structures (Computer science)
3. Computer algorithms. I. Title.

QA76.73.J38 D695 2000   00-023893
005.13'3--dc21

To my wife, Bogna

Contents

12 MEMORY MANAGEMENT 565

APPENDIX

Preface

The study of data structures, a fundamental component of a computer science education, serves as the foundation upon which many other computer science fields are built. Some knowledge of data structures is a must for students who wish to do work in design implementation, testing, or maintenance of virtually any software system. The scope and presentation of material in *Data Structures and Algorithms in Java* provide students with the knowledge necessary to perform such work.

This book highlights three important aspects of data structures. First, a very strong emphasis is placed on the connection between data structures and their algorithms, including analyzing algorithms' complexity. Second, data structures are presented in the object-oriented setting in accordance with the current design and implementation paradigm. In particular, the information-hiding principle to advance encapsulation and decomposition is stressed. Finally, an important component of the book is data structure implementation, which leads to the choice of Java as the programming language.

The language Java, an object-oriented descendant of C and C++, has gained popularity in industry and academia as an excellent programming language due to widespread use of the Internet. Because of its consistent use of object-oriented features and the security of the language, Java is also useful and natural for introducing data structures. Currently, C++ is the primary language of choice for teaching data structures. However, because of the wide use of Java in application programming and the object-oriented characteristics of the language, using Java to teach a data structures and algorithms course, even on the introductory level, is well justified.

This book provides the material for a course that includes the topics listed under CS2 and CS7 of the old ACM curriculum. It also meets the requirements for most of the courses C_A 202, C_D 202, and C_F 204 of the new ACM curriculum.

Most chapters include a case study that illustrates a complete context in which certain algorithms and data structures can be used. These case studies were chosen from different areas of computer science such as interpreters, symbolic computation, and file processing, to indicate the wide range of applications to which topics under discussion may apply.

Brief examples of Java code are included throughout the book to illustrate the practical importance of data structures. However, theoretical analysis is equally important. Thus, presentations of algorithms are integrated with analyses of efficiency.

Great care is taken in the presentation of recursion because even advanced students have problems with it. Our experience has shown that recursion can be explained best if the run-time stack is taken into consideration. Changes to the stack are shown when tracing a recursive function not only in the chapter on recursion but in other chapters as well. For example, a surprisingly short method for tree traversal may remain a mystery if work done by the system on the run-time stack is not included in the explanation. Standing aloof from the system and retaining only a purely theoretical perspective when discussing data structures and algorithms are not necessarily helpful. This book also includes comprehensive chapters on data compression and memory management.

The thrust of this book is data structures, and other topics are treated here only as much as necessary to ensure a proper understanding of this subject. Algorithms are discussed from the perspective of data structures so that the reader will not find a comprehensive discussion of different kinds of algorithms and all the facets that a full presentation of algorithms requires. However, as mentioned, recursion is covered in depth. In addition, complexity analysis of algorithms is presented in some detail.

Chapters 1–8 present a number of different data structures and the algorithms that operate on them. The efficiency of each algorithm is analyzed, and improvements to the algorithm are suggested.

☐ Chapter 1 presents the basic principles of object-oriented programming, an introduction to dynamic memory allocation and the use of pointers, and a rudimentary introduction to Java.

☐ Chapter 2 describes some methods used to assess the efficiency of algorithms.

☐ Chapter 3 contains an introduction to linked lists.

☐ Chapter 4 presents stacks and queues and their applications.

☐ Chapter 5 contains a detailed discussion of recursion. Different types of recursion are discussed and a recursive call is dissected.

☐ Chapter 6 discusses binary trees, including implementation, traversal, and search. This chapter also includes balanced trees.

☐ Chapter 7 details more generalized trees such as tries, 2–4 trees, and B-trees.

☐ Chapter 8 presents graphs.

Chapters 9–12 show different applications of data structures introduced in the previous chapters. They emphasize the data structure aspects of each topic under consideration.

☐ Chapter 9 analyzes sorting in detail, and several elementary and nonelementary methods are presented.

☐ Chapter 10 discusses hashing, one of the most important areas in searching. Various techniques are presented with an emphasis on the utilization of data structures.

▢ Chapter 11 discusses data compression algorithms and data structures.

▢ Chapter 12 presents various techniques and data structures for memory management.

▢ Appendix A discusses in greater detail big-O notation, introduced in Chapter 2.

Each chapter contains a discussion of the material illustrated with appropriate diagrams and tables. Except for Chapter 2, all chapters include a case study, which is an extended example using the features discussed in that chapter. Following the text of the chapters is a set of exercises of varying degrees of difficulty. Except for Chapter 2, all chapters also include programming assignments and an up-to-date bibliography of relevant literature.

Chapters 1–6 (excluding Sections 2.9, 3.4, 6.4.3, 6.7, and 6.8) contain the core material that forms the basis of any data structures course. These chapters should be studied in sequence. The remaining six chapters can be taken in any order. A one-semester course could include Chapters 1–6, 9, and Sections 10.1 and 10.2. The entire book could also be part of a two-semester sequence.

The source code for the text example programs is available via the Web site at `www.mathcs.duq.edu/drozdek/DSinJava`.

ACKNOWLEDGMENTS

I would like to thank the following reviewers, whose comments and advice helped me to improve this book:

James Ball, Indiana State University

Li-hsiang Cheo, William Paterson University of New Jersey

Julius Dichter, University of Bridgeport

Le Gruenwald, University of Oklahoma

George Harrison, Norfolk State University

Craig Morgenstern, Texas Christian University

Jong-Min Park, San Diego State University

However, the ultimate content is my responsibility, and I would appreciate hearing from readers about any shortcomings or strengths. My e-mail address is drozdek@duq.edu.

Adam Drozdek

Object-Oriented Programming Using Java

1.1 RUDIMENTARY JAVA

This chapter introduces the reader to elementary Java. Java is an immense language and programming environment, and it is impossible to touch upon all Java-related issues within the confines of one chapter. This chapter introduces only those aspects of Java that are necessary for understanding the Java code offered in this book. The reader familiar with Java can skip this chapter.

A Java program is a sequence of statements that have to be formed in accordance with the predefined syntax. A statement is the smallest executable unit in Java. Each statement ends with a semicolon. Compound statements, or blocks, are marked by delimiting them with braces, { and }.

1.1.1 Variable Declarations

Each variable must be declared before it can be used in a program. It is declared by specifying its type and its name. Variable names are strings of any length of letters, digits, underscores, and dollar signs that begin with a letter, underscore, or dollar sign. However, a letter is any Unicode letter (a character above 192), not only 1 of the 26 letters in the English alphabet. Local variables must be initialized. Java is case sensitive so that variable n is different from variable N.

A type of variable is either one of the eight built-in basic types, a built-in or user-defined class type, or an array. Here are built-in types and their sizes:

Type	Size	Range
boolean	1 bit	true, false
char	16 bits	Unicode characters
byte	8 bits	[-128, 127]
short	16 bits	[-32768, 32767]
int	32 bits	[-2147483648, 2147483647]
long	64 bits	[-9223372036854775808, 9223372036854775807]
float	32 bits	[-3.4E38, 3.4E38]
double	64 bits	[-1.7E308, 1.7E308]

Note that the sizes of the types are fixed, which is extremely important for portability of programs. In C/C++, the size of integer and long integer is system dependent. Unlike C/C++, Boolean is not a numeric type, and no arithmetic operations can be performed on Boolean variables. But as in C/C++, characters are considered integers (in Java, they are unsigned integers) so that they can be operands of arithmetic operations.

Integer operations are performed with 32-bit precision (for long integers, it is 64-bit precision); therefore, operations on byte and short variables require a cast. For example, the statements

```
byte a, b = 1, c = 2;
a = b + c;
```

give a compilation error, "incompatible type for =. Explicit cast is needed to convert int to byte." The addition b + c gives an integer value which must be cast to execute the assignment to the byte variable a. To avoid the problem, the assignment should be changed to

```
a = (byte) (b + c);
```

An overflow resulting from an arithmetic operation (unless it is division by zero) is not indicated so that the programmer must be aware that, for two integers,

```
int i = 2147483647, j = i + 1;
```

the value of j is −2147483648.

Java does not provide modifiers signed and unsigned, but it has other modifiers.

An important difference between C/C++ and Java is characters that are 8-bits long in C/C++ and 16-bits long in Java. With the usual 8-bit characters, only 256 different characters can be represented. To address the problem of representing characters of languages other than English, the set of available codes must be significantly extended. The problem is not only with representing letters with diacritical marks (e.g., Polish letter ń, Rumanian letter ţ, or Danish letter ø) but also with non-Latin characters such as Cyrillic, Greek, Japanese, Chinese, and so on. By allowing a character variable to be of two bytes, the number of different characters represented now equals 65,536.

To assign a specific Unicode character to a character variable, 'u' followed by four hexadecimal digits can be used; for example,

```
char ch = '\u12ab';
```

However, high Unicode codes should be avoided, because as of now, few systems display them. Therefore, although the assignment to ch just given is legal, printing the value of ch results in displaying a question mark.

Other ways of assigning literal characters to character variables is by using a character surrounded with single quotes,

```
ch = 'q';
```

and using a character escape sequence such as

```
ch = '\n';
```

to assign an end-of-line character; other possibilities are: `'\t'` (tab), `'\b'` (backspace), `'\r'` (carriage return), `'\f'` (formfeed), `'\''` (single quote), `'\"'` (double quote), `'\\'` (backslash). Unlike C/C++, `'\b'` (bell) and `'\v'` (vertical tab) are not included. Moreover, an octal escape sequence "\ddd" can be used as in

```
ch = '\123'; // decimal 83, ASCII of 'S';
```

where ddd represents an octal number $[0, 377]$.

Integer literals can be expressed as decimal numbers by any sequence of digits 0 through 9,

```
int i = 123;
```

as octal numbers by 0 followed by any sequence of digits 0 through 7,

```
int j = 0123; // decimal 83;
```

or as hexadecimal numbers by "0x" followed by any sequence of hexadecimal numbers 0 through 9 and A through F (lower- or uppercase),

```
int k = 0x123a; // decimal 4666;
```

Literal integers are considered 32 bits long; therefore, to convert them to 64-bit numbers, they should be followed by an 'L':

```
long p = 0x123aL;
```

note that uppercase L should be used rather than lowercase l because the latter can be easily confounded with number 1.

Floating-point numbers are any sequences of digits 0 through 9 before and after a period; the sequences can be empty: 2., .2, 1.2. In addition, the number can be followed by a letter e and a sequence of digits possibly preceded by a sign: 4.5e+6 ($= 4.5 \cdot 10^6 = 4500000.0$), $102.055e-3 = 102.055 \cdot 10^{-3} = .102055$). Floating-point literals are 64-bit numbers by default; therefore, the declaration and assignment

```
float x = 123.45;
```

result in a compilation error, "incompatible type for declaration. Explicit cast needed to convert double to float," which can be eliminated by appending the modifier f (or F) at the end of the number,

```
float x = 123.45f;
```

A modifier d or D can be appended to double numbers, but this is not necessary.

1.1.2 Operators

Value assignments are executed with the assignment operator =, which can be used one at a time or can be strung together with other assignment operators, as in

```
x = y = z = 1;
```

which means that all three variables are assigned the same value, number 1. Java uses shorthands for cases when the same value is updated; for example,

```
x = x + 1;
```

can be shortened to

```
x += 1;
```

Java also uses autoincrement and autodecrement prefix and postfix operators, as in ++n, n++, --m, and n--, which are shorthands of assignments n = n + 1 and n = n - 1, where n can be any number, including a floating-point number. The difference between prefix and postfix operators is that, for the prefix operator, a variable is incremented (or decremented) first and then an operation is performed in which the increment takes place. For a postfix operator, autoincrement (or autodecrement) is the last operation performed; for example, after executing assignments

```
x = 5;
y = 6 + ++x;
```

y equals 12, whereas after executing

```
x = 5;
y = 6 + x++;
```

y equals 11. In both cases, x equals 6 after the second statement is completely executed.

Java allows performing operations on individual bits with bitwise operators: & (bitwise and), | (bitwise or), ^ (bitwise xor), << (left shift), >> (right shift), >>> (zero filled shift right), ~ (bitwise complement). Shorthands &=, |=, ^=, <<=, >>=, and >>>= are also possible. Except for the operator >>>, the other operators are also in C/C++. The operator >> shifts out a specified number of rightmost (least significant) bits and shifts in the same number of 0s for positive numbers and 1s for negative numbers. For example, the value of m after the assignments

```
int n = -4;
int m = n >> 1;
```

is −1 because −4 in n is two-complement representation as the sequence of 32 bits 11 . . . 1100, which after shifting to the right by one bit gives in m the pattern 11 . . . 1110, which is a two-complement representation of −2. To have 0s shifted in also for negative numbers, the operator >>> should be used,

```
int n = −4;
int m = n >> 1;
```

in which case, the pattern 11 . . . 1100 in n is transformed into the pattern 01 . . . 1110 in m, which is the number 2147483646 (one less that the maximum value for an integer).

1.1.3 Decision Statements

One decision statement is an if statement

```
if (condition)
        do something;
[else  do something else;]
```

in which the word if is followed by a condition surrounded by parentheses, by the body of the if clause, which is a block of statements, and by an optional else clause, which is the word else followed by a block of statements. A condition must return a Boolean value (in C/C++, it can return any value). A condition is formed with relational operators <, <=, ==, !=, >=, > that take two arguments and return a Boolean value and with logical operators that take one (!) or two (&&, ||) Boolean arguments and return a Boolean value.

An alternative to an if-else statement is the conditional operator of the form

```
condition ?  do-if-true  :  do-if-false;
```

The conditional operator returns a value, whereas an if-statement does not, so the former can be used, for example, in assignments, as in

```
n = i <= 0 ? 10 : 20;
```

Another decision statement is a switch statement which is a shorthand for nested if statements. Its form is as follows:

```
switch (integer expression) {
        case value1: block1; break;
         . . . . . .
        case valueN: blockN; break;
        default: default block;
}
```

The test expression following switch must be an integer expression so that any expression of type byte, char, short, and int can be used. The value of the expression is compared to the values that follow the word case. If a match is found, the block of statements following this value is executed, and upon encountering break, the `switch` statement is exited. Note that if the word `break` is missing, then execution is continued for the block of the next `case` clause. After executing the statement

```
switch (i) {
    case 5 : x + 10; break;
    case 6 : x = 20;
    case 7 : x *= 2; break;
    default : x = 30;
}
```

the value of x is 10 if i equals 5, 40 if i equals 6, it is doubled if i equals 7, and 30 for any other value of i.

1.1.4 Loops

The first loop available in Java is the `while` loop:

```
while (condition)
    do something;
```

The condition must be a Boolean expression.

The second loop is a `do-while` loop:

```
do
    do something;
while (condition);
```

The loop continues until the Boolean condition is false.

The third loop is the `for` loop:

```
for (initialization; condition; increment)
    do something;
```

The initialization part may also declare variables, and these variables exist only during execution of the loop.

A loop can be exited before all the statements in its body are executed with an unlabeled `break` statement. We have already seen a `break` statement used in the `switch` statement. In the case of nested loops, when a `break` statement is encountered, the current loop is exited so that the outer loop can be continued. An unlabeled `continue` statement causes the loop to skip the remainder of its body and begin the next iteration.

1.1.5 Exception Handling

If an error is detected during execution of a Java program, Java throws an exception after which the program is terminated and an error message is displayed informing the user which exception was raised (that is, what type of error occurred and where in the program it happened). However, the user may handle the error in the program should one occur, at least by making the program ignore it so that execution of the program can continue. But if an exception is raised, a special course of actions can be undertaken and then the program can continue. Catching an error is possible by a try-catch mechanism.

A general format of the try-catch statement is

```
try {
    do something;
} catch (exception-type exception-name) {
    do something;
}
```

The number of catch clauses is not limited to one. There can be as many as needed, each one for a particular exception.

In this statement, execution of the body of the try clause is tried, and if an exception occurs, control is transferred to the catch clause to execute its body. Then execution of the program continues with a statement following the try-catch statement, unless it contains the throw clause which causes an exit from the method.

Consider the following method:

```
public int f1(int[] a, int n) throws ArrayIndexOutOfBoundsException {
    return n * a[n+2];
}
```

The throws clause in the heading of the method is a warning to the user of the method that a particular exception can occur, and if not handled properly, the program crashes. To prevent that from happening, the user may include the try-catch statement in the caller of f1():

```
public void f2() {
    int[] a = {1,2,3,4,5};
    try {
        for (int i = 0; i < a.length; i++)
            System.out.print(f1(a,i) + " ");
    } catch (ArrayIndexOutOfBoundsException e) {
        System.out.println("Exception caught in f2()");
        throw e;
    }
}
```

The catch clause prints a message, but it does not perform any fixing operation on the array a, although it could. In this example, the catch clause also includes the throw statement, although this is not very common. In this way, the exception is not only caught and handled in f2(), but a caller of f2() is forced to handle it as well, as in the method f3():

```
public void f3() {
    try {
        f2();
    } catch (ArrayIndexOutOfBoundsException e) {
        System.out.println("Exception caught in f3()");
    }
}
```

If the caller of `f2()` does not handle the exception, the program crashes, although the exception was caught in `f2()`. The same fate meets a program if a caller of `f1()` does not catch the exception:

```
public void f4() {
    int[] a = {1,2,3,4,5};
    for (int i = 0; i < a.length; i++)
        System.out.print(f1(a,i) + " ");
}
```

Note that the behavior of the program in all these cases is the same (that is, handling an exception, passing it to another method, or crashing the program) if the `throws` clause is not included in the heading of `f1()` so that `f1()` could simply be:

```
public int f1(int[] a, int n) {
    return n * a[n+2];
}
```

The `throws` clause is thus a very important signal for the user to a possible problem that may occur when calling a particular method.

Not all types of exception can be ignored as the exception raised by `f1()` is ignored by `f4()`. Most of the time, exceptions have to be handled in the program; otherwise, the program does not compile. This, for instance, is the case with `IOException` thrown by I/O methods; therefore, these methods are usually called inside `try-catch` clauses.

◨ ## 1.2 OBJECT-ORIENTED PROGRAMMING IN JAVA

1.2.1 Encapsulation

Object-oriented programming (OOP) revolves around the concept of an object. Objects, however, are created using a class definition. A *class* is a template in accordance to which objects are created. A class is a piece of software that includes data specification and functions operating on these data and possibly on the data belonging to other class instances. Functions defined in a class are called *methods,* and variables used in a class are called *class variables, class scope variables* (to distinguish them from variables local to method or blocks), *instance variables, data fields,* or simply *fields.* This combining of the data and related operations is called data *encapsulation.* An object is an instance of a class, an entity created using a class definition.

In contradistinction to functions in languages that are not object-oriented languages (OOL), objects make the connection between data and methods much tighter and more meaningful. In non-OOLs, declarations of data and definitions of functions could be interspersed throughout the entire program, and only the program documentation indicates that there is a connection between them. In OOLs, a connection is established right at the outset; in fact, the program is based on this connection. An object encompasses related data and operations, and because there may be many objects used in the same program, the objects communicate by exchanging messages, thereby revealing to each other only as much, or rather as little, detail about their internal structure as necessary for adequate communication. Structuring programs in terms of objects allows us to accomplish several goals.

First, this strong coupling of data and operations can be used much better in modeling a fragment of the world, which is emphasized especially by software engineering. Not surprisingly, OOP has its roots in simulation, that is, in modeling real-world events. The first OOL was Simula; it was developed in the 1960s in Norway.

Second, objects allow for easier error finding because operations are localized to the confines of their objects. Even if side effects can occur, they are easier to trace.

Third, objects allow us to conceal certain details of their operations from other objects so that these operations may not be adversely affected by other objects. This is known as the *information-hiding* principle. In languages that are not object-oriented, this principle can be found to some extent in the case of local variables, or as in Pascal, in local functions and procedures, which can only be used and accessed by the function defining them. This is, however, a very tight hiding or no hiding at all. Sometimes we may need to use (again, as in Pascal) a function *f2* defined in *f1* outside of *f1,* but we cannot. Sometimes we may need to access some data local to *f1* without exactly knowing the structure of these data, but in non-OOLs, we cannot. Hence, some modification is needed, and it is accomplished in OOLs.

An object in OOL is like a watch. As users, we are interested in what the hands show, but not in the inner workings of the watch. We are aware that there are gears and springs inside the watch, but we usually know very little about why all these parts are in a particular configuration. Because of that, we should not have access to this mechanism so that we do not damage it, inadvertently or on purpose. Therefore, this mechanism is hidden from us, we have no immediate access to it, and thereby the watch is protected and works better than when its mechanism is open for everyone to see.

Hence, an object is like a black box whose behavior is very well defined, and we use the object because we know what it does, not because we have an insight into how it does it. This opacity of objects is extremely useful for maintaining them independently of each other. If communication channels between the objects are well defined, then changes made inside an object can affect other objects only as much as these changes affect the communication channels. Knowing the kind of information sent out and received by an object, the object can be replaced more easily by another object more suitable in a particular situation: A new object can perform the same task differently but more quickly in a certain hardware environment. Hence, an object discloses only as much as is needed for the user to utilize it. It has a public part which can be accessed by any user when the user sends a message matching any of the method names revealed by the object. In this public part, the object displays to the user buttons which can be pushed to invoke the object's operations. The user knows only the names of these operations and the expected behavior.

Information hiding tends to blur the dividing line between data and operations. In Pascal-like languages, the distinction between data and functions/procedures is clear and rigid. They are defined differently and their roles are very distinct. OOLs put data and methods together, and to the user of the object, this distinction is much less noticeable. To some extent, this is an incorporation of features of functional languages. LISP, one of the earliest programming languages, allows the user to treat data and functions on a par, since the structure of both is the same.

We have already made a distinction between particular objects and object types or classes. We write methods to be used with different variables, and by analogy, we do not want to be forced to write as many object declarations as the number of objects required by the program. Certain objects are of the same type and we would like only to use a reference to a general object specification. For single variables, we make a distinction between type declaration and variable declaration. In the case of objects, a distinction is made between a class declaration and its instantiation which is an object. Consider the following program:

```
class C {
    C() {
        this("",1,0);
    }
    C(String s) {
        this(s,1,0);
    }
    C(String s, int i) {
        this(s,i,0);
    }
    C(String s, int i, double d) {
        dataField1 = new String(s);
        dataField2 = i;
        dataField3 = d;
    }
    void method1() {
        System.out.println(dataField1 + " " + dataField2 + " " + dataField3);
    }
    void method2(int i) {
        method2(i,"unknown");
    }
    void method2(int i, String s) {
        dataField2 = i;
        System.out.println(i + " received from " + s);
    }
    private String dataField1;
    private int dataField2;
    private double dataField3;
    public static void main (String args[]) {
        C object1 = new C("object1",100,2000),
          object2 = new C("object2"), object3 = new C();
        object1.method2(123);
        object1.method1();
```

```
            object2.method2(123,"object2");
     }
}
```

The program contains a declaration of class C. Inside method main( ), objects of class type C are generated by declaring and instantiating them,

```
C object1 = new C("object1",100,2000),
   object2 = new C("object2"), object3 = new C();
```

It is very important to see that object declarations do not create objects so that the two lines:

```
C object1;
object1.method1();
```

result in a compilation error. The object variable object1 has to be assigned an object, which can be done directly in declaration by initializing the variable with the operator new,

```
C object1 = new C(. . .);
```

Message passing is an equivalent to a function call in traditional languages. However, to stress the fact that in OOLs the methods are relative to objects, this new term is used. For example, the call to method1( ) with respect to object1,

```
object1.method1();
```

is to be seen as the message method1( ) sent to object1. Upon receiving the message, the object invokes its method. Messages can acquire parameters so that

```
object1.method2(123);
```

is the message method2( ) with parameter 123 received by object1.

The lines containing these messages are in a method of the current object or another object. Therefore, the receiver of the message is identifiable, but not necessarily the sender. If object1 receives the message method1( ), it does not know where the message originated. It only responds to it by displaying the information method1( ) encompasses. The same goes for method2( ). Therefore, the sender may prefer sending a message that also includes its identification, as in

```
object1.method2(123,"object1");
```

The declaration of class C contains the method main( ), which as in C/C++, is the starting point for execution of programs. Unlike in C/C++, main( ) must be included inside a class; it cannot be a stand-alone method. In this way, after class C is stored in a file C.java, the file can be compiled with the instruction

```
javac C.java
```

and then the program can be run with

```
java C
```

The `javac` instruction can be applied to any file containing Java code, but the `java` instruction requires that the class with which it is invoked includes method `main()`. The example of class `C` shows only one class, but as we shall see throughout the book, the number of classes is usually not limited to one; however, one of the classes must include the method `main()` to make the program executable.

The signature of the method `main()` is always the same:

```
public static void main(String[] args)
```

It returns no value (`void`) and allows for taking command line arguments from the interpreter by storing them in an array of strings. The `public` modifier belongs to the category of access modifiers. Java uses four access modifiers (three plus one unnamed) which are related to the concept of package. A package is a collection of classes that are located in one subdirectory. A package is a counterpart of a C/C++ library.

Methods and fields declared `public` can be used by any other object.

The `protected` modifier means that a method or a field is accessible only to the class containing it and to derived classes.

The `private` modifier indicates methods and fields that can be used only by this class.

A default modifier is no modifier at all, which indicates access to methods and fields to all objects in the package.

There are two more modifiers that need to be listed. A method and field declared `static` are the same for all instances (objects) of the class. A `final` method of field cannot be changed by derived classes (see Section 1.2.3, Inheritance).

A very important aspect of OOP in Java is the possibility of declaring generic classes. For example, if we need to declare a class that uses an array for storing some items, then we may declare this class as

```
class IntClass {
    int[] storage = new int[50];
    . . . . . . . . . . . . . . . . .
}
```

However, in this way, we limit the usability of this class to integers only; hence, if a class is needed that performs the same operations as `IntClass`, but it operates on double numbers, then a new declaration is needed, such as

```
class DoubleClass {
    double[] storage = new double[50];
    . . . . . . . . . . . . . . . . .
}
```

If `storage` is to hold objects of a particular class, then another class must be declared. It is much better to declare a generic class and decide during the run of the program to which type of items it is referring. Java allows us to declare a class in this way, and the declaration for the example is

```
class GenClass {
    Object[] storage = new Object[50];
```

```
Object find(int n) {
    return storage[n];
}
. . . . . . . . . . . . . . . . .
}
```

Then the decision is made how to create two specific objects

```
GenClass intObject = new GenClass();
GenClass doubleObject = new GenClass();
```

This generic class manifests itself in different forms depending on the way information is stored in it or retrieved from it. To treat it as an object holding an array of integers, the following way of accessing data can be used:

```
int k = ((Integer) intObject.find(n)).intValue();
```

To retrieve data from doubleObject, the return value has to be cast as Double. The same cast can also be used for intObject so that objects respond differently in different situations. One generic declaration suffices for enabling such different forms.

1.2.1.1 Arrays

Arrays are Java objects, but to the user, they are objects to a very limited extent. There is no keyword with which all arrays are declared. They may be considered instances of an understood array class. The lack of a keyword for all arrays also means that no subclasses can be created (see Section 1.2.3).

Arrays are declared with empty brackets after the name of the type or the name of the array itself. These two declarations are equivalent:

```
int[] a;
```

and

```
int a[];
```

A declaration of a basic data type also creates an item of the specified type. As for all objects, an array declaration does not create an array. An array can be created with the operator new, and very often declaration and initialization are combined, as in

```
int[] a = new int[10];
```

This creates an array of ten cells that are indexed with numbers 0 through 9; that is, the first cell is a[0] and the last cell a[9]. An array can also be created by specifying the value of its cells,

```
int[] b = {5, 4, 2, 1};
```

which creates a four-cell array of integers.

Unlike C/C++, it is impossible to access a cell that is out of bounds. An attempt to do so, as with the assignment

```
a[10] = 5;
```

results in a run-time error `ArrayIndexOutOfBoundsException`. To avoid this, the length of the array can be checked before performing an assignment with the variable `length` associated with each array, `a.length`.

In Java 1.2, the class `Arrays` is added with several useful methods to be applied to arrays, in particular `binarySearch()`, `equals()`, `fill()`, and `sort()`. For example, to sort an array, it is enough to import class `java.util.Arrays` and execute one of the versions of the method sort, for example,

```
Arrays.sort(a);
```

1.2.1.2 *Wrapper Classes*

Except for basic data types, everything in Java is an object. For this reason, many classes in the `java.util` package operate on items of type `Object`. To include basic data types in this category so that the utility classes can also operate on them, the so-called wrapper classes are introduced to provide object versions of basic data types. For example, the `Integer` class is an object wrapper for the type `int`. The class provides several methods. The `Integer` class includes the following methods: `getInteger()` to convert a string into an `Integer`, `parseInt()` to convert a string into an `int`, `convert()` to convert a string into a number when the radix is not known, `toString()` to convert an integer into a string, and sequence of methods to convert an integer into other basic types: `intValue()`, `longValue()`, and so on.

1.2.2   Abstract Data Types

Before a program is written, the programmer should have a fairly good idea how to accomplish the task being implemented by the program. Hence, an outline of the program containing its requirements should precede the coding process. The larger and more complex the project, the more detailed the outline phase should be. The implementation details should be delayed to the later stages of the project. In particular, the details of the particular data structures to be used in the implementation should not be specified at the beginning.

From the start, it is important to specify each task in terms of input and output. At the beginning stages, we should be more concerned with what the program should do, not how it should or could be done. Behavior of the program is more important than the gears of the mechanism accomplishing it. For example, if an item is needed to accomplish some tasks, the item is specified in terms of operations performed on it rather than in terms of its inner structure. These operations may act upon this item by modifying it, searching for some details in it, or storing something in it. After these operations are precisely specified, the implementation of the program may start. The implementation decides which data structure should be used to make execution most efficient in terms of time and space. An item specified in terms of operations is called an *abstract data type*. In Java, an abstract data type can be part of a program in the form of an interface.

Interfaces, successors of protocols in Objective-C, are similar to classes, but they can contain only constants (`final` variables) and method prototypes or signatures, that is, specifications of method names, types of parameters, and types of return values. Methods are thus not defined, and the task of defining methods is passed to a class that `implements` an interface (that is, implements as public all the methods listed in the interface). One class can implement more than one interface, the same interface can be implemented by more than one class, and the classes implementing one interface do not have to be related in any way to each other. Therefore, at the first stage of program design, interfaces can be specified, and the specifics of implementation of their methods are left until later for the implementation classes. And because an interface can extend another interface, a top-down design can become part of the program in a very natural way. This allows the program developer to concentrate first on big issues when designing a program, but also allows a user of a particular implementation of an interface to be certain that all the methods listed in the interface are implemented. In this way, the user is assured that no method listed in the interface is left out in any of the implementation classes, and all instances of implementation classes respond to the same method calls.

The rigidity of interfaces is somewhat relaxed in abstract classes. A class declared `abstract` can include defined methods, that is, not only method signatures but also method bodies. A method that is specified only by its signature must also be declared as `abstract`. A class can make an abstract class specific by extending it. Here is an example:

```
public interface I {
    void If1(int n);
}
class A implements I {
    public void If1(int n) {
        System.out.println("AIf1 " + n);
    }
}
public abstract class AC {
    abstract void ACf1(int n);
    void ACf2(int n) {
        System.out.println("ACf2 " + n);
    }
}
class B extends AC {
    void ACf1(int n) {
        System.out.println("BACf1 " + n);
    }
}
```

1.2.3 Inheritance

OOLs allow for creating a hierarchy of classes so that objects do not have to be instantiations of a single class. Before discussing the problem of inheritance, consider the following class definitions:

```java
class BaseClass {
    public BaseClass() {
    }
    void f(String s) {
        System.out.println("Method f() in BaseClass called from " + s);
        h("BaseClass");
    }
    protected void g(String s) {
        System.out.println("Method g() in BaseClass called from " + s);
    }
    private void h(String s) {
        System.out.println("Method h() in BaseClass called from " + s);
    }
}
class Derived1Level1 extends BaseClass {
    public void f(String s) {
        System.out.println("Method f() in Derived1Level1 called from " + s);
        g("Derived1Level1");
        h("Derived1Level1");
    }
    public void h(String s) {
        System.out.println("Method h() in Derived1Level1 called from " + s);
    }
}
class Derived2Level1 extends BaseClass {
    public void f(String s) {
        System.out.println("Method h() in Derived2Level1 called from " + s);
        g("Derived2Level1");
//      h("Derived2Level1"); // No method matching h() found in class BaseClass
    }
}
class DerivedLevel2 extends Derived1level1 {
    public void f(String s) {
        System.out.println("Method h() in DerivedLevel2 called from " + s);
        g("DerivedLevel2");
        h("DerivedLevel2");
        super.f("DerivedLevel2");
    }
}
class testInheritance {
    void run() {
        BaseClass bc = new BaseClass ();
        Derived1Level1 d1l1 = new Derived1Level1();
        Derived2Level1 d2l1 = new Derived2Level1();
        DerivedLevel2 dl2 = new DerivedLevel2();
        bc.f("main(1)");
```

```
//       bc.g("main(2)");   // No method matching g() found in class BaseClass.
//       bc.h("main(3)");   // No method matching h() found in class BaseClass.
         d1l1.f("main(4)");
//       d1l1.g("main(5)"); // No method matching g() found in class Derived1Level1.
         d1l1.h("main(6)");
         d2l1.f("main(7)");
//       d2l1.g("main(8)"); // No method matching g() found in class Derived2Level1.
//       d2l1.h("main(9)"); // No method matching h() found in class Derived2Level1.
         dl2.f("main(10)");
//       dl2.g("main(11)"); // No method matching g() found in class DerivedLevel2.
         dl2.h("main(12)");
    }
}
```

The execution of

```
(new testInheritance()).run();
```

produces the following output:

```
Method f() in BaseClass called from main(1)
Method h() in BaseClass called from BaseClass
Method f() in Derived1Level1 called from main(4)
Method g() in BaseClass called from Derived1Level1
Method h() in Derived1Level1 called from Derived1Level1
Method h() in Derived1Level1 called from main(6)
Method h() in Derived2Level1 called from main(7)
Method g() in BaseClass called from Derived2Level1
Method h() in DerivedLevel2 called from main(10)
Method g() in BaseClass called from DerivedLevel2
Method h() in Derived1Level1 called from DerivedLevel2
Method f() in Derived1Level1 called from DerivedLevel2
Method g() in BaseClass called from Derived1Level1
Method h() in Derived1Level1 called from Derived1Level1
Method h() in Derived1Level1 called from main(12)
```

The class BaseClass is called a *base class* or a *superclass,* and other classes are called *subclasses* or *derived classes* because they are derived from the superclass in that they can use the data fields and methods specified in BaseClass as protected, public, or have no access modifier. They inherit all these fields and methods from their base class so that they do not have to repeat the same definitions. However, a derived class can override the definition of a non-final method by introducing its own definition. In this way, both the base class and the derived class have some measure of control over their methods.

The base class can decide which methods and data fields can be revealed to derived classes so that the principle of information hiding holds not only with respect to the user of the base class but also to the derived classes. Moreover, the derived class can decide which parts of the public and protected methods and data fields to retain and use and which to modify. For example, both Derived1Level1 and

`Derived2Level1` redefine method `f()` by giving their own versions of `f()`. However, the access to the method with the same name in the parent class is still possible by preceding the method name with the keyword `super` as shown in the call of `super.f()` from `f()` in `DerivedLevel2`.

A derived class can add new methods and fields of its own. Such a class can become a base class for other classes that can be derived from it so that the inheritance hierarchy can be deliberately extended. For example, the class `Derived1Level1` is derived from `BaseClass`, but at the same time, it is the base class for `DerivedLevel2`.

Protected methods or fields of the base class are accessible only to derived classes and not to nonderived classes. For this reason, both `Derived1Level1` and `Derived2Level1` can call `BaseClass`'s protected method `g()`, but a call to this method from `run()` in `testInheritance` is rendered illegal.

Unlike C++, which supports multiple inheritance, inheritance in Java has to be limited to one class only so that it is not possible to declare a new class with the declaration

```
class Derived2Level2 extends Derived1Level1, Derived2Level1 { ... }
```

In addition, a class declared `final` cannot be extended (the wrapper classes are examples of `final` classes).

1.2.4 Polymorphism

Polymorphism refers to the ability of acquiring many forms. In the context of OOP, this means that the same method name denotes many methods that are members of different objects. This is accomplished by so-called *dynamic binding*, when the type of a method to be executed can be delayed until run time. This is distinguished from *static binding*, when the type of response is determined at compilation time, as in the case of the `IntObject` and `DoubleObject` presented in Section 1.2.1. Both of these objects are declared as objects whose storage fields hold data of type `Object` and not integer or double. The conversion is performed dynamically, but outside the object itself. For dynamic binding, consider the following declarations:

```
class A {
    public void process() {
        System.out.println("Inside A");
    }
}
class ExtA extends A {
    public void process() {
        System.out.println("Inside ExtA");
    }
}
```

then the code

```
A object = new A();
object.process();
```

```
object = new ExtA();
object.process();
```

results in the output

```
Inside A
Inside ExtA
```

This is due to dynamic binding: The system checks dynamically the type of object to which a variable is currently referring and chooses the method appropriate for this type. Thus, although the variable `object` is declared to be of type A, it is assigned in the second assignment an object of type ExtA and executes the method `process()` which is defined in class ExtA rather than the method by the same name defined in class A.

This is also true for interfaces. For example, if the declarations

```
interface B {
    void process();
}
class ImplB1 implements B {
    public void process() {
        System.out.println("Inside ImplB1");
    }
}
class ImplB2 implements B {
    public void process() {
        System.out.println("Inside ImplB2");
    }
}
```

are followed by the statements

```
B object = new ImplB1();
object.process();
object = new ImplB2();
object.process();
```

then the output is

```
Inside ImplB1
Inside ImplB2
```

notwithstanding the fact that `object` is of type B. The system recognizes that, for the first call of `process()`, `object` refers to an object of type ImplB1, and in the second call, it refers to an object of type ImplB2.

Polymorphism is thus a powerful tool in OOP. It is enough to send a standard message to many different objects without specifying how the message will be followed. There is no need to know of what type the objects are. The receiver is responsible for interpreting the message and following it. The sender does not have to modify the message depending on the type of receiver. There is no need for `switch` or `if-else` statements. Also, new units can be added to a complex program without the need of recompiling the entire program.

Dynamic binding allows for empowering the definition of `GenClass`. Assume that the definition of this class also includes a method for finding a position of a particular piece of information. If the information is not found, −1 is returned. The definition is now

```
class GenClass {
    Object[] storage = new Object[50];
    int find(Object el) {
        for (int i = 0; i < 50; i++)
            if (storage[i] != null && storage[i].equals(el))
                return i;
        return -1;
    }
    void store(Object el) {
        . . . . . . . .
    }
    . . . . . . . .
}
```

The method `find()` returns the correct result if wrappers of basic types are used— `Character()`, `Integer()`, etc.—but what happens if we want to store in an instance of `GenClass` nonstandard objects? Consider the following declaration

```
class SomeInfo {
    SomeInfo (int n) {
        this.n = n;
    }
    private int n;
}
```

The problem is now, what happens, if for a declaration

```
GenClass object = new GenClass();
```

we execute:

```
object.store(new SomeInfo(17));
System.out.println(object.find(new SomeInfo(17)));
```

As it turns out, −1 is printed to indicate an unsuccessful search. The result is caused by the method `equals()`. The system is using a built-in method for type `Object` which returns true if *references* of the compared variables are the same, not the *contents* of objects to which they refer. To overcome this limitation, the method `equals()` must be redefined by overriding the standard definition by a new definition. Therefore, the definition of `SomeInfo` is incomplete and it should be extended to

```
class SomeInfo {
    SomeInfo (int n) {
```

```
        this.n = n;
    }
    public boolean equals(Object si) {
        return n == ((SomeInfo) si).n;
    }
    private int n;
}
```

With this new definition, find( ) returns the position of the object holding number 17. The reason this works properly is that all classes are extensions of the class Object. This extension is done implicitly by the system so that the declaration of SomeInfo is really

```
class SomeInfo extends Object {
    . . . . . . . .
}
```

The qualifier extends Object is understood in the original definition and does not have to be made explicit. In this way, the standard method equals( ) is overridden by redefinition of this method in the class SomeInfo and by the power of dynamic binding. When executing the call object.find(new SomeInfo(17)), the system uses method equals( ) defined in the class SomeInfo because an instance of this class is an argument in the method call. Thus, inside find( ), the local variable becomes a reference to an object of type SomeInfo, although it is defined as a parameter of type Object. The problem is, however, that such a quick adjustment can only be done for the built-in methods for Object, in particular, equals( ) and toString( ). Only slightly more complicated is the case when we want to define a generic class that makes comparisons possible. A more realistic example of polymorphism is given in the case study.

⬛ 1.3 INPUT AND OUTPUT

The java.io package provides several classes for reading and writing data. To use the classes, the package has to be explicitly included with the statement

```
import java.io.*;
```

In this section, we briefly introduce classes for reading from standard device (keyboard), writing to standard device (monitor), and processing I/O on files. There are also a number of other classes that are particularly important for interacting with the network, such as buffered, filtered, and piped streams.

To print anything on the screen, two statements are sufficient:

```
System.out.print(message);
System.out.println(message);
```

The two statements differ in that the second version outputs the end-of-line character after printing a message. The message printed by the statement is a string. The string can be composed of literal strings, string variables, and strings generated by the method toString() for a particular object; all components of the print statement are concatenated with the operator +. For example, having declared the class C:

```
class C {
    int i = 10;
    char a = 'A';
    public String toString() {
        return "(" + i + " " + a + ")";
    }
}
```

and an object

```
C obj = new C();
```

a printing statement

```
System.out.println("The object: " + obj);
```

outputs

```
The object: (10 A)
```

Note that if toString() were not defined in C, the output would be

```
The object: C@1cc789
```

The reason is that class C is by default an extension of the class Object whose method toString() prints the address of a particular object. Therefore, it is almost always critical that toString() is redefined in a user class to have a more meaningful output than an address.

Reading input is markedly more cumbersome. Data are read from standard input with the input stream System.in. To that end, the method read() can be used, which returns an integer. To read a line, the user must define a new method, for example,

```
public static String readLine() {
    int ch;
    String s = "";
    while (true) {
        try {
            ch = System.in.read();
            if (ch == -1 || (char)ch == '\n') //end of file or end of line;
                break;
            else if ((char)ch != '\r')           // ignore carriage return;
                s = s + (char)ch;
        } catch(IOException e) {
        }
    }
    return s;
}
```

Because `read()` is defined as a method that throws an `IOException`, the exception has to be handled with the `try-catch` clause.

Note that `ch` must be an integer to detect the end of file (which is Ctrl-z entered from the PC keyboard). The end-of-field marker is the number –1, and characters are really unsigned integers. If `ch` were declared as a character, then the assignment statement would have to be

```
ch = (char) System.in.read();
```

with which the end-of-line marker –1 would be stored as number 65535 in `ch`, whereby the subcondition `ch == -1` would be evaluated to false and the system would wait for further input.

Fortunately, the task can be accomplished differently by first declaring an input stream with the declarations:

```
static InputStreamReader cin = new InputStreamReader(System.in);
static BufferedReader br = new BufferedReader(cin);
```

or with one declaration:

```
static BufferedReader br = new BufferedReader(new InputStreamReader(System.in));
```

and then a built-in method `readLine()` can be called to assign a value to a string `s`:

```
try {
        s = br.readLine();
} catch(IOException e) {
}
```

To read a number, an input must be read as a string and then converted into a number. For example, if input is in string `s`, then the conversion can be performed with

```
try {
    i = Integer.valueOf(s.trim()).intValue();
} catch (NumberFormatException e) {
    System.out.println("Not a number");
}
```

Note that the assignment

```
i = Integer.valueOf(s.trim());
```

is insufficient if `i` is an integer because `Integer.valueOf()` returns an object of type `Integer`, not an integer of type `int`, so that the integer value must be extracted from the object with the method `intValue()`.

To perform input and output on a file, the `RandomAccessFile` class should be used. A file is created with the constructor

```
RandomAccessFile(name, mode);
```

The constructor opens a file with the specified name either for reading only or for reading and writing. The mode is specified by either the letter w or letters rw, for instance,

```
RandomAccessFile = raf new RandomAccessFile("myFile", "rw");
```

We can move anywhere in the file, but to know that we are within the file, we can use the method `length()` that returns the size of the file measured in bytes. The method `getFilePointer()` returns the current position in the file. The method `seek(pos)` moves the file pointer to the position specified by an integer `pos`.

Reading is done by the method `read()` that returns a byte as an integer, by `read(b)` that fills entirely a byte array `b`, by `read(b,off,len)` that fills `len` cells of the byte array `b` starting from cell `off`, and by `readLine()` to read one line of input. Other reading methods return a value specified by their names: `readBoolean()`, `readByte()`, `readShort()`, `readChar()`, `readInt()`, `readLong()`. All these reading methods have corresponding writing methods, for example, `write()`, `write(b)`, `read(b,off,len)`, etc. plus the method `writeBytes(s)` to write a string `s` as a sequence of bytes.

After file processing is finished, the file should be closed with the `close()` method:

```
raf.close();
```

⌨ 1.4 JAVA AND POINTERS

In this section, a problem of implementing Java objects is analyzed.

Although Java does not use explicit pointers and does not allow the programmer to use them, object access is implemented in terms of pointers. An object occupies some memory space starting from a certain memory location. A pointer to this object is a variable that holds the address of the object, and this address is the starting position of the object in memory. In many languages, *pointer* is a technical term for a type of variable; therefore, the term is avoided in discussing Java programs and usually the term *reference* is used instead.

Consider the following declarations:

```
class Node {
    String name;
    int age;
}
```

With declarations

```
Node p = null, q = new Node("Bill",20);
```

two reference variables are created, `p` and `q`. The variable `p` is initialized to `null`. The pointer `null` does not point anywhere. It is not able to point to any object of any type; therefore, `null` is compatible with and can be assigned to a reference variable of any type. After execution of the assignment

```
p = null;
```

FIGURE **1.1**   Object reference variables p and q: (a) logic of reference of q to an object; (b) implementation of this reference.

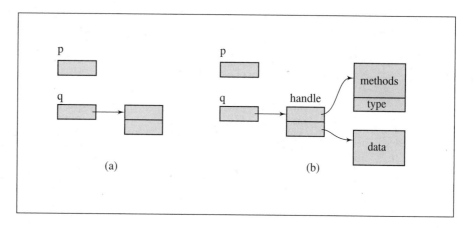

(a)   (b)

we may not say that p refers to null or points to null but that p becomes null or p is null. The variable p is created to be used in the future as a reference to an object, but currently, it does not refer to any. The variable q is a reference to an object that is an instance of class Node. Forced by the built-in method new, the operating system through its memory manager allocates enough space for one unnamed object that can be accessed, for now, only through the reference variable q. This reference is a pointer to the address of the memory chunk allocated for the object just created, as shown in Figure 1.1a. Figure 1.1a represents the logic of object reference, whose implementation can vary from one system to another and is usually much more intricate than the simple logic presented in this figure. For example, in Sun's implementation of Java, q refers to a handle which is a pair of pointers: one to the method table of the object and its type (which is a pointer to the class whose instance the object is) and the other to the object's data (Figure 1.1b). In Microsoft's implementation, q refers to the object's data with the type and method table pointed to by a hidden field of the object q. For simplicity, the subsequent illustrations use the form reflecting the logic of object reference, as in Figure 1.1a.

Keeping in mind how object access is implemented in Java helps explain the results of reference comparisons in Java. Consider the following code:

```
p = new Node("Bill",20);
System.out.print(p == q);
```

The printing statement outputs false because we compare references to two different objects; that is, we compare two different references (addresses), not the objects. To compare the objects' contents, their data fields have to be compared one by one using a method defined just for this reason. If Node includes the method

FIGURE **1.2**   Illustrating the necessity of using the method `clone()`.

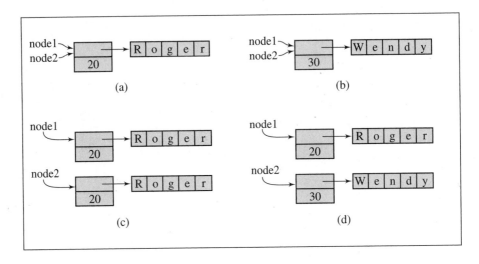

```
public boolean equals(Node n) {
      return name.equals(n.name) && age == n.age;
}
```

then the printing statement

```
System.out.print(p.equals(q));
```

outputs `true`. (This can be accomplished much more elegantly in C++ by overloading the equality operator `==`, that is, by defining a method which allows for application of this operator to instances of class `Node`.)

The realization that object variables are really references to objects helps explain the need for caution with the use of the assignment operator. The intention of the declarations

```
Node node1 = new Node("Roger",20), node2 = node1;
```

is to create objects `node1`, assign values to the two fields in `node1`, and then create object `node2` and initialize its fields to the same values as in `node1`. These objects are to be independent entities so that assigning values to one of them should not affect values in the other. However, after the assignments

```
node2.name = "Wendy";
node2.age  = 30;
```

the printing statement

```
System.out.println(node1.name+" "+node1.age+" "+node2.name+" "+ node2.age);
```

generates the output

```
Wendy 30 Wendy 30
```

Both the ages and names in the two objects are the same. What happened? Because node1 and node2 are pointers, the declarations of node1 and node2 result in the situation illustrated in Figure 1.2a. After the assignments to the two fields of node1, the situation is as in Figure 1.2b. To prevent this from happening, we have to create a new copy of the object referenced by node1 and then make node2 to become a reference to this copy. This can be done by defining the method clone() marked in the interface Cloneable. A new definition of Node is now:

```java
class Node implements Cloneable {
    String name;
    int age;
    Node(String n, int a) {
        name = n; age = a;
    }
    Node() {
        this("",0);
    }
    public Object clone() {
        return new Node(name,age);
    }
    public boolean equals(Node n) {
        return name.equals(n.name) && age == n.age;
    }
}
```

With this definition, the declarations should be

```java
Node node1 = new Node("Roger",20), node2 = (Node) node1.clone();
```

which results in the situation shown in Figure 1.2c so that the two assignments

```java
node2.name = "Wendy";
node2.age  = 30;
```

affect only the second object (Figure 1.2d).

The Java pointers are screened from the programmer. There is no pointer type in Java. The lack of an explicit pointer type is motivated by the desire to eliminate harmful behavior of programs. First, it is not possible in Java to have a nonnull reference to a nonexisting object. If a reference variable is not null, it always points to an object because the programmer cannot destroy an object referenced by a variable. An object can be destroyed in Pascal through the use of the function dispose() and in C++ through delete. The reason for using dispose() or delete is the need to return to the memory manager memory space occupied by an unneeded object. Directly after execution of dispose() or delete, pointer variables hold addresses of objects already returned to the memory manager. If these variables are not set to null or to the address of an object accessible from the program, the so-called *dangling reference problem* arises, which can lead to a program crash. In Java, the dangling reference problem does not arise. If a reference variable p changes its reference from one object to another, and the old object is not referenced by any other variable q, then the space occupied by the object is reclaimed automatically by the operating system through garbage collection (see Chapter 12). There is no equivalent in Java of `dispose()` or `delete`. Unneeded objects are simply abandoned and included in the pool of free memory cells automatically by the garbage collector during execution of the user program.

Another reason for not having explicit pointers in Java is a constant danger of having a reference to a memory location that has nothing to do with the logic of the program. This would be possible through the pointer arithmetic that is not allowed in Java, where such assignments as

```
(p + q).ch = 'b';
(++p).n = 6;
```

are illegal.

Interestingly, although explicit pointers are absent in Java, Java relies on pointers more heavily than C/C++. An object declaration is always a declaration of reference to an object; therefore, an object declaration

```
Node p;
```

should be followed by initializing the variable p either by explicitly using a constructor, as in

```
p = new Node();
```

or by assigning a value from an already initialized variable, as in

```
p = q;
```

Because an array is also an object, the declaration

```
int a[10];
```

is illegal; this declaration is considered an attempt to define a variable whose name is `a[10]`. A declaration has to be followed with initialization, which is often combined with the declaration, as in

```
int[] a = new int[10];
```

In this way, Java does not allow for variables that name objects directly. Thus, the dot notation used to access fields of the object, as in `p.name`, is really an indirect reference to the field name because p is not the name of the object with field name, but a reference to (address of) this object. Fortunately, the programmer does not have to be very concerned about this distinction because it is all the matter of language implementation. But as mentioned, an understanding of these implementation details helps explain the results of some operations, as illustrated earlier by the operator `==`.

1.5 VECTORS IN `java.util`

One of the most useful classes in the `java.util` package is the class `Vector`. A vector is the data structure with a contiguous block of memory just like an array. Because memory locations are contiguous, they can be randomly accessed so that the access time of any element of the vector is constant. Storage is managed automatically so that on an attempt to insert an element into a full vector, a larger memory block is allocated for the vector, the vector elements are copied to the new block, and the old block is released. Vector is thus a flexible array, that is, an array whose size can be dynamically changed.

The class hierarchy in the package `java.util` is as follows:

$$\text{Object} \Rightarrow \text{AbstractCollection} \Rightarrow \text{AbstractList} \Rightarrow \text{Vector}$$

Figure 1.3 lists alphabetically the methods of class `Vector`. Some of these methods are inherited from `AbstractList`; others are from `AbstractCollection`. Figure 1.3 lists most of the methods of class. Only methods `iterator()` and `listIterator()` inherited from class `AbstractList` and methods `finalize()`, `getClass()`, `notify()`, `notifyAll()`, and `wait()` inherited from class `Object` are not included.

FIGURE **1.3**   An alphabetical list of member functions in the class `java.util.Vector`.

Method	Operation
`void add(ob)`	insert object `ob` at the end of the list
`void add(pos, ob)`	insert object `ob` at position `pos` after shifting elements at positions following `pos` by one position; raise `ArrayIndexOutOfBoundsException` if `pos` is out of range
`boolean addAll(col)`	add all the elements from the collection `col` to the end of the list; return `true` if `col` is not empty
`boolean addAll(pos, col)`	add all the elements from the collection `col` at the position `pos` of the list after shifting the objects following position `pos`; raise `ArrayIndexOutOfBoundsException` if `pos` is out of range
`void addElement(ob)`	insert object `ob` at the end of the list; same as `add(ob)`
`int capacity()`	return the number of objects that can be stored in the vector
`void clear()`	remove all the objects from the list
`Object clone()`	return a clone of the vector
`boolean contains(ob)`	return `true` if the list contains the object `ob`
`boolean containsAll(col)`	return `true` if the list contains all of the objects in the collection `col`
`void copyInto(objArr[])`	copy objects from the vector to the object array `objArr`; throw `IndexOutOfBoundsException` if the array is not large enough to accommodate all objects from the vector

FIGURE **1.3**   *(continued)*

`Object elementAt(pos)`	return the object at position `pos`; raise `ArrayIndexOutOf-BoundsException` if `pos` is out of range; same as `get(pos)`
`Enumeration elements()`	return an `Enumeration` object that enumerates all the objects in the vector
`void ensureCapacity(minCap)`	extend the size of the vector to accommodate at least `minCap` objects; do nothing if the size of the vector exceeds the minimum capacity `minCap`
`boolean equals(lst)`	return `true` if the current list and object `lst` contain equal objects in the same order
`Object firstElement()`	return the first element in the vector; raise `NoSuchElementException` if the vector is empty
`Object get(pos)`	return the object at position `pos`; raise `ArrayIndexOutOf-BoundsException` if `pos` is out of range
`int hashCode()`	return the hash code for the vector
`int indexOf(ob)`	return the position of the first occurrence of object `ob` in the list; return −1 if `ob` is not found
`int indexOf(ob, pos)`	return the position of the first occurrence of object `ob` in the list beginning the search at position `pos`; return −1 if `ob` is not found
`void insertElementAt(ob, pos)`	insert object `ob` at position `pos` after shifting elements at positions following `pos` by one position; raise `ArrayIndexOut-OfBoundsException` if `pos` is out of range; same as `add(ob,pos)`
`boolean isEmpty()`	return `true` if the list contains no elements, `false` otherwise
`Object lastElement()`	return the last element in the vector; raise `NoSuchElementException` if the vector is empty
`int lastIndexOf(ob)`	return the position of the last occurrence of object `ob` in the list; return −1 if `ob` is not found
`int lastIndexOf(ob, pos)`	return the position of the last occurrence of object `ob` in the list beginning the backward search at position `pos`; return -1 if `ob` is not found
`boolean remove(ob)`	remove the first occurrence of `ob` in the list and return `true` if `ob` was in the list
`Object remove(pos)`	remove the object at position `pos`; raise `ArrayIndexOutOf-BoundsException` if `pos` is out of range
`boolean removeAll(col)`	remove from the list all the objects contained in collection `col`; return `true` if any element was removed

FIGURE **1.3**   (*continued*)

`boolean removeElement(ob)`	remove from the vector the first occurrence of `ob`; return `true` if an occurrence of `ob` was found; same as `remove(ob)`
`void removeElementAt(pos)`	remove the object at position `pos`; raise `ArrayIndexOutOf-BoundsException` if `pos` is out of range
`void removeAllElements()`	remove all the objects from the list; same as `clear()`
`void removeRange(first, last)`	remove objects starting at position `first` and ending at `last-1` and then shift all the succeeding objects to fill the hole (protected method)
`boolean retainAll(col)`	remove from the list all objects that are not in the collection `col`; return `true` if any object was removed
`Object set(pos, ob)`	assign object `ob` to position `pos` and return the object that occupied this position before the assignment; raise `ArrayIndex-OutOfBoundsException` if `pos` is out of range
`void setElementAt(ob, pos)`	assign object `ob` to position `pos`; raise `ArrayIndexOutOf-BoundsException` if `pos` is out of range
`void setSize(sz)`	set size of the vector to `sz`; if current size is greater than `sz`, add new cells with null objects; if the current size is smaller than `sz`, discard the overflowing objects
`int size()`	return the number of object in the list
`List subList(first, last)`	return the sublist of the list (not its copy) containing elements from `first` to `last-1`; raise `ArrayIndexOutOfBoundsEx-ception` if either `first` or `last` is out of range and `Ille-galArgumentException` if `last` < `first`
`Object[] toArray()`	copy all objects from the list to a newly created array and return the array
`Object[] toArray(arr[])`	copy all objects from the list to the array `arr` if `arr` is large enough or to a newly created array and return the array
`String toString()`	return a string representation of the vector that contains the string representation of all the objects
`void trimToSize()`	change the capacity of the vector to the number of objects currently stored in it
`Vector()`	construct an empty vector
`Vector(col)`	construct a vector with objects copied from collection `col`
`Vector(initCap)`	construct a vector with the specified initial capacity
`Vector(initCap, capIncr)`	construct a vector with the specified initial capacity and capacity increment

FIGURE **1.4**   A program demonstrating the operation of vector member functions.

```
import java.io.*;
import java.util.Vector;

class testVectors {
    public static void main(String a[]) {
        Vector v1 = new Vector();            // v1 = [], size = 0, capacity = 10
        for (int j = 1; j <= 5; j++)
            v1.addElement(new Integer(j));   // v1 = [1, 2, 3, 4, 5], size = 5,
                                             // capacity = 10
        System.out.println("v1 = " + v1);
        Integer i = new Integer(3);
        System.out.println(v1.indexOf(i) + " " + v1.indexOf(i,4));    // 2 -1
        System.out.println(v1.contains(i) + " " + v1.lastIndexOf(i)); // true 2
        Vector v2 = new Vector(3,4);         // v2 = [], size = 0, capacity = 3
        for (int j = 4; j <= 8; j++)
            v2.addElement(new Integer(j));   // v2 = [4, 5, 6, 7, 8], size = 5,
                                             // capacity = 7
        v2.ensureCapacity(9);                // v2 = [4, 5, 6, 7, 8], size = 5,
                                             // capacity = 11
        Vector v3 = new Vector(2);           // v3 = [], size = 0, capacity = 2
        v3.setSize(4);                       // v3 = [null, null, null, null],
                                             // size = cap = 4
        v3.setElementAt(new Integer(9),1);   // v3 = [null, null, null, 9]
        v3.setElementAt(new Integer(5),3);   // v3 = [null, 9, null, 5]
        v3.insertElementAt(v3.elementAt(3),1); // v3 = [null, 5, 9, null, 5],
                                             // size = 5, cap = 8
        v3.ensureCapacity(9);                // v3 = [null, 5, 9, null, 5],
                                             // size = 5, cap = 16
        v3.removeElement(new Integer(9));    // v3 = [null, 5, null, 5]
        v3.removeElementAt(v3.size()-2);     // v3 = [null, 5, 5]
        java.util.Enumeration ev = v3.elements();
        while (ev.hasMoreElements())
            System.out.print(ev.nextElement() + " ");
        System.out.println();
        v3.removeElementAt(0);               // v3 = [5, 5]
        v3.addAll(v1);                       // v3 = [5, 5, 1, 2, 3, 4, 5]
        v3.removeAll(v2);                    // v3 = [1, 2, 3] = v3 - v2
        v3.addAll(2,v1);                     // v3 = [1, 2, 1, 2, 3, 4, 5, 3]
        v3.retainAll(v2);                    // v3 = [4, 5] = intersection(v3,v2)
        v1.subList(1,3).clear();             // v1 = [1, 4, 5]
        Vector v4 = new Vector(), v5;
        v4.addElement(new Node("Jill",23));
        v5 = (Vector) v4.clone();            // v4 = [(Jill, 23)]
        ((Node)v5.firstElement()).age = 34; // v4 = v5 = [(Jill, 34)]
    }
}
```

An application of these methods is illustrated in Figure 1.4. The contents of affected vectors are shown as comments on the line in which the methods are called. The contents of vectors are output with an implicit call to the method `toString()` in

```
System.out.println("v1 = " + v1);
```

but in the program in Figure 1.4, only one such line is shown.

To use the class `Vector`, the program has to include the `import` instruction

```
import java.util.Vector;
```

Vector `v1` is declared empty, and then new elements are inserted with the method `addElement()`. Adding a new element to a vector is usually fast unless the vector is full and has to be copied to a new block. But if the vector has some unused cells, it can accommodate a new element immediately in constant time.

The status of the vector can be tested with two methods: `size()`, which returns the number of elements currently in the vector, and `capacity()`, which returns the number of cells in the vector. If the vector's capacity is greater than its size, then a new element can be inserted at the end of the vector immediately. How frequently a vector is filled and has to be copied depends on the interplay between these two parameters, size and capacity, and the third parameter, capacity increment. By default, a new empty vector has capacity 10, and its capacity is doubled every time all its size reaches the current capacity. For a large vector, this may lead to wasted space. For example, a full vector containing 50,000 elements has 100,000 cells after a new element arrives, but the user may never include more elements than 50,001. In such a situation, the method `trimToSize()` should be used to reduce the waste.

When the user is reasonably sure of the maximum number of elements inserted in a vector, the method `ensureCapacity()` should be used to set capacity to the desired number so that all insertions are immediate. Otherwise, the user may set the capacity increment to a certain value so that when the vector is full, it is not doubled but increased by the capacity increment. Consider the declaration of vector `v2`:

```
Vector v2 = new Vector (3,4);
```

Initially, capacity is set to 3, and because the capacity increment equals 4, the capacity of the vector after inserting the fourth element equals 7. With this capacity, the statement

```
v2.ensureCapacity(9);
```

raises the capacity to 11 because it uses the capacity increment. Because for vector `v3` capacity increment is not specified in its declaration, then when its capacity equals 8, the statement

```
v3.ensureCapacity(9);
```

causes the capacity to be doubled to 16.

The method `ensureCapacity()` affects only the capacity of the vector, not its content. The method `setSize()` affects its content and possibly the capacity. For example, the empty vector `v2` of capacity 2 changes to `v2` = [null, null, null, null] after execution of

```
v2.setSize(4);
```

and its capacity equals 4.

The contents of `v2` are potentially dangerous if a method is executed that expects nonnull objects. For example, `v2.toString()` used in a printing statement raises `NullPointerException`. (To print a vector safely, a loop should be used in which `v.elementAt(i)` is printed.)

The method `addElement()` adds an element at the end of the vector. The insertion of an element in any other position can be performed with `insertElementAt()`. This reflects the fact that adding a new element inside the vector is a complex operation because it requires that all the elements are moved by one position to make room for the new element.

The method `elements()` puts vector elements in an object of `Enumeration` type. The loop shown in the program works the same for any data structure that returns an `Enumeration` object. In this way, data contained in different data structures become comparable by, as it were, equalizing the data structures themselves by using the common ground, the type `Enumeration`.

The method `clone()` should be used carefully. The method clones the array implementing the vector, but not the objects in the array. After the method is finished, the cloned vector includes references to the same objects as the vector from which it was cloned. In Figure 1.4, vector `v4` contains one object of type `Node` (as defined in Section 1.4), and then vector `v5`, a clone of `v4`, references the very same object from position 0. This is evident after the object is updated through reference `v5`; both `v4` and `v5` now reference the same updated object.

⬛ 1.6 DATA STRUCTURES AND OBJECT-ORIENTED PROGRAMMING

Although the computer operates on bits, we do not usually think in these terms; in fact, we would not like to. Although an integer is a sequence of 32 bits, we prefer seeing an integer as an entity with its own individuality which is reflected in operations that can be performed on integers but not on variables of other types. As an integer uses bits as its building blocks, so other objects can use integers as their atomic elements. Some data types are already built into a particular language, but some data types can be, and need to be, defined by the user. New data types have a distinctive structure, a new configuration of their elements, and this structure determines the behavior of objects of these new types. The task given to the data structures domain is to explore such new structures and investigate their behavior in terms of time and space requirements. Unlike the object-oriented approach, where we start with behavior and then try to find the most suitable data type which allows for an efficient performance of desirable operations, we now start with a data type specification with some data structure and then look at what it can do, how it does it, and how efficiently. The data structures field is designed for building tools to be incorporated in and used by application programs and for finding data structures that can perform certain operations speedily and without imposing too much burden on computer memory. This field is interested in building classes by concentrating on the mechanics of these classes, on their gears and cogs, which in most cases are not visible to the user of the classes. The data structures field investigates the operability of these classes and its improvement by modifying the data structures to be found inside the classes, since it has direct access to them. It sharpens tools and advises the user to what purposes they can be applied. Because of inheritance, the user can add some more operations to these classes and try to squeeze from them more than the class designer did.

The data structures field performs best if done in the object-oriented fashion. In this way, it can build the tools it intends without the danger that these tools will be inadvertently misused in the application. By encapsulating the data structures into a class and making public only what is necessary for proper usage of the class, the data structures field can develop tools whose functioning is not compromised by unnecessary tampering.

◧ 1.7 CASE STUDY: RANDOM ACCESS FILE

From the perspective of the operating systems, files are collections of bytes, regardless of their contents. From the user's perspective, files are collections of words, numbers, data sequences, records, and so on. If the user wants to access the fifth word in a text file, a searching procedure goes sequentially through the file staring at position 0 and checks all of the bytes along the way. It counts the number of sequences of blank characters, and after it skips four such sequences (or five if a sequence of blanks begins the file), it stops because it encounters the beginning of the fifth nonblank sequence or the fifth word. This word can begin at any position of the file. It is impossible to go to a particular position of any text file and be certain that this is a starting position of the fifth word of the file. Ideally, we want to go directly to a certain position of the file and be sure that the fifth word begins in it. The problem is caused by the lengths of the preceding words and sequences of blanks. If we know that each word occupies the same amount of space, then it is possible to go directly to the fifth word by going to the position $4 \cdot length(\text{word})$. But because words are of various lengths, this can be accomplished by assigning the same number of bytes to each word; if a word is shorter, some padding characters are added to fill up the remaining space; if it is longer, then the word is trimmed. In this way, a new organization is imposed on the file. The file is now treated not merely as a collection of bytes, but as a collection of records; in our example, each record consists of one word. If a request comes to access the fifth word, the word can be directly accessed without looking at the preceding words. With the new organization, we created a random access file.

A random access file allows for direct access of each record. The records usually include more items than one word. The preceding example suggests one way of creating a random access file, namely, by using fixed-length records. Our task in this case study is to write a generic program that generates a random access file for any type of record. The workings of the program are illustrated for a file containing personal records, each record consisting of five fields (social security number, name, city, year of birth, and salary), and for a student file that stores student records. The latter records have the same fields as personal records plus information about academic major. This allows us to illustrate inheritance.

In this case study, a generic random access file program inserts a new record to a file, finds a record in the file, and modifies a record. The name of the file has to be supplied by the user, and if the file is not found, it is created; otherwise, it is open for reading and writing. The program is shown in Figure 1.5.

The program uses a class `IOmethods` and the interface `DbObject`. A user-defined class that specifies one record in the database is the extension `IOmethods` of and implementation of `DbObject`.

The class `Database` is generic so that it can operate on any random access file. Its generic character relies on polymorphism. Consider the method `find()`, which determines whether a record is in the file. It performs the search sequentially comparing each retrieved record `tmp` to the sought record `d` using the method `equals()` defined for the particular class (or rather, redefined because the method is inherited from the class `Object` from which any other class is derived). The object `d` is passed in as a parameter to `find()`. But `d` must not be changed because its value is needed for comparison. Therefore, another object is needed to read data from the file. This object is created with the method `copy()`, which takes a one-cell array as a parameter and assigns the reference to a copy of `d` created by `new` in `copy()` to the only cell of the array. If parameter `copy()` were of type `DbObject`, not `DbObject[]`, the reference would be discarded because the parameter would be passed by value. Now, the array is also passed by value, but its cell is changed permanently. The cell `tmp[0]` now contains a copy of `d`, in particular, its type, so that the system uses methods of the particular class; for example, `tmp[0].readFromFile()` is taken from class `Personal` if `d` is an object of this type, and from `Student` if `d` is a `Student` object.

The method `find()` uses to some extent the fact that the file is random by scrutinizing it record by record, not byte by byte. To be sure, the records are built out of bytes and all the bytes belonging to a particular record have to be read, but only the bytes required by the equality operator are participating in the comparison.

The method `modify()` updates information stored in a particular record. The record is first retrieved from the file, also using sequential search, and the new information is read from the user using the method `readFromFile()` defined for a particular class. To store the updated record `tmp[0]` in the file, `modify()` forces the file pointer `database` to go back to the beginning of the record `tmp[0]` that has just been read; otherwise, the record following `tmp[0]` in the file would be overwritten. The starting position of `tmp` can be determined immediately because each record occupies the same number of bytes; therefore, it is enough to jump back the number of bytes occupied by one record. This is accomplished by calling `database.seek(database.getFilePointer()-d.size())`, where `size()` must be defined for the particular class.

The generic `Database` class includes two more methods. Method `add()` places a record at the end of file. Method `printDb()` prints the contents of the file.

To see the class `Database` in action, we have to define a specific class which specifies the format of one record in a random access file. As an example, we define the class `Personal` with five fields, `SSN`, `name`, `city`, `year`, and `salary`. The first three fields are strings, but only `SSN` is always of the same size. To have slightly more flexibility with the other two strings, two constants, `nameLen` and `cityLen`, are defined.

FIGURE **1.5**   Listing of a program to manage random access files.

```
//*********************** DbObject.java ***********************

import java.io.*;

public interface DbObject {
    public void writeToFile(RandomAccessFile out) throws IOException;
    public void readFromFile(RandomAccessFile in) throws IOException;
    public void readFromConsole() throws IOException;
    public void writeLegibly() throws IOException;
    public void readKey() throws IOException;
    public void copy(DbObject[] db);
    public int size();
}


//*********************** Personal.java ***********************

import java.io.*;

public class Personal extends IOmethods implements DbObject {
    protected final int nameLen = 10, cityLen = 10;
    protected String SSN, name, city;
    protected int year;
    protected long salary;
    protected final int size = 9*2 + nameLen*2 + cityLen*2 + 4 + 8;
    Personal() {
    }
    Personal(String ssn, String n, String c, int y, long s) {
        SSN = ssn; name = n; city = c; year = y; salary = s;
    }
    public int size() {
        return size;
    }
    public boolean equals(Object pr) {
        return SSN.equals(((Personal)pr).SSN);
    }
    public void writeToFile(RandomAccessFile out) throws IOException {
        writeString(SSN,out);
        writeString(name,out);
        writeString(city,out);
        out.writeInt(year);
        out.writeLong(salary);
    }
```

FIGURE **1.5** *(continued)*

```java
    public void writeLegibly() {
        System.out.print("SSN = " + SSN + ", name = " + name.trim()
                + ", city = " + city.trim() + ", year = " + year
                + ", salary = " + salary);
    }
    public void readFromFile(RandomAccessFile in) throws IOException {
        SSN = readString(9,in);
        name = readString(nameLen,in);
        city = readString(cityLen,in);
        year = in.readInt();
        salary = in.readLong();
    }
    public void readKey() throws IOException {
        System.out.print("Enter SSN: ");
        SSN = readLine();
    }
    public void readFromConsole() throws IOException {
        System.out.print("Enter SSN: ");
        SSN = readLine();
        System.out.print("Name: ");
        name = readLine();
        for (int i = name.length(); i < nameLen; i++)
            name += ' ';
        System.out.print("City: ");
        city = readLine();
        for (int i = city.length(); i < cityLen; i++)
            city += ' ';
        System.out.print("Birthyear: ");
        year = Integer.valueOf(readLine().trim()).intValue();
        System.out.print("Salary: ");
        salary = Long.valueOf(readLine().trim()).longValue();
    }
    public void copy(DbObject[] d) {
        d[0] = new Personal(SSN,name,city,year,salary);
    }
}

//********************** Student.java **********************

import java.io.*;

public class Student extends Personal {
```

FIGURE **1.5**   *(continued)*

```java
    public int size() {
        return super.size() + majorLen*2;
    }
    protected String major;
    protected final int majorLen = 10;
    Student() {
        super();
    }
    Student(String ssn, String n, String c, int y, long s, String m) {
        super(ssn,n,c,y,s);
        major = m;
    }
    public void writeToFile(RandomAccessFile out) throws IOException {
        super.writeToFile(out);
        writeString(major,out);
    }
    public void readFromFile(RandomAccessFile in) throws IOException {
        super.readFromFile(in);
        major = readString(majorLen,in);
    }
    public void readFromConsole() throws IOException {
        super.readFromConsole();
        System.out.print("Enter major: ");
        major = readLine();
        for (int i = major.length(); i < nameLen; i++)
            major += ' ';
    }
    public void writeLegibly() {
        super.writeLegibly();
        System.out.print(", major = " + major.trim());
    }
    public void copy(DbObject[] d) {
        d[0] = new Student(SSN,name,city,year,salary,major);
    }
}

//*********************** Database.java ***********************

import java.io.*;

public class Database {
    private RandomAccessFile database;
```

Continues

FIGURE **1.5**   *(continued)*

```java
    private String fName = new String();;
    private IOmethods io = new IOmethods();
    Database() throws IOException {
        System.out.print("File name: ");
        fName = io.readLine();
    }
    private void add(DbObject d) throws IOException {
        database = new RandomAccessFile(fName,"rw");
        database.seek(database.length());
        d.writeToFile(database);
        database.close();
    }
    private void modify(DbObject d) throws IOException {
        DbObject[] tmp = new DbObject[1];
        d.copy(tmp);
        database = new RandomAccessFile(fName,"rw");
        while (database.getFilePointer() < database.length()) {
            tmp[0].readFromFile(database);
            if (tmp[0].equals(d)) {
                tmp[0].readFromConsole();
                database.seek(database.getFilePointer()-d.size());
                tmp[0].writeToFile(database);
                database.close();
                return;
            }
        }
        database.close();
        System.out.println("The record to be modified is not in the
database");
    }
    private boolean find(DbObject d) throws IOException {
        DbObject[] tmp = new DbObject[1];
        d.copy(tmp);
        database = new RandomAccessFile(fName,"r");
        while (database.getFilePointer() < database.length()) {
            tmp[0].readFromFile(database);
            if (tmp[0].equals(d)) {
                database.close();
                return true;
            }
        }
    }
    database.close();
```

FIGURE **1.5**　　*(continued)*

```
        return false;
    }
    private void printDb(DbObject d) throws IOException {
        database = new RandomAccessFile(fName,"r");
        while (database.getFilePointer() < database.length()) {
            d.readFromFile(database);
            d.writeLegibly();
            System.out.println();
        }
        database.close();
    }
    public void run(DbObject rec) throws IOException {
        String option;
        System.out.println("1. Add 2. Find 3. Modify a record; 4. Exit");
        System.out.print("Enter an option: ");
        option = io.readLine();
        while (true) {
            if (option.charAt(0) == '1') {
                rec.readFromConsole();
                add(rec);
            }
            else if (option.charAt(0) == '2') {
                rec.readKey();
                System.out.print("The record is ");
                if (find(rec) == false)
                    System.out.print("not ");
                System.out.println("in the database");
            }
            else if (option.charAt(0) == '3') {
                rec.readKey();
                modify(rec);
            }
            else if (option.charAt(0) != '4')
                System.out.println("Wrong option");
            else return;
            printDb(rec);
            System.out.print("Enter an option: ");
            option = io.readLine();
        }
    }
}
```

Continues

FIGURE **1.5**   *(continued)*

```
//*********************  UseDatabase.java  ************************

import java.io.*;

public class UseDatabase {
    static public void main(String a[]) throws IOException {
//      (new Database()).run(new Personal());
        (new Database()).run(new Student());
    }
}
```

Storing data from one object requires particular care, which is the task of method `writeToFile()`. The SSN field is the simplest to handle. A social security number always includes nine digits; therefore, the output operator << can be used. However, the lengths of names and cities vary from record to record, and yet the sections of a record in the data file designated for these two fields should always have the same length. To guarantee this, the method `readFromConsole()` adds trailing blanks to the strings.

Another problem is posed by the numerical fields, `year` and `salary`, particularly the latter field. If salary is written to the file with the method `printLong()`, then the salary 50000 is written as a five-byte-long string '50000', and the salary 100000 as a six-byte-long string '100000', which violates the condition that each record in the random access file should be of the same length. To avoid the problem, the numbers are stored in binary form. For example, 50000 is represented in the field `salary` as the string of 32 bits, 00000000000000001100001101010000. We can now treat this sequence of bits as representing not a long number, but a string of four characters, 00000000, 00000000, 11000011, 01010000, that is, the characters whose ASCII codes are, in decimal, numbers 0, 0, 195, and 80. In this way, regardless of the value of salary, the value is always stored in four bytes. This is accomplished in Java with the method `writeLong()`.

This method of storing records in a data file poses a readability problem, particularly in the case of numbers. For example, 50000 is stored as four bytes: two null characters, a special character, and a capital P. For a human reader, it is far from obvious that these characters represent 50000. Therefore, a special routine is needed to output records in readable form. This is accomplished by the method `writeLegibly()`, which explains why this program uses two methods for reading records and two for writing records: One is for maintaining data in a random access file, and the other is for reading and writing data in readable form.

To test the flexibility of the `Database` class, another user class is defined, class `Student`. This class is also used to show one more example of inheritance.

Class Student uses the same data fields as class Personal by being defined as a class derived from Personal plus one more field, a string field major. Processing input and output on objects of class type Student is very similar to that for class Personal, but the additional field has to be accounted for. This is done by redefining methods from the base class and at the same time reusing them. Consider the method writeToFile() for writing student records in a data file in fixed-length format:

```
public void writeToFile(RandomAccessFile out) throws IOException{
    super.writeToFile(out);
    writeString(major,out);
}
```

The method uses the base class' writeTofile() to initialize the five fields, SSN, name, city, year, and salary, and initializes the field major. Note that a special variable super must be used to indicate clearly that writeToFile() being defined for class Student calls writeToFile() already defined in base class Personal. However, class Student inherits without any modification method readKey() and the method equals() because both in Personal and in Student objects the same key is used to uniquely identify any record, namely, SSN.

1.8 EXERCISES

1. What should be the type of constructors defined in classes?

2. Assume that classA includes a private variable k, a variable m with no modifier, a private protected variable n, a protected variable p, and a public variable q. Moreover, classB is derived from classA, classC is not derived from classA, and all three classes are in the same package. In addition, classD is derived from classA, classE is not derived from classA, and classA is in a different package than classD and classE. Which of the five variables defined in classA can be used by any of the four other classes?

3. What happens if the declaration of C:

```
class C {
    void process1(char ch) {
        System.out.println("Inside process1 in C " + ch);
    }
    void process2(char ch) {
        System.out.println("Inside process2 in C " + ch);
    }
    void process3(char ch) {
        System.out.println("Inside process3 in C " + ch);
        process2(ch);
    }
}
```

is followed by the following declaration of its extension:

```java
class ExtC extends C {
    void process1(int n) {
        System.out.println("Inside process1 in ExtC " + n);
    }
    void process2(char ch) {
        System.out.println("Inside process2 in ExtC " + ch);
    }
    void process4(int n) {
        System.out.println("Inside process4 in Ext C " + n);
    }
}
```

Which methods are invoked if the declaration of three objects

```java
ExtC object1 = new ExtC();
C object2 = new ExtC(), object3 = new ExtC();
```

is followed by these statements:

```java
object1.process1(1000);
object1.process4(2000);
object2.process1(3000);
object2.process4(4000);
object3.process1('P');
object3.process2('Q');
object3.process3('R');
```

4. For the declaration of I1:

```java
interface I1 {
    int I1f1();
    void I1f2(int i);
}
```

identify the errors.

(a) in the declaration of the interface I2:

```java
interface I2 extends I1 {
    double I2f1();
    void I2f2(int i);
    int I1f1();
    double I2f1() { return 10; }
    private int AC1f4();
    private int n = 10;
}
```

(b) in the declaration of class `CI1`:

```
class CI1 implements I1 {
     int I1f1() { . . . . . }
     void I1f2(int i) { . . . . . }
     int CI1f3() { . . . . . }
}
```

(c) and in the declaration of object `c6`:

```
I1 c6 = new I1();
```

5. Identify the errors:

(a)
```
abstract class AC1 {
     int AC1f1() { . . . . }
     void AC1f2(int i) { . . . . }
     int AC1f3();
}
```

(b) `interface C6 extends CAC1 { . . . }`

where `CAC1` is a class.

(c) `class CAC1AC2 extends AC1, AC2 { . . . }`

where `AC1` and `AC2` are two abstract classes.

(d) `AC1 c7 = new AC1();`

where `AC1` is an abstract class.

6. What happens if the class `SomeInfo` instead of the definition of `equals()` from Section 1.2.4 uses the following definition of this method:

```
public boolean equals(SomeInfo si) {
     return n == si.n;
}
```

📖 1.9 PROGRAMMING ASSIGNMENTS

1. Write a `Fraction` class which defines adding, subtracting, multiplying, and dividing fractions. Then write a method for reducing factors and methods for inputting and outputting fractions.

2. Write a class `Quaternion` which defines the four basic operations of quaternions and the two I/O operations. Quaternions, as defined in 1843 by William Hamilton and published in his *Lectures on Quaternions* in 1853, are an extension of complex numbers. Quaternions are quadruples of real numbers, $(a,b,c,d) = a + bi + cj + dk$, where $1 = (1,0,0,0)$, $i = (0,1,0,0)$, $j = (0,0,1,0)$, and $k = (0,0,0,1)$ and the following equations hold:

$$i^2 = j^2 = k^2 = -1$$

$$ij = k, \; jk = i, \; ki = j, \; ji = -k, \; kj = -i, \; ik = -j$$

$$(a + bi + cj + dk) + (p + qi + rj + sk)$$

$$= (a + p) + (b + q)i + (c + r)j + (d + s)k$$

$$(a + bi + cj + dk) \cdot (p + qi + rj + sk)$$

$$= (ap - bq - cr - ds) + (aq + bp + cs - dr)i$$

$$+ (ar + cp + dq - bs)j + (as + dp + br - cq)k.$$

Use these equations in implementing a quaternion class.

3. Write a program to reconstruct a text from a concordance of words. This was a real problem of reconstructing some unpublished texts of the Dead Sea Scrolls using concordances. For example, here is William Wordsworth's poem, *Nature and the Poet*, and a concordance of words corresponding with the poem.

So pure the sky, so quiet was the air!
So like, so very like, was day to day!
Whene'er I look'd, thy image still was there;
It trembled, but it never pass'd away.

The 33-word concordance is as follows:

1:1 so quiet was the *air!
1:4 but it never pass'd *away.
1:4 It trembled, *but it never
1:2 was *day to day!
1:2 was day to *day!
1:3 thy *image still was there;
. . . .
1:2 so very like, *was day
1:3 thy image still *was there;
1:3 *Whene'er I look'd,

In this concordance, each word is shown in context of up to five words, and the word referred to on each line is preceded with an asterisk. For larger concordances, two numbers have to be included, a number corresponding with a poem and a number of the line where the words can be found. For example, assuming that 1 is the number of *Nature and the Poet*, line "1:4 but it never pass'd *away." means that the word "away" is found in this poem in line 4. Note that punctuation marks are included in the context.

Write a program that loads a concordance from a file and creates a vector where each cell is associated with one line of the concordance. Then, using a binary search, reconstruct the text.

4. Modify the program from the case study by maintaining an order during insertion of new records into the data file. This requires defining the method compareTo() in Personal and in Student to be used in a modified method add() in Database. The method finds a proper position for a record d, moves all the records in the file to make room for d, and writes d into the file. With the new organization of the data file,

find() and modify() can also be modified. For example, find() stops sequential search when it encounters a record greater than the record looked for (or reaches the end of file). A more efficient strategy can use binary search, discussed in Section 2.7.

5. Write a program that maintains an order in the data file indirectly. Use a vector of file position pointers (obtained through getFilePointer()) and keep the vector in sorted order without changing the order of records in the file.

6. Modify the program from the case study to remove records from the data file. Define method isNull() in classes Personal and Student to determine that a record is null. Define also method writeNullToFile() in the two classes to overwrite a record to be deleted by a null record. A null record can be defined as having a non-numeric character (a tombstone) in the first position of the SSN field. Then define method remove() in Database (very similar to modify()), which locates the position of a record to be deleted and overwrites it with the null record. After a session is finished, a Database method purge() destructor should be invoked which copies nonnull records to a new data file, deletes the old data file, and renames the new data file with the name of the old data file.

Bibliography

Object-Oriented Programming

Cardelli, Luca and Wegner, Peter. "On Understanding Types, Data Abstraction, and Polymorphism," *Computing Surveys* 17 (1985), 471–522.

Ege, Raimund K., *Programming in an Object-Oriented Environment*, San Diego: Academic Press, 1992.

Khoshafian, Setrag and Razmik, Abnous, *Object Orientation: Concepts, Languages, Databases, User Interfaces*, New York: Wiley, 1995.

Meyer, Bertrand, *Object-Oriented Software Construction*, Upper Saddle River, NJ: Prentice Hall, 1997.

Java

Naughton, Patrick, *The Java Handbook*, Berkeley, CA: Osborne McGraw-Hill, 1996.

Weber, Joe (ed.), *Using Java 1.2*, Indianapolis, IN: Que, 1998.

Weiss, Mark A., *Data Structures and Problem Solving Using Java*, Reading, MA: Addison-Wesley, 1998.

Complexity Analysis

2.1 COMPUTATIONAL AND ASYMPTOTIC COMPLEXITY

The same problem can frequently be solved with algorithms that differ in efficiency. The differences between the algorithms may be immaterial for processing a small number of data items, but these differences grow proportionally with the amount of data. To compare the efficiency of algorithms, a measure of the degree of difficulty of an algorithm called *computational complexity* was developed by Juris Hartmanis and Richard E. Stearns.

Computational complexity indicates how much effort is needed to apply an algorithm or how costly it is. This cost can be measured in a variety of ways and the particular context determines its meaning. This book concerns itself with the two efficiency criteria: time and space. The factor of time is more important than that of space, so efficiency considerations usually focus on the amount of time elapsed when processing data. However, the most inefficient algorithm run on a Cray computer can execute much faster than the most efficient algorithm run on a PC, so run time is always system-dependent. For example, to compare a hundred algorithms, all of them would have to be run on the same machine. Furthermore, the results of run-time tests depend on the language in which a given algorithm is written even if the tests are performed on the same machine. If programs are compiled, they execute much faster than when they are interpreted. A program written in C or Pascal may be 20 times faster than the same program encoded in BASIC or LISP.

To evaluate an algorithm's efficiency, real-time units such as microseconds and nanoseconds should not be used. Rather, logical units that express a relationship between the size n of a file or an array and the amount of time t required to process the data should be used. If there is a linear relationship between the size n and time t, that is, $t_1 = cn_1$, then an increase of data by a factor of 5 results in the increase of the execution time by the same factor, if $n_2 = 5n_1$, then $t_2 = 5t_1$. Similarly, if $t_1 = \log_2 n$, then doubling n increases t by only one unit of time. Therefore, if $t_2 = \log_2(2n)$, then $t_2 = t_1 + 1$.

A function expressing the relationship between n and t is usually much more complex, and calculating such a function is important only in regard to large bodies of data; any terms which do not substantially change the function's magnitude should be eliminated from the function. The resulting function gives only an approximate measure of efficiency of the original function. However, this approximation is sufficiently close to the original, especially for a function that processes large quantities of data. This measure of efficiency is called *asymptotic complexity* and is used when disregarding certain terms of a function to express the efficiency of an algorithm or when calculating a function is difficult or impossible and only approximations can be found. To illustrate the first case, consider the following example:

$$f(n) = n^2 + 100n + \log_{10}n + 1000 \tag{2.1}$$

For small values of n, the last term, 1000, is the largest. When n equals 10, the second (100n) and last (1000) terms are on equal footing with the other terms making the same contribution to the function value. When n reaches the value of 100, the first and the second terms make the same contribution to the result. But when n becomes larger than 100, the contribution of the second term becomes less significant. Hence, for large values of n, due to the quadratic growth of the first term (n^2), the value of the function f depends mainly on the value of this first term, as Figure 2.1 demonstrates. Other terms can be disregarded in the long run.

⬚ 2.2 BIG-O NOTATION

The most commonly used notation for specifying asymptotic complexity, that is, for estimating the rate of function growth, is the big-O notation introduced in 1894 by Paul Bachmann. Given two positive-valued functions f and g, consider the following definition:

Definition 1: $f(n)$ is $O(g(n))$ if there exist positive numbers c and N such that $f(n) \leq cg(n)$ for all $n \geq N$.

This definition reads: f is big-O of g if there is a positive number c such that f is not larger than cg for sufficiently large ns, that is, for all ns larger than some number N. The relationship between f and g can be expressed by stating either that $g(n)$ is an upper bound on the value of $f(n)$ or that, in the long run, f grows at most as fast as g.

The problem with this definition is that, first, it states only that there must exist certain c and N, but it does not give any hint how to calculate these constants. Second, it does not put any restrictions on these values and gives little guidance in situations when there are many candidates. In fact, there are usually infinitely many pairs of cs and Ns that can be given for the same pair of functions f and g. For example, for

$$f(n) = 2n^2 + 3n + 1 = O(n^2) \tag{2.2}$$

where $g(n) = n^2$, candidate values for c and N are shown in Figure 2.2.

FIGURE **2.1**   The growth rate of all terms of function $f(n) = n^2 + 100n + \log_{10}n + 1000$.

n	$f(n)$	n^2		$100n$		$\log_{10}n$		1000	
	Value	Value	%	Value	%	Value	%	Value	%
1	1,101	1	0.1	100	9.1	0	0.0	1000	90.82
10	2,101	100	4.76	1,000	47.6	1	0.05	1000	47.62
100	21002	10,000	47.6	10,000	47.6	2	0.991	1000	4.76
1,000	1,101,003	1,000,000	90.8	100,000	9.1	3	0.0003	1000	0.09
10,000	101,001,004	100,000,000	99.0	1,000,000	0.99	4	0.0	1000	0.001
100,000	10,010,001,005	10,000,000,000	99.9	10,000,000	0.099	5	0.0	1000	0.00

FIGURE **2.2**   Different values of c and N for function $f(n) = 2n^2 + 3n + 1 = O(n^2)$ calculated according to the definition of big-O.

c	≥ 6	$\geq 3\frac{3}{4}$	$\geq 3\frac{1}{9}$	$\geq 2\frac{13}{16}$	$\geq 2\frac{16}{25}$	$\cdots$	$\rightarrow$	2
N	1	2	3	4	5	$\cdots$	$\rightarrow$	∞

We obtain these values by solving the inequality:

$$2n^2 + 3n + 1 \leq cn^2$$

or equivalently

$$2 + \frac{3}{n} + \frac{1}{n^2} \leq c$$

for different ns. The first inequality results in substituting the quadratic function from Equation 2.2 for $f(n)$ in the definition of the big-O notation and n^2 for $g(n)$. Since it is one inequality with two unknowns, different pairs of constants c and N for the same function $g(= n^2)$ can be determined. To choose the best c and N, it should be determined for which N a certain term in f becomes the largest and stays the largest. In Equation 2.2, the only candidates for the largest term are $2n^2$ and $3n$; these terms can be compared using the inequality $2n^2 > 3n$ that holds for $n > 1$. Thus, $N = 2$ and $c \geq 3\frac{3}{4}$, as Figure 2.2 indicates.

What is the practical significance of the pairs of constants just listed? All of them are related to the same function $g(n) = n^2$ and to the same $f(n)$. For a fixed g, an infinite

FIGURE **2.3**   Comparison of functions for different values of c and N from Figure 2.2.

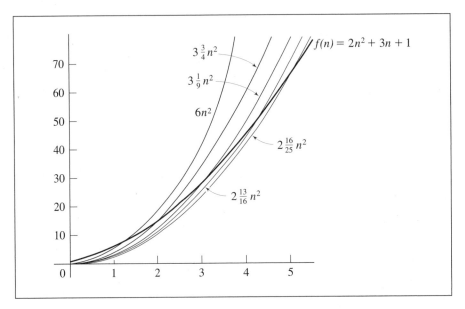

number of pairs of cs and Ns can be identified. The point is that f and g grow at the same rate. The definition states, however, that g is almost always greater than or equal to f if it is multiplied by a constant c. "Almost always" means for all ns not less than a constant N. The crux of the matter is that the value of c depends on which N is chosen and vice versa. For example, if 1 is chosen as the value of N—that is, if g is multiplied by c so that $cg(n)$ will not be less than f right away—then c has to be equal to 6 or greater. If $cg(n)$ is greater than or equal to $f(n)$ starting from $n = 2$, then it is enough that c is equal to 3.75. The constant c has to be at least $3\frac{1}{9}$ if $cg(n)$ is not less than $f(n)$ starting from $n = 3$. Figure 2.3 shows the graphs of the functions f and g. The function g is plotted with different coefficients c. Also, N is always a point where the functions $cg(n)$ and f intersect each other.

The inherent imprecision of the big-O notation goes even further, since there can be infinitely many functions g for a given function f. For example, the f from Equation 2.2 is big-O not only of n^2, but also of n^3, n^4, $\ldots$, n^k, $\ldots$ for any $k \geq 2$. To avoid this embarrassment of riches, the smallest function g is chosen, n^2 in this case.

The approximation of function f can be refined using big-O notation only for the part of the equation suppressing irrelevant information. For example, in Equation 2.1, the contribution of the third and last terms to the value of the function can be omitted (see Equation 2.3).

$$f(n) = n^2 + 100n + O(\log_{10} n) \tag{2.3}$$

Similarly, the function f in Equation 2.2 can be approximated as

$$f(n) = 2n^2 + O(n) \tag{2.4}$$

📖 2.3 PROPERTIES OF BIG-O NOTATION

Big-O notation has some helpful properties that can be used when estimating the efficiency of algorithms.

Fact 1. (transitivity) If $f(n)$ is $O(g(n))$ and $g(n)$ is $O(h(n))$, then $f(n)$ if $O(h(n))$. (This can be rephrased as $O(O(g(n)))$ is $O(g(n))$.)

Proof: According to the definition, $f(n)$ is $O(g(n))$ if there exist positive numbers c_1 and N_1 such that $f(n) \leq c_1 g(n)$ for all $n \geq N_1$, and $g(n)$ is $O(h(n))$ if there exist positive numbers c_2 and N_2 such that $g(n) \leq c_2 h(n)$ for all $n \geq N_2$.

Hence, $c_1 g(n) \leq c_1 c_2 h(n)$ for $n \geq N$ where N is the larger of N_1 and N_2. If we take $c = c_1 c_2$, then $f(n) \leq ch(n)$ for $n \geq N$, which means that f is big-O of h.

Fact 2. If $f(n)$ is $O(h(n))$ and $g(n)$ is $O(h(n))$, then $f(n) + g(n)$ is $O(h(n))$.

Proof: After setting c equal to $c_1 + c_2$, $f(n) + g(n) \leq ch(n)$.

Fact 3. The function an^k is $O(n^k)$.

Proof: For the inequality $an^k \leq cn^k$ to hold, $c \geq a$ is necessary.

Fact 4. The function n^k is $O(n^{k+j})$ for any positive j.

Proof: The statement holds if $c = N = 1$.

It follows from all these facts that every polynomial is big-O of n raised to the largest power, or

$$f(n) = a_k n^k + a_{k-1} n^{k-1} + \cdots + a_1 n + a_0 \text{ is } O(n^k)$$

It is also obvious that in the case of polynomials, $f(n)$ is $O(n^{k+j})$ for any positive j.

One of the most important functions in the evaluation of the efficiency of algorithms is the logarithmic function. In fact, if it can be stated that the complexity of an algorithm is on the order of the logarithmic function, the algorithm can be regarded as very good. There are an infinite number of functions that can be considered better than the logarithmic function, among which only a few, such as $O(\lg \lg n)$ or $O(1)$, have practical bearing. Before we show an important fact about logarithmic functions, let us state without proof:

Fact 5. If $f(n) = cg(n)$, then $f(n)$ is $O(g(n))$.

Fact 6. The function $\log_a n$ is $O(\log_b n)$ for any positive numbers a and $b \neq 1$.

This correspondence holds between logarithmic functions. Fact 6 states that regardless of their bases, logarithmic functions are big-O of each other; that is, all these functions have the same rate of growth.

Proof: Letting $\log_a n = x$ and $\log_b n = y$, we have, by the definition of logarithm, $a^x = n$ and $b^y = n$.

Taking ln of both sides results in

$$x \ln a = \ln n \text{ and } y \ln b = \ln n$$

Thus

$$x \ln a = y \ln b,$$

$$\ln a \log_a n = \ln b \log_b n,$$

$$\log_a n = \frac{\ln b}{\ln a} \log_b n = c \log_b n$$

which proves that $\log_a n$ and $\log_b n$ are multiples of each other. By Fact 5, $\log_a n$ is $O(\log_b n)$.

Because the base of the logarithm is irrelevant in the context of big-O notation, we can always use just one base and Fact 6 can be written as

Fact 7. $\log_a n$ is $O(\lg n)$ for any positive $a \neq 1$, where $\lg n = \log_2 n$.

♠ 2.4 Ω AND Θ NOTATIONS

Big-O notation refers to the upper bounds of functions. There is a symmetrical definition for a lower bound in the definition of big-Ω:

Definition 2: The function $f(n)$ is $\Omega(g(n))$ if there exist positive numbers c and N such that $f(n) \geq cg(n)$ for all $n \geq N$.

This definition reads: f is Ω (big-omega) of g if there is a positive number c such that f is at least equal to cg for almost all ns. In other words, $cg(n)$ is a lower bound on the size of $f(n)$, or, in the long run, f grows at least at the rate of g.

The only difference between this definition and the definition of big-O notation is the direction of the inequality; one definition can be turned into the other by replacing "$\geq$" by "$\leq$." There is an interconnection between these two notations expressed by the equivalence

$$f(n) \text{ is } \Omega(g(n)) \text{ iff } g(n) \text{ is } O(f(n))$$

Ω notation suffers from the same profusion problem as does big-O notation: There is an unlimited number of choices for the constants c and N. For Equation 2.2, we are looking for such a c, for which $2n^2 + 3n + 1 \geq cn^2$, which is true for any $n \geq 0$, if $c \leq 2$, where 2 is the limit for c in Figure 2.2. Also, if f is an Ω of g and $h \leq g$, then f is an Ω of h; that is, if for f we can find one g such that f is an Ω of g, then we can find infinitely many. For example, the function 2.2 is an Ω of n^2 but also of n, $n^{1/2}$, $n^{1/3}$, $n^{1/4}$, ..., and also of $\lg n$, $\lg \lg n$, ..., and of many other functions. For practical purposes, only the closest Ωs are the most interesting, the largest lower bounds. This restriction is made implicitly each time we choose an Ω of a function f.

There are an infinite number of possible lower bounds for the function f; that is, there is an infinite set of gs such that $f(n)$ is $\Omega(g(n))$ as well as an unbounded number of possible upper bounds of f. This may be somewhat disquieting, so we restrict our attention to the smallest upper bounds and the largest lower bounds. Note that there is a common ground for big-O and Ω notations indicated by the equalities in the definitions of these notations: Big-O is defined in terms of "≤" and Ω in terms of "≥"; "=" is included in both inequalities. This suggests a way of restricting the sets of possible lower and upper bounds. This restriction can be accomplished by the following definition of Θ (theta) notation:

Definition 3: $f(n)$ is $\Theta(g(n))$ if there exist positive numbers c_1, c_2, and N such that $c_1 g(n) \leq f(n) \leq c_2 g(n)$ for all $n \geq N$.

This definition reads: f has an order of magnitude g, f is on the order of g, or both functions grow at the same rate in the long run. We see that $f(n)$ is $\Theta(g(n))$ if $f(n)$ is $O(g(n))$ and $f(n)$ is $\Omega(g(n))$.

The only function just listed that is both big-O and Ω of the function 2.2 is n^2. However, it is not the only choice and there are still an infinite number of choices, since the functions $2n^2, 3n^2, 4n^2, \ldots$ are also Θ of function 2.2. But it is rather obvious that the simplest, n^2, will be chosen.

When applying any of these notations (big-O, Ω, and Θ), do not forget that they are approximations that hide some detail which in many cases may be considered important.

⏻ 2.5 POSSIBLE PROBLEMS

All the notations serve the purpose of comparing the efficiency of various algorithms designed for solving the same problem. However, if only big-Os are used to represent the efficiency of algorithms, then some of them may be rejected prematurely. The problem is that in the definition of big-O notation, f is considered big-O of g if the inequality $f(n) \leq cg(n)$ holds in the long run for all natural numbers with a few exceptions. The number of ns violating this inequality is always finite. It is enough to meet the condition of the definition. As Figure 2.2 indicates, this number of exceptions can be reduced by choosing a sufficiently large c. However, this may be of little practical significance if the constant c in $f(n) \leq cg(n)$ is prohibitively large, say 10^8, although the function g taken by itself seems to be promising.

Consider that there are two algorithms to solve a certain problem and suppose that the number of operations required by these algorithms is $10^8 n$ and $10n^2$. The first function is big-O of n and the second is big-O of n^2. Using just the big-O information, the second algorithm is rejected because it grows too fast. It is true but, again, in the long run, since for $n \leq 10^7$, which is 10 million, the second algorithm performs fewer operations than the first. Although 10 million is not an unheard-of number of elements to be processed by an algorithm, in most cases the number is much lower, and in these cases the second algorithm is preferable.

For these reasons, it may be desirable to use one more notation that includes constants which are very large for practical reasons. Udi Manber proposes a double-O (OO) notation to indicate such functions: f is $OO(g(n))$ if it is big-O of $g(n)$ and the constant c is too large to have practical significance. Thus, $10^8 n$ is $OO(n)$. However, the definition of "too large" depends on the particular application.

◻ 2.6 EXAMPLES OF COMPLEXITIES

Algorithms can be classified by their time or space complexities, and in this respect, several classes of such algorithms can be distinguished, as Figure 2.4 illustrates. Their growth is also displayed in Figure 2.5. For example, an algorithm is called *constant* if its execution time remains the same for any number of elements; it is called *quadratic* if its execution time is $O(n^2)$. For each of these classes, a number of operations is shown along with the real time needed for executing them on a machine able to perform 1 million operations per second, or one operation per microsecond (μsec). The table in Figure 2.4 indicates that some ill-designed algorithms, or algorithms whose complexity cannot be improved, have no practical application on available computers. To process 1 million items with a quadratic algorithm, over 11 days are needed,

FIGURE **2.4**   Classes of algorithms and their execution times on a computer executing 1 million operations per second (1 sec = 10^6 μsec = 10^3 msec).

Class	Complexity	Number of Operations and Execution Time (1 instr/μsec)					
n		10		10^2		10^3	
constant	$O(1)$	1	1 μsec	1	1 μsec	1	1 μsec
logarithimic	$O(\lg n)$	3.32	3 μsec	6.64	7 μsec	9.97	10 μsec
linear	$O(n)$	10	10 μsec	10^2	100 μsec	10^3	1 msec
$O(n \lg n)$	$O(n \lg n)$	33.2	33 μsec	664	664 μsec	9970	10 msec
quadratic	$O(n^2)$	10^2	100 μsec	10^4	10 msec	10^6	1 sec
cubic	$O(n^3)$	10^3	1 msec	10^6	1 sec	10^9	16.7 min
exponential	$O(2^n)$	1024	10 msec	10^{30}	$3.17 * 10^{17}$ yrs	10^{301}	
n		10^4		10^5		10^6	
constant	$O(1)$	1	1 μsec	1	1 μsec	1	1 μsec
logarithmic	$O(\lg n)$	13.3	13 μsec	16.6	7 μsec	19.93	20 μsec
linear	$O(n)$	10^4	10 msec	10^5	0.1 sec	10^6	1 sec
$O(n \lg n)$	$O(n \lg n)$	$133 * 10^3$	133 msec	$166 * 10^4$	1.6 sec	$199.3 * 10^5$	20 sec
quadratic	$O(n^2)$	10^8	1.7 min	10^{10}	16.7 min	10^{12}	11.6 days
cubic	$O(n^3)$	10^{12}	11.6 days	10^{15}	31.7 yr	10^{18}	31,709 yr
exponential	$O(2^n)$	10^{3010}		10^{30103}		10^{301030}	

F I G U R E **2.5**   Typical functions applied in big-O estimates.

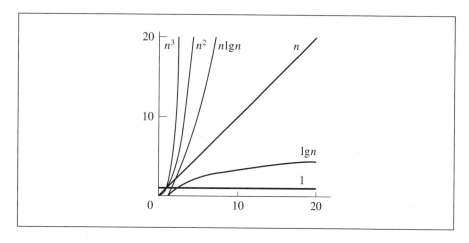

and for a cubic algorithm, thousands of years. Even if a computer can perform one operation per nanosecond (1 billion operations per second), the quadratic algorithm finishes in only 16.7 seconds, but the cubic algorithm requires over 31 years. Even a 1000-fold improvement in execution speed has very little practical bearing for this algorithm. Analyzing the complexity of algorithms is of extreme importance and cannot be abandoned on account of the argument that we have entered an era when, at relatively little cost, a computer on our desktop can execute millions of operations per second. The importance of analyzing the complexity of algorithms, in any context but in the context of data structures in particular, cannot be overstressed. The impressive speed of computers is of limited use if the programs that run on them use inefficient algorithms.

◫ 2.7 FINDING ASYMPTOTIC COMPLEXITY: EXAMPLES

Asymptotic bounds are used to estimate the efficiency of algorithms by assessing the amount of time and memory needed to accomplish the task for which the algorithms were designed. This section illustrates how this complexity can be determined.

In most cases, we are interested in time complexity, which usually measures the number of assignments and comparisons performed during the execution of a program. Chapter 9, which deals with sorting algorithms, considers both types of operations; this chapter considers only the number of assignment statements.

Begin with a simple loop to calculate the sum of numbers in an array:

```
for(i = sum = 0; i < n; i++)
    sum += a[i];
```

First, two variables are initialized, then the for loop iterates n times, and during each iteration, it executes two assignments, one of which updates sum and the other updates i. Thus, there are $2 + 2n$ assignments for the complete run of this for loop; its asymptotic complexity is $O(n)$.

Complexity usually grows if nested loops are used, as in the following code, which outputs the sums of all the subarrays that begin with position 0:

```
for(i = 0; i < n; i++) {
    for(j = 1, sum = a[0]; j <= i; j++)
        sum += a[j];
    System.out.println ("sum for subarray 0 through "+i+" is" + sum);
}
```

Before the loops start, i is initialized. The outer loop is performed n times, executing in each iteration an inner for loop, print statement, and assignment statements for i, j, and sum. The inner loop is executed i times for each $i \in \{1, \ldots, n-1\}$ with two assignments in each iteration: one for sum and one for j. Therefore, there are $1 + 3n + \sum_{i=1}^{n-1} 2i = 1 + 3n + 2(1 + 2 + \cdots + n - 1) = 1 + 3n + n(n-1) = O(n) + O(n^2) = O(n^2)$ assignments executed before the program is completed.

For nested loops, complexity usually grows in comparison with one loop, but it does not have to grow at all. For example, we may request printing sums of numbers in the last five cells of the subarrays starting in position 0. We adopt the foregoing code and transform it to

```
for(i = 4; i < n; i++) {
    for(j = i-3, sum = a[i-4]; j <= i; j++)
        sum += a[j];
    System.out.println ("sum for subarray "+(i - 4)+" through "+i+" is"+ sum);
}
```

For each i, the inner loop is executed only four times; for each iteration of the outer loop, there are 11 assignments. This number does not depend on the size of the array. The program makes $1 + 11(n - 4) = O(n)$ assignments, although the use of nested loops suggests something else.

Analysis of these two examples is relatively uncomplicated because the number of times the loops executed did not depend on the ordering of the arrays. Computation of asymptotic complexity is more involved if the number of iterations is not always the same. This point can be illustrated with a loop used to determine the length of the longest subarray with the numbers in increasing order. For example, in [1 8 1 2 5 0 11 12], it is three, the length of subarray [1 2 5]. The code is

```
for(i = 0, length = 1; i < n-1; i++) {
    for(i1 = i2 = k = i; k < n-1 && a[k] < a[k+1]; k++,i2++);
    if(length < i2 - i1 + 1)
        length = i2 - i1 + 1;
    System.out.println ("the length of the longest ordered subarray is" + length);
}
```

Notice that if all numbers in the array are in decreasing order, the outer loop is executed $n - 1$ times, but in each iteration, the inner loop executes just one time. Thus, the algorithm is $O(n)$. The algorithm is least efficient if the numbers are in increasing order. In this case, the outer for loop is executed $n - 1$ times, and the inner loop is executed i times for each $i \in \{1, \ldots, n-1\}$. Thus, the algorithm is $O(n^2)$. In most cases, the arrangement of data is less orderly, and measuring the efficiency in these cases is of great importance. However, it is far from trivial to determine the efficiency in the average cases.

A last example used to determine the computational complexity is the *binary search algorithm,* which is used to locate an element in an ordered array. If it is an array of numbers and we try to locate number k, then the algorithm accesses the middle element of the array first. If that element is equal to k, then the algorithm returns its position; if not, the algorithm continues. In the second trial, only half of the original array is considered: the first half, if k is smaller than the middle element, and the second otherwise. Now, the middle element of the chosen subarray is accessed and compared to k. If it is the same, the algorithm completes successfully. Otherwise, the subarray is divided into two halves, and if k is larger than this middle element, the first half is discarded; otherwise, the first half is retained. This process of halving and comparing continues until k is found or the array can no longer be divided into two subarrays. This relatively simple algorithm can be coded as follows:

```
int binarySearch(int[] arr, int key) {
    int lo = 0, mid, hi = arr.length-1;
    while (lo <= hi) {
        mid = (lo + hi)/2;
        if (key < arr[mid])
            hi = mid - 1;
        else if (arr[mid] < key)
            lo = mid + 1;
        else return mid;   // success: return the index of
    }                      //   the cell occupied by key;
    return -1;             // failure: key is not in the array;
}
```

If key is in the middle of the array, the loop executes only one time. How many times does the loop execute in the case where key is not in the array? First the algorithm looks at the entire array of size n, then at one of its halves of size $\frac{n}{2}$, then at one of the halves of this half, of size $\frac{n}{2^2}$, and so on, until the array is of size 1. Hence, we have the sequence $n, \frac{n}{2}, \frac{n}{2^2}, \ldots, \frac{n}{2^m}$, and we want to know the value of m. But the last term of this sequence $\frac{n}{2^m}$ equals 1, from which we have $m = \lg n$. So the fact that k is not in the array can be determined after $\lg n$ iterations of the loop.

◻ 2.8 THE BEST, AVERAGE, AND WORST CASES

The last two examples in the preceding section indicate the need for distinguishing at least three cases for which the efficiency of algorithms has to be determined. The *worst case* is when an algorithm requires a maximum number of steps, and the *best case* is when the number of steps is the smallest. The *average case* falls between these extremes. In simple cases, the average complexity is established by considering possible inputs to an algorithm, determining the number of steps performed by the algorithm for each input, adding the number of steps for all the inputs, and dividing by the number of inputs. This definition, however, assumes that the probability of occurrence of each input is the same, which is not always the case. To consider the probability explicitly, the average complexity is defined as the average over the number of steps executed when processing each input weighted by the probability of occurrence of this input, or,

$$C_{avg} = \sum_i p(input_i) \, steps(input_i)$$

This is the definition of expected value which assumes that all the possibilities can be determined and that the probability distribution is known, which simply determines a probability of occurrence of each input, $p(input_i)$. The probability function p satisfies two conditions: It is never negative, $p(input_i) \geq 0$, and all probabilities add up to 1, $\sum_i p(input_i) = 1$.

As an example, consider searching sequentially an unordered array to find a number. The best case is when the number is found in the first cell. The worst case is when the number is in the last cell or is not in the array at all. In this case, all the cells are checked to determine this fact. And the average case? We may make the assumption that there is an equal chance for the number to be found in any cell of the array; that is, the probability distribution is uniform. In this case, there is a probability equal to $\frac{1}{n}$ that the number is in the first cell, a probability equal to $\frac{1}{n}$ that it is in the second cell, . . . , and finally, a probability equal to $\frac{1}{n}$ that it is in the last, nth cell. This means that the probability of finding the number after one try equals $\frac{1}{n}$, the probability of finding it after two tries equals $\frac{1}{n}$, . . . , and the probability of finding it after n tries also equals $\frac{1}{n}$. Therefore, we can average all these possible numbers of tries over the number of possibilities and conclude that it takes on the average

$$\frac{1 + 2 + \ldots + n}{n} = \frac{n+1}{2}$$

steps to find a number. But if the probabilities differ, then the average case gives a different outcome. For example, if the probability of finding a number in the first cell equals $\frac{1}{2}$, the probability of finding it in the second cell equals $\frac{1}{4}$, and the probability of locating it in any of the remaining cells is the same and equal to

$$\frac{1 - \frac{1}{2} - \frac{1}{4}}{n-2} = \frac{1}{4(n-2)}$$

then, on the average, it takes

$$\frac{1}{2} + \frac{2}{4} + \frac{3 + \ldots n}{4(n-2)} = 1 + \frac{n(n+1) - 6}{8(n-2)} = 1 + \frac{n+3}{8}$$

steps to find a number, which is approximately four times better than $\frac{n+1}{2}$ found previously for the uniform distribution. Note that the probabilities of accessing a particular cell have no impact on the best and last cases.

The complexity for the three cases was relatively easy to determine for sequential search, but usually it is not that straightforward. Particularly, the complexity of the average case can pose difficult computational problems. If the computation is very complex, approximations are used, and that is where we find the big-O, Ω, and Θ notations most useful.

As an example, consider the average case for binary search. Assume that the size of the array is a power of 2 and that a number to be searched has an equal chance to be in any of the cells of the array. Binary search can locate it either after one try in the middle of the array, or after two tries in the middle of the first half of the array, or after two tries in the middle of the second half, or after three tries in the middle of the first quarter of the array, or ... or after three tries in the middle of the fourth quarter, or after four tries in the middle of the first eighth of the array, or ... or after four tries in the middle of the eighth eighth of the array, or ... or after try $\lg n$ in the first cell, or after try $\lg n$ in the third cell, or ... or, finally, after try $\lg n$ in the last cell. That is, the number of all possible tries equals

$$1 \cdot 1 + 2 \cdot 2 + 4 \cdot 3 + 8 \cdot 4 + \ldots + \frac{n}{2} \lg n = \sum_{i=0}^{\lg n-1} 2^i (i+1)$$

which has to be divided by $\frac{1}{n}$ to determine the average case complexity. What is this sum equal to? We know that it is between 1 (the best case result) and $\lg n$ (the worst case) determined in the preceding section. But is it closer to the best case—say, $\lg \lg n$—or to the worst case—for instance, $\frac{\lg n}{2}$, or $\lg \frac{n}{2}$? The sum does not lend itself to a simple conversion into a closed form; therefore, its estimation should be used. Our conjecture is that the sum is not less than the sum of powers of 2 in the specified range multiplied by a half of $\lg n$, that is,

$$s_1 = \sum_{i=0}^{\lg n-1} 2^i (i+1) \geq \frac{\lg n}{2} \sum_{i=0}^{\lg n-1} 2^i = s_2$$

The reason for this choice is that s_2 is a power series multiplied by a constant factor, and thus, it can be presented in closed form very easily, namely,

$$s_2 = \frac{\lg n}{2} \sum_{i=0}^{\lg n-1} 2^i = \frac{\lg n}{2} \left(1 + 2 \frac{2^{\lg n-1} - 1}{2-1} \right) = \frac{\lg n}{2} (n-1)$$

which is $\Omega(n \lg n)$. Because s_2 is the lower bound for the sum s_1 under scrutiny—that is, s_1 is $\Omega(s_2)$—then so is $\frac{s_2}{n}$, the lower bound of the sought average case complexity $\frac{s_1}{n}$—that is, $\frac{s_1}{n} = \Omega(\frac{s_2}{n})$. Because $\frac{s_2}{n}$ is $\Omega(\lg n)$, so must be $\frac{s_1}{n}$. Because $\lg n$ is an assessment of the complexity of the worst case, the average case's complexity equals $\Theta(\lg n)$.

There is still one unresolved problem: Is $s_1 \geq s_2$? To determine this, we conjecture that the sum of each pair of terms positioned symmetrically with respect to the center of the sum s_1 is not less than the sum of the corresponding terms of s_2. That is,

$$2^0 \cdot 1 + 2^{\lg n - 1} \lg n \geq 2^0 \frac{\lg n}{2} + 2^{\lg n - 1} \frac{\lg n}{2}$$

$$2^1 \cdot 2 + 2^{\lg n - 2}(\lg n - 1) \geq 2^1 \frac{\lg n}{2} + 2^{\lg n - 2} \frac{\lg n}{2}$$

...

$$2^j(j+1) + 2^{\lg n - 1 - j}(\lg n - j) \geq 2^j \frac{\lg n}{2} + 2^{\lg n - 1 - j} \frac{\lg n}{2}$$

..

where $j \leq \frac{\lg n}{2} - 1$. The last inequality, which represents every other inequality, is transformed into

$$2^{\lg n - 1 - j}\left(\frac{\lg n}{2} - j\right) \geq 2^j\left(\frac{\lg n}{2} - j - 1\right)$$

and then into

$$2^{\lg n - 1 - 2j} \geq \frac{\frac{\lg n}{2} - j - 1}{\frac{\lg n}{2} - j} = 1 - \frac{1}{\frac{\lg n}{2} - j} \tag{2.5}$$

All of these transformations are allowed because all the terms that moved from one side of the conjectured inequality to another are nonnegative and thus do not change the direction of inequality. Is the inequality true? Because $j \leq \frac{\lg n}{2} - 1$, $2^{\lg n - 1 - 2j} \geq 2$, and the right-hand side of the inequality (2.5) is always less than 1, the conjectured inequality is true.

This concludes our investigation of the average case for binary search. The algorithm is relatively straightforward, but the process of finding the complexity for the average case is rather grueling, even for uniform probability distributions. For more complex algorithms, such calculations are significantly more challenging.

◻ 2.9 AMORTIZED COMPLEXITY

In many situations, data structures are subject to a sequence of operations rather than one operation. In this sequence, one operation possibly performs certain modifications that have an impact on the run time of the next operation in the sequence. One way of assessing the worst case run time of the entire sequence is to add worst case efficiencies for each operation. But this may result in an excessively large and unrealistic bound on the actual run time. To be more realistic, amortized analysis can be used to find the average complexity of a worst case sequence of operations. By analyzing sequences of operations rather than isolated operations, amortized analysis takes into account interdependence between operations and their results. For example, if an array is sorted and only a very few new elements are added, then resorting this array should be much faster than sorting it for the first time because, after the new additions, the array is nearly sorted. Thus, it should be quicker to put all elements in perfect order than in a completely disorganized array. Without taking this correlation into account, the run time of the two sorting operations can be considered twice the worst case efficiency. Amortized analysis, on the other hand, decides that the second sorting is hardly applied in the worst case situation so that the combined complexity of the two sorting operations is much less than double the worst case complexity. Consequently, the average for the worst case sequence of sorting, a few insertions, and sorting again is lower according to amortized analysis that according to worst case analysis, which disregards the fact that the second sorting is applied to an array operated on already by a previous sorting.

It is important to stress that amortized analysis is analyzing sequences of operations, or if single operations are analyzed, it is done in view of their being part of the sequence. The cost of operations in the sequence may vary considerably, but how frequently particular operations occur in the sequence is important. For example, for the sequence of operations $op_1, op_2, op_3, \ldots$, the worst case analysis renders the computational complexity for the entire sequence equal to

$$C(op_1, op_2, op_3, \ldots) = C_{worst}(op_1) + C_{worst}(op_2) + C_{worst}(op_3) + \ldots$$

whereas the average complexity determines it to be

$$C(op_1, op_2, op_3, \ldots) = C_{avg}(op_1) + C_{avg}(op_2) + C_{avg}(op_3) + \ldots$$

Although specifying complexities for a sequence of operations, neither worst case analysis nor average case analysis was looking at the position of a particular operation in the sequence. These two analyses considered the operations as executed in isolation and the sequence as a collection of isolated and independent operations. Amortized analysis changes the perspective by looking at what happened up until a particular point in the sequence of operations and then determines the complexity of a particular operation,

$$C(op_1, op_2, op_3, \ldots) = C(op_1) + C(op_2) + C(op_3) + \ldots$$

where C can be the worst, the average, the best case complexity, or very likely, a complexity other than the three depending on what happened before. To find amortized complexity in this way may be, however, too complicated. Therefore, another approach is used. The knowledge of the nature of particular processes and possible changes of a data structure is used to determine the function C which can be applied to each operation of the sequence. The function is chosen in such a manner that it considers quick operations as slower than they really are and time-consuming operations as quicker than they actually are. It is as though the cheap (quick) operations are charged more time units to generate credit to be used for covering the cost of expensive operations that are charged below their real cost. It is like letting the government charge us more for social security than necessary so that at the end of the fiscal year the overpayment can be received back and used to cover the expenses of something else. The art of amortized analysis lies in finding an appropriate function C so that it overcharges cheap operations sufficiently to cover expenses of undercharged operations. The overall balance must be nonnegative. If a debt occurs, there must be a prospect of paying it.

Consider the operation of adding a new element to the vector implemented as a flexible array. The best case is when the size of the vector is less than its capacity because adding a new element amounts to putting it in the first available cell. The cost of adding a new element is thus $O(1)$. The worst case is when size equals capacity, in which case there is no room for new elements. In this case, new space must be allocated, the existing elements are copied to the new space, and only then can the new element be added to the vector. The cost of adding a new element is $O(size(vector))$. It is clear that the latter situation is less frequent than the former, but this depends on another parameter, capacity increment, which refers to how much the vector is increased when overflow occurs. In the extreme case, it can be incremented by just one cell, so in the sequence of m consecutive insertions, each insertion causes overflow and requires $O(size(vector))$ time to finish. Clearly, this situation should be delayed. One solution is to allocate, say, 1 million cells for the vector, which in most cases does not cause an overflow, but the amount of space is excessively large and only a small percentage of space allocated for the vector may be expected to be in actual use. Another solution to the problem is to double the space allocated for the vector if overflow occurs. In this case, the pessimistic $O(size(vector))$ performance of the insertion operation may be expected to occur only infrequently. By using this estimate, it may be claimed that, in the best case, the cost of inserting m items is $O(m)$, but it is impossible to claim that, in the worst case, it is $O(m \cdot size(vector))$. Therefore, to see better what impact this performance has on the sequence of operations, the amortized analysis should be used.

In amortized analysis, the question is asked: What is the expected efficiency of a sequence of insertions? We know that the best case is $O(1)$ and the worst case is $O(size(vector))$, but also we know that the latter case occurs only occasionally and leads to doubling the size of the vector. In which case, what is the expected efficiency of one insertion in the series of insertions? Note that we are interested only in sequences of insertions, excluding deletions and modifications, to have the worst case scenario. The outcome of amortized analysis depends on the assumed amortized cost of one insertion. It is clear that if

$$amCost(push(x)) = 1$$

where 1 represents the cost of one insertion, then we are not gaining anything from this analysis because easy insertions are paying for themselves right away, and the insertions causing overflow and thus copying have no credit to use to make up for their high cost. Is

$$amCost(push(x)) = 2$$

a reasonable choice? Consider the table in Figure 2.6a. It shows the change in vector capacity and the cost of insertion when size grows from 0 to 18; that is, the table indicates the changes in the vector during the sequence of 18 insertions into an initially empty vector. For example, if there are four elements in the vector (size = 4), then before inserting the fifth element, the four elements are copied at the cost of four units and then the new fifth element is inserted in the newly allocated space for the vector. Hence, the cost of the fifth insertion is 4 + 1. But to execute this insertion, two units allocated for the fifth insertion are available plus one unit left from the previous fourth insertion. This means that this operation is two units short to pay for itself. Thus, in the units left column, −2 is entered to indicate the debt of two units. The table indicates that the debt decreases and becomes zero, one cheap insertion away from the next expensive insertion. This means that the operations are almost constantly executed in the red, and more important, if a sequence of operations finishes before the debt is paid off, then the balance indicated by amortized analysis is negative, which is inadmissible in the case of algorithm analysis. Therefore, the next best solution it to assume that

$$amCost(push(x)) = 3$$

The table in Figure 2.6b indicates that we are never in debt and that the choice of three units for amortized cost is not excessive because right after an expensive insertion, the accumulated units are almost depleted.

FIGURE **2.6**

(a) Size	Capacity	Amortized Cost	Cost	Units Left	(b) Size	Capacity	Amortized Cost	Cost	Units Left
0	0				0	0			
1	1	2	0 + 1	1	1	1	3	0 + 1	2
2	2	2	1 + 1	1	2	2	3	1 + 1	3
3	4	2	2 + 1	0	3	4	3	2 + 1	3
4	4	2	1	1	4	4	3	1	5
5	8	2	4 + 1	−2	5	8	3	4 + 1	3
6	8	2	1	−1	6	8	3	1	5
7	8	2	1	0	7	8	3	1	7
8	8	2	1	1	8	8	3	1	9
9	16	2	8 + 1	−6	9	16	3	8 + 1	3
10	16	2	1	−5	10	16	3	1	5
:	:	:	:	:	:	:	:	:	:
16	16	2	1	1	16	16	3	1	17
17	32	2	16 + 1	−14	17	32	3	16 + 1	3
18	32	2	1	−13	18	32	3	1	5
:	:	:	:	:	:	:	:	:	:

In this example, the choice of a constant function for amortized cost is adequate, but usually it is not. Define as *potential* a function that assigns a number to a particular state of a data structure *ds* that is a subject of a sequence of operations. The amortized cost is defined as a function

$$amCost(op_i) = cost(op_i) + potential(ds_i) - potential(ds_{i-1})$$

which is the real cost of executing the operation op_i plus the change in potential in the data structure *ds* as a result of execution of op_i. This definition holds for one single operation of a sequence of *m* operations. If amortized costs for all the operations are added, then the amortized cost for the sequence

$$amCost(op_1, \ldots, op_m) = \sum_{i=1}^{m} (amCost(op_i) + potential(ds_i) - potential(ds_{i-1}))$$

$$= \sum_{i=1}^{m} amCost(op_i) + potential(ds_m) - potential(ds_0)$$

In most cases, the potential function is initially zero and is always nonnegative so that amortized time is an upper bound of real time. This form of amortized cost is used later in the book.

Amortized cost of including new elements in a vector can now be phrased in terms of the new form for the function *amCost*:

$$amCost(push_i()) = \begin{cases} 0 & \text{if } size_i = capacity_i \text{ (vector is full)} \\ 2size_i - capacity_i & \text{otherwise} \end{cases}$$

To see that the function works as intended, consider three cases. The first case is when a cheap pushing follows cheap pushing (vector is not extended right before the current push and is not extended as a consequence of the current push) and

$$amCost(push_i()) = 1 + 2size_{i-1} + 2 - capacity_{i-1} - 2size_{i-1} + capacity_i = 3$$

because the capacity does not change, $size_i = size_{i-1} + 1$, and the actual cost equals 1. For expensive pushing following cheap pushing,

$$amCost(push_i()) = size_{i-1} + 2 + 0 - 2size_{i-1} + capacity_{i-1} = 3$$

because $size_{i-1} + 1 = capacity_{i-1}$ and the actual cost equals $size_i + 1 = size_{i-1} + 2$, which is the cost of copying the vector elements plus adding the new element. For cheap pushing following expensive pushing,

$$amCost(push_i()) = 1 + 2size_i - capacity_i - 0 = 3$$

because $2(size_i - 1) = capacity_i$ and actual cost equals 1. Note that the fourth case, expensive pushing following expensive pushing, occurs only twice, when capacity changes from zero to one and from one to zero. In both cases, amortized cost equals 3.

◨ 2.10 Exercises

1. Explain the meaning of the following expressions:
   a. $f(n)$ is $O(1)$.
   b. $f(n)$ is $\Theta(1)$.
   c. $f(n)$ is $n^{O(1)}$.

2. Assuming that $f_1(n)$ is $O(g_1(n))$ and $f_2(n)$ is $O(g_2(n))$, prove the following statements:
   a. $f_1(n) + f_2(n)$ is $O(\max(g_1(n),g_2(n)))$.
   b. If a number k can be determined such that for all $n > k$, $g_1(n) \le g_2(n)$, then $O(g_1(n)) + O(g_2(n))$ is $O(g_2(n))$.
   c. $f_1(n) * f_2(n)$ is $O(g_1(n) * g_2(n))$ (rule of product).
   d. $O(cg(n))$ is $O(g(n))$.
   e. c is $O(1)$.

3. Prove the following statements:
   a. $\sum_{i=1}^{n} i^2$ is $O(n^3)$ and more generally, $\sum_{i=1}^{n} i^k$ is $O(n^{k+1})$.
   b. $an^k/\lg n$ is $O(n^k)$ but $an^k/\lg n$ is not $\Theta(n^k)$.
   c. $n^{1.1} + n\lg n$ is $\Theta(n^{1.1})$.
   d. 2^n is $O(n!)$ and $n!$ is not $O(2^n)$.
   e. 2^{n+a} is $O(2^n)$.
   f. 2^{2n+a} is not $O(2^n)$.
   g. $2^{\sqrt{\lg n}}$ is $O(n^a)$.

4. Make the same assumptions as in Exercise 2 and, by finding counterexamples, refute the following statements:
   a. $f_1(n) - f_2(n)$ is $O(g_1(n) - g_2(n))$.
   b. $f_1(n)/f_2(n)$ is $O(g_1(n)/g_2(n))$.

5. Find functions f_1 and f_2 such that both $f_1(n)$ and $f_2(n)$ are $O(g(n))$, but $f_1(n)$ is not $O(f_2)$.

6. Is it true that
   a. if $f(n)$ is $\Theta(g(n))$, then $2^{f(n)}$ is $\Theta(2^{g(n)})$?
   b. $f(n) + g(n)$ is $\Theta(\min(f(n),g(n)))$?
   c. 2na is $O(2^n)$?

7. The algorithm presented in this chapter for finding the length of the longest subarray with the numbers in increasing order is inefficient, since there is no need to continue to search for another array if the length already found is greater than the length of the subarray to be analyzed. Thus, if the entire array is already in order, we can

discontinue the search right away, converting the worst case into the best. The change needed is in the outer loop, which now has one more test:

```
for(i = 0, length = 1; i < n-1 && length < n==i; i++)
```

What is the worst case now? Is the efficiency of the worst case still $O(n^2)$?

8. Find the complexity of the function used to find the kth integer in an unordered array of integers

```
int selectkth(int a[], int k, int n) {
    int i, j, mini, tmp;
    for (i = 0; i < k; i++) {
        mini = i;
        for (j = i+1; j < n; j++)
            if (a[j]<a[mini])
                mini = j;
        tmp = a[i];
        a[i] = a[mini];
        a[mini] = tmp;
    }
    return a[k-1];
}
```

9. Determine the complexity of the following implementations of the algorithms for adding, multiplying, and transposing $n \times n$ matrices:

```
for(i = 0; i < n; i++)
    for(j = 0; j < n; j++)
        a[i][j] = b[i][j] + c[i][j];

for(i = 0; i < n; i++)
    for(j = 0; j < n; j++)
        for(k = a[i][j] = 0; k < n; k++)
            a[i][j] += b[i][k] * c[k][j];

for(i = 0; i < n - 1; i++)
    for(j = i+1; j < n; j++) {
        tmp = a[i][j];
        a[i][j] = a[j][i];
        a[j][i] = tmp;
    }
```

10. Find the computational complexity for the following four loops:

    a.
    ```
    for (cnt1 = 0, i = 1; i <= n; i++)
        for (j = 1; j <= n; j++)
            cnt1++;
    ```

b.
```
for (cnt2 = 0, i = 1; i <= n; i++)
    for (j = 1; j <= i; j++)
        cnt2++;
```

c.
```
for (cnt3 = 0, i = 1; i <= n; i *= 2)
    for (j = 1; j <= n; j++)
        cnt3++;
```

d.
```
for (cnt4 = 0, i = 1; i <= n; i *= 2)
    for (j = 1; j <= i; j++)
        cnt4++;
```

11. Find the average case complexity of sequential search in an array if the probability of accessing the last cell equals $\frac{1}{2}$, the probability of the next to last cell equals $\frac{1}{4}$, and the probability of locating a number in any of the remaining cells is the same and equal to $\frac{1}{4(n-2)}$.

12. Consider a process of incrementing a binary n-bit counter. An increment causes some bits to be flipped: Some 0s are changed to 1s, some 1s to 0s. In the best case, counting involves only one bit switch; for example, when 000 is changed to 001, sometimes all the bits are changed, as when incrementing 011 to 100.

Number	Flipped Bits
000	
001	1
010	2
011	1
100	3
101	1
110	2
111	1

Using worst case assessment, we may conclude that the cost of executing $m = 2^n - 1$ increments is $O(mn)$. Use amortized analysis to show that the cost of executing m increments is $O(m)$.

Bibliography

Computational Complexity

Hartmanis, Juris and Hopcroft, John E., "An Overview of the Theory of Computational Complexity," *Journal of the ACM* 18 (1971), 444–475.

Hartmanis, Juris and Stearns, Richard E., "On the Computational Complexity of Algorithms," *Transactions of the American Mathematical Society* 117 (1965), 284–306.

Preparata, Franco P., "Computational Complexity," in Pollack, S. V. (ed.), *Studies in Computer Science*, Washington: The Mathematical Association of America, 1982, 196–228.

Big-O, Ω, and Θ Notations

Brassard, G., "Crusade for a Better Notation," *SIGACT News* 17 (1985), 60–64.

Knuth, Donald, *The Art of Computer Programming, Vol. 2: Seminumerical Algorithms*, Reading, MA: Addison-Wesley, 1998.

Knuth, Donald, "Big Omicron and Big Omega and Big Theta," *SIGACT News*, April–June, 8 (1976), 18–24.

Vitanyi, P. M. B. and Meertens, L., "Big Omega versus the Wild Functions," *SIGACT News* 16 (1985), 56–59.

OO Notation

Manber, Udi, *Introduction to Algorithms: A Creative Approach*, Reading, MA: Addison-Wesley, 1989.

Amortized Analysis

Heileman, Gregory L., *Discrete Structures, Algorithms, and Object-Oriented Programming*, New York: McGraw-Hill, 1996, Chs. 10–11.

Tarjan, Robert E., "Amortized Computational Complexity," *SIAM Journal on Algebraic and Discrete Methods* 6 (1985), 306–318.

Linked Lists

An array is a very useful data structure provided in programming languages. However, it has at least two limitations: (1) changing the size of the array requires creating a new array and then copying all data from the array with the old size to the array with the new size and (2) the data in the array are next to each other sequentially in memory, which means that inserting an item inside the array requires shifting some other data in this array. This limitation can be overcome by using *linked structures*. A linked structure is a collection of nodes storing data and links to other nodes. In this way, nodes can be located anywhere in memory, and passing from one node of the linked structure to another is accomplished by storing the reference(s) to other node(s) in the structure. Although linked structures can be implemented in a variety of ways, the most flexible implementation is by using a separate object for each node.

3.1 SINGLY LINKED LISTS

If a node contains a data field that is a reference to another node, then many nodes can be strung together using only one variable to access the entire sequence of nodes. Such a sequence of nodes is the most frequently used implementation of a *linked list*, which is a data structure composed of nodes, each node holding some information and a reference to another node in the list. If a node has a link only to its successor in this sequence, the list is called a *singly linked list*. An example of such a list is shown in Figure 3.1. Note that only one variable p is used to access any node in the list. The last node on the list can be recognized by the null reference field.

FIGURE **3.1** A singly linked list.

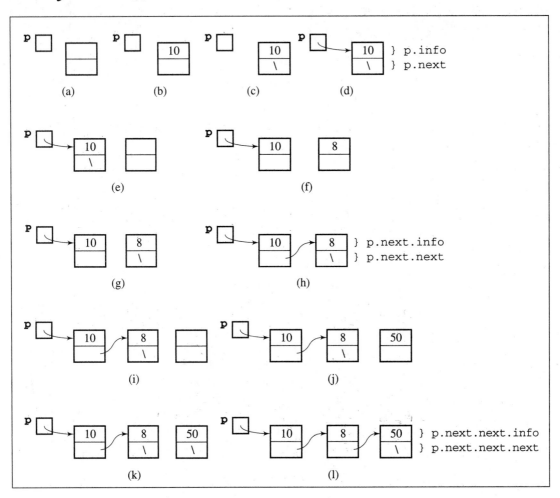

(a)   (b)   (c)   (d)

(e)   (f)

(g)   (h)

(i)   (j)

(k)   (l)

Each node in the list in Figure 3.1 is an instance of the following class definition:

```
public class IntNode {
    public int info;
    public IntNode next;
    public IntNode(int i) {
        this(i,null);
    }
    public IntNode(int i, IntNode n) {
        info = i; next = n;
    }
}
```

A node includes two data fields: `info` and `next`. The `info` field is used to store information, and this field is important to the user. The `next` field is used to link together nodes to form a linked list. It is an auxiliary field used to maintain the linked list. It is indispensable for implementation of the linked list but less important (if at all) from the user's perspective. Note that `IntNode` is defined in terms of itself because one data field, `next`, is a reference to a node of the same type that is just being defined. This circularity, however, is permitted in Java.

The definition of a node also includes two constructors. The second constructor takes two arguments, one to initialize the `info` field and another to initialize the `next` field. The first constructor takes one argument and is defined in terms of the second constructor. The reserved word `this` is used to refer to the current object, and this word can appear anywhere this object can be used. Therefore, `this(i,null)` means the same as `IntNode(i,null)`; that is, the first constructor invokes the second constructor by having `null` as the value of the second argument. As the result of executing the first constructor, the `info` field is initialized to `i` and the `next` field to `null`.

Now, let us create the linked list in Figure 3.1l. One way to create this three-node linked list is to first generate the node containing number 10, then the node containing 8, and finally the node containing 50. Each node has to be initialized properly and incorporated into the list. To see it, each step is illustrated in Figure 3.1 separately.

First, we execute the declaration and assignment

```
IntNode p = new IntNode(10);
```

which creates the first node on the list and makes the variable p a reference to this node. This is done in four steps. In the first step, a new `IntNode` is created (Figure 3.1a), in the second step, the `info` field of this node is set to 10 (Figure 3.1b), and in the third step, the node's `next` field is set to `null` (Figure 3.1c). The null reference is marked with a slash in the reference field. Note that the slash in the `next` field is not a slash character. That is, the second and third steps—initialization of fields of the new `IntNode`—are performed by invoking the constructor `IntNode(10)`, which in turn invokes the constructor `IntNode(10,null)`. The fourth step is making p a reference to the newly created node (Figure 3.1d). This reference is the address of the node, and it is shown as an arrow from the variable p to the new node.

The second node is created with the assignment

```
p.next = new IntNode(8);
```

where `p.next` is the `next` field of the node pointed by p (Figure 3.1d). As before, four steps are executed:

1. creating a new node (Figure 3.1e),

2. assigning by the constructor number 8 to the `info` field of this node (Figure 3.1f) and

3. `null` to its `next` field (Figure 3.1g), and finally

4. including the new node in the list by making the `next` field of the first node a reference to the new node (Figure 3.1h).

The linked list is now extended by adding a third node with the assignment

```
p.next.next = new IntNode(50);
```

where p.next.next is the next field of the second node. This cumbersome notation has to be used because the list is accessible only through the variable p.

In processing the third node, four steps are also executed: creating the node (Figure 3.1i), initializing its two fields (Figure 3.1j–k), and then incorporating the node in the list (Figure 3.1l).

Our linked list example illustrates a certain inconvenience in using references: The longer the linked list, the longer the chain of nexts to access the nodes at the end of the list. In this example, p.next.next.next allows us to access the next field of the 3rd node on the list. But what if it were the 103rd or, worse, the 1003rd node on the list? Typing 1003 nexts, as in p.next ... next, would be daunting. If we missed one next in this chain, then a wrong assignment is made. Also, the flexibility of using linked lists is diminished. Therefore, other ways of accessing nodes in linked lists are needed. One way is always to keep two references to the linked list: one to the first node and one to the last, as shown in Figure 3.2.

FIGURE **3.2**   An implementation of a singly linked list of integers.

```
//*********************  IntNode.java  *************************
//          a node in an integer singly linked list class

public class IntNode {
    public int info;
    public IntNode next;
    public IntNode(int i) {
        this(i,null);
    }
    public IntNode(int i, IntNode n) {
        info = i; next = n;
    }
}


//*********************  IntSLList.java  ************************
//          singly linked list class to store integers

public class IntSLList {
    private IntNode head, tail;
    public IntSLList() {
        head = tail = null;
    }
    public boolean isEmpty() {
        return head == null;
    }
```

FIGURE **3.2**   (*continued*)

```
    public void addToHead(int el) {
        head = new IntNode(el,head);
        if (tail == null)
            tail = head;
    }
    public void addToTail(int el) {
        if (!isEmpty()) {
            tail.next = new IntNode(el);
            tail = tail.next;
        }
        else head = tail = new IntNode(el);
    }
    public int deleteFromHead() { // delete the head and return its info;
        int el = head.info;
        if (head == tail)    // if only one node on the list;
            head = tail = null;
        else head = head.next;
        return el;
    }
    public int deleteFromTail() { // delete the tail and return its info;
        int el = tail.info;
        if (head == tail)    // if only one node on the list;
            head = tail = null;
        else {                    // if more than one node on the list,
            IntNode tmp;    // find the predecessor of tail;
            for (tmp = head; tmp.next != tail; tmp = tmp.next);
            tail = tmp;       // the predecessor of tail becomes tail;
            tail.next = null;
        }
        return el;
    }
    public void printAll() {
        for (IntNode tmp = head; tmp != null; tmp = tmp.next)
            System.out.print(tmp.info + " ");
    }
    public boolean isInList(int el) {
        IntNode tmp;
        for (tmp = head; tmp != null && tmp.info != el; tmp = tmp.next);
        return tmp != null;
    }
```

Continues

FIGURE **3.2** (*continued*)

```
public void delete(int el) {  // delete the node with an element el;
    if (!isEmpty())
        if (head == tail && el == head.info) // if only one
            head = tail = null;               // node on the list;
        else if (el == head.info) // if more than one node on the
            head = head.next;     // list; and el is in the head node;
        else {                    // if more than one node in the list
            IntNode pred, tmp;    // and el is in a non-head node;
            for (pred = head, tmp = head.next;
                 tmp != null && tmp.info != el;
                 pred = pred.next, tmp = tmp.next);
            if (tmp != null) {    // if el was found;
                pred.next = tmp.next;
                if (tmp == tail) // if el is in the last node;
                    tail = pred;
            }
        }
}
```

FIGURE **3.3** A singly linked list of integers.

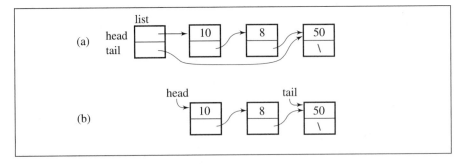

A singly linked list implementation in Figure 3.2 uses two classes: one class, IntNode, for nodes of the list, and another, IntSLList, for access to the list. The class IntSLList defines two data fields, head and tail, which are references to the first and the last nodes of a list. An example of a list is shown in Figure 3.3. The list is declared with the statement

```
IntSLList list = new IntSLList();
```

FIGURE **3.4**   Inserting a new node at the beginning of a singly linked list.

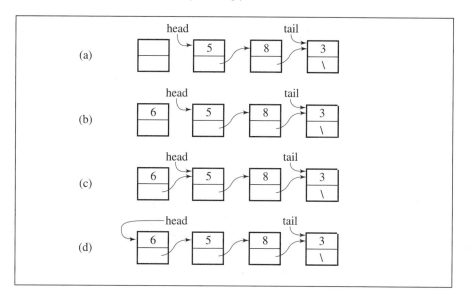

The first object in Figure 3.3a is not part of the list; it allows for having access to the list. For simplicity, in subsequent figures, only nodes belonging to the list are shown, the access node is omitted, and the head and tail fields are marked as in Figure 3.3b.

Besides the head and tail fields, the class IntSLList also defines methods that allow us to manipulate the lists. We now look more closely at some basic operations on linked lists presented in Figure 3.2.

3.1.1 Insertion

Adding a node at the beginning of a linked list is performed in four steps.

1. An empty node is created. It is empty in the sense that the program performing insertion does not assign any values to the fields of the node (Figure 3.4a).

2. The node's info field is initialized to a particular integer (Figure 3.4b).

3. Because the node is being included at the front of the list, the next field becomes a reference to the first node on the list, that is, the current value of head (Figure 3.4c).

4. The new node precedes all the nodes on the list, but this fact has to be reflected in the value of head; otherwise, the new node is not accessible. Therefore, head is updated to become the reference to the new node (Figure 3.4d).

The four steps are executed by the method addToHead() (Figure 3.2). The method executes the first three steps indirectly by calling the constructor Node(el,head). The last step is executed directly in the method by assigning the address (reference) of the newly created node to head.

FIGURE 3.5   Inserting a new node at the end of a singly linked list.

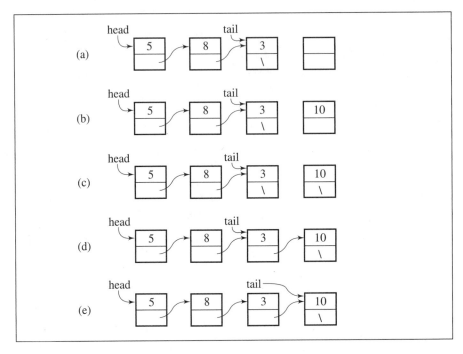

The method `addToHead()` singles out one special case, namely, inserting a new node in an empty linked list. In an empty linked list, both `head` and `tail` are null; therefore, both become references to the only node of the new list. When inserting in a nonempty list, only `head` needs to be updated.

The process of adding a new node to the end of the list has five steps.

1. An empty node is created (Figure 3.5a).

2. The node's `info` field is initialized to an integer `el` (Figure 3.5b).

3. Because the node is being included at the end of the list, the `next` field is set to null (Figure 3.5c).

4. The node is now included in the list by making the next field of the last node of the list a reference to the newly created node (Figure 3.5d).

5. The new node follows all the nodes of the list, but this fact has to be reflected in the value of `tail`, which now becomes the reference to the new node (Figure 3.5e).

All these steps are executed in the `if` clause of the `addToTail()` method (Figure 3.2). The `else` clause of this method is executed only if the linked list is empty. If this case were not included, the program would crash because in the `if` clause we make an assignment to the `next` field of the node referred by `tail`. In the case of an empty linked list, it is a reference to a nonexisting field of a nonexisting node, which leads to raising the `NullPointerException`.

FIGURE **3.6**   Deleting a node from at the beginning of a singly linked list.

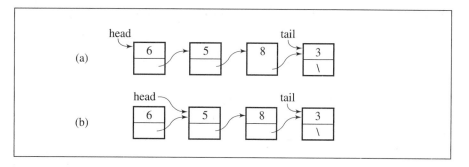

The process of inserting a new node at the beginning of the list is very similar to the process of inserting a node at the end of the list. This is so because the implementation of `IntSLList` uses two reference fields: `head` and `tail`. For this reason, both `addtoHead()` and `addToTail()` can be executed in constant time $O(1)$; that is, regardless of the number of nodes in the list, the number of operations performed by these two methods does not exceed some constant number c. Note that because the `head` reference allows us to have access to a linked list, the `tail` reference is not indispensable; its only role is to have immediate access to the last node of the list. With this access, a new node can be easily added at the end of the list. But as illustrated by a linked list implementation of `SLList` in Figure 3.9, the tail reference does not have to be used. In this case, adding a node at the end of the list is more complicated because we first have to reach the last node in order to attach a new node to it. This requires scanning the list and requires $O(n)$ steps to finish; that is, it is linearly proportional to the length of the list. The process of scanning lists is illustrated when discussing deletion of the last node.

3.1.2 Deletion

One deletion operation consists in deleting a node at the beginning of the list and returning the value stored in it. This operation is implemented by the method `delete-FromHead()`. In this operation the information from the first node is temporarily stored in a local variable `el`, and then `head` is reset so what was the second node becomes the first node. In this way, the former first `node` is abandoned to be processed later by the garbage collector (Figure 3.6). Note that the former first node still accesses the linked list, but the node itself is inaccessible. Thus, it is considered nonexistent. Because the head node is immediately accessible, `deleteFromHead()` takes constant time $O(1)$ to perform its task.

Unlike before, there are now two special cases to consider. One case is when we attempt to remove a node from an empty linked list. If such an attempt is made, the program crashes because of the `NullPointerException`, which we don't want to happen. The caller should also know that such an attempt was made to perform certain action. After all, if the caller expects a number to be returned from the call to deleteFromHead() and no number can be returned, then the caller may be unable to accomplish some other operations.

There are at least two ways of solving the problem. One solution is to use the throws clause as in

```
public int deleteFromHead() throws NullPointerException {
    . . . . . . . . . .
}
```

The throws clause is expected to have a matching try-catch clause in the caller (or caller's caller, etc.) catches the exception as in:

```
void f() {
    . . . . . . . . .
    try {
        n = list.deleteFromHead();
    } catch (NullPointerException npe) {
        System.out.println("Empty list");
    . . . . . . . . .
}
```

This solution gives the caller a control over the abnormal situation without making it lethal to the program. The user is responsible for providing an exception handler in the form of the try-catch clause, with the solution appropriate in the particular case. If the clause is not provided, then the program crashes when the exception is thrown. The method f() may only print a message that a list is empty when an attempt is made to delete a number from an empty list, another method g() may assign a certain value for n in such a case, and yet another method h() may find such a situation detrimental to the program and abort the program altogether.

The idea that the user is responsible for providing an action in the case of an exception is also presumed in the implementation given in Figure 3.2. The method assumes that the list is not empty. To prevent the program from crashing, the method isEmpty() is added to the IntSLList class, and the user should use it as in:

```
if (!list.isEmpty())
    n = list.deleteFromHead();
else do not remove;
```

Note that including a similar if statement in deleteFromHead() does not solve the problem. Consider this code:

```
public int deleteFromHead() {
    if (!isEmpty()) {              // if non-empty list;
        int el = head.info;
        . . . . . . . . .
        return el;
    }
    else return 0;
}
```

FIGURE **3.7**   Deleting a node from the end of a singly linked list.

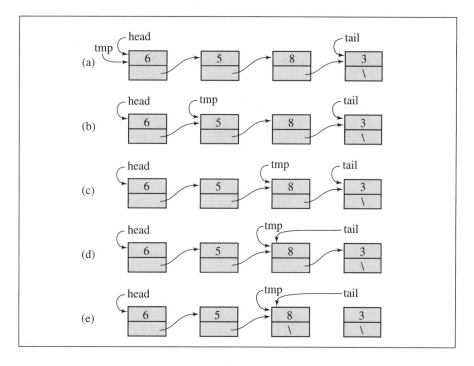

If an `if` statement is added, then the `else` clause must also be added; otherwise, the program does not compile because "return required at end of int deleteFromHead()." But now, if 0 is returned, the caller does not know whether the returned 0 is the sign of failure or if it is a literal 0 retrieved from the list. To avoid any confusion, the caller must use an `if` statement to test whether the list is empty before calling `deleteFromHead()`. In this way, one `if` statement would be redundant.

The second special case in `deleteFromHead()` is when the list has only one node to be removed. In this case, the list becomes empty, which requires setting `head` and `tail` to null.

The second deletion operation consists in deleting a node from the end of the list, and it is implemented as a method `deleteFromTail()`. The problem is that after removing a node, `tail` should refer to the new tail of the list; that is, `tail` has to be moved backward by one node. But moving backward is impossible because there is no direct link from the last node to its predecessor. Hence, this predecessor has to be found by searching from the beginning of the list and stopping right before `tail`. This is accomplished with a temporary variable `tmp` used to scan the list within the `for` loop. The variable `tmp` is initialized to the head of the list, and then in each iteration of the loop, it is advanced to the next node. If the list is as in Figure 3.7a, then `tmp` first refers to the head node holding number 6; after executing the assignment `tmp = tmp.next`, `tmp` refers to the second node (Figure 3.7b). After the second iteration and executing the same assignment, `tmp` refers to the third node (Figure 3.7c). Because this node is also the next to last node, the loop is exited, after which `tail` becomes the reference to the next to last node (Figure 3.7d), and then the `next` field of this node is set to null (Figure 3.7e). After the last assignment, what was the last node is now detached from the list and inaccessible from it. In due course, this node is claimed by the garbage collector.

Note that in the `for` loop, a temporary variable was used to scan the list. If the loop were simplified to

```
for ( ; head.next != tail; head = head.next);
```

then the list is scanned only once, and the access to the beginning of the list is lost because `head` was permanently updated to the next to last node, which is about to become the last node. It is absolutely critical that, in cases such as this, a temporary variable is used so that the access to the beginning of the list is kept intact.

In removing the last node, the two special cases are the same as in `deleteFrom-Head()`. If the list is empty, then nothing can be removed, but what should be done in this case is decided in the user program just as in the case `deleteFromHead()`. The second case is when a single-node list becomes empty after removing its only node, which also requires setting `head` and `tail` to null.

The most time-consuming part in `deleteFromTail()` is finding the next to last node performed by the `for` loop. It is clear that the loop performs $n - 1$ iterations in a list of n nodes, which is the main reason this method takes $O(n)$ time to delete the last node.

The two discussed deletion operations remove a node from the head or from the tail (that is, always from the same position) and return an integer that happens to be in the node being removed. A different approach is when we want to delete a node that holds a particular integer regardless of the position of this node in the list. It may be right at the beginning, at the end, or anywhere inside the list. Briefly, a node has to be located first and then detached from the list by linking the predecessor of this node directly to its successor. Because we do not know where the node may be, the process of finding and deleting a node with a certain integer is much more complex than the deletion operations discussed so far. The method `delete()` (Figure 3.2) is an implementation of this process.

A node is removed from inside a list by linking its predecessor to its successor. But because the list has only forward links, the predecessor of a node is not reachable from the node. One way to accomplish the task is to find the node to be removed, first by scanning the list and then scanning it again to find its predecessor. Another way is presented in `delete()`, as shown in Figure 3.8. Assume that we want to delete a node that holds number 8. The method uses two reference variables, `pred` and `tmp`, which are initialized in the `for` loop so that they point to the first and second nodes of the list, respectively (Figure 3.8a). Because the node `tmp` has number 5, the first iteration is executed in which both `pred` and `tmp` are advanced to the next nodes (Figure 3.8b). Because the condition of the `for` loop is now true (`tmp` points to the node with 8), the loop is exited and an assignment `pred.next = tmp.next` is executed (Figure

FIGURE **3.8**   Deleting a node from a singly linked list.

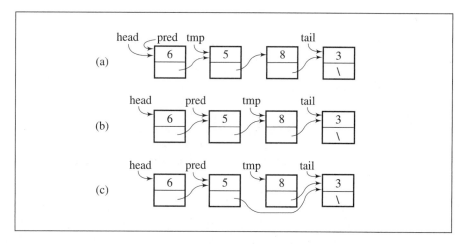

3.8c). This assignment effectively excludes the node with 8 from the list. Although the node is still accessible from variable `tmp`, it will not be accessible after the method `delete()` is exited because `tmp` is local to the method. Hence, it ceases to exist after exiting this method. As before, the now inaccessible node with number 8 will be processed by the garbage collector.

The preceding paragraph discussed only one case. Here are the remaining cases:

1. An attempt to remove a node from an empty list, in which case the method is immediately exited.

2. Deleting the only node from a one-node linked list: Both `head` and `tail` are set to null.

3. Removing the first node of the list with at least two nodes, which requires updating `head`.

4. Removing the last node of the list with at least two nodes, leading to the update of `tail`.

5. An attempt to delete a node with a number that is not in the list: Do nothing.

It is clear that the best case for `delete()` is when the head node is to be deleted, which takes $O(1)$ time to accomplish. The worst case is when the last node needs to be deleted, which reduces `delete()` to `deleteFromTail()` and to its $O(n)$ performance. What is the average case? It depends on how many iterations the `for` loop executes. Assuming that any node on the list has an equal chance to be deleted, the loop performs no iteration if it is the first node, one iteration if it is the second node, . . . , and finally $n - 1$ iterations if it is the last node. For a long sequence of deletions, one deletion requires on the average

$$\frac{0+1+\ldots+(n-1)}{n} = \frac{\frac{(n-1)n}{2}}{n} = \frac{n-1}{2}$$

That is, on the average, delete() executes $O(n)$ steps to finish, just like in the worst case.

3.1.3 Search

The insertion and deletion operations modify linked lists. The searching operation scans an existing list to learn whether or not a number is in it. We implement this operation with the Boolean method isInList(). The method uses a temporary variable tmp to go through the list starting from the head node. The number stored in each node is compared to the number being sought, and if the two numbers are equal, the loop is exited; otherwise, tmp is updated to tmp.next so that the next node can be investigated. After reaching the last node and executing the assignment tmp = tmp.next, tmp becomes null, which is used as an indication that the number el is not in the list. That is, if tmp is not null, the search was discontinued somewhere inside the list because el was found. That is why isInList() returns the result of comparison tmp != 0: If tmp is not null, el was found and true is returned. If tmp is null, the search was unsuccessful and false is returned.

With reasoning very similar to that used to determine the efficiency of delete(), isInList() takes $O(1)$ time in the best case and $O(n)$ in the worst and average cases.

In the foregoing discussion, the operations on nodes have been stressed. However, a linked list is built for the sake of storing and processing information, not for the sake of itself. Therefore, the approach used in this section is limited in that the list can only store integers. If we wanted a linked list for float numbers or arrays of numbers, then a new class has to be declared with a new set of methods, all of them resembling the ones discussed here. However, it is more advantageous to declare such a class only once without deciding in advance what type of data will be stored in it. One solution is to declare the info field as Object. This is an adequate solution if the linked list is used for the type of storage and retrieval operations that are position oriented: insert at the beginning or retrieve from the end. But for the method delete(), which first relies on finding a node with specific information or for such operations as retrieving the largest element, inserting the information in ascending order, or just finding a particular piece of information in the list, the type Object does not allow us to do it for the reasons indicated in Section 1.4: Comparison amounts to comparing references to data, not the data themselves. Hence, the desired comparison methods have to be defined each time a linked list is accommodated to storing a particular data type. This way of defining generic linked lists is shown in Figure 3.9. For the rest of the chapter, linked lists of integers are used to simplify coding and to show clearly the linked list's operations.

FIGURE **3.9**   Implementation of a generic singly linked list.

```java
//********************* SLLNode.java *****************************

public class SLLNode {
    public Object info;
    public SLLNode next;
    public SLLNode() {
        next = null;
    }
    public SLLNode(Object el) {
        info = el; next = null;
    }
    public SLLNode(Object el, SLLNode ptr) {
        info = el; next = ptr;
    }
}

/********************* SLLList.java *************************
 *       generic singly linked list class with head only
 */

public class SLLList {
    protected SLLNode head = null;
    public SLLList() {
    }
    public boolean isEmpty() {
        return head == null;
    }
    public Object first() {
        return head.info;
    }
    public void printAll(java.io.PrintStream out) {
        for (SLLNode tmp = head; tmp != null; tmp = tmp.next)
            out.print(tmp.info.toString());
    }
    public void add(Object el) {
        head = new SLLNode(el,head);
    }
    public Object find(Object el) {
        SLLNode tmp = head;
```

Continues

FIGURE **3.9**   (*continued*)

```
            for ( ; tmp != null && !el.equals(tmp.info); tmp = tmp.next);
            if (tmp == null)
                return null;
            else return tmp.info;
        }
    public Object deleteHead() { // remove the head and return its info;
        Object el = head.info;
        head = head.next;
        return el;
    }
    public void delete(Object el) {     // find and remove el;
        if (head != null)              // if non-empty list;
            if (el.equals(head.info)) // if head needs to be removed;
                head = head.next;
            else {
                SLLNode pred = head, tmp = head.next;
                for ( ; tmp != null && !(tmp.info.equals(el));
                        pred = pred.next, tmp = tmp.next);
                if (tmp != null)       // if found
                    pred.next = tmp.next;
            }
    }
}
```

◻ 3.2 DOUBLY LINKED LISTS

The method deleteFromTail() indicates a problem inherent to singly linked lists. The nodes in such lists contain only references to the successors; therefore, there is no immediate access to the predecessors. For this reason, deleteFromTail() was implemented with a loop which allowed us to find the predecessor of tail. Although this predecessor is, so to speak, within sight, it is out of reach. We have to scan the entire list to stop right in front of tail to delete it. For long lists and for frequent executions of deleteFromTail(), this may be an impediment to swift list processing. To avoid this problem, the linked list is redefined so that each node in the list has two reference fields, one to the successor and one to the predecessor. A list of this type is called a *doubly linked list* and is illustrated in Figure 3.10. An implementation of a doubly linked list of integers is shown in Figure 3.11.

FIGURE **3.10**   A doubly linked list.

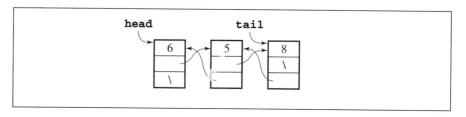

Methods for processing doubly linked lists are slightly more complicated than their singly linked lists counterparts because there is one more reference field to be maintained. Only two methods are discussed: a method to insert a node at the end of a doubly linked list and a method to remove a node from the end (Figure 3.11).

To add a node to a list, the node has to be created, its fields properly initialized, and then the node needs to be incorporated into the list. Inserting a node at the end of a doubly linked list is illustrated in Figure 3.12. The process is performed in six steps:

1. A new node is created (Figure 3.12a) and then its three fields are initialized:

2. the `info` field to the number `el` being inserted (Figure 3.12b),

3. the `next` field to null (Figure 3.12c),

4. and the `prev` field to the value of `tail` so that this field points to the last node in the list (Figure 3.12d). But now, the new node should become the last node; therefore,

5. `tail` is set to reference the new node (Figure 3.12e). But the new node is not yet accessible from its predecessor; to rectify this,

6. the `next` field of the predecessor is set to reference the new node (Figure 3.12f).

A special case concerns the last step. It is assumed in this step that the newly created node has a predecessor, so it accesses its `prev` field. It should be obvious that for an empty linked list, the new node is the only node in the list and that it has no predecessor. In this case, both `head` and `tail` refer to this node, and the sixth step is now setting `head` to refer to this node. Note that step four—setting the `prev` field to the value of `tail`—is executed properly because for an initially empty list, `tail` is null. Thus, null becomes the value of the `prev` field of the new node.

Deleting the last node from the doubly linked list is straightforward because there is direct access from the last node to its predecessor and no loop is needed to remove the last node. When deleting a node from the list in Figure 3.13a, temporary variable `el` is set to the value in the last node, then tail is set to its predecessor (Figure 3.13b), and the last node is cut off from the list by setting the `next` field of the next to last node to null. In this way, the next to last node becomes the last node, and the formerly last node is abandoned (Figure 3.13c). Although this node accesses the list, the node is inaccessible from the list. Hence, it will be claimed by the garbage collector. The last step is returning the value stored in the removed node.

FIGURE **3.11**   An implementation of a doubly linked list.

```
/*********************** IntDLLNode.java ***************************/

public class IntDLLNode {
    public int info;
    public IntDLLNode next, prev;
    public IntDLLNode(int el) {
        this(el,null,null);
    }
    public IntDLLNode(int el, IntDLLNode n, IntDLLNode p) {
        info = el; next = n; prev = p;
    }
}

/*********************** IntDLLList.java ***************************/

public class IntDLLList {
    private IntDLLNode head, tail;
    public IntDLLList() {
        head = tail = null;
    }
    public boolean isEmpty() {
        return head == null;
    }
    public void addToTail(int el) {
        if (!isEmpty()) {
            tail = new IntDLLNode(el,null,tail);
            tail.prev.next = tail;
        }
        else head = tail = new IntDLLNode(el);
    }
    public int removeFromTail() {
        int el = tail.info;
        if (head == tail)   // if only one node in the list;
            head = tail = null;
        else {                    // if more than one node in the list;
            tail = tail.prev;
            tail.next = null;
        }
        return el;
    }
    . . . . . . . . . .
}
```

FIGURE **3.12**   Adding a new node at the end of a doubly linked list.

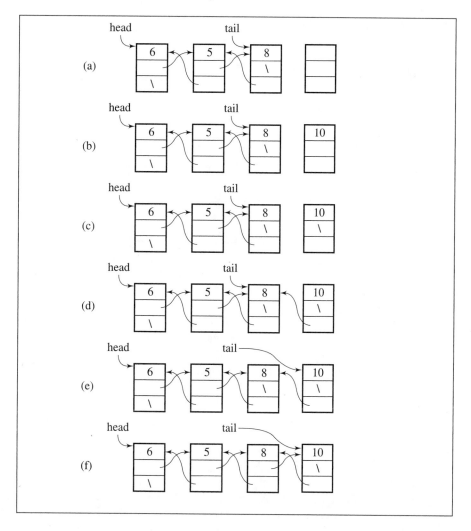

An attempt to delete a node from an empty list may result in a program crash. Therefore, the user has to check whether the list is not empty before making an attempt of deleting the last node from it to extract information from the node. As for singly linked list's `deleteFromHead()`, the caller should have an `if` statement

```
if (!list.isEmpty())
    n = list.deleteFromTail();
else  do not remove;
```

The second special case is the deletion of the only node from a single-node linked list. In this case, both `head` and `tail` are set to null.

FIGURE **3.13**   Deleting a node from the end of a doubly linked list.

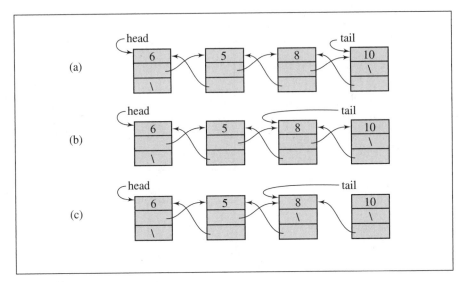

Because of the immediate accessibility of the last node, both `addToTail()` and `deleteFromTail()` execute in constant time $O(1)$.

Methods for operating at the beginning of the doubly linked list are easily obtained from the two methods just discussed by changing `head` to `tail` and vice versa, changing `next` to `prev` and vice versa, and exchanging the order of parameters when executing `new`.

⌐   3.3 CIRCULAR LISTS

In some situations, a *circular list* is needed in which nodes form a ring: The list is finite and each node has a successor. An example of such a situation is when several processes are using the same resource for the same amount of time, and we have to assure that no process accesses the resource before all other processes did. Therefore, all processes—let their numbers be 6, 5, 8, and 10 as in Figure 3.14—are put on a circular list accessible through `current`. After one node of the list is accessed and the process number is retrieved from the node to activate this process, `current` moves to the next node so that the next process can be activated the next time.

In an implementation of a circular singly linked list, we can use only one permanent reference, `tail`, to the list even though operations on the list require access to the tail and its predecessor, the head. To that end, a linear singly linked list discussed in Section 3.1 uses two permanent references, `head` and `tail`.

Figure 3.15a shows a sequence of insertions at the front of the circular list, and Figure 3.15b illustrates insertions at the end of the list. As an example of a method

FIGURE **3.14**   A circular singly linked list.

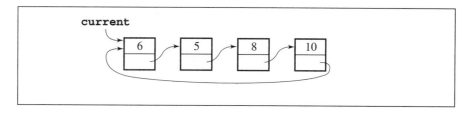

FIGURE **3.15**   Inserting nodes at the front of circular singly linked list (a) and at its end (b).

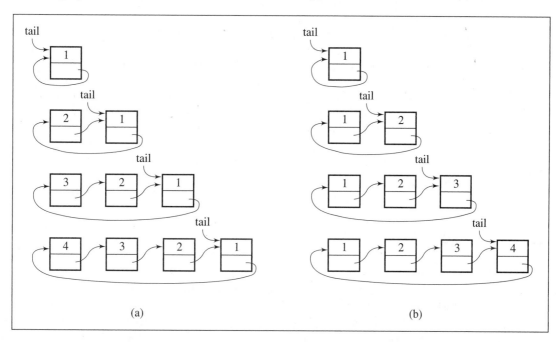

operating on such a list, we present a method to insert a node at the tail of a circular singly linked list:

```
public void addToTail(int el) {
    if (isEmpty()) {
        tail = new IntNode(el);
        tail.next = tail;
    }
    else {
        tail.next = new IntNode(el,tail.next);
        tail = tail.next;
    }
}
```

FIGURE **3.16**   A circular doubly linked list.

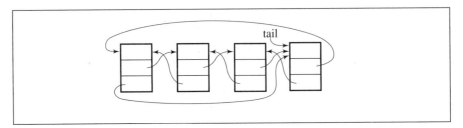

The implementation just presented is not without its problems. A method for deletion of the tail node requires a loop so that `tail` can be set after deletion to its predecessor. This makes this method delete the tail node in $O(n)$ time. Moreover, processing data in the reverse order (printing, searching, etc.) is not very efficient. To avoid the problem and still be able to insert and delete nodes at the front and at the end of the list without using a loop, a doubly linked circular list can be used. The list forms two rings: one going forward through `next` fields and one going backward through `prev` fields. Figure 3.16 illustrates such a list accessible through the last node. Deleting the node from the end of the list can be done easily because there is direct access to the next to last node that needs to be updated in the case of such a deletion. In this list, both insertion and deletion of the tail node can be done in $O(1)$ time.

⏏ 3.4 SKIP LISTS

Linked lists have one serious drawback: They require sequential scanning to locate an element searched for. The search starts from the beginning of the list and stops when either an element searched for is found or the end of the list is reached without finding this element. Ordering elements on the list can speed up searching, but sequential search is still required. Therefore, we may think about lists which allow for skipping certain nodes to avoid sequential processing. A *skip list* is an interesting variant of the ordered linked list which makes such a nonsequential search possible (Pugh 1990).

In a skip list of n nodes, for each k and i such that $1 \leq k \leq \lfloor \lg n \rfloor$ and $1 \leq i \leq \lfloor n/2^{k-1} \rfloor - 1$, the node in position $2^{k-1} \cdot i$ points to the node in position $2^{k-1} \cdot (i + 1)$. This means that every second node points to the node two positions ahead, every fourth node points to the node four positions ahead, and so on, as shown in Figure 3.17a. This is accomplished by having different numbers of reference fields in nodes on the list: Half of the nodes have just one reference field, one-fourth of the nodes have two reference fields, one-eighth of the nodes have three reference fields, and so on. The number of reference fields indicates the *level* of each node, and the number of levels is $maxLevel = \lfloor \lg n \rfloor + 1$.

FIGURE **3.17**   A skip list with (a) evenly and (b) unevenly spaced nodes of different levels; (c) the skip list with reference nodes clearly shown.

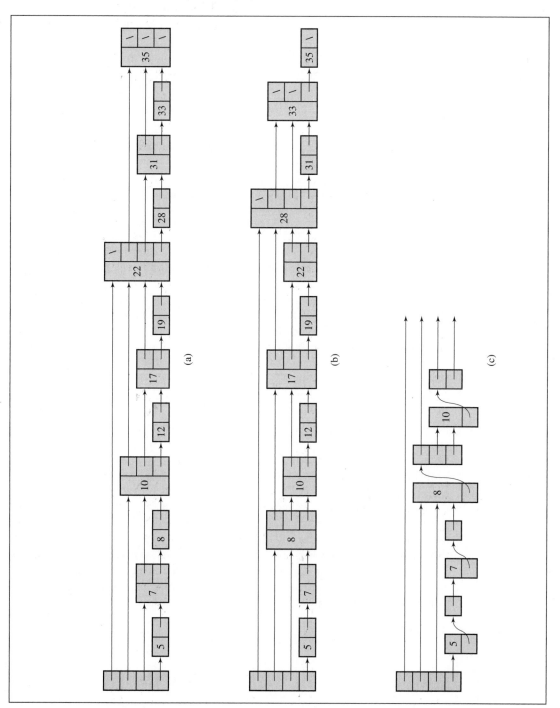

Searching for an element *el* consists of following the references on the highest level until an element is found which finishes the search successfully. In the case of reaching the end of the list or encountering an element *key* that is greater than *el,* the search is restarted from the node preceding the one containing *key,* but this time staring from a reference on a lower level than before. The search continues until *el* is found, or the first-level references are followed to reach the end of the list or to find an element greater than *el.* Here is a pseudocode for this algorithm:

```
find(element el)
    p = the nonnull list on the highest level i;
        while el not found and i >= 0
            if p.key < el
                p = a sublist that begins in the predecessor of p on level --i;
            else if p.key > el
                if p is the last node on level i
                    p = a nonnull sublist that begins in p on the highest level < i;
                    i = the number of the new level;
                else p = p.next;
```

For example, if we look for number 16 in the list in Figure 3.17b, then level four is tried first, which is unsuccessful because the first node on this level has 28. Next, we try the third-level sublist starting from the root: It first leads to 8 and then to 17. Hence, we try the second-level sublist that originates in the node holding 8: It leads to 10 and then again to 17. The last try is by starting the first-level sublist which begins in node 10; this sublist's first node has 12, the next number is 17, and since there is no lower level, the search is pronounced unsuccessful. The path through which the list passed during this searching process is indicated in Figure 3.17c with a dashed line. Code for the searching method is given in Figure 3.18.

Searching appears to be efficient. However, the design of skip lists can lead to very inefficient insertion and deletion procedures. To insert a new element, all nodes following the node just inserted have to be restructured; the number of reference fields and the value of references have to be changed. In order to retain some of the advantages which skip lists offer with respect to searching and to avoid problems with restructuring the lists when inserting and deleting nodes, the requirement on the positions of nodes of different levels is now abandoned and only the requirement on the number of nodes of different levels is kept. For example, the list in Figure 3.17a becomes the list in Figure 3.17b: Both lists have six nodes in level one (with one reference field), three nodes in level two, two nodes in level three, and one node in level four. The new list is searched exactly the same way as the original list. Inserting does not require list restructuring, and nodes are generated so that the distribution of the nodes on different levels is kept adequate. How can this be accomplished?

FIGURE **3.18**   An implementation of a skip list.

```
/*********************** IntSkipListNode.java *********************/

public class IntSkipListNode {
    public int key;
    public IntSkipListNode[] next;
    IntSkipListNode(int i, int n) {
        key = i;
        next = new IntSkipListNode[n];
        for (int j = 0; j < n; j++)
            next[j] = null;
    }
}

/*********************** IntSkipList.java **********************/

import java.util.Random;

public class IntSkipList {
    private int maxLevel;
    private IntSkipListNode[] root;
    private int[] powers;
    private Random rd = new Random();
    IntSkipList() {
        this(4);
    }
    IntSkipList (int i) {
        maxLevel = i;
        root = new IntSkipListNode[maxLevel];
        powers = new int[maxLevel];
        for (int j = 0; j < maxLevel; j++)
            root[j] = null;
        choosePowers();
    }
    public void choosePowers() {
        powers[maxLevel-1] = (2 << (maxLevel-1)) - 1;     // 2^maxLevel - 1
        for (int i = maxLevel - 2, j = 0; i >= 0; i--, j++)
            powers[i] = powers[i+1] - (2 << j);           // 2^(j+1)
    }
    public int chooseLevel() {
        int i, r = Math.abs(rd.nextInt()) % powers[maxLevel-1] + 1;
        for (i = 1; i < maxLevel; i++)
```

FIGURE **3.18**   (*continued*)

```
                 if (r < powers[i])
                     return i-1; // return a level < the highest level;
             return i-1;         // return the highest level;
         }
     public int skipListSearch (int key) {
         int lvl;
         IntSkipListNode prev, curr;            // find the highest non-null
         for (lvl = maxLevel-1; lvl >= 0 && root[lvl] == null; lvl--);  // level;
         prev = curr = root[lvl];
         while (true) {
             if (key == curr.key)               // success if equal;
                 return curr.key;
             else if (key < curr.key) {         // if smaller, go down,
                 if (lvl == 0)                   // if possible,
                     return 0;
                 else if (curr == root[lvl])    // by one level
                     curr = root[--lvl];        // starting from the
                 else curr = prev.next[--lvl]; // predecessor which
             }                                  // can be the root;
             else {                             // if greater,
                 prev = curr;                   // go to the next
                 if (curr.next[lvl] != null)    // non-null node
                     curr = curr.next[lvl];     // on the same level
                 else {                         // or to a list on a lower level;
                     for (lvl--; lvl >= 0 && curr.next[lvl] == null; lvl--);
                     if (lvl >= 0)
                         curr = curr.next[lvl];
                     else return 0;
                 }
             }
         }
     }
     public void skipListInsert (int key) {
         IntSkipListNode[] curr = new IntSkipListNode[maxLevel];
         IntSkipListNode[] prev = new IntSkipListNode[maxLevel];
         IntSkipListNode newNode;
         int lvl, i;
         curr[maxLevel-1] = root[maxLevel-1];
         prev[maxLevel-1] = null;
         for (lvl = maxLevel - 1; lvl >= 0; lvl--) {
             while (curr[lvl] != null && curr[lvl].key < key) { // go to the next
                 prev[lvl] = curr[lvl];                 // if smaller;
```

Figure **3.18**   (*continued*)

```
                curr[lvl] = curr[lvl].next[lvl];
            }
            if (curr[lvl] != null && curr[lvl].key == key) // don't include
                return;                          // duplicates;
            if (lvl > 0)                         // go one level down
                if (prev[lvl] == null) {         // if not the lowest
                    curr[lvl-1] = root[lvl-1]; // level, using a link
                    prev[lvl-1] = null;          // either from the root
                }
                else {                           // or from the predecessor;
                    curr[lvl-1] = prev[lvl].next[lvl-1];
                    prev[lvl-1] = prev[lvl];
                }
        }
        lvl = chooseLevel();                 // generate randomly level
                                             // for newNode;
        newNode = new IntSkipListNode(key,lvl+1);
        for (i = 0; i <= lvl; i++) {         // initialize next fields of
            newNode.next[i] = curr[i];       // newNode and reset to newNode
            if (prev[i] == null)             // either fields of the root
                root[i] = newNode;           // or next fields of newNode's
            else prev[i].next[i] = newNode; // predecessors;
        }
    }
}
```

Assume that *maxLevel* = 4. For 15 elements, the required number of nodes on level one is eight, on level two is four, on level three is two, and in level one is one. Each time a node is inserted, a random number r between 1 and 15 is generated, and if $r <$ 9, then a node of level one is inserted. If $r < 13$, a second-level node is inserted, if $r <$ 15, it is a third-level node, and if $r = 15$, the node of level four is generated and inserted. If *maxLevel* = 5, then for 31 elements the correspondence between the value of r and the level of node is as follows:

r	Level of Node to Be Inserted
31	5
29–30	4
25–28	3
17–24	2
1–16	1

To determine such a correspondence between *r* and the level of node for any *maxLevel*, the method `choosePowers()` initializes the array `powers[]` by putting lower bounds for each range. For example, for *maxLevel* = 4, the array is [1 9 13 15], and for *maxLevel* = 5, it is [1 17 25 29 31]. `chooseLevel()` uses `powers[]` to determine the level of the node about to be inserted. Figure 3.18 contains the code for `choosePowers()` and `chooseLevel()`. Note that the levels range between 0 and *maxLevel*-1 (and not between 1 and *maxLevel*) so that the array indexes can be used as levels. For example, the first level is level zero.

But we also have to address the question of implementing a node. The easiest way is to make each node have *maxLevel* reference fields, but this is wasteful. We need only as many reference fields per one node as the level of the node requires. To accomplish this, the `next` field of each node is not a reference to the next node, but to an array of reference(s) to the next node(s). The size of this array is determined by the level of the node. The `IntSkipListNode` and `SkipList` classes are declared as in Figure 3.18. In this way, the list in Figure 3.17b is really a list whose first four nodes are shown in Figure 3.17c. Only now can an inserting procedure be implemented, as in Figure 3.18.

How efficient are skip lists? In the ideal situation, which is exemplified by the list in Figure 3.17a, the search time is $O(\lg n)$. In the worst situation, when all lists are on the same level, the skip list turns into a regular singly linked list, and the search time is $O(n)$. However, the latter situation is unlikely to occur; in the random skip list, the search time is of the same order as the best case, that is, $O(\lg n)$. This is an improvement over the efficiency of searching regular linked lists. It also turns out that skip lists fare extremely well in comparison with more sophisticated data structures, such as self-adjusting trees or AVL trees (cf. Sections 6.7.3, 6.8), and therefore they are a viable alternative to these data structures (see also the table in Figure 3.21).

◻ 3.5 SELF-ORGANIZING LISTS

The introduction of skip lists was motivated by the need to speed up the searching process. Although singly and doubly linked lists require sequential search to locate an element or to see that it is not in the list, we can improve the efficiency of the search by dynamically organizing the list in a certain manner. This organization depends on the configuration of data; thus, the stream of data requires reorganizing the nodes already on the list. There are many different ways to organize the lists, and this section describes four of them.

1. *Move-to-front method.* After the desired element is located, put it at the beginning of the list (Figure 3.19a).

2. *Transpose method.* After the desired element is located, swap it with its predecessor unless it is at the head of the list (Figure 3.19b).

3. *Count method.* Order the list by the number of times elements are being accessed (Figure 3.19c).

4. *Ordering method.* Order the list using certain criteria natural for information under scrutiny (Figure 3.19d).

FIGURE **3.19**   Accessing an element on a linked list and changes on the list depending on the self-organiza-tion technique applied: (a) move-to-front method, (b) transpose method, (c) count method, and (d) ordering method, in particular, alphabetical ordering which leads to no change. In the case when the desired element is not in the list, (e) the first three methods add a new node with this element at the end of the list and (f) the ordering method maintains an order on the list.

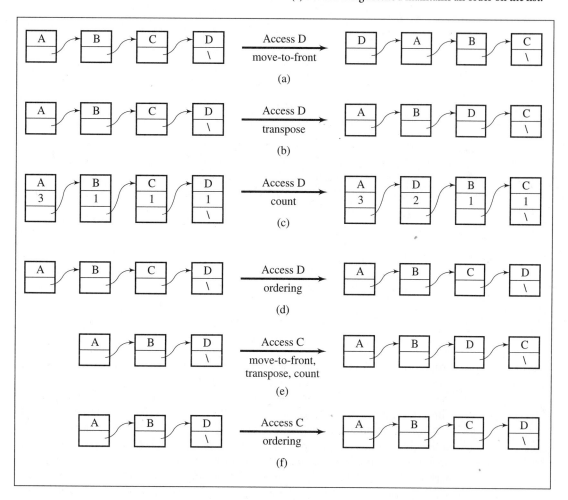

In the first three methods, new information is stored in a node added to the end of the list (Figure 3.19e); in the fourth method, new information is stored in a node inserted somewhere in the list to maintain the order of the list (Figure 3.19f). An ex-ample of searching for elements in a list organized by these different methods is shown in Figure 3.20.

With the first three methods, we try to locate the elements most likely to be looked for near the beginning of the list, most explicitly with the move-to-front method and most cautiously with the transpose method. The ordering method already uses some

---

FIGURE **3.20**   Processing the stream of data, A C B C D A D A C A C C E E, by different methods of organizing linked lists. Linked lists are presented in an abbreviated form; for example, the transformation shown in Figure 3.19a is abbreviated as transforming list A B C D into list D A B C.

Element Searched for	Plain	Move-to-Front	Transpose	Count	Ordering
A:	A	A	A	A	A
C:	A C	A C	A C	A C	A C
B:	A C B	A C B	A C B	A C B	A B C
C:	A C B	C A B	C A B	C A B	A B C
D:	A C B D	C A B D	C A B D	C A B D	A B C D
A:	A C B D	A C B D	A C B D	C A B D	A B C D
D:	A C B D	D A C B	A C D B	D C A B	A B C D
A:	A C B D	A D C B	A C D B	A D C B	A B C D
C:	A C B D	C A D B	C A D B	C A D B	A B C D
A:	A C B D	A C D B	A C D B	A C D B	A B C D
C:	A C B D	C A D B	C A D B	A C D B	A B C D
C:	A C B D	C A D B	C A D B	C A D B	A B C D
E:	A C B D E	C A D B E	C A D B E	C A D B E	A B C D E
E:	A C B D E	E C A D B	C A D E B	C A E D B	A B C D E

properties inherent to the information stored in the list. For example, if we are storing nodes pertaining to people, then the list can be organized alphabetically by the name of the person or the city or in ascending or descending order using, say, birthday or salary. This is particularly advantageous when searching for information which is not in the list, since the search can terminate without scanning the entire list. Searching all the nodes of the list, however, is necessary in such cases using the other three methods. The count method can be subsumed in the category of the ordering methods if frequency is part of the information. In many cases, however, the count itself is an additional piece of information required solely to maintain the list; hence, it may not be considered "natural" to the information at hand.

Analyses of the efficiency of these methods customarily compare their efficiency to that of *optimal static ordering*. With this ordering, all the data are already ordered by the frequency of their occurrence in the body of data so that the list is used only for searching, not for inserting new items. Therefore, this approach requires two passes through the body of data, one to build the list and another to use the list for search alone.

To experimentally measure the efficiency of these methods, the number of all actual comparisons was compared to the maximum number of possible comparisons. The latter number is calculated by adding the lengths of the list at the moment of processing each element. For example, in the table in Figure 3.20, the body of data contains 14 letters, 5 of them being different, which means that 14 letters were processed. The length of the list before processing each letter is recorded, and the result, $0 + 1 + 2 + 3 + 3 + 4 + 4 + 4 + 4 + 4 + 4 + 4 + 4 + 5 = 46$, is used to compare the number of all made comparisons to this combined length. In this way, we know what percentage of the list was scanned during the entire process. For all the list organizing methods except optimal ordering, this combined length is the same; only the number of comparisons can change. For example, when using the move-to-front technique for the data in the table in Figure 3.20, 33 comparisons were made, which is 71.7% when compared to 46. The latter number gives the worst possible case, the combined length of intermediate lists every time all the nodes in the list are looked at. Plain search, with no reorganization, required only 30 comparisons, which is 65.2%.

These samples are in agreement with theoretical analyses which indicate that count and move-to-front methods are, in the long run, at most twice as costly as the optimal static ordering; the transpose method approaches, in the long run, the cost of the move-to-front method. In particular, with amortized analysis, it can be established that the cost of accessing a list element with the move-to-front method is at most twice the cost of accessing this element on the list that uses optimal static ordering.

In a proof of this statement, the concept of inversion is used. For two lists containing the same elements, an inversion is defined to be a pair of elements (x, y) such that on one list x precedes y and on the other list y precedes x. For example, the list (C, B, D, A) has four inversions with respect to list (A, B, C, D): (C, A), (B, A), (D, A), and (C, B). Define the amortized cost to be the sum of actual cost and the difference between the number of inversions before accessing an element and after accessing it,

$$amCost(x) = cost(x) + (inversionsBeforeAccess(x) - inversionsAfterAccess(x))$$

To assess this number, consider an optimal list $OL = (A, B, C, D)$ and a move-to-front list $MTF = (C, B, D, A)$. The access of elements usually changes the balance of inversions. Let $displaced(x)$ be the number of elements preceding x in MTF but following x in OL. For example, $displaced(A) = 3$, $displaced(B) = 1$, $displaced(C) = 0$, and $displaced(D) = 0$. If $pos_{MTF}(x)$ is the current position of x in MTF, then $pos_{MTF}(x) - 1 - displaced(x)$ is the number of elements preceding x in both lists. It is easy to see that for D this number equals 2, and for the remaining elements it is 0. Now, accessing an element x and moving it to the front of MTF creates $pos_{MTF}(x) - 1 - displaced(x)$ new inversions and removes $displaced(x)$ other inversions so that the amortized time to access x is

$$amCost(x) = pos_{MTF}(x) + pos_{MTF}(x) - 1 - displaced(x) - displaced(x) = 2(pos_{MTF}(x) - displaced(x)) - 1$$

where $cost(x) = pos_{MTF}(x)$. Accessing A transforms MTF $= (C, B, D, A)$ into (A, C, B, D) and $amCost(A) = 2(4 - 3) - 1 = 1$. For B, the new list is (B, C, D, A) and $amCost(B) = 2(2 - 1) - 1 = 1$. For C, the list does not change and $amCost(C) = 2(1 - 0) - 1 = 1$. Finally, for D, the new list is (D, C, B, A) and $amCost(D) = 2(3 - 0) - 1 = 5$. However, the number of common elements preceding x on the two lists cannot exceed the number of all the elements preceding x on OL; therefore, $pos_{MTF}(x) - 1 - displaced(x) \leq pos_{OL}(x) - 1$, so that

$$amCost(x) \leq 2pos_{OL}(x) - 1$$

The amortized cost of accessing an element x in MTF is in excess of $pos_{OL}(x) - 1$ units to its actual cost of access on OL. This excess is used to cover an additional cost of accessing elements in MTF for which $pos_{MTF}(x) > pos_{OL}(x)$, that is, elements that require more accesses on MTF than on OL.

FIGURE **3.21**   Measuring the efficiency of different methods using formula (number of data comparisons)/(combined length) expressed in percentages.

Different Words/ All Words	149/423	550/2847	156/347	609/1510	1163/5866	2013/23065
Optimal	26.4	17.6	28.5	24.5	16.2	10.0
Plain	71.2	56.3	70.3	67.1	51.7	35.4
Move-to-Front	49.5	31.3	61.3	54.5	30.5	18.4
Transpose	69.5	53.3	68.8	66.1	49.4	32.9
Count	51.6	34.0	61.2	54.7	32.0	19.8
Alphabetical Order	45.6	55.7	50.9	48.0	50.4	50.0
Skip List	12.3	5.5	15.1	6.6	4.8	3.8

It is important to stress that the amortized costs of single operations are meaningful in the context of sequences of operations. A cost of an isolated operation may seldom equal its amortized cost; however, in a sufficiently long sequence of accesses, each access on the average takes at most $2pos_{OL}(x) - 1$ time.

Figure 3.21 contains sample runs of the self-organizing lists. The first two columns of numbers refer to files containing programs, and the remaining columns refer to files containing English text. Except for alphabetical ordering, all methods improve their efficiency with the size of the file. The move-to-front and count methods are almost the same in their efficiency, and both outperform the transpose, plain, and ordering methods. The poor performance for smaller files is due to the fact that all of the methods are busy including new words to the lists, which requires an exhaustive search of the lists. Later, the methods concentrate on organizing the lists to reduce the number of searches. The table in Figure 3.21 also includes data for a skip list. There is an overwhelming difference between the skip list's efficiency compared to the other methods. However, keep in mind that in the table in Figure 3.21, only comparisons of data are included with no indication of the other operations needed for execution of the analyzed methods. In particular, there is no indication of how many references are used and relinked, which, when included, may make the difference between various methods less dramatic.

These sample runs show that for lists of modest size, the linked list suffices. With the increase in the amount of data and in the frequency with which they have to be accessed, more sophisticated methods and data structures need to be used.

□ 3.6 SPARSE TABLES

In many applications, the choice of a table seems to be the most natural one, but space considerations may preclude this choice. This is particularly true if only a small fraction of the table is actually used. A table of this type is called a *sparse table* since the table is populated sparsely by data and most of its cells are empty. In this case, the table can be replaced by a system of linked lists.

As an example, consider the problem of storing grades for all students in a university for a certain semester. Assume that there are 8000 students and 300 classes. A natural implementation is a two-dimensional array *grades* where student numbers are indexes of the columns and class numbers are indexes of the rows (see Figure 3.22). An association of student names and numbers is represented by the one-dimensional array *students* and an association of class names and numbers by the array *classes*. The names do not have to be ordered. If order is required, then another array can be used where each array element is occupied by an object with two fields, name and number,[1] or the original array can be sorted each time an order is required. This, however, leads to the constant reorganization of *grades* and is not recommended.

Each cell of *grades* stores a grade obtained by each student after finishing a class. If signed grades such as A–, B+, or C+ are used, then two characters (that is, four bytes) are required to store each grade. To reduce the table size by one-half, the array *gradeCodes* in Figure 3.22c associates each grade with a codeword which requires only one byte of storage.

The entire table (Figure 3.22d) occupies 8000 students · 300 classes · 1 byte = 2.4 million bytes. This table is very large but is sparsely populated by grades. Assuming that, on the average, students take four classes a semester, each column of the table has only four cells occupied by grades, and the rest of the cells, 296 cells or 98.7%, are unoccupied and wasted.

A better solution is to use two pairs of parallel two-dimensional arrays: In one, *classesTaken1* and *classesTaken2* represent all the classes taken by every student; in the other, *studentsInClasses1* and *studentsInClasses2* represent all students participating in each class (Figure 3.23). Moreover, *classesTaken1* contains class numbers, *studentsInClasses1* contains student numbers, and *classesTaken2* and *studentsInClasses2* contain grades. We assume that a student can take at most eight classes and that there can be at most 250 students signed up for a class. We need two pairs of arrays, since with one array only it is very time consuming to produce lists. For example, if only *classesTaken1* and *classesTaken2* were used, then printing a list of all students taking a particular class would very much require an exhaustive search of these two arrays.

Assume that short integers are used to store student and class numbers which occupy two bytes to store an integer. With this new structure, three bytes are needed for each cell. Therefore, the tables *classesTaken1* and *classesTaken2* occupy 8000 students · 8 classes · 3 bytes = 192,000 bytes, and tables *studentsInClasses1* and *studentsInClasses2* occupy 300 classes · 250 students · 3 bytes = 225,000 bytes, and all the tables require a total of 417,000 bytes, less than one-fifth the number of bytes required for the sparse table in Figure 3.22.

Although this is a much better implementation than before, it still suffers from a wasteful use of space; seldom if ever will both arrays be full since most classes have fewer than 250 students and most students take fewer than eight classes. This structure is also inflexible: If a class can be taken by more than 250 students, a problem occurs

---

[1]This is called an *index-inverted table*.

FIGURE **3.22**   Arrays and sparse table used for storing student grades.

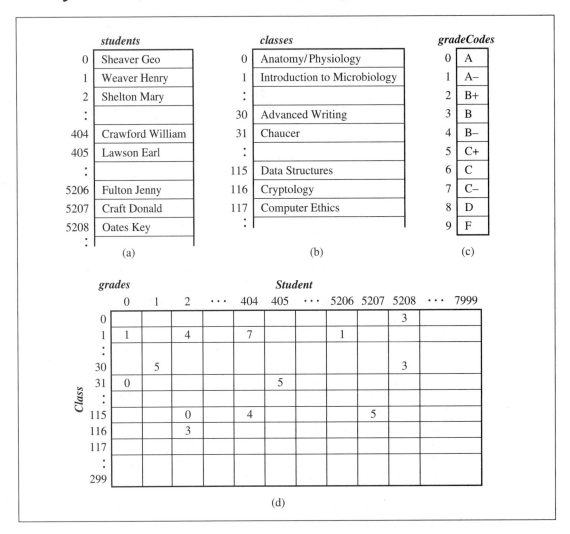

(a)   (b)   (c)

(d)

which has to be circumvented in an artificial way. One way is to create a nonexistent class which holds students from the overflowing class. Another way is to recompile the program with a new table size, which may not be practical at a future time. Another more flexible solution is needed.

Two one-dimensional arrays of linked lists can be used as in Figure 3.24. Each cell of the array *class* is a reference to a linked list of students taking a class, and each cell of the array *student* indicates a linked list of classes taken by a student. The linked lists contain nodes of five fields: student number, class number, grade, a reference to the next student, and a reference to the next class. Assuming that each reference requires only four bytes, one node occupies thirteen bytes, and the entire structure can be stored in 8000 students · 4 classes (on the average) · 13 bytes = 416,000 bytes, which is

FIGURE 3.23   Two-dimensional arrays for storing student grades.

classesTaken1

	0	1	2	...	404	405	...	5206	5207	5208	...7999
0	1	30	1		1	31		1	115	0	
1	31		115		115	64		33	121	30	
2	124		116		218	120		86	146	208	
3	136				221			121	156	211	
4					285			203		234	
5					292						
6											
7											

classesTaken2

	0	1	2	...	404	405	...	5206	5207	5208	...7999
0	1	5	4		7	5		1	5	3	
1	0		0		4	5		1	5	3	
2	0		3		6	4		0	3	2	
3	2				5			2	0	3	
4					3			2		1	
5					3						
6											
7											

(a)

studentsInClass1

	0	1	...	30	31	...	115	116	... 299
0	5208	0		1	0		2	2	
1		2		5208	405		404		
2		404					5207		
3		5206							
249									

studentsInClass2

	0	1	...	30	31	...	115	116	... 299
0	3	0		5	0		0	3	
1		0		3	5		4		
2		7					5		
3		1							
249									

(b)

FIGURE **3.24**   Student grades implemented using linked lists.

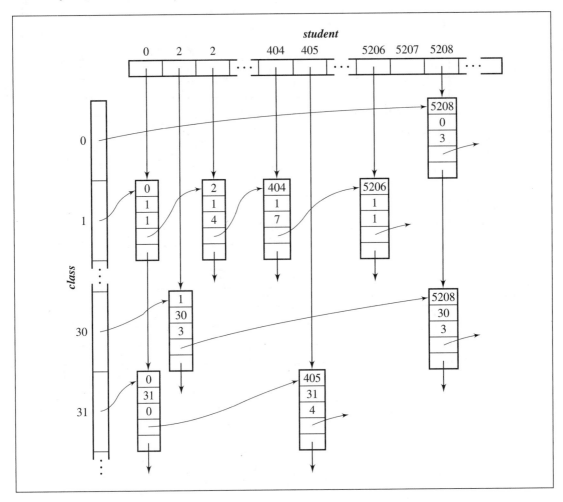

approximately 17% of the space required for the first implementation and roughly the same amount of space of the second. But now, no space is used unnecessarily, there is no restriction imposed on the number of students per class, and the lists of students taking a class can be printed immediately, even faster than in the first approach.

⊡ 3.7 LINKED LISTS IN `java.util`

The `LinkedList` class in the `java.util` package is an implementation of various operations on the nodes of a linked list. The `LinkedList` class implements a list as a generic doubly linked list with references to the head and to the tail. An instance of such a list that stores integers is presented in Figure 3.10.

The class hierarchy in the package `java.util` is as follows:

> `Object` ⇒ `AbstractCollection` ⇒ `AbstractList`
> ⇒ `AbstractSequentialList` ⇒ `LinkedList`

`AbstractList` is a direct superclass of `Vector` and `ArrayList`. `ArrayList` is an array implementation of the linked list so that for all practical purposes it is more similar to the class `Vector` than to the class `LinkedList`.

The methods included in the `LinkedList` class are represented in Figure 3.25, but the methods `finalize()`, `getClass()`, `notify()`, `notifyAll()`, and `wait()` inherited from class `Object` are not included.

The workings of most of the methods have already been illustrated in the case of the class `Vector` (Figure 1.4 and the discussion of these methods in Section 1.5). A demonstration of some of the linked list methods is presented in Figure 3.26.

New elements can be added at the beginning of the list with `addFirst()`, at the end of the list with `addLast()`, and anywhere inside the list with `add()`. Elements can be retrieved from the list, without removing them from it, with `getFirst()`, `getLast()`, and `get()`. Elements can also be removed permanently from the list with several removal methods. An important issue is, however, to perform user-defined operations on individual elements of the list. For example, list elements can be printed with the method `toString()`, which prints the list by starting with the left bracket, prints elements of the list in sequence in the way specified by their own version of `toString()` (whether a built-in version or redefined by the user), separates

---

FIGURE **3.25**   An alphabetical list of methods in the class `LinkedList`.

Method	Operation
`void add(ob)`	insert object `ob` at the end of the list
`void add(pos, ob)`	insert object `ob` at position `pos` after shifting elements at positions following `pos` by one position; raise `IndexOutOf-BoundsException` if `pos` is out of range
`boolean addAll(col)`	add all the elements from the collection `col` to the end of the list; return `true` if the list was modified
`boolean addAll(pos, col)`	add all the elements from the collection `col` at the position `pos` of the list after shifting the objects following position `pos`; raise `IndexOutOfBoundsException` if `pos` is out of range
`void addFirst(ob)`	insert object `ob` at the beginning of the list
`void addLast(ob)`	insert object `ob` at the end of the list; same as `add(ob)`
`void clear()`	remove all the objects from the list

Continues

FIGURE **3.25** *(continued)*

`Object clone()`	return the copy of the list without cloning its elements
`boolean contains(ob)`	return `true` if the list contains the object `ob`
`boolean containsAll(col)`	return `true` if the list contains all of the objects in the collection `col`
`boolean equals(lst)`	return `true` if the current list and object `lst` contain equal objects in the same order
`Object get(pos)`	return the object at position `pos`; raise `IndexOutOfBoundsException` if `pos` is out of range
`Object getFirst()`	return the first object in the list
`Object getLast()`	return the first object in the list; raise `NoSuchElementException` if the list is empty
`int hashCode()`	return the hash code for the list
`int indexOf(ob)`	return the position of the first occurrence of object `ob` in the list; return −1 if `ob` is not found
`boolean isEmpty()`	return `true` if the list contains no elements, `false` otherwise
`Iterator iterator()`	generate and return an iterator for the list
`int lastIndexOf(ob)`	return the position of the last occurrence of object `ob` in the list; return −1 if `ob` is not found
`LinkedList()`	create an empty linked list
`LinkedList(col)`	create a list with copies of elements from collection `col`
`ListIterator listIterator()`	generate and return a list iterator for the list initialized to position 0
`ListIterator listIterator(n)`	generate and return a list iterator for the list initialized to position n; raise `IndexOutOfBoundsException` if n is out of range
`boolean remove(ob)`	remove the first occurrence of `ob` in the list and return `true` if `ob` was in the list
`Object remove(pos)`	remove the object at position `pos`; raise `IndexOutOfBoundsException` if `pos` is out of range
`boolean removeAll(col)`	remove from the list all the objects contained in collection `col`; return `true` if any element was removed
`Object removeFirst()`	remove and return the first object on the list; raise `NoSuchElementException` if the list is empty
`Object removeLast()`	remove and return the last object on the list; raise `NoSuchElementException` if the list is empty

FIGURE **3.25**   *(continued)*

`void removeRange(first,last)`	remove from the list all the objects from position `first` to position `last-1`
`boolean retainAll(col)`	remove from the list all objects that are not in the collection `col`; return `true` if any object was removed
`Object set(pos, ob)`	assign object `ob` to position `pos` and return the object that occupied this position before the assignment; raise `IndexOutOf-BoundsException` if `pos` is out of range
`int size()`	return the number of object in the list
`List subList(first, last)`	return the sublist of the list (not its copy) containing elements from `first` to `last-1`; raise `IndexOutOfBoundsException` if either `first` or `last` is out of range and `IllegalArgumentException` if `last < first`
`Object[] toArray()`	copy all objects from the list to a newly created array and return the array
`Object[] toArray(arr[])`	copy all objects from the list to the array `arr` if `arr` is large enough or to a newly created array and return the array
`String toString()`	return a string representation of the list that contains the string representation of all the objects

all elements by commas, and ends printing with the right bracket. For example, the list consisting of numbers 1, 2, and 3 is printed as [1, 2, 3]. How can the output format be changed? One way is to redefine the method `toString()`. But this approach works just for printing. How can we find the largest element on the list? Or how can elements meeting certain conditions be counted? Or how can they be updated? These problems can be solved by processing the first element of the list and putting it at the end until all elements are processed.

Such a situation in the case of vectors uses the subscript operation: To access the element at position 5 of vector `v`, we simply use the expression `v[5]`. A similar role for linked lists is played by the method `get()`. But if we have two accesses in the row, say, `lst.get(5)`, `lst.get(6)`, then the search for position five begins from the beginning of the list for the first statement and again from the beginning of the list for the second statement. Instead, a temporary array can be created with the method `toArray()`. But this approach incurs unnecessary overhead in terms of space needed for the array and time needed to create it. A better approach is to use an iterator.

Iterators are objects that allow for access of elements of particular collections. The class `Iterator` defines three methods: `next()` to retrieve the next element of the collection for which the iterator is defined, `hasNext()` to check whether any elements are left for processing, and an optional `remove()` to remove from the

FIGURE **3.26**   A program demonstrating the operation of `LinkedList` methods.

```java
import java.io.*;
import java.util.LinkedList;

class testLists {
    public static void main(String[] ar) {
        LinkedList lst1 = new LinkedList();        // lst1 = []
        lst1.addFirst(new Integer(4));             // lst1 = [4]
        lst1.addFirst(new Integer(5));             // lst1 = [5, 4]
        lst1.addLast(new Integer(6));              // lst1 = [5, 4, 6]
        lst1.addLast(new Integer(5));              // lst1 = [5, 4, 6, 5]
        System.out.println("lst1: " + lst1.toString()); // lst1 = [5, 4, 6, 5]
        System.out.println(lst1.lastIndexOf(new Integer(5)));// 3
        System.out.println(lst1.indexOf(new Integer(5)));    // 0
        System.out.println(lst1.indexOf(new Integer(7)));    // -1
        lst1.remove(new Integer(5));               // lst1 = [4, 6, 5]
        LinkedList lst2 = new LinkedList(lst1);    // lst2 = [4, 6, 5]
        lst2.add(2,new Integer(8));                // lst2 = [4, 6, 8, 5]
        lst2.remove(new Integer(5));               // lst2 = [4, 6, 8]
        lst2.remove(1);                            // lst2 = [4, 8]
        System.out.println(lst2.getFirst() + " " + lst2.getLast()); // 4 8
        System.out.println(lst2.set(1,new Integer(7)));   // 8, lst2 = [4, 7]
        Integer[] a1, b = {new Integer(1), new Integer(2)};// b = [1, 2]
        for (int i = 0; i < b.length; i++)
            System.out.print(b[i] + " ");
        System.out.println();
        a1 = (Integer[]) lst2.toArray(b);          // a1 = b = [4, 7]
        for (int i = 0; i < b.length; i++)
            System.out.print(b[i] + " ");
        System.out.println();
        a1 = (Integer[]) lst1.toArray(b);          // a1 = [4, 6, 5], b = [4, 7]
        for (int i = 0; i < b.length; i++)
            System.out.print(b[i] + " ");
        System.out.println();
        for (int i = 0; i < a1.length; i++)
            System.out.print(a1[i] + " ");
        System.out.println();
        Object[] a2 = lst1.toArray();
        for (int i = 0; i < a2.length; i++)        // a2 = [4, 6, 5]
            System.out.print(a2[i] + " ");         // 4 6 5
        System.out.println();
```

FIGURE **3.26** (*continued*)

```
    for (int i = 0; i < lst1.size(); i++)
        System.out.print(lst1.get(i) + " ");  // 4 6 5
    System.out.println();
    for (java.util.Iterator it = lst1.iterator(); it.hasNext(); )
        System.out.print(it.next() + " ");    // 4 6 5
    System.out.println();
  }
}
```

collection the most recently accessed element. An example of application of an iterator is given in Figures 3.26 and 3.29.

◻ 3.8 Concluding Remarks

Linked lists have been introduced to overcome limitations of arrays by allowing dynamic allocation of necessary amounts of memory. Also, linked lists allow easy insertion and deletion of information since such operations have a local impact on the list. To insert a new element at the beginning of an array, all elements in the array have to be shifted to make room for the new item; hence, insertion has a global impact on the array. Deletion is the same. So should we always use linked lists instead of arrays?

Arrays have some advantages over linked lists, namely that they allow random accessing. To access the tenth node in a linked list, all nine preceding nodes have to be passed. In the array, we can go to the tenth cell immediately. Therefore, if an immediate access of any element is necessary, then an array is a better choice. This was the case with binary search and it will be the case with most sorting algorithms (see Chapter 9). But if we are constantly accessing only some elements—the first, the second, the last, and the like—and if changing the structure is the core of an algorithm, then using a linked list is a better option. A good example is a queue, which is discussed in the next chapter.

Another advantage in the use of arrays is space. To hold items in arrays, the cells have to be of the size of the items. In linked lists, we store one item per node and the node also includes at least one reference field; in doubly linked lists, the node contains two reference fields. For large linked lists, a significant amount of memory is needed to store the references. Therefore, if a problem does not require many shifts of data, then having an oversized array may not be wasteful at all if its size is compared to the amount of space needed for the linked structure storing the same data as the array.

◨ 3.9 Case Study: A Library

This case study is a program that can be used in a small library to include new books in the library, to check out books to people, and to return them.

As this program is a practice in the use of linked lists, almost everything is implemented in terms of such lists. But to make the program more interesting, it uses linked lists of linked lists that also contain cross-references (see Figure 3.27).

First, there could be a list including all authors of all books in the library. However, searching through such a list can be time-consuming, so the search can be sped up by choosing at least one of the two following strategies:

▲ The list can be ordered alphabetically, and the search can be interrupted if we find the name, if we encounter an author's name greater than the one we are searching for, or if we reach the end of list.

▲ We can use an array of references to the author structures and indexed with letters; each slot of the array points to the linked list of authors whose names start with the same letter.

The best strategy is to combine both approaches. However, in this case study, only the second approach is used, and the reader is urged to amplify the program by adding the first approach. Note that the articles *a, an,* and *the* at the beginning of the titles should be disregarded during the sorting operation.

The program uses an array `catalog` of all the authors of the books included in the library and an array `people` of all the people who have used the library at least once. Both arrays are indexed with letters so that, for instance, position `catalog['F']` refers to a linked list of all the authors whose names start with F.

Because we can have several books by the same author, one of the fields of the author node refers to the list of books of this author that can be found in the library. Similarly, because each person can check out several books, the person node contains a reference to the list of books currently checked out by this person. This fact is indicated by setting the `person` field of the checked-out book to the node pertaining to the person who is taking the book out.

Books can be returned, and that fact should be reflected by removing the appropriate `checkedOutBook` nodes from the list of the checked-out books of the person who returns them. The `person` field in the node related to the book that is being returned has to be reset to null.

The program defines four classes: `Author`, `Book`, `Person`, and `CheckedOut-Book`. Java's `LinkedList` class is used to define three more classes: `AuthorList`, `BookList`, and `PersonList`. To use the `LinkedList` class to generate and process a specific linked list, the generic methods need to be accommodated to a specific class. In particular, because the way of comparing instances of the first four library classes and the way of displaying them vary from one class to another, each of the four classes includes a definition of the method `equals()` to override the generic definition used in class `Object`. To display data, two classes override the generic method `isString()`. However, this allows us to print information extracted from one node of a linked list.

FIGURE **3.27**   Linked lists indicating library status.

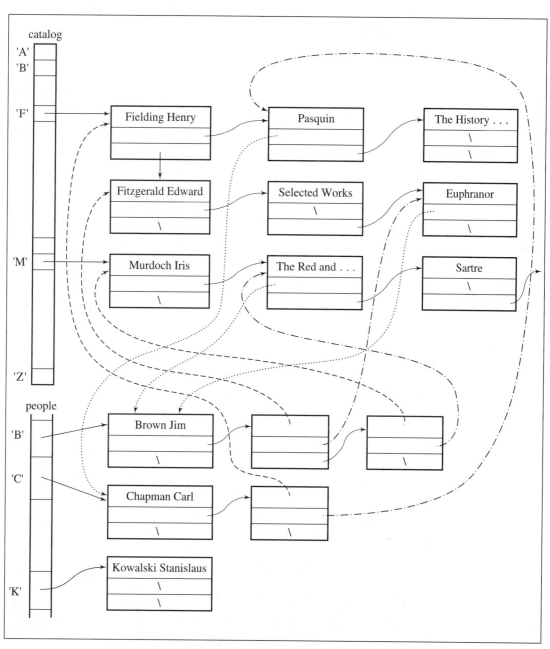

For two classes, however, a method is needed to print linked lists L_1 of linked lists L_2 (e.g., a list of people, each node of which refers to a linked list of checked-out books). It is possible to convert for each node of L_1 to string not only information contained directly in the node but also all the information on the linked list accessed from the node. This is a way of overriding the method `toString()` defined for `LinkedList`. For some variety, the three classes derived from `LinkedList` define their own versions of the `display()` method. `AuthorList` displays the list of authors by first converting the list into an array and then processing the array with the subscripting operator. `BookList` uses the `get()` method to access the elements of the list of books. Finally, `PersonList` uses an iterator to perform the same task. Note that `BookList` is used generically to create two types of lists: a linked list of books in `Author` objects and checked-out books in `Person` objects.

The program allows the user to choose one of the five operations: including a book, checking a book out, returning it, showing the current status of the library, and exiting the program. The operation is chosen after a menu is displayed and a proper number is entered. The cycle of displaying the menu and executing an elected operation ends with choosing the exit option. Here is an example of the status for a situation shown in Figure 3.27.

```
Library has the following books:

Fielding Henry
     * Pasquin - checked out to Chapman Carl
     * The History of Tom Jones
Fitzgerald Edward
     * Selected Works
     * Euphranor - checked out to Brown Jim
Murdoch Iris
     * The Red and the Green - checked out to Brown Jim
     * Sartre
     * The Bell

The following people are using the library:

Brown Jim has the following books
     * Fitzgerald Edward, Euphranor
     * Murdoch Iris, The Red and the Green
Chapman Carl has the following books
     * Fielding Henry, Pasquin
Kowalski Stanislaus has no books
```

Note that the diagram in Figure 3.27 reflects only the logic of the use of the linked lists and thus is significantly simplified. In a more realistic diagram, we need to take into account the fact that object data fields do not hold objects but only references to them. Also, each object that is an instance of the generic `LinkedList` class refers to a linked list in which each node refers to an object. A fragment of Figure 3.27 is shown in Figure 3.28 with implementation details shown more explicitly. The listing for the library program is shown in Figure 3.29.

FIGURE **3.28**   Fragment of structure from Figure 3.27 with all the objects used in the implementation.

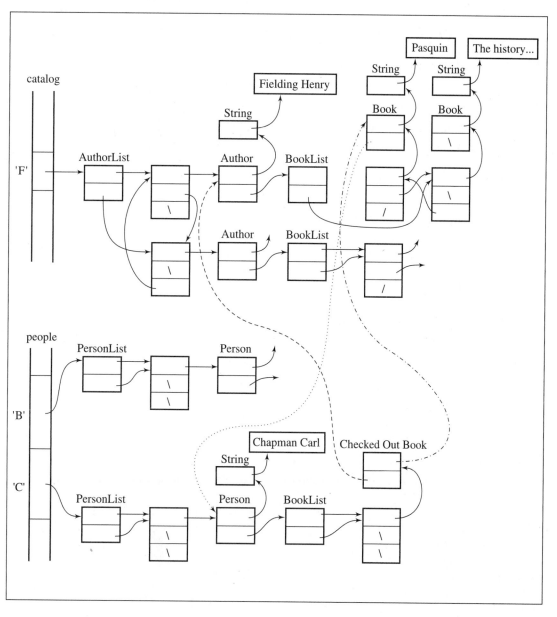

FIGURE **3.29**   The library program.

```
/*************************  Library.java  *************************/
import java.io.*;
import java.util.LinkedList;

class Author {
    String name;
    BookList books = new BookList();
    Author() {
    }
    public boolean equals(Object node) {
        return name.equals(((Author) node).name);
    }
    void display() {
        System.out.println(name);
        books.display();
    }
}

class Book {
    String title;
    Person person = null;
    Book() {
    }
    public boolean equals(Object node) {
        return title.equals(((Book) node).title);
    }
    public String toString() {
        return "    * " + title +
            (person != null ? " - checked out to " + person.name : "") + "\n";
    }
}

class CheckedOutBook {
    Author author = null;
    Book book = null;
    CheckedOutBook() {
    }
    public boolean equals(Object node) {
        return book.title.equals(((CheckedOutBook) node).book.title) &&
                author.name.equals(((CheckedOutBook) node).author.name);
    }
    public String toString() {
```

FIGURE **3.29**   (*continued*)

```java
            return "    * " + author.name + ", " + book.title + "\n";
        }
    }


    class Person {
        String name;
        BookList books = new BookList();
        Person() {
        }
        public boolean equals(Object node) {
            return name.equals(((Person) node).name);
        }
        void display() {
            if (!books.isEmpty()) {
                System.out.println(name + " has the following books:");
                books.display();
            }
            else System.out.print(name + " has no books");
        }
    }


    class AuthorList extends LinkedList {
        AuthorList() {
            super();
        }
        void display() {
            Object[] authors = toArray();
            for (int i = 0; i < authors.length; i++)
                ((Author)authors[i]).display();
        }
    }


    class BookList extends LinkedList {
        BookList() {
            super();
        }
        void display() {
            for (int i = 0; i < size(); i++)
                System.out.print(get(i).toString());
        }
    }
```

Continues

FIGURE **3.29**   (*continued*)

```
class PersonList extends LinkedList {
    PersonList() {
        super();
    }
    void display() {
        for (java.util.Iterator it = iterator(); it.hasNext(); )
            ((Person)it.next()).display();
    }
}

class Library {
    static AuthorList[] catalog = new AuthorList[(int)('Z'+1)];
    static PersonList[] people = new PersonList[(int)('Z'+1)];
    static String input;
    static InputStreamReader cin = new InputStreamReader(System.in);
    static BufferedReader buffer = new BufferedReader(cin);
    static String getString(String msg) {
        System.out.print(msg + " ");
        System.out.flush();
        try {
            input = buffer.readLine();
        } catch(IOException io) {
        }
        return input.substring(0,1).toUpperCase() + input.substring(1);
    }
    static void status() {
        System.out.println("Library has the following books:\n ");
        for (int i = (int) 'A'; i <= (int) 'Z'; i++)
            if (!catalog[i].isEmpty())
                catalog[i].display();
        System.out.println("\nThe following people are using the library:\n ");
        for (int i = (int) 'A'; i <= (int) 'Z'; i++)
            if (!people[i].isEmpty())
                people[i].display();
    }
    static void includeBook() {
        Author newAuthor = new Author();
        int oldAuthor;
        Book newBook = new Book();
        newAuthor.name = getString("Enter author's name:");
        newBook.title  = getString("Enter the title of the book:");
```

FIGURE **3.29**   (*continued*)

```
        oldAuthor = catalog[(int) newAuthor.name.charAt(0)].indexOf(newAuthor);
        if (oldAuthor == -1) {
            newAuthor.books.add(newBook);
            catalog[(int) newAuthor.name.charAt(0)].add(newAuthor);
        }
        else ((Author)catalog[(int) newAuthor.name.charAt(0)].get(oldAuthor)).
            books.add(newBook);
    }
    static void checkOutBook() {
        Person person = new Person(), personRef = new Person();
        Author author = new Author(), authorRef = new Author();
        Book   book   = new Book(), bookRef = new Book();
        int personIndex, bookIndex = -1, authorIndex = -1;
        CheckedOutBook bookToCheckOut = new CheckedOutBook();
        person.name = getString("Enter person's name:");
        while (authorIndex == -1) {
            author.name = getString("Enter author's name:");
            authorIndex = catalog[(int) author.name.charAt(0)].indexOf(author);
            if (authorIndex == -1)
                System.out.println("Misspelled author's name");
        }
        while (bookIndex == -1) {
            book.title = getString("Enter the title of the book:");
            authorRef =
              (Author) catalog[(int) author.name.charAt(0)].get(authorIndex);
            bookIndex = authorRef.books.indexOf(book);
            if (bookIndex == -1)
                System.out.println("Misspelled title");
        }
        bookRef = (Book) authorRef.books.get(bookIndex);
        bookToCheckOut.author = authorRef;
        bookToCheckOut.book   = bookRef;
        personIndex = people[(int) person.name.charAt(0)].indexOf(person);
        if (personIndex == -1) {        // a new person in the library;
            person.books.add(bookToCheckOut);
            people[(int) person.name.charAt(0)].add(person);
            bookRef.person =
                  (Person) people[(int) person.name.charAt(0)].getFirst();
        }
        else {
            personRef = (Person) people[(int) person.name.charAt(0)].get(personIndex);
```

FIGURE **3.29** (*continued*)

```
                personRef.books.add(bookToCheckOut);
                bookRef.person = personRef;
        }
    }
    static void returnBook() {
        Person person = new Person();
        CheckedOutBook checkedOutBook = new CheckedOutBook();
        Book book = new Book();
        Author author = new Author(), authorRef = new Author();
        int personIndex = -1,  bookIndex = -1, authorIndex = -1;
        while (personIndex == -1) {
            person.name = getString("Enter person's name:");
            personIndex = people[(int) person.name.charAt(0)].indexOf(person);
            if (personIndex == -1)
                System.out.println("Misspelled person's name");
        }
        while (authorIndex == -1) {
            author.name = getString("Enter author's name:");
            authorIndex = catalog[(int) author.name.charAt(0)].indexOf(author);
            if (authorIndex == -1)
                System.out.println("Misspelled author's name");
        }
        while (bookIndex == -1) {
            book.title = getString("Enter the title of the book:");
            authorRef =
                (Author) catalog[(int) author.name.charAt(0)].get(authorIndex);
            bookIndex = authorRef.books.indexOf(book);
            if (bookIndex == -1)
                System.out.println("Misspelled title");
        }
        checkedOutBook.author = authorRef;
        checkedOutBook.book  = (Book) authorRef.books.get(bookIndex);
        ((Book)authorRef.books.get(bookIndex)).person = null;
        ((Person)people[(int) person.name.charAt(0)].get(personIndex)).
                books.remove(checkedOutBook);
    }
    static char menu() {
        return getString("\nEnter one of the following options:\n" +
                "1. Include a book in the catalog\n" +
                "2. Check out a book\n" +
                "3. Return a book\n4. Status\n5. Exit\n" +
                "Your option:").charAt(0);
```

FIGURE **3.29**   (*continued*)

```
    }
    public static void main(String args[]) {
        for (int i = 0; i <= (int) 'Z'; i++) {
            catalog[i] = new AuthorList();
            people[i] = new PersonList();
        }
        while (true)
            switch (menu()) {
                case '1': includeBook();  break;
                case '2': checkOutBook(); break;
                case '3': returnBook();   break;
                case '4': status();       break;
                case '5': return;
                default: System.out.println("Wrong option, try again.");
            }
    }
}
```

▯ 3.10 EXERCISES

1. Assume that a circular doubly linked list has been created, as in Figure 3.30. After each of the following assignments, indicate changes made in the list by showing which links have been modified. Process these assignments in sequence; that is, the second assignment should make changes in the list modified by the first assignment, and so on.

   ```
   list.next.next.next = list.prev;
   list.prev.prev.prev = list.next.next.next.prev;
   list.next.next.next.prev = list.prev.prev.prev;
   list.next.prev.next = list.next.next.next;
   ```

2. How many nodes does the shortest linked list have? The longest linked list?

3. The linked list in Figure 3.1l was created in Section 3.2 with three assignments. Create this list with only one assignment.

4. Merge two ordered singly linked lists of integers into one ordered list.

5. Delete an *i*th node on a linked list. Be sure that such a node exists.

FIGURE **3.30**   A circular doubly linked list.

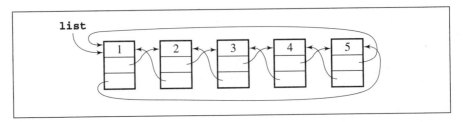

6. Delete from list L_1 nodes whose positions are to be found in an ordered list L_2. For instance, if $L_1 = $ (A B C D E) and $L_2 = $ (2 4 8), then the second and the fourth nodes are to be deleted from list L_1 (the eighth node does not exist), and after deletion, $L_1 = $ (A C E).

7. Delete from list L_1 nodes occupying positions indicated in ordered lists L_2 and L_3. For instance, if $L_1 = $ (A B C D E), $L_2 = $ (2 4 8), and $L_3 = $ (2 5), then after deletion, $L_1 = $ (A C).

8. Delete from an ordered list L nodes occupying positions indicated in list L itself. For instance, if $L = $ (1 3 5 7 8), then after deletion, $L = $ (1 7).

9. Suggest an array implementation of linked lists.

10. Write a method to check whether two singly linked lists have the same contents.

11. Write a method to reverse a singly linked list using only one pass through the list.

12. Write a method to insert a new node into a singly linked list (a) before and (b) after a node referred by p in this list (possibly the first or the last). Do not use a loop in either operation.

13. Attach a singly linked list to the end of another singly linked list.

14. Put numbers in a singly linked list in ascending order. Use this operation to find the median in the list of numbers.

15. How can a singly linked list be implemented so that insertion requires no test for whether head is null?

16. Insert a node exactly in the middle of a doubly linked list.

17. Write code for class `IntCircularSLList` for a circular singly linked list that includes equivalents of the methods listed in Figure 3.2.

18. Write code for class `IntCircularDLList` for a circular doubly linked list that includes equivalents of the methods listed in Figure 3.2.

19. How likely is the worst case for searching a skip list to occur?

20. Consider the move-to-front, transpose, count, and ordering methods.

a. In what case is a list maintained by these methods not changed?

    b. In what case do these methods require an exhaustive search of lists for each search, assuming that only elements in the list are searched for?

21. In the discussion of self-organizing lists, only the number of comparisons was considered as the measure of different methods' efficiency. This measure can, however, be greatly affected by a particular implementation of the list. Discuss how the efficiency of the move-to-front, transpose, count, and ordering methods are affected in the case when the list is implemented as

    a. an array

    b. a singly linked list

    c. a doubly linked list

22. For doubly linked lists, there are two variants of the move-to-front and transpose methods (Valiveti and Oommen 1993). A *move-to-end* method moves a node being accessed to the end opposite from which the search started. For instance, if the doubly linked list is a list of items *A B C D* and the search starts from the left end to access node *C*, then the reorganized list is *A B D C*. If the search for *C* started from the right end, the resulting list is *C A B D*.

The *swapping* technique transposes a node with its predecessor also with respect to the end from which the search started. Assuming that only elements of the list are in the data, what is the worst case for a move-to-end doubly linked list when the search is made alternately from the left and from the right? For a swapping list?

23. What is the maximum number of comparisons for optimal search for the 14 letters shown in Figure 3.20?

24. Adapt the binary search to linked lists. How efficient can this search be?

25. In the second implementation of storing student grades, two pairs of two-dimensional arrays are used: *classesTaken1* and *classesTaken2*, and *studentsInClasses1* and *studentsInClasses2* (Figure 3.23). Why not use just two arrays, *classesTaken* and *studentsInClasses*, of objects with two data fields?

◪ 3.11 PROGRAMMING ASSIGNMENTS

1. Farey fractions of level one are defined as sequence $(\frac{0}{1}, \frac{1}{1})$. This sequence is extended in level two to form a sequence $(\frac{0}{1}, \frac{1}{2}, \frac{1}{1})$, sequence $(\frac{0}{1}, \frac{1}{3}, \frac{1}{2}, \frac{2}{3}, \frac{1}{1})$ at level three, sequence $(\frac{0}{1}, \frac{1}{4}, \frac{1}{3}, \frac{1}{2}, \frac{2}{3}, \frac{3}{4}, \frac{1}{1})$ at level four, so that at each level n, a new fraction $\frac{a+b}{c+d}$ is inserted between two neighbor fractions $\frac{a}{c}$ and $\frac{b}{d}$ only if $c + d \leq n$. Write a program which for a number n entered by the user creates—by constantly extending it—a linked list of fractions at level n and then displays them.

2. Write a simple airline ticket reservation program. The program should display a menu with the following options: reserve a ticket, cancel a reservation, check whether a ticket is reserved for a particular person, and display the passengers. The information is maintained on an alphabetized linked list of names. In a simpler version of the program, assume that tickets are reserved for only one flight. In a fuller version, place no limit on the number of flights. Create a linked list of flights with each node including a reference to a linked list of passengers.

3. Read Section 12.1 about sequential-fit methods. Implement the discussed methods with linked lists and compare their efficiency.

4. Write a program to simulate managing files on disk. Define the disk as a one-dimensional array `disk` of size `numOfSectors*sizeOfSector`, where `sizeOfSector` indicates the number of characters stored in one sector. (For the sake of debugging, make it a very small number.) A pool of available sectors is kept in a linked list `sectors` of three-field structures: two fields to indicate ranges of available sectors and one `next` field. Files are kept in a linked list `files` of four-field structures: file name, the number of characters in the file, a reference to a linked list of sectors where the contents of the file can be found, and the `next` field.

a. In the first part, implement methods to save and delete files. Saving files requires claiming a sufficient number of sectors from `pool`, if available. The sectors may not be contiguous, so the linked list assigned to the file may contain several nodes. Then the contents of the file have to be written to the sectors assigned to the file. Deletion of a file only requires removing the nodes corresponding with this file (one from `files` and the rest from its own linked list of sectors) and transferring the sectors assigned to this file back to `pool`. No changes are made in `disk`.

b. File fragmentation slows down file retrieval. In the ideal situation, one cluster of sectors is assigned to one file. However, after many operations with files, it may not be possible. Extend the program to include a method `together()` to transfer files to contiguous sectors, that is, to create a situation illustrated in Figure 3.31. Fragmented files `file1` and `file2` occupy only one cluster of sectors after `together()` is finished. However, particular care should be taken not to overwrite sectors occupied by other files. For example, `file1` requires eight sectors; five sectors are free at the beginning of `pool`, but sectors 5 and 6 are occupied by `file2`. Therefore, a file f occupying such sectors has to be located first by scanning `files`. The contents of these sectors must be transferred to unoccupied positions, which requires updating the sectors belonging to f in the linked list; only then can the released sectors be utilized. One way of accomplishing this is by copying from the area into which one file is copied chunks of sectors of another file into an area of the disk large enough to accommodate these chunks. In the example in Figure 3.31, contents of `file1` first are copied to sectors 0 through 4, and then copying is temporarily suspended because sector 5 is occupied. Thus, contents of sectors 5 and 6 are moved to sectors 12 and 14, and the copying of `file1` is resumed.

FIGURE **3.31**   Linked lists used to allocate disk sectors for files: (a) a pool of available sectors; two files (b) before and (c) after putting them in contiguous sectors; the situation in sectors of the disk (d) before and (e) after this operation.

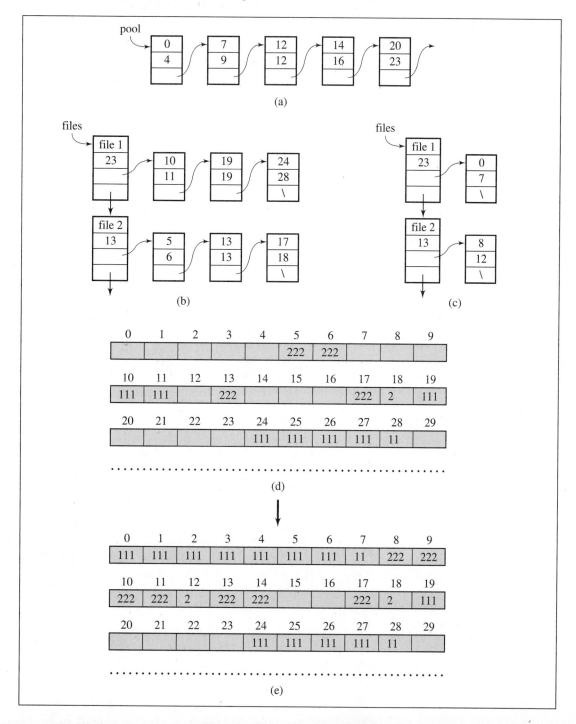

5. Write a simple line editor. Keep the entire text on a linked list, one line in a separate node. Start the program with entering EDIT file, after which a prompt appears along with the line number. If the letter I is entered with a number *n* following it, then insert the text to be followed before line *n*. If I is not followed by a number, then insert the text before the current line. If D is entered with two numbers *n* and *m*, one *n*, or no number following it, then delete lines *n* through *m*, line *n*, or the current line. Do the same with the command L, which stands for listing lines. If A is entered, then append the text to the existing lines. Entry E signifies exit and saving the text in a file. Here is an example:

```
EDIT testfile
1> The first line
2>
3> And another line
4> I 3
3> The second line
4> One more line
5> L
1> The first line
2>
3> The second line
4> One more line
5> And another line   // This is now line 5, not 3;
5> D 2                // line 5, since L was issued from line 5;
4> L                  // line 4, since one line was deleted;
1> The first line
2> The second line    // this and the following lines
3> One more line      // now have new numbers;
4> And another line
4> E
```

6. Extend the case study program in this chapter to have it store all the information in the file Library.dat at exit and initialize all the linked lists using this information at the invocation of the program. Also, extend it by adding more error checking, such as not allowing the same book to be checked out at the same time to more than one person or not including the same person more than once in the library.

7. Test the efficiency of skip lists. In addition to the methods given in this chapter, implement skipListDelete() and then compare the number of node accesses in searching, deleting, and inserting for large numbers of elements. Compare this efficiency with the efficiency of linked lists and ordered linked lists. Test your program on a randomly generated order of operations to be executed on the elements. These elements should be processed in random order. Then try your program on nonrandom samples.

Bibliography

Bentley, Jon L. and McGeoch, Catherine C., "Amortized Analyses of Self-Organizing Sequential Search Heuristics," *Communications of the ACM* 28 (1985), 404–411.

Foster, John M., *List Processing,* London: MacDonald, 1967.

Hansen, Wilfred J., "A Predecessor Algorithm for Ordered Lists," *Information Processing Letters* 7 (1978), 137–138.

Hester, James H. and Hirschberg, Daniel S., "Self-Organizing Linear Search," *Computing Surveys* 17 (1985), 295–311.

Pugh, William, "Skip Lists: A Probabilistic Alternative to Balanced Trees," *Communications of the ACM* 33 (1990), 668–676.

Rivest, Ronald, "On Self-Organizing Sequential Search Heuristics," *Communications of the ACM* 19 (1976), No. 2, 63–67.

Sleator, Daniel D. and Tarjan, Robert E., "Amortized Efficiency of List Update and Paging Rules," *Communications of the ACM* 28 (1985), 202–208.

Valiveti, R. S. and Oommen, B. J., "Self-Organizing Doubly Linked Lists," *Journal of Algorithms* 14 (1993), 88–114.

Wilkes, Maurice V., "Lists and Why They Are Useful," *Computer Journal* 7 (1965), 278–281.

Stacks and Queues

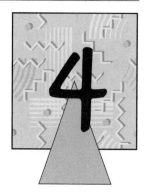

A s the first chapter explained, abstract data types allow us to delay the specific implementation of a data type until it is well understood what operations are required to operate on the data. In fact, these operations determine which implementation of the data type is most efficient in a particular situation. This situation is illustrated by two data types, stacks and queues, which are described by a list of operations. Only after the list of the required operations is determined do we present some possible implementations and compare them.

4.1 STACKS

A *stack* is a linear data structure which can be accessed only at one of its ends for storing and retrieving data. Such a stack resembles a stack of trays in a cafeteria: New trays are put on the top of the stack and taken off the top. The last tray put on the stack is the first tray removed from the stack. For this reason, a stack is called an *LIFO* structure: last in/first out.

A tray can be taken only if there are trays on the stack, and a tray can be added to the stack only if there is enough room, that is, if the stack is not too high. Therefore, a stack is defined in terms of operations which change its status and operations which check this status. The operations are as follows:

▲ *clear()*—Clear the stack.

▲ *isEmpty()*—Check to see if the stack is empty.

▲ *isFull()*—Check to see if the stack is full.

▲ *push(el)*—Put the element *el* on the top of the stack.

▲ *pop()*—Take the topmost element from the stack.

▲ *topEl()*—Return the topmost element in the stack without removing it.

FIGURE **4.1**   A series of operations executed on a stack.

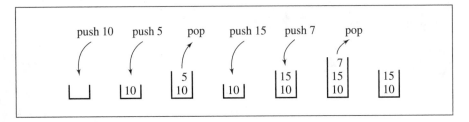

A series of *push()* and *pop()* operations is shown in Figure 4.1. After pushing number 10 onto an empty stack, the stack contains only this number. After pushing 5 on the stack, the number is placed on top of 10 so that, when the popping operation is executed, 5 is removed from the stack, because it arrived after 10, and 10 is left on the stack. After pushing 15 and then 7, the topmost element is 7, and this number is removed when executing the popping operation, after which the stack contains 10 at the bottom and 15 above it.

Generally, the stack is very useful in situations when data have to be stored and then retrieved in reverse order. One application of the stack is in matching delimiters in a program. This is an important example because delimiter matching is part of any compiler: No program is considered correct if the delimiters are mismatched.

In Java programs, we have the following delimiters: parentheses '(' and ')', square brackets '[' and ']', curly brackets '{' and '}', and comment delimiters '/*' and '*/'. Here are examples of Java statements that use delimiters properly:

```
a = b + (c − d ) * (e − f);
g[10] = h[i[9]] + (j + k) * l;
while (m < (n[8] + o)) { p = 7; /* initialize p */ r = 6; }
```

These examples are statements in which mismatching occurs:

```
a = b + (c − d) * (e − f));
g[10] = h[i[9]] + j + k) * l;
while (m < (n[8] + o]) { p = 7; /* initialize p */ r = 6; }
```

A particular delimiter can be separated from its match by other delimiters; that is, delimiters can be nested. Therefore, a particular delimiter is matched up only after all the delimiters following it and preceding its match have been matched. For example, in the condition of the loop

```
while (m < (n[8] + o))
```

the first opening parenthesis must be matched with the last closing parenthesis, but this is done only after the second opening parenthesis is matched with the next to last closing parenthesis; this, in turn, is done after the opening square bracket is matched with the closing bracket.

The delimiter matching algorithm reads a character from a Java program and stores it on a stack if it is an opening delimiter. If a closing delimiter is found, the delimiter is compared to a delimiter popped off the stack. If they match, processing continues. If not, processing discontinues by signaling an error. The processing of the Java program ends successfully after the end of the program is reached and the stack is empty. Here is the algorithm:

```
delimiterMaching(file)
     read character ch from file;
     while not end of file
        if ch is '(', '[', or '{'
             push(ch);
        else if ch is '/'
             read the next character;
             if this character is '*'
                  push(ch);
             else ch = the character read in;
                  continue; // go to the beginning of the loop;
        else if ch is ')', ']', or '}'
             if ch and popped off delimiter do not match
                  failure;
        else if ch is '*'
             read the next character;
             if this character is '/' and popped off delimiter is not '/'
                  failure;
             else ch = the character read in;
                  push back the popped off delimiter;
                  continue;
     // else ignore other characters;
        read next character ch from file;
     if stack is empty
        success;
     else failure;
```

Figure 4.2 shows the processing that occurs when applying this algorithm to the statement

```
s=t[5]+u/(v*(w+y));
```

The first column in Figure 4.2 shows the contents of the stack at the end of the loop before the next character is input from the program file. The first line shows the initial situation in the file and on the stack. Variable ch is initialized to the first character of the file, letter s, and in the first iteration of the loop, the character is simply ignored. This situation is shown in the second row in Figure 4.2. Then the next character, equal sign, is read. It is also ignored and so is the letter t. After reading the left bracket, the bracket is pushed onto the stack so that the stack now has one element, the left bracket. Reading digit 5 does not change the stack, but after the right bracket becomes the value of ch, the topmost element is popped off the stack and compared with ch. Because the popped off element (left bracket) matches ch (right bracket), the processing of input continues. After reading and discarding the letter u, a slash is read and the algorithm checks whether it is part of the comment delimiter by reading

FIGURE **4.2**   Processing the statement s= t[5]+u / (v*(w+y)); with the algorithm
`delimiterMatching()`.

Stack	Nonblank Character Read	Input Left
empty		s = t[5] + u / (v * (w + y));
empty	s	= t[5] + u / (v * (w + y));
empty	=	t[5] + u / (v * (w + y));
empty	t	[5] + u / (v * (w + y));
[	[	5] + u / (v * (w + y));
[	5	] + u / (v * (w + y));
empty	]	+ u / (v * (w + y));
empty	+	u / (v * (w + y));
empty	u	/ (v * (w + y));
empty	/	(v * (w + y));
(	(	v * (w + y));
(	v	* (w + y));
(	*	(w + y));
((	(	w + y));
((	w	+y));
((	+	y));
((	y	));
(	)	);
empty	)	;
empty	;	

the next character, a left parenthesis. Because the character read in is not an asterisk,
the slash is not a beginning of a comment, so ch is set to left parenthesis. In the next
iteration, this parenthesis is pushed onto the stack and processing continues, as
shown in Figure 4.2. After reading the last character, a semicolon, the loop is exited
and the stack is checked. Because it is empty (no unmatched delimiters are left), success is pronounced.

As another example of stack application, consider adding very large numbers. The largest magnitude of integers is limited, so we are not able to add 18,274,364,583,929,273,748,459,595,684,373 and 8,129,498,165,026,350,236, since integer variables cannot hold such large values, let alone their sum. The problem can be solved if we treat these numbers as strings of numerals, store the numbers corresponding to these numerals on two stacks, and then perform addition by popping numbers from the stacks. The pseudocode for this algorithm is as follows:

```
AddingLargeNumbers()
    read the numerals of the first number and store the numbers corresponding to
    them on one stack;
    read the numerals of the second number and store the numbers corresponding
    to them on another stack;
    result = 0;
    while at least one stack is not empty
        pop a number from each nonempty stack and add them to result;
        push the unit part on the result stack;
        store carry in result;
    push carry on the result stack if it is not zero;
    pop numbers from the result stack and display them;
```

Figure 4.3 shows an example of application of this algorithm. In this example, number 592 and 3784 are added.

1. First, numbers corresponding to digits composing the first number are pushed onto operandStack1 and numbers corresponding to digits of 3784 are pushed onto operandStack2. Note the order of digits on the stacks.

2. Numbers 2 and 4 are popped from the stacks, and the result, 6, is pushed onto resultStack.

3. Numbers 9 and 8 are popped from the stacks, and the unit part of their sum, 7, is pushed onto resultStack; the tens part of the result, 1, is retained as a carry in the variable result for subsequent addition.

4. Numbers 5 and 7 are popped from the stacks, added to the carry, and the unit part of the result, 3, is pushed onto resultStack, and the carry, 1, becomes a value of the variable result.

5. One stack is empty, so a number is popped from the nonempty stack, added to carry, and the result is stored on resultStack.

6. Both operand stacks are empty, so the numbers from resultStack are popped and printed as the final result.

Another important example is a stack used by the Java Virtual Machine (JVM). Java's popularity and power lie in the portability of its programs. This is ensured by compiling Java programs into bytecodes which are executable on a specific machine, the Java Virtual Machine. JVM is distinct in that it has no hardware realization; there is no palpable JVM with a JVM chip. It is an abstract construct; therefore, to execute a Java program, byte-codes have to be interpreted on a particular platform. Thus, in this process, the command

```
javac MyJavaProgram.java
```

FIGURE **4.3**   An example of adding numbers 592 and 3784 using stacks.

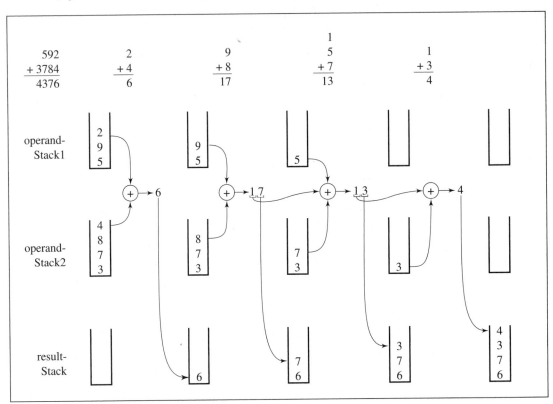

transforms each class and interface *C* included in `MyJavaProgram` into bytecodes that are stored in *C*.`class` file, and then the command

```
java MyClass
```

transforms MyClass (that includes `main()`)into machine code executable on a particular computer. In this way, a particular system needs to have an interpreter to execute a stream of bytecodes received through the Internet.

What is interesting in the context of this chapter is that the JVM is stack based. Each JVM thread has a private *Java stack* that contains *frames* for all currently active methods (only one method in a thread can be currently active; other active methods are suspended). A new frame is pushed every time a new method is invoked, and a frame is popped every time a method completes its execution. Each frame includes an array containing all local variables and an execution environment that includes, among other things, a link to the frame of the caller and information for catching exceptions.

Interestingly, each frame also includes an *operand stack*, which is used by JVM instructions as a source of arguments and a repository of results. For instance, if bytecode

FIGURE **4.4**   Vector implementation of a stack.

```java
public class Stack {
    private java.util.Vector pool = new java.util.Vector();
    public Stack() {
    }
    public Stack(int n) {
        pool.ensureCapacity(n);
    }
    public void clear() {
        pool.clear();
    }
    public boolean isEmpty() {
        return pool.isEmpty();
    }
    public Object topEl() {
        return pool.lastElement();
    }
    public Object pop() {
        return pool.remove(pool.size()-1);
    }
    public void push(Object el) {
        pool.addElement(el);
    }
    public String toString() {
        return pool.toString();
    }
}
```

96, which is the instruction iload, is followed by a bytecode *index*, which is an index into the array that in the current frame holds local variables, then iload loads, or pushes, an integer value from the local variable in position *index* in the array onto the operand stack. Another example is the instruction imul, whose bytecode equals 104. If imul is encountered, then the two topmost elements, which must be integers, are popped off the operand stack, multiplied, and the integer result is pushed onto the stack. The interpreter is also responsible for passing the final value generated by the current method to the operand stack of its caller.

Consider now implementation of our abstract stack data structure. We used push and pop operations as though they were readily available, but they also have to be implemented as methods operating on the stack.

A natural implementation for a stack is a flexible array, that is, a vector. Figure 4.4 contains a generic stack class definition that can be used to store any type of object. Also, a linked list can be used for implementation of a stack (Figure 4.5).

FIGURE **4.5**   Implementing a stack as a linked list.

```java
public class LLStack {
    private java.util.LinkedList list = new java.util.LinkedList();
    public LLStack() {
    }
    public void clear() {
        list.clear();
    }
    public boolean isEmpty() {
        return list.isEmpty();
    }
    public Object topEl() {
        return list.getLast();
    }
    public Object pop() {
        return list.removeLast();
    }
    public void push(Object el) {
        list.add(el);
    }
    public String toString() {
        return list.toString();
    }
}
```

Figure 4.6 shows the same sequence of push and pop operations as Figure 4.1 with the changes that take place in the stack implemented as a vector (Figure 4.6b) and as a linked list (Figure 4.6c). The linked list implementation more closely matches the abstract stack in that it includes only the elements that are on the stack because the number of nodes in the list is the same as the number of stack elements. In the vector implementation, the capacity of the stack can often surpass its size.

The vector implementation, like the linked list implementation, does not force the programmer to make a commitment at the beginning of the program concerning the size of the stack. If the size can be reasonably assessed in advance, then the predicted size can be used as a parameter for the stack constructor to create in advance a vector of the specified capacity. In this way, an overhead is avoided to copy the vector elements to a new larger location when pushing a new element to the stack for which size equals capacity.

It is easy to see that in the vector and linked list implementations, popping and pushing are executed in constant time $O(1)$. However, in the vector implementation, pushing an element onto a full stack requires allocating more memory and copies the elements from the existing vector to a new vector. Therefore, in the worst case, pushing takes $O(n)$ time to finish.

FIGURE **4.6**   A series of operations executed on an abstract stack (a) and the stack implemented with an array (b) and with a linked list (c).

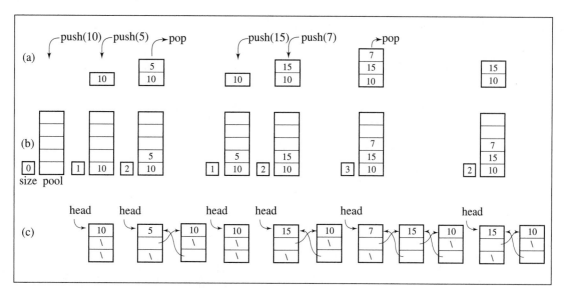

4.1.1 Stacks in `java.util`

A generic stack class implemented in the `java.util` package is an extension of class `Vector` to which one constructor and five methods are added (Figure 4.7). A stack can be created with this declaration and initialization:

```
java.util.Stack stack = new java.util.Stack();
```

Note that the return type of `push()` is not `void`, but `Object`: the object being pushed is the return value of the method. To check the topmost element without removing it from the stack, the method `peek()` has to be used. Both `push()` and `peek()` return the original topmost element, not its copy, so that the update of the topmost elements is possible using these methods. Having defined the class `C` with a public double field `d`, the topmost object can be updated as follows:

```
((C)stack.push(newC())).d = 12.3;
((C)stack.peek()).d = 45.6;
```

The Java implementation of the stack is potentially fatal because this is really not a stack, but a structure with stack-related methods. Class `Stack` is simply an extension of class `Vector`; therefore, it inherits all vector-related methods. With the declaration just given, it is possible to have such statements as:

```
stack.setElementAt(new Integer(5),1);
stack.removeElementAt(3);
```

which violate the integrity of the stack. A stack is a structure in which elements are accessed at one end only, which is not true for the `Stack` class. For this reason, class

FIGURE **4.7**   A list of methods in `java.util.Stack`

Method	Operation
`boolean empty()`	return `true` if the stack includes no element and `false` otherwise
`Object peek()`	return the top element on the stack; throw `EmptyStackException` for empty stack
`Object pop()`	remove the top element of the stack and return it; throw `EmptyStackException` for empty stack
`Object push(el)`	insert `el` at the top of the stack and return it
`int search(el)`	return the position of `el` on the stack (the first position is at the top; –1 in case of failure)
`Stack()`	create an empty stack

`java.util.Stack` is not used in this book. The integrity of the stack can be retained and advantages of vectors utilized if a stack is implemented not as an extension of class `Vector`, but when it uses a vector as a data field, as suggested in Figure 4.4.

▢ 4.2 QUEUES

A *queue* is simply a waiting line that grows by adding elements to its end and shrinks by taking elements from its front. Unlike a stack, a queue is a structure in which both ends are used: one for adding new elements and one for removing them. Therefore, the last element has to wait until all elements preceding it on the queue are removed. A queue is an FIFO structure: first in/first out.

Queue operations are similar to stack operations. The following operations are needed to properly manage a queue:

▲ *clear()*—Clear the queue.

▲ *isEmpty()*—Check to see if the queue is empty.

▲ *isFull()*—Check to see if the queue is full.

▲ *enqueue(el)*—Put the element *el* at the end of the queue.

▲ *dequeue()*—Take the first element from the queue.

▲ *firstEl()*—Return the first element in the queue without removing it.

A series of *enqueue()* and *dequeue()* operations is shown in Figure 4.8. This time—unlike for stacks—the changes have to be monitored both at the beginning of the queue and at the end. The elements are enqueued on one end and dequeued from the other. For example, after enqueuing 10 and then 5, the dequeue operation removes 10 from the queue (Figure 4.8).

FIGURE **4.8**   A series of operations executed on a queue.

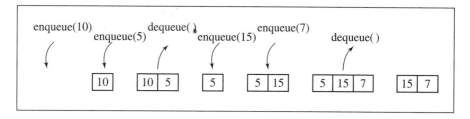

For an application of a queue, consider the following poem written by Lewis Carroll:

Round the wondrous globe I wander wild,

Up and down-hill—Age succeeds to youth—

Toiling all in vain to find a child

Half so loving, half so dear as Ruth.

The poem is dedicated to Ruth Dymes, which is indicated not only by the last word of the poem, but also by reading in sequence the first letter of each line, which also spells Ruth. This type of poem is called an acrostic and it is characterized by initial letters that form a word or phrase when taken in order. To see whether a poem is an acrostic, we devise a simple algorithm that reads a poem, echoprints it, retrieves and stores the first letter from each line on a queue, and after the poem is processed, all the stored first letters are printed in order. Here is an algorithm:

```
acrosticIndicator()
    while  not finished
        read a line of poem;
        enqueue the first letter of the line;
        output the line;
    while  queue is not empty
        dequeue and print a letter;
```

There is a more significant example to follow, but first consider the problem of implementation.

One possible queue implementation is an array, although this may not be the best choice. Elements are added to the end of the queue, but they may be removed from its beginning, thereby releasing array cells. These cells should not be wasted. Therefore, they are utilized to enqueue new elements, whereby the end of the queue may occur at the beginning of the array. This situation is better pictured as a circular array as Figure 4.9c illustrates. The queue is full if the first element immediately precedes in the counterclockwise direction the last element. However, because a circular array is implemented with a "normal" array, the queue is full if either the first element is in the first cell and the last element is in the last cell (Figure 4.9a) or if the first element is right after the last (Figure 4.9b). Similarly, *enqueue()* and *dequeue()* have to consider the

FIGURE **4.9**   (a–b) Two possible configurations in an array implementation of a queue when the queue is full. (c) The same queue viewed as a circular array. (f) Enqueuing number 6 to a queue storing 2, 4, and 8. (d–e) The same queue seen as a one-dimensional array with the last element (d) at the end of the array and (e) in the middle.

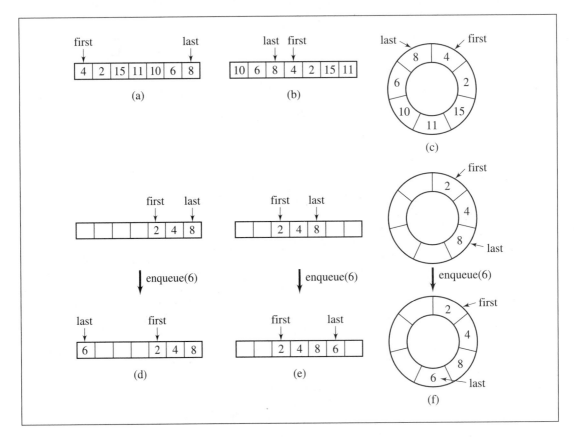

possibility of wrapping around the array when adding or removing elements. For example, *enqueue()* can be viewed as operating on a circular array (Figure 4.9c), but in reality, it is operating on a one-dimensional array. Therefore, if the last element is in the last cell and if any cells are available at the beginning of the array, a new element is placed there (Figure 4.9d). If the last element is in any other position, then the new element is put after the last, space permitting (Figure 4.9e). These two situations must be distinguished when implementing a queue viewed as a circular array (Figure 4.9f).

Figure 4.10 contains possible implementations of methods which operate on queues. A more natural queue implementation is a singly linked list as offered in the previous chapter (Figure 4.11).

In both suggested implementations, enqueuing and dequeuing can be executed in constant time $O(1)$. In the singly linked list implementation, it can be done in $O(1)$

FIGURE **4.10**   Array implementation of a queue.

```java
public class ArrayQueue {
    private int first, last, size;
    private Object[] storage;
    public ArrayQueue() {
        this(100);
    }
    public ArrayQueue(int n) {
        size = n;
        storage = new Object[size];
        first = last = -1;
    }
    public boolean isFull()  {
        return first == 0 && last == size-1 || first == last + 1;
    }
    public boolean isEmpty() {
        return first == -1;
    }
    public void enqueue(Object el) {
        if (last == size-1 || last == -1) {
            storage[0] = el;
            last = 0;
            if (first == -1)
                first = 0;
        }
        else storage[++last] = el;
    }
    public Object dequeue() {
        Object tmp = storage[first];
        if (first == last)
            last = first = -1;
        else if (first == size-1)
            first = 0;
        else first++;
        return tmp;
    }
    public void printAll() {
        for (int i = 0; i < size; i++)
            System.out.print(storage[i] + " ");
    }
}
```

FIGURE **4.11**   Linked list implementation of a queue.

```
/******************** QueueNode.java ***********************
 *                     generic queue node
 */

public class QueueNode {
    public Object info;
    public QueueNode next = null;
    public QueueNode(Object el) {
        info = el;
    }
}


/*********************** Queue.java ************************
 *                     generic queue
 */

public class Queue {
    private QueueNode head, tail;
    public Queue() {
        head = tail = null;
    }
    public boolean isEmpty() {
        return head == null;
    }
}
```

time, because `head` and `tail` are used and because dequeuing is executed at the head.

Figure 4.12 shows the same sequence of enqueue and dequeue operations as Figure 4.8 and indicates the changes in the queue implemented as an array (Figure 4.12b) and as a linked list (Figure 4.12c). The linked list keeps only the numbers that the logic of the queue operations indicated by Figure 4.12a requires. The array includes all the numbers until it fills up the array, after which new numbers are included starting from the beginning of the array.

Queues are frequently used on simulations to the extent that a well-developed and mathematically sophisticated theory of queues exists, called queuing theory, in which various scenarios are analyzed and models are built which use queues. In queuing processes, there are a number of customers coming to servers to receive service. The throughput of the server may be limited. Therefore, customers have to wait in queues before they are served and spend some amount of time while they are being

FIGURE **4.11** (*continued*)

```java
    public void clear() {
        head = tail = null;
    }
    public Object firstEl() {
        return head.info;
    }
    public void enqueue(Object el) {
        if (!isEmpty()) {
            tail.next = new QueueNode(el);
            tail = tail.next;
        }
        else head = tail = new QueueNode(el);
    }
    public Object dequeue() { // remove the head and return its info;
        if (!isEmpty()) {
            Object el = head.info;
            if (head == tail)      // if only one node on the list;
                head = tail = null;
            else head = head.next;
            return el;
        }
        else return null;
    }
}
```

served. By customers, we mean not only people but also objects. For example, parts on an assembly line in the process of being assembled into a machine, trucks waiting for service at a weighing station on an interstate, or barges waiting for a sluice to be opened so they can pass through a channel also wait in queues. The most familiar examples are lines in stores, post offices, or banks. The type of problems posed in simulations are: How many servers are needed to avoid long queues? How large must the waiting space be to put the entire queue in it? Is it cheaper to increase this space or to open one more server?

As an example, consider Bank One which, over a period of 3 months, recorded the number of customers coming to the bank and the amount of time needed to serve them. The table in Figure 4.13a shows the number of customers who arrived during 1-minute intervals throughout the day. For 15% of such intervals, no customer arrived, for 20%, only one arrived, etc. Currently, six clerks are employed, no lines are ever observed, and the bank management wants to know whether six clerks are too

FIGURE **4.12**   A series of operations executed on an abstract queue (a) and the stack implemented with an array (b) and with a linked list (c).

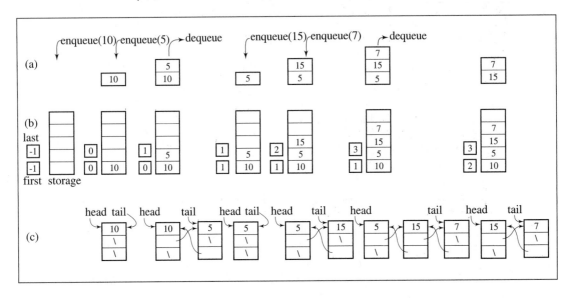

FIGURE **4.13**   Bank One example: (a) data for number of arrived customers per 1-minute interval and (b) transaction time in seconds per customer.

Number of customers per minute	Percentage of one-minute intervals	Range		The amount of of time needed for service in seconds	Percentage of customers	Range
0	15	1–15		0	0	—
1	20	16–35		10	0	—
2	25	36–60		20	0	—
3	10	61–70		30	10	1–10
4	30	71–100		40	5	11–15
		(a)		50	10	16–25
				60	10	26–35
				70	0	—
				80	15	36–50
				90	25	51–75
				100	10	76–85
				110	15	86–100
					(b)	

many. Would five suffice? Four? Maybe even three? Can lines be expected at any time? To answer these questions, a simulation program is written which applies the recorded data and checks different scenarios.

The number of customers depends on the value of a randomly generated number between 1 and 100. The table in Figure 4.13a identifies five ranges of numbers from 1 to 100, based on the percentages of 1-minute intervals that had 0, 1, 2, 3, or 4 customers. If the random number is 21, then the number of customers is 1; if the random number is 90, then the number of customers is 4. This method simulates the rate of customers arriving at Bank One.

In addition, analysis of the recorded observations indicates that no customer required 10-second or 20-second transactions, 10% required 30 seconds, etc., as indicated in Figure 4.13b. The table in 4.13b includes ranges for random numbers to generate the length of a transaction in seconds.

Figure 4.14 contains the code simulating customer arrival and transaction time at Bank One. The program uses three arrays. `arrivals[]` records the percentages of 1-minute intervals depending on the number of the arrived customers. The array `service[]` is used to store the distribution of time needed for service. The amount of time is obtained by multiplying the index of a given array cell by 10. For example, `service[3]` is equal to 10, which means that 10% of the time a customer required $3 \cdot 10$ seconds for service. The array `clerks[]` records the length of transaction time in seconds.

FIGURE **4.14**   Bank One example: implementation code.

```java
import java.util.Random;

class BankSimulation {
    static Random rd = new Random();
    static int Option(int percents[]) {
        int i = 0, perc, choice = Math.abs(rd.nextInt()) % 100 + 1;
        for (perc = percents[0]; perc < choice; perc += percents[i+1], i++);
        return i;
    }
    public static void main(String args[]) {
        int[] arrivals = {15,20,25,10,30};
        int[] service = {0,0,0,10,5,10,10,0,15,25,10,15};
        int[] clerks = {0,0,0,0};
        int clerksSize = clerks.length;
        int customers, t, i, numOfMinutes = 100, x;
        double maxWait = 0.0, thereIsLine = 0.0, currWait = 0.0;
        Queue simulQ = new Queue();
        for (t = 1; t <= numOfMinutes; t++) {
            System.out.print(" t = " + t);
```

FIGURE **4.14**   *(continued)*

```
             for (i = 0; i < clerksSize; i++)// after each minute subtract
                 if (clerks[i] < 60)          // at most 60 seconds from time
                     clerks[i] = 0;           // left to service the current
                 else clerks[i] -= 60;        // customer by clerk i;
             customers = Option(arrivals);
             for (i = 0; i < customers; i++) { // enqueue all new customers
                 x = Option(service)*10;      // (or rather service time
                 simulQ.enqueue(new Integer(x));        // they require);
                 currWait += x;
             }
             // dequeue customers when clerks are available:
             for (i = 0; i < clerksSize && !simulQ.isEmpty(); )
                 if (clerks[i] < 60) {
                     x = ((Integer) simulQ.dequeue()).intValue();
                         // assign more than one customer
                     clerks[i] += x;          // to a clerk if service time
                     currWait  -= x;          // is still below 60 sec;
                 }
                 else i++;
             if (!simulQ.isEmpty()) {
                 thereIsLine++;
                 System.out.print(" wait = " + ((long)(currWait/6.0)) / 10.0);
                 if (maxWait < currWait)
                     maxWait = currWait;
             }
             else System.out.print(" wait = 0;");
         }
         System.out.println("\nFor " + clerksSize + " clerks, there was a line "
             + thereIsLine/numOfMinutes*100.0 + "% of the time;\n"
             + "maximum wait time was " + maxWait/60.0 + " min.");
     }
 }
```

For each minute (represented by the variable t), the number of arriving customers is randomly chosen, and for each customer, the transaction time is also randomly determined. The method `option()` generates a random number, finds the range into which it falls, and then outputs the position, which is either the number of customers or the tenth the number of seconds.

Executions of this program indicate that six and five clerks are too many. With four clerks, service is performed smoothly; 20% of the time there is a short line of waiting customers. However, three clerks are always busy and there is always a long line of customers waiting. Bank management would certainly decide to employ four clerks.

◨ 4.3 PRIORITY QUEUES

In many situations, simple queues are inadequate, as when first in/first out scheduling has to be overruled using some priority criteria. In a post office example, a handicapped person may have priority over others. Therefore, when a clerk is available, a handicapped person is served instead of someone from the front of the queue. On roads with tollbooths, some vehicles may be put through immediately, even without paying (police cars, ambulances, fire engines, etc.). In a sequence of processes, process P_2 may need to be executed before process P_1 for the proper functioning of a system, even though P_1 was put on the queue of waiting processes before P_2. In situations like these, a modified queue, or *priority queue,* is needed. In priority queues, elements are dequeued according to their priority and their current queue position.

The problem with a priority queue is in finding an efficient implementation which allows relatively fast enqueuing and dequeuing. Since elements may arrive randomly to the queue, there is no guarantee that the front elements will be the most likely to be dequeued and that the elements put at the end will be the last candidates for dequeuing. The situation is complicated because a wide spectrum of possible priority criteria can be used in different cases such as frequency of use, birthday, salary, position, status, and others. It can also be the time of scheduled execution on the queue of processes, which explains the convention used in priority queue discussions in which higher priorities are associated with lower numbers indicating priority.

Priority queues can be represented by two variations of linked lists. In one type of linked list, all elements are entry ordered, and in another, order is maintained by putting a new element in its proper position according to its priority. In both cases, the total operational times are $O(n)$ because, for an unordered list, adding an element is immediate but searching is $O(n)$, and in a sorted list, taking an element is immediate but adding an element is $O(n)$.

Another queue representation uses a short ordered list and an unordered list, and a threshold priority is determined (Blackstone et al. 1981). The number of elements in the sorted list depends on a threshold priority. This means that in some cases this list can be empty and the threshold may change dynamically to have some elements in this list. Another way is to have always the same number of elements in the sorted list; the number $\sqrt{n}$ is a good candidate. Enqueuing takes on the average $O(\sqrt{n})$ time and dequeuing is immediate.

Another implementation of queues was proposed by J. O. Hendriksen (1977, 1983). It uses a simple linked list with an additional array of references to this list to find a range of elements in the list in which a newly arrived element should be included.

Experiments by Douglas W. Jones (1986) indicate that a linked list implementation, in spite of its $O(n)$ efficiency, is best for ten elements or less. The efficiency of the two-list version depends greatly on the distribution of priorities, and it may be excellent or as poor as that of the simple list implementation for large numbers of elements. Hendriksen's implementation, with its $O(\sqrt{n})$ complexity, operates consistently well with queues of any size.

☐ 4.4 CASE STUDY: EXITING A MAZE

Consider the problem of a trapped mouse that tries to find its way to an exit in a maze (Figure 4.15a). The mouse hopes to escape from the maze by systematically trying all the routes. If it reaches a dead end, it retraces its steps to the last position and begins at least one more untried path. For each position, the mouse can go in one of four directions: right, left, down, up. Regardless of how close it is to the exit, it always tries the open paths in this order, which may lead to some unnecessary detours. By retaining information that allows for resuming the search after a dead end is reached, the mouse uses a method called *backtracking*. This method is discussed further in the next chapter.

The maze is implemented as a two-dimensional character array in which passages are marked with 0s, walls by 1s, exit position by the letter e, and the initial position of the mouse by the letter m (Figure 4.15b). In this program, the maze problem is slightly generalized by allowing the exit to be in any position of the maze (picture the exit position as having an elevator that takes the mouse out of trap) and allowing passages to be on the borderline. To protect itself from falling off the array by trying to continue its path when an open cell is reached on one of the borderlines, the mouse also has to constantly check whether it is in such a borderline position or not. To avoid it, the program automatically puts a frame of 1s around the maze entered by the user.

The program uses two stacks: one to initialize the maze and another to implement backtracking.

The user enters a maze one line at a time. The maze entered by the user can have any number of rows and any number of columns. The only assumption the program makes is that all rows are of the same lengths and that it uses only these characters: any number of 1s, any number of 0s, one e, and one m. The rows are pushed on the stack mazeRows in the order they are entered after attaching one 1 at the beginning and one 1 at the end. After all rows are entered, the size of the array store can be determined, and then the rows from the stack are transferred to the array.

A second stack, mazeStack, is used in the process of escaping the maze. To remember untried paths for subsequent tries, the positions of the untried neighbors of the current position (if any) are stored on a stack and always in the same order, first upper neighbor, then lower, then left, and finally right. After stacking the open avenues on the stack, the mouse takes the topmost position and tries to follow it by first storing untried neighbors and then trying the topmost position and so forth until it reaches the exit or exhausts all possibilities and finds itself trapped. To avoid falling into an infinite loop of trying paths which have already been investigated, each visited position of the maze is marked with a period.

Here is a pseudocode of an algorithm for escaping a maze:

FIGURE **4.15**   (a) A mouse in a maze; (b) two-dimensional character array representing this situation.

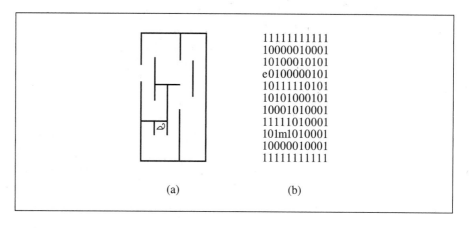

```
                                    11111111111
                                    10000010001
                                    10100010101
                                    e0100000101
                                    10111110101
                                    10101000101
                                    10001010001
                                    11111010001
                                    101m1010001
                                    10000010001
                                    11111111111

         (a)                             (b)
```

```
exitMaze()
    initialize stack, exitCell, entryCell, currentCell = entryCell;
    while currentCell is not exitCell
        mark currentCell as visited;
        push onto the stack the unvisited neighbors of currentCell;
        if stack is empty
            failure;
        else pop off a cell from the stack and make it currentCell;
    success;
```

The stack stores coordinates of positions of cells. This could be done, for instance, by using two integer stacks for *x* and *y* coordinates. Another possibility is to use one integer stack with both coordinates stored in one integer variable with the help of the shifting operation. In the program in Figure 4.17, a class MazeCell is used with two data fields, x and y, so that one mazeStack is used for storing MazeCell objects.

Consider an example shown in Figure 4.16. The program actually prints out the maze after each step made by the mouse.

0.   After the user enters the maze

```
1100
000e
00m1
```

the maze is immediately surrounded with a frame of 1s

```
111111
111001
1000e1
100m11
111111
```

FIGURE **4.16** An example of processing a maze.

						(2 4)	
stack:		(3 1)	(2 1)	(2 2)	(2 3)	(1 3)	(1 3)
	(3 2)	(2 2)	(2 2)	(2 2)	(2 2)	(2 2)	(2 2)
	(2 3)	(2 3)	(2 3)	(2 3)	(2 3)	(2 3)	(2 3)

currentCell: (3 3)   (3 2)   (3 1)   (2 1)   (2 2)   (2 3)   (2 4)

maze:
```
        111111   111111   111111   111111   111111   111111   111111
        111001   111001   111001   111001   111001   111001   111001
        1000e1   1000e1   1000e1   1..00e1  1..0e1   1...e1   1...e1
        100m11   10.m11   1..m11   1..m11   1..m11   1..m11   1..m11
        111111   111111   111111   111111   111111   111111   111111
```

(a)   (b)   (c)   (d)   (e)   (f)   (g)

entryCell and currentCell are initialized to (3 3) and exitCell to (2 4) (Figure 4.16a).

1. Because currentCell is not equal to exitCell, all four neighbors of the current cell (3 3) are tested, and only two of them are candidates for processing, namely, (3 2) and (2 3); therefore, they are pushed onto the stack. The stack is checked to see whether it contains any position, and because it is not empty, the topmost position (3 2) becomes current (Figure 4.16b).

2. currentCell is still to equal to exitCell; therefore, the two viable options accessible from (3 2) are pushed onto the stack, namely, positions (2 2) and (3 1). Note that the position holding the mouse is not included in the stack. After the current position is marked as visited, the situation in the maze is as in Figure 4.16c. Now, the topmost position, (3 1), is popped off the stack, and it becomes the value of currentCell. The process continues until the exit is reached, as shown step by step in Figure 4.16d–f.

Note that in step four (Figure 4.16d), the position (2 2) is pushed onto the stack, although it is already there. However, this poses no danger, because when the second instance of this position is popped from the stack, all the paths leading from this position have already been investigated using the first instance of this position on the stack. Note also that the mouse makes a detour, although there is a shorter path from its initial position to the exit.

Figure 4.17 contains code implementing the maze exiting algorithm. The program uses the stack defined in this chapter. If the user wants to use the stack from java.util, the line

```
Stack stack = new Stack();
```

should be replaced by

```
java.util.Stack stack = new java.util.Stack();
```

FIGURE **4.17**   Listing of the program for maze processing.

```
//*************************  Maze.java  *****************************
import java.io.*;

class MazeCell {
    int x, y;
    MazeCell() {
    }
    MazeCell(int i, int j) {
        x = i; y = j;
    }
    boolean equals(MazeCell cell) {
        return x == cell.x && y == cell.y;
    }
}

class Maze {
    int rows = 0, cols = 0;
    char[][] store;
    MazeCell currentCell, exitCell = new MazeCell(), entryCell = new MazeCell();
    final char exitMarker = 'e', entryMarker = 'm', visited = '.';
    final char passage = '0', wall = '1';
    Stack mazeStack = new Stack();
    Maze() {
        int row = 0, col = 0;
        Stack mazeRows = new Stack();
        InputStreamReader isr = new InputStreamReader(System.in);
        BufferedReader buffer = new BufferedReader(isr);
        String str;
        System.out.println("Enter a rectangular maze using the following "
                + "characters:\nm - entry\ne - exit\n1 - wall\n0 - passage\n"
                + "Enter one line at at time; end with Ctrl-z:");
        try {
            str = buffer.readLine();
            while (str != null) {
                row++;
                cols = str.length();
                str = "1" + str + "1";  // put 1s in the borderline cells;
                mazeRows.push(str);
                if (str.indexOf(exitMarker) != -1) {
                    exitCell.x = row;
```

Continues

FIGURE **4.17**   (*continued*)

```
                    exitCell.y = str.indexOf(exitMarker);
            }
            if (str.indexOf(entryMarker) != -1) {
                entryCell.x = row;
                entryCell.y = str.indexOf(entryMarker);
            }
            str = buffer.readLine();
        }
    } catch(IOException eof) {
    }
    rows = row;
    store = new char[rows+2][];       // create a 1D array of char arrays;
    store[0] = new char[cols+2];      // a borderline row;
    for ( ; !mazeRows.isEmpty(); row--)
        store[row] = ((String) mazeRows.pop()).toCharArray();
    store[rows+1] = new char[cols+2]; // another borderline row;
    for (col = 0; col <= cols+1; col++) {
        store[0][col] = wall;         // fill the borderline rows with 1s;
        store[rows+1][col] = wall;
    }
}
void display(PrintStream out) {
    for (int row = 0; row <= rows+1; row++)
        out.println(store[row]);
    out.println();
}
void pushUnvisited(int row, int col) {
    if (store[row][col] == passage || store[row][col] == exitMarker)
        mazeStack.push(new MazeCell(row,col));
}
void exitMaze(PrintStream out) {
    int row = 0, col = 0;
    currentCell = entryCell;
    out.println();
    while (!currentCell.equals(exitCell)) {
        row = currentCell.x;
        col = currentCell.y;
        display(System.out);          // print a snapshot;
        if (!currentCell.equals(entryCell))
            store[row][col] = visited;
        pushUnvisited(row-1,col);
        pushUnvisited(row+1,col);
```

FIGURE **4.17**   (*continued*)

```
            pushUnvisited(row,col-1);
            pushUnvisited(row,col+1);
            if (mazeStack.isEmpty()) {
                display(out);
                out.println("Failure");
                return;
            }
            else currentCell = (MazeCell) mazeStack.pop();
        }
        display(out);
        out.println("Success");
    }
    static public void main (String args[]) {
        (new Maze()).exitMaze(System.out);
    }
}
```

No other changes need to be made, although according to Figure 4.7, `java.util.Stack()` uses method `empty()`, but the program in Figure 4.17 uses method `isEmpty()`. This occurs because the method `isEmpty()` is inherited by `java.util.Stack()` from `java.util.Vector()`.

🔼 4.5 EXERCISES

1. Reverse the order of elements on stack S
   a. using two additional stacks
   b. using one additional queue
   c. using one additional stack and some additional variables

2. Put the elements on the stack S in ascending order using one additional stack and some additional variables.

3. Transfer elements from stack S_1 to stack S_2 so that the elements from S_2 are in the same order as on S_1
   a. using one additional stack
   b. using no additional stack but only some additional variables

4. Suggest an implementation of a stack to hold elements of two different types, such as structures and float numbers.

5. A possible definition of a linked list based stack can be given as follows:

```
public class LLStack2 extends LinkedList {
    public Object pop() {
        return removeLast();
    }
    public void push(Object el) {
        add(el);
    }
    . . . . .
    }
}
```

It appears to be simpler than the definition of LLStack in Figure 4.5. What is the problem with the definition of LLStack2?

6. Using additional variables, order all elements on a queue using also

   a. two additional queues

   b. one additional queue

7. In this chapter, two different implementations were developed for a stack: class Stack and class LLStack. The names of methods in both classes suggest that the same data structure is meant; however, a tighter connection between these two classes can be established. Define an abstract base class for a stack and derive from it both class Stack and class LLStack.

8. In the class Stack, no test is made in push() for stack overflow. The test should be made by the user to avoid abnormal program termination. Similarly, no test for stack underflow is made in pop() and in topEl(). The tests can be incorporated in all these methods in a variety of ways. Here are some examples.

   a. `void push(Object el, boolean pushed) { ... }`

      In this definition, pushed is set by push() to false if stack is full and to true if el can be pushed onto the stack. The variable pushed is tested by the user after push() is finished.

   b. `boolean push (Object el) { ... }`

      In this version, the return value plays the same role as pushed in the previous version. push() returns true if el was pushed successfully, false otherwise.

   c. `void push(Object el) { if (isFull()) Runtime.getRuntime.exit(0)`
      `                                   else ...}`

      Interrupt the program when an attempt is made to push an element onto a full stack, possibly printing an error message, and push the element on the stack otherwise.

   What are the disadvantages of these definitions?

9. Define a stack in terms of a queue, that is; create a class

```
class StackQ {
    Queue pool = new Queue();
    . . . . . . . . . . .
    public void push(Object el) {
        pool.enqueue(el);
    . . . . . . . . .
```

10. Define a queue in terms of a stack.

11. A generic queue class defined in terms of a vector:

```
public class QueueV
    private java.util.Vector list = new java.util.Vector();
    public Object dequeue() {
    . . . . . . . . . .
```

Is this a viable solution?

12. Modify the program from the case study to print out the path without dead ends and, possibly, with detours. For example, for an input maze

```
1111111
1e00001
1110111
1000001
100m001
1111111
```

the program from the case study outputs the processed maze

```
1111111
1e....1
111.111
1.....1
1..m..1
1111111
Success
```

The modified program should, in addition, generate the path from the exit to the mouse:

[1 1] [1 2] [1 3] [2 3] [3 3] [3 4] [3 5] [4 5] [4 4] [4 3]

which leaves out two dead ends, [1 4] [1 5] and [3 2] [3 1] [4 1] [4 2], but retains a detour, [3 4] [3 5] [4 5] [4 4].

13. Modify the program from the previous exercise so that it prints the maze with the path without dead ends; the path is indicated by dashes and vertical bars to show the

changes of direction of the path; for the input maze from the previous exercise, the modified program should output

```
1111111
1e--..1
111|111
1..|--1
1..m-|1
1111111
```

🔲 4.6 PROGRAMMING ASSIGNMENTS

1. Write a program that determines whether or not an input string is a palindrome, that is, whether or not it can be read the same way forward and backward. At each point, you can read only one character of the input string; do not use an array to first store this string and then analyze it (except, possibly, in a stack implementation). Consider using multiple stacks.

2. Write a program to convert a number from decimal notation to a number expressed in a number system whose base (or radix) is a number between 2 and 9. The conversion is performed by repetitious division by the base to which a number is being converted and then taking the remainders of division in the reverse order. For example, in converting to binary, number 6 requires three such divisions: $6/2 = 3$ remainder 0, $3/2 = 1$ remainder 1, and finally, $1/2 = 0$ remainder 1. The remainders 0, 1, and 1 are put in the reverse order so that the binary equivalent of 6 is equal to 110.

   Modify your program so that it can perform a conversion in the case when the base is a number between 11 and 27. Number systems with bases greater than 10 require more symbols. Therefore, use capital letters. For example, a hexadecimal system requires 16 digits: 0, 1, . . ., 9, A, B, C, D, E, F. In this system, decimal number 26 is equal to 1A in hexadecimal notation, since $26/16 = 1$ remainder 10 (that is, A), and $1/16 = 0$ remainder 1.

3. Write a program that implements the algorithm `delimiterMatching()` from Section 4.1.

4. Write a program that implements the algorithm `addingLargeNumbers()` from Section 4.1.

5. Write a program to perform the four basic arithmetic operations, +, −, ·, and /, on very large integers; the result of division should also be an integer. Apply these operations to compute 123^{45}, or the hundredth number in the sequence $1 * 2 + 3, 2 * 3^2 + 4, 3 * 4^3 + 5, . . .$ Also apply them to compute the Gödel numbers of arithmetic expressions.

   The Gödel numbering function GN first establishes a correspondence between basic elements of language and numbers:

Symbol	Gödel Number GN
$=$	1
$+$	2
$\star$	3
$-$	4
$/$	5
$($	6
$)$	7
$\wedge$	8
0	9
S	10
x_i	$11 + 2 \star i$
X_i	$12 + 2 \star i$

where S is the successor function. Then, for any formula $F = s_1 s_2 \ldots s_n$:

$$GN('s_1 s_2 \ldots s_n') = 2^{GN(s_1)} \star 3^{GN(s_2)} \star \ldots \star p_n^{GN(s_n)}$$

where p_n is the nth prime. For example,

$$GN(1) = GN(S0) = 2^{10} \star 3^9$$

and

$$GN('x_1 + x_3 = x_4') = 2^{11+2} \star 3^2 \star 5^{11+6} \star 7^1 \star 11^{11+8}$$

In this way, every arithmetic expression can be assigned a unique number. This method has been used by Gödel to prove theorems, known as Gödel's theorems, which are of extreme importance for the foundations of mathematics.

6. Write a program for adding very large floating-point numbers. Extend this program to other arithmetic operations.

Bibliography

Queues

Sloyer, Clifford, Copes, Wayne, Sacco, William, and Starck, Robert, *Queues: Will This Wait Never End!* Providence, RI: Janson, 1987.

Priority Queues

Blackstone, John H., Hogg, Gary L., and Phillips, Don T., "A Two-List Synchronization Procedure for Discrete Event Simulation," *Communications of the ACM* 24 (1981), 825–829.

Hendriksen, James O., "An Improved Events List Algorithm," *Proceedings of the 1977 Winter Simulation Conference,* Piscataway, NJ: IEEE, 1977, 547–557.

Hendriksen, James O., "Event List Management—A Tutorial," *Proceedings of the 1983 Winter Simulation Conference,* Piscataway, NJ: IEEE, 1983, 543–551.

Jones, Douglas W., "An Empirical Comparison of Priority-Queue and Event-Set Implementations," *Communications of the ACM* 29 (1986), 300–311.

Java Virtual Machine

Joshi, Daniel I., Lemay, Laura, and Perkins, Charles L., *Teach Yourself Java in Café in 21 Days*, Indianapolis, IN: Sams.net Publishing, 1996, Ch. 21.

Lindholm, Tim and Yellin, Frank, *The Java Virtual Machine Specification*, Reading, MA: Addison-Wesley, 1999.

Meyer, Jon and Downing, Troy, *Java Virtual Machine*, Cambridge, MA: O'Reilly, 1997.

Recursion

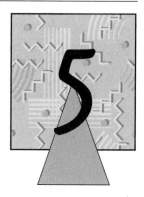

5.1 Recursive Definitions

One of the basic rules for defining new objects or concepts is that the definition should contain only such terms that have already been defined or that are obvious. Therefore, an object which is defined in terms of itself is a serious violation of this rule—a vicious circle. On the other hand, there are many programming concepts that define themselves. As it turns out, formal restrictions imposed on definitions such as existence and uniqueness are satisfied and no violation of the rules takes place. Such definitions are called *recursive definitions* and are used primarily to define infinite sets. When defining such a set, giving a complete list of elements is impossible, and for large finite sets, it is inefficient. Thus, a more efficient way has to be devised to determine if an object belongs to a set.

A recursive definition consists of two parts. In the first part, called the *anchor* or the *ground case*, the basic elements that are the building blocks of all other elements of the set are listed. In the second part, rules are given that allow for the construction of new objects out of basic elements or objects that have already been constructed. These rules are applied again and again to generate new objects. For example, to construct the set of natural numbers, one basic element, 0 is singled out, and the operation of incrementing by 1 is given as:

1. $0 \in \mathbf{N}$;
2. if $n \in \mathbf{N}$, then $(n + 1) \in \mathbf{N}$;
3. there are no other objects in the set $\mathbf{N}$.

(More axioms are needed to ensure that only the set that we know as the natural numbers can be constructed by these rules.)

According to these rules, the set of natural numbers **N** consists of the following items: $0, 0 + 1, 0 + 1 + 1, 0 + 1 + 1 + 1$, etc. Although the set **N** contains objects (and only such objects) that we call natural numbers, the definition results in a somewhat unwieldy list of elements. Can you imagine doing arithmetic on large numbers using such a specification? Therefore, it is more convenient to use the following definition, which encompasses the whole range of Arabic numeric heritage:

1. $0, 1, 2, 3, 4, 5, 6, 7, 8, 9 \in$ **N**;

2. if $n \in$ **N**, then $n0, n1, n2, n3, n4, n5, n6, n7, n8, n9 \in$ **N**;

3. these are the only natural numbers.

Then the set **N** includes all possible combinations of the basic building blocks 0 through 9.

Recursive definitions serve two purposes: *generating* new elements, as already indicated, and *testing* whether or not an element belongs to a set. In the case of testing, the problem is solved by reducing it to a simpler problem, and if the simpler problem is still too complex it is reduced to an even simpler problem, and so on, until it is reduced to a problem indicated in the anchor. For instance, is 123 a natural number? According to the second condition of the definition introducing the set **N**, $123 \in$ **N** if $12 \in$ **N** and the first condition already says that $3 \in$ **N**; but $12 \in$ **N** if $1 \in$ **N** and $2 \in$ **N**, and they both belong to **N**.

The ability to decompose a problem into simpler subproblems of the same kind is sometimes a real blessing, as we shall see in the discussion of quicksort in a later chapter, or a curse, as we shall see shortly in this chapter.

Recursive definitions are frequently used to define functions and sequences of numbers. For instance, the factorial function, !, can be defined in the following manner:

$$n! = \begin{cases} 1 & \text{if } n = 0 \text{ (anchor)} \\ n \cdot (n-1)! & \text{if } n > 0 \text{ (inductive step)} \end{cases}$$

Using this definition, we can generate the sequence of numbers

$$1, 1, 2, 6, 24, 120, 720, 5040, 40320, 362880, 3628800, \ldots$$

which includes the factorials of the numbers $0, 1, 2, \ldots, 10, \ldots$

Another example is the definition

$$f(n) = \begin{cases} 1 & \text{if } n = 0 \\ f(n-1) + \dfrac{1}{f(n-1)} & \text{if } n > 0 \end{cases}$$

which generates the sequence of rational numbers

$$1, 2, \frac{5}{2}, \frac{29}{10}, \frac{941}{290}, \frac{969581}{272890}, \ldots$$

Recursive definitions of sequences have one undesirable feature: To determine the value of an element s_n of a sequence, we first have to compute the values of some or all of the previous elements, $s_1, \ldots, s_{n-1}$. For example, calculating the value of 3! requires us to first compute the values of 0!, 1!, and 2!. Computationally, this is undesirable since it forces us to make calculations in a roundabout way. Therefore, we want to find an equivalent definition or formula that makes no references to other elements of the sequence. Generally, finding such a formula is a difficult problem that cannot always be solved. But the formula is preferable to a recursive definition because it simplifies the computational process and allows us to find the answer for an integer n without computing the values for integers $0, 1, \ldots, n-1$. For example, a definition of the sequence g,

$$g(n) = \begin{cases} 1 & \text{if } n = 0 \\ 2 \cdot g(n-1) & \text{if } n > 0 \end{cases}$$

can be converted into the simple formula

$$g(n) = 2^n$$

In the foregoing discussion, recursive definitions have been dealt with only theoretically, as a definition used in mathematics. Naturally, our interest is in computer science. One area where recursive definitions are used extensively is in the specification of the grammars of programming languages. Every programming language manual contains—either as an appendix or throughout the text—a specification of all valid language elements. Grammar is specified either in terms of block diagrams or in terms of the Backus-Naur form (BNF). For example, the syntactic definition of a statement in the Java language can be presented in the block diagram form:

statement ⟶ while ⟶ (⟶ expression ⟶) ⟶ statement

if ⟶ (⟶ expression ⟶) ⟶ statement ⟶ else ⟶ statement ⟶

or in BNF:

$$\langle statement \rangle ::= \text{while } (\langle expression \rangle) \langle statement \rangle \mid$$
$$\text{if } (\langle expression \rangle) \langle statement \rangle \mid$$
$$\text{if } (\langle expression \rangle) \langle statement \rangle \text{else} \langle statement \rangle \mid$$
$$\ldots$$

The language element $\langle statement \rangle$ is defined recursively, in terms of itself. Such definitions naturally express the possibility of creating such syntactic constructs as nested statements or expressions.

Recursive definitions are also used in programming. The good news is that virtually no effort is needed to make the transition from a recursive definition of a function to its implementation in Java. We simply make a translation from the formal definition into Java syntax. Hence, for example, a Java equivalent of factorial is the method

```java
int factorial (int n) {
   if (n == 0)
        return 1;
   else return n * factorial (n - 1);
}
```

The problem now seems to be more critical since it is far from clear how a method calling itself can possibly work, let alone return the correct result. This chapter shows that it is possible for such a method to work properly. Recursive definitions on most computers are eventually implemented using a run-time stack, although the whole work of implementing recursion is done by the operating system, and the source code includes no indication of how it is performed. E. W. Dijkstra introduced the idea of using a stack to implement recursion. To better understand recursion and to see how it works, it is necessary to discuss the processing of method calls and to look at operations carried out by the system at method invocation and method exit.

🔲 5.2 METHOD CALLS AND RECURSION IMPLEMENTATION

What happens when a method is called? If the method has formal parameters, they have to be initialized to the values passed as actual parameters. In addition, the system has to know where to resume execution of the program after the method has finished. The method can be called by other methods or by the main program (the method main()). The information indicating where it has been called from has to be remembered by the system. This could be done by storing the return address in main memory in a place set aside for return addresses, but we do not know in advance how much space might be needed, and allocating too much space for that purpose alone is not efficient.

For a method call, more information has to be stored than just a return address. Therefore, dynamic allocation using the run-time stack is a much better solution. It needs to be stressed that the run-time stack is maintained by a particular operating system. At the end of Section 4.1, a Java stack used by the Java Virtual Machine was briefly described. Java stack and run-time stack are two different entities. They are similar in that their role in processing method calls is basically the same; therefore, they store similar information that enables this processing, although they store this information differently. The role of the interpreter java is to convert information bytecodes in .class files so that the run-time stack takes over the function of the Java stack, which is only an abstract construct. The subsequent discussion is presented in terms of the run-time stack rather than the Java stack, which in no way changes the logic of processing method calls, in particular, recursive calls.

What information should be preserved when a method is called? First, automatic (local) variables must be stored. If method f1() which contains a declaration of an automatic variable x calls method f2() which locally declares the variable x, the system has to make a distinction between these two variables x. If f2() uses a variable x, then its own x is meant; if f2() assigns a value to x, then x belonging to f1() should be left unchanged. When f2() is finished, f1() can use the value assigned to its private x before f2() was called. This is especially important in the context of the present chapter, when `f1()` is the same as `f2()`, when a method calls itself recursively. How does the system make a distinction between these two variables `x`?

The state of each method, including `main()`, is characterized by the contents of all automatic variables, by the values of the method's parameters, and by the return address indicating where to restart its caller. The data area containing all this information is called an *activation record* or *stack frame* and is allocated on the run-time stack. An activation record exists for as long as a method owning it is executing. This record is a private pool of information for the method, a repository that stores all information necessary for its proper execution and how to return to where it was called from. Activation records usually have a short lifespan because they are dynamically allocated at method entry and deallocated upon exiting. Only the activation record of `main()` outlives every other activation record.

An activation record usually contains the following information:

▲ Values for all parameters to the method, location of the first cell if an array is passed or a variable is passed by reference, and copies of all other data items.

▲ Local (automatic) variables which can be stored elsewhere, in which case, the activation record contains only their descriptors and pointers to the locations where they are stored.

▲ The return address to resume control by the caller, the address of the caller's instruction immediately following the call.

▲ A dynamic link, which is a pointer to the caller's activation record.

▲ The returned value for a method not declared as `void`. Since the size of the activation record may vary from one call to another, the returned value is placed right above the activation record of the caller.

As mentioned above, if a method is called either by `main()` or by another method, then its activation record is created on the run-time stack. The run-time stack always reflects the current state of the method. For example, suppose that `main()` calls method `f1()`, `f1()` calls `f2()`, and `f2()` in turn calls `f3()`. If `f3()` is being executed, then the state of the run-time stack is as shown in Figure 5.1. By the nature of the stack, if the activation record for `f3()` is popped by moving the stack pointer right below the return value of `f3()`, then `f2()` resumes execution and now has free access to the private pool of information necessary for reactivation of its execution. On the other hand, if `f3()` happens to call another method `f4()`, then the run-time stack increases its height since the activation record for `f4()` is created on the stack and the activity of `f3()` is suspended.

Creating an activation record whenever a method is called allows the system to handle recursion properly. Recursion is calling a method that happens to have the same name as the caller. Therefore, a recursive call is not literally a method calling itself, but rather an instantiation of a method calling another instantiation of the same original. These invocations are represented internally by different activation records and are thus differentiated by the system.

FIGURE **5.1**   Contents of the run-time stack when `main()` calls method `f1()`, `f1()` calls `f2()`, and `f2()` calls `f3()`.

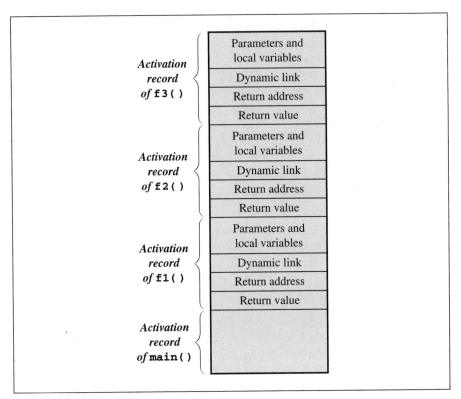

5.3 ANATOMY OF A RECURSIVE CALL

The function that defines raising any number x to a nonnegative integer power n is a good example of a recursive function. The most natural definition of this function is given by:

$$x^n = \begin{cases} 1 & \text{if } n = 0 \\ x \cdot x^{n-1} & \text{if } n > 0 \end{cases}$$

A Java method for computing x^n can be written directly from the definition of a power:

```
/* 102 */ double power (double x, int n) {
/* 103 */     if (n == 0)
/* 104 */         return 1.0;
          // else
```

```
/* 105 */                return x * power(x,n-1);
          }
```

What if we called the method with a negative n? To avoid this problem, we can add another test in the method, such as if (n < 0), and return a special value, say, –1, or print an error message, or we can make sure before power() is called that $n \geq 0$.

Using this definition, the value of x^4 can be computed in the following way:

$$x^4 = x \cdot x^3 = x \cdot (x \cdot x^2) = x \cdot (x \cdot (x \cdot x^1)) = x \cdot (x \cdot (x \cdot (x \cdot x^0)))$$
$$= x \cdot (x \cdot (x \cdot (x \cdot 1))) = x \cdot (x \cdot (x \cdot (x))) = x \cdot (x \cdot (x \cdot x))$$
$$= x \cdot (x \cdot x \cdot x) = x \cdot x \cdot x \cdot x$$

The repetitive application of the inductive step eventually leads to the anchor which is the last step in the chain of recursive calls. The anchor produces 1 as a result of raising x to the power of zero; the result is passed back to the previous recursive call. Now, that call, whose execution has been pending, returns its result, $x \cdot 1 = x$. The third call, which has been waiting for this result, computes its own result, namely, $x \cdot x$, and returns it. Next, this number $x \cdot x$ is received by the second call which multiplies it by x and returns the result, $x \cdot x \cdot x$, to the first invocation of power(). This call receives $x \cdot x \cdot x$, multiplies it by x, and returns the final result. In this way, each new call increases the level of recursion, as follows:

call 1	$x^4 = x \cdot x^3$	$= x \cdot x \cdot x \cdot x$
call 2	$x \cdot x^2$	$= x \cdot x \cdot x$
call 3	$x \cdot x^1$	$= x \cdot x$
call 4	$x \cdot x^0$	$= x \cdot 1 = x$
call 5	1	

or alternatively, as

call 1	power(x,4)
call 2	power(x,3)
call 3	power(x,2)
call 4	power(x,1)
call 5	power(x,0)
call 5	1
call 4	x
call 3	$x \cdot x$
call 2	$x \cdot x \cdot x$
call 1	$x \cdot x \cdot x \cdot x$

What does the system do as the method is being executed? As we already know, the system keeps track of all calls on its run-time stack. Each line of code is assigned a number by the system,[1] and if a line is a method call, then its number is a return address. The address is used by the system to remember where to resume execution after the method has completed. For this example, assume that the lines in the method

---

[1]This is not quite precise since the system uses machine code rather than source code to execute programs. This means that one line of source program is usually implemented by several machine instructions.

power() are assigned the numbers 102 through 105 and that it is called in main()
from the statement

```
        static public void main(String args[] {
            { ...
/* 136 */   y = power(5.6,2);
                ...
        }
```

A trace of the recursive calls is relatively simple, as indicated by this diagram

```
call 1              power(5.6,2)
call 2                  power(5.6,1)
call 3                      power(5.6,0)
call 3                      1
call 2                  5.6
call 1              31.36
```

since most of the operations are performed on the run-time stack.

When the method is invoked for the first time, four items are pushed onto the run-time stack: the return address 136, the actual parameters 5.6 and 2, and one location reserved for the value returned by power(). Figure 5.2a represents this situation. (In this and subsequent diagrams, SP is a stack pointer, AR is an activation record, and question marks stand for locations reserved for the returned values. To distinguish values from addresses, the latter are parenthesized, although addresses are numbers exactly like method arguments.)

Now the method power() is executed. First, the value of the second argument, 2, is checked, and power() tries to return the value of $5.6 \cdot$ power(5.6,1) because that argument is not 0. This cannot be done immediately since the system does not know the value of power(5.6,1); it must be computed first. Therefore, power() is called again with the arguments 5.6 and 1. But before this call is executed, the run-time stack receives new items, and its contents are shown in Figure 5.2b.

Again, the second argument is checked to see if it is 0. Since it is equal to 1, power() is called for the third time, this time with the arguments 5.6 and 0. Before the method is executed, the system remembers the arguments and the return address by putting them on the stack, not forgetting to allocate one cell for the result. Figure 5.2c contains the new contents of the stack.

Again, the question arises: Is the second argument equal to zero? Because it finally is, a concrete value—namely, 1.0—can be returned and placed on the stack, and the method is finished without making any additional calls. At this point, there are two pending calls on the run-time stack—the calls to power()—that have to be completed. How is this done? The system first eliminates the activation record of power() that has just finished. This is performed logically by popping all its fields (the result, two arguments, and the return address) off the stack. We say "logically" since physically all these fields remain on the stack and only the SP is decremented appropriately. This is important because we do not want the result to be destroyed since it has not been used yet. Before and after completion of the last call of power(), the stack looks the same, but the SP's value is changed (see Figures 5.2d and 5.2e).

FIGURE **5.2**   Changes to the run-time stack during execution of `power(5.6,2)`.

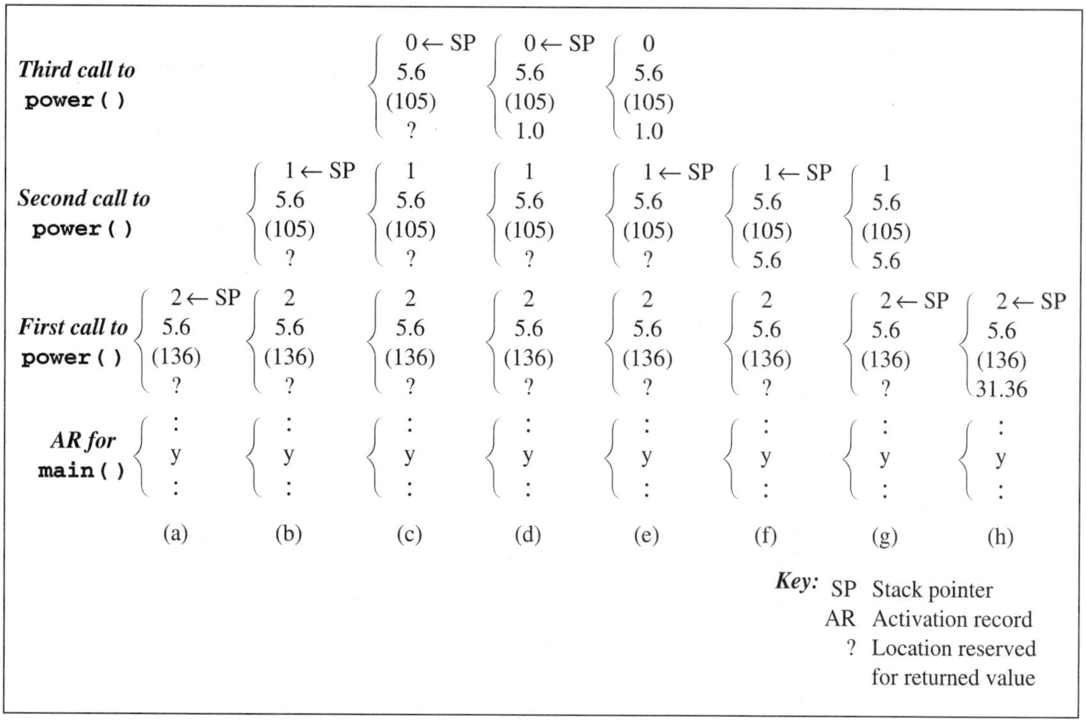

Third call to `power()`			0 ← SP 5.6 (105) ?	0 ← SP 5.6 (105) 1.0	0 5.6 (105) 1.0			
Second call to `power()`		1 ← SP 5.6 (105) ?	1 5.6 (105) ?	1 5.6 (105) ?	1 ← SP 5.6 (105) ?	1 ← SP 5.6 (105) 5.6	1 5.6 (105) 5.6	
First call to `power()`	2 ← SP 5.6 (136) ?	2 5.6 (136) ?	2 5.6 (136) ?	2 5.6 (136) ?	2 5.6 (136) ?	2 5.6 (136) ?	2 ← SP 5.6 (136) ?	2 ← SP 5.6 (136) 31.36
AR for `main()`	⋮ y ⋮	⋮ y ⋮	⋮ y ⋮	⋮ y ⋮	⋮ y ⋮	⋮ y ⋮	⋮ y ⋮	⋮ y ⋮
	(a)	(b)	(c)	(d)	(e)	(f)	(g)	(h)

Key: SP Stack pointer
AR Activation record
? Location reserved
    for returned value

Now the second call to `power()` can complete since it waited for the result of the call `power(5.6,0)`. This result, 1.0, is multiplied by 5.6 and stored in the field allocated for the result. After that, the system can pop the current activation record off the stack by decrementing the SP, and it can finish the execution of the first call to `power()` that needed the result for the second call. Figure 5.2f shows the contents of the stack before changing the SP's value, and Figure 5.2g shows the contents of the stack after this change. At this moment, `power()` can finish its first call by multiplying the result of its second call, 5.6, by its first argument, also 5.6. The system now returns to the method that invoked `power()`, and the final value, 31.36, is assigned to y. Right before the assignment is executed, the content of the stack looks like Figure 5.2h.

The method `power()` can be implemented differently, without using any recursion, by using a loop:

```
double nonRecPower(double x, int n) {
   double result = 1;
   if (n > 0)
   for (result = x; n > 1; --n)
        result *= x;
   return result;
}
```

Do we gain anything by using recursion instead of a loop? The recursive version seems to be more intuitive since it is similar to the original definition of the power function. The definition is simply expressed in Java without losing the original structure of the definition. The recursive version increases program readability, improves self-documentation, and simplifies coding. In our example, the code of the nonrecursive version is not substantially larger than in the recursive version, but for most recursive implementations, the code is shorter than it is in the nonrecursive implementations.

☐ 5.4 TAIL RECURSION

All recursive definitions contain a reference to a set or function being defined. There are, however, a variety of ways such a reference can be implemented. This reference can be done in a straightforward manner or in an intricate fashion, just once or many times. There may be many possible levels of recursion or different levels of complexity. In the following sections, some of these types are discussed, starting with the simplest case, *tail recursion.*

Tail recursion is characterized by the use of only one recursive call at the very end of a method implementation. In other words, when the call is made, there are no statements left to be executed by the method; the recursive call is not only the last statement but there are no earlier recursive calls, direct or indirect. For example, the method `tail()` defined as

```
void tail (int i) {
  if (i > 0) {
    System.out.print (i + "");
    tail(i-1);
  }
}
```

is an example of a method with tail recursion, whereas the method `nonTail()` defined as

```
void nonTail (int i) {
  if (i > 0) {
    nonTail(i-1);
    System.out.print (i + "");
    nonTail(i-1);
  }
}
```

is not. Tail recursion is simply a glorified loop and can be easily replaced by one. In this example, it is replaced by substituting a loop for the `if` statement and incrementing or decrementing the variable `i` in accordance with the level of recursion. In this way, `tail()` can be expressed by an iterative method:

```
void iterativeEquivalentOfTail (int i) {
   for ( ; i > 0; i--)
   System.out.print(i+ "");


}
```

Is there any advantage in using tail recursion over iteration? For languages such as Java, there may be no compelling advantage, but in a language such as Prolog, which has no explicit loop construct (loops are simulated by recursion), tail recursion acquires a much greater weight. In languages endowed with a loop or its equivalents, such as an `if` statement combined with a `goto` statement or labeled statement, tail recursion is not a recommended feature.

◨ 5.5 Nontail Recursion

Another problem that can be implemented in recursion is printing an input line in reverse order. Here is a simple recursive implementation:

```
/* 200 */ void reverse() {
/* 201 */       char ch = getChar();
/* 202 */       if (ch != '\n') {
/* 203 */             reverse();
/* 204 */             System.out.print(ch);
              }
        }
```

Where is the trick? It does not seem possible that the method does anything. But it turns out that, by the power of recursion, it does exactly what it was designed for. `main()` calls `reverse()` and the input is the string: "ABC." First, an activation record is created with cells for the variable `ch` and the return address. There is no need to reserve a cell for a result, since no value is returned, which is indicated by using `void` in front of the method's name. A user-defined method `getChar()` reads in the first character, "A." Figure 5.3a shows the contents of the run-time stack right before `reverse()` calls itself recursively for the first time.

The second character is read in and checked to see if it is the end-of-line character, and if not, `reverse()` is called again. But in either case, the value of `ch` is pushed onto the run-time stack along with the return address. Before `reverse()` is called for a third time (the second time recursively), there are two more items on the stack (see Figure 5.3b).

Note that the method is called as many times as the number of characters contained in the input sting, including the end-of-line character. In our example, `reverse()` is called four times, and the run-time stack during the last call is shown in Figure 5.3d.

On the fourth call, `getChar()` finds the end-of-line character and `reverse()` executes no other statement. The system retrieves the return address from the activation record and discards this record by decrementing SP by the proper number of bytes. Execution resumes from line 204, which is a print statement. Because the activation record of the third call is now active, the value of `ch`, the letter "C," is output as

FIGURE **5.3**   Changes on the run-time stack during the execution of reverse().

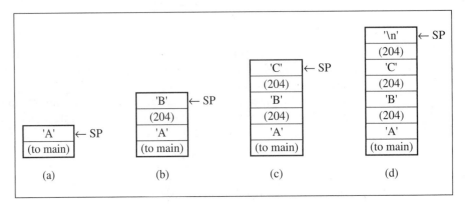

(a)   (b)   (c)   (d)

the first character. Next, the activation record of the third call to reverse() is discarded and now SP points to where "B" is stored. The second call is about to be finished, but the first "B" is assigned to ch and then the statement on line 204 is executed, which results in printing "B" on the screen right after "C." Finally, the activation record of the first call to reverse() is reached. Then "A" is printed, and what can be seen on the screen is the string "CBA." The first call is finally finished and the program continues execution in main().

Compare the recursive implementation with a nonrecursive version of the same method:

```
void simpleIterativeReverse() {
        String stack = new String();
        int top = 0;
        try { stack = buffer.readLine();
        } catch (IOException io) {
        }
        for (top = stack.length() - 1; top >= 0; top--)
            System.out.print(stack.charAt(top));
    }
```

The method is quite short and, perhaps, a bit more cryptic than its recursive counterpart. What is the difference then? Keep in mind that the brevity and relative simplicity of the second version are due mainly to the fact that we want to reverse a string or array of characters. This means that methods like length() and readLine() from the standard Java library can be used. If we are not supplied with such methods, then our iterative method has to be implemented differently:

```
void iterativeReverse() {
        char[] stack = new char[80];
        int top = 0;
```

```
        stack[top] = getChar();
        while (stack[top] != '\n')
            stack[++top] = getChar();
        for (top -= 1; top >= 0; top--)
            System.out.print(stack[top]);
    }
```

The `while` loop replaces `getLine()` and the autoincrement of variable `top` replaces `length()`. The `for` loop is about the same as before. This discussion is not purely theoretical because reversing an input line consisting of integers uses the same implementation as `iterativeReverse()` after changing the data type of `stack` from `char` to `int` and modifying the `while` loop.

Note that the variable name `stack` used for the array is not accidental. We are just making explicit what is done implicitly by the system. Our stack takes over the run-time stack's duty. Its use is necessary here since one simple loop does not suffice, as in the case of tail recursion. In addition, the statement `System.out.print()` from the recursive version has to be accounted for. Note also that the variable `stack` is local to the method `iterativeReverse()`. However, if it were a requirement to have a stack object `st`, then this implementation can be written as

```
void nonRecursiveReverse() {
    Stack st = new Stack();
    char ch = getChar();
    while (ch != '\n') {
        st.push(new Character(ch));
        ch = getChar();
    }
    while (!st.isEmpty())
        System.out.print((Character) st.pop());
}
```

After comparing `iterativeReverse()` to `nonRecursiveReverse()`, we can conclude that the first version is better because it is faster, no method calls are made, and the method is self-sufficient, whereas `nonRecursiveReverse()` calls at least one method during each loop iteration, slowing down execution.

One way or the other, the transformation of recursion into iteration usually involves the explicit handling of a stack. Furthermore, when converting a method from a recursive into an iterative version, program clarity can be diminished and the brevity of program formulation lost. Iterative versions of recursive Java methods are not as verbose as in other programming languages, so program brevity may not be an issue.

To conclude this section, consider a construction of the von Koch snowflake. The curve was constructed in 1904 by Swedish mathematician Helge von Koch as an example of a continuous and nondifferentiable curve with an infinite length and yet encompassing a finite area. Examples of von Koch snowflakes are presented in Figure 5.4. As in real snowflakes, these curves have six petals, but to facilitate the algorithm, it is treated as a combination of three identical curves drawn in different angles and joined together. One such curve is drawn in the following fashion:

FIGURE **5.4**   Examples of von Koch snowflakes.

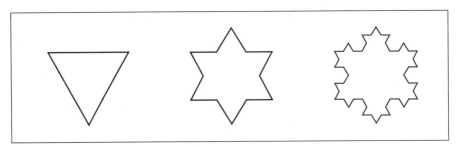

FIGURE **5.5**   The process of drawing four sides of one segment of the von Koch snowflake.

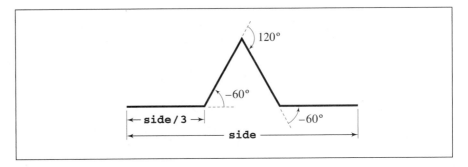

1. Divide an interval *side* into three even parts.
2. Move one-third of *side* in the direction specified by *angle*.
3. Turn to the right 60° (i.e., turn –60°) and go forward one-third of *side*.
4. Turn to the left 120° and proceed forward one-third of *side*.
5. Turn right 60° and again draw a line one-third of *side* long.

    The result of these five steps is summarized in Figure 5.5. This line, however, becomes more jagged if every one of the four intervals became a miniature of the whole curve, that is, if the process of drawing four lines were made for each of these *side*/3 long intervals. As a result, sixteen intervals *side*/9 long would be drawn. The process may be continued indefinitely—at least in theory. Computer graphics resolution prevents us from going too far because if lines are smaller than the diameter of a pixel, we just see one dot on the screen.

    The five steps that instead of drawing one line of length *side* draw four lines each of length one-third of *side* form one cycle only. Each of these four lines can also be compound lines drawn by the use of the described cycle. This is a situation in which recursion is well suited, which is reflected by the following pseudocode:

```
drawFourLines (side, level)
   if (level = 0)
      draw a line;
   else
      drawFourLines(side/3, level-1);
      turn left 60°;
      drawFourLines(side/3, level-1);
      turn right 120°;
      drawFourLines(side/3, level-1);
      turn left 60°;
      drawFourLines(side/3, level-1);
```

This pseudocode can be rendered almost without change into Java code. However, remember that a line drawn must not be of deliberate length, because the snowflake drawn will not be a closed line. Therefore, the original line is divided in three parts, each of which is divided in three parts also, level-1 times. Figure 5.6 contains the Java code for this example.

FIGURE **5.6**   Recursive implementation of the von Koch snowflake.

```java
import java.awt.*;

class vonKoch extends Frame {
    vonKoch(int x, int y, double s, int lvl) {
        super("vonKochs");
        currPt = new Point(x,y);
        level = lvl;
        side = s;
        resize(600,400);
        setForeground(Color.white);
        setBackground(Color.red);
        show();
    }
    double side, angle = 0.0;
    int level;
    Point currPt, pt = new Point();
    void right(double x) {
        angle += x;
    }
    void left (double x) {
        angle -= x;
    }
    void drawFourLines(double side, int level, Graphics g) {
```

Continues

FIGURE **5.6**   *(continued)*

```
        if (level == 0) {
            // arguments to sin() and cos() must be angles given
            // in radians, thus, the angles given in degrees must be
            // multiplied by PI/180;
            pt.x = ((int)(Math.cos(angle*Math.PI/180)*side)) + currPt.x;
            pt.y = ((int)(Math.sin(angle*Math.PI/180)*side)) + currPt.y;
            g.drawLine(currPt.x, currPt.y, pt.x, pt.y);
            currPt.x = pt.x;
            currPt.y = pt.y;
        }
        else {
            drawFourLines(side/3.0,level-1,g);
            left (60);
            drawFourLines(side/3.0,level-1,g);
            right(120);
            drawFourLines(side/3.0,level-1,g);
            left (60);
            drawFourLines(side/3.0,level-1,g);
        }
    }
    public void paint(Graphics g) {
        for (int i = 1; i <= 3; i++) {
            drawFourLines(side,level,g);
            right(120);
        }
    }
    static public void main(String[] a) {
        new vonKoch(200,  150,  200, 3);
    }
}
```

🞂 5.6 INDIRECT RECURSION

The preceding sections discussed only direct recursion, where a method f() called itself. However, f() can call itself indirectly via a chain of other calls. For example, f() can call g(), and g() can call f(). This is the simplest case of indirect recursion. The chain of intermediate calls can be of an arbitrary length, as in:

```
f() -> f1() -> f2() -> ... -> fn() -> f()
```

FIGURE **5.7**   A tree of recursive calls for sin (x).

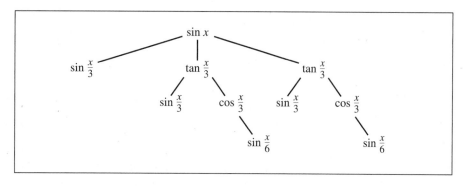

There is also the situation when $f()$ can call itself indirectly through different chains. Thus, in addition to the chain just given, another chain might also be possible. For instance

```
f() -> g1() -> g2() -> ... -> gm() -> f()
```

This situation can be exemplified by three methods used for decoding information. `receive()` stores the incoming information in a buffer, `decode()` converts it into legible form, and `store()` stores it in a file. `receive()` fills the buffer and calls `decode()`, which in turn, after finishing its job, submits the buffer with decided information to `store()`. After `store()` accomplishes its tasks, it calls `receive()` to intercept more encoded information using the same buffer. Therefore, we have the chain of calls

```
receive() -> decode() -> store() -> receive() -> decode() -> ...
```

which is finished when no new information arrives. These three methods work in the following manner:

```
receive(buffer)
    while buffer is not filled up
        if information is still incoming
            get a character and store it in buffer;
        else exit();
        decode(buffer);


decode(buffer)
    decode information in buffer;
    store(buffer);


store(buffer)
    transfer information from buffer to file;
    receive(buffer);
```

A more mathematically oriented example concerns formulas calculating the trigonometric functions sine, cosine, and tangent:

$$\sin(x) = \sin\left(\frac{x}{3}\right) \cdot \frac{\left(3 - \tan^2\left(\frac{x}{3}\right)\right)}{\left(1 + \tan^2\left(\frac{x}{3}\right)\right)}$$

$$\tan(x) = \frac{\sin(x)}{\cos(x)}$$

$$\cos(x) = 1 - \sin\left(\frac{x}{2}\right)$$

As usual in the case of recursion, there has to be an anchor in order to avoid falling into an infinite loop of recursive calls. In the case of sine, we can use the following approximation:

$$\sin(x) \approx x - \frac{x^3}{6}$$

where small values of x give a better approximation. To compute the sine of a number x such that its absolute value is greater than an assumed tolerance, we have to compute $\sin\left(\frac{x}{3}\right)$ directly, $\sin\left(\frac{x}{3}\right)$ indirectly through tangent, and also indirectly, $\sin\left(\frac{x}{3}\right)$ through tangent and cosine. If the absolute value of $\frac{x}{3}$ is sufficiently small, which does not require other recursive calls, we can represent all the calls as a tree, as in Figure 5.7.

☐ 5.7 NESTED RECURSION

A more complicated case of recursion is found in definitions in which a function is not only defined in terms of itself but is also used as one of the parameters. The following definition is an example of such a nesting:

$$h(n) = \begin{cases} 0 & \text{if } n = 0 \\ n & \text{if } n > 4 \\ h(2 + h(2n)) & \text{if } n \leq 4 \end{cases}$$

Function h has a solution for all $n \geq 0$. This fact is obvious for all $n > 4$ and $n = 0$, but it has to be proven for $n = 1, 2, 3,$ and 4. Thus, $h(2) = h(2 + h(4)) = h(2 + h(2 + h(8))) = 12$. (What are the values of $h(n)$ for $n = 1, 3,$ and 4?)

Another example of nested recursion is a very important function originally suggested by Wilhelm Ackermann in 1928 and later modified by Rozsa Peter:

$$A(n,m) = \begin{cases} m+1 & \text{if } n = 0 \\ A(n-1,1) & \text{if } n > 0, m = 0 \\ A(n-1, A(n,m-1)) & \text{otherwise} \end{cases}$$

This function is interesting because of its remarkably rapid growth. It grows so fast that it is guaranteed not to have a representation by a formula that uses arithmetic operations such as addition, multiplication, and exponentiation. To illustrate the rate of growth of the Ackermann function, we need only show that

$$A(3,m) = 2^{m+3} - 3$$
$$A(4,m) = 2^{2^{\cdot^{\cdot^{2^{16}}}}} - 3$$

with a stack of m 2s in the exponent; $A(4,1) = 2^{2^{16}} - 3 = 2^{65536} - 3$, which exceeds even the number of atoms in the universe (which is 10^{80} according to current theories).

The definition translates very nicely into Java, but the task of expressing it in a nonrecursive form is truly troublesome.

◻ 5.8 EXCESSIVE RECURSION

Logical simplicity and readability are used as an argument supporting the use of recursion. The price for using recursion is slowing down execution time and storing on the run-time stack more things than required in a nonrecursive approach. If recursion is too deep (for example, computing $5.6^{100,000}$), then we can run out of space on the stack and our program terminates abnormally by raising an unrecoverable `stackOverflowError`. But usually, the number of recursive calls is much smaller than 100,000, so the danger of overflowing the stack may not be imminent.[2] However, if some recursive function repeats the computations for some parameters, the run time can be prohibitively long even for very simple cases.

Consider Fibonacci numbers. A sequence of Fibonacci numbers is defined as follows:

$$\text{Fib}(n) = \begin{cases} n & \text{if } n < 2 \\ \text{Fib}(n-2) + \text{Fib}(n-1) & \text{otherwise} \end{cases}$$

The definition states that if the first two numbers are 0 and 1, then any number in the sequence is the sum of its two predecessors. But these predecessors are in turn sums of their predecessors, and so on, to the beginning of the sequence. The sequence produced by the definition is

$$0, 1, 1, 2, 3, 5, 8, 13, 21, 34, 55, 89, \ldots$$

How can this definition be implemented in Java? It takes almost term-by-term translation to have a recursive version, which is

```
int Fib (int n) {
   if (n < 2)
      return n;
   else return Fib(n-2) + Fib(n-1);
}
```

---

[2]Even if we try to compute the value of $5.6^{100,000}$ using an iterative algorithm, we are not completely free from a troublesome situation since the number is much too large to fit even a variable of double length. Thus, although the program would not crash, the computed value would be incorrect (why?), which may be even more dangerous than a program crash.

The method is simple and easy to understand but extremely inefficient. To see it, compute `Fib(6)`, the seventh number of the sequence, which is 8. Based on the definition, the computation runs as follows:

```
Fib(6) =                         Fib(4)                        + Fib(5)
       =      Fib(2)                +           Fib(3)         + Fib(5)
       = Fib(0)+Fib(1)              +           Fib(3)         + Fib(5)
       =    0   +   1               +           Fib(3)         + Fib(5)
       =        1          + Fib(1)+    Fib(2)                 + Fib(5)
       =        1          + Fib(1)+Fib(0)+Fib(1)             + Fib(5)
```

etc.

This is just the beginning of our calculation process, and even here there are certain shortcuts. All these calculations can be expressed more concisely in the form of the tree shown in Figure 5.8. Tremendous inefficiency results because `Fib()` is called 25 times to determine the seventh element of the Fibonacci sequence. The source of this inefficiency is the repetition of the same calculations because the system forgets what has already been calculated. For example, `Fib()` is called eight times with parameter $n = 1$ to decide that 1 can be returned. For each number of the sequence, the method computes all its predecessors without taking into account that it suffices to do this only once. To find `Fib(6)` = 8, it computes `Fib(5)`, `Fib(4)`, `Fib(3)`, `Fib(2)`, `Fib(1)`, and `Fib(0)` first. To determine these values, `Fib(4)`,..., `Fib(0)` have to be computed to know the value of `Fib(5)`. Independently of this, the chain of computations `Fib(3)`,..., `Fib(0)` is executed to find `Fib(4)`.

We can prove that the number of additions required to find `Fib(n)` using a recursive definition is equal to $\text{Fib}(n + 1) - 1$. Counting two calls per one addition plus the very first call means that `Fib()` is called $2 \cdot \text{Fib}(n + 1) - 1$ times to compute `Fib(n)`. This number can be exceedingly large for fairly small ns, as the table in Figure 5.9 indicates.

It takes almost a quarter of a million calls to find the twenty-sixth Fibonacci number, and nearly 3 million calls to determine the thirty-first! This is too heavy a price for the simplicity of the recursive algorithm. As the number of calls and the run time grow exponentially with n, the algorithm has to be abandoned except for very small numbers.

An iterative algorithm may be produced rather easily as follows:

```
int iterativeFib (int n) {
    if (n < 2)
        return n;
    else {
        int i = 2, tmp, current = 1, last = 0;
        for ( ; i <= n; ++i) {
            tmp = current;
            current += last;
            last = tmp;
        }
        return current;
    }
}
```

FIGURE **5.8**   The tree of calls for `Fib(6)`.

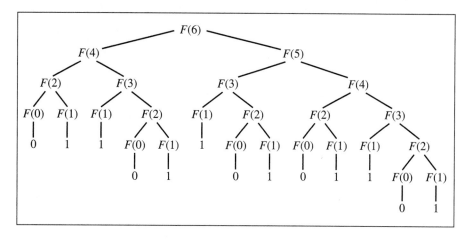

FIGURE **5.9**   Number of addition operations and number of recursive calls to calculate Fibonacci numbers.

n	Fib(n+1)	Number of Additions	Number of Calls
6	13	12	25
10	89	88	177
15	987	986	1973
20	10946	10945	21891
25	121393	121392	242785
30	1346269	1346268	2692537

For each n > 1, the method loops n − 1 times making three assignments per iteration and only one addition, disregarding the autoincrement of i (see Figure 5.10).

However, there is another, numerical method for computing Fib(n), using a formula discovered by A. de Moivre:

$$\text{Fib}(n) = \frac{\phi^n - \hat{\phi}^n}{\sqrt{5}}$$

where $\phi = \frac{1}{2}(1 + \sqrt{5})$ and $\hat{\phi} = 1 - \phi = \frac{1}{2}(1 - \sqrt{5}) \approx -0.618034$. Because $-1 < \hat{\phi} < 0$, $\hat{\phi}^n$ becomes very small when n grows. Therefore, it can be omitted from the formula and

$$\text{Fib}(n) = \frac{\phi^n}{\sqrt{5}}$$

FIGURE **5.10**   Comparison of iterative and recursive algorithms for calculating Fibonacci numbers.

n	Number of Additions	Assignments	
		Iterative Algorithm	Recursive Algorithm
6	5	15	25
10	9	27	177
15	14	42	1973
20	19	57	21891
25	24	72	242785
30	29	87	2692537

approximated to the nearest integer. This leads us to the third implementation for computing a Fibonacci number:

```
long deMoivreFib (int n)
{
return Math.round(Math.exp(n*Math.log(1.6180339897) - Math.log(2.2360679775)));
}
```

Try to justify this implementation using the definition of logarithm.

☐ 5.9 BACKTRACKING

In solving some problems, a situation arises where there are different ways leading from a given position, none of them known to lead to a solution. After trying one path unsuccessfully, we return to this crossroads and try to find a solution using another path. However, we must ensure that such a return is possible and that all paths can be tried. This technique is called *backtracking*, and it allows us to systematically try all available avenues from a certain point after some of them lead to nowhere. Using backtracking, we can always return to a position which offers other possibilities for successfully solving the problem. This technique is used in artificial intelligence, and one of the problems in which backtracking is very useful is the eight queens problem.

The eight queens problem attempts to place eight queens on a chessboard in such a way that no queen is attacking any other. The rules of chess say that a queen can take another piece if it lies on the same row, on the same column, or on the same diagonal as the queen (see Figure 5.11). To solve this problem, we try to put the first queen on the board, then the second so that it cannot take the first, then the third so that it is not in conflict with the two already placed, and so on, until all of the queens are placed. What happens if, for instance, the sixth queen cannot be

FIGURE **5.11**   The eight queens problem.

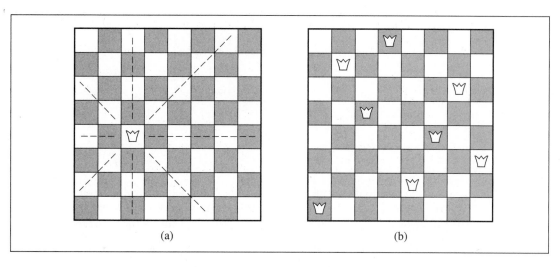

(a)   (b)

placed in a nonconflicting position? We choose another position for the fifth queen and try again with the sixth. If this does not work the fifth queen is moved again. If all the possible positions for the fifth queen have been tried, the fourth queen is moved and then the process restarts. This process requires a great deal of effort, most of which is spent backtracking to the first crossroads offering some untried avenues. In terms of code, however, the process is rather simple due to the power of recursion which is a natural implementation of backtracking. Pseudocode for this backtracking algorithm is as follows (the last line pertains to backtracking):

```
putQueen(row)
    for every position col on the same row
        if position col is available
            place the next queen in position col;
            if (row < 8)
                putQueen(row+1);
            else success;
            remove the queen from position col;
```

This algorithm finds all possible solutions without regard to the fact that some of them are symmetrical.

The most natural approach for implementing this algorithm is to declare an 8×8 array board of 1s and 0s representing a chessboard. The array is initialized to 1s, and each time a queen is put in a position (r, c), board[r][c] is set to 0. Also, a method must set to 0, as not available, all positions on row r, in column c, and on both diagonals that cross each other in position (r, c). When backtracking, the same positions (that is, positions on corresponding row, column, and diagonals) have to be set back to 1, as again available. Since we can expect hundreds of attempts to find

FIGURE **5.12**   A 4 × 4 chessboard.

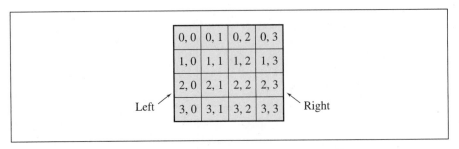

available positions for queens, the setting and resetting process is the most time-consuming part of the implementation; for each queen, between 22 and 28 positions have to be set and then reset, 15 for row and column, and between 7 and 13 for diagonals.

In this approach, the board is viewed from the perspective of the player who sees the entire board along with all the pieces at the same time. However, if we focus solely on the queens, we can consider the chessboard from their perspective. For the queens, the board is not divided into squares, but into rows, columns, and diagonals. If a queen is placed on a single square, it resides not only on this square, but on the entire row, column, and diagonal, treating them as its own temporary property. A different data structure can be utilized to represent this.

To simplify the problem for the first solution, we use a 4 × 4 chessboard instead of the regular 8 × 8 board. Later, we can make the rather obvious changes in the program to accommodate a regular board.

Figure 5.12 contains the 4 × 4 chessboard. Notice that indexes in all fields in the indicated left diagonal all add up to three, $r + c = 3$; this number is associated with this diagonal. There are seven left diagonals, 0 through 6. Indexes in the fields of the indicated right diagonal all have the same difference, $r - c = -1$, and this number is unique among all right diagonals. Therefore, right diagonals are assigned numbers –3 through 3. The data structure used for all left diagonals is simply an array indexed by numbers 0 through 6. For right diagonals, it is also an array, but it cannot be indexed by negative numbers. Therefore, it is an array of seven cells, but to account for negative values obtained from the formula $r - c$, the same number is always added to it so as not to cross the bounds of this array.

An analogous array is also needed for columns, but not for rows, since a queen i is moved along row i and all queens $< i$ have already been placed in rows $< i$. Figure 5.13 contains the code to implement these arrays. The program is short due to recursion, which hides some of the goings-on from the user's sight.

Figures 5.14 through 5.17 document the steps taken by putQueen() to place four queens on the chessboard. Figure 5.14 contains the move number, queen number and row and column number for each attempt to place a queen. Figure 5.15 contains the changes to the arrays positionInRow, column, leftDiagonal, and rightDiagonal. Figure 5.16 shows the changes to the run-time stack during the

F IGURE **5.13**   Eight queens problem implementation.

```java
import java.io.*;

class Queens {
    static final boolean available = true;
    static final int squares = 4, norm = squares - 1;
    static int[] positionInRow = new int[squares];
    static boolean[] column = new boolean[squares];
    static boolean[] leftDiagonal  = new boolean[squares*2 - 1];
    static boolean[] rightDiagonal = new boolean[squares*2 - 1];
    static int howMany = 0;
    Queens() {
        for (int i = 0; i < squares; i++) {
            positionInRow[i] = -1;
            column[i] = available;
        }
        for (int i = 0; i < squares*2 - 1; i++)
            leftDiagonal[i] = rightDiagonal[i] = available;
    }
    static void PrintBoard(PrintStream out) {
        . . . . . . . .
    }
    static void PutQueen(int row) {
        for (int col = 0; col < squares; col++)
            if (column[col] == available &&
                leftDiagonal [row+col] == available &&
                rightDiagonal[row-col+norm] == available) {
                positionInRow[row] = col;
                column[col] = !available;
                leftDiagonal[row+col] = !available;
                rightDiagonal[row-col+norm] = !available;
                if (row < squares-1)
                    PutQueen(row+1);
                else PrintBoard(System.out);
                column[col] = available;
                leftDiagonal[row+col] = available;
                rightDiagonal[row-col+norm] = available;
            }
    }
    static public void main(String args[]) {
        Queens queens = new Queens();
        queens.PutQueen(0);
        System.out.println(howMany + " solutions found.");
    }
}
```

FIGURE **5.14** Steps leading to the first successful configuration of four queens as found by the method putQueen().

Move	Queen	row	col	
{1}	1	0	0	
{2}	2	1	2	failure
{3}	2	1	3	
{4}	3	2	1	failure
{5}	1	0	1	
{6}	2	1	3	
{7}	3	2	0	
{8}	4	3	2	

FIGURE **5.15** Changes in the four arrays used by method putQueen().

positionInRow	column	leftDiagonal	rightDiagonal	row
(0, 2, ,)	(!a, a, !a, a)	(!a, a, a, !a, a, a, a)	(a, a, !a, !a, a, a, a)	0, 1
{1}{2}	{1} {2}	{1} {2}	{2}{1}	{1}{2}
(0, 3, 1,)	(!a, !a, a, !a)	(!a, a, a, !a, !a, a, a)	(a, !a, a, !a, !a, a, a)	1, 2
{1}{3}{4}	{1}{4} {3}	{1} {4}{3}	{3} {1}{4}	{3}{4}
(1, 3, 0, 2)	(!a, !a, !a, !a)	(a, !a, !a, a, !a, !a, a)	(a, !a, !a, a, !a, !a, a)	0, 1, 2, 3
{5}{6}{7}{8}	{7}{5}{8}{6}	{5}{7} {6}{8}	{6}{5} {8}{7}	{5}{6}{7}{8}

eight steps. All changes to the run-time stack are depicted by an activation record for each iteration of the for loop, which mostly lead to a new invocation of putQueen(). Each activation record stores a return address and the values of row and col. Figure 5.17 illustrates the changes to the chessboard. A detailed description of each step follows.

{1} We start by trying to put the first queen in the upper left corner (0, 0). Since it is the very first move, the condition in the if statement is met, and the queen is placed in this square. After the queen is placed, the column 0, the main right diagonal, and the leftmost diagonal are marked as unavailable. In Figure 5.15, {1} is put underneath cells reset to !available in this step.

FIGURE **5.16**   Changes on the run-time stack for the first successful completion of putQueen().

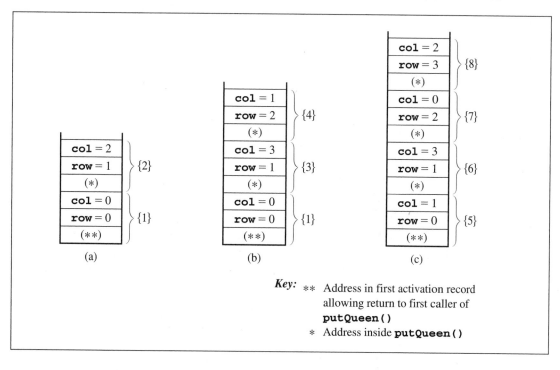

(a)   (b)   (c)

Key: ** Address in first activation record allowing return to first caller of **putQueen()**
* Address inside **putQueen()**

FIGURE **5.17**   Changes to the chessboard leading to the first successful configuration.

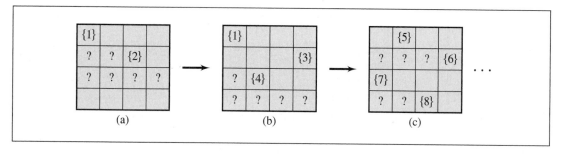

(a)   (b)   (c)

{2} Since row<3, putQueen() calls itself with row+1, but before its execution, an activation record is created on the run-time stack (see Figure 5.16a). Now we check the availability of a field on the second row (i.e., row==1). For col==0, column 0 is guarded, for col==1, main right diagonal is checked, and for col==2, all three parts of the if statement condition are true. Therefore, the second queen is placed in position (1,2), and this fact is immediately reflected in the proper cells of all four arrays. Again, row<3. putQueen() is called trying to locate the third queen in row 2. After

FIGURE **5.18**   Trace of calls to putQueen( ) to place four queens.

```
putQueen(0);
  col = 0;
  putQueen(1);
    col = 0;
    col = 1;
    col = 2;
    putQueen(2)
      col = 0;
      col = 1;
      col = 2;
      col = 3;
    col = 3;
    putQueen(2);
      col = 0;
      col = 1;
      putQueen(3);
        col = 0;
        col = 1;
        col = 2;
        col = 3;
      col = 2;
      col = 3;
  col = 1;
  putQueen(1);
    col = 0;
    col = 1;
    col = 2;
    col = 3;
    putQueen(2)
      col = 0;
      putQueen(3)
        col = 0;
        col = 1;
        col = 2;
        success;
```

all the positions in this row, 0 through 3, are tested, no available position is found, the for loop is exited without executing the body of the if statement, and this call to putQueen( ) is complete. But this call was executed by putQueen( ) dealing with the second row, to which control is now returned.

{3} Values of `col` and `row` are restored and the execution of the second call of `putQueen()` continues by resetting some fields in three arrays back to `available`, and since `col==2`, the `for` loop can continue iteration. The test in the `if` statement allows the second queen to be placed on the board, this time in position $(1, 3)$.

{4} Afterward, `putQueen()` is called again with `row==2`, the third queen is put in $(2, 1)$, and after the next call to `putQueen()`, an attempt to place the fourth queen is unsuccessful (see Figure 5.17b). No calls are made, the call from step {3} is resumed, and the third queen is once again moved, but no position can be found for it. At the same time, `col` becomes 3, and the `for` loop is finished.

{5} As a result, the first call of `putQueen()` resumes execution by placing the first queen in position $(0, 1)$.

{6–8} This time execution continues smoothly and we obtain a complete solution.

Figure 5.18 contains a trace of all calls leading to the first successful placement of four queens on a 4×4 chessboard.

⚑ 5.10 CONCLUDING REMARKS

After looking at all these examples (and one more to follow), what can be said about recursion as a programming tool? Like any other topic in data structures, it should be used with good judgment. There are no general rules for when to use it and when not to use it. Each particular problem decides. Recursion is usually less efficient than its iterative equivalent. But if a recursive program takes 100 milliseconds (ms) for execution, for example, and the iterative version only 10 ms, then although the latter is ten times faster, the difference is hardly perceivable. If there is an advantage in the clarity, readability, and simplicity of the code, the difference in the execution time between these two versions can be disregarded. Recursion is often simpler that the iterative solution and more consistent with the logic of the original algorithm. The factorial and power methods are such examples, and we will see more interesting cases in chapters to follow.

Although every recursive method can be converted into an iterative version, the conversion is not always a trivial task. In particular, it may involve explicitly manipulating a stack. That is where the time-space trade-off comes into play: Using iteration often necessitates the introduction of a new data structure to implement a stack, whereas a recursion relieves the programmer of this task by handing it over to the system. One way or the other, if nontail recursion is involved, very often a stack has to be maintained by the programmer or by the system. But the programmer decides who carries the load.

Two situations can be presented in which a nonrecursive implementation is preferable even if recursion is a more natural solution. First, iteration should be used in the so-called real-time systems where an immediate response is vital for proper functioning of the program. For example, in military environments, in the space shuttle, or in certain types of scientific experiments, it may matter whether the response time is 10 ms or 100 ms. Second, the programmer is encouraged to avoid recursion in programs that are executed hundreds of times. The best example of this kind of program is a compiler.

But these remarks should not be treated too stringently, because sometimes a recursive version is faster than a nonrecursive implementation. Hardware may have built-in stack operations that considerably speed up methods operating on the run-time stack, such as recursive methods. Running a simple routine implemented recursively and iteratively and comparing the two run times can help to decide if recursion is advisable—in fact, recursion can execute faster than iteration. Such a test is especially important if tail recursion comes into play. However, when a stack cannot be eliminated from the iterative version, the use of recursion is usually recommended, since the execution time for both versions does not differ substantially—certainly not by a factor of 10.

Recursion should be eliminated if some part of the work is unnecessarily repeated to compute the answer. The Fibonacci series computation is a good example of such a situation. It shows that the ease of using recursion can sometimes be deceptive, and this is where iteration can grapple effectively with run-time limitations and inefficiencies. Whether a recursive implementation leads to unnecessary repetitions may not be immediately apparent; therefore, drawing a tree of calls similar to Figure 5.8 can be very helpful. This tree shows that `Fib(n)` is called many times with the same argument n. A tree drawn for power or factorial methods is reduced to a linked list with no repetitions in it. If such a tree is very deep (that is, it has many levels), then the program can endanger the run-time stack with an overflow. If the tree is shallow and bushy, with many nodes on the same level, then recursion seems to be a good approach—only if the number of repetitions is very moderate.

⚓ 5.11 CASE STUDY: A RECURSIVE DESCENT INTERPRETER

All programs written in any programming language have to be translated into a representation that the computer system can work on. However, this is not a simple process. Depending on the system and programming language, the process may consist of translating one executable statement at a time and immediately executing it, which is called *interpretation*, or translating the entire program first and then executing it, which is called *compilation*. Whichever strategy is used, the program should not contain sentences or formulas that violate the formal specification of the programming language in which the program is written. For example, if we want to assign a value to a variable, we must put the variable first, then the equal sign, and then a value after it.

Writing an interpreter is by no means a trivial task. As an example, this case study is a sample interpreter for a limited programming language. Our language consists only of assignment statements; it contains no declarations, `if-else` statements, loops, methods, etc. For this limited language, we would like to write a program that accepts any input and

▲ determines if it contains valid assignment statements (this process is known as parsing); and simultaneously,

▲ evaluates all expressions.

Our program is an interpreter in that it not only checks whether the assignment statements are syntactically correct, but also executes the assignments.

The program is to work in the following way. If we enter the assignment statements

```
var1 = 5;
var2 = 3 + var1;
var3 = 44/2.5 * (var2 + var1);
```

then the system can be prompted for the value of each variable separately. For instance, after entering

```
print var3;
```

the system should respond by printing

```
var3 = 228.8
```

Evaluation of all variables stored so far may be requested by entering

```
status;
```

and the following values should be printed in our example:

```
var3 = 228.8; var2 = 8.0; var1 = 5.0
```

All current values are to be stored on `idList` and updated if necessary. Thus, if

```
var2 = var2 * 5;
```

is entered, then

```
print var2;
```

should return

```
var2 = 40.0
```

The interpreter prints a message if any undefined identifier is used and if statements and expressions do not conform to common grammatical rules such as unmatched parentheses, two identifiers in a row, etc.

The program can be written in a variety of ways, but to illustrate recursion, we choose a method known as *recursive descent*. This consists of several mutually recursive methods according to the diagrams in Figure 5.19.

These diagrams serve to define a statement and its parts. For example, a term is a factor or a factor followed by either the multiplication symbol "*" or the division symbol "/" and then another factor. A factor, in turn, is either an identifier, a number, an expression enclosed in a pair of matching parentheses, or a negated factor. In this method, a statement is looked at in more and more detail. It is broken down into its components, and if the components are compound, they are separated into their constituent parts until the simplest language elements are found: numbers, variable names, operators, and parentheses. Thus, the program recursively descends from a global overview of the statement to more detailed elements.

The diagrams in Figure 5.19 indicate that recursive descent is a combination of direct and indirect recursion. For example, a factor can be a factor preceded by a

FIGURE **5.19**   Diagrams of methods used by the recursive descent interpreter.

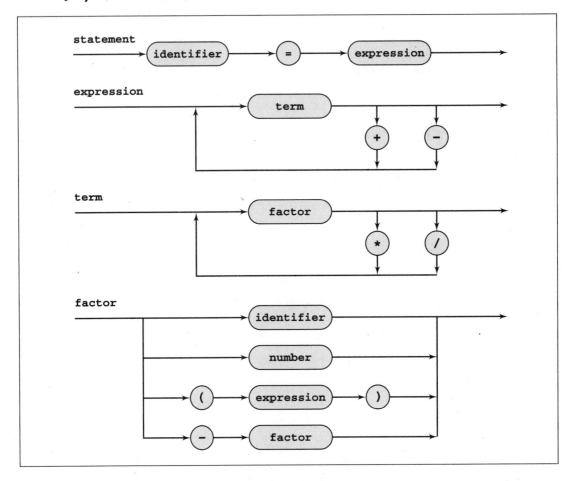

minus, an expression can be a term, a term can be a factor, a factor can be an expression that, in turn, can be a term, until the level of identifiers or numbers is found. Thus, an expression can be composed of expressions, a term of terms, and a factor of factors.

How can the recursive descent interpreter be implemented? The simplest approach is to treat every word in the diagrams as a method name. For instance, term( ) is a method returning a double number. This method always calls factor( ) first, and if the nonblank character currently being looked at is either "*" or "/", then term( ) calls factor( ) again. Each time, the value already accumulated by term( ) is either multiplied or divided by the value returned by the subsequent call of term( ) to factor( ). Every call of term( ) can invoke another call to term( ) indirectly through the chain term( ) -> factor( ) -> expression( ) -> term( ). Pseudocode for the method term( ) looks like the following:

```
term()
    f1 = factor();
    check current character ch;
    while ch is either / or *
        f2 = factor();
        f1 = f1 * f2 or f1 / f2;
    return f1;
```

The method expression() has exactly the same structure, and the pseudocode for factor() is:

```
factor()
    process all +s and – s preceding a factor;
    if current character ch is a letter
        store in id all consecutive letters and/or digits starting with ch;
        return value assigned to id;
    else if ch is a digit
        store in id all consecutive digits starting from ch;
        return number represented by string id;
    else if ch is (
        e = expression();
        if ch is )
            return e;
```

We have tacitly assumed that ch is a variable visible to all the methods in a class that encompasses term() and factor(), and this variable is used for scanning an input character by character.

However, in the pseudocode, we assumed that only valid statements are entered for evaluation. What happens if a mistake is made, such as entering two equal signs, mistyping a variable name, or forgetting an operator? In the interpreter, parsing is simply discontinued after printing an error message. Figure 5.20 contains the complete code for our interpreter.

FIGURE **5.20**   Implementation of a simple language interpreter.

```java
import java.io.*;

class Id {
    private String id;
    double value;
    Id(String s, double d) {
        id = s; value = d;
    }
}
```

FIGURE **5.20**   *(continued)*

```
    public boolean equals(Object node) {
        return id.equals(((Id)node).id);
    }
    public String toString() {
        return id + " = " + value + "; ";
    }
}

class Interpreter {
    static String input;
    static InputStreamReader isr = new InputStreamReader(System.in);
    static BufferedReader buffer = new BufferedReader(isr);
    static java.util.LinkedList idList = new java.util.LinkedList();
    static char ch;
    static int i = 0;
    static public void addOrModify(String id, double e) {
        Id tmp = new Id(new String(id),e);
        int pos;
        if ((pos = idList.indexOf(tmp)) != -1)
            ((Id)idList.get(pos)).value = e;
        else idList.add(tmp);
    }
    static double findValue(String id) {
        int pos;
        if ((pos = idList.indexOf(new Id(id,0.0))) != -1)
            return ((Id)idList.get(pos)).value;
        else issueError("Unknown variable " + id);
        return 0.0;  // this statement will never be reached;
    }
    static void issueError(String s) {
        System.out.println(s);
        Runtime.getRuntime().exit(-1);
    }
    static void skipblanks() {
        while (Character.isSpace(ch))
            readCh();
    }
    static String getLine() {
        i = 0;
        System.out.flush();
        try {
            input = buffer.readLine();
```

FIGURE **5.20** *(continued)*

```
        } catch(IOException io) {
            System.out.println("Problem with input.");
        }
        return input;
    }
    static void readCh() {
        if (i < input.length())
            ch = input.charAt(i++);
        else issueError("Incomplete expression");
    }
    /** readId() reads strings of letters, underscores, dollar signs, and
     *  digits that start with a letter, an underscore, or a dollar sign.
     *  Examples of identifiers are: var1, x, _pqr123xyz, $aName, etc.
     */
    static String readId() {
        String id = "";
        skipblanks();
        if (Character.isJavaLetter(ch)) {
            while (Character.isJavaLetterOrDigit(ch)) {
                id += ch;
                readCh(); // don't skip blanks;
            }
        }
        else issueError("Identifier expected");
        return id;
    }
    static double factor() {
        double var, minus = 1.0;
        readCh();
        skipblanks();
        while (ch == '+' || ch == '-') { // take all '+'s and '-'s.
            if (ch == '-')
                minus *= -1.0;
            readCh();
        }
        if (Character.isDigit(ch) || ch == '.') { // factor can be a number
            String number = new String();
            while (Character.isDigit(ch)) {
                number += ch;
                readCh();
```

Continues

FIGURE **5.20**   *(continued)*

```
                }
                if (ch == '.') {
                    number += ch;
                    readCh();
                }
                while (Character.isDigit(ch)) {
                    number += ch;
                    readCh();
                }
                var = Double.valueOf(number).doubleValue();
            }
            else if (ch == '(') {            // or a parenthesized expression,
                var = expression();
                skipblanks();
                if (ch == ')')
                    readCh();
                else issueError("Right paren left out");
            }
            else {
                String id = readId();        // or an identifier.
                var = findValue(id);
            }
            skipblanks();
            return minus * var;
        }
        static double term() {
            double f = factor();
            while (true) {
                switch (ch) {
                    case '*' : f *= factor(); break;
                    case '/' : f /= factor(); break;
                    default  : return f;
                }
            }
        }
        static double expression() {
            double t = term();
            while (true) {
                switch (ch) {
                    case '+' : t += term(); break;
```

FIGURE **5.20**   *(continued)*

```
                case '-' : t -= term(); break;
                default  : return t;
            }
        }
    }
    static void getStatement() {
        System.out.print("Enter a statement: ");
        getLine();
        readCh();
        String str = readId();
        if (str.toUpperCase().equals("STATUS")) {
            java.util.Iterator it = idList.iterator();
            while (it.hasNext())
                System.out.println(it.next());
        }
        else if (str.toUpperCase().equals("PRINT")) {
            str = readId();
            System.out.println(str + " = " + findValue(str));
        }
        else if (str.toUpperCase().equals("END"))
            Runtime.getRuntime().exit(0);
        else {
            skipblanks();
            if (ch == '=') {
                double e = expression();
                if (ch != ';')
                   issueError("There are some extras in the statement");
                else addOrModify(str,e);
            }
            else issueError("'=' is missing");
        }
    }
    public static void main(String args[]) {
        System.out.println("The program processes statements in the "
            + "following format:\n"
            + "\t<id> = <expr>;\n\tprint <id>;\n\tstatus;\n\tend;\n");
        while (true)         // exit caused by an error or entering
            getStatement(); // 'end;' in getStatement();
    }
}
```

☐ 5.12 EXERCISES

1. The set of natural numbers **N** defined at the beginning of this chapter includes the numbers 10, 11, . . . , 20, 21, . . . , and also the numbers 00, 000, 01, 001, . . . Modify this definition to allow only numbers with no leading zeros.

2. Write a recursive method that calculates and returns the length of a linked list.

3. What is the output for the following version of `reverse()`:

```
void reverse() {
   int ch = getChar();
   if (ch != '\n')
        reverse();
   System.out.print(ch);
}
```

4. An early application of recursion can be found in the sixteenth century in John Napier's method of finding logarithms. The method was as follows:

   start with two numbers `n, m` *and their logarithms* `logn, logm` *if they are known;*
   `while` *not done*
       for a geometric mean of two earlier numbers find a logarithm which is an arithmetic mean of two earlier logarithms, that is, `logk =` `(logn+logm)` `/2 for k =` $\sqrt{nm}$;
       proceed recursively for pairs `(n,`$\sqrt{nm}$`) and (`$\sqrt{nm}$`,m);`

   For example, the 10-based logarithms of 100 and 1000 are numbers 2 and 3, the geometric mean of 100 and 1000 is 316.23, and the arithmetic mean of their logarithms, 2 and 3, is 2.5. Thus, the logarithm of 316.23 equals 2.5. The process can be continued: The geometric mean of 100 and 316.23 is 177.83 whose logarithm is equal to $(2 + 2.5)/2 = 2.25$.

   a. Write a recursive method `logarithm()` that outputs logarithms until the difference between adjacent logarithms is smaller than a certain small number.

   b. Modify this method so that a new method `logarithmOf()` finds a logarithm of a specific number x between 100 and 1000. Stop processing if you reach a number y such that $y - x < \epsilon$ for some ϵ.

   c. Add a method which calls `logarithmOf()` after determining between what powers of 10 a number x falls so that it does not have to be a number between 100 and 1000.

5. The algorithms for both versions of the power function given in this chapter are rather simpleminded. Is it really necessary to make eight multiplications to compute x^8? It can be observed that $x^8 = (x^4)^2$, $x^4 = (x^2)^2$, and $x^2 = x \cdot x$; that is, only three multiplications are needed to find the value of x^8. Using this observation, improve both algorithms for computing x^n. Hint: A special case is needed for odd exponents.

6. Execute by hand the methods `tail()` and `nonTail()` for the parameter values of 0, 2, and 4. Definitions of these methods are given in Section 5.4.

7. Write a method that recursively converts a string of numerals into an integer. For instance, `convert("1234")` would return the integer 1234.

8. Write a recursive method to compute the binomial coefficient according to the definition

$$\binom{n}{k} = \begin{cases} 1 & \text{if } k = 0 \text{ or } k = n \\ \binom{n-1}{k-1} + \binom{n-1}{k} & \text{otherwise} \end{cases}$$

9. Write a recursive method to add the first n terms of the series

$$1 + \frac{1}{2} - \frac{1}{3} + \frac{1}{4} - \frac{1}{5} \cdots$$

10. Write a recursive method `GCD(n,m)` that returns the greatest common divisor of two integers n and m according to the following definition:

$$GCD(n,m) = \begin{cases} m & \text{if } m \le n \text{ and } n \bmod m = 0 \\ GCD(m,n) & \text{if } n < m \\ GCD(m,n \bmod m) & \text{otherwise} \end{cases}$$

11. Give a recursive version of the following method:

```
void cubes (int n) {
   for (int i = 1; i <=n; i++)
       system.out.print (i * i * i + "");
}
```

12. Check recursively if the following objects are palindromes:

a. a word

b. a sentence (ignoring blanks, lower- and uppercase differences, and punctuation marks so that "Madam, I'm Adam" is accepted as a palindrome)

13. For a given character recursively,

a. Check if it is in a string.

b. Count all of its occurrences in a string.

c. Remove all of its occurrences from a string.

14. Write equivalents of the last three methods for substrings.

15. What changes would have to be made in the method presented in Figure 5.6 to draw a line as in Figure 5.21? Try it, and experiment with other possibilities to generate other curves.

16. Create a tree of calls for $\sin(x)$ assuming that only $\frac{x}{18}$ (and smaller values) do not trigger other calls.

FIGURE **5.21**   Lines to be drawn with modified program in Figure 5.6.

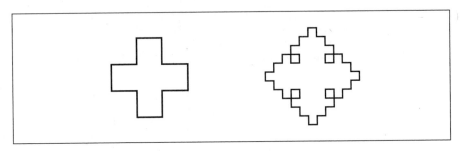

17. Write recursive and nonrecursive methods to print out a nonnegative integer in binary. The methods should not use bitwise operations.

18. The nonrecursive version of the method for computing Fibonacci numbers uses information accumulated during computation, whereas the recursive version does not. However, it does not mean that no recursive implementation can be given which can collect the same information as the nonrecursive counterpart. In fact, such an implementation can be obtained directly from the nonrecursive version. What would it be? Consider using two methods instead of one; one would do all the work, the other would only invoke it with the proper parameters.

19. The method `putQueen()` does not recognize that certain configurations are symmetric. Adapt method `putQueen()` for a full 8 × 8 chessboard, write the method `printBoard()`, and run a program for solving the eight queens problem so that it does not print symmetric solutions.

20. Finish the trace of execution of `putQueen()` shown in Figure 5.18.

21. Execute the following program by hand from the case study, using these two entries:

    a. `v = x + y*w - z`

    b. `v = x * (y - w) --z`

    Indicate clearly which methods are called at which stage of parsing these sentences.

22. Extend our interpreter so that it can also process exponentiation, ^. Remember that exponentiation has precedence over all other operations so that `2 — 3^4 * 5` is the same as `2 — ((3^4) * 5)`. Notice also that exponentiation is a right-associative operator (unlike addition and subtraction); that is, `2^3^4` is the same as `2^(3^4)` and not `(2^3)^4`.

23. In Java, the division operator, /, returns an integer result when it is applied to two integers; for instance, `11/5` equals 2. However, in our interpreter, the result is `2.2`. Modify this interpreter so that division works the same way as in Java.

24. Our interpreter is unforgiving when a mistake is made by the user, since it finishes execution if a problem is detected. For example, when the name of a variable is mistyped when requesting its value, the program notifies the user and exits and destroys the list of identifiers. Modify the program so that it continues execution after finding an error.

25. Write the shortest program you can that uses recursion.

◪ 5.13 PROGRAMMING ASSIGNMENTS

1. Compute the standard deviation σ for n values x_k stored in an array `data` and for the equal probabilities $\frac{1}{n}$ associated with them. The standard deviation is defined as

$$\sigma = \sqrt{V}$$

where the variance, V, is defined by

$$V = \frac{1}{n-1}\Sigma_k(x_k - \bar{x})^2$$

and the mean, $\bar{x}$, by

$$\bar{x} = \frac{1}{n}\Sigma_k x_k$$

Write recursive and iterative versions of both V and $\bar{x}$ and compute the standard deviation using both versions of the mean and variance. Run your program for $n = 500$, 1000, 1500, and 2000 and compare the run times.

2. Write a program to do symbolic differentiation. Use the following formulas:

$$\text{Rule 1: } (fg)' = fg' + f'g$$

$$\text{Rule 2: } (f+g)' = f' + g'$$

$$\text{Rule 3: } \left(\frac{f}{g}\right)' = \frac{f'g - fg'}{g^2}$$

$$\text{Rule 4: } (ax^n)' = nax^{n-1}$$

An example of application of these rules is given below with differentiation with respect to x:

$$\left(5x^3 + \frac{6x}{y} - 10x^2y + 100\right)'$$

$$= (5x^3)' + \left(\frac{6x}{y}\right)' + (-10x^2y)' + (100)' \qquad \text{by Rule 2}$$

$$= 15x^2 + \left(\frac{6x}{y}\right)' + (-10x^2y)' \qquad \text{by Rule 4}$$

$$= 15x^2 + \frac{(6x)'y - (6x)y'}{y^2} + (-10x^2y)' \qquad \text{by Rule 3}$$

$$= 15x^2 + \frac{6y}{y^2} + (-10x^2y)' \qquad\qquad \text{by Rule 4}$$

$$= 15x^2 + \frac{6y}{y^2} + (-10x^2)y' + (-10x^2)'y \qquad \text{by Rule 1}$$

$$= 15x^2 + \frac{6}{y} - 20xy \qquad\qquad\qquad \text{by Rule 4}$$

First, run your program for polynomials only, and then add formulas for derivatives for trigonometric functions, logarithms, etc. that extend the range of functions handled by your program.

3. An $n \times n$ square consists of black and white cells arranged in a certain way. The problem is to determine the number of white areas and the number of white cells in each area. For example, a regular 8×8 chessboard has 32 one-cell white areas; the square in Figure 5.22a consists of ten areas, two of them of ten cells, and eight of two cells; the square in Figure 5.22b has five white areas of one, three, twenty-one, ten, and two cells.

   Write a program that, for a given $n \times n$ square, outputs the number of white areas and their sizes. Use an $(n + 2) \times (n + 2)$ array with properly marked cells. Two additional rows and columns constitute a frame of black cells surrounding the entered square to simplify your implementation. For instance, the square in Figure 5.22b is stored as the square in Figure 5.22c.

   Traverse the square row by row and, for the first unvisited cell encountered, invoke a method that processes one area. The secret is in using four recursive calls in this method for each unvisited white cell and marking it with a special symbol as visited (counted).

4. Write a program for *pretty printing* Java programs, that is, for printing programs with consistent use of indentation, the number of spaces between tokens such as key words, parentheses, brackets, operators, etc., the number of blank lines between blocks of code (classes, methods, etc.), aligning braces with key words, aligning `else` statements with the corresponding `if` statements, and so on. The program takes as input a Java file and prints code in this file according to the rules incorporated in the pretty printing program. For example, the code

```
if (n == 1) { n = 2 * m;
if (m < 10)
objectA.methodA (n,m-1); else objectA.methodA (n,m-2); } else n = 3 * m;
```

should be transformed into

```
if (n == 1) {
    n = 2 * m;
    if (m < 10)
        objectA.methodA (n,m-1);
    else objectA.methodA (n,m-2);
}
else n = 3 * m;
```

FIGURE **5.22**   (a–b) Two $n \times n$ squares of black and white cells and (c) an $(n + 2) \times (n + 2)$ array implementing square (b).

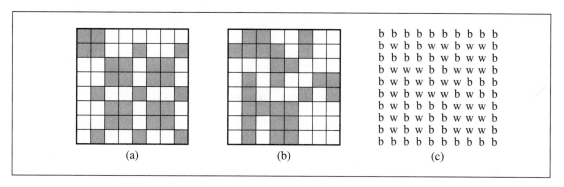

(a)	(b)

```
b b b b b b b b b b
b w b b w w b w w b
b b b b b w b w w b
b w w w b b w w w b
b w b w b w w b b b
b w b w w w b w b b
b w b b b b w w w b
b w b w b b w w w b
b w b w b w w w w b
b b b b b b b b b b
```

(c)

5. An excellent example of a program that can be greatly simplified by the use of recursion is the Chapter 4 case study, escaping a maze. As already explained, in each maze cell the mouse stores on the maze stack up to four cells neighboring the cell in which it is currently located. The cells put on the stack are the ones that should be investigated after reaching a dead end. It does the same for each visited cell. Write a program that uses recursion to solve the maze problem. Use the following pseudocode:

```
exitCell(currentCell)
    if currentCell is the exit
        success;
    else exitCell(the passage above currentCell);
         exitCell(the passage below currentCell);
         exitCell(the passage left to currentCell);
         exitCell(the passage right to currentCell);
```

Bibliography

Recursion and Applications of Recursion

Barron, David W., *Recursive Techniques in Programming,* New York: Elsevier, 1975.

Berlioux, Pierre, and Bizard, Philippe, *Algorithms: The Construction, Proof, and Analysis of Programs,* New York: Wiley, 1986, Chs. 4–6.

Bird, Richard S., *Programs and Machines,* New York: Wiley, 1976.

Burge, William H., *Recursive Programming Techniques,* Reading, MA: Addison-Wesley, 1975.

Lorentz, Richard, *Recursive Algorithms,* Norwood, NJ: Ablex, 1994.

Roberts, Eric, *Thinking Recursively,* New York: Wiley, 1986.

Rohl, Jeffrey S., *Recursion via Pascal,* Cambridge: Cambridge University Press, 1984.

Transformations Between Recursion and Iteration

Auslander, M. A., and Strong, H. R., "Systematic Recursion Removal," *Communications of the ACM* 21 (1978), 127–134.

Bird, R. S., "Notes on Recursion Elimination," *Communications of the ACM* 20 (1977), 434–439.

Dijkstra, Edsger W., "Recursive Programming," *Numerische Mathematik* 2 (1960), 312–318.

Algorithm to Solve the Eight Queens Problem

Wirth, Niklaus, *Algorithms and Data Structures*, Englewood Cliffs, NJ: Prentice Hall, 1986.

Binary Trees

6.1 TREES, BINARY TREES, AND BINARY SEARCH TREES

Linked lists usually provide greater flexibility than arrays, but they are linear structures and it is difficult to use them to organize a hierarchical representation of objects. Although stacks and queues reflect some hierarchy, they are limited to only one dimension. To overcome this limitation, we create a new data type called a *tree* that consists of *nodes* and *arcs*. Unlike natural trees, these trees are depicted upside down with the *root* at the top and the *leaves* at the bottom. The root is a node that has no parent; it can have only child nodes. Leaves, on the other hand, have no children, or rather, their children are null. A tree can be defined recursively as the following:

1. An empty structure is an empty tree.

2. If $t_1, \ldots, t_k$ are disjoint trees, then the structure whose root has as its children the roots of $t_1, \ldots, t_k$ is also a tree.

3. Only structures generated by rules 1 and 2 are trees.

Figure 6.1 contains examples of trees. Each node has to be reachable from the root through a unique sequence of arcs, called a *path*. The number of arcs in a path is called the *length* of the path. The *level* of a node is the length of the path from the root to the node plus 1, which is the number of nodes in the path. The *height* of a nonempty tree is the maximum level of a node in the tree. The empty tree is a legitimate tree of height 0 (by definition), and a single node is a tree of height 1. This is the only case in which a node is both the root and a leaf. The level of a node must be between 1 (the level of the root) and the height of the tree, which in the extreme case is the level of the only leaf in a degenerate tree resembling a linked list.

FIGURE **6.1**   Examples of trees.

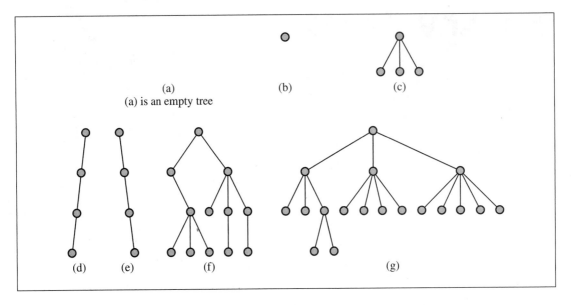

(a)   (b)   (c)

(a) is an empty tree

(d)   (e)   (f)   (g)

FIGURE **6.2**   Hierarchical structure of a university shown as a tree.

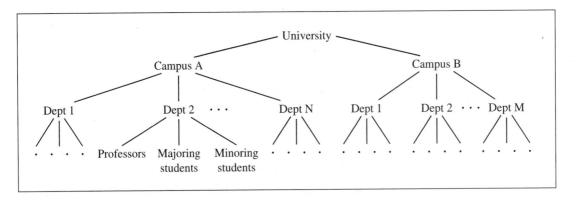

Figure 6.2 contains an example of a tree that reflects the hierarchy of a university. Other examples are genealogical trees, trees reflecting the grammatical structure of sentences, and trees showing the taxonomic structure of organisms, plants, or characters. Virtually all areas of science make use of trees to represent hierarchical structures.

The definition of a tree does not impose any condition on the number of children of a given node. This number can vary from 0 to any integer. In hierarchical trees, this is a welcome property. For example, the university has only two branches, but each

FIGURE **6.3** Transforming (a) a linked list into (b) a tree.

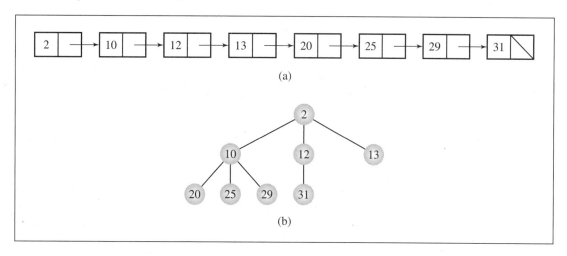

campus can have a different number of departments. Such trees are used in database management systems, especially in the hierarchical model. But representing hierarchies is not the only reason for using trees. In fact, in the discussion to follow, that aspect of trees is treated rather lightly, mainly in the discussion of expression trees. This chapter focuses on tree operations that allow us to accelerate the search process.

Consider a linked list of *n* elements. To locate an element, the search has to start from the beginning of the list, and the list must be scanned until the element is found or the end of the list is reached. Even if the list is ordered, the search of the list always has to start from the first node. Thus, if the list has 10,000 nodes and the information in the last node is to be accessed, then all 9999 of its predecessors have to be traversed, an obvious inconvenience. If all the elements are stored in an *orderly tree,* a tree where all elements are stored according to some predetermined criterion of ordering, the number of tests can be reduced substantially even when the element to be located is the one furthest away. For example, the linked list in Figure 6.3a can be transformed into the tree in Figure 6.3b.

Was a reasonable criterion of ordering applied to construct this tree? To test whether 31 is in the linked list, eight tests have to be performed. Can this number be reduced further if the same elements are ordered from top to bottom and from left to right in the tree? What would an algorithm be like that forces us to make three tests only: one for the root, 2, one for its middle child, 12, and one for the only child of this child, 31? The number 31 could be located on the same level as 12, or it could be a child of 10. With this ordering of the tree, nothing really interesting is achieved in the context of searching. (The heap discussed later in this chapter uses this approach.) Consequently, a better criterion must be chosen.

Again, note that each node can have any number of children. In fact, there are algorithms developed for trees with a deliberate number of children (see the next chapter),

Figure **6.4**   Examples of binary trees.

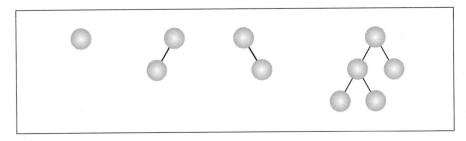

but this chapter discusses only binary trees. A *binary tree* is a tree whose nodes have two children (possibly empty), and each child is designated as either a left child or a right child. For example, the trees in Figure 6.4 are binary trees, whereas the university tree in Figure 6.2 is not. An important characteristic of binary trees, which is used later in assessing an expected efficiency of sorting algorithms, is the number of leaves.

As already defined, the level of a node is the number of arcs traversed from the root to the node plus one. According to this definition, the root is at level 1, its immediate children are at level 2, and so on. If all the nodes at all levels except the last had two nonnull children, then there would be $1 = 2^0$ node at level 1, $2 = 2^1$ nodes at level 2, $4 = 2^2$ nodes at level 3, and generally, 2^i nodes at level $i + 1$. A tree satisfying this condition is referred to as a *complete binary tree*. In this tree, all nonterminal nodes have both their children, and all leaves are at the same level. Consequently, in all binary trees, there are at most 2^i nodes at level $i + 1$. In Chapter 9, we calculate the number of leaves in a *decision tree*, which is a binary tree in which all nodes have either zero or two nonempty children. Because leaves can be interspersed throughout a decision tree and appear at each level except level 1, no generally applicable formula can be given to calculate the number of nodes because it may vary from tree to tree. But the formula can be approximated by noting first that

> For all the nonempty binary trees whose nonterminal nodes have exactly two nonempty children, the number of leaves m is greater than the number of nonterminal nodes k and $m = k + 1$.

If a tree has only a root, this observation holds trivially. If it holds for a certain tree, then after attaching two leaves to one of the already existing leaves, this leaf turns into a nonterminal node, whereby m is decremented by 1 and k is incremented by 1. However, because two new leaves have been grafted onto the tree, m is incremented by 2. After these two increments and one decrement, the equation $(m - 1) + 2 = (k + 1) + 1$ is obtained and $m = k + 1$, which is exactly the result aimed at (see Figure 6.5). It implies that an $i + 1$-level complete decision tree has 2^i leaves, and on account of the preceding observation, it also has $2^i - 1$ nonterminal nodes, which makes $2^i + 2^i - 1 = 2^{i+1} - 1$ nodes in total (see also Figure 6.35).

In this chapter, the *binary search trees*, also called *ordered binary trees*, are of particular interest. A binary search tree has the following property: For each node n of the

FIGURE **6.5**   Adding a leaf to tree (a), preserving the relation of the number of leaves to the number of nonterminal nodes (b).

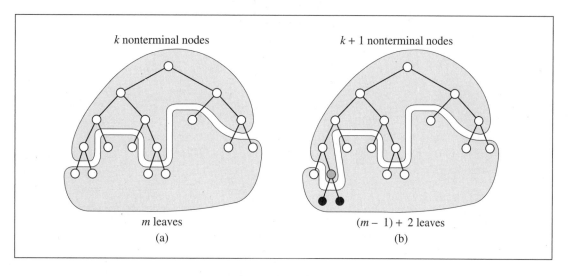

FIGURE **6.6**   Examples of binary search trees.

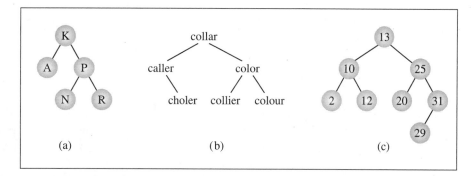

tree, all values stored in its left subtree (the tree whose root is the left child) are less than value v stored in n, and all values stored in the right subtree are greater than v. For reasons to be discussed later, storing multiple copies of the same value in the same tree is avoided. An attempt to do so can be treated as an error. The meanings of "less than" or "greater than" depend on the type of values stored in the tree: It is "$<$" and "$>$" for numerical values and alphabetical order in the case of strings. The trees in Figure 6.6 are binary search trees. Note that Figure 6.6c contains a tree with the same data as the linked list in Figure 6.3a whose searching was to be optimized.

FIGURE **6.7**   Array representation of the tree in Figure 6.6c.

Index	Info	Left	Right
0	13	4	2
1	31	6	−1
2	25	7	1
3	12	−1	−1
4	10	5	3
5	2	−1	−1
6	29	−1	−1
7	20	−1	−1

⌐ 6.2 IMPLEMENTING BINARY TREES

Binary trees can be implemented in at least two ways: as arrays and as linked structures. To implement a tree as an array, a node is declared as a structure with an information field and two "reference" fields. These reference fields contain the indexes of the array cells in which the left and right children are stored, if there are any. For example, the tree from Figure 6.6c can be represented as the array in Figure 6.7. The root is always located in the first cell, cell 0, and −1 indicates a null child. In this representation, the two children of node 13 are located in positions 4 and 2, and the right child of node 31 is null.

However, this implementation may be inconvenient, as is often the case with static allocation, since the size of the array has to become part of the program and must be known in advance. It is a problem because the data may overflow the array if too little space is allocated, or memory space may be wasted if too much space is allocated. This is important because trees often change and it may be hard to predict how many nodes will be created during program execution. However, sometimes an array implementation of a tree is convenient and desirable. It is used when discussing the heap sort, although an array of data rather than an array of structures is used there. But usually, a dynamic data structure is a more efficient way to represent a tree. This chapter's examples use dynamic data structures.

In the new implementation, only trees of integers are discussed. The use of a generic tree (that is, a tree for storing any type of data) is illustrated in the case study at the end of this chapter.

In the new implementation, a node is an instance of a class composed of an information field and two reference fields. This node is used and operated on by methods in another class that pertains to the tree as a whole (see Figure 6.8).

Figure **6.8**   Implementation of a generic binary search tree.

```
/*********************  IntBSTNode.java  *************************
 *                 binary search tree of integers
 */

public class IntBSTNode {
    protected int key;
    protected IntBSTNode left, right;
    public IntBSTNode() {
        left = right = null;
    }
    public IntBSTNode(int el) {
        this(el,null,null);
    }
    public IntBSTNode(int el, IntBSTNode lt, IntBSTNode rt) {
        key = el; left = lt; right = rt;
    }
    public void visit() {
        System.out.print(key + " ");
    }
}

/*********************  IntBST.java  *************************
 *                 binary search tree of integers
 */

public class IntBST {
    protected IntBSTNode root;
    public IntBST() {
        root = null;
    }
    public IntBSTNode search(IntBSTNode p, int el) {
        return search(p, root);
    }
    public IntBSTNode search(IntBSTNode p, int el) { . . . } // Figure 6.9
    public void breadthFirst() { . . . }                    // Figure 6.10
    public void preorder() {
        preorder(root);
    }
    protected void preorder(IntBSTNode p) { . . . }         // Figure 6.11
    public void inorder() {
```

Continues

FIGURE **6.8**   (*continued*)

```
        inorder(root);
    }
    protected void inorder(IntBSTNode p) { . . . }          //  Figure 6.11
    public void postorder() {
        postorder(root);
    }
    protected void postorder(IntBSTNode p) { . . . }         //  Figure 6.11
    public void iterativePreorder() { . . . }                //  Figure 6.15
    public void iterativeInorder() { . . . }                 //  Figure 6.17
    public void iterativePostorder() { . . . }               //  Figure 6.16
    public void MorrisInorder() { . . . }                    //  Figure 6.20
    public void insert(int el) { . . . }                     //  Figure 6.23
    public void deleteByMerging(int el) { . . . }            //  Figure 6.29
    public void deleteByCopying(BaseObject el) { . . . }     //  Figure 6.32
    . . . . . . . . . . . . . . . . . . . .
}
```

◩ 6.3 SEARCHING A BINARY SEARCH TREE

An algorithm for locating an element in this tree is quite straightforward as indicated by its implementation in Figure 6.9. For every node, compare the key to be located with the value stored in the node currently referred. If the key is less than the value, go to the left subtree and try again. If it is greater than that value, try the right subtree. If it is the same, obviously the search can be discontinued. The search is also aborted if there is no way to go, indicating that the key is not in the tree. For example, to locate the number 31 in the tree in Figure 6.6c, only three tests are performed. First, the tree is checked to see if the number is in the root node. Next, because 31 is greater than 13, the root's right child containing the value 25 is tried. Finally, since 31 is again greater than the value of the currently tested node, the right child is tried again, and the value 31 is found.

The worst case for this binary tree is when it is searched for the numbers 26, 27, 28, 29, or 30 because those searches each require four tests (why?). In the case of all other integers, the number of tests is fewer than four. It can now be seen why an element should only occur in a tree once. If it occurs more than once, then two approaches are possible. One approach locates the first occurrence of an element and disregards the others. In this case, the tree contains redundant nodes that are never used for their own sake; they are accessed only for testing. In the second approach, all occurrences of an element may have to be located. Such a search always has to finish with a leaf. For example, to locate all instances of 13 in the tree, the root node 13 has

FIGURE **6.9**   A function for searching binary search tree.

```
public IntBSTNode search(IntBSTNode p, int el) {
    while (p != null)
        if (el == p.key)
            return p;
        else if (el < p.key)
            p = p.left;
        else p = p.right;
    return null;
}
```

to be tested, then its right child 25, and finally the node 20. The search proceeds along the worst-case scenario: when the leaf level has to be reached in expectation that some more occurrences of the desired element can be encountered.

The complexity of searching is measured by the number of comparisons performed during the searching process. This number depends on the number of nodes encountered on the unique path leading from the root to the node being searched for. Therefore, the complexity is the length of the path leading to this node plus 1. Complexity depends on the shape of the tree and the position of the node in the tree.

The *internal path length* (IPL) is the sum of all path lengths of all nodes, which is calculated by summing $\sum (i-1)l_i$ over all levels i, where l_i is the number of nodes on level i. A position of a node in the tree is determine by the path length. An average position, called an *average path length,* is given by the formula IPL/n, which depends on the shape of the tree. In the worst case, when the tree turns into a linked list, $path_{worst} = \frac{1}{n}\sum_{i=1}^{n}(i-1) = \frac{n-1}{2} = O(n)$, and a search can takes n time units.

The best case occurs when all leaves in the tree of height h are in at most two levels, and only nodes in the next to last level can have one child. To simplify the computation, we approximate the average path length for such a tree, $path_{best}$ by the average path of a complete binary tree of the same height.

By looking at simple examples, we can determine that for the complete binary tree of height h, IPL $= \sum_{i=1}^{h-1} i2^i$. From this and from the fact that $\sum_{i=1}^{h-1} 2^i = 2^h - 2$, we have

$$\text{IPL} = 2\text{IPL} - \text{IPL} = (h-1)2^h - \sum_{i=1}^{h-1} 2^i = (h-2)2^h + 2$$

As has already been established, the number of nodes in the complete binary tree $n = 2^h - 1$, so

$$path_{best} = \text{IPL}/n = \left((h-2)2^h + 2\right)/(2^h - 1) \approx h - 2$$

which is in accordance with the fact that, in this tree, one-half of the nodes are in the leaf level with path length $h - 1$. Also, in this tree, the height $h = \lg(n + 1)$, so $path_{best} = \lg(n + 1) - 2$; the average path length in a perfectly balanced tree is $\lceil \lg(n + 1)\rceil - 2 = O(\lg n)$ where $\lceil x\rceil$ is the closest integer greater than x.

The average case in an average tree is somewhere between $\frac{n-1}{2}$ and $\lg(n+1) - 2$. Is a search for a node in an average position in a tree of average shape closer to $O(n)$ or $O(\lg n)$? First, the average shape of the tree has to be represented computationally.

The root of a binary tree can have an empty left subtree and a right subtree with all $n - 1$ nodes. It also can have one node in the left subtree and $n - 2$ nodes in the right and so on. Finally, it can have an empty right subtree with all remaining nodes in the left. The same reasoning can be applied to both subtrees of the root, to the subtrees of these subtrees, down to the leaves. The average internal path length is the average over all these differently shaped trees.

Assume that the tree contains nodes 1 through n. If i is the root, then its left subtree has $i - 1$ nodes, and its right subtree has $n - i$ nodes. If $path_{i-1}$ and $path_{n-i}$ are average paths in these subtrees, then the average path of this tree is

$$path_n(i) = ((i-1)(path_{i-1} + 1) + (n-i)(path_{n-i} + 1))/n$$

Assuming that elements are coming randomly to the tree, the root of the tree can be any number i, $1 \le i \le n$. Therefore, the average path of an average tree is obtained by averaging all values of $path_n(i)$ over all values of i. This gives the formula

$$path_n = \frac{1}{n}\sum_{i=1}^{n} path_n(i) = \frac{1}{n^2} \sum_{i=1}^{n} ((i-1)(path_{i-1} + 1) + (n-i)(path_{n-i} + 1))$$

$$= \frac{2}{n^2} \sum_{i=1}^{n-1} i(path_i + 1)$$

from which, and from $path_1 = 0$, we obtain $2 \ln n = 2 \ln 2 \lg n = 1.386 \lg n$ as an approximation for $path_n$ (see Section A.4 in Appendix A). This is an approximation for the average number of comparisons in an average tree. This number is $O(\lg n)$, which is closer to the best case than to the worst case. This number also indicates that there is little room for improvement, since $path_{best}/path_n \approx .7215$, and the average path length in the best case is different by only 27.85% from the expected path length in the average case. Searching in a binary tree is, therefore, very efficient in most cases, even without balancing the tree. However, this is true only for randomly created trees because, in highly unbalanced and elongated trees whose shapes resemble linked lists, search time is $O(n)$, which is unacceptable considering that $O(\lg n)$ efficiency can be achieved.

⬛ 6.4 TREE TRAVERSAL

Tree traversal is the process of visiting each node in the tree exactly one time. Traversal may be interpreted as putting all nodes on one line or linearizing a tree.

The definition of traversal specifies only one condition—visiting each node only one time—but it does not specify the order in which the nodes are visited. Hence, there are as many tree traversals as there are permutations of nodes; for a tree with n nodes, there are $n!$ different traversals. Most of them, however, are rather chaotic and do not indicate much regularity so that implementing such traversals lacks generality: For each n, a separate set of traversal procedures must be implemented, and only a few of them can be used for a different number of data. For example, two possible traversals of the tree in Figure 6.6c that may be of some use are the sequence 2, 10, 12, 20, 13, 25, 29, 31 and the sequence 29, 31, 20, 12, 2, 25, 10, 13. The first sequence lists even numbers and then odd numbers in ascending order. The second sequence lists all nodes from level to level right to left, starting from the lowest level up to the root. The sequence 13, 31, 12, 2, 10, 29, 20, 25 does not indicate any regularity in the order of numbers or in the order of the traversed nodes. It is just a random jumping from node to node that in all likelihood is of no use. Nevertheless, all these sequences are the results of three legitimate traversals out of 8! = 40,320. In the face of such an abundance of traversals and the apparent uselessness of most of them, we would like to restrict our attention to two classes only, namely, breadth-first and depth-first traversals.

6.4.1 Breadth-First Traversal

Breadth-first traversal is visiting each node starting from the lowest (or highest) level and moving down (or up) level by level, visiting nodes on each level from left to right (or from right to left). There are thus four possibilities, and one such possibility—a top-down, left-to-right, breadth-first traversal of the tree in Figure 6.6c—results in the sequence 13, 10, 25, 2, 12, 20, 31, 29.

Implementation of this kind of traversal is straightforward when a queue is used. Consider a top-down left-to-right, breadth-first traversal. After a node is visited, its children, if any, are placed at the end of the queue, and the node at the beginning of the queue is visited. Considering that for a node on level n, its children are on level $n + 1$, by placing these children at the end of the queue, they are visited after all nodes from level n are visited. Thus, the restriction that all nodes on level n must be visited before visiting any nodes on level $n + 1$ is accomplished.

An implementation of the corresponding method is shown in Figure 6.10.

6.4.2 Depth-First Traversal

Depth-first traversal proceeds as far as possible to the left (or right), then backs up until the first crossroad, goes one step to the right (or left), and again as far as possible to the left (or right). We repeat this process until all nodes are visited. This definition, however, does not clearly specify exactly when nodes are visited: before proceeding down the tree or after backing up? There are some variations of the depth-first traversal.

There are three tasks of interest in this type of traversal:

V—visiting a node

L—traversing the left subtree

R—traversing the right subtree

An orderly traversal takes place if these tasks are performed in the same order for each node. The three tasks can themselves be ordered in 3! = 6 ways, so there are six possible ordered depth-first traversals:

VLR VRL
LVR RVL
LRV RLV

FIGURE **6.10**   Top-down, left-to-right, breadth-first traversal implementation.

```java
public void breadthFirst() {
    IntBSTNode p = root;
    Queue queue = new Queue;
    if (p != null) {
        queue.enqueue(p);
        while (!queue.isempty()) {
            p = (IntBSTNode) queue.dequeue();
            p.visit;
            if (p.left != null)
                queue.enqueue(p.left);
            if (p.right != null)
                queue.enqueue(p.right);
        }
    }
}
```

FIGURE **6.11**   Depth-first traversal implementation.

```java
protected void preorder(IntBSTNode p) {
    if (p != null) {
        p.visit();
        preorder(p.left);
        preorder(p.right);
    }
}
protected void inorder(IntBSTNode p) {
    if (p != null) {
        inorder(p.left);
        p.visit();
        inorder(p.right);
    }
}
protected void postorder(IntBSTNode p) {
    if (p != null) {
        postorder(p.left);
        postorder(p.right);
        p.visit();
    }
}
```

FIGURE **6.12**   Inorder tree traversal.

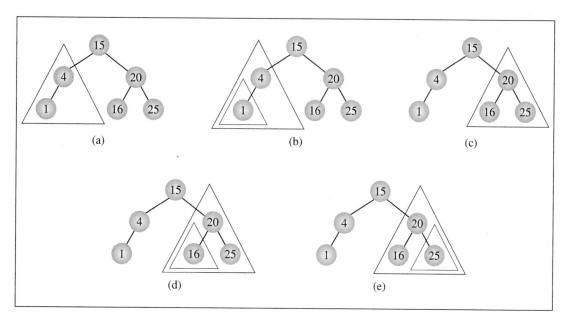

(a)   (b)   (c)

(d)   (e)

If the number of different orders still seems like a lot, it can be reduced to three traversals where the move is always from left to right and attention is focused on the first column. The three traversals are given these standard names:

VLR—preorder tree traversal

LVR—inorder tree traversal

LRV—postorder tree traversal

Short and elegant methods can be implemented directly from the symbolic descriptions of these three traversals, as shown in Figure 6.11.

These methods may seem too simplistic, but their real power lies in recursion, in fact, double recursion. The real job is done by the system on the run-time stack. This simplifies coding but lays a heavy burden upon the system. To better understand this process, inorder tree traversal is discussed in some detail.

In inorder traversal, the left subtree of the current node is visited first, then the node itself, and finally, the right subtree. All of this, obviously, holds if the tree is not empty. Before drawing aside the run-time curtain by analyzing the run-time stack, the output given by the inorder traversal is determined by referring to Figure 6.12. The following steps correspond to the letters in that figure:

(a)   Node 15 is the root on which `inorder()` is called for the first time. The method calls itself for node 15's left child, node 4.

(b)   Node 4 is not null, so `inorder()` is called on node 1. Because node 1 is a leaf (that is, both its subtrees are empty), invocations of `inorder()` on the subtrees do not result

FIGURE **6.13**   Details of several of the first steps of inorder traversal.

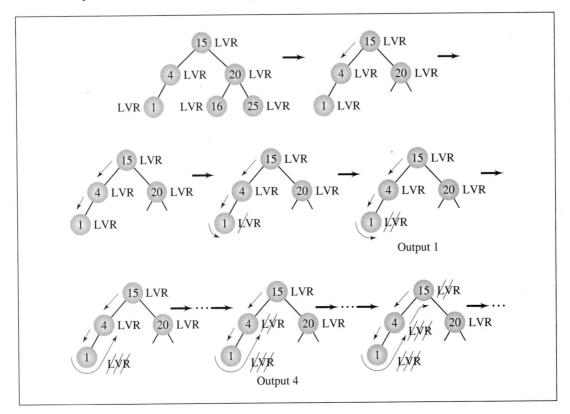

in other recursive calls of `inorder()`, as the condition in the `if` statement is not met. Thus, after immediate return from `inorder()` called for empty left subtree, node 1 is visited; afterwards a quick call to `inorder()` is executed for the null right subtree of node 1. After resuming the call for node 4, node 4 is visited. Node 4 has a null right subtree; hence, `inorder()` is called only to check that, and right after resuming the call for node 15, node 15 is visited.

(c)   Node 15 has a right subtree so, `inorder()` is called for node 20.

(d)   `inorder()` is called for node 16, the node is visited, and then on its null left subtree, which is followed by visiting node 16. After a quick call to `inorder()` on the null right subtree of node 16 and return to the call on node 20, node 20 is also visited.

(e)   `inorder()` is called on node 25, then on its empty left subtree, then node 25 is visited, and finally `inorder()` is called on node 25's empty right subtree.

If the visit includes printing the value stored in a node, then the output is:

```
1 4 15 16 20 25
```

The key to the traversal is that the three tasks, L, V, and R, are performed for each node separately. This means that the traversal of the right subtree of a node is held pending until the first two tasks, L and V, are accomplished. If the latter two are finished, they can be crossed out as in Figure 6.13.

To present the way `inorder()` works, the behavior of the run-time stack is observed. The numbers in comments in Figure 6.14 indicate return addresses shown on the left-hand side of the code for `inorder()`.

```
void inorder(IntBSTNode node) {
                if (node != null) {
/* 1 */             inorder(node.left);
/* 2 */             node.visit();
/* 3 */             inorder(node.right);
/* 4 */         }
        }
```

A rectangle with an up arrow and a number indicates the current value of node pushed onto the stack. For example, ↑4 means that node refers to the node of the tree whose value is the number 4. Figure 6.14 shows the changes of the run-time stack when `inorder()` is executed for the tree in Figure 6.12.

(a) Initially, the run-time stack is empty (or rather it is assumed that the stack is empty by disregarding what has been stored on it before the first call to `inorder()`).

(b) Upon the first call, the return address of `inorder()` and the value of node, ↑15, are pushed onto the run-time stack. The tree, referred to by node, is not empty, the condition in the `if` statement is satisfied, and `inorder()` is called again with node 4.

(c) Before it is executed, the return address, (2), and current value of node, ↑4, are pushed onto the stack. Since node is not null, `inorder()` is about to be invoked for node's left child, ↑1.

(d) First, the return address, (2), and the node's value are stored on the stack.

(e) `inorder()` is called with node 1's left child. The address (2) and the current value of parameter node, null, are stored on the stack. Since node is null, `inorder()` is exited immediately; upon exit, the activation record is removed from the stack.

(f) The system goes now to its run-time stack, restores the value of the node, ↑1, executes the statement under (2) and prints the number 1. Since node is not completely processed, the value of node and address (2) are still on the stack.

(g) With the right child of node ↑1, the statement under (3) is executed, which is the next call to `inorder()`. First, however, the address (4) and node's current value, null, are pushed onto the stack. Because node is null, `inorder()` is exited; upon exit, the stack is cleaned up.

(h) The system now restores the old value of the node, ↑1, and executes statement (4).

(i) Since this is `inorder()`'s exit, the system removes the current activation record and refers again to the stack, restores the node's value, ↑4, and resumes execution from statement (2). This prints the number 4 and then calls `inorder()` for the right child of node, which is null.

FIGURE **6.14**   Changes in the run-time stack during inorder traversal.

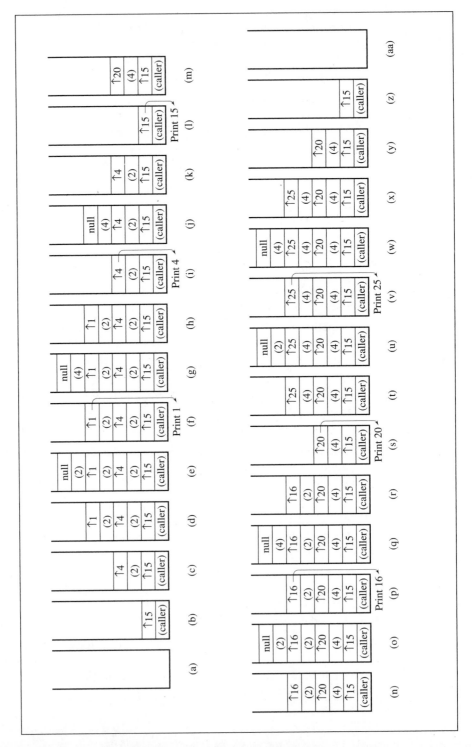

FIGURE **6.15**   A non-recursive implementation of preorder tree traversal.

```
public void iterativePreorder() {
    IntBSTNode p = root;
    Stack travStack = new Stack();
    if (p != null) {
        travStack.push(p);
        while (!travStack.isEmpty()) {
            p = (IntBSTNode) travStack.pop();
            p.visit();
            if (p.right != null)
                travStack.push(p.right);
            if (p.left  != null)          // left child pushed after right
                travStack.push(p.left);// to be on the top of the
                                          // stack;
        }
    }
}
```

These steps are just the beginning. All of the steps are shown in Figure 6.14.

At this point, consider the problem of a nonrecursive implementation of the three traversal algorithms. As indicated in Chapter 5, a recursive implementation has a tendency to be less efficient than a nonrecursive counterpart. If two recursive calls are used in a method, then the problem of possible inefficiency doubles. Can recursion be eliminated from the implementation? The answer has to be positive because if it is not eliminated in the source code, the system does it for us anyway. So the question should be rephrased: Is it expedient to do so?

Look first at a nonrecursive version of the preorder tree traversal shown in Figure 6.15. The method `iterativePreorder()` is twice as large as `preorder()`, but it is still short and legible. However, it uses a stack heavily. Therefore, supporting methods are necessary to process the stack, and the overall implementation is not so short. Although two recursive calls are omitted, there are now up to four calls per iteration of `while` loop: up to two calls of `push()`, one call of `pop()`, and one call of `visit()`. This can hardly be considered an improvement in efficiency.

In the recursive implementations of the three traversals, note that the only difference is in the order of the lines of code. For example, in `preorder()`, first a node is visited, and then there are calls for the left and right subtrees. On the other hand, in `postorder()`, visiting a node succeeds both calls. Can we so easily transform the nonrecursive version of a left-to-right preorder traversal into a nonrecursive left-to-right postorder traversal? Unfortunately, no. In `iterativePreorder()`, visiting occurs before both children are pushed onto the stack. But this order does not really matter. If the children are pushed first and then the node is visited, that is, if `p.visit`

FIGURE **6.16**   A non-recursive implementation of postorder tree traversal.

```
public void iterativePostorder() {
    BSTNode p = root, q = root;
    Stack travStack = new Stack();
    while (p != null) {
        for ( ; p.left != null; p = p.left)
            travStack.push(p);
        while (p != null && (p.right == null || p.right == q)) {
            p.visit();
            q = p;
            if (travStack.isEmpty())
                return;
            p = (BSTNode) travStack.pop();
        }
        travStack.push(p);
        p = p.right;
    }
}
```

is placed after both calls to push(), the resulting implementation is still a preorder traversal. What matters here is that visit() has to follow pop() and the latter has to precede both calls of push(). Therefore, nonrecursive implementations of inorder and postorder traversals have to be developed independently.

A nonrecursive version of postorder traversal can be obtained rather easily if we observe that the sequence generated by a left-to-right postorder traversal (a LRV order) is the same as the reversed sequence generated by a right-to-left preorder traversal (a VRL order). In this case, the implementation of iterativePreorder() can be adopted to create iterativePostorder(). This means that two stacks have to be used, one to visit each node in the reverse order after a right-to-left preorder traversal is finished. It is, however, possible to develop a function for postorder traversal that pushes onto the stack a node that has two descendants, once before traversing its left subtree and once before traversing its right subtree. An auxiliary reference is used to distinguish between these two cases. Nodes with one descendant are pushed only once, and leaves do not need to be pushed at all (Figure 6.16).

A nonrecursive inorder tree traversal is also a complicated matter. One possible implementation is given in Figure 6.17. In this case, we can clearly see the power of recursion: iterativeInorder() is almost unreadable, and without thorough explanation, it is not easy to determine the purpose of this method. On the other hand, recursive inorder() immediately demonstrates a purpose and logic. Therefore, iterativeInorder() can be defended in one case only: if it is shown that there is a substantial gain in execution time and that the method is called often in a program. Otherwise, inorder() is preferable to its iterative counterpart.

FIGURE **6.17**   A non-recursive implementation of inorder tree traversal.

```
public void iterativeInorder() {
    IntBSTNode p = root;
    Stack travStack = new Stack();
    while (p != null) {
        while(p != null) {                         // stack the right child (if any)
            if (p.right != null)                   // and the node itself when going
                travStack.push(p.right); // to the left;
            travStack.push(p);
            p = p.left;
        }
        p = (IntBSTNode) travStack.pop();// pop a node with no left child
        while (!travStack.isEmpty() && p.right == null) {// visit it and all
            p.visit();                    // nodes with no right child;
            p = (IntBSTNode) travStack.pop();
        }
        p.visit();                                 // visit also the first node with
        if (!travStack.isEmpty())          // a right child (if any);
            p = (IntBSTNode) travStack.pop();
        else p = null;
    }
}
```

6.4.3 Stackless Depth-First Traversal

Threaded Trees

The traversal methods analyzed in the preceding section were either recursive or non-recursive, but both kinds used a stack either implicitly or explicitly to store information about nodes whose processing has not been finished. In the case of recursive methods, the run-time stack was utilized. In the case of nonrecursive variants, an explicitly defined and user-maintained stack was used. The concern is that some additional time has to be spent to maintain the stack, and some more space has to be set aside for the stack itself. In the worst case, when the tree is unfavorably skewed, the stack may hold information about almost every node of the tree, a serious concern for very large trees.

It is more efficient to incorporate the stack as part of the tree. This is done by incorporating *threads* in a given node. Threads are references to the predecessor and successor of the node according to an inorder traversal, and trees whose nodes use threads are called *threaded trees*. Four reference fields are needed for each node in the tree, which again takes up valuable space.

The problem can be solved by overloading existing reference fields. In trees, left or right references are references to children, but they can also be used as references to predecessors

FIGURE **6.18**   (a) A threaded tree and (b) an inorder traversal's path in a threaded tree with right successors only.

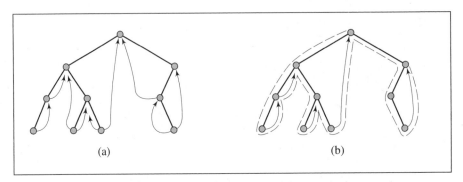

(a)   (b)

and successors, thereby being overloaded with meaning. To distinguish these meanings, a new data member has to be used to indicate the current meaning of the references.

Because a reference can refer to one node at a time, the left reference is either a reference to the left child or to the predecessor. Analogously, the right reference refers to either to the right subtree or to the successor (Figure 6.18a).

Figure 6.18a suggests that both references to predecessors and to successors have to be maintained, which is not always the case. It may be sufficient to use only one thread as shown in the implementation of the inorder traversal of a threaded tree, which requires only references to successors (Figure 6.18b).

The method is relatively simple. The dashed line in Figure 6.18b indicates the order in which p accesses nodes in the tree. Note that only one variable, p, is needed to traverse the tree. No stack is needed; therefore, space is saved. But is it really? As indicated, nodes require a field indicating how the right reference is being used. In the implementation of `threadedInorder()`, the Boolean field `successor` plays this role as shown in Figure 6.19. Hence, `successor` requires only one bit of computer memory, insignificant in comparison to other fields. However, the Java Virtual Machine does not use type Boolean, and Boolean variables are fields and represented as integers, which is four bytes (Boolean arrays are a slightly different matter). If so, the `successor` field needs at least four bytes, which defeats the argument about saving space by using threaded trees.

Threaded trees can also be used for preorder and postorder traversals. In preorder traversal, the current node is visited first and then traversal continues with its left descendant, if any, or right descendant, if any. If the current node is a leaf, threads are used to go through the chain of its already visited inorder successors to restart traversal with the right descendant of the last successor.

Postorder traversal is only slightly more complicated. First, a dummy node is created that has the root as its left descendant. In the traversal process, a variable can be used to check the type of the current action. If the action is left traversal and the current node has a left descendant, then the descendant is traversed; otherwise, the action is changed to right traversal. If the action is right traversal and the current node has a

FIGURE **6.19**   Implementation of the generic threaded tree and the inorder traversal of a threaded tree.

```
/******************** IntThreadedTreeNode.java ********************
 *                 binary search threaded tree of integers
 */

class IntThreadedTreeNode {
    protected int key;
    protected boolean sucessor;
    protected IntThreadedTreeNode left, right;
    public IntThreadedTreeNode() {
        left = right = null; sucessor = false;
    }
    public IntThreadedTreeNode(int el) {
        this(el,null,null);
    }
    public IntThreadedTreeNode(int el, IntThreadedTreeNode lt,
                                       IntThreadedTreeNode rt) {
        key = el; left = lt; right = rt; sucessor = false;
    }
    public void visit() {
        System.out.print(key + " ");
    }
}

/********************** IntThreadedTree.java **********************
 *                 binary search threaded tree of integers
 */

public class IntThreadedTree {
    private IntThreadedNode root;
    public IntThreadedTree() {
        root = null;
    }
    protected void threadedInorder() {
        IntThreadedNode prev, p = root;
        if (p != null) {                    // process only nonempty trees;
            while (p.left != null)          // go to the leftmost node;
                p = p.left;
            while (p != null) {
                p.visit();
                prev = p;
```

Continues

FIGURE **6.19**   (*continued*)

```
            p = p.right;              // go to the right node and only
            if (p != null && !prev.sucessor)// if it is a descendant
                while (p.left != null)// go to the leftmost node,
                    p = p.left;       // otherwise visit the
                                      // successor;
        }
    }
}
public void threadedInsert(int el) {
//  Figure 6.24
    }
}
```

right nonthread descendant, then the descendant is traversed and the action is changed to left traversal; otherwise, the action changes to visiting a node. If the action is visiting a node, then the current node is visited, and afterward, its postorder successor has to be found. If the current node's parent is accessible through a thread (that is, current node is parent's left child), then traversal is set to continue with the right descendant of the parent. If the current node has no right descendant, then it is the end of the right-extended chain of nodes. First, the beginning of the chain is reached through the thread of the current node, then the right references of nodes in the chain are reversed, and finally, the chain is scanned backward, each node is visited, and then right references are restored to their previous setting.

Traversal Through Tree Transformation

The first set of traversal algorithms analyzed earlier in this chapter needed a stack to retain some information necessary for successful processing. Threaded trees incorporated a stack as part of the tree at the cost of extending the nodes by one field to make a distinction between the interpretation of the right reference as a reference to the child or to the successor. Two such tag fields are needed if both successor and predecessor are considered. However, it is possible to traverse a tree without using any stack or threads. There are many such algorithms, all of them made possible by making temporary changes in the tree during traversal. These changes consist of re-assigning new values to some reference fields. However, the tree may temporarily lose its tree structure which needs to be restored before traversal is finished. The technique is illustrated by an elegant algorithm devised by Joseph M. Morris applied to inorder traversal.

First, it is easy to notice that inorder traversal is very simple for degenerate trees, in which no node has a left child (see Figure 6.1e). No left subtree has to be considered

FIGURE **6.20** Implementation of the Morris algorithm for inorder traversal.

```
public void MorrisInorder() {
    IntBSTNode p = root, tmp;
    while (p != null)
        if (p.left == null) {
            p.visit();
            p = p.right;
        }
        else {
            tmp = p.left;
            while (tmp.right != null && // go to the rightmost node of
                   tmp.right != p)   // the left subtree or
                tmp = tmp.right;     // to the temporary parent of p;
            if (tmp.right == null) {// if 'true' rightmost node was
                tmp.right = p;       // reached, make it a temporary
                p = p.left;          // parent of the current root,
            }
            else {                   // else a temporary parent has been
                p.visit();           // found; visit node p and then cut
                tmp.right = null;    // the right pointer of the current
                p = p.right;         // parent, whereby it ceases to be
            }                        // a parent;
        }
}
```

for any node. Therefore, the usual three steps, LVR (visit left subtree, visit node, visit right subtree), for each node in inorder traversal turn into two steps, VR. No information needs to be retained about the current status of the node being processed before traversing its left child, simply because there is no left child. Morris's algorithm takes into account this observation by temporarily transforming the tree so that the node being processed has no left child; hence, this node can be visited and its right subtree processed. The algorithm can be summarized as follows:

```
MorrisInorder()
    while not finished
        if node has no left descendant
            visit it;
            go to the right;
        else make this node right child of the rightmost node in its left descendant;
            go to this left descendant;
```

FIGURE **6.21**   Tree traversal with the Morris method.

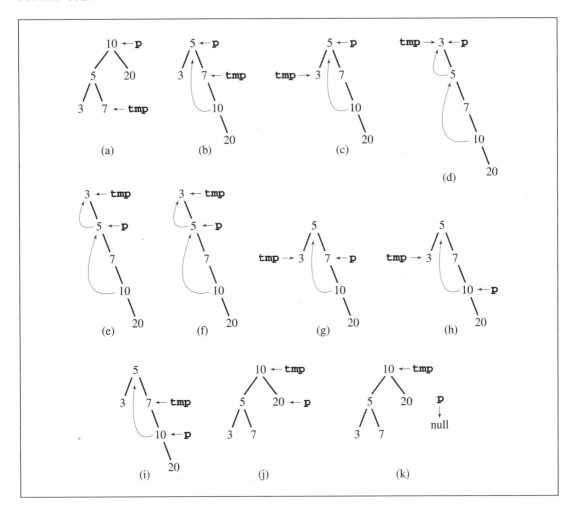

This algorithm successfully traverses the tree but only once, since it destroys its original structure. Therefore, some information has to be retained to allow the tree to restore its original form. This is achieved by retaining the left reference of the node moved down its right subtree, as in the case of nodes 10 and 5 in Figure 6.21.

An implementation of the algorithm is shown in Figure 6.20, and the details of the execution are illustrated in Figure 6.21. The following description is divided into actions performed in consecutive iterations of the outer while loop:

1. Initially, p refers to the root, which has a left child. As a result, the inner while loop takes tmp to node 7, which is the rightmost node of the left child of node 10, referred by p (Figure 6.21a). Since no transformation has been done, tmp has no right child,

and in the inner `if` statement, the root, node 10, is made the right child of `tmp`. Node 10 retains its left reference to node 5, its original left child. Now, the tree is not a tree anymore, since it contains a cycle (Figure 6.21b). This completes the first iteration.

2. Reference `p` refers to node 5, which also has a left child. First, `tmp` reaches the largest node in this subtree, which is 3 (Figure 6.21c), and then the current root, node 5, becomes the right child of node 3 while retaining contact with node 3 through its left reference (Figure 6.21d).

3. Because node 3, referred by `p`, has no left child, in the third iteration, this node is visited, and `p` is reassigned to its right child, node 5 (Figure 6.21e).

4. Node 5 has a nonnull left reference, so `tmp` finds a temporary parent of node 5, which is the same node currently referred by `tmp` (Figure 6.21f). Next, node 5 is visited, and configuration of the tree in Figure 6.21b is reestablished by setting the right reference of node 3 to null (Figure 6.21g).

5. Node 7, referred to now by `p`, is visited, and `p` moves down to its right child (6.21h).

6. `tmp` is updated to refer to the temporary parent of node 10 (Figure 6.21i). Next, node 10 is visited and then reestablished to its status of root by nullifying the right reference of node 7 (Figure 6.21j).

7. Finally, node 20 is visited without further ado, since it has no left child, nor has its position been altered.

This completes the execution of Morris's algorithm. Notice that there are seven iterations of the outer `while` loop for only five nodes in the tree in Figure 6.21. This is due to the fact that there are two left children in the tree, so the number of extra iterations depends on the number of left children in the entire tree. The algorithm performs worse for trees with a large number of such children.

Preorder traversal is easily obtainable from inorder traversal by moving `visit()` from inner `else` clause to the inner `if` clause. In this way, a node is visited before a tree transformation.

Postorder traversal can also be obtained from inorder traversal by first creating a dummy node whose left descendant is the tree being processed and whose right descendant is null. Then this temporarily extended tree is a subject of traversal as in inorder traversal except that in the inner `else` clause, after finding a temporary parent, nodes between `p->left` (included) and `p` (excluded) extended to the right in a modified tree are processed in the reverse order. To process them in constant time, the chain of nodes is scanned down and right references are reversed to refer to parents of nodes. Then the same chain is scanned upward, each node is visited, and the right references are restored to their original setting.

How efficient are the traversal procedures discussed in this section? All of them run in $\Theta(n)$ time, threaded implementation requires $\Theta(n)$ more space for threads than nonthreaded binary search trees, and both recursive and iterative traversals require $O(n)$ additional space (on the run-time stack or user-defined stack). Several dozens of runs on randomly generated trees of 5000 nodes indicate that for preorder and inorder traversal routines (recursive, iterative, Morris, and threaded), the difference in the execution time is only on the order of 5–10%. Morris traversals have one undeniable advantage over other types of traversals: They do not require additional space. Recursive traversals rely on the run-time stack which can be overflowed when traversing trees of large height. Iterative traversals also use a stack, and although the stack can be overflowed as well, the problem is not as imminent as in the case of the run-time stack. Threaded trees use nodes that are larger than the nodes used by non-threaded trees, which usually should not pose a problem. But both iterative and threaded implementations are much less intuitive than their recursive counterparts; therefore, the clarity of implementation and comparable run time clearly favors in most situations recursive implementations over other implementations.

◻ 6.5 INSERTION

Searching a binary tree does not modify the tree. It scans the tree in a predetermined way to access some or all of the keys in the tree, but the tree itself remains undisturbed after such an operation. Tree traversals can change the tree but they may also leave it in the same condition. Whether or not the tree is modified depends on the actions prescribed by visit(). There are certain operations that always make some systematic changes in the tree, such as adding nodes, deleting them, modifying elements, merging trees, and balancing trees to reduce their height. This section deals only with inserting a node into a binary search tree.

To insert a new node, called *n_node*, a tree node, called *t_node*, with a dead end has to be reached, and the new node has to be attached to it. A *t_node* is found using the same technique that tree searching used; the key of the *n_node* to be inserted is compared to the value of a node, denoted as *c_node*, currently being examined during a tree scan. If it is less than that value, the left child (if any) is tried; otherwise, the right child is tested. If the child of the *c_node* to be tested is empty, the scanning is discontinued and the *n_node* becomes this child. The procedure is illustrated in Figure 6.22. Figure 6.23 contains the algorithm to insert a node.

In analyzing the problem of traversing binary trees, three approaches have been presented: traversing with the help of a stack, traversing with the aid of threads, and traversing through tree transformation. The first approach does not change the tree during the process. The third approach changes it, but restores it to the same condition as before it started. Only the second approach needs some preparatory operations on the tree to become feasible: It requires threads. These threads may be created each time before the traversal procedure starts its task and removed each time it is finished. If the traversal is performed infrequently, this becomes a viable option. Another approach is to maintain the threads in all operations on the tree when inserting a new element in the binary search tree.

The method for inserting a node in a threaded tree is a simple extension of insert() for regular binary search trees to adjust threads whenever applicable. This method is for inorder tree traversal and it only takes care of successors, not predecessors.

A node with a right child has a successor some place in its right subtree. Therefore, it does not need a successor thread. Such threads are needed to allow climbing the tree, not going down it. A node with no right child has its successor somewhere

FIGURE **6.22**   Inserting nodes into binary search trees.

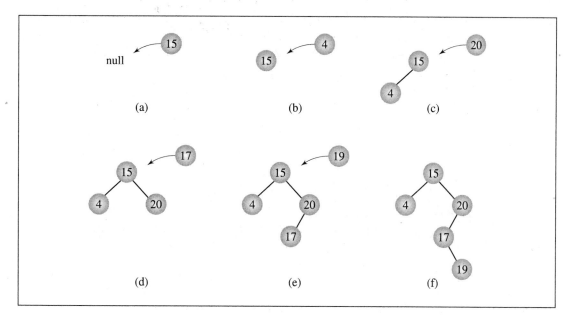

FIGURE **6.23**   Implementation of the insertion algorithm.

```
public void insert(int el) {
    IntBSTNode p = root, prev = null;
    while (p != null) {  // find a place for inserting new node;
        prev = p;
        if (p.key < el)
             p = p.right;
        else p = p.left;
    }
    if (root == null)    // tree is empty;
         root = new IntBSTNode(el);
    else if (prev.key < el)
         prev.right = new IntBSTNode(el);
    else prev.left  = new IntBSTNode(el);
}
```

FIGURE **6.24**   Implementation of the algorithm to insert node nto a threaded tree.

```java
public void threadedInsert(int el) {
    IntThreadedNode newNode = new IntThreadedNode(el);
    if (root == null) {                    // tree is empty
         root = newNode;
         return;
    }
    IntThreadedNode p = root, prev = null;
    while (p != null) {                    // find a place to insert newNode;
         prev = p;
         if (el < p.key)
             p = p.left;
         else if (!p.hasSuccessor)     // go to the right only if it is
             p = p.right;              // a descendant, not a successor;
         else break;                   // don't follow successor link;
    }
    if (el < prev.key) {               // if newNode is left child of
         prev.left  = newNode;         // its parent, the parent
         newNode.hasSuccessor = true;// also becomes its successor;
         newNode.right = prev;
    }
    else if (prev.hasSuccessor) {      // if parent of the newNode
         newNode.hasSuccessor = true;// is not the rightmost node,
         prev.hasSuccessor = false;   // make parent's successor
         newNode.right = prev.right;  // newNode's successor,
         prev.right = newNode;
    }
    else prev.right = newNode;         // otherwise it has no successor;
}
```

above it. Except for one node, all nodes with no right children will have threads to their successors. If a node becomes the right child of another node, it inherits the successor from its new parent. If a node becomes a left child of another node, this parent becomes its successor. Figure 6.24 contains the implementation of this algorithm, threadedInsert(). The first few insertions are shown in Figure 6.25.

FIGURE **6.25**   Inserting nodes into a threaded tree.

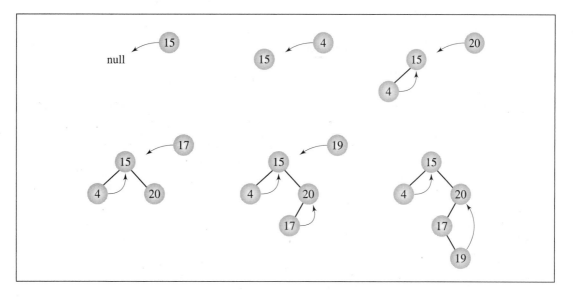

6.6 DELETION

Deleting a node is another operation necessary to maintain a binary search tree. The level of complexity in performing the operation depends on the position of the node to be deleted in the tree. It is by far more difficult to delete a node having two subtrees than to delete a leaf; the complexity of the deletion algorithm is proportional to the number of children the node has. There are three cases of deleting a node from the binary search tree:

1. The node is a leaf; it has no children. This is the easiest case to deal with. The appropriate reference of its parent is set to null and the space occupied by the deleted node is later claimed by the garbage collector as in Figure 6.26.

2. The node has one child. This case is not complicated. The parent's reference to the node is reset to refer to the node's child. In this way, the node's children are lifted up by one level and all great-great-. . . grandchildren lose one "great" from their kinship designations. For example, the node containing 20 (see Figure 6.27) is deleted by setting the right reference of its parent containing 15 to refer to 20's only child, which is 16.

3. The node has two children. In this case, no one-step operation can be performed since the parent's right or left reference cannot refer to both node's children at the same time. This section discusses two different solutions to this problem.

FIGURE **6.26**   Deleting a leaf.

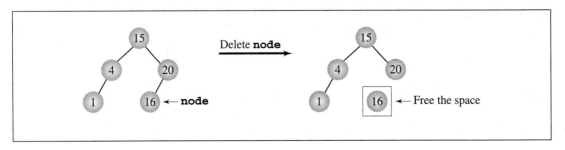

FIGURE **6.27**   Deleting a node with one child.

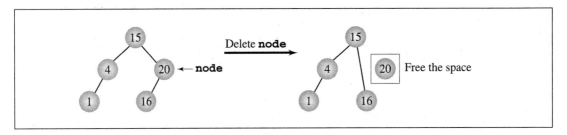

6.6.1 Deletion by Merging

This solution makes one tree out of the two subtrees of the node and then attaches it to the node's parent. This technique is called *deleting by merging.* But how can we merge these subtrees? By the nature of binary search trees, every value of the right subtree is greater than every value of the left subtree, so the best thing to do is to find in the left subtree the node with the greatest value and make it a parent of the right subtree. Symmetrically, the node with the lowest value can be found in the right subtree and made a parent of the left subtree.

The desired node is the rightmost node of the left subtree. It can be located by moving along this subtree and taking right references until null is encountered. This means that this node will not have a right child, and there is no danger of violating the property of binary search trees in the original tree by setting that rightmost node's right reference to the right subtree. The same could be done by setting the left reference of the leftmost node of the right subtree to the left subtree. Figure 6.28 depicts this operation. Figure 6.29 contains the implementation of the algorithm.

Figure 6.30 shows each step of this operation. It shows what changes are made when DeleteByMerging() is executed. The numbers in this figure correspond to numbers put in comments in the code in Figure 6.29.

FIGURE **6.28**   Summary of deleting by merging.

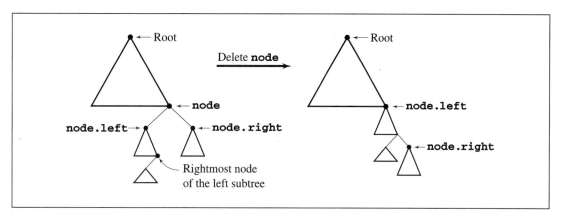

FIGURE **6.29**   Implementation of algorithm for deleting by merging.

```
public void deleteByMerging(int el) {
    IntBSTNode tmp, node, p = root, prev = null;
    while (p != null && p.key != el) { // find the node p
        prev = p;                      // with element el;
        if (p.key < el)
            p = p.right;
        else p = p.left;
    }
    node = p;
    if (p != null && p.key == el) {
        if (node.right == null) // node has no right child: its left
            node = node.left;   // child (if any) is attached to its
                                // parent;
        else if (node.left == null) // node has no left child: its right
            node = node.right; // child is attached to its parent;
        else {                  // be ready for merging subtrees;
            tmp = node.left;    // 1. move left
            while (tmp.right != null) // 2. and then right as far as
                tmp = tmp.right;     //    possible;
            tmp.right =         // 3. establish the link between the
                node.right;     //    the rightmost node of the left
                                //    subtree and the right subtree;
            node = node.left;   // 4.
```

Continues

FIGURE **6.29**   (*continued*)

```
        }
        if (p == root)
             root = node;
        else if (prev.left == p)
             prev.left = node;
        else prev.right = node;
    }
    else if (root != null)
        System.out.println("key " + el + " is not in the tree");
    else System.out.println("the tree is empty");
}
```

FIGURE **6.30**   Details of deleting by merging.

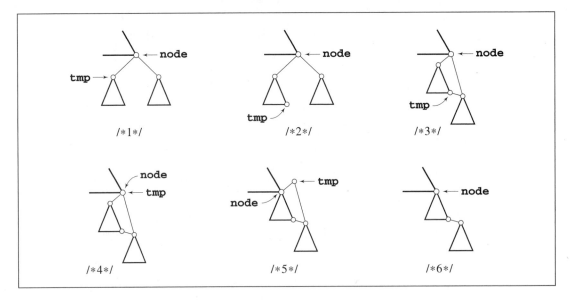

The algorithm for deletion by merging may result in increasing the height of the tree. In some cases, the new tree may be highly unbalanced, as Figure 6.31a illustrates. Sometimes the height may be reduced (see Figure 6.31b). This algorithm is not necessarily inefficient, but it is certainly far from perfect. There is a need for an algorithm that does not give the tree the chance to increase its height when deleting one of its nodes.

FIGURE **6.31**   The height of a tree can be (a) extended or (b) reduced after deleting by merging.

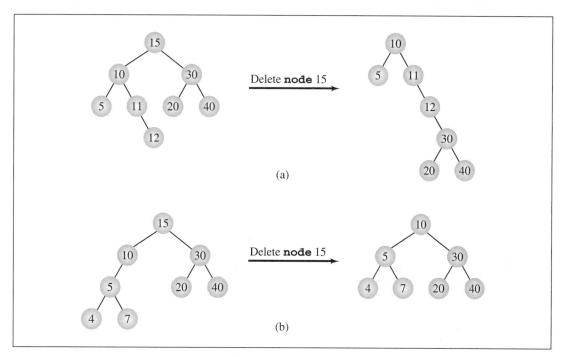

6.6.2 Deletion by Copying

Another solution, called *deletion by copying,* was proposed by Thomas Hibbard and Donald Knuth. If the node has two children, it can be reduced to one of two simple cases: The node is a leaf or the node has only one nonempty child. This can be done by replacing the key being deleted with its immediate predecessor (or successor). As already indicated in the discussion of deletion by merging, a key's predecessor is the key in the rightmost node in the left subtree (and analogically, its immediate successor is the key in the leftmost node in the right subtree). First, the predecessor has to be located. This is done, again, by moving one step to the left by first reaching the root of the node's left subtree and then moving as far to the right as possible. Next, the key of the located node replaces the key to be deleted. And that is where one of two simple cases comes into play. If the rightmost node is a leaf, the first case applies; however, if it has one child, the second case is relevant. In this way, deletion by copying removes a key k_1 by overwriting it by another key k_2 and then removing the node that holds k_2, whereas deletion by merging consisted of removing a key k_1 along with the node that holds it.

An implementation of this algorithm is in Figure 6.32. A step-by-step trace is shown in Figure 6.33, and the numbers under the diagrams refer to the numbers indicated in comments included in the implementation of `deleteByCopying()`.

FIGURE **6.32**   Implementation of algorithm for deleting by copying.

```
public void deleteByCopying(BaseObject el) {
    BSTNode node, p = root, prev = null;
    while (p != null && !p.key.equals(el)) { // find the node p
        prev = p;                            // with element el;
        if (p.key.isLessThan(el))
            p = p.right;
        else p = p.left;
    }
    node = p;
    if (p != null && p.key.equals(el)) {
        if (node.right == null)           // node has no right child;
            node = node.left;
        else if (node.left == null)       // no left child for node;
            node = node.right;
        else {
            BSTNode tmp = node.left;       // node has both children;
            BSTNode previous = node;       // 1.
            while (tmp.right != null) {     // 2. find the rightmost
                previous = tmp;            //     position in the
                tmp = tmp.right;           //     left subtree of node;
            }
            node.key = tmp.key;            // 3. overwrite the reference
                                           //     of the key being deleted;
            if (previous == node)          // if node's left child's
                previous.left = tmp.left;  // right subtree is null;
            else previous.right = tmp.left; // 4.
        }
        if (p == root)
            root = node;
        else if (prev.left == p)
            prev.left = node;
        else prev.right = node;
    }
    else if (root != null)
        System.out.println("key " + el.toString() + " is not in the tree");
    else System.out.println("the tree is empty");
}
```

FIGURE **6.33**   Deleting by copying.

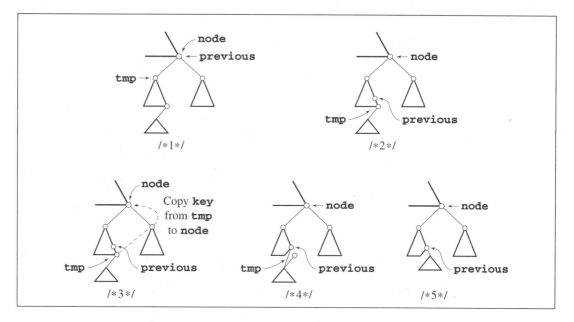

This algorithm does not increase the height of the tree, but it still causes a problem if it is applied many times along with insertion. The algorithm is asymmetric; it always deletes the node of the immediate predecessor of information in node, possibly reducing the height of the left subtree and leaving the right subtree unaffected. Therefore, the right subtree of node can grow after later insertions, and if the information in node is again deleted, the height of the right tree remains the same. After many insertions and deletions, the entire tree becomes right unbalanced, with the right tree bushier and larger than the left subtree.

To circumvent this problem, a simple improvement can make the algorithm symmetrical. The algorithm can alternately delete the predecessor of the information in node from the left subtree and delete its successor from the right subtree. The improvement is significant. Simulations performed by Jeffrey Eppinger show that an expected internal path length for many insertions and asymmetric deletions is $\Theta(n \lg^3 n)$ for n nodes, and when symmetric deletions are used, the expected IPL becomes $\Theta(n \lg n)$. Theoretical results obtained by J. Culberson confirm these conclusions. According to Culberson, insertions and asymmetric deletions give $\Theta(n\sqrt{n})$ for the expected IPL and $\Theta(\sqrt{n})$ for the average search time (average path length), whereas symmetric deletions lead to $\Theta(\lg n)$ for the average search time, and as before, $\Theta(n \lg n)$ for the average IPL.

These results may be of moderate importance for practical applications. Experiments show that for a 2048-node binary tree, only after 1.5 million insertions and asymmetric deletions does the IPL become worse than in a randomly generated tree.

Theoretical results are only fragmentary because of the extraordinary complexity of the problem. Arne Jonassen and Donald Knuth analyzed the problem of random insertions and deletions for a tree of only three nodes, which required using Bessel functions and bivariate integral equations, and the analysis turned out to rank among "the more difficult of all exact analyses of algorithms that have been carried out to date." Therefore, the reliance on experimental results is not surprising.

6.7 BALANCING A TREE

At the beginning of this chapter, two arguments were presented in favor of trees: They are well suited to represent the hierarchical structure of a certain domain, and the search process is much faster using trees instead of linked lists. The second argument, however, does not always hold. It all depends on what the tree looks like. Figure 6.34 shows three binary search trees. All of them store the same data, but obviously, the tree in Figure 6.34a is the best and Figure 6.34c is the worst. In the worst case, three tests are needed in the former and six tests are needed in the latter to locate an object. The problem with the trees in Figures 6.34b and 6.34c is that they are somewhat unsymmetrical, or lopsided; that is, objects in the tree are not distributed evenly to the extent that the tree in Figure 6.34c practically turned into a linked list, although, formally, it is still a tree. Such a situation does not arise in balanced trees.

A binary tree is *height-balanced* or simply *balanced* if the difference in height of both subtrees of any node in the tree is either zero or one. For example, for node K in Figure 6.34b, the difference between the heights of its subtrees being equal to one is acceptable. But for node B this difference is three, which means that the entire tree is unbalanced. For the same node B in 6.34c, the difference is the worst possible, namely, five. Also, a tree is considered *perfectly balanced* if it is balanced and all leaves are to be found on one level or two levels.

Figure 6.35 shows how many nodes can be stored in binary trees of different heights. Since each node can have two children, the number of nodes on a certain level is double the number of parents residing on the previous level (except, of course, the root). For example, if 10,000 elements are stored in a perfectly balanced tree, then the tree is of height $\lceil \lg(10,001) \rceil = \lceil 13.289 \rceil = 14$. In practical terms, this means that if 10,000 elements are stored in a perfectly balanced tree, then at most 14 nodes have to be checked to locate a particular element. This is a substantial difference compared to the 10,000 tests needed in a linked list (in the worst case). Therefore, it is worth the effort to build a balanced tree or modify an existing tree so that it is balanced.

There are a number of techniques to properly balance a binary tree. Some of them consist of constantly restructuring the tree when elements arrive and lead to an unbalanced tree. Some of them consist of reordering the data themselves and then building a tree, if an ordering of the data guarantees that the resulting tree is balanced. This section presents a simple technique of this kind.

The linked listlike tree of Figure 6.34c is the result of a particular stream of data. Thus, if the data arrive in ascending or descending order, then the tree resembles a linked list. The tree in Figure 6.34b is lopsided because the first element that arrived was the letter B, which precedes almost all other letters, except A; the left subtree of B is guar-

FIGURE **6.34**   Different binary search trees with the same information.

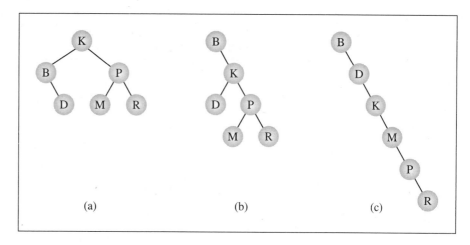

(a)   (b)   (c)

FIGURE **6.35**   Maximum number of nodes in binary trees of different heights.

Height	Nodes at one level	Nodes at all levels
1	$2^0 = 1$	$1 = 2^1 - 1$
2	$2^1 = 2$	$3 = 2^2 - 1$
3	$2^2 = 4$	$7 = 2^3 - 1$
4	$2^3 = 8$	$15 = 2^4 - 1$
⋮		
11	$2^{10} = 1024$	$2047 = 2^{11} - 1$
⋮		
14	$2^{13} = 8192$	$16383 = 2^{14} - 1$
⋮		
h	2^{h-1}	$n = 2^h - 1$
⋮		

anteed to have just one node. The tree in Figure 6.34a looks very good, since the root contains an element near the middle of all the possible elements, and P is more or less in the middle of K and Z. This leads us to an algorithm based on binary search technique.

When data arrive, store all of them in an array. If all possible data arrived, sort the array using one of the efficient algorithms discussed in Chapter 9. Now, designate for the root the middle element in the array. The array now consists of two subarrays: one between the beginning of the array and the element just chosen for the root and one between the root and the end of the array. The left child of the root is taken from the

FIGURE **6.36**   Creating a binary search tree from an ordered array.

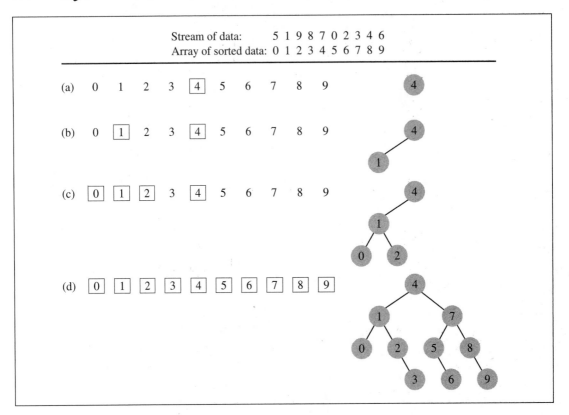

middle of the first subarray, its right child an element in the middle of the second. In this way, building the level of the children of the root is finished. The next level, with children of children of the root, is constructed in the same fashion using four subarrays and the middle elements from each of them.

In this description, first the root is inserted into an initially empty tree, then its left child, then its right child, and so on level by level. An implementation of this algorithm is greatly simplified if the order of insertion is changed: First insert the root, then its left child, then left child of this left child, and so on. This allows for using the following simple recursive implementation:

```
void balance(int data[], int first, int last) {
    if (first <= last) {
        int middle = (first + last)/2;
        insert(data[middle]);
        balance(data,first,middle-1);
        balance(data,middle+1,last);
    }
}
```

FIGURE **6.37**   Right rotation of child Ch about parent Par.

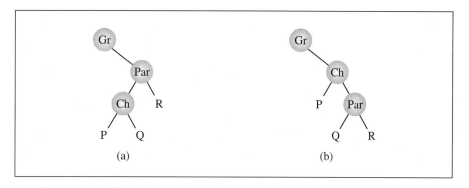

(a)   (b)

An example of application of `balance()` is shown in Figure 6.36. First, number 4 is inserted (Figure 6.36a), then 1 (Figure 6.36b), then 0 and 2 (Figure 6.36c), and finally, 6, 5, 7, and 8 (Figure 6.36d).

This algorithm has one serious drawback: All data must be put in an array before the tree can be created. They can be stored in the array directly from the input. In this case, the algorithm may be unsuitable when the tree has to be used while the data to be included in the tree are still coming. But the data can be transferred from an unbalanced tree to the array using inorder traversal. The tree can now be deleted and recreated using `balance()`. This at least does not require using any sorting algorithm to put data in order.

6.7.1 The DSW Algorithm

The algorithm discussed in the previous section was somewhat inefficient in that it required an additional array which needed to be sorted before the construction of a perfectly balanced tree began. To avoid sorting, it required deconstructing and then reconstructing the tree, which is inefficient except for relatively small trees. There are, however, algorithms that require little additional storage for intermediate variables and use no sorting procedure. The very elegant DSW algorithm was devised by Colin Day and later improved by Quentin F. Stout and Bette L. Warren.

The building block for tree transformations in this algorithm is the *rotation*. There are two types of rotation, left and right, which are symmetrical to one another. The right rotation of the node `Ch` about its parent `Par` is performed according to the following algorithm:

```
rotateRight (Gr, Par, Ch)
    if Par is not the root of the tree // i.e., if Gr is not null
        grandparent Gr of child Ch becomes Ch's parent by replacing Par;
    right subtree of Ch becomes left subtree of Ch's parent Par;
    node Ch acquires Par as its right child;
```

FIGURE **6.38**   Transforming a binary search tree into a backbone.

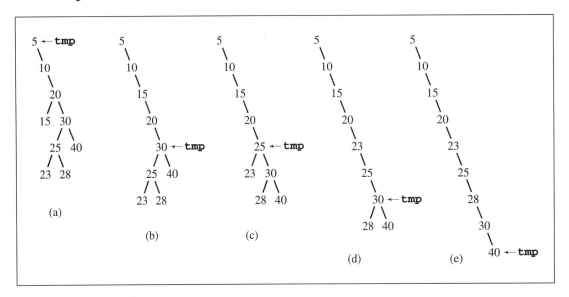

The steps involved in this compound operation are shown in Figure 6.37. The third step is the core of the rotation, when Par, the parent node of child Ch, becomes the child of Ch, when the roles of a parent and its child change. However, this exchange of roles cannot affect the principal property of the tree, namely, that it is a search tree. The first and the second steps of rotateRight() are needed to ensure that, after the rotation, the tree remains a search tree.

Basically, the DSW algorithm transfigures an arbitrary binary search tree into a linked listlike tree called a *backbone* or *vine*. Then this elongated tree is transformed in a series of passes into a perfectly balanced tree by repeatedly rotating every second node of the backbone about its parent.

In the first phase, a backbone is created using the following routine:

```
createBackbone(root, n)
    tmp = root;
    while (tmp != null)
        if tmp has a left child
            rotate this child about tmp; // hence the left child
                                         // becomes parent of tmp;
            set tmp to the child which just became parent;
        else set tmp to its right child;
```

This algorithm is illustrated in Figure 6.38. Note that a rotation requires knowledge about the parent of tmp, so another reference has to be maintained when implementing the algorithm.

In the best case, when the tree is already a backbone, the `while` loop is executed n times and no rotation is performed. In the worst case, when the root does not have a right child, the `while` loop executes $2n - 1$ times with $n - 1$ rotations performed, where n is the number of nodes in the tree; that is, the run time of the first phase is $O(n)$. In this case, for each node except the one with the smallest value, the left child of `tmp` is rotated about `tmp`. After all rotations are finished, `tmp` refers to the root, and after n iterations, it descends down the backbone to become null.

In the worst case, the `while` loop is executive $2n - 1$ times with $n - 1$ rotations performed where n is the number of nodes in the tree; the run time of the first phase is $O(n)$.

In the second phase, the backbone is transformed into a tree, but this time, the tree is perfectly balanced by having leaves only on two adjacent levels. In each pass down the backbone, every second node is rotated about its parent. One such pass decreases the size of the backbone by one-half. Only the first pass may not reach the end of the backbone: It is used to account for the difference between the number n of nodes in the current tree and the number $2^{\lfloor \lg(n+1) \rfloor} - 1$ of nodes in the closest complete binary tree where $\lfloor x \rfloor$ is the closest integer less than x. That is, the overflowing nodes are treated separately.

```
createPerfectTree(n)
    m = 2^⌊lg(n+1)⌋−1;
    make n-m rotations starting from the top of backbone;
    while (m > 1)
        m = m/2;
        make m rotations starting from the top of backbone;
```

Figure 6.39 contains an example. The backbone in Figure 6.38e has nine nodes and is preprocessed by one pass outside the loop to be transformed into the backbone shown in Figure 6.39b. Now, two passes are executed. In each backbone, the nodes to be promoted by one level by left rotations are shown as squares; their parents, about which they are rotated, are circles.

To compute the complexity of the tree building phase, observe that the number of iterations performed by the while loop equals

$$(2^{\lg(m+1)-1} - 1) + \cdots + 15 + 7 + 3 + 1 = \sum_{i=1}^{\lg(m+1)-1} (2^i - 1) = m - \lg(m+1)$$

The number of rotations can now be given by the formula

$$n - m + (m - \lg(m+1)) = n - \lg(m+1) = n - \lfloor \lg(n+1) \rfloor$$

that is, the number of rotations is $O(n)$. Because creating a backbone also required at most $O(n)$ rotations, the cost of global rebalancing with the DSW algorithm is optimal in terms of time because it grows linearly with n and requires a very small and fixed amount of storage.

6.7.2 AVL Trees

The previous two sections discussed algorithms which rebalanced the tree globally; each and every node could have been involved in rebalancing either by moving data

FIGURE **6.39**   Transforming a backbone into a perfectly balanced tree.

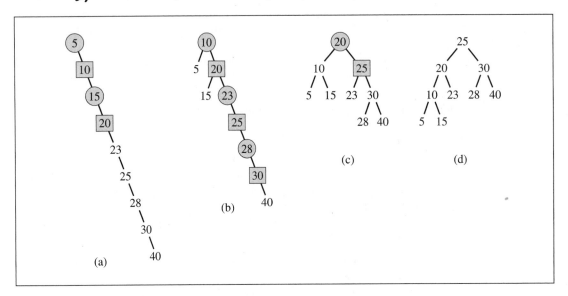

from nodes or by reassigning new values to reference fields. Tree rebalancing, however, can be performed locally if only a portion of the tree is affected when changes are required after an element is inserted into or deleted from the tree. One classical method has been proposed by Adel'son-Vel'skii and Landis, which is commemorated in the name of the tree modified with this method: the AVL tree.

An *AVL tree* (originally called an *admissible tree*) is one in which the height of left and right subtrees of every node differ by at most one. For example, all the trees in Figure 6.40 are AVL trees. Numbers in the nodes indicate the *balance factors* which are the differences between the heights of the left and right subtrees. A balance factor is the height of the right subtree minus the height of the left subtree. For an AVL tree, all balance factors should be +1, 0, or −1. Notice that the definition of the AVL tree is the same as the definition of the balanced tree. However, the concept of the AVL tree always implicitly includes the techniques for balancing the tree. Moreover, unlike the two methods previously discussed, the technique for balancing AVL trees does not guarantee that the resulting tree is perfectly balanced.

The definition of an AVL tree indicates that the minimum number of nodes in a tree is determined by the recurrence equation

$$AVL_h = AVL_{h-1} + AVL_{h-2} + 1$$

where $AVL_0 = 0$ and $AVL_1 = 1$ are the initial conditions.[1] As shown by Adel'son-Vel'skii and Landis, this formula leads to the following bounds on the height *h* of an AVL tree depending on the number of nodes *n*:

---

[1]Numbers generated by this recurrence formula are called *Leonardo numbers*.

FIGURE **6.40**   Examples of AVL trees.

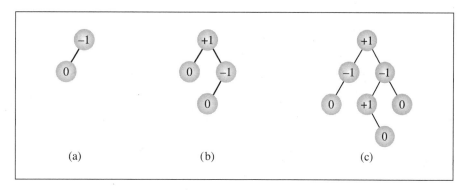

(a)   (b)   (c)

$$\lg(n + 1) \le h < 1.44\lg(n + 2) - 0.328$$

Therefore, h is bounded by $O(\lg n)$; the worst case search requires $O(\lg n)$ comparisons. For a perfectly balanced binary tree of the same height, $h = \lceil\lg(n + 1)\rceil$. Therefore, the search time in the worst case in an AVL tree is 44% worse (it requires 44% more comparisons) than in the best case tree configuration. Empirical studies indicate that the average number of searches is much closer to the best case than to the worst and is equal to $\lg n + 0.25$ for large n (Knuth 1998). Therefore, AVL trees are definitely worth studying.

If the balance factor of any node in an AVL tree becomes less than -1 or greater than 1, the tree has to be balanced. An AVL tree can become out of balance in four situations, but only two of them need to be analyzed; the remaining two are symmetrical. The first case, the result of inserting a node in the right subtree of the right child, is illustrated in Figure 6.41. The heights of the participating subtrees are indicated within these subtrees. In the AVL tree in Figure 6.41a, a node is inserted somewhere in the right subtree of Q (Figure 6.41b), which disturbs the balance of the tree P. In this case, the problem can be easily rectified by rotating node Q about its parent P (Figure 6.41c) so that the balance factor of both P and Q becomes zero, which is even better than at the outset.

The second case, the result of inserting a node in the left subtree of the right child, is more complex. A node is inserted into the tree in Figure 6.42a; the resulting tree is shown in Figure 6.42b and in more detail in Figure 6.42c. To bring the tree back into balance, a double rotation is performed. The balance of the tree P is restored by rotating R about node Q (Figure 6.42d) and then by rotating R again, this time about node P (Figure 6.42e).

In these two cases, the tree P is considered a stand-alone tree. However, P can be part of a larger AVL tree; it can be a child of some other node in the tree. If a node is entered into the tree and the balance of P is disturbed and then restored, does extra work need to be done to the predecessor(s) of P? Fortunately not. Note that the heights of the trees in Figures 6.41c and 6.42e resulting from the rotations are the same as the heights of the trees before insertion (Figures 6.41a and 6.42a) and are

FIGURE **6.41**   Balancing a tree after insertion of a node in the right subtree of node Q.

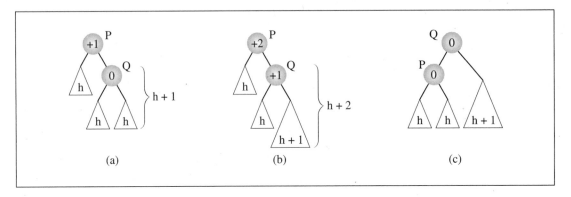

FIGURE **6.42**   Balancing a tree after insertion of a node in the left subtree of node Q.

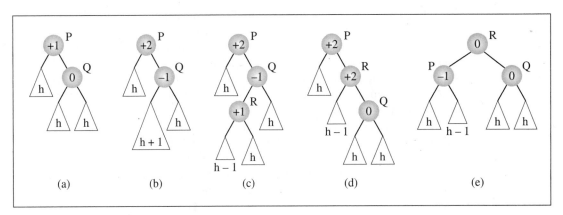

equal to $h + 2$. This means that the balance factor of the parent of the new root (Q in Figure 6.41c and R in Figure 6.42e) remains the same as it was before the insertion, and the changes made to the subtree P are sufficient to restore the balance of the entire AVL tree. The problem is in finding a node P for which the balance factor becomes unacceptable after a node has been inserted into the tree.

This node can be detected by moving up toward the root of the tree from the position in which the new node has been inserted and by updating the balance factors of the nodes encountered. Then, if a node with a ±1 balance factor is encountered, the balance factor may be changed to ±2, and the first node whose balance factor is changed in this way becomes the root P of a subtree for which the balance has to be restored. Note that the balance factors do not have to be updated above this node since they remain the same.

FIGURE **6.43** An example of inserting a new node (b) in an AVL tree (a), which requires one rotation (c) to restore the height balance.

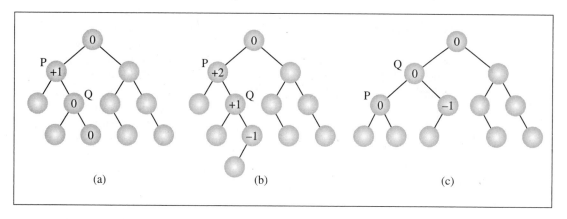

(a)   (b)   (c)

FIGURE **6.44** In an AVL tree (a) a new node is inserted (b) requiring no height adjustments.

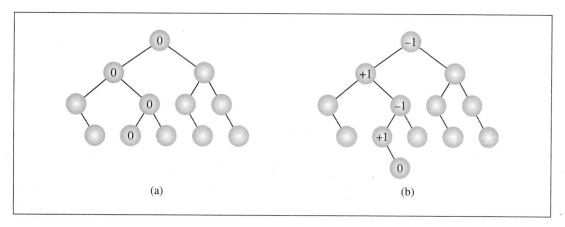

(a)   (b)

In Figure 6.43a, a path is marked with one balance factor equal to +1. Insertion of a new node at the end of this path results in an unbalanced tree (Figure 6.43b), and the balance is restored by one left rotation (Figure 6.43c).

However, if the balance factors on the path from the newly inserted node to the root of the tree are all zero, all of them have to be updated, but no rotation is needed for any of the encountered nodes. In Figure 6.44a, the AVL tree has a path of all zero balance factors. After a node has been appended to the end of this path (Figure 6.44b), no changes are made in the tree except for updating the balance factors of all nodes along this path.

Deletion may be more time-consuming than insertion. First, we apply `delete-ByCopying()` to delete a node. This technique allows us to reduce the problem of deleting a node with two descendants to deleting a node with at most one descendant.

After a node has been deleted from the tree, balance factors are updated from the parent of the deleted node up to the root. For each node in this path whose balance factor becomes ±2, a single or double rotation has to be performed to restore the balance of the tree. Importantly, the rebalancing does not stop after the first node P is found for which the balance factor would become ±2, as is the case with insertion. This also means that deletion leads to at most $O(\lg n)$ rotations, since in the worst case, every node on the path from the deleted node to the root may require rebalancing.

Deletion of a node does not have to necessitate an immediate rotation because it may improve the balance factor of its parent (by changing it from ±1 to 0), but it may also worsen the balance factor for the grandparent (by changing it from ±1 to ±2). We illustrate only those cases that require immediate rotation. There are four such cases (plus four symmetric cases). In each of these cases, we assume that the left child of node P is deleted.

In the first case, the tree in Figure 6.45a turns after deletion into the tree in Figure 6.45b. The tree is rebalanced by rotating Q about P (Figure 6.45c). In the second case, P has a balance factor equal to +1, and its right subtree Q has a balance factor equal to 0 (Figure 6.45d). After deleting a node in the left subtree of P (Figure 6.45e), the tree is rebalanced by the same rotation as in the first case (Figure 6.45f). In this way, cases one and two can be processed together in an implementation after checking that the balance factor of Q is +1 or 0. If Q is –1, we have two other cases, which are more complex. In the third case, the left subtree R of Q has a balance factor equal to –1 (Figure 6.45g). To rebalance the tree, first R is rotated about Q and then about P (Figures 6.45h–i). The fourth case differs from the third in that R's balance factor equals +1 (Figure 6.45j), in which case the same two rotations are needed to restore the balance factor of P (Figures 6.45k–l). Cases three and four can be processed together in a program processing AVL trees.

The previous analyses indicate that insertions and deletions require at most 1.44 $\lg(n + 2)$ searches. Also, insertion can require one single or one double rotation, and deletion can require 1.44 $\lg(n + 2)$ rotations in the worst case. But as also indicated, the average case requires $\lg(n) + .25$ searches, which reduces the number of rotations in case of deletion to this number. To be sure, insertion in the average case may lead to one single/double rotation. Experiments also indicate that deletions in 78% of cases require no rebalancing at all. On the other hand, only 53% of insertions do not bring the tree out of balance (Karlton et al. 1976). Therefore, the more time-consuming deletion occurs less frequently than the insertion operation, not markedly endangering the efficiency of rebalancing AVL trees.

AVL trees can be extended by allowing the difference in height $\Delta > 1$ (Foster 1973). Not unexpectedly, the worst-case height increases with Δ and

$$h = \begin{cases} 1.81 \lg(n) - 0.71 & \text{if } \Delta = 2 \\ 2.15 \lg(n) - 1.13 & \text{if } \Delta = 3 \end{cases}$$

As experiments indicate, the average number of visited nodes increases by one-half in comparison to pure AVL trees ($\Delta = 1$), but the amount of restructuring can be decreased by a factor of 10.

FIGURE **6.45**   Rebalancing an AVL tree after deleting a node.

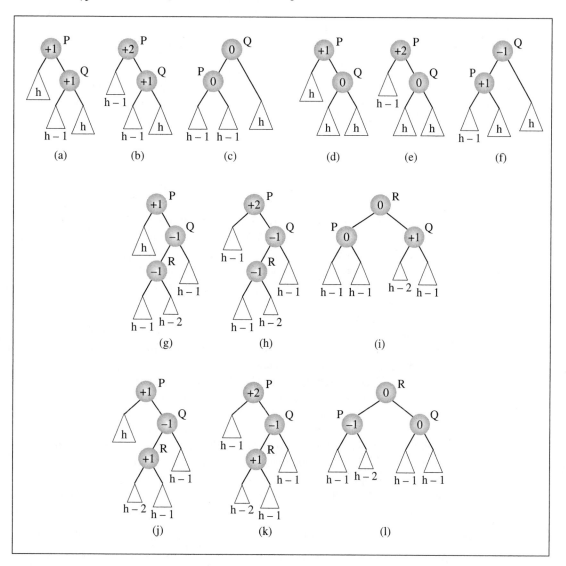

🔲 *6.8* SELF-ADJUSTING TREES

The main concern in balancing trees is to keep them from becoming lopsided and, ideally, to allow leaves to occur only at one or two levels. Therefore, if a newly arriving element endangers the tree balance, the problem is immediately rectified by restructuring the tree locally (the AVL method) or by re-creating the tree (the DSW method). However, we may question whether or not such a restructuring is always necessary. Binary

FIGURE **6.46**   Restructuring a tree by using (a) a single rotation or (b) moving to the root when accessing node *R*.

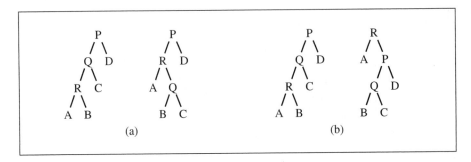

(a)   (b)

search trees are used to insert, retrieve, and delete elements quickly, and the speed of performing these operations is the issue, not the shape of the tree. Performance can be improved by balancing the tree, but this is not the only method that can be used.

Another approach begins with the observation that not all elements are used with the same frequency. For example, if an element on the tenth level of the tree is used only infrequently, then the execution of the entire program is not greatly impaired by accessing this level. However, if the same element is constantly being accessed, then it makes a big difference whether it is on the tenth level or close to the root. Therefore, the strategy in self-adjusting trees is to restructure trees only by moving up the tree those elements that are used more often, creating a kind of "priority tree." The frequency of accessing nodes can be determined in a variety of ways. Each node can have a counter field which records the number of times the element has been used for any operation. Then the tree can be scanned to move the most frequently accessed elements toward the root. In a less sophisticated approach, it is assumed that an element being accessed has a good chance of being accessed again soon. Therefore, it is moved up the tree. No restructuring is performed for new elements. This assumption may lead to promoting elements which are occasionally accessed, but the overall tendency is to move up elements with a high frequency of access, and for the most part, these elements will populate the first few levels of the tree.

6.8.1 Self-Restructuring Trees

A strategy proposed by Brian Allen and Ian Munro and by James Bitner consists of two possibilities:

1. Single rotation: Rotate a child about its parent if an element in a child is accessed unless it is the root (Figure 6.46a).

2. Moving to the root: Repeat the child-parent rotation until the element being accessed is in the root (Figure 6.46b).

Using the single rotation strategy, frequently accessed elements are eventually moved up close to the root so that later accesses are faster than previous ones. In the move-to-the-root strategy, it is assumed that the element being accessed has a high

FIGURE **6.47**   (a–e) Moving element *T* to the root and then (e–i) moving element *S* to the root.

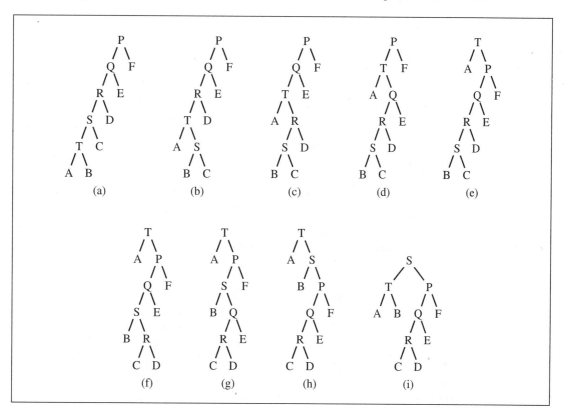

probability to be accessed again, so it percolates right away up to the root. Even if it is not used in the next access, the element remains close to the root. These strategies, however, do not work very well in unfavorable situations, when the binary tree is elongated as in Figure 6.47. In this case, the shape of the tree improves slowly. Nevertheless, it has been determined that the cost of moving a node to the root converges to the cost of accessing the node in optimal tree times 2 ln 2; that is, it converges to $(2 \ln 2)\lg n$. The result holds for any probability distribution (that is, independently of the probability that a particular request is issued). However, the average search time when all requests are equally likely is for the single rotation technique equal to $\sqrt{\pi n}$.

6.8.2 Splaying

A modification of the move-to-the-root strategy is called *splaying*, which applies single rotations in pairs in an order depending on the links between the child, parent, and grandparent (Sleator and Tarjan 1985). First, three cases are distinguished depending on the relationship between a node R being accessed and its parent Q and grandparent P (if any) nodes:

Case 1: Node R's parent is the root.

Case 2: Homogeneous configuration: Node R is the left child of its parent Q, and Q is the left child of its parent P, or R and Q are both right children.

Case 3: Heterogeneous configuration: Node R is the right child of its parent Q, and Q is the left child of its parent P, or R is the left child of Q, and Q is the right child of P.

The algorithm to move a node R being accessed to the root of the tree is as follows:

```
splaying(P,Q,R)
    while R is not the root
        if R's parent is the root
                perform a singular splay, rotate R about its parent (Figure 6.48a);
        else if R is in homogeneous configuration with its predecessors
            perform a homogeneous splay, first rotate Q about P
            and then R about Q (Figure 6.48b);
        else // if R is in heterogeneous configuration
             // with its predecessors
            perform a heterogeneous splay, first rotate R about Q
            and then about P (Figure 6.48c);
```

The difference in restructuring a tree is illustrated in Figure 6.49, where the tree from Figure 6.47a is used to access node T located at the fifth level. The shape of the tree is immediately improved. Then, node R is accessed (Figure 6.49c) and the shape of the tree becomes even better (Figure 6.49d).

Although splaying is a combination of two rotations except when next to the root, these rotations are not always used in the bottom-up fashion, as in self-adjusting trees. For the homogeneous case (left-left or right-right), first the parent and the grandparent of the node being accessed are rotated, and only afterward are the node and its parent rotated. This has the effect of moving an element to the root and flattening the tree, which has a positive impact on the accesses to be made.

The number of rotations may seem excessive, and it certainly would be if an accessed element happened to be in a leaf every time. In the case of a leaf, the access time is usually $O(\lg n)$, except for some initial accesses when the tree is not balanced. But accessing elements close to the root may make the tree unbalanced. For example, in the tree in Figure 6.49a, if the left child of the root is always accessed, then eventually, the tree would also be elongated, this time extending to the right.

To establish the efficiency of accessing a node in a binary search tree that utilizes the splaying technique, an amortized analysis will be used.

Consider a binary search tree t. Let $nodes(x)$ be the number of nodes in the subtree whose root is x, $rank(x) = \lg(nodes(x))$, so that $rank(root(t)) = \lg(n)$, and $potential(t) = \sum_{x \text{ is a node of } t} rank(x)$. It is clear that $nodes(x) + 1 \le nodes(parent(x))$;

FIGURE **6.48**   Examples of splaying.

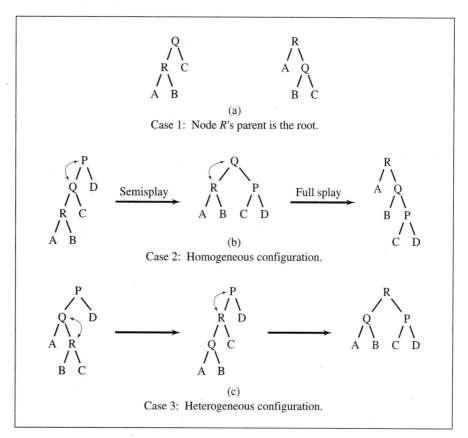

(a)
Case 1: Node *R*'s parent is the root.

Semisplay   Full splay

(b)
Case 2: Homogeneous configuration.

(c)
Case 3: Heterogeneous configuration.

FIGURE **6.49**   Restructuring a tree with splaying (a–c) after accessing *T* and (c–d) then *R*.

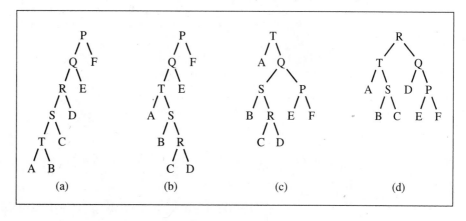

(a)   (b)   (c)   (d)

therefore, $rank(x) < rank(parent(x))$. Let the amortized cost of accessing node x be defined as the function

$$amCost(\text{x}) = cost(x) + potential_s(t) - potential_0(t)$$

where $potential_s(t)$ and $potential_0(t)$ are the potentials of the tree before access takes place and after it is finished. It is very important to see that one rotation changes ranks only of the node x being accessed, its parent, and its grandparent. This is the reason for basing the definition of the amortized cost of accessing node x on the change in the potential of the tree, which amounts to the change of ranks of the nodes involved in splaying operations that promote x to the root. We can state now a lemma specifying the amortized cost of one access.

Access lemma (Sleator and Tarjan 1985). For the amortized time to splay the tree t at a node x,

$$amCost(x) < 3(\lg(n) - rank(x)) + 1$$

The proof of this conjecture is divided into three parts, each dealing with the different case indicated in Figure 6.48. Let $par(x)$ be a parent of x and $gpar(x)$ a grandparent of x (in Figure 6.48, $x = R$, $par(x) = Q$, and $gpar(x) = P$).

Case 1: One rotation is performed. This can be only the last splaying step in the sequence of such steps which move node x to the root of the tree t, and if there are a total of s splaying steps in the sequence, then the amortized cost of the last splaying step s is

$$amCost_s(x) = cost_s(x) + potential_s(t) - potential_{s-1}(t)$$

$$= 1 + (rank_s(x) - rank_{s-1}(x)) + (rank_s(par(x)) - rank_{s-1}(par(x)))$$

where $cost_s(x) = 1$ represents the actual cost, the cost of the one splaying step (which in this step is limited to one rotation); $potential_{s-1}(t) = rank_{s-1}(x) + rank_{s-1}(par(x)) + C$ and $potential_s(t) = rank_s(x) + rank_s(par(x)) + C$, because x and $par(x)$ are the only nodes whose ranks are modified. Now because $rank_s(x) = rank_{s-1}(par(x))$

$$amCost_s(x) = 1 - rank_{s-1}(x) + rank_s(par(x))$$

and because $rank_s(par(x)) < rank_s(x)$

$$amCost_s(x) < 1 - rank_{s-1}(x) + rank_s(\text{x}).$$

Case 2: Two rotations are performed during a homogeneous splay. As before, number 1 represents the actual cost of one splaying step.

$$amCost_i(x) = 1 + (rank_i(x) - rank_{i-1}(x)) + (rank_i(par(x)) - rank_{i-1}(par(x))) + (rank_i(gpar(x)) - rank_{i-1}(gpar(x)))$$

Because $rank_i(x) = rank_{i-1}(gpar(x))$

$$amCost_i(x) = 1 - rank_{i-1}(x) + rank_i(par(x)) - rank_{i-1}(par(x)) + rank_i(gpar(x))$$

Because $rank_i(gpar(x)) < rank_i(par(x)) < rank_i(x)$

$$amCost_i(x) < 1 - rank_{i-1}(x) - rank_{i-1}(par(x)) + 2rank_i(x)$$

and because $rank_{i-1}(x) < rank_{i-1}(par(x))$, that is, $-rank_{i-1}(par(x)) < -rank_{i-1}(x)$

$$amCost_i(x) < 1 - 2rank_{i-1}(x) + 2rank_i(x).$$

To eliminate number 1, consider the inequality $rank_{i-1}(x) < rank_{i-1}(gpar(x))$; that is, $1 \le rank_{i-1}(gpar(x)) - rank_{i-1}(x)$. From this, we obtain

$$amCost_i(x) < rank_{i-1}(gpar(x)) - rank_{i-1}(x) - 2rank_{i-1}(x) + 2rank_i(x)$$

$$amCost_i(x) < rank_{i-1}(gpar(x)) - 3rank_{i-1}(x) + 2rank_i(x)$$

and because $rank_i(x) = rank_{i-1}(gpar(x))$

$$amCost_i(x) < -3rank_{i-1}(x) + 3rank_i(x)$$

Case 3: Two rotations are performed during a heterogeneous splay. The only difference in this proof is making the assumption that $rank_i(gpar(x)) < rank_i(x)$ and $rank_i(par(x)) < rank_i(x)$ instead of $rank_i(gpar(x)) < rank_i(par(x)) < rank_i(x)$, which renders the same result.

The total amortized cost of accessing a node x equals the sum of amortized costs of all the spaying steps executed during this access. If the number of steps equals s, then at most one (the last) step requires only one rotation (case 1) and thus

$$amCost(x) = \sum_{i=1}^{s} amCost_i(x) = \sum_{i=1}^{s-1} amCost_i(x) + amCost_s(x)$$

$$< \sum_{i=1}^{s-1} 3(rank_i(x) - rank_{i-1}(x)) + rank_s(x) - rank_{s-1}(x) + 1$$

Because $rank_s(x) > rank_{s-1}(x)$,

$$amCost(x) < \sum_{i=1}^{s-1} 3(rank_i(x) - rank_{i-1}(x)) + 3(rank_s(x) - rank_{s-1}(x)) + 1$$

$$= 3(rank_s(x) - rank_0(x)) + 1 = 3(\lg n - rank_0(x)) + 1 = O(\lg n)$$

This indicates that the amortized cost of an access to a node in a tree that is restructured with the splaying technique equals $O(\lg n)$, which is the same as the worst case in balanced trees. However, to make the comparison more adequate, we should compare a sequence of m accesses to nodes rather than one access because, with the amortize cost, one isolated access can still be on the order of $O(n)$. The efficiency of a tree that applies splaying is thus comparable to that of a balanced tree for a sequence of accesses and equals $O(m \lg n)$. ❏

Splaying is a strategy focusing upon the elements rather than the shape of the tree. It may perform well in situations in which some elements are used much more frequently than others. If elements near the root are accessed with about the same frequency as elements on the lowest levels, then splaying may not be the best choice. In this case, a strategy which stresses balancing the tree rather than frequency is better; a modification of the splaying method is a more viable option.

FIGURE **6.50**   (a–c) Accessing *T* and restructuring the tree with semisplaying; (c–d) accessing *T* again.

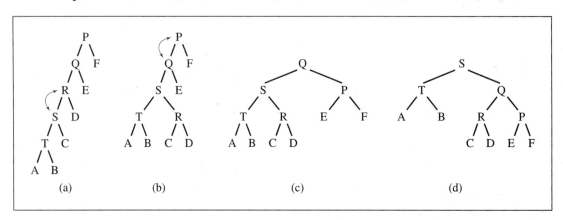

Semisplaying is a modification that requires only one rotation for a homogeneous splay and continues splaying with the parent of the accessed node, not with the node itself. It is illustrated in Figure 6.48b. After *R* is accessed, its parent *Q* is rotated about *P* and splaying continues with *Q*, not with *R*. Rotation of *R* about *Q* is not performed, as would be the case for splaying.

Figure 6.50 illustrates the advantages of semisplaying. The elongated tree from Figure 6.49a becomes more balanced with semisplaying after accessing *T* (Figures 6.50a–c), and after *T* is accessed again, the tree in Figure 6.50d has basically the same number of levels as the tree in Figure 6.50c. (It may have one more level if *E* or *F* was a subtree higher than any of subtrees *A*, *B*, *C*, or *D*.) For implementation of this tree strategy, see the case study at the end of this chapter.

🔲 6.9 HEAPS

A particular kind of binary tree, called a *heap*, has the following two properties:

1. The value of each node is not less than the values stored in each of its children.

2. The tree is perfectly balanced, and the leaves in the last level are all in the leftmost positions.

To be exact, these two properties define a *max heap*. If "less" in the first property is replaced with "greater," then the definition specifies a *min heap*. This means that the root of a max heap contains the largest element, whereas the root of a min heap contains the smallest. A tree has the *heap property* if each nonleaf has the first property. Due to the second condition, the number of levels in the tree is $O(\lg n)$.

The trees in Figure 6.51a are all heaps; the trees in Figure 6.51b violate the first property, and the trees in Figure 6.51c violate the second.

FIGURE **6.51**   Examples of (a) heaps and (b–c) nonheaps.

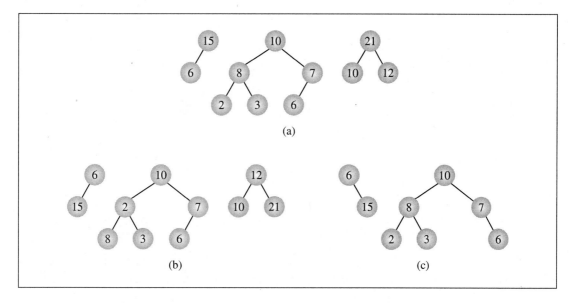

FIGURE **6.52**   The array [2 8 6 1 10 15 3 12 11] seen as a tree.

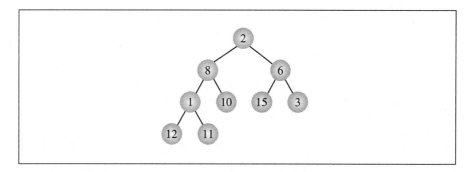

Interestingly, heaps can be implemented by arrays. For example, the array `data` = [2 8 6 1 10 15 3 12 11] can represent the nonheap tree in Figure 6.52. The elements are placed at sequential locations representing the nodes from top to bottom and in each level from left to right. The second property reflects the fact that the array is packed, with no gaps. Now, a heap can be defined as an array `heap` of length n in which

$$\texttt{heap[i]} \geq \texttt{heap[2 · i + 1]}, \text{for } 0 \leq i < \frac{n-1}{2}$$

FIGURE **6.53**   Different heaps constructed with the same elements.

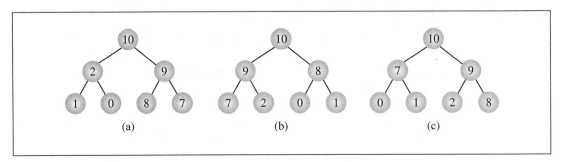

(a)   (b)   (c)

and

$$\text{heap[i]} \geq \text{heap[2} \cdot \text{i + 2]}, \text{for } 0 \leq i < \frac{n-2}{2}$$

Elements in a heap are not perfectly ordered. We know only that the largest element is in the root node and that, for each node, all its descendants are less than or equal to that node. But the relation between sibling nodes or, to continue the kinship terminology, between uncle and nephew nodes is not determined. The order of the elements obeys a linear line of descent, disregarding lateral lines. For this reason, all the trees in Figure 6.53 are legitimate heaps, although the heap in Figure 6.53b is ordered best.

6.9.1 Heaps as Priority Queues

A heap is an excellent way to implement a priority queue. Section 4.e used linked lists to implement priority queues, structures for which the complexity was expressed in terms of $O(n)$ or $O(\sqrt{n})$. For large n, this may be too ineffective. On the other hand, a heap is a perfectly balanced tree; hence, reaching a leaf requires $O(\lg n)$ searches. This efficiency is very promising. Therefore, heaps can be used to implement priority queues. To this end, however, two procedures have to be implemented to enqueue and dequeue elements on a priority queue.

To enqueue an element, the element is added at the end of the heap as the last leaf. Restoring the heap property in the case of enqueuing is achieved by moving from the last leaf toward the root.

The algorithm for enqueuing is as follows:

```
heapEnqueue(el)
    put el at the end of heap;
    while el is not in the root and el > parent(el)
        swap el with its parent;
```

For example, the number 15 is added to the heap in Figure 6.54a as the next leaf (Figure 6.54b), which destroys the heap property of the tree. To restore this property, 15 has to be moved up the tree until either it ends up in the root or finds a parent that

FIGURE **6.54**   Enqueuing an element to a heap.

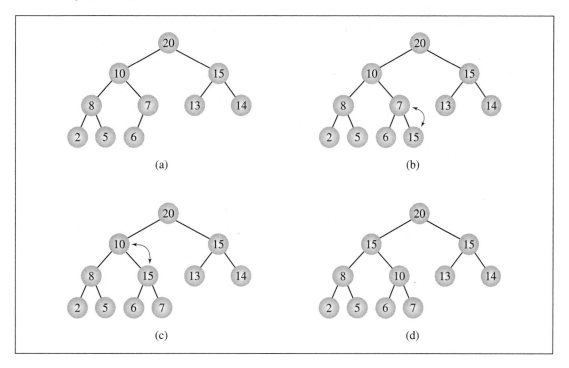

(a)   (b)

(c)   (d)

is not less than 15. In this example, the latter case occurs, and 15 has to be moved only twice without reaching the root.

Dequeuing an element from the heap consists of removing the root element from the heap, since by the heap property it is the element with the greatest priority. Then the last leaf is put in its place, and the heap property almost certainly has to be restored, this time by moving from the root down the tree.

The algorithm for dequeuing is as follows:

```
heapDequeue()
    extract the element from the root;
    put the element from the last leaf in its place;
    remove the last leaf;
    // both subtrees of the root are heaps;
    p = the root;
    while p is not a leaf and p < any of its children
        swap p with the larger child;
```

For example, 20 is dequeued from the heap in Figure 6.55a and 6 is put in its place (Figure 6.55b). To restore the heap property, 6 is swapped first with its larger child, number 15 (Figure 6.55c), and once again with the larger child, 14 (Figure 6.55d).

FIGURE **6.55**   Dequeuing an element from a heap.

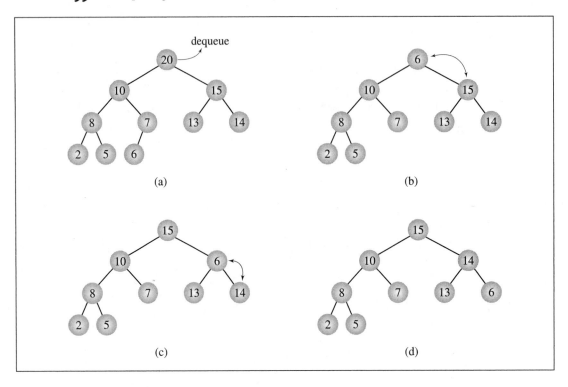

FIGURE **6.56**   Implementation of algorithm to move the root element down a tree.

```
void moveDown(Object[] data, int first, int last) {
    int largest = 2*first + 1;
    while (largest <= last) {
        if (largest < last && // first has two children (at 2*first+1 and
                              //    2*first+2)
            ((Comparable)data[largest]).compareTo(data[largest+1]) < 0)
                largest++;
        if (((Comparable)data[first]).compareTo(data[largest]) < 0) {
            swap(data,first,largest);        // if necessary, swap values
            first = largest;                 // and move down;
            largest = 2*first + 1;
        }
        else largest = last + 1;// to exit the loop: the heap property
                              // isn't violated by data[first]
    }
}
```

The last three lines of the dequeuing algorithm can be treated as a separate algorithm that restores the heap property only if it has been violated by the root of the tree. In this case, the root element is moved down the tree until it finds a proper position. This algorithm, which is the key to the heap sort, is presented in one possible implementation in Figure 6.56.

6.9.2 Organizing Arrays as Heaps

Heaps can be implemented as arrays, and in that sense, each heap is an array, but all arrays are not heaps. In some situations, however, most notably in heap sort (cf. Section 9.3.2), we need to convert an array into a heap (that is, reorganize the data in the array so that the resulting organization represents a heap). There are several ways to do this, but in light of the preceding section the simplest way is to start with an empty heap and sequentially include elements into a growing heap. This is a top-down method and it was proposed by John Williams; it extends the heap by enqueuing new elements in the heap.

Figure 6.57 contains a complete example of the top-down method. First, the number 2 is enqueued in the initially empty heap (6.57a). Next, 8 is enqueued by putting it at the end of the current heap (6.57b) and then swapping with its parent (6.57c). Enqueuing the third and fourth elements, 6 (6.57d) and then 1 (6.57e), necessitates no swaps. Enqueuing the fifth element, 10, amounts to putting it at the end of the heap (6.57f), then swapping it with its parent, 2 (6.57g), and then with its new parent, 8 (6.57h) so that eventually 10 percolates up to the root of the heap. All remaining steps can be traced in Figure 6.57.

To check the complexity of the algorithm, observe that in the worst case, when a newly added element has to be moved up to the root of the tree, $\lfloor \lg k \rfloor$ exchanges are made in a heap of k nodes. Therefore, if n elements are enqueued, then in the worst case

$$\sum_{k=1}^{n} \lfloor \lg k \rfloor \leq \sum_{k=1}^{n} \lg k = \lg 1 + \cdots + \lg n = \lg(1 \cdot 2 \cdot \cdots \cdot n) = \lg(n!) = O(n \lg n)$$

exchanges are made during execution of the algorithm and the same number of comparisons. (For the fact that $\lg(n!)$ is $O(n \lg n)$, see Section A.2 in Appendix A.) It turns out, however, that we can do better than that.

In another algorithm, developed by Robert Floyd, a heap is built bottom-up. In this approach, small heaps are formed and repetitively merged into larger heaps in the following way:

```
FloydAlgorithm(data[])
    for (i = index of the last nonleaf; i >= 0; i--)
        restore the heap property for the tree whose root is data[i] by calling
        moveDown(data,i,n-1);
```

Figure 6.58 contains an example of transforming the array data[ ] = [2 8 6 1 10 15 3 12 11] into a heap.

We start from the last nonleaf node, which is data[n/2-1], n being the array size. If data[n/2-1] is less than one of its children, it is swapped with the larger child. In the tree in Figure 6.58a, this is the case for data[3] = 1 and data[7] = 12.

FIGURE **6.57**   Organizing an array as a heap with a top-down method.

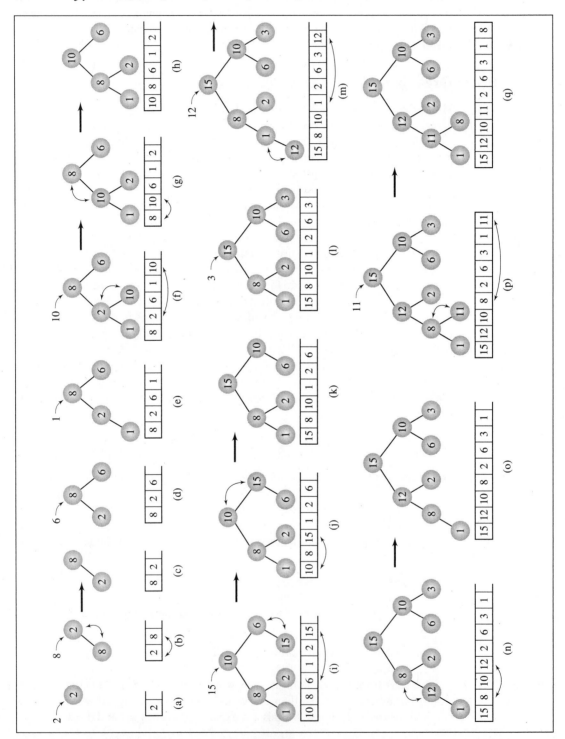

FIGURE **6.58**   Transforming the array [2 8 6 1 10 15 3 12 11] into a heap with a bottom-up method.

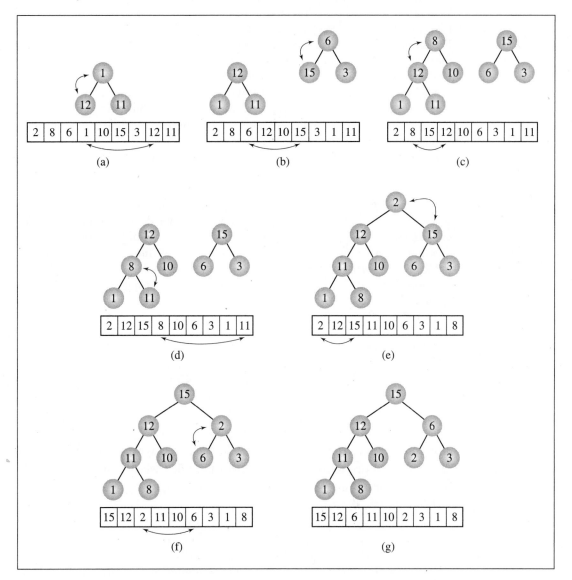

After exchanging the elements, a new tree is created, shown in Figure 6.58b. Next the element `data[n/2-2]` = `data[2]` = 6 is considered. Because it is smaller than its child `data[5]` = 15, it is swapped with that child and the tree is transformed to that in Figure 6.58c. Now `data[n/2-3]` = `data[1]` = 8 is considered. Since it is smaller than one of its children, which is `data[3]` = 12, an interchange occurs, leading to the tree in Figure 6.58d. But now it can be noticed that the order established in the subtree whose root was 12 (Figure 6.58c) has been somewhat disturbed since 8 is smaller than its new child 11. This simply means that it does not suffice to compare a node's value with its children's, but a similar comparison needs to be done with grandchildren's, great-grandchildren's, etc. until the node finds its proper position. Taking this into consideration, the next swap is made, after which the tree in Figure 6.58e is created. Only now is the element `data[n/2-4]` = `data[0]` = 2 compared with its children, which leads to two swaps (Figures 6.58f).

Assume that the heap being created is a complete binary tree, that is, it includes n = $2^k - 1$ nodes for some k. To create the heap, `moveDown()` is called $\frac{n+1}{2}$ times, once for each nonleaf. In the worst case, `moveDown()` moves data from the next to last level, consisting of $\frac{n+1}{4}$ nodes, down by one level to the level of leaves by performing $\frac{n+1}{4}$ swaps. Therefore, all nodes from this level make $1 \cdot \frac{n+1}{4}$ moves. Data from the second to last level, which has $\frac{n+1}{8}$ nodes, are moved two levels down to reach the level of the leaves. Thus, nodes from this level perform $2 \cdot \frac{n+1}{8}$ moves and so on up to the root. The root of the tree as the tree becomes a heap is moved, again in the worst case, $\lg(n+1) - 1 = \lg\frac{n+1}{2}$ levels down the tree to end up in one of the leaves. Since there is only one root, this contributes $\lg\frac{n+1}{2} \cdot 1$ moves. The total number of movements can be given by this sum

$$\sum_{i=2}^{\lg(n+1)} \frac{n+1}{2^i}(i-1) = (n+1)\sum_{i=2}^{\lg(n+1)} \frac{i-1}{2^i}$$

which is $O(n)$ since the series $\sum_{i=2}^{\infty}\frac{i}{2^i}$ converges to 1.5 and $\sum_{i=2}^{\infty}\frac{i}{2^i}$ converges to 0.5. For an array that is not a complete binary tree, the complexity is all the more bounded by $O(n)$. The worst case for comparisons is twice this value, which is also $O(n)$, because for each node in `moveDown()`, both children of the node are compared to each other to choose the larger. That, in turn, is compared to the node. Therefore, for the worst case, Williams's method performs better than Floyd's.

The performance for the average case is much more difficult to establish. It has been found that Floyd's heap construction algorithm requires on average $1.88n$ comparisons (Knuth 1998; Doberkat 1984), and the number of comparisons required by Williams's algorithm in this case is between $1.75n$ and $2.76n$ and the number of swaps is $1.3n$ (Hayward and McDiarmid 1991; McDiarmid and Reed 1989). Thus, in the average case, the two algorithms perform at the same level.

◪ 6.10 POLISH NOTATION AND EXPRESSION TREES

One of the applications of binary trees is an unambiguous representation of arithmetical, relational, or logical expressions. In the early 1920s, a Polish logician, Jan Łukasiewicz (pronounced: wook-a-sie-vich), invented a special notation for propositional logic that allows us to eliminate all parentheses from formulas. However, Łukasiewicz's notation, called *Polish notation,* results in less readable formulas than the parenthesized originals and it was not widely used. However, it proved useful after the emergence of computers, especially for writing compilers and interpreters.

To maintain readability and prevent the ambiguity of formulas, extra symbols such as parentheses have to be used. However, if avoiding ambiguity is the only goal, then these symbols can be omitted at the cost of changing the order of symbols used in the formulas. This is exactly what the compiler does. It rejects everything that is not essential to retrieve the proper meaning of formulas, rejecting it as "syntactic sugar."

How does this notation work? Look first at the following example. What is the value of this algebraic expression?

$$2 - 3 \cdot 4 + 5$$

The result depends on the order in which the operations are performed. If we multiply first and then subtract and add, the result is –5 as expected. If subtraction is done first, then addition and multiplication, as in

$$(2 - 3) \cdot (4 + 5)$$

the result is –9. But if we subtract after we multiply and add, as in

$$2 - (3 \cdot 4 + 5)$$

then the result of evaluation is –15. If we see the first expression, then we know in what order to evaluate it. But the computer does not know that, in such a case, multiplication has precedence over addition and subtraction. If we want to override the precedence, then parentheses are needed.

Compilers need to generate assembly code in which one operation is executed at a time and the result is retained for other operations. Therefore, all expressions have to be broken down unambiguously into separate operations and put into their proper order. That is where Polish notation is useful. It allows us to create an *expression tree,* which imposes an order on the execution of operations. For example, the first expression, $2 - 3 \cdot 4 + 5$, which is the same as $2 - (3 \cdot 4) + 5$, is represented by the tree in Figure 6.59a. The second and the third expressions correspond to the trees in Figures 6.59b and 6.59c. It is obvious now that in both Figures 6.59a and 6.59c we have to first multiply 3 by 4 to obtain 12. But 12 is subtracted from 2, according to the tree in Figure 6.59a, and added to 5, according to Figure 6.59c. There is no ambiguity involved in this tree representation. The final result can be computed only if intermediate results are calculated first.

Notice also that trees do not use parentheses and yet no ambiguity arises. We can maintain this parentheses-free situation if the expression tree is linearized (that is, if

FIGURE **6.59**   Examples of three expression trees and results of their traversals.

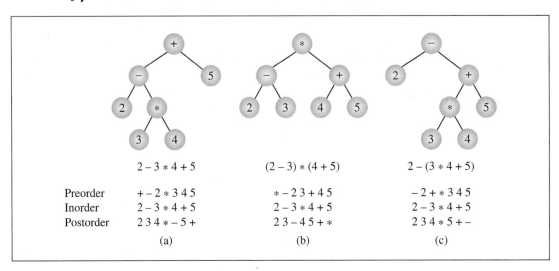

	(a)	(b)	(c)
	$2 - 3 * 4 + 5$	$(2 - 3) * (4 + 5)$	$2 - (3 * 4 + 5)$
Preorder	$+ - 2 * 3\,4\,5$	$* - 2\,3 + 4\,5$	$- 2 + * 3\,4\,5$
Inorder	$2 - 3 * 4 + 5$	$2 - 3 * 4 + 5$	$2 - 3 * 4 + 5$
Postorder	$2\,3\,4 * - 5 +$	$2\,3 - 4\,5 + *$	$2\,3\,4 * 5 + -$

the tree is transformed into an expression using a tree traversal method). The three traversal methods relevant in this context are preorder, inorder, and postorder tree traversals. Using these traversals, nine outputs are generated, as shown in Figure 6.59. Interestingly, inorder traversal of all three trees results in the same output, which is the initial expression that caused all the trouble. What it means is that inorder tree traversal is not suitable for generating unambiguous output. But the other two traversals are. They are different for different trees and are therefore useful for the purpose of creating unambiguous expressions and sentences.

Because of the importance of these different conventions, special terminology is used. Preorder traversal generates *prefix notation,* inorder traversal generates *infix notation,* and postorder traversal generates *postfix notation.* Note that we are accustomed to infix notation. In infix notation, an operator is surrounded by its two operands. In prefix notation, the operator precedes the operands, and in postfix notation the operator follows the operands. Some hand calculators operate on expressions in postfix notation. Also, some programming languages are using Polish notation. For example, Forth uses postfix notation. LISP and, to a large degree, LOGO use prefix notation.

6.10.1 Operations on Expression Trees

Binary trees can be created in two different ways: top-down or bottom-up. In the implementation of insertion, the first approach was used. This section applies the second approach by creating expression trees bottom-up while scanning infix expressions from left to right.

The most important part of this construction process is retaining the same precedence of operations as in the expression being scanned, as exemplified in Figure 6.59.

If parentheses are not allowed, the task is simple, as parentheses allow for many levels of nesting. Therefore, an algorithm should be powerful enough to process any number of nesting levels in an expression. A natural approach is a recursive implementation. We modify the recursive descent interpreter discussed in Chapter 5's case study and outline a recursive descent expression tree constructor.

As Figure 6.59 indicates, a node contains either an operator or an operand, the latter being either an identifier or a number. To simplify the task, all of them can be represented as strings in an instance of the class defined as

```
class ExprTreeNode {
    String key;
    ExprTreeNode left, right;
    ExprTreeNode(String k) {
        this(k,null,null);
    }
    ExprTreeNode(String k, ExprTreeNode pt1, ExprTreeNode pt2) {
        key = new String(k); left = pt1; right = pt2;
    }
    . . . . . . . . . . . . .
}
```

Expressions that are converted to trees use the same syntax as expressions in the case study in Chapter 5. Therefore, the same syntax diagrams can be used. Using these diagrams, a class `ExprTree` can be created in which member functions for processing a factor and term have the following pseudocode (a function for processing an expression has the same structure as the function processing a term):

```
class ExprTree {
    protected ExprTreeNode root;
    ExprTreeNode factor() {
        if (token is a number, id or operator)
            return new ExprTreeNode(token);
        else if (token is '(') {
            ExprTreeNode p = expr();
            if (token is ')')
                return p;
            else error;
        }
    }
    ExprTreeNode term() {
        String oper;
        ExprTreeNode p1, p2;
        p1 = factor();
        while (token is '*' or '/') {
            oper = token;
            p2 = factor();
            p1 = new ExprTreeNode(oper,p1,p2);
        }
```

```
                            return p1;
                        }
                        · · · · ·
                }
```

The tree structure of expressions is very suitable for generating assembly code or intermediate code in compilers, as shown in this pseudocode of a function from `ExprTree` class:

```
void generateCode() {
    generateCode(root);
}
String generateCode(ExprTreeNode p) {
    if (p.key is a number or id)
        return p.key;
    else if (p.key.charAt(0) == '+') {
        String result = newTemporaryVar();
        output "+\t" + generateCode(p.left) +
            "\t" + generateCode(p.right) + "\t" + result;
        return result;
    }
    · · · · · · · ·
}
```

With these methods, an expression

$$(var2 + n) * (var2 + var1)/5$$

is transformed into an expression tree shown in Figure 6.60, and from this tree, `generateCode()` generates the following intermediate code:

add	var2	n	_tmp_3
add	var2	var1	_tmp_4
mul	_tmp_3	_tmp_4	_tmp_2
div	_tmp_2	5	_tmp_1

Expression trees are also very convenient for performing other symbolic operations, such as differentiation. Rules for differentiation (given in the programming assignments in Chapter 5) are shown in the form of tree transformations in Figure 6.61 and in the following pseudocode:

```
differentiate(p,x) {
    if (p == 0)
        return 0;
    if (p.key is the id x)
        return new ExprTreeNode("1");
    if (p.key is another id or a number)
        return new ExprTreeNode("0");
    if (p.key is '+' or '-') {
        return new ExprTreeNode(p.key,differentiate(p.left,x),
                            differentiate(p.right,x));
```

Figure **6.60**   An expression tree.

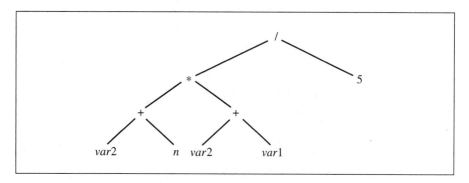

Figure **6.61**   Tree transformations for differentiation of multiplication and division.

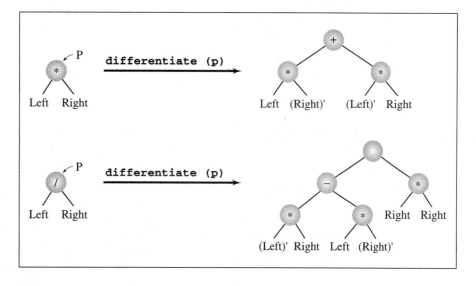

```
if (p.key is '*')
    ExprTreeNode *q = new ExprTreeNode("+");
    q.left = new ExprTreeNode("*",p.left,new ExprTreeNode(*p.right));
    q.left.right = differentiate(q.left.right,x);
    q.right = new ExprTreeNode("*",new ExprTreeNode(*p.left),p.right);
    q.right.left = differentiate(q.right.left,x);
    return q;
  . . . . . . . . .
}
```

Here p is a pointer to the expression to be differentiated with respect to x.
The rule for division is left as an exercise.

FIGURE **6.62** Semisplay tree used for computing word frequencies.

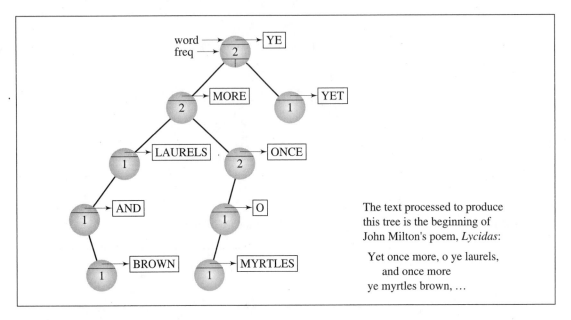

The text processed to produce this tree is the beginning of John Milton's poem, *Lycidas*:

Yet once more, o ye laurels,
and once more
ye myrtles brown, …

⬚ 6.11 CASE STUDY: COMPUTING WORD FREQUENCIES

One tool in establishing authorship of text in cases when the text is not signed, or it is attributed to someone else, is using word frequencies. If it is known that an author A wrote text T_1 and the distribution of word frequencies in a text T_2 under scrutiny is very close to the frequencies in T_1, then it is likely that T_2 was written by author A.

Regardless of how reliable this method is for literary studies, our interest lies in writing a program that scans a text file and computes the frequency of the occurrence of words in this file. For the sake of simplification, punctuation marks are disregarded and case sensitivity is disabled. Therefore, the word *man's* is counted as two words, *man* and *s,* although in fact it may be one word (for possessive) and not two words (contraction for *man is* or *man has*). But contractions are counted separately; for example, *s* from *man's* is considered a separate word. Similarly, separators in the middle of words such as hyphens cause portions of the same words to be considered separate words. For example, *pre-existence* is split into *pre* and *existence*. Also, by disabling case sensitivity, *Good* in the phrase *Mr. Good* is considered as another occurrence of the word *good*. On the other hand, *Good* used in its normal sense at the beginning of a sentence is properly included as another occurrence of *good*.

This program focuses not so much on linguistics as on building a self-adjusting binary search tree using the semisplaying technique. If a word is encountered in the file for the first time, it is inserted in the tree. Otherwise, the semisplaying is started from the node corresponding to this word.

FIGURE **6.63**　　　Implementation of word frequency computation.

```
/*************************** SplayingNode.java ************************
 *                   node for generic splaying tree class
 */

public class SplayingNode {
    protected BaseObject el;
    protected SplayingNode left, right, parent;
    public SplayingNode() {
        left = right = parent = null;
    }
    public SplayingNode(BaseObject el) {
        this(el,null,null,null);
    }
    public SplayingNode(BaseObject ob, SplayingNode lt, SplayingNode rt,
SplayingNode pr) {
        el = ob; left = lt; right = rt; parent = pr;
    }
}

/************************** SplayTree.java ***********************
 *                   generic splaying tree class
 */

public class SplayTree {
    private SplayingNode root = null;
    public SplayTree() {
        super();
    }
    private void continueRotation(SplayingNode gr, SplayingNode par,
                              SplayingNode ch, SplayingNode desc) {
        if (gr != null) { // if p has a grandparent;
            if (gr.right == ch.parent)
                gr.right = ch;
            else gr.left  = ch;
        }
        else root = ch;
        if (desc != null)
            desc.parent = par;
        par.parent = ch;
        ch.parent = gr;
    }
```

FIGURE **6.63** (*continued*)

```
private void rotateR(SplayingNode p) {
    p.parent.left = p.right;
    p.right = p.parent;
    continueRotation(p.parent.parent,p.right,p,p.right.left);
}
private void rotateL(SplayingNode p) {
    p.parent.right = p.left;
    p.left = p.parent;
    continueRotation(p.parent.parent,p.left,p,p.left.right);
}
private void semisplay(SplayingNode p) {
    while (p != root) {
        if (p.parent.parent == null)     // if p's parent is the root;
            if (p.parent.left == p)
                rotateR(p);
            else rotateL(p);
        else if (p.parent.left == p)    // if p is a left child;
            if (p.parent.parent.left == p.parent) {
                rotateR(p.parent);
                p = p.parent;
            }
            else {
                rotateR(p); // rotate p and its parent;
                rotateL(p); // rotate p and its new parent;
            }
        else                            // if p is a right child;
            if (p.parent.parent.right == p.parent) {
                rotateL(p.parent);
                p = p.parent;
            }
            else {
                rotateL(p); // rotate p and its parent;
                rotateR(p); // rotate p and its new parent;
            }
            if (root == null)        // update the root;
                root = p;
    }
}
public Object search(BaseObject el) {
    SplayingNode p = root;
    while (p != null) {
        if (p.el.equals(el)) {        // if el is in the tree,
```

FIGURE **6.63** (*continued*)

```
                    semisplay(p);           // move it upward;
                    return p.el;
            }
            else if (el.isLessThan(p.el))
                    p = p.left;
            else p = p.right;
        }
        return null;
    }
    public void insert(BaseObject el) {
        SplayingNode p = root, prev = null, newNode;
        while (p != null) {  // find a place for inserting a new node;
             prev = p;
             if (el.isLessThan(p.el))
                    p = p.left;
             else p = p.right;
        }
        if ((newNode = new SplayingNode(el,null,null,prev)) == null) {
             System.err.println("No room for new nodes");
             Runtime.getRuntime().exit(0);
        }
        if (root == null)            // if tree is empty
             root = newNode;
        else if (el.isLessThan(prev.el))
             prev.left  = newNode;
        else prev.right = newNode;
    }
    protected void inorder() {
        inorder(root);
    }
    protected void inorder(SplayingNode p) {
        if (p != null) {
             inorder(p.left);
             visit(p);
             inorder(p.right);
        }
    }
    protected void visit(SplayingNode p) {
    }
}
```

Continues

F I G U R E **6.63**   (*continued*)

```
/********************  WordSplaying.java  ********************/

import java.io.*;

class Word extends BaseObject {
    String word;
    int freq = 1;
    Word() {
    }
    Word(String s) {
        word = s;
    }
    public boolean equals(Object ir) {
        return word.equals(((Word)ir).word);
    }
    public boolean isLessThan(BaseObject ir) {
        return word.compareTo(((Word)ir).word) < 0;
    }
    public String toString() {
        return word + ": " + freq + " ";
    }
}

class WordSplay extends SplayTree {
    WordSplay() {
        differentWords = wordCnt = 0;
    }
    private int differentWords, // counter of different words in text file;
                wordCnt;        // counter of all words in the same file;
    protected void visit(SplayingNode p) {
        differentWords++;
        wordCnt += ((Word)p.el).freq;
    }
    void run(InputStream fIn, String fileName) {
        int ch = 1;
        String s;
        Word p;
        try {
            while (ch > -1) {
                while (true)
                    if (ch > -1 && !Character.isLetter((char)ch)) // skip
                        ch = fIn.read();                          // nonletters;
                    else break;
```

FIGURE **6.63**   (*continued*)

```
                    if (ch == -1)
                        break;
                    s = "";
                    while (ch > -1 && Character.isLetter((char)ch)) {
                        s += Character.toUpperCase((char)ch);
                        ch = fIn.read();
                    }
                    if ((p = (Word)search(new Word(s))) == null)
                        insert(new Word(s));
                    else ((Word)p).freq++;
                }
        } catch (IOException io) {
        }
        inorder();
        System.out.println("\n\nFile " + fileName
                + " contains " + wordCnt + " words among which "
                + differentWords + " are different\n");
    }
}

class WordSplaying {
    static public void main(String args[]) {
        String fileName = "";
        InputStream fIn;
        InputStreamReader isr = new InputStreamReader(System.in);
        BufferedReader buffer = new BufferedReader(isr);
        try {
            if (args.length == 0) {
                System.out.print("Enter a file name: ");
                fileName = buffer.readLine();
                fIn = new FileInputStream(fileName);
            }
            else {
                fIn = new FileInputStream(args[0]);
                fileName = args[0];
            }
            (new WordSplay()).run(fIn,fileName);
            fIn.close();
        } catch(IOException io) {
            System.err.println("Cannot open " + fileName);
        }
    }
}
```

Another concern is storing all predecessors when scanning the tree. It is achieved by using a pointer to the parent. In this way, from each node we can access any predecessor of this node up to the root of the tree.

Figure 6.62 shows the structure of the tree using the content of a short file, and Figure 6.63 contains the complete code. The program reads a word, which is any sequence of alphanumeric characters that starts with a letter (spaces, punctuation marks, etc. are discarded) and checks whether the word is in the tree. If so, the semi-splaying technique is used to reorganize the tree and then the word's frequency count is incremented. Note that this movement toward the root is accomplished by changing links of the nodes involved, not by physically transferring information from one node to its parent and then to its grandparent and so on. If a word is not found in the tree, it is inserted in the tree by creating a new leaf for it. After all words are processed, an inorder tree traversal goes through the tree to count all the nodes and add all frequency counts to print as the final result the number of words in the tree and the number of words in the file.

This program also illustrates the use of a generic binary search tree. Because scanning this tree requires using comparison, the approach used in Chapter 3's case study cannot be followed. The meaning of comparison varies from one data type to another; therefore, when defining a tree, the comparison has to be used in a generic way, and only when creating a specific tree is the generic comparison overridden by a definition pertaining to the data type for which the tree was created. This is accomplished by first defining class `BaseObject` with two generic methods, `isLessThan()` and `visit()`. This class represents a generic information field in a tree node. Therefore, a generic tree node `BSTNode` is defined in terms of `BaseObject`, and only then is a generic binary search tree class `BST` is defined using `BSTNode`. Now the methods in BST class are defined with generic `isLessThan()` and `visit()`. Next, a generic `SplayTree` class is defined as an extension of `BST`, and then, a specific splaying tree, `WordTree`, is defined in terms of a specific information type `InfoNode`. The `InfoNode` class includes definitions of methods that override generic definitions either in `Object` (`equals()` and `toString()`) or in `BaseObject` (`isLessThan()` and `visit()`).

◻ 6.12 Exercises

1. The method `search()` given in Section 6.3 is well suited for searching binary *search* trees. Try to adopt all four traversal algorithms so that they become search procedures for any binary tree.

2. Write methods to count the number of nodes in a binary tree, the number of leaves, the number of right children, and the height of the tree.

3. Write a method that checks whether or not a binary tree is perfectly balanced.

4. Design an algorithm to test whether a binary tree is a binary search tree.

6. Write a method to delete all leaves from a binary tree.

FIGURE **6.64**   An example of a binary search tree.

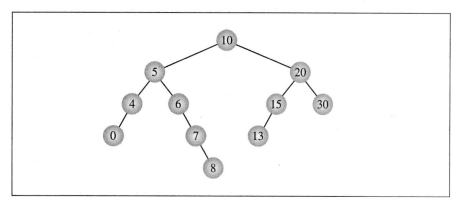

7. Apply `preorder()`, `inorder()`, and `postorder()` to the tree in Figure 6.64 if `p.visit` in `IntBSTNode` is defined as:

a. ```
if (left != null && key - left.key < 2)
    left.key += 2;
```

b. ```
if (left == null)
    right = null;
```

c. ```
if (left == null)
    left = new IntBSTNode(key-1);
```

d. ```
{   IntBSTNode tmp = right;
    right = left;
    left = tmp;
}
```

7. Show a tree for which the preorder and inorder traversals generate the same sequence.

8. Figure 6.59 indicates that the inorder traversal for different trees can result in the same sequence. Is this possible for the preorder or postorder traversals? If it is, show an example.

9. Draw all possible binary search trees for the three elements *A, B,* and *C.*

10. What are the minimum and maximum numbers of leaves in a balanced tree of height *h?*

11. Write a method to create a mirror image of a binary tree.

12. Consider an operation *R* that for a given traversal method *t* processes nodes in the opposite order than *t* and an operation *C* that processes nodes of the mirror image of

a given tree using traversal method t. For the tree traversal methods—preorder, inorder, and postorder—determine which of the following nine equalities are true:

$$
\begin{aligned}
R(\text{preorder}) &= C(\text{preorder}) \\
R(\text{preorder}) &= C(\text{inorder}) \\
R(\text{preorder}) &= C(\text{postorder}) \\
R(\text{inorder}) &= C(\text{preorder}) \\
R(\text{inorder}) &= C(\text{inorder}) \\
R(\text{inorder}) &= C(\text{postorder}) \\
R(\text{postorder}) &= C(\text{preorder}) \\
R(\text{postorder}) &= C(\text{inorder}) \\
R(\text{postorder}) &= C(\text{postorder})
\end{aligned}
$$

13. Using inorder, preorder, and postorder tree traversal, visit only leaves of a tree. What can you observe? How can you explain this phenomenon?

14. (a) Write a method which prints sideways each binary tree with proper indentation, as in Figure 6.65a. (b) Adopt this method to print a threaded tree sideways; if appropriate, print the key in the successor node, as in Figure 6.65b.

15. Outline methods for inserting and deleting a node in a threaded tree in which threads are put only in the leaves in the way illustrated by Figure 6.66.

16. The tree in Figure 6.66b includes threads lining predecessors and successors according to the postorder traversal. Are these threads adequate to perform threaded preorder, inorder, and postorder traversals?

17. Apply the method `balance()` to the English alphabet to create a balanced tree.

18. A sentence Dpq that uses a Sheffer's alternative is false only if both p and q are true. In 1925, J. Łukasiewicz simplified Nicod's axiom from which all theses of propositional logic can be derived. Transform the Nicod-Łukasiewicz axiom into an infix parenthesized sentence and build a binary tree for it. The axiom is $DDpDqrDDsDssDDsqD$-$DpsDps$.

19. Write an algorithm for printing a parenthesized infix expression from an expression tree. Do not include redundant parentheses.

20. Hibbard's (1962) algorithm to delete a key from a binary search tree requires that if the node containing the key has a right child, then the key is replaced by the smallest key in the right subtree; otherwise, the node with the key is removed. In what respect is Knuth's algorithm (`deleteByCopying()`) an improvement?

21. Which tree of four nodes is the worst case for generating a backbone in the DSW algorithm? Execute this procedure in this tree by hand.

22. Define a binary search tree in terms of the inorder traversal.

23. A *Fibonacci tree* can be considered the worst case AVL tree in that it has the smallest number of nodes among AVL trees of height h. Draw Fibonacci trees for $h = 1,2,3,4$ and justify the name of the tree.

FIGURE **6.65**   Printing a binary search tree (a) and a threaded tree (b) sideways.

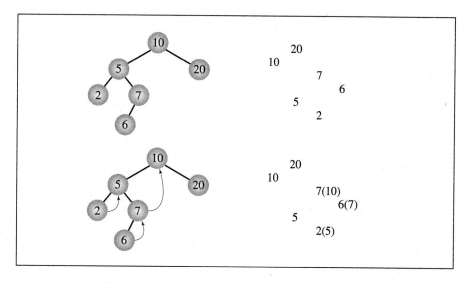

FIGURE **6.66**   Examples of threaded trees.

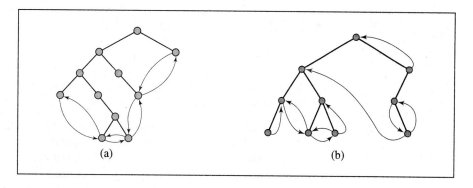

(a)   (b)

24.   *One-sided height-balanced trees* are AVL trees in which only two balance factors are allowed: −1 and 0 or 0 and +1 (Zweben and McDonald 1978). What is the rationale for introducing this type of tree?

25.   In *lazy deletion*, nodes to be deleted are retained in the tree and only marked as deleted. What are the advantages and disadvantages of this approach?

26.   What is the number of comparisons and swaps in the best case for creating a heap using (a) Williams's method and (b) Floyd's method?

27. A crossover between Floyd's and Williams's methods for constructing a heap is a method in which an empty position occupied by an element is moved down to the bottom of the tree and then the element is moved up, as in Williams's method, the tree from the position that was just moved down. A pseudocode of this function is as follows:

```
i = (n-1)/2; // position of the last parent in the array of n elements;

while (i >= 0)
    // Floyd's phase:
    tmp = array[i];
    consider element array[i] empty and move it down to the bottom
        swapping it every time with larger child;
    put tmp in the leaf at which this process ended;
    // Williams's phase:
    while tmp is not the root and it is larger than its parent
        swap tmp with its parent;
    i--; // go to the preceding parent;
```

It has been shown that this algorithm requires $1.65n$ comparisons in the average case (McDiarmid and Reed 1989). Show changes in the array [2 8 6 1 10 15 3 12 11] during execution of the algorithm. What is the worst case?

◻ 6.13 Programming Assignments

1. Write a program that accepts an arithmetic expression written in prefix (Polish) notation, builds an expression tree, and then traverses the tree to evaluate the expression. The evaluation should start after a complete expression has been entered.

2. A binary tree can be used to sort n elements of an array data. First, create a complete binary tree, a tree with all leaves at one level, whose height $h = \lceil \lg n \rceil + 1$, and store all elements of the array in the first n leaves. In each empty leaf, store an element E greater than any element in the array. Figure 6.67a shows an example for data = {8, 20, 41, 7, 2}, $h = \lceil \lg(5) \rceil + 1 = 4$, and $E = 42$. Then, starting from the bottom of the tree, assign to each node the minimum of its two children values, as in Figure 6.67b, so that the smallest element e_{min} in the tree is assigned to the root. Next, until the element E is assigned to the root, execute a loop that in each iteration stores E in the leaf, with the value of e_{min}, and that, also starting from the bottom, assigns to each node the minimum of its two children. Figure 6.67c displays this tree after one iteration of the loop.

3. Implement a menu-driven program for managing a software store. All information about the available software is stored in a file software. This information includes the name, version, quantity, and price of each package. When it is invoked, the program automatically creates a binary search tree with one node corresponding to one software package and includes as its key the name of the package and its version.

FIGURE **6.67**   Binary tree used for sorting.

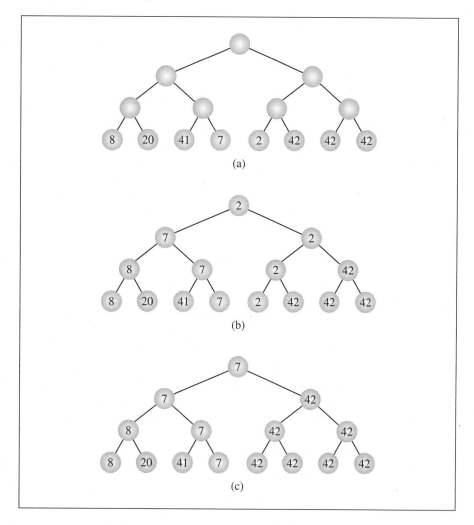

Another field in this node should include the position of the record in the file `software`. The only access to the information stored in `software` should be through this tree.

The program should allow the file and tree to be updated when new software packages arrive at the store and when some packages are sold. The tree is updated in the usual way. All packages are entry ordered in the file `software`; if a new package arrives, then it is put at the end of the file. If the package already has an entry in the tree (and the file), then only the quantity field is updated. If a package is sold out, the corresponding node is deleted from the tree, and the quantity field in the file is changed to 0. For example, if the file has these entries:

```
Adobe Photoshop              4.0        21        250
Norton Utilities W95         3.0        10         45
Norton Utilities DOS/WIN     8.0         6         40
Visual J++                   1.0        19         40
Visual J++                   1.1        27         40
```

then after selling all six copies of *Norton Utilities DOS/WIN 8.0,* the file is

```
Adobe Photoshop              4.0        21        250
Norton Utilities W95         3.0        10         45
Norton Utilities DOS/WIN     8.0         0         40
Visual J++                   1.0        19         40
Visual J++                   1.1        27         40
```

If an exit option is chosen from the menu, the program cleans up the file by moving entries from the end of the file to the positions marked with 0 quantities. For example, the previous file becomes

```
Adobe Photoshop              4.0        21        250
Norton Utilities W95         3.0        10         45
Visual J++                   1.1        27         40
Visual J++                   1.0        19         40
```

4. Implement algorithms for constructing expression trees and for differentiating the expressions they represent. Extend the program to simplify expression trees. For example, two nodes can be eliminated from the subtrees representing $a \pm 0$, $a \cdot 1$, or $\frac{a}{1}$.

5. Write a cross-reference program which constructs a binary search tree with all words included from a text file and records the line numbers on which these words were used. These line numbers should be stored on linked lists associated with the nodes of the tree. After the input file has been processed, print in alphabetical order all words of the text file along with the corresponding list of numbers of the lines in which the words occur.

6. Perform an experiment with alternately applying insertion and deletion of random elements in a randomly created binary search tree. Apply asymmetric and symmetric deletions (discussed in this chapter); for both these variants of the deletion algorithm, alternate deletions strictly with insertions and alternate these operations randomly. This gives four different combinations. Also, use two different random number generators to ensure randomness. This leads to eight combinations. Run all of these combinations for trees of heights 500, 1000, 1500, and 2000. Plot the results and compare them with the expected IPLs indicated in this chapter.

7. Each unit in a Latin textbook contains a Latin-English vocabulary of words which have been used for the first time in a particular unit. Write a program that converts a set of such vocabularies stored in file `Latin` into a set of English-Latin vocabularies. Make the following assumptions:

   a. Unit names are preceded by a percentage symbol.

   b. There is only one entry per line.

c. A Latin word is separated by a colon from its English equivalent(s); if there is more than one equivalent, they are separated by a comma.

To output English words in alphabetical order, create a binary search tree for each unit containing English words and linked lists of Latin equivalents. Make sure that there is only one node for each English word in the tree. For example, there is only one node for *and,* although *and* is used twice in *unit 6:* with words *ac* and *atque.* After the task has been completed for a given unit (that is, the content of the tree has been stored in an output file), delete the tree along with all linked lists from computer memory before creating a tree for the next unit.

Here is an example of a file containing Latin-English vocabularies:

```
%Unit 5
ante : before, in front of, previously
antiquus : ancient
ardeo : burn, be on fire, desire
arma : arms, weapons
aurum : gold
aureus : golden, of gold

%Unit 6
animal : animal
Athenae : Athens
atque : and
ac : and
aurora : dawn

%Unit 7
amo : love
amor : love
annus : year
Asia : Asia
```

From these units, the program should generate the following output:

```
%Unit 5
ancient : antiquus
arms : arma
be on fire : ardeo
before : ante
burn : ardeo
desire : ardeo
gold: aurum
golden : aureus
in front of : ante
of gold : aureus
previously : ante
weapons : arma
```

```
%Unit 6
Athens : Athenae
and : ac, atque
animal : animal
dawn : aurora

%Unit 7
Asia : Asia
love : amor, amo
year : annus
```

Bibliography

Insertions and Deletions

Culberson, Joseph, "The Effect of Updates in Binary Search Trees," *Proceedings of the 17th Annual Symposium on Theory of Computing* (1985), 205–212.

Eppinger, Jeffrey L., "An Empirical Study of Insertion and Deletion in Binary Search Trees," *Communications of the ACM* 26 (1983), 663–669.

Hibbard, Thomas N., "Some Combinatorial Properties of Certain Trees with Applications to Searching and Sorting," *Journal of the ACM* 9 (1962), 13–28.

Jonassen, Arne T. and Knuth, Donald E., "A Trivial Algorithm Whose Analysis Isn't," *Journal of Computer and System Sciences* 16 (1978), 301–322.

Knuth, Donald E., "Deletions That Preserve Randomness," *IEEE Transactions of Software Engineering*, SE-3 (1977), 351–359.

Tree Traversals

Berztiss, Alfs, "A Taxonomy of Binary Tree Traversals," *BIT* 26 (1986), 266–276.

Burkhard, W. A., "Nonrecursive Tree Traversal Algorithms," *Computer Journal* 18 (1975), 227–230.

Morris, Joseph M., "Traversing Binary Trees Simply and Cheaply," *Information Processing Letters* 9 (1979), 197–200.

Balancing Trees

Baer, J. L. and Schwab, B., "A Comparison of Tree-Balancing Algorithms," *Communications of the ACM* 20 (1977), 322–330.

Chang, Hsi and Iyengar, S. Sitharama, "Efficient Algorithms to Globally Balance a Binary Search Tree," *Communications of the ACM* 27 (1984), 695–702.

Day, A. Colin, "Balancing a Binary Tree," *Computer Journal* 19 (1976), 360–361.

Martin, W. A. and Ness, D. N., "Optimizing Binary Trees Grown with a Sorting Algorithm," *Communications of the ACM* 1 (1972), 88–93.

Stout, Quentin F. and Warren, Bette L., "Tree Rebalancing in Optimal Time and Space," *Communications of the ACM* 29 (1986), 902–908.

AVL Trees

Adel'son-Vel'skii, G. M. and Landis, E. M., "An Algorithm for the Organization of Information," *Soviet Mathematics* 3 (1962), 1259–1263.

Foster, Caxton C., "A Generalization of AVL Trees," *Communications of the ACM* 16 (1973), 512–517.

Karlton, P. L., Fuller, S. H., Scroggs, R. E., and Kaehler, E. B., "Performance of Height-Balanced Trees," *Communications of the ACM* 19 (1976), 23–28.

Knuth, Donald, *The Art of Computer Programming, Vol. 3: Sorting and Searching,* Reading, MA: Addison-Wesley, 1998.

Zweben, S. H. and McDonald, M. A., "An Optimal Method for Deletion in One-Sided Height Balanced Trees," *Communications of the ACM* 21 (1978), 441–445.

Self-Adjusting Trees

Allen, Brian and Munro, Ian, "Self-Organizing Binary Search Trees," *Journal of the ACM* 25 (1978), 526–535.

Bitner, James R., "Heuristics That Dynamically Organize Data Structures," *SIAM Journal on Computing* 8 (1979), 82–110.

Sleator, Daniel D. and Tarjan, Robert E., "Self-Adjusting Binary Search Trees," *Journal of the ACM* 32 (1985), 652–686.

Heaps

Bollobés, B. and Simon, I., "Repeated Random Insertion into a Priority Queue Structure," *Journal of Algorithms* 6 (1985), 466–477.

Doberkat, E. E., "An Average Case of Floyd's Algorithm to Construct Heaps," *Information and Control* 61 (1984), 114–131.

Floyd, Robert W., "Algorithm 245: Treesort 3," *Communications of the ACM* 7 (1964), 701.

Frieze, A., "On the Random Construction of Heaps," *Information Processing Letters* 27 (1988), 103.

Gonnett, Gaston H. and Munro, Ian, "Heaps on Heaps," *SIAM Journal on Computing* 15 (1986), 964–971.

Hayward, Ryan and McDiarmid, Colin, "Average Case Analysis of Heap Building by Repeated Insertion," *Journal of Algorithms* 12 (1991), 126–153.

McDiarmid, C. J. H. and Reed, B. A., "Building Heaps Fast," *Journal of Algorithms* 10 (1989), 351–365.

Weiss, Mark A., *Data Structures and Algorithm Analysis*, Redwood City, CA: Benjamin/Cummings, 1992, Ch. 6.

Williams, J. W. J., "Algorithm 232: Heapsort," *Communications of the ACM* 7 (1964), 347–348.

Multiway Trees

A t the beginning of the preceding chapter, a general definition of a tree was given, but the thrust of that chapter was binary trees, in particular, binary search trees. A tree was defined as either an empty structure or a structure whose children are disjoint trees $t_1, \ldots, t_k$. According to this definition, each node of this kind of tree can have more than two children. This tree is called a *multiway tree of order m*, or an *m-way tree*.

In a more useful version of a multiway tree, an order is imposed on the keys residing in each node. A *multiway search tree of order m*, or an *m-way search tree*, is a multiway tree in which

1. Each node has m children and $m - 1$ keys.

2. The keys in each node are in ascending order.

3. The keys in the first i children are smaller than the ith key.

4. The keys in the last $m - i$ children are larger than the ith key.

The m-way search trees play the same role among m-way trees that binary search trees play among binary trees, and they are used for the same purpose: fast information retrieval and update. The problems they cause are similar. The tree in Figure 7.1 is a 4-way tree in which accessing the keys can require a different number of tests for different keys: The number 35 can be found in the second node tested, and 55 is in the fifth node checked. The tree, therefore, suffers from a known malaise: It is unbalanced. This problem is of particular importance if we want to use trees to process data on secondary storage such as disks or tapes where each access is costly. Constructing such trees requires a more careful approach.

FIGURE **7.1**   A 4-way tree.

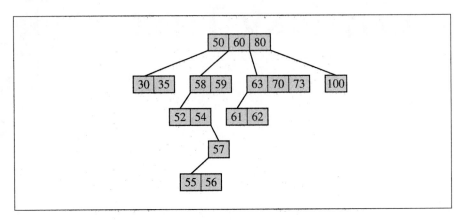

7.1 THE FAMILY OF B-TREES

The basic unit of I/O operations associated with a disk is a block. When information is read from a disk, the entire block containing this information is read into memory, and when information is stored on a disk, an entire block is written to the disk. Each time information is requested from a disk, this information has to be located on the disk, the head has to be positioned above the part of the disk where the information resides, and the disk has to be spun so that the entire block passes underneath the head to be transferred to memory. This means that there are several time components for data access:

access time = seek time + rotational delay (latency) + transfer time

This process is extremely slow compared to transferring information within memory. The first component, *seek time,* is particularly slow because it depends on the mechanical movement of the disk head to position the head at the correct track of the disk. *Latency* is the time required to position the head above the correct block, and on the average, it is equal to the time needed to make one-half of a revolution. For example, the time to transfer 5KB (kilobytes) from a disk requiring 40 ms (milliseconds) to locate a track, making 3000 revolutions per minute and with a data transfer rate of 1000KB per second is

access time = 4 ms + 10 ms + 5 ms = 55 ms

This example indicates that transferring information to and from the disk is on the order of milliseconds. On the other hand, the CPU processes data on the order of microseconds, 1000 times faster, or on the order of nanoseconds, 1 million times faster, or even faster. We can see that processing information on secondary storage can significantly decrease the speed of a program.

FIGURE **7.2**   Nodes of a binary tree can be located in different blocks on a disk.

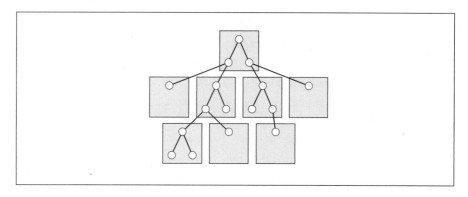

If a program constantly uses information stored in secondary storage, the characteristics of this storage have to be taken into account when designing the program. For example, a binary search tree can be spread over many different blocks on a disk, as in Figure 7.2, so that an average of two blocks have to be accessed. When the tree is used frequently in a program, these accesses can significantly slow down the execution time of the program. Also, inserting and deleting keys in this tree require many block accesses. The binary search tree, which is such an efficient tool when it resides entirely in memory, turns out to be an encumbrance. In the context of secondary storage, its otherwise good performance counts very little because the constant accessing of disk blocks that this method causes severely hampers this performance.

It is also better to access a large amount of data at one time than to jump from one position on the disk to another to transfer small portions of data. For example, if 10KB have to be transferred, then using the characteristics of the disk given earlier, we see that

$$access\ time = 40\ ms + 10\ ms + 10\ ms = 60\ ms$$

However, if this information is stored in two 5KB pieces, then

$$access\ time = 2 \cdot (40\ ms + 10\ ms + 5\ ms) = 110\ ms$$

which is nearly twice as long as in the previous case. The reason is that each disk access is very costly; if possible, the data should be organized to minimize the number of accesses.

7.1.1 B-Trees

In database programs where most information is stored on disks or tapes, the time penalty for accessing secondary storage can be significantly reduced by the proper choice of data structures. *B-trees* (Bayer and McCreight 1972) are one such approach.

A B-tree operates closely with secondary storage and can be tuned to reduce the impediments imposed by this storage. One important property of B-trees is the size of each node which can be made as large as the size of a block. The number of keys in one node can vary depending on the sizes of the keys, organization of the data (are only keys kept in the nodes or entire records?), and of course, on the size of a block. Bock size varies for each system. It can be 512 bytes, 4KB, or more; block size is the size of each node of a B-tree. The amount of information stored in one node of the B-tree can be rather large.

A *B-tree of order m* is a multiway search tree with the following properties:

1. The root has at least two subtrees unless it is a leaf.

2. Each nonroot and each nonleaf node holds $k-1$ keys and k references to subtrees where $\lceil m/2 \rceil \le k \le m$.

3. Each leaf node holds $k-1$ keys where $\lceil m/2 \rceil \le k \le m$.

4. All leaves are on the same level.[1]

According to these conditions, a B-tree is always at least half full, has few levels, and is perfectly balanced.

A node of a B-tree is usually implemented as a `class` containing an array of $m-1$ cells for keys, an m-cell array of references to other nodes, and possibly other information facilitating tree maintenance, such as the number of keys in a node and a leaf/nonleaf flag, as in

```
class BTreeNode {
    int m = 4;
    boolean leaf = true;
    int keyTally = 1;
    int keys[] = new int[m-1];
    BTreeNode references[] = new BTreeNode[m];
    BTreeNode(int key) {
        keys[0] = key;
        for (int i = 0; i < m; i++)
            references[i] = null;
    }
}
```

Usually, m is large (50–500) so that information stored in one page or block of secondary storage can fit into one node. Figure 7.3a contains an example of a B-tree of order 7 which stores codes for some items. In this B-tree, the keys appear to be the only objects of interest. In most cases, however, such codes would only be fields of larger structures, possibly variant records (unions). In these cases, the array `keys` is an array of objects, each having a unique identifier field (such as the identifying code in Figure 7.3a) and an address field, the address of the entire record on secondary storage as in Figure 7.3b.[2] If the contents of one such node also reside in secondary

---

[1] In this definition, the order of a B-tree specifies the *maximum* number of children. Sometimes nodes of a B-tree of order m are defined as having k keys and $k+1$ references where $m \le k \le 2m$, which specifies the *minimum* number of children.

[2] Figure 7.3 reflects the logic of the situation; in actual implementation, the array `keys` is an array of references to objects, and each object has a key field and an address field.

FIGURE **7.3**   One node of a B-tree of order 7 (a) without and (b) with an additional indirection.

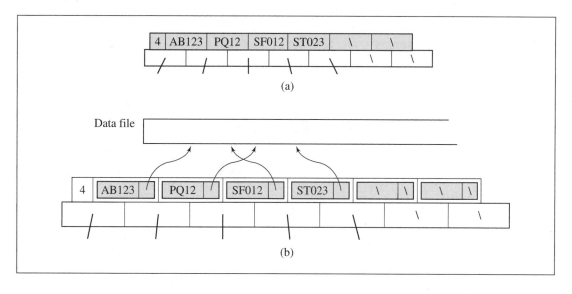

FIGURE **7.4**   A B-tree of order 5 shown in an abbreviated form.

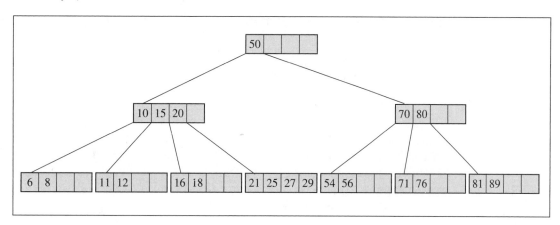

storage, each key access would require two secondary storage accesses. In the long run, this is better than keeping the entire records in the nodes, since in this case, the nodes can hold a very small number of such records. The resulting B-tree is much deeper, and search paths through it are much longer than in a B-tree with the addresses of records.

From now on, B-trees will be shown in an abbreviated form without explicitly indicating `keyTally` or the reference fields, as in Figure 7.4.

Searching in a B-Tree

The worst case of searching is when a B-tree has the smallest allowable number of references per nonroot node, $q = \lceil m/2 \rceil$, and the search has to reach a leaf (either for a successful or an unsuccessful search). In this case, in a B-tree of height h, there are

$$1 \text{ key in the root } +$$

$$2(q-1) \text{ keys on the second level } +$$

$$2q(q-1) \text{ keys on the third level } +$$

$$2q^2(q-1) \text{ keys on the fourth level } +$$

$$\vdots$$

$$2q^{h-2}(q-1) \text{ keys in the leaves (level } h) =$$

$$1 + \left(\sum_{i=0}^{h-2} 2q^i \right) (q-1) \text{ keys in the B-tree}$$

With the formula for the sum of the first n elements in a geometric progression,

$$\sum_{i=0}^{n} q^i = \frac{q^{n+1} - 1}{q - 1}$$

the number of keys in the worst-case B-tree can be expressed as

$$1 + 2(q-1) \left(\sum_{i=0}^{h-2} q^i \right) = 1 + 2(q-1) \left(\frac{q^{h-1} - 1}{q-1} \right) = -1 + 2q^{h-1}$$

The relation between the number of n of keys in any B-tree and the height of the B-tree is then expressed as

$$n \geq -1 + 2q^{h-1}$$

Solving this inequality for the height h results in

$$h \leq \log_q \frac{n+1}{2} + 1$$

This means that for a sufficiently large order m, the height is small even for a large number of keys stored in the B-tree. For example, if $m = 200$ and $n = 2,000,000$, then $h \leq 4$; in the worst case, finding a key in this B-tree requires four seeks. If the root can be kept in memory at all times, this number can be reduced to only three seeks into secondary storage.

An algorithm for finding a key in a B-tree is simple and coded as follows:

```
public BTreeNode BTreeSearch(int key) {
    return BTreeSearch(key,root);
}
protected BTreeNode BTreeSearch(int key, BTreeNode node) {
    if (node != null) {
        int i = 1;
        for ( ; i <= node.keyTally && node.keys[i-1] < key; i++);
        if (i > node.keyTally || node.keys[i-1] > key)
            return BTreeSearch(key,node.references[i-1]);
```

```
        else return node;
    }
    else return null;
}
```

Inserting a Key in a B-Tree

Both the insertion and deletion operations appear to be somewhat challenging if we remember that all leaves have to be at the last level. Not even balanced binary trees require that. Implementing insertion becomes easier when the strategy of building a tree is changed. When inserting a node in a binary search tree, the tree is always built from top to bottom, resulting in unbalanced trees. If the first incoming key is the smallest, then this key is put in the root, and the root does not have a left subtree unless special provisions are made to balance the tree.

But a tree can be built from the bottom up so that the root is an entity always in flux, and only at the end of all insertions can we know for sure the contents of the root. This strategy is applied to inserting keys into B-trees. In this process, given an incoming key, we go directly to a leaf and place it there, if there is room. When the leaf is full, another leaf is created, the keys are divided between these leaves, and one key is promoted to the parent. If the parent is full, the process is repeated until the root is reached and a new root created.

To approach the problem more systematically, there are three common situations encountered when inserting a key in a B-tree.

1. A key is placed in a leaf that still has some room, as in Figure 7.5. In a B-tree of order 5, a new key, 7, is placed in a leaf, preserving the order of the keys in the leaf so that key 8 must be shifted to the right by one position.

2. The leaf in which a key should be placed is full, as in Figure 7.6. In this case, the leaf is *split*, creating a new leaf, and half of the keys are moved from the full leaf to the new leaf. But the new leaf has to be incorporated into the B-tree. The last key of the old leaf is moved to the parent, and a reference to the new leaf is placed in the parent as well. The same procedure can be repeated for each internal node of the B-tree so that each such split adds one more node to the B-tree. Moreover, such a split guarantees that each leaf never has less than $\lceil m/2 \rceil - 1$ keys.

FIGURE **7.5**   A B-tree (a) before and (b) after insertion of the number 7 to a leaf which has available cells.

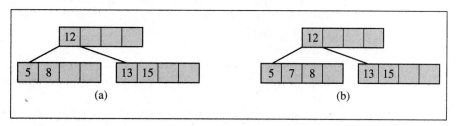

FIGURE **7.6**   Inserting the number 6 into a full leaf.

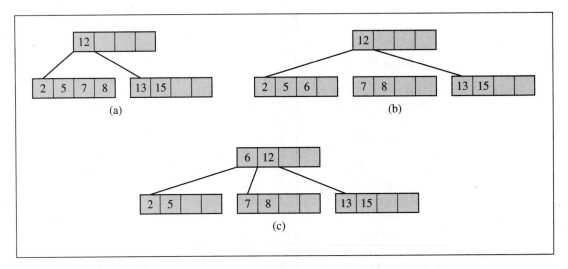

3. A special case arises if the root of the B-tree is full. In this case, a new root and a new sibling of the existing root have to be created. This split results in two new nodes in the B-tree. For example, after inserting the key 13 in the third leaf in Figure 7.7a, the leaf is split (as in case 2), a new leaf is created and the key 15 is about to be moved to the parent, but the parent has no room for it (7.7b). So the parent is split (7.7c), but now two B-trees have to be combined into one. This is achieved by creating a new root and moving the last key from the old root to it (7.7d). It should be obvious that it is the only case in which the B-tree increases in height.

An algorithm for inserting keys in B-trees follows:

```
BTreeInsert (K)
   find a leaf node to insert K;
   while (true)
      find a proper position in array keys for K;
      if node is not full
         insert K and increment keyTally;
         return;
      else split node in node1 and node2; // node1 = node, node2 is new;
         distribute keys and references evenly between node1 and node2 and
         initialize properly their keyTally's;
         K = the last key of node1;
         if node was the root
            create a new root as parent of node1 and node2;
            put K and references to node1 and node2 in the root, and set its keyTally to 1;
            return;
         else node = its parent; // and now process the node's parent;
```

FIGURE **7.7**   Inserting the number 13 into a full leaf.

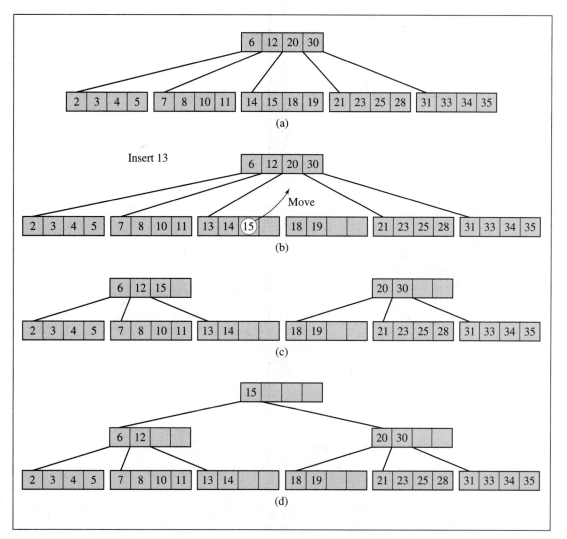

Figure 7.8 shows the growth of a B-tree of order 5 in the course of inserting new keys. Note that at all times the tree is perfectly balanced.

A variation of this insertion strategy uses *presplitting:* When a search is made from the top down for a particular key, each visited node that is already full is split. In this way, no split has to be propagated upward.

How often are node splits expected to occur? A split of the root node of a B-tree creates two new nodes. All other splits add only one more node to the B-tree. During the construction of a B-tree of p nodes, $p - h$ splits have to be performed, where h is the height of the B-tree. Also, in a B-tree of p nodes, there are at least

FIGURE **7.8**   Building a B-tree of order 5 with the `BTreeInsert()` algorithm.

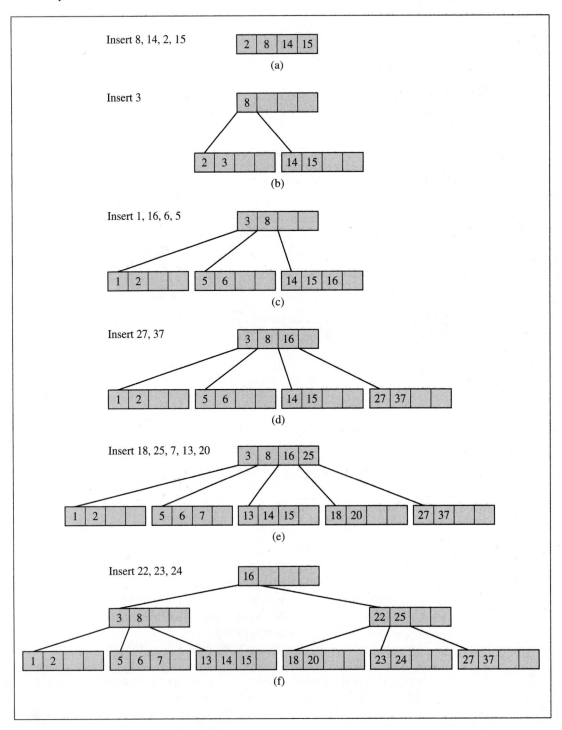

$$1 + (\lceil m/2 \rceil - 1)(p - 1)$$

keys. The rate of splits with respect to the number of keys in the B-tree can be given by

$$\frac{p - h}{1 + (\lceil m/2 \rceil - 1)(p - 1)}$$

After dividing the numerator and denominator by $p - h$ and observing that $\frac{1}{p-h} \to 0$ and $\frac{p-1}{p-h} \to 1$ with the increase of p, the average probability of a split is

$$\frac{1}{\lceil m/2 \rceil - 1}$$

For example, for $m = 10$, this probability is equal to .25, for $m = 100$, it is .02, and for $m = 1000$, it is .002, and expectedly so: The larger the capacity of one node, the less frequently splits occur.

Deleting a Key from a B-Tree

Deletion is to a great extent a reversal of insertion, although it has more special cases. Care has to be taken to avoid allowing any node to be less than half full after a deletion. This means that nodes sometimes have to be merged.

In deletion, there are two main cases: deleting a key from a leaf and deleting a key from a nonleaf node. In the latter case, we will use a procedure similar to `deleteByCopying()` used for binary search trees (Section 6.6).

1. Deleting a key from a leaf.

    1.1 If after deleting a key *K*, the leaf is at least half full and only keys greater than *K* are moved to the left to fill the hole (see Figures 7.9a–b). This is the inverse of insertion's case 1.

    1.2 If after deleting *K*, the number of keys in the leaf is less than $\lceil m/2 \rceil - 1$, causing an *underflow*.

    1.2.1 If there is a left or right sibling with the number of keys exceeding the minimal $\lceil m/2 \rceil - 1$, then all keys from this leaf and this sibling are *redistributed* between them by moving the separator key from the parent to the leaf and moving one key from the sibling to the parent (see Figures 7.9b–c).

    1.2.2 If the leaf underflows and the number of keys in its siblings is $\lceil m/2 \rceil - 1$, then the leaf and a sibling are *merged;* the keys from the leaf, from its sibling, and the separating key from the parent are all put in the leaf, and the sibling node is discarded. The keys in the parent are moved if a hole appears (see Figures 7.9c–d). This can initiate a chain of operations if the parent underflows. The parent is now treated as though it were a leaf, and either step 1.2.2 is repeated until step 1.2.1 can be executed or the root of the tree has been reached. This is the inverse of insertion's case 2.

FIGURE **7.9**   Deleting keys from a B-tree.

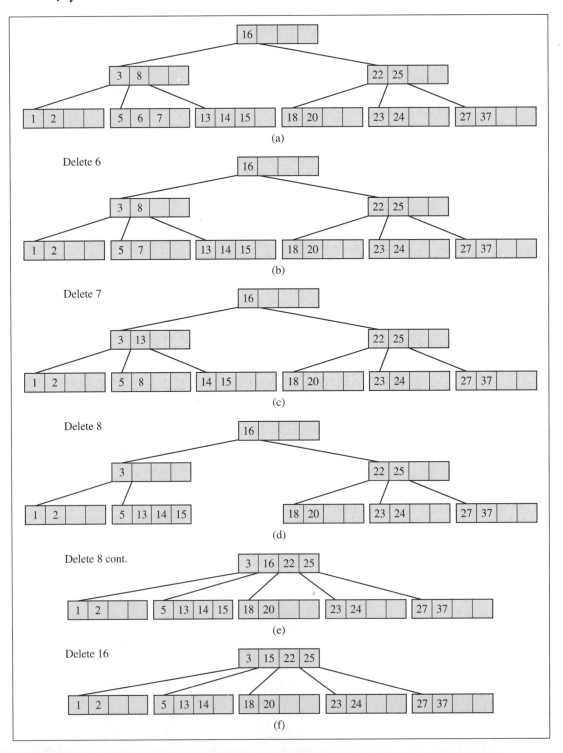

1.2.2.1 A particular case results in merging a leaf or nonleaf with its sibling when its parent is the root with only one key. In this case, the keys from the node and its sibling, along with the only key of the root, are put in the node which becomes a new root, and both the sibling and the old root nodes are discarded. This is the only case when two nodes disappear at one time. Also, the height of the tree is decreased by one (see Figures 7.9c–e). This is the inverse of insertion's case 3.

2.   Deleting a key from a nonleaf. This may lead to problems with tree reorganization. Therefore, deletion from a nonleaf node is reduced to deleting a key from a leaf. The key to be deleted is replaced by its immediate successor (the predecessor could also be used), which can only be found in a leaf. This successor key is deleted from the leaf, which brings us to the preceding case 1 (see Figures 7.9e–f).

Here is the deletion algorithm:

```
BTreeDelete (K)
    node = BTreeSearch(K,root);
    if (node != null)
        if node is not a leaf
            find a leaf with the closest successor S of K;
            copy S over K in node;
            node = the leaf containing S;
            delete S from node;
        else delete K from node;
        while (true)
            if node does not underflow
                return;
            else if there is a sibling of node with enough keys
                redistribute the keys between node and its sibling;
                return;
            else if node's parent is the root
                if the parent has only one key
                    merge node, its sibling, and the parent to form a new root;
                else merge node and its sibling;
                return;
            else merge node and its sibling;
                node = its parent;
```

B-trees, according to their definition, are guaranteed to be at least 50% full, so it may happen that 50% of space is basically wasted. How often does this happen? If it happens too often, then the definition must be reconsidered or some other restrictions imposed on this B-tree. Analyses and simulations, however, indicate that after a series of numerous random insertions and deletions, the B-tree is approximately 69% full (Yao 1978), after which the changes in the percentage of occupied cells are very small. But it is very unlikely that the B-tree will ever be filled to the brim, so some additional stipulations are in order.

FIGURE **7.10** Overflow in a B*-tree is circumvented by redistributing keys between an overflowing node and its sibling.

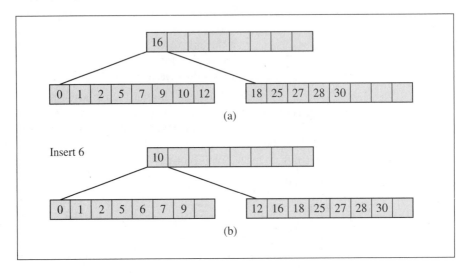

7.1.2 B*-Trees

Since each node of a B-tree represents a block of secondary memory, accessing one node means one access of secondary memory, which is expensive compared to accessing keys in the node residing in primary memory. Therefore, the fewer nodes that are created, the better.

A B*-tree is a variant of the B-tree introduced by Donald Knuth and named by Douglas Comer. In a B*-tree, all nodes except the root are required to be at least two-thirds full, not just half full as in a B-tree. More precisely, the number of keys in all nonroot nodes in a B-tree of order m is now k for $\lfloor \frac{2m-1}{3} \rfloor \leq k \leq m-1$. The frequency of node splitting is decreased by delaying a split, and when the time comes, by splitting two nodes into three, not one into two. The average utilization of B*-tree is 81% (Leung, 1984).

A split in a B*-tree is delayed by attempting to redistribute the keys between a node and its sibling when the node overflows. Figure 7.10 contains an example of a B*-tree of order 9. The key 6 is to be inserted into the left node, which is already full. Instead of splitting the node, all keys from this node and its sibling are evenly divided and the median key, key 10, is put into the parent. Notice that this not only evenly divides the keys, but also the free spaces so that the node which was full is now able to accommodate one more key.

If the sibling is also full, a split occurs: One new node is created, the keys from the node and its sibling (along with the separating key from the parent) are evenly divided among three nodes, and two separating keys are put into the parent (see Figure 7.11). All three nodes participating in the split are guaranteed to be two-thirds full.

FIGURE **7.11**   If a node and its sibling are both full in a B*-tree, a split occurs: A new node is created and keys are distributed between three nodes.

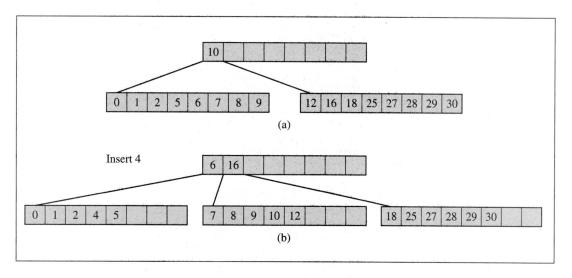

Note that, as may be expected, this increase of a *fill factor* can be done in a variety of ways, and some database systems allow the user to choose a fill factor between .5 and 1. In particular, a B-tree whose nodes are required to be at least 75% full is called a B**-tree (McCreight 1977). The latter suggests a generalization: A B^n-tree is a B-tree whose nodes are required to be $\frac{n+1}{n+2}$ full.

7.1.3   B$^+$-Trees

Since one node of a B-tree represents one secondary memory page or block, the passage from one node to another requires a time-consuming page change. Therefore, we would like to make as few node accesses as possible. What happens if we request that all the keys in the B-tree be printed in ascending order? An inorder tree traversal can be used which is easy to implement, but for nonterminal nodes, only one key is displayed at a time and then another page has to be accessed. Therefore, we would like to enhance B-trees to allow us to access data sequentially in a faster manner than using inorder traversal. A *B$^+$-tree* offers a solution (Wedekind 1974).[3]

In a B-tree, references to data are made from any node of the tree, but in a B$^+$-tree, these references are made only from the leaves. The internal nodes of a B$^+$-tree are indexes for fast access of data; this part of the tree is called an *index set*. The leaves have a different structure than other nodes of the B$^+$-tree, and usually they are linked

---

[3] Wedekind, who considered these trees to be only "a slight variation" of B-trees, called them B*-trees.

FIGURE **7.12**   An example of a B$^+$-tree of order 4.

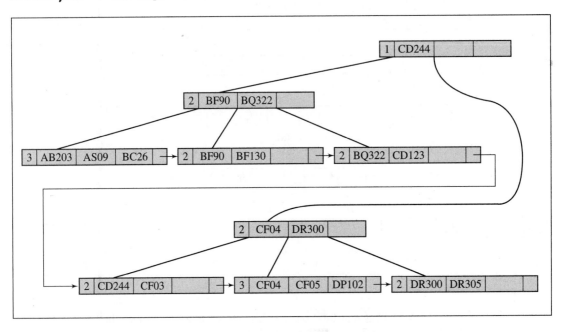

sequentially to form a *sequence set* so that scanning this list of leaves results in data given in ascending order. Hence, a B$^+$-tree is truly a B plus tree: It is an index implemented as a regular B-tree plus a linked list of data. Figure 7.12 contains an example of a B$^+$-tree. Note that internal nodes store keys, references to other nodes, and a key count. Leaves store keys, references to records in a data file associated with the keys, and references to the next leaf.

Operations on B$^+$-trees are not very different from operations on B-trees. Inserting a key into a leaf which still has some room requires putting the keys of this leaf in order. No changes are made in the index set. If a key is inserted into a full leaf, the leaf is split, the new leaf node is included in the sequence set, keys are distributed evenly between the old and the new leaves, and the first key from the new node is copied (not moved, as in a B-tree) to the parent. If the parent is not full, this may require local reorganization of the keys of the parent (see Figure 7.13). If the parent is full, the splitting process is performed the same way as in B-trees. After all, the index set is a B-tree.

Deleting a key from a leaf leading to no underflow requires putting the remaining keys in order. No changes are made to the index set. In particular, if a key which occurs only in a leaf is deleted, then it is simply deleted from the leaf but can remain in the internal node. The reason is that it still serves as a proper guide when navigating down the B$^+$-tree because it still properly separates keys between two adjacent children even if the separator itself does not occur in either of the children. The deletion of key 6 from the tree in Figure 7.13b results in the tree in Figure 7.14a. Note that the number 6 is not deleted from an internal node.

FIGURE **7.13**   An attempt to insert the number 6 in the first leaf of a B⁺-tree.

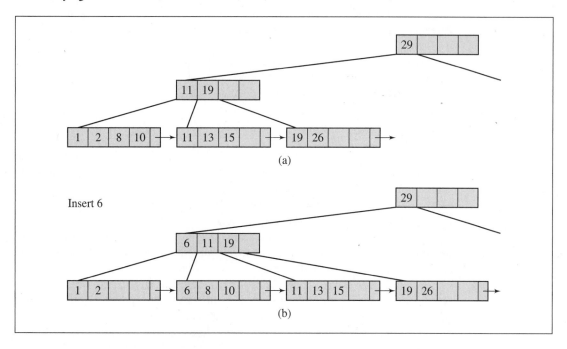

FIGURE **7.14**   Actions after deleting the number 6 from the B⁺-tree in Figure 7.13b.

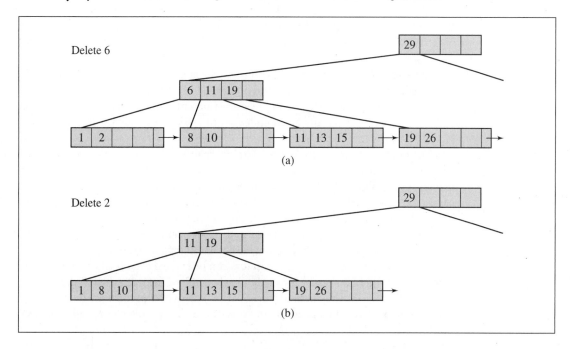

When the deletion of a key from a leaf causes an underflow, then either the keys from this leaf and the keys of a sibling are redistributed between this leaf and its sibling or the leaf is deleted and the remaining keys are included in its sibling. Figure 7.14b illustrates the latter case. After deleting the number 2, an underflow occurs and two leaves are combined to form one leaf. The first key from the right sibling of the node remaining after merging is copied to the parent node, and keys in the parent are put in order. Both these operations require updating the separator in the parent. Also, removing a leaf may trigger merges in the index set.

7.1.4 Prefix B⁺-Trees

If a key occurred in a leaf and in an internal node of a B⁺-tree, then it is enough to delete it only from the leaf because the key retained in the node is still a good guide in subsequent searches. So it really does not matter whether a key in an internal node is in any leaf or not. What counts is that it is an acceptable separator for keys in adjacent children; for example, for two keys K_1 and K_2, the separator s must meet the condition $K_1 < s \leq K_2$. This property of the separator keys is also retained if we make keys in internal nodes as small as possible by removing all redundant contents from them and still have a properly working B⁺-tree.

A *simple prefix B⁺-tree* (Bayer and Unterauer 1977) is a B⁺-tree in which the chosen separators are the shortest prefixes that allow us to distinguish two neighboring index keys. For example, in Figure 7.12, the left child of the root has two keys, BF90 and BQ322. If a key is less than BF90, the first leaf is chosen; if it is less than BQ322, the second leaf is the right pick. But observe that we also have the same results, if instead of BF90, keys BF9 or just BF are used and instead of BQ322, one of three prefixes of this key is used: BQ32, BQ3, or just BQ. After choosing the shortest prefixes of both keys, if any key is less than BF, the search ends up in the first leaf, and if the key is less than BQ, the second leaf is chosen; the result is the same as before. Reducing the size of the separators to the bare minimum does not change the result of the search. It only makes separators smaller. As a result, more separators can be placed in the same node, whereby such a node can have more children. The entire B⁺-tree can have fewer levels, which reduces the branching factor and makes processing the tree faster.

This reasoning does not stop at the level of parents of the leaves. It is carried over to any other level so that the entire index set of a B⁺-tree is filled with prefixes (see Figure 7.15).

The operations on simple prefix B⁺-trees are much the same as the operations on B⁺-trees with certain modifications to account for prefixes used as separators. In particular, after a split, the first key from the new node is neither moved nor copied to the parent, but the shortest prefix is found which differentiates it from the prefix of the last key in the old node; and then the shortest prefix is placed in the parent. For deletion, however, some separators retained in the index set may turn out to be too long, but to make deletion faster, they do not have to be immediately shortened.

The idea of using prefixes as separators can be carried even further if we observe that prefixes of prefixes can be omitted in lower levels of the tree, which is the idea behind a *prefix B⁺-tree*. This method works particularly well if prefixes are long and repetitious. Figure 7.16 contains an example. Each key in the tree has a prefix AB12XY,

FIGURE **7.15**   A B$^+$-tree from Figure 7.12 presented as a simple prefix B$^+$-tree.

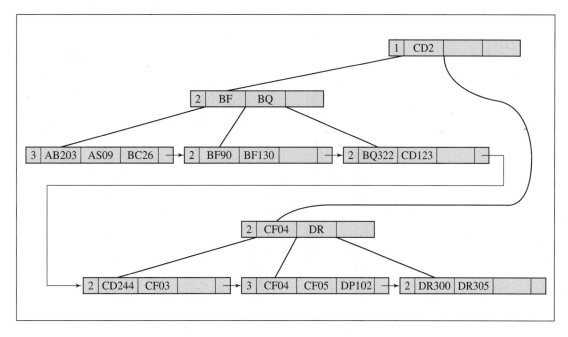

and this prefix appears in all internal nodes. This is redundant; Figure 7.16b shows the same tree with "AB12XY" stripped from prefixes in children of the root. To restore the original prefix, the key from the parent node, except for its last character, becomes the prefix of the key found in the current node. For example, the first cell of the child of the root in Figure 7.16b has the key "08." The last character of the key in the root is discarded and the obtained prefix, "AB12XY," is put in front of "08." The new prefix, "AB12XY08," is used to determine the direction of the search.

How efficient are prefix B$^+$-trees? Experimental runs indicate that there is almost no difference in the time needed to execute algorithms in B$^+$-trees and simple prefix B$^+$-trees, but prefix B$^+$-trees need 50–100% more time. In terms of disk accesses, there is no difference between these trees in the number of times the disk is accessed for trees of 400 nodes or less. For trees of 400–800 nodes, both simple prefix B$^+$-trees and prefix B$^+$-trees require 20–25% fewer accesses (Bayer and Unterauer 1977). This indicates that simple prefix B$^+$-trees are a viable option, but prefix B$^+$-trees remain largely of theoretical interest.

7.1.5 Bit-Trees

A very interesting approach is, in a sense, taking to the extreme the prefix B$^+$-tree method. In this method, bytes are used to specify separators. In *bit-trees,* the bit level is reached (Ferguson 1992).

FIGURE **7.16**   (a) A simple prefix B$^+$-tree and (b) its abbreviated version presented as a prefix B$^+$-tree.

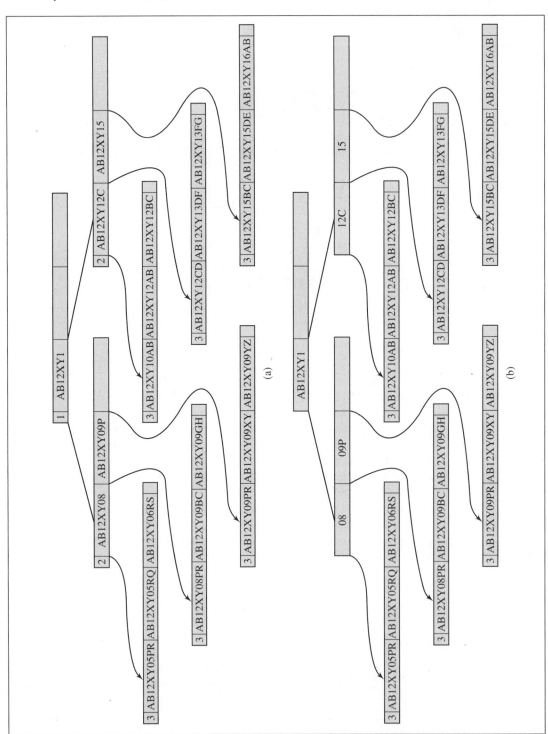

FIGURE **7.17**   A leaf of a bit-tree.

Position in leaf	$i-1$	i	$i+1$	$i+2$	$i+3$
D-bits	$\cdots$	5	7	3	5 $\cdots$
Records in data file					
Key	"K"	"N"	"O"	"R"	"V"
Key code	01001011	01001110	01001111	01010010	01010110

Data file

The bit-tree is based on the concept of a *distinction bit* (*D-bit*). A distinction bit $D(K,L)$ is the number of the most significant bit which differs in two keys K and L, and $D(K,L) = key\text{-}length\text{-}in\text{-}bits - 1 - \lfloor \lg(K \text{ xor } L) \rfloor$. For example, the D-bit for the letters "K" and "N", whose ASCII codes are 0100**1**011 and 0100**1**110, is 5, the position at which the first difference between these keys has been detected; $D(\text{"K"},\text{"N"}) = 8 - 1 - \lfloor \lg 5 \rfloor = 5$.

A bit-tree uses D-bits to separate keys in the leaves only; the remaining part of the tree is a prefix B$^+$-tree. This means that the actual keys and entire records from which these keys are extracted are stored in a data file so that the leaves can include much more information than would be the case when the keys were stored in them. The leaf entries refer to the keys indirectly by specifying distinction bits between keys corresponding to neighboring locations in the leaf (see Figure 7.17).

Before presenting an algorithm for processing data with bit-trees, some useful properties of D-bits need to be discussed. All keys in the leaves are kept in ascending order. Therefore, $D_i = D(K_{i-1}, K_i)$ indicates the leftmost bit that is different in these keys; this bit is always 1 since $K_{i-1} < K_i$ for $1 \le i < m$ (= order of the tree). For example, $D(\text{"N"},\text{"O"}) = D(01001110, 01001111) = 7$, and the bit in position 7 is on, all preceding bits in both keys being the same.

Let j be the first position in a leaf for which $D_j < D_i$ and $j > i$; D_j is the first D-bit smaller than a preceding D_i. In this case, for all keys between positions i and j in this leaf, the D_i bit is 1. In the example in Figure 7.17, $j = i + 2$, since D_{i+2} is the first D-bit following position i that is smaller than D_i. Bit 5 in key "O" in position $i + 1$ is 1 as it is 1 in key "N" in position i.

The algorithm for searching a key using a bit-tree leaf is

```
bitTreeSearch(K)
    R = record R₀;
    for (i = 1; i < m; i++)
        if the Dᵢ bit in K is 1
```

```
        R = R_i;
    else skip all following D-bits until a smaller D-bit is found;
read record R from data file;
if K == key from record R
    return R;
else return -1;
```

Using this algorithm, we can search for "V" assuming that, in Figure 7.17, $i - 1 = 0$ and $i + 3$ is the last entry in the leaf. R is initialized to R_0, and i to 1.

1. In the first iteration of the for loop, bit $D_1 = 5$ in key "V" $= 01010110$ is checked, and because it is 1, R is assigned R_1.

2. In the second iteration, bit $D_2 = 7$ is tested. It is 0, but nothing is skipped, as required by the else statement, since right away a D-bit is found which is smaller than 7.

3. The third iteration: bit $D_3 = 3$ is 1, so R becomes R_3.

4. In the fourth iteration, bit $D_4 = 5$ is checked again, and because it is 1, R is assigned R_5. This is the last entry in the leaf; the algorithm is finished and R_5 is properly returned.

What happens if the desired key is not in the data file? We can try to locate "S" $= 01010011$ using the same assumptions on $i - 1$ and $i + 3$. Bit $D_1 = 5$ is 0, so the position with D-bit 7 is skipped, and since bit $D_3 = 3$ in "S" is 1, the algorithm would return record R_3. To prevent this, bitTreeSearch() checks whether the record it found really corresponds with the desired key. If not, a negative number is returned to indicate failure.

7.1.6 R-Trees

Spatial data are the kind of objects which are utilized frequently in many areas. Computer-assisted design, geographical data, and VLSI design are examples of domains in which spatial data are created, searched, and deleted. This type of data requires special data structures to be processed efficiently. For example, we may request that all counties in an area specified by geographical coordinates be printed or that all buildings in walking distance from city hall be identified. Many different data structures have been developed to accommodate this type of data. One example is an *R-tree* (Guttman 1984).

An R-tree of order m is a B-treelike structure containing at least m entries in one node for some $m \leq$ maximum number allowable per one node (except the root). Hence, an R-tree is not required to be at least half full.

A leaf in an R-tree contains entries of the form (*rect,id*) where $rect = ([x_0,y_0], \ldots, [x_{n-1},y_{n-1}])$ is an n-dimensional rectangle and *id* is a reference to a record in a data file. *rect* is the smallest rectangle containing object *id*. For example, the entry in a leaf corresponding to an object X on a Cartesian plane as in Figure 7.18 is the pair $(([10,100], [5,52]), X)$.

A nonleaf node cell entry has the form (*rect,child*) where *rect* is the smallest rectangle encompassing all the rectangles found in *child*. The structure of an R-tree is not identical to the structure of a B-tree: The former can be viewed as a series of n keys and n references corresponding to these keys.

FIGURE **7.18**   An area *X* on the Cartesian plane enclosed tightly by the rectangle ([10,100], [5,52]). The rectangle parameters and the area identifier are stored in a leaf of an R-tree.

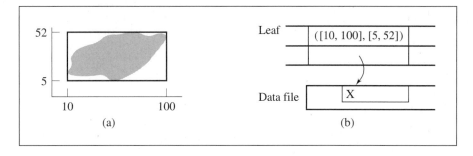

Inserting new rectangles in an R-tree is made in B-tree fashion, with splits and re-distribution. A crucial operation is finding a proper leaf in which to insert a rectangle *rect*. When moving down the R-tree, the subtree chosen in the current node is the one that corresponds to the rectangle requiring the least enlargement to include *rect*. If a split occurs, new encompassing rectangles have to be created. The detailed algorithm is more involved since, among other things, it is not obvious how to divide rectangles of a node being split. The algorithm should generate rectangles which enclose rectangles of the two resulting nodes and are minimal in size.

Figure 7.19 contains an example of inserting four rectangles to an R-tree. After inserting the first three rectangles, R_1, R_2, and R_3, only the root is full (Figure 7.19a). Inserting R_4 causes a split, resulting in the creation of two encompassing rectangles (Figure 7.19b). Inserting R_7 changes nothing, and inserting R_8 causes rectangle R_6 to be extended to accommodate R_8 (Figure 7.19c). Figure 7.19d shows another split after entering R_9 in the R-tree. R_6 is discarded, and R_{10} and R_{11} are created.

A rectangle *R* can be contained in many other encompassing rectangles, but it can be stored only once in a leaf. Therefore, a search procedure may take a wrong path at some level *h* when it sees that *R* is enclosed by another rectangle found in a node on this level. For example, rectangle R_3 in Figure 7.19d is enclosed by both R_{10} and R_{11}. Since R_{10} is before R_{11} in the root, the search accesses the middle leaf when looking for R_3. However, if R_{11} preceded R_{10} in the root, following the path corresponding with R_{11} would be unsuccessful. For large and high R-trees, this overlapping becomes excessive.

A modification of R-trees, called an R^+-*tree*, removes this overlap (Stonebraker, Sellis, and Hanson 1986; Sellis, Roussopoulos, and Faloutsos 1987). The encompassing rectangles are no longer overlapping, and each encompassing rectangle is associated with all the rectangles it intersects. But now the data rectangle can be found in more than one leaf. For example, Figure 7.20 shows an R^+-tree constructed after the data rectangle R_9 was inserted into the R-tree in Figure 7.19c. Figure 7.20 replaces Figure 7.19d. Note that R_8 can be found in two leaves, since it is intersected by two encompassing rectangles, R_{10} and R_{11}. Operations on an R^+-tree make it difficult to ensure without further manipulation that nodes are at least half full.

FIGURE **7.19**   Building an R-tree.

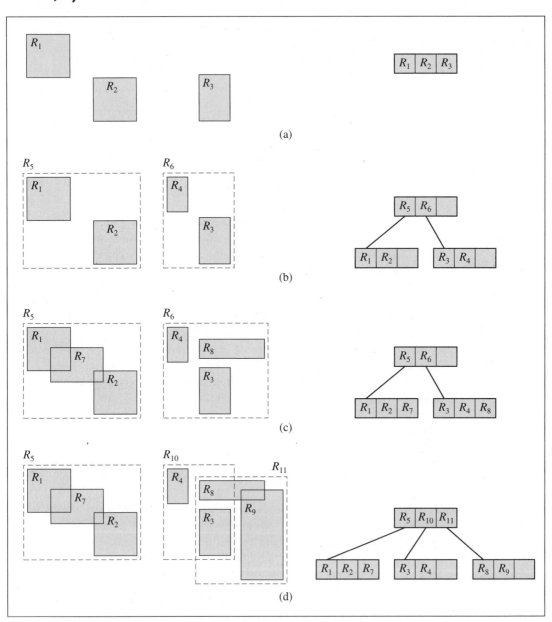

(a)

(b)

(c)

(d)

FIGURE **7.20**   An R$^+$-tree representation of the R-tree in Figure 7.19d after inserting the rectangle R_9 in the tree in Figure 7.19c.

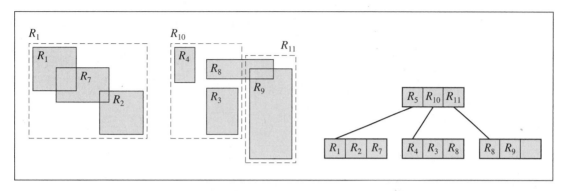

7.1.7 2–4 Trees

This section discusses a special case of B-tree, a B-tree of order 4. This B-tree was first discussed by Rudolf Bayer who called it a *symmetric binary B-tree* (Bayer 1972), but it is usually called a *2–3–4 tree* or just a *2–4 tree*. A 2–4 tree seems to offer no new perspectives, but quite the opposite is true. In B-trees, the nodes are large to accommodate the contents of one block read from secondary storage. In 2–4 trees, on the other hand, only one, two, or at most three elements can be stored in one node. Unless the elements are very large, so large that three of them can fill up one block on a disk, there seems to be no reason for even mentioning B-trees of such a small order. Although B-trees have been introduced in the context of handling data on secondary storage, it does not mean that they have to be used only for that purpose.

We spent an entire chapter discussing binary trees, in particular, binary search trees, and developing algorithms that allow quick access to the information stored in these trees. Can B-trees offer a better solution to the problem of balancing or traversing binary trees? We now return to the topics of binary trees and processing data in memory.

B-trees are well-suited to challenge the algorithms used for binary search trees, since a B-tree by its nature has to be balanced. No special treatment is needed in addition to building a tree: Building a B-tree balances it at the same time. Instead of using binary search trees, we may use B-trees of small order such as 2–4 trees. However, if these trees are implemented as structures similarly to B-trees, there are three locations per node to store up to three keys and four locations per node to store up to four references. In the worst case, half of these cells are unused, and on the average, 69% are unused. Since space is much more at a premium in main memory than in secondary storage, we would like to avoid this wasted space. Therefore, 2–4 trees are transformed into binary tree form in which each node holds only one key. Of course, the transformation has to be done in a way that permits an unambiguous restoration of the original B-tree form.

To represent a 2–4 tree as a binary tree, two types of links between nodes are used: One type indicates links between nodes representing keys belonging to the same node of a 2–4 tree, and another represents regular parent-children links. Bayer called

FIGURE **7.21**   (a) A 3-node represented (b–c) in two possible ways by red-black trees and (d–e) in two possible ways by horizontal-vertical trees. (f) A 4-node represented (g) by a red-black tree and (h) by a horizontal-vertical tree.

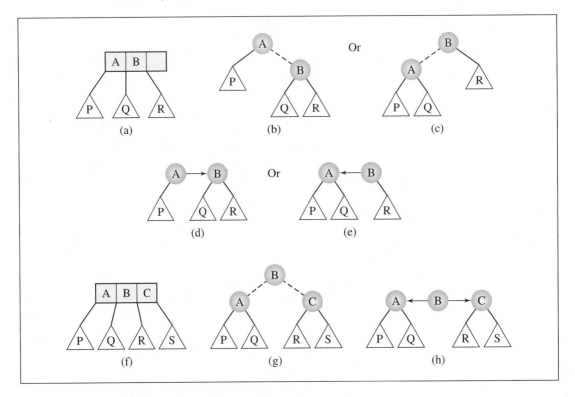

them *horizontal* and *vertical* pointers or, more cryptically, ρ-pointers and δ-pointers; Guibas and Sedgewick in their dichromatic framework use the names *red* and *black* pointers. Not only are the names different, but the trees are also drawn a bit differently. Figure 7.21 shows nodes with two and three keys, which are called *3-nodes* and *4-nodes*, and their equivalent representations. Figure 7.22 shows a complete 2–4 tree and its binary tree equivalents. Note that the red links are drawn with dashed lines. The red-black tree better represents the exact form of a binary tree; the horizontal-vertical trees are better in retaining the shape of 2–4 trees and in having leaves shown as though they were on the same level. Also, horizontal-vertical trees lend themselves easily to representing B-trees of any order, the red-black trees not so.

Both red-black trees and horizontal-vertical trees are binary trees. Each node has two references which can be interpreted in two ways. To make a distinction between the interpretation applied in a given context, a flag for each of the references is used.

The operations performed on horizontal-vertical trees should be the same as on binary trees, although their implementation is much more involved. Only searching is the same: To find a key in a horizontal-vertical tree, no distinction is made between

FIGURE **7.22**   (a) A 2–4 tree represented (b) by a red-black tree and (c) by a binary tree with horizontal and vertical pointers.

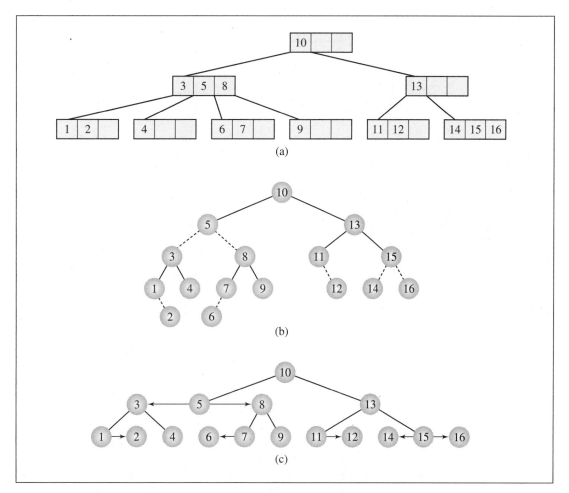

the different types of references. We can use the same searching procedure as for binary search trees: If the key is found, stop. If the key in the current node is larger than the one we are looking for, we go to the left subtree; otherwise, we go to the right subtree.

Before discussing insertion, note that horizontal-vertical trees have the following properties:

▲   The path from the root to any leaf contains the same number of vertical links.

▲   No path from the root can have two horizontal links in a row.

Insertions restructure the tree by adding one more node and one more link to the tree. Should it be a horizontal or vertical link? Deletions restructure the tree as well by

FIGURE **7.23**   (a–b) Split of a 4-node attached to a node with one key in a 2–4 tree. (c–d) The same split in a horizontal-vertical tree equivalent to these two nodes.

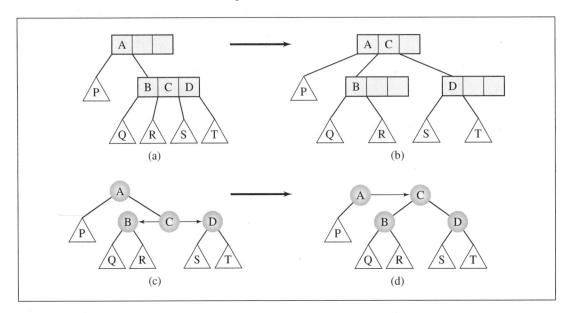

removing one node and one link, but this may lead to two consecutive horizontal links. These operations are not as straightforward as for binary search trees, since some counterparts of node splitting and node merging have to be represented in horizontal-vertical trees.

A good idea when splitting 2–4 trees, as already indicated in the discussion of B-trees is to split nodes when going down the tree while inserting a key. If a 4-node is encountered, it is split before descending further down the tree. Because this splitting is made from the top down, a 4-node can be a child of either a 2-node or a 3-node (with the usual exception: unless it is the root). Figures 7.23a and 7.23b contain an example. Splitting the node with keys *B, C,* and *D* requires creating a new node. The two nodes involved in splitting (Figure 7.23a) are 4/6 full and three nodes after splitting are 4/9 full (6/8 and 7/12, respectively, for reference fields). Splitting nodes in 2–4 trees results in poor performance. However, if the same operations are performed on their horizontal-vertical tree equivalents, the operation is remarkably efficient. In Figures 7.23c and 7.23d, the same split is performed on a horizontal-vertical tree, and the operation requires changing only two flags from horizontal to vertical and one from vertical to horizontal: Only three bits are reset!

Resetting these three flags suggests the following algorithm:

```
flagFlipping(node)
```
   if node's *both links are horizontal*
      reset the flag corresponding to the link from node's *parent to* node *to horizontal;*
      reset flags in node *to vertical;*

FIGURE **7.24**   (a–b) Split of a 4-node attached to a 3-node in a 2–4 tree and (c–d) a similar operation performed on one possible horizontal-vertical tree equivalent to these two nodes.

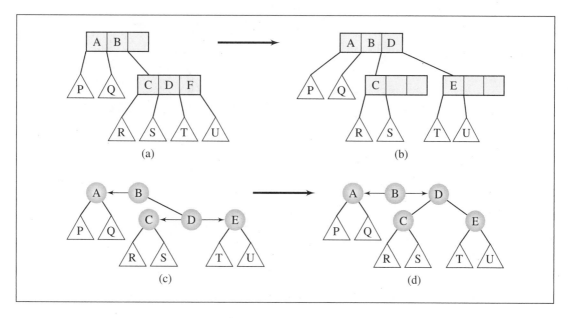

For the second case, when 4-node is a child of a 3-node and the links are as in Figure 7.24a, the split results in the 2–4 tree as in Figure 7.24b; applying *flagFlipping* to a horizontal-vertical tree equivalent requires that only three bits are reset (Figures 7.24c and 7.24d).

Figure 7.21 indicates that the same node of a 2–4 tree can have two equivalents in a horizontal-vertical tree. Therefore, the situation in Figure 7.24a can be reflected not only by the tree in Figure 7.24c, but also by the tree in Figure 7.24a. If we proceed as before, by changing three flags as in Figure 7.24d, the tree in Figure 7.25b ends up with two consecutive horizontal links, which has no counterpart in any 2–4 tree. In this case, the three flag flips have to be followed by a rotation; namely, node *B* is rotated about node *A*, two flags are flipped, and the tree in Figure 7.25c is the same as in Figure 7.24d.

Figure 7.26a contains another way in which a 4-node is attached to a 3-node in a 2–4 tree before splitting. Figure 7.26b shows the tree after splitting. Applying *flagFlipping* to the tree in Figure 7.26c yields the tree in Figure 7.26d with two consecutive horizontal links. To restore the horizontal-vertical tree property, two rotations and four flag flips are needed: Node *C* is rotated about node *E*, which is followed by two flag flips (Figure 7.26e), and then node *C* about node *A*, which is also followed by two flag flips. This all leads to the tree in Figure 7.26f.

We presented four configurations leading to a split. This number has to be doubled if the mirror images of the situation just analyzed are added. The number of special cases is rather high, and this fact is reflected in the following insertion algorithm.

FIGURE **7.25**   Fixing a horizontal-vertical tree that has consecutive horizontal links.

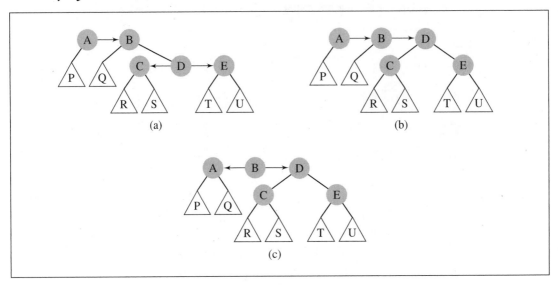

```
HVTreeInsert(K)
    create newNode and initialize it;
    if HVTree is empty
        root = newNode;
        return;
    for (p = root, prev = null; p != null;)
        if p has both flags set to 0  // horizontal
            set them to 1;            // vertical
                mark prev's link connecting it with p as 0;
            if links connecting parent of prev with prev and prev with p are both marked 0
                if both these links are left or both are right
                    rotate prev about its parent;
                else rotate p about prev and then p about its new parent;
            prev = p;
            if (p.key > K)
                p = p.left;
            else p = p.right;
    attach newNode to prev;
    mark prev's flag corresponding to its link to newNode to 0;
    if link from prev's parent to prev is marked 0
        rotate prev about its parent or
        first rotate newNode about prev and then newNode about its new parent;
```

FIGURE **7.26**   A 4-node attached to a 3-node in a 2–4 tree.

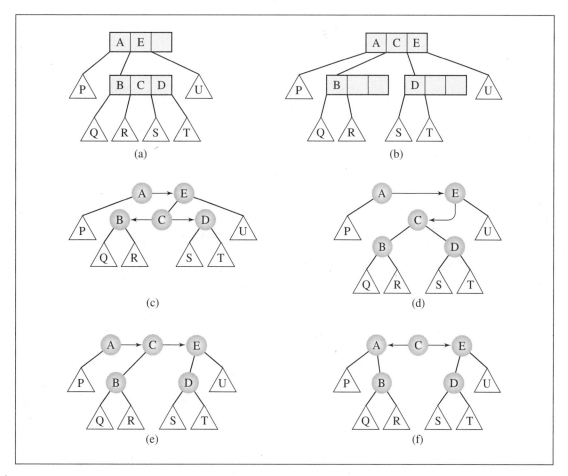

Figure 7.27 contains an example of inserting a sequence of numbers. Note that a double rotation has to be made in the tree in Figure 7.27h while 6 is being inserted. First, 9 is rotated about 5 and then 9 is rotated about 11.

How efficient is a horizontal-vertical tree in comparison with balanced trees? Since the minimum number n of nodes in a horizontal-vertical tree of height h is different for even and odd heights, the correspondence between n and h was proven to be

$$\lg(n+1) \le h \le 2\lg(n+2) - 2$$

The upper bound on the height of a horizontal-vertical tree is approximately 2 lg n, which is more than the same bound for AVL trees, 1.44 lg n. Hence, the

FIGURE **7.27**   Building a horizontal-vertical tree by inserting numbers in this sequence: 10, 11, 12, 13, 4, 5, 8, 9, 6, 14.

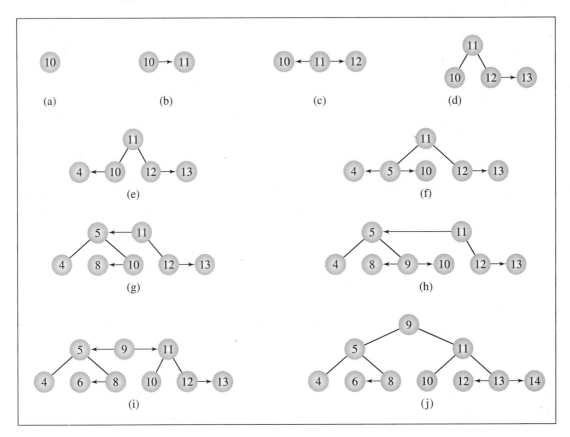

horizontal-vertical tree may appear less useful than an AVL tree. However, the horizontal-vertical tree requires less tree restructuring during node insertion than the AVL tree. Moreover, this restructuring may be limited to resetting only three bits, whereas in an AVL tree, at least one rotation has to take place when rebalancing the tree. Therefore, AVL trees are preferable in programs which require little tree restructuring and use the tree primarily for information retrieval. When, on the other hand, there is a great deal of node insertion and deletion, a horizontal-vertical tree is a more prudent choice.

The horizontal-vertical trees also include AVL trees. An AVL tree can be transformed into an horizontal-vertical tree by converting the links connecting the roots of subtrees of even height with children of these roots of odd height into horizontal links. Figure 7.28 illustrates this conversion.

FIGURE **7.28**   An example of converting (a) an AVL tree into (b) an equivalent horizontal-vertical tree.

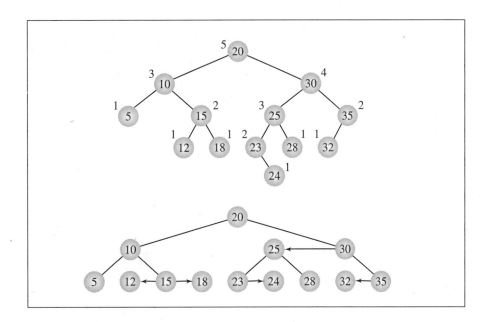

7.1.8 Sets in `java.util`

A set is an object that stores unique elements. In Java, there are two implementations available. The class `HashSet` implements the set with a hash table and a hash function (see Chapter 10). Another implementation is provided in the class `TreeSet`, which keeps elements of a set in a sorted order. Methods of `TreeSet` are listed in Figure 7.29. Most of the methods have already been encountered in classes `Vector` and `LinkedList`. However, because of the need for constant checking during insertion to determine whether an element being inserted is already in the set, the insertion operation has to be implemented specifically for that task. Although a vector could be a possible implementation of a set, the insertion operation requires $O(n)$ time to finish. For an unordered vector, all the elements of the vector have to be tested before an insertion takes place. For an ordered vector, checking whether an element is in the vector takes $O(\lg n)$ time with binary search, but a new element requires shifting all greater elements so that the new element can be placed in a proper cell of the vector, and the complexity of this operation in the worst case is $O(n)$. To speed up execution of insertion (and also deletion), `TreeSet` uses a red-black tree for implementation of a set. This guarantees $O(\lg n)$ time for insertion and deletion.

Class hierarchy in `java.util` is as follows

Object ⇒ AbstractCollection ⇒ AbstractSet ⇒ TreeSet

The operation of some methods for integer sets is illustrated in Figure 7.30.

FIGURE **7.29**   Methods of the class `TreeSet`.

Method	Operation
`void add(ob)`	insert object `ob` to the set if it is not already there
`boolean addAll(col)`	add all the elements from the collection `col` to the set; return `true` if the set was modified
`void clear()`	remove all the objects from the set
`Object clone()`	return the copy of the set without cloning its elements
`Comparator comparator()`	return the comparator used to order the set or `null` if the `compareTo()` method is defined for the elements of the set
`boolean contains(ob)`	return `true` if the set contains the object `ob`
`boolean containsAll(col)`	return `true` if the set contains all of the objects in the collection `col`
`boolean equals(set)`	return `true` if the current set and object `set` contain equal objects in the same order
`Object first()`	return the smallest object of the set
`SortedSet headSet(ob)`	return the subset with objects smaller than `ob`
`int hashCode()`	return the hash code for the set
`boolean isEmpty()`	return `true` if the set contains no elements, `false` otherwise
`Iterator iterator()`	generate and return an iterator for the set
`Object last()`	return the largest object of the set
`boolean remove(ob)`	remove the object `ob` from the set and return `true` if `ob` was in the set
`boolean removeAll(col)`	remove from the set all the objects contained in collection `col`; return `true` if any element was removed
`boolean retainAll(col)`	remove from the set all objects that are not in the collection `col`; return `true` if any object was removed
`int size()`	return the number of object in the set
`SortedSet subSet(first, last)`	return the subset of the set (not its copy) containing elements that are not smaller than `first` and smaller than `last`
`SortedSet tailSet(ob)`	return the subset with objects not smaller than `ob`
`Object[] toArray()`	copy all objects from the set to a newly created array and return the array
`Object[] toArray(arr[])`	copy all objects from the set to the array `arr` if `arr` is large enough or to a newly created array and return the array

FIGURE **7.29**   (*continued*)

`String toString()`	return a string representation of the set that contains the string representation of all the objects
`TreeSet()`	create an empty set for elements that implement `Comparable`
`TreeSet(col)`	create a set with copies of elements from collection `col` sorted according to the method `compareTo()`
`TreeSet(comp)`	create an empty set sorted according to the comparator `comp`
`TreeSet(sortedSet)`	create a set with copies of elements from `sortedSet` using the sorted set's order

FIGURE **7.30**   An example of application of the `TreeSet` methods.

```java
import java.io.*;
import java.util.TreeSet;

class Person {
    String name;
    int age;
    Person(String s, int i) {
        name = s; age = i;
    }
    Person() {
        this("",0);
    }
    public String toString() {
        return "(" + name + ", " + age  + ")";
    }
}

class PersonByName extends Person implements Comparable {
    PersonByName(String s, int i) {
        super(s,i);
    }
    PersonByName() {
        super();
    }
```

Continues

FIGURE **7.30**   (*continued*)

```
    PersonByName(Person p) {
        super(p.name,p.age);
    }
    public int compareTo(Object p) {
        return name.compareTo(((Person)p).name);
    }
}

class PersonByAge extends Person implements Comparable {
    PersonByAge(String s, int i) {
        super(s,i);
    }
    PersonByAge() {
        super();
    }
    PersonByAge(Person p) {
        super(p.name,p.age);
    }
    public int compareTo(Object p) {
        return age - ((Person)p).age;
    }
}

class PersonComparator implements java.util.Comparator {
    public int compare(Object ob1, Object ob2) {
        if (ob1 == ob2)
            return 0;
        else if(ob1 == null)
            return -1;
        else if (ob2 == null)
            return 1;
        else return ((Person)ob1).name.compareTo(((Person)ob2).name);
    }
}

class testSets {
    public static void main(String[] ar) {
        TreeSet set1 = new TreeSet();           // set1 = []
        set1.add(new Integer(4));               // set1 = [4]
        set1.add(new Integer(5));               // set1 = [4, 5]
        set1.add(new Integer(6));               // set1 = [4, 5, 6]
        set1.add(new Integer(5));               // set1 = [4, 5, 6]
        System.out.println("set1 = " + set1);// set1 = [4, 5, 6]
```

FIGURE **7.30** (*continued*)

```
        System.out.println(set1.contains(new Integer(5)));    // true
        System.out.println(set1.contains(new Integer(7)));    // false
        System.out.println(set1.first() + " " + set1.last()); // 4 6
        System.out.println(set1.headSet(new Integer(5)));    // [4]
        System.out.println(set1.tailSet(new Integer(5)));    // [5, 6]
        TreeSet set2 = new TreeSet(set1);      // set2 = [4, 5, 6]
        set2.remove(new Integer(5));           // set2 = [4, 6]
        set1.removeAll(set2);                  // set1 = [5]
        set1.addAll(set2);                     // set1 = [4, 5, 6]

        TreeSet pSet1 = new TreeSet(), pSet2 = new TreeSet();
        Person[] p = {new Person("Gregg",25), new Person("Ann",30),
                   new Person("Bill",20),  new Person("Gregg",35),
                   new Person("Kay",30)};
        for (int i = 0; i < p.length; i++)
            pSet1.add(new PersonByName(p[i]));
        // pSet1 = [(Ann,30), (Bill,20), (Gregg,25), (Kay,30)]
        for (int i = 0; i < p.length; i++)
            pSet2.add(new PersonByAge(p[i]));
        // pSet2 = [(Bill,20), (Gregg,25), (Ann,30), (Gregg,35)]
        java.util.Iterator it = pSet2.iterator();
        it.next();
        ((Person)it.next()).age = 50;
        // pSet2 = [(Bill,20), (Gregg,50), (Ann,30), (Gregg,35)]
        pSet2.add(new PersonByAge("Craig",40));
        // pSet2 = [(Bill,20), (Craig,40), (Gregg,50), (Ann,30), (Gregg,35)]
        for (int i = 0; i < p.length; i++)
            System.out.println(p[i] + " "
                                   + pSet2.contains(new PersonByAge(p[i])));
        // (Gregg,25) false
        // (Ann,30) false
        // (Bill,20) true
        // (Gregg,35) false
        // (Kay,30) false
        TreeSet pSet3 = new TreeSet(new PersonComparator());
        for (int i = 0; i < p.length; i++)
            pSet3.add(p[i]);
        pSet3.add(null);
        pSet3.add(null);
        System.out.println("pSet3 = " + pSet3);
        // pSet3 = [null, (Ann,30), (Bill,20), (Gregg,25), (Kay,30)]
    }
}
```

A new number is inserted into a set if it is not already there. For example, an attempt to insert number 5 into the set st1 = (4 5 6) is unsuccessful.

A more interesting situation arises for compound objects whose order is determined by the values of some of its fields. Consider the class Person defined in Figure 7.30. Any attempt to add a new object of type Person raises the ClassCastException. Because TreeSet is an ordered structure, an ordering relation must be provided to determine the order of elements in the set. For simple objects, such as objects of type Integer, the relation is already provided by the system. But for user-defined classes the relation has to be also user-defined.

For the class Person, which contains two fields—a string field name and an integer field age—the order of objects can be determined by the first field, by the second, or by both. For the sake of example, two classes are derived from Person—PersonByName and PersonByAge—which inherit the same data fields from Person but define the ordering relation differently. The definition is accomplished by defining the method compareTo() from interface Comparable. For this reason, both PersonByName and PersonByAge are declared as implementations of Comparable. Now, two sets are created, pSet1 with person objects ordered by name and pSet2 with objects ordered by age. For this reason, each name appears in pSet1 only once so that the object ("Gregg,"35) from the array p[ ] is not included, whereas in pSet2 each age is unique, so that object ("Kay,"30) is not included.

It is very important that operations on the objects in the set do not disturb the order of these elements in the set because it may adversely affect subsequent operations. For example, after changing the age of Gregg in pSet1 to 50, the object (Craig,40) is included in front of the updated object ("Gregg,"50). Moreover, searching may result in incorrect results. For all the objects from the array p[ ], only the one preceding the updated object is found. The remaining objects are considered absent from pSet1. The reason is the tree implementation of the set. For each node of the tree, the search decides whether to continue searching for a particular key in the left subtree or in the right subtree. After the key in the node is increased, the search is sometimes directed to left subteee, although before modification of the node, it would be directed to the right subtree.

Another concern is the inclusion of a null object in the set. An attempt to include a null object in pSet1 or pSet2 results in the NullPointerException. The reason is the syntax of the compareTo() method, which is ob1.compareTo(ob2). If ob1 is null, then the program crashes. To circumvent the problem, comparison must be introduced not as redefinition of compareTo() from Comparable, but as redefinition of compare() from class Comparator. The method compareTo() is redefined inside of a class that is used to generate objects. The method compare() is redefined outside of a class that is used to generate objects and inside a comparator class that implements the interface Comparator. In Figure 7.30, PersonComparator is defined to compare objects of type Person. To let the system know that compare() should be used instead of compareTo(), a new set is declared with the constructor TreeSet(comp), where comp is a comparator, not with TreeSet() as in the case of pSet1 and pSet2.

7.1.9 Maps in `java.util`

Maps are tables that can be indexed with any type of data. Hence, they are a generalization of arrays because arrays can be indexed only with constants and variables of ordinal types, such as characters and nonnegative integers, but not with strings or double numbers.

Maps use keys that are used as indexes and elements to be accessed through the keys. Like indexes in arrays, keys in maps are unique in that one key is associated with one element only. Thus, maps are also a generalization of sets. Like sets, maps are implemented as red-black trees. But unlike trees implementing sets that store elements only, trees implementing maps store pairs <key, element> called entries which can be operated on by methods specified in the interface `Map.Entry` (Figure 7.31a). The pairs are ordered by an ordering relation defined for keys, not for elements. Therefore, a particular element is found in the tree by locating a particular node using the key which is associated with this element and extracting the element in this node. Unlike in sets, elements can now be modified without disturbing the order in the tree, because the tree is ordered by keys, not elements, which also means that keys in the tree cannot be modified.

Methods of the class `TreeMap` are listed in Figure 7.31b. Class hierarchy in `java.util` is as follows

$$\texttt{Object} \Rightarrow \texttt{AbstractMap} \Rightarrow \texttt{TreeMap}$$

Operation of some methods for integer sets is illustrated in Figure 7.32. The map `cities` is indexed with objects of type `Person`. The map is initialized with three pairs <`Person` object, string>. The assignment

```
cities.put(new PersonByName("Gregg",30)] = "Austin";
```

FIGURE **7.31**   (a) Methods in the interface `Map.Entry`; (b) methods of the class `TreeMap`.

(a) Method	Operation
`boolean equals()`	return `true` if the map entry equals another object
`Object getKey()`	return the key of the map entry
`Object getValue()`	return the value of the map entry
`int hashCode()`	return the hash code for the map entry
`Object setValue(val)`	replace the value of the map entry by `val` and return the old value
(b) Method	**Operation**
`void clear()`	remove all the objects from the map
`Object clone()`	return the copy of the map without cloning its elements
`Comparator comparator()`	return the comparator used to order the map or `null` if the `compareTo()` method is defined for the elements of the map

FIGURE **7.31** *(continued)*

`boolean containsKey(key)`	return `true` if the map contains the object `key`; raise `NullPointerException` if `key` is null
`boolean containsValue(val)`	return `true` if the map contains the object `val`; raise `NullPointerException` if `val` is null
`Set entrySet()`	return a set containing all the pairs (key, value) in the map
`boolean equals(map)`	return `true` if the current map and object `map` contain equal objects in the same order
`Object firstKey()`	return the smallest key of the map
`Object get(key)`	return the object associated with `key`
`int hashCode()`	return the hash code for the map
`SortedMap headMap(key)`	return the submap with objects associated with keys not smaller than `key`
`boolean isEmpty()`	return `true` if the map contains no elements, `false` otherwise
`Set keySet()`	return a set containing all the keys of the map
`Object lastKey()`	return the largest object of the map
`Object put(key, value)`	put the pair (`key`, `value`) in the map; return a value associated with `key` if there is any in the map, `null` otherwise
`void putAll(map)`	add objects from `map` to the current map
`Object remove(key)`	remove the pair (`key`,value) from the map and return the value associated currently with `key` in the map or `null` otherwise
`int size()`	return the number of object in the map
`SortedMap subMap(first, last)`	return the submap of the map (not its copy) containing elements that are not smaller than `first` and smaller than `last`
`SortedMap tailMap(ob)`	return the submap with objects associated with keys smaller than key
`String toString()`	return a string representation of the map that contains the string representation of all the objects
`TreeMap()`	create an empty map for elements that implement `Comparable`
`TreeMap(m)`	create a map with copies of elements from map `m` sorted according to the method `compareTo()`
`TreeMap(comp)`	create an empty map sorted according to the comparator `comp`
`TreeMap(sortedMap)`	create a map with copies of elements from `sortedMap` using the sorted map's order
`Collection values()`	return `Collection` with all the values contained in the map

FIGURE **7.32**   An example of application of the `TreeMap` methods.

```java
import java.io.*;
import java.util.*;

class testMaps {
    public static void main(String[] ar) {
        TreeMap cities = new TreeMap();
        cities.put(new PersonByName("Gregg",25),"Pittsburgh");
        cities.put(new PersonByName("Ann",30),"Boston");
        cities.put(new PersonByName("Bill",20),"Belmont");
        System.out.println(cities);
        // {(Ann,30)=Boston, (Bill,20)=Belmont, (Gregg,25)=Pittsburgh}
        cities.put(new PersonByName("Gregg",30),"Austin");
        // cities = {(Ann,30)=Boston, (Bill,20)=Belmont, (Gregg,25)=Austin}
        System.out.println(cities.containsKey(new PersonByName("Ann",30)));
        // true
        System.out.println(cities.containsValue("Austin"));
        // true
        System.out.println(cities.firstKey() + " " + cities.lastKey());
        // (Ann,30) (Gregg,25)
        System.out.println(cities.get(new PersonByName("Ann",30)));
        // Boston
        System.out.println(cities.entrySet());
        // [(Ann,30)=Boston, (Bill,20)=Belmont, (Gregg,25)=Pittsburgh]
        System.out.println(cities.keySet());
        // [(Ann,30), (Bill,20), (Gregg,25)]
        System.out.println(cities.remove(new PersonByName("Bill",20)));
        // Belmont
        // cities = {(Ann,30)=Boston, (Gregg,25)=Pittsburgh}

        Map.Entry me = (Map.Entry)cities.entrySet().iterator().next();
        // first entry
        System.out.println(me.getKey());               // (Ann,30)
        System.out.println(me.getValue());             // Boston
        System.out.println(me.setValue("Harrisburg")); // Boston
        System.out.println(cities);
        // cities = {(Ann,30)=Harrisburg, (Gregg,25)=Pittsburgh}
    }
}
```

uses a new object as an index, but the subscript of the method `put()` is so defined for maps that it inserts the pair <key, element> if it is not in the map, as in the case of this assignment. Note that this time the object has a different value in the `age` field than the existing entry for Gregg in the map, but both `PersonByName("Gregg",25)` and `PersonByName("Gregg",30)` are treated as the same object because the definition of `compareTo()` in the definition of class `PersonByName` takes only the name field into account.

The program in Figure 7.32 illustrates the way the methods specified in the interface `Map.Entry` can be used. The set of entries of the underlying map can be created with the `entrySet()` method and then the `Map.Entry` methods can be applied individually to the desired entries. Note that updating the entry set returned by the `entrySet()` method affects the map itself.

The program in Figure 7.32 is shown only to illustrate unconventional indexing. For this particular example, it would probably be more natural to include a city as another data member in each object. A more useful example concerns social security numbers and objects of type `PersonByName`. If we wanted to create an array (or a vector) so that SSNs could be used as indexes, the array would need 1 billion cells because the largest SSN equals 999999999. But with maps, we can have only as many entries as the number of `PersonByName` objects used in the program. For example, we can declare a map `SSN`

```
TreeMap SSN = new TreeMap();
```

and then execute a number of assignments

```
SSN.put(new Integer(123456789), new PersonByName("Gregg",25));
SSN.put(new Integer(111111111), new PersonByName("Ann",30));
SSN.put(new Integer(222222222), new PersonByName("Bill",20));
```

In this way, `SSN` has only three entries, although keys are very large numbers

```
SSN = {111111111= ("Ann",20), 123456789=("Gregg",25), 222222222=("Bill", 20)}
```

Information is now very easily accessible and modifiable by using SSNs as the access keys.

⌐ 7.2 TRIES

The preceding chapter showed that traversing a binary tree was guided by full key comparisons; each node contained a key which was compared to another key to find a proper path through the tree. The discussion of prefix B-trees indicated that this is not necessary and that only a portion of a key is required to determine the path. However, finding a proper prefix became an issue, and maintaining prefixes of an acceptable form and size made the process for insertion and deletion more complicated than in standard B-trees. A tree that uses parts of the key to navigate the search is called a *trie*. The name of the tree is appropriate, as it is a portion of the word re*trie*val with convoluted pronunciation: To distinguish a tree from a trie in speech, trie is pronounced "try."

Each key is a sequence of characters, and a trie is organized around these characters rather than entire keys. For simplicity, assume that all the keys are made out of five capital letters: A, E, I, P, R. There are many words which can be generated out of these five letters, but our examples will use only a handful of them.

Figure 7.33 shows a trie for words which are indicated in the vertical rectangles; this form was first used by E. Fredkin. These rectangles represent the leaves of the trie, which are nodes with actual keys. The internal nodes can be viewed as arrays of references to subtries. At each level i, the position of the array is checked which corresponds to the ith letter of the key being processed. If the reference in this position is null, the key is not in the trie which may mean a failure or a signal for key insertion. If not, we continue processing until a leaf containing this key is found. For example, we check for the word "ERIE." At the first level of the trie, the reference corresponding to the first letter of this word, "E," is checked. The reference is not null, so we go to the second level of the trie, to the child of the root accessible from position "E"; now the reference in the position indicated by the second letter, "R," is tested. It is not null either, so we descend down the trie one more level. At the third level, the third letter, "I," is used to access a reference in this node. The reference refers to a leaf containing the word "ERIE." Thus, we conclude that the search is successful. If the desired word was "ERIIE," we would fail because we would access the same leaf as before, and obviously, the two words are different. If the word were "ERPIE," we would access the same node whose one leaf contains "ERIE," but this time "P" would be used to check the corresponding reference in the node. Since the reference is null, we would conclude that "ERPIE" is not in the trie.

There are at least two problems. First, how do we make a distinction between two words when one is a prefix of the other? For example, "ARE" is a prefix in "AREA." Thus, if we are looking for "ARE" in the trie, we must not follow the path leading to "AREA." To that end, a special character is used in each node guaranteed not to be used in any word, in this case, a sharp sign, "#." Now, while searching for "ARE" and after processing "A," "R," and "E," we find ourselves in a node at the fourth level of the trie, whose leaves are "ARE" and "AREA." Since we processed all letters of the key "ARE," we check the reference corresponding to the end of words, "#," and since it is not empty, we conclude that the word is in the trie.

This last example points to another problem. Is it really necessary to store entire words in the trie? After we reached the fourth level when searching for "ARE" and the reference for "#" is not null, do we have to go to the leaf to make a comparison between the key "ARE" and the contents of the leaf, also "ARE"? Not necessarily, and the example of prefix B-trees suggests the solution. The leaves may contain only the unprocessed suffices of the words.

This example restricted the number of letters used to five, but in a more realistic setting, all letters are used so that each node has 27 references (including "#"). The height of the trie is determined by the longest prefix, and for English words, the prefix should not be a long string. For most words, the matter is settled after several node visits, probably 5–7. This is true for 10,000 English words in the trie, and for 100,000. A corresponding perfectly balanced binary search tree for 10,000 words has a height $\lceil \lg 10{,}000 \rceil = 14$. Since most words are stored on the lowest levels of this tree, then on the average, the search takes 13 node visits. (The average path length in a perfectly balanced tree of height h is $\lceil \lg h \rceil - 2$.) This is double the number of visits in the trie.

FIGURE **7.33**   A trie of some words composed of the five letters A, E, I, R, and P. The sharp sign # indicates the end of a word which can be a prefix of another word.

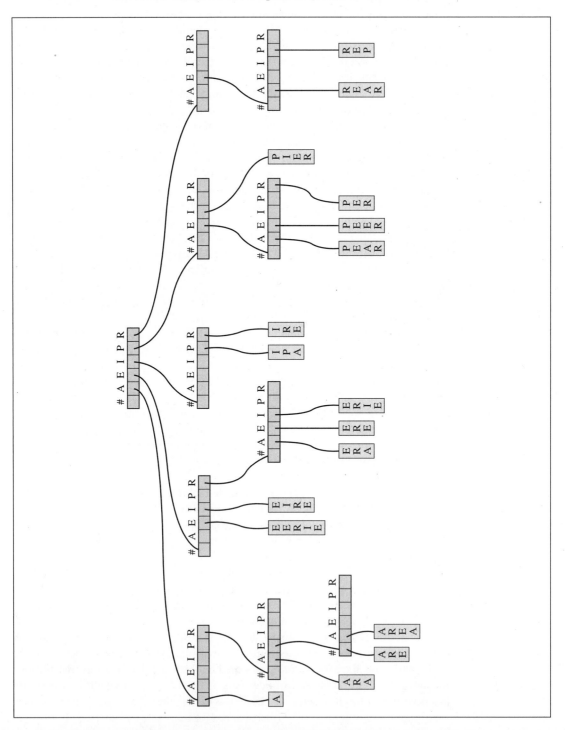

For 100,000 words, the average number of visits in the tree increases by 3 since $\lceil \lg 100,000 \rceil = 17$; in the trie this number can increase by 1 or 2. Besides, when making a comparison in the binary search tree, the comparison is made between the key searched for and the key in the current node, whereas in the trie only one character is used in each comparison except when comparing with a key in a leaf. Therefore, in situations where the speed of access is vital, such as in spell checkers, a trie is a very good choice.

Due to the fact that the trie has two types of nodes, inserting a key into a trie is a bit more complicated than inserting it into a binary search tree.

```
trieInsert(K)
    i = 0;
    p = the root;
    while not inserted
        if the end of word k is reached
            set the end-of-word marker in p to true;
        else if (p.ptrs[K[i]] == 0)
            create a leaf containing K and put its address in p.ptrs[K[i]];
        else if reference p.ptrs[K[i]] refers to a leaf
            K_L = key in leaf p.ptrs[K[i]]
            do create a nonleaf and put its address in p.ptrs[K[i]];
                p = the new nonleaf;
            while (K[i] == K_L[i++]);
            create a leaf containing K and put its address in p.ptrs[K[--i]];
            if the end of word k is reached
                set the end-of-word marker in p to true;
            else create a leaf containing K_L and put its address in p.ptrs[K_L[i]];
        else p = p.ptrs[K[i++]];
```

The inner do loop in this algorithm is needed when a prefix in the word K and in the word K_L is longer than the number of nodes in the path leading to the current node p. For example, before "REP" is inserted in the trie in Figure 7.33, the word "REAR" is stored in a leaf corresponding to the letter "R" of the root of the trie. If "REP" is now being inserted, it is not enough to replace this leaf by a nonleaf, since the second letters of both these words are the same letter "E." Hence, one more nonleaf has to be created on the third level of the trie, and two leaves containing the words "REAR" and "REP" are attached to this nonleaf.

If we compare tries with binary search trees, we see that for tries, the order in which keys are inserted is irrelevant, whereas this order determines the shape of binary search trees. However, tries can be skewed by words or, rather, by the type of prefixes in words being inserted. The length of the longest identical prefix in two words determines the height of the trie. Therefore, the height of the trie is equal to the length of the longest prefix common to two words plus one (for a level to discriminate between the words with this prefix) plus one (for the level of leaves). The trie in Figure 7.33 has height five since the longest identical prefix, "ARE," is merely three letters long.

The main problem tries pose is the amount of space they require; a substantial amount of this space is basically wasted. Many nodes may have only a couple of

FIGURE **7.34**   The trie in Figure 7.33 with all unused reference fields removed.

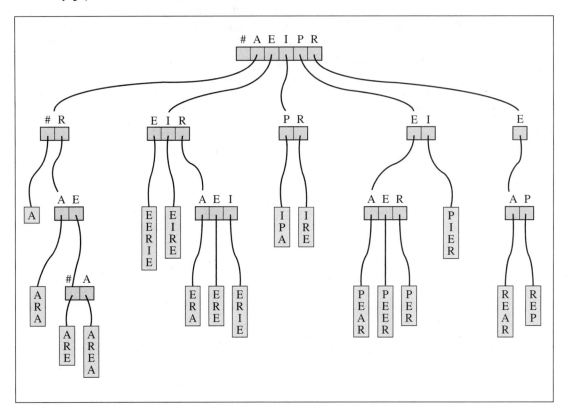

nonnull references, and yet the remaining 25 references must reside in memory. There is a burning need to decrease the amount of required space.

One way to reduce the size of a node is by storing only those references which are actually in use, as in Figure 7.34 (Briandais 1959). However, the introduced flexibility concerning the size of each node somewhat complicates the implementation. Such tries can be implemented in the spirit of 2–4 tree implementation. All sibling nodes can be put on a linked list accessible from the parent node, as in Figure 7.35. One node of the previous trie corresponds now to a linked list. This means that random access of references stored in arrays is no longer possible, and the linked lists have to be scanned sequentially, although not exhaustively, since alphabetical order is most likely maintained. The space requirements are not insignificant either because each node now contains two references.

Another way to reduce the space requirements is by changing the way words are tested (Rotwitt and Maine 1971). A trie *a tergo* can be built in which the reverses of words are inserted. In our example, the number of nodes is about the same, but a trie *a tergo* representation for such words as "logged," "loggerhead," "loggia," and "logging" has leaves on the third level, not on the seventh, as in a forward trie. Admittedly, for some frequently used endings, such as "tion," "ism," and "ics," the problem reappears.

FIGURE **7.35**   The trie from Figure 7.34 implemented as a binary tree.

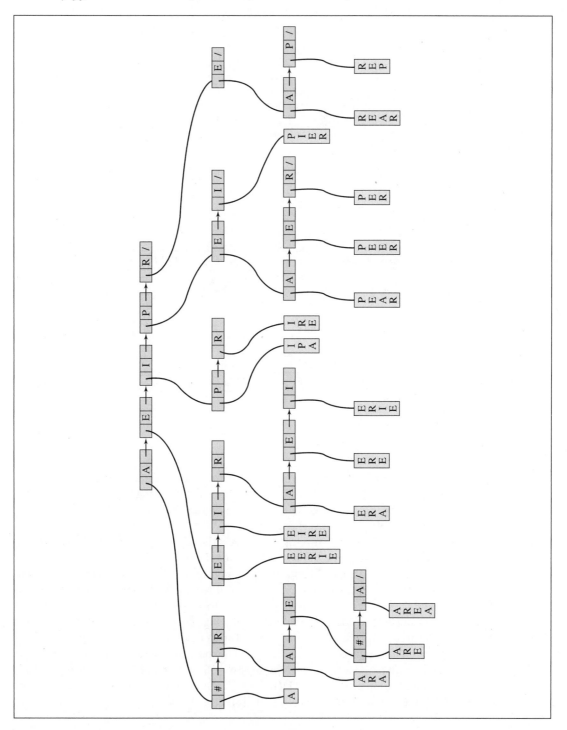

FIGURE **7.36**   A part of a trie (a) before and (b) after compression using the `compressTrie()` algorithm and (c) after compressing it in an optimal way.

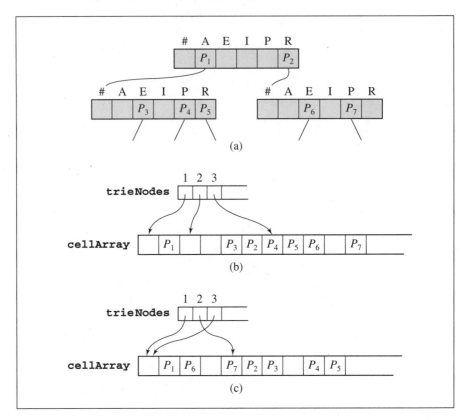

A variety of other orders can be considered, and checking every second character proved to be very useful (Bourne and Ford 1961), but solving the problem of an optimal order cannot be solved in its generality, since the problem turns out to be extremely complex (Comer and Sethi 1977).

Another way to save space is to compress the trie. One method creates a large cellArray out of all the arrays in all nonleaf nodes by interleaving these arrays so that the references remain intact. The starting positions of these arrays are recorded in the encompassing `cellArray`. For example, the three nodes shown in Figure 7.36a containing references p_1 through p_7 to other nodes of the trie (including leaves) are put one by one into `cellArray` in a nonconflicting way, as in Figure 7.36b. The problem is how to do that efficiently timewise and spacewise so that the algorithm is fast and the resulting array occupies substantially less space than all nonleaf nodes combined. In this example, all three nodes require $3 \cdot 6 = 18$ cells, and `cellArray` has 11 cells, so the compression rate is $(18 - 11)/18$, 39%. However, if the cells are stored as in Figure 7.36c, the compression rate is $(18 - 10)/18$, 44%.

It turns out that the algorithm which compresses the trie is exponential in the number of nodes and inapplicable for large tries. Other algorithms may not render the optimal compression rate but are faster (cf. Al-Suwaiyel and Horowitz 1984). One such algorithm is `compressTrie()`.

```
compressTrie()
    set to null all nodeNum*cellNum cells of cellArray;
    for each node
        for each position j of cellArray
            if after superimposing node on cellArray[j],···,cellArray[j+cellNum-1]
                no cell containing a reference is superimposed on a cell with a reference
            copy reference cells from node to corresponding cells starting from cellArray[j];
            record j in trieNodes as the position of node in cellArray;
            break;
```

This is the algorithm that was applied to the trie in Figure 7.36a to render the arrays in Figure 7.36b. Searching such a compressed trie is similar to searching a regular trie. However, node accesses are mediated through the array `trieNodes`. If $node_1$ refers to $node_2$, the position of $node_2$ has to be found in this array and then $node_2$ can be accessed in `cellArray`.

The problem with using a compressed trie is that the search can lead us astray. For instance, a search for a word starting with the letter P is immediately discontinued in the trie in Figure 7.36a, since the reference field corresponding to this letter in the root node is null. On the other hand, in the compressed version of the same trie (Figure 7.36b), in the field corresponding to P, reference P_3 can be found. But the misguided path is detected only after later encountering a null reference field or, after reaching a leaf, by comparing the key in this leaf with the key used in searching.

One more way to compress tries is by creating a C-trie which is a bit-version of the original trie (Maly 1976). In this method, the nodes of one level of the C-trie are stored in consecutive locations of memory, and the addresses of the first nodes of each level are stored in a table of addresses. Information stored in particular nodes allows us to access the children of these nodes by computing the offsets from these nodes to their children.

Each node has four fields: a leaf/nonleaf flag, end-of-word on/off field (which functions as our sharp-sign field), a K-field of *cellNum* bits corresponding to the cells with characters, and a C-field which gives the number of 1s in all the K-fields that are on the same level and precede this node. The latter integer is the number of nodes in the next level preceding the first child of this node.

The leaves store actual keys (or suffixes of keys) if they fit into the K-field+C-field. If not, the key is stored in some table and the leaf contains a reference to its position in this table. The end-of-word field is used to distinguish between these two cases. A fragment of the C-trie version of the trie from Figure 7.33 is shown in Figure 7.37. All nodes are the same size. It is assumed that the leaf can store up to three characters.

To search a key in the C-trie, the offsets have to be computed very carefully. Here is an outline of the algorithm:

FIGURE **7.37**　　A fragment of the C-trie representation of the trie from Figure 7.33.

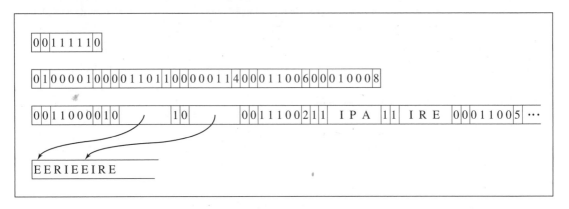

```
CTrieSearch(K)
    for (i = 1, p = the root; ; i++)
        if p is a leaf
            if K is equal to the key(p)
                success;
            else failure;
        else if the end of word k is reached
            if end-of-word field is on
                success;
            else failure;
        else if the bit corresponding to character K[i] is off
            failure;
        else p = address(the first node of level i+1)
                +C-field(p)* size(one node)  // to skip all children of nodes
                                             // in front of p on level i;
            +(number of 1-bits in K-field(p) to the left of the bit  // to skip
                corresponding to K[i])* size(one node)  // some children of p;
```

For example, to find "EERIE" in the C-trie in Figure 7.37, we first check in the root the bit corresponding to the first letter, "E." Since the bit is on and the root is not a leaf, we go to the second level. On the second level, the address of the node to be tested is determined by adding the address of the first node on this level to the length of one node, the first, in order to skip it. The bit of this nonleaf node corresponding to the second letter of our word, also an "E," is on, so we proceed to the third level. The address of the node to be tested is determined by adding the address of the first node of the third level to the size of one node (the first node of level three). We now access a leaf node with the end-of-word field set to 0. The table of words is accessed to make a comparison between the key looked for and the key in the table.

The compression is significant. One node of the original trie of 27 references of 2 bytes each occupies 54 bytes. One node of the C-trie requires $1 + 1 + 27 + 32 = 61$ bits which can be stored in 9 bytes. But it is not without a price. This algorithm requires putting nodes of one level tightly together, but storing one node at a time in memory by using new does not guarantee that the nodes are put in consecutive locations, especially in a multiuser environment. Therefore, the nodes from one level have to be generated first in temporary storage and only then can a chunk of memory be requested which is large enough to accommodate all these nodes. This problem also indicates that the C-trie is ill-suited for dynamic updates. If the trie is generated only once, the C-trie is an excellent variation to be utilized. If, however, the trie needs to be frequently updated, this technique for trie compression should be abandoned.

♠   7.3 Concluding Remarks

The survey of multiway trees in this chapter is by no means exhaustive. The number of different types of multiway trees is very large. Our intention is to highlight the variety of uses to which these trees can be applied and show how the same type of tree can be applied to different areas. Of particular interest is a B-tree with all its variations. B$^+$-trees are commonly used in the implementation of indexes in today's relational databases. They allow very fast random access to the data, and they also allow fast sequential processing of the data.

The application of B-trees is not limited to processing information from secondary storage, although it was the original motivation in introducing these trees. A variant of B-trees, 2–4 trees, although unsuitable for processing information in secondary storage, turns out to be very useful in processing information in memory.

Also of particular use are tries, a different type of tree. With many variations, they have a vast scope of applications, and our case study illustrates one very useful application of tries.

♠   7.4 Case Study: Spell Checker

An indispensable utility for any word processor is a spell checker which allows the user to find as many spelling mistakes as possible. Depending on the sophistication of the spell checker, the user may even see possible corrections. Spell checkers are used mostly in an interactive environment; the user can invoke them at any time when using the word processor, make corrections on the fly, and exit even before processing the entire file. This requires writing a word processing program and, in addition to it, a spell checker module. This case study focuses on the use of tries. Therefore, the spell checker will be a stand-alone program to be used outside a word processor. It will process a text file in batch mode not allowing word-by-word corrections after possible errors are detected.

The core of a spell checker is a data structure allowing efficient access to words in a dictionary. Such a dictionary most likely has thousands of words, so access has to be very fast to process a text file in a reasonable amount of time. Out of many possible

FIGURE **7.38**   An implementation of a trie that uses pseudoflexible arrays. The trie has the same words as the trie in Figure 7.33.

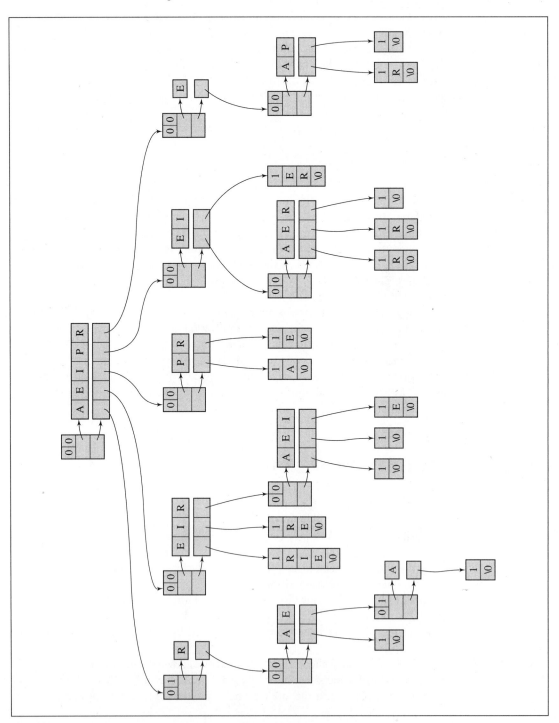

data structures, the trie is chosen to store the dictionary words. The trie is first created after the spell checker is invoked using the file dictionary, and afterward, the actual spell checking takes place.

For a large number of dictionary words, the size of the trie is very important because it should reside in main memory without recourse to virtual memory. But as we have already observed in this chapter, tries with fixed length nodes, as in Figure 7.33, are too wasteful. In most cases, only a fraction of the positions in each node is utilized, and the further away from the root, the smaller this fraction becomes (the root may be the only node with 26 children). Creating linked lists corresponding to all utilized letters for each node reduces wasted space, as in Figure 7.35. This approach has two disadvantages: The space required for the reference fields can be substantial, and the linked lists force us to use sequential search. An improvement over the last solution is to reserve only as much space as required by the letters used by each node without resorting to the use of linked lists. We could use the type Vector as an implementation of flexible arrays (arrays automatically growable), but it incurs an additional overhead: Vectors store objects. Thus, to store an integer in one, the integer has to be cast to the Integer class and then stored. The same is true for extracting values from vectors. Therefore, we will use pseudoflexible arrays by substituting larger arrays for existing arrays, copying the content of the old arrays to the new, and returning the old arrays to the operating system.

The key to the use of such pseudoflexible arrays is the implementation of a node. There are three types of nodes: TrieNode with leaf/nonleaf flag and its subclasses, TrieLeaf and TrieNonLeaf. TrieNonLeaf node has three fields: an end-of-word flag, a reference to a string, and a reference to an array of references to an array of nodes. These references can be references to both leaves and nonleaves, and this is a reason why the superclass TrieNode is also used. The array is declared as an array of TrieNode so that assigning instances of its subclasses does not cause a compilation error. Figure 7.38 contains the trie utilizing the nodes of this structure. If a string attached to a certain node has to be extended, a new string is created which contains the contents of the old string with a new letter inserted into the proper position, a function performed by addCell(). The letters in each node are kept in alphabetical order.

The method insert() is an implementation of the algorithm trieInsert() discussed earlier in this chapter. Since the position of each letter may vary from one node to another, this position has to be determined each time, a function performed by position(). Should a letter be absent in a node, position() returns –1, which allows insert() to undertake the proper action.

Also, the discussion of tries in this chapter assumed that the leaves of the tries store full keys. This is not necessary because the prefixes of all words are implicitly stored in the trie and can be reconstructed by garnering all the letters on the path leading to the leaf. For example, to access the leaf with the word "ERIE," two nonleaves have to be passed though references corresponding to the letters "E" and "R." Therefore, it is enough to store the suffix "IE" in the leaf instead of the entire word "ERIE." By doing this, only 13 letters of suffixes of these words have to be retained in these leaves out of the 58 letters stored in all leaves of the trie in Figure 7.33, a substantial improvement.

We also included the method sideView(), which prints the content of a trie sideways. The output generated by this method when applied to the trie in Figure 7.38 is as follows:

```
          >>REP|
           >REA|R
         >PI|ER
          >>PER|
           >PEE|R
           >PEA|R
        >IR|E
        >IP|A
          >ERI|E
         >>ERE|
         >>ERA|
       >EI|RE
       >EE|RIE
            >>AREA|
            >>ARE||
          >>ARA|
      >>A||
```

Two angle brackets and a single vertical bar at the end indicate words for which the endOfWord flag has been set in a corresponding node and, with two vertical bars indicate words that have an empty leaf. The vertical bar in remaining words separates a prefix reconstructed when scanning the trie and a suffix that was extracted from a leaf.

Spell checking works in a straightforward fashion by examining each word of a text file and printing out all misspelled words along with the line numbers where the misspelled words are found. Figure 7.39 contains the complete code of the spell checker.

FIGURE **7.39**   Implementation of a spell checker using tries.

```
/*********************  Trie.java  *****************************
 *
 */

class TrieNode {
    boolean isLeaf;
}

class TrieNonLeaf extends TrieNode {
    boolean endOfWord = false;
    String letters;
    TrieNode[] ptrs = new TrieNode[1];
    TrieNonLeaf() {
        isLeaf = false;
    }
```

FIGURE **7.39**   *(continued)*

```
    TrieNonLeaf(char ch) {
        letters = new String();
        letters += ch;
        isLeaf = false;
    }
}

class TrieLeaf extends TrieNode {
    String suffix;
    TrieLeaf() {
        isLeaf = true;
    }
    TrieLeaf(String suffix) {
        this.suffix = new String(suffix);
        isLeaf = true;
    }
}

class Trie {
    protected TrieNonLeaf root;
    protected final int notFound = -1;
    public Trie() {
    }
    public Trie(String word) {
        root = new TrieNonLeaf(word.charAt(0)); // initialize the root
        createLeaf(word.charAt(0),word.substring(1),root); // to avoid later
    }                                               // test;
    public void sideView() {
        sideView(0,root,new String()); // assumption: the root is not null;
    }
    protected void sideView(int depth, TrieNode p, String prefix) {
        if (p.isLeaf) {
            for (int j = 1; j <= depth; j++)
                System.out.print("   ");
            System.out.println(" >" + prefix + "|" + ((TrieLeaf)p).suffix);
        }
        else {
            for (int i = ((TrieNonLeaf)p).letters.length()-1; i >= 0; i--) {
                if (((TrieNonLeaf)p).ptrs[i] != null) {
                    // add the letter corresponding to position i to prefix;
                    prefix = prefix.substring(0,depth) +
```

Continues

FIGURE **7.39**   *(continued)*

```
                        ((TrieNonLeaf)p).letters.charAt(i);
                  sideView(depth+1,((TrieNonLeaf)p).ptrs[i],prefix);
            }
            else { // if empty leaf;
                for (int j = 1; j <= depth+1; j++)
                    System.out.print("  ");
                System.out.println(">>" + prefix.substring(0,depth) +
                        ((TrieNonLeaf)p).letters.charAt(i) + "|");
            }
        }
        if (((TrieNonLeaf)p).endOfWord) {
            for (int j = 1; j <= depth+1; j++)
                System.out.print("  ");
            System.out.println(">>" + prefix.substring(0,depth) + "||");
        }
    }
}
protected int position(TrieNonLeaf p, char ch) {
    int i = 0;
    for ( ; i < p.letters.length() && p.letters.charAt(i) != ch; i++);
    if (i < p.letters.length())
         return i;
    else return notFound;
}
public boolean found(String word) {
    TrieNode p = root;
    int pos, i = 0;
    while (true)
        if (p.isLeaf) {                    // node p is a leaf
            TrieLeaf lf = (TrieLeaf) p;    // where the matching
            if (word.substring(i).equals(lf.suffix)) // suffix of
                return true;               // word should be found;
            else return false;
        }
        else if ((pos = position((TrieNonLeaf)p,word.charAt(i))) != notFound
                && i+1 == word.length())   // the end of word has to
            if (((TrieNonLeaf)p).ptrs[pos] == null) // correspond with
                return true;               // an empty leaf
            else if(!(((TrieNonLeaf)p).ptrs[pos]).isLeaf &&
                    ((TrieNonLeaf)((TrieNonLeaf)p).ptrs[pos]).endOfWord)
                return true;               // or the endOfWord marker on;
            else return false;
```

FIGURE **7.39**   *(continued)*

```
            else if (pos != notFound && ((TrieNonLeaf)p).ptrs[pos] != null) {
                p = ((TrieNonLeaf)p).ptrs[pos];// continue path,
                i++;                          // if possible,
            }
            else return false;                       // otherwise failure;
    }
    protected void addCell(char ch, TrieNonLeaf p, int stop) {
        int i;
        int len = p.letters.length();
        char[] s = new char[len+1];
        TrieNode[] tmp = p.ptrs;
        p.ptrs = new TrieNode[len+1];
        for (i = 0; i < len+1; i++)
            p.ptrs[i] = null;
        if (stop < len)           // if ch does not follow all letters in p,
            for (i = len; i >= stop+1; i--) { // copy from tmp letters > ch;
                p.ptrs[i] = tmp[i-1];
                s[i] = p.letters.charAt(i-1);
            }
        s[stop] = ch;
        for (i = stop-1; i >= 0; i--) {        // and letters < ch;
            p.ptrs[i] = tmp[i];
            s[i] = p.letters.charAt(i);
        }
        p.letters = new String(s);
    }
    protected void createLeaf(char ch, String suffix, TrieNonLeaf p) {
        int pos = position(p,ch);
        TrieLeaf lf = null;
        if (suffix != null && suffix.length() > 0) // don't create any leaf
            lf = new TrieLeaf(suffix);              // if there is no suffix;
        if (pos == notFound) {
            for (pos = 0; pos < p.letters.length() &&
                         p.letters.charAt(pos) < ch; pos++);
            addCell(ch,p,pos);
        }
        p.ptrs[pos] = lf;
    }
    public void insert(String word) {
        TrieNonLeaf p = root;
        TrieLeaf lf;
```

Continues

FIGURE **7.39**   *(continued)*

```
    int offset, pos, i = 0;
    while (true) {
        if (i == word.length()) {       // if the end of word reached, then
            if (p.endOfWord)            // set endOfWord to true;
                System.out.println("duplicate entry1: " + word);
            p.endOfWord = true;        // set endOfWord to true;
            return;
        }                              // if position in p indicated
        pos = position(p,word.charAt(i));
        if (pos == notFound) {         // by the first letter of word
            createLeaf(word.charAt(i),word.substring(i+1),p);
                                       // does not exist, create
            return;                    // a leaf and store in it the
        }                              // unprocessed suffix of word;
        else if (pos != notFound &&    // empty leaf in position pos;
                p.ptrs[pos] == null) {
            if (i+1 == word.length()) {
                System.out.println("duplicate entry1: " + word);
                return;
            }
            p.ptrs[pos] = new TrieNonLeaf(word.charAt(i+1));
            ((TrieNonLeaf)(p.ptrs[pos])).endOfWord = true;
            // check whether there is any suffix left:
            String s = (word.length() > i+2) ? word.substring(i+2) : null;
            createLeaf(word.charAt(i+1),s,(TrieNonLeaf)(p.ptrs[pos]));
            return;
        }
        else if (pos != notFound &&     // if position pos is
                p.ptrs[pos].isLeaf) {   // occupied by a leaf,
            lf = (TrieLeaf) p.ptrs[pos]; // hold this leaf;
            if (lf.suffix.equals(word.substring(i+1))) {
                System.out.println("duplicate entry2: " + word);
                return;
            }
            offset = 0;
            // create as many nonleaves as the length of identical
            // prefix of word and the string in the leaf (for cell 'R',
            // leaf "EP", and word "REAR", two such nodes are created);
            do {
                pos = position(p,word.charAt(i+offset));
                // word = "ABC", leaf = "ABCDEF" => leaf = "DEF";
                if (word.length() == i+offset+1) {
                    p.ptrs[pos] = new TrieNonLeaf(lf.suffix.charAt(offset));
```

FIGURE **7.39**   *(continued)*

```
                    p = (TrieNonLeaf) p.ptrs[pos];
                    p.endOfWord = true;
                    createLeaf(lf.suffix.charAt(offset),
                              lf.suffix.substring(offset+1),p);
                    return;
                }
                // word = "ABCDEF", leaf = "ABC" => leaf = "DEF";
                else if (lf.suffix.length() == offset ) {
                    p.ptrs[pos] = new TrieNonLeaf(word.charAt(i+offset+1));
                    p = (TrieNonLeaf) p.ptrs[pos];
                    p.endOfWord = true;
                    createLeaf(word.charAt(i+offset+1),
                              word.substring(i+offset+2),p);
                    return;
                }
                p.ptrs[pos] = new TrieNonLeaf(word.charAt(i+offset+1));
                p = (TrieNonLeaf) p.ptrs[pos];
                offset++;
            } while (word.charAt(i+offset) == lf.suffix.charAt(offset-1));
            offset--;
            // word = "ABCDEF", leaf = "ABCPQR" =>
            //     leaf('D') = "EF", leaf('P') = "QR";
            // check whether there is any suffix left:
            // word = "ABCD", leaf = "ABCPQR" =>
            //     leaf('D') = null, leaf('P') = "QR";
            String s = null;
            if (word.length() > i+offset+2)
                s = word.substring(i+offset+2);
            createLeaf(word.charAt(i+offset+1),s,p);
            // check whether there is any suffix left:
            // word = "ABCDEF", leaf = "ABCP" =>
            //     leaf('D') = "EF", leaf('P') = null;
            if (lf.suffix.length() > offset+1)
                s = lf.suffix.substring(offset+1);
            else s = null;
            createLeaf(lf.suffix.charAt(offset),s,p);
            return;
        }
        else {
            p = (TrieNonLeaf) p.ptrs[pos];
            i++;
```

Figure **7.39**   *(continued)*

```
            }
        }
    }
}

/*********************  SpellCheck.java  *****************************
 *
 */

import java.io.*;

class SpellCheck {
    static int lineNum = 1;
    static String s;
    static int ch;
    static void readWord(InputStream fIn) {
        try {
            while (true)
                if (ch > -1 && !Character.isLetter((char)ch)) { // skip
                    ch = fIn.read();                     // nonletters;
                    if (ch == '\n')
                        lineNum++;
                }
                else break;
            if (ch == -1)
                return;
            s = "";
            while (ch > -1 && Character.isLetter((char)ch)) {
                s += Character.toUpperCase((char)ch);
                ch = fIn.read();
            }
        } catch (IOException io) {
            System.out.println("Problem with input.");
        }
    }
    static public void main(String args[]) {
        String fileName = "";
        InputStream fIn, dictionary;
        InputStreamReader isr = new InputStreamReader(System.in);
        BufferedReader buffer = new BufferedReader(isr);
        Trie trie = null;
        try {
```

FIGURE **7.39**   *(continued)*

```
            dictionary = new FileInputStream("dictionary");
            readWord(dictionary);
            trie = new Trie(s.toUpperCase());  // initialize root;
            while (ch > -1) {
                readWord(dictionary);
                if (ch == -1)
                    break;
                trie.insert(s);
            }
            dictionary.close();
        } catch(IOException io) {
            System.err.println("Cannot open dictionary");
        }
        System.out.println("\nTrie sideview: ");
        trie.sideView();
        ch = ' ';
        lineNum = 1;
        try {
            if (args.length == 0) {
                System.out.print("Enter a file name: ");
                fileName = buffer.readLine();
                fIn = new FileInputStream(fileName);
            }
            else {
                fIn = new FileInputStream(args[0]);
                fileName = args[0];
            }
            System.out.println("Misspelled words:");
            while (true) {
                readWord(fIn);
                if (ch == -1)
                    break;
                if (!trie.found(s))
                    System.out.println(s + " on line " + lineNum);
            }
            fIn.close();
        } catch(IOException io) {
            System.err.println("Cannot open " + fileName);
        }
    }
}
```

⬛ 7.5 EXERCISES

1. What is the maximum number of nodes in a multiway tree of height h?

2. How many keys can a B-tree of order m and of height h hold?

3. Write a method that prints out the contents of a B-tree in ascending order.

4. The root of a B*-tree requires special attention since it has no sibling. A split does not render two nodes two-thirds full plus a new root with one key. Suggest some solutions to this problem.

5. Are B-trees immune to the order of the incoming data? Construct B-trees of order 3 (two keys per node) first for the sequence 1, 5, 3, 2, 4 and then for the sequence 1, 2, 3, 4, 5. Is it better to initialize B-trees with ordered data or with data in random order?

6. Draw all ten different B-trees of order 3 which can store 15 keys and make a table that for each of these trees shows the number of nodes and the average number of visited nodes (Rosenberg and Snyder 1981). What generalization can you make about them? Would this table indicate that (a) the smaller the number of nodes, the smaller the average number of visited nodes and (b) the smaller the average number of visited nodes, the smaller the number of nodes? What characteristics of the B-tree should we concentrate on to make them more efficient?

7. In all our considerations concerning B-trees, we assumed that the keys are unique. However, this does not have to be the case since multiple occurrences of the same key in a B-tree do not violate the B-tree property. If these keys refer to different objects in the data file (e.g., if the key is a name, and many people can have the same name), how would you implement such data file references?

8. What is the maximum height of a B^+-tree with n keys?

9. Occasionally, in a simple prefix B^+-tree, a separator can be as large as a key in a leaf. For example, if the last key in one leaf is "Herman" and the first key in the next leaf is "Hermann," then "Hermann" must be chosen as a separator in the parent of these leaves. Suggest a procedure to enforce the shorter separator.

10. Write a method that determines the shortest separator for two keys in a simple prefix B^+-tree.

11. Is it a good idea to use abbreviated forms of prefixes in the leaves of prefix B^+-trees?

12. If in two different positions, i and j, $i < j$, of a leaf in a bit-tree two D-bits are found such that $D_j = D_i$, what is the condition on at least one of the D-bits D_k for $i < k < j$?

13. If key K_i is deleted from a leaf of a bit-tree, then the D-bit between K_{i-1} and K_{i+1} has to be modified. What is the value of this D-bit if the values D_i and D_{i+1} are known? Make deletions in the leaf in Figure 7.17 to make an educated guess and then generalize this observation. In making a generalization, consider two cases: (a) $D_i < D_{i+1}$ and (b) $D_i > D_{i+1}$.

14. Write an algorithm that, for an R-tree, finds all entries in the leaves whose rectangles overlap a search rectangle *R*.

15. In the discussion of B-trees, which are comparable in efficiency to binary search trees, why are only B-trees of small order used and not B-trees of large order?

16. What is the worst case of inserting a key into a 2–4 tree?

17. What is the complexity of the `compressTrie()` algorithm in the worst case?

18. Can the leaves of the trie compressed with `compressTrie()` still have abbreviated versions of the words, namely, parts which are not included in the nonterminal nodes?

19. In the examples of tries analyzed in this chapter, we dealt with only 26 capital letters. A more realistic setting includes lowercase letters as well. However, some words require a capital letter at the beginning (names), and some require the entire word to be capitalized (acronyms). How can we solve this problem without including both lowercase and capital letters in the nodes?

20. A variant of a trie is a *digital tree* which processes information on the level of bits. Since there are only two bits, only two outcomes are possible. Digital trees are binary. For example, to test whether the word "BOOK" is in the tree, we do not use the first letter, "B," in the root to determine to which of its children we should go, but the first bit, 0, of the first letter (ASCII(B) = 01000010), on the second level, the second bit, and so on before we get to the second letter. Is it a good idea to use a digital tree for a spell checking program, as was discussed in the case study?

⌨ 7.6 Programming Assignments

1. Extend our spell checking program to suggest the proper spelling of a misspelled word. Consider these types of misspellings: changing the order of letters (copmuter), omitting a letter (computr), adding a letter (compueter), dittography, i.e., repeating a letter (computter), and changing a letter (compurer). For example, if the letter *i* is exchanged with the letter *i* + 1, then the level *i* of the trie should be processed before level *i* + 1.

2. A *point quadtree* is a 4-way tree used to represent points on a plane (Samet 1989). A node contains a pair of coordinates (*latitude,longitude*) and references to four children which represent four quadrants, NW, NE, SW, and SE. These quadrants are generated by the intersection of the vertical and horizontal lines passing through point (*lat,lon*) of the plane. Write a program that accepts the names of cities and their geographical locations (*lat,lon*) and inserts them into the quadtree. Then, the program should give the names of all cities located within distance *d* from a location (*Lat,Lon*) or, alternatively, within distance *d* from a city *C*.

Figure 7.40 contains an example. Locations on the map in Figure 7.40a are inserted into the quadtree in Figure 7.40b in the order indicated by the encircled numbers shown next to the city names. For instance, when inserting Pittsburgh into the quadtree, we check in which direction it is with respect to the root. The root stores the

FIGURE **7.40** A map indicating (a) coordinates of some cities and (b) a quadtree containing the same cities.

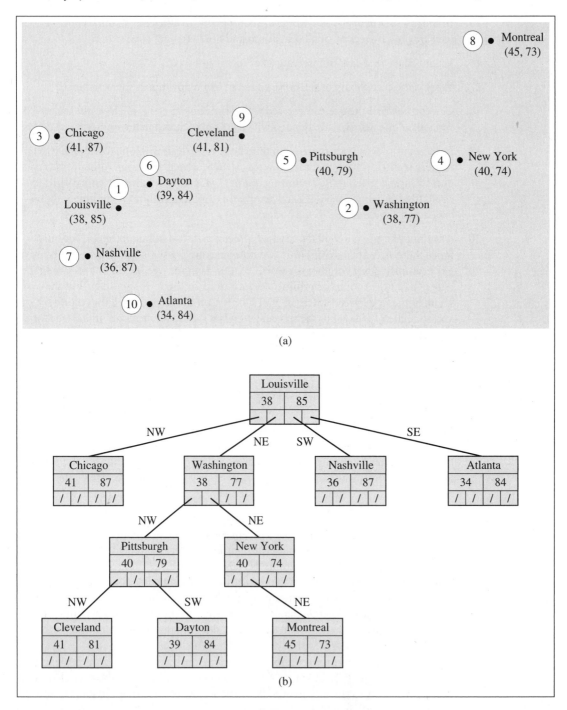

(a)

(b)

FIGURE **7.41** (a) A trie with words having long identical prefixes and (b) a Patricia tree with the same words.

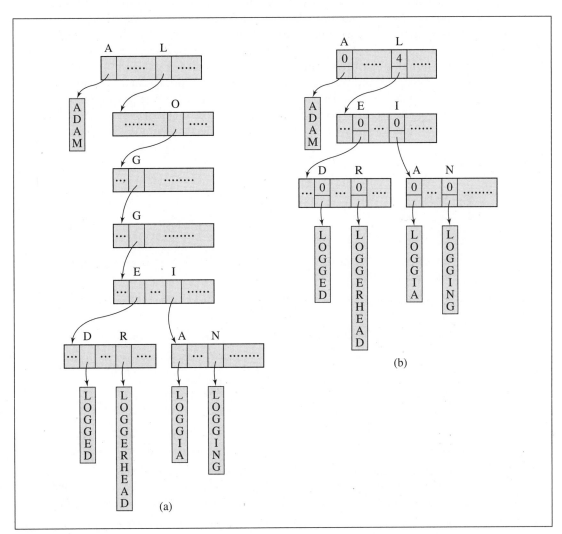

coordinates of Louisville, and Pittsburgh is NE from it; that is, it belongs to the second child of the root. But this child already stores a city, Washington. Therefore, we ask the same question concerning Pittsburgh with respect to the current node, the second child of the root: In which direction with respect to this city is Pittsburgh? This time the answer is NW. Therefore, we go to the first child of the current node. The child is a null node, and therefore, the Pittsburgh node can be inserted here.

3. Figure 7.33 indicates one source of inefficiency for tries: The path to "REAR" and "REP" leads through a node which has just one child. For longer identical prefixes, the number of such nodes can be even longer. Implement a spell checker with a variation of the trie, called the *multiway Patricia tree* (Morrison 1968),[4] which curtails the paths in the trie by avoiding nodes with only one child. It does this by indicating for each branch how many characters should be skipped to make a test. For example, a trie from Figure 7.41a is transformed into a Patricia tree in Figure 7.41b. The paths leading to the four words with prefix "LOGG" are shortened at the cost of recording in each node the number of characters to be omitted starting from the current position in a string. Now, because certain characters are not tested along the way, the final test should be between a key searched for and the *entire* key found in a specific leaf.

Bibliography

B-Trees

Bayer, R., "Symmetric Binary B-Trees: Data Structures and Maintenance Algorithms," *Acta Informatica* 1 (1972), 290–306.

Bayer, R. and McCreight, E., "Organization and Maintenance of Large Ordered Indexes," *Acta Informatica* 1 (1972), 173–189.

Bayer, Rudolf and Unterauer, Karl, "Prefix B-Trees," *ACM Transactions on Database Systems* 2 (1977), 11–26.

Comer, Douglas, "The Ubiquitous B-Tree," *Computing Surveys* 11 (1979), 121–137.

Ferguson, David E., "Bit-Tree: A Data Structure for Fast File Processing," *Communications of the ACM* 35 (1992), No. 6, 114–120.

Folk, Michael J., Zoellick, Bill, and Riccardi, Greg, *File Structures: An Object-Oriented Approach with C++,* Reading, MA: Addison-Wesley, 1998, Chs. 9, 10.

Guibas, L. J., and Sedgwick, R., A Dichromatic Framework for Balanced Trees, *Proceedings of the 19th Annual IEEE Symposium on the Foundation of Computer Science* 1978, 8–21.

Guttman, Antonin, "R-Trees: A Dynamic Index Structure for Spatial Searching," *ACM SIGMOD '84 Proc. of Annual Meeting, SIGMOD Record* 14 (1984), 47–57 [also in Stonebraker, Michael (ed.), *Readings in Database Systems,* San Mateo CA: Kaufmann, 1988, 599–609].

Johnson, Theodore and Shasha, Dennis, "B-Trees with Inserts and Deletes: Why Free-at-Empty Is Better Than Merge-at-Half," *Journal of Computer and System Sciences* 47 (1993) 45–76.

Leung, Clement H. C., Approximate Storage Utilization of B-trees: A Simple Derivation and Generalizations, *Information Processing Letters* 19 (1984), 199–201.

McCreight, Edward M., "Pagination of B*-Trees with Variable-Length Records," *Communications of the ACM* 20 (1977), 670–674.

Rosenberg, Arnold L. and Snyder, Lawrence, "Time- and Space-Optimality in B-Trees," *ACM Transactions on Database Systems* 6 (1981), 174–193.

---

[4] The original Patricia tree was a binary tree, and the test were made on the level of bits.

Sedgewick, Robert, *Algorithms,* Reading, MA: Addison-Wesley, 1988, Ch. 15.

Sellis, Timos, Roussopoulos, Nick, and Faloutsos, Christos, "The R$^+$-Tree: A Dynamic Index for Multi-Dimensional Objects," *Proceedings of the 13th Conference on Very Large Databases* (1987), 507–518.

Stonebraker, M., Sellis, T. and Hanson, E., "Analysis of Rule Indexing Implementations in Data Base Systems," *Proceedings of the First International Conference on Expert Database Systems,* Charleston, SC, 1986, 353–364.

Wedekind, H., "On the Selection of Access Paths in a Data Base System," in Klimbie, J. W. and Koffeman, K. L. (eds.), *Data Base Management,* Amsterdam: North-Holland, 1974, 385–397.

Yao, Andrew Chi-Chih, "On Random 2–3 Trees," *Acta Informatica* 9 (1978), 159–170.

Tries

Al-Suwaiyel, M. and Horowitz, E., "Algorithms for Trie Compaction," *ACM Transactions on Database Systems* 9 (1984), 243–263.

Bourne, Charles P. and Ford, Donald F., "A Study of Methods for Systematically Abbreviating English Words and Names," *Journal of the ACM* 8 (1961), 538–552.

de la Briandais, Rene, "File Searching Using Variable Length Keys," *Proceedings of the Western Joint Computer Conference,* 1959, 295–298.

Comer, Douglas and Sethi, Ravi, "The Complexity of Trie Index Construction," *Journal of the ACM* 24 (1977), 428–440.

Fredkin, Edward, "Trie Memory," *Communications of the ACM* 3 (1960), 490–499.

Maly, Kurt, "Compressed Tries," *Communications of the ACM* 19 (1976), 409–415.

Morrison, Donald R., "Patricia Trees," *Journal of the ACM* 15 (1968), 514–534.

Rotwitt, T. and de Maine, P. A. D., "Storage Optimization of Tree Structured Files Representing Descriptor Sets," *Proceedings of the ACM SIGFIDET Workshop on Data Description, Access and Control,* New York, 1971, 207–217.

Quadtrees

Finkel, R. A., Bentley, J. L., "Quad Trees: A Data Structure for Retrieval on Composite Keys," *Acta Informatica* 4 (1974), 1–9.

Samet, Hanan, *The Design and Analysis of Spatial Data Structures,* Reading, MA: Addison-Wesley, 1989.

Graphs

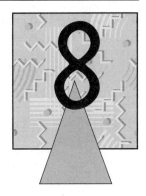

In spite of the flexibility of trees and the many different tree applications, trees, by their nature, have one limitation, namely, they can only represent relations of a hierarchical type, such as relations between parent and child. Other relations are only represented indirectly, such as the relation of being a sibling. A generalization of a tree, a *graph*, is a data structure in which this limitation is lifted. Intuitively, a graph is a collection of vertices (or nodes) and the connections between them. Generally, no restriction is imposed on the number of vertices in the graph or on the number of connections one vertex can have to other vertices. Figure 8.1 contains examples of graphs. Graphs are versatile data structures that can represent a large number of different situations and events from diverse domains. Graph theory has grown into a sophisticated area of mathematics and computer science in the last 200 years since it was first studied. Many results are of theoretical interest, but in this chapter, some selected results of interest to computer scientists are presented. Before discussing different algorithms and their applications, several definitions need to be introduced.

A *simple graph* $G = (V, E)$ consists of a nonempty set V of *vertices* and a possibly empty set E of *edges,* each edge being a set of two vertices from V. The number of vertices and edges is denoted by $|V|$ and $|E|$, respectively. A *directed graph*, or a *digraph*, $G = (V, E)$ consists of a nonempty set V of vertices and a set E of edges (also called *arcs*), where each edge is a pair of vertices from V. The difference is that one edge of a simple graph is of the form $\{v_i, v_j\}$, and for such an edge, $\{v_i, v_j\} = \{v_j, v_i\}$. In a digraph, each edge is of the form (v_i, v_j), and in this case, $(v_i, v_j) \neq (v_j, v_i)$. Unless necessary, this distinction in notation will be disregarded, and an edge between vertices v_i and v_j will be referred to as $edge(v_i v_j)$.

These definitions are restrictive in that they do not allow for two vertices to have more than one edge. A *multigraph* is a graph in which two vertices can be joined by multiple edges. Geometric interpretation is very simple (see Figure 8.1e). Formally,

FIGURE **8.1**   Examples of graphs: (a–d) simple graphs; (c) a complete graph K_4; (e) a multigraph; (f) a pseudograph; (g) a circuit in a digraph; (h) a cycle in the digraph.

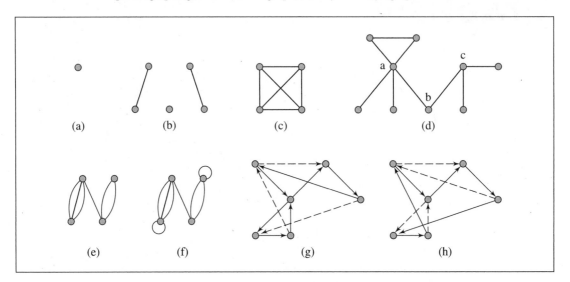

the definition is as follows: A multigraph $G = (V,E,f)$ is composed of a set of vertices V, a set of edges E, and a function $f: E \rightarrow \{\{v_i,v_j\} : v_i,v_j \in V$ and $v_i \neq v_j\}$. A *pseudograph* is a multigraph with the condition $v_i \neq v_j$ removed, which allows for *loops* to occur; in a pseudograph, a vertex can be joined with itself by an edge (Figure 8.1f).

A *path* from v_1 to v_n is a sequence of edges $edge(v_1 v_2)$, $edge(v_2 v_3)$, ... , $edge(v_{n-1} v_n)$ and is denoted as path $v_1, v_2, v_3, \ldots, v_{n-1}, v_n$. If $v_1 = v_n$ and no edge is repeated, then the path is called a *circuit* (Figure 8.1g). If all vertices in a circuit are different, then it is called a *cycle* (Figure 8.1h).

A graph is called a *weighted graph* if each edge has an assigned number. Depending on the context in which such graphs are used, the number assigned to an edge is called its weight, cost, distance, length, or some other name.

A graph with n vertices is called *complete* and is denoted K_n if for each pair of distinct vertices there is exactly one edge connecting them; that is, each vertex can be connected to any other vertex (Figure 8.1c). The number of edges in such a graph $|E| =$

$$\binom{|V|}{2} = \frac{|V|!}{2!(|V|-2)!} = \frac{|V|(|V|-1)}{2} = O(|V|^2).$$

A *subgraph* G' of graph $G = (V,E)$ is a graph (V',E') such that $V' \subseteq V$ and $E' \subseteq E$. A subgraph *induced* by vertices V' is a graph (V',E') such that an edge $e \in E$ if $e \in E'$.

Two vertices v_i and v_j are called *adjacent* if the $edge(v_i v_j)$ is in E. Such an edge is called *incident with* the vertices v_i and v_j. The *degree* of a vertex v, $deg(v)$, is the number of edges incident with v. If $deg(v) = 0$, then v is called an *isolated vertex*. The definition of a graph indicating that the set of edges E can be empty allows for a graph consisting only of isolated vertices.

♤ 8.1 GRAPH REPRESENTATION

There are a variety of ways to represent a graph. A simple representation is given by an *adjacency list* which specifies all vertices adjacent to each vertex of the graph. This list can be implemented as a table, in which case it is called a *star representation,* which can be forward or reverse, as illustrated in Figure 8.2b, or as a linked list (Figure 8.2c).

Another representation is a matrix which comes in two forms: an adjacency matrix and an incidence matrix. An *adjacency matrix* of graph $G = (V,E)$ is a binary $|V| \times |V|$ matrix such that each entry of this matrix

$$a_{ij} = \begin{cases} 1 & \text{if there exists an } edge(v_i v_j) \\ 0 & \text{otherwise} \end{cases}$$

An example is shown in Figure 8.2d. Note that the order of vertices $v_1, \ldots, v_{|V|}$ used for generating this matrix is arbitrary; therefore, there are $n!$ possible adjacency matrices for the same graph G. Generalization of this definition to also cover multigraphs can be easily accomplished by transforming the definition into the following form:

$$a_{ij} = \text{number of edges between } v_i \text{ and } v_j$$

Another matrix representation of a graph is based on the incidence of vertices and edges and is called an *incidence matrix.* An incidence matrix of graph $G = (V,E)$ is a $|V| \times |E|$ matrix such that

$$a_{ij} = \begin{cases} 1 & \text{if edge } e_j \text{ is incident with vertex } v_i \\ 0 & \text{otherwise} \end{cases}$$

Figure 8.2e contains an example of an incidence matrix. In an incidence matrix for a multigraph, some columns are the same, and a column with only one 1 indicates a loop.

Which representation is best? It depends on the problem at hand. If our task is to process vertices adjacent to a vertex v, then the adjacency list requires only $deg(v)$ steps, whereas the adjacency matrix requires $|V|$ steps. On the other hand, inserting or deleting a vertex adjacent to v requires linked list maintenance for an adjacency list (if such an implementation is used); for a matrix, it requires only changing 0 to 1 for insertion, or 1 to 0 for deletion, in one cell of the matrix.

♤ 8.2 GRAPH TRAVERSALS

As in trees, traversing a graph consists of visiting each vertex only one time. The simple traversal algorithms used for trees cannot be applied here because graphs may include cycles; hence, the tree traversal algorithms would result in infinite loops. To prevent that from happening, each visited vertex can be marked to avoid revisiting it. However, graphs can have isolated vertices, which means that some parts of the graph are left out if unmodified tree traversal methods are applied.

FIGURE **8.2**   Graph representations. (a) A graph represented as (b–c) an adjacency list, (d) an adjacency matrix, and (e) an incidence matrix.

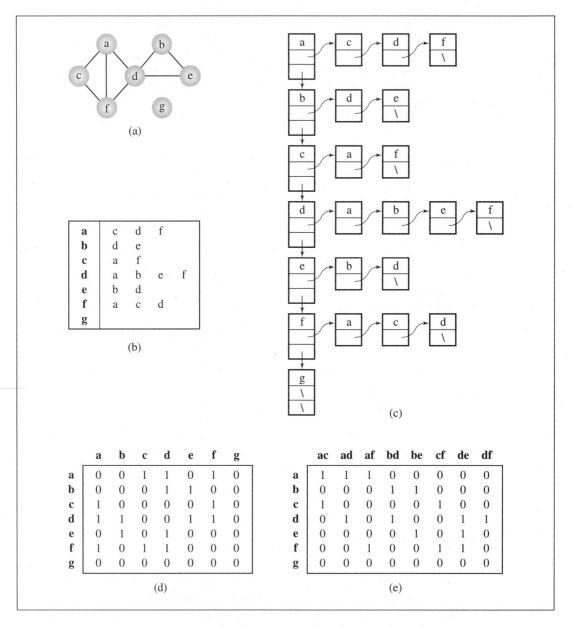

An algorithm for traversing a graph, known as the depth-first search algorithm, was developed by John Hopcroft and Robert Tarjan. In this algorithm, each vertex v is visited and then each unvisited vertex adjacent to v is visited. If a vertex v has no adjacent vertices or all of its adjacent vertices have been visited, we backtrack to the predecessor of v. The traversal is finished if this visiting and backtracking process leads to the first vertex where the traversal started. If there are still some unvisited vertices in the graph, the traversal continues restarting for one of the unvisited vertices.

Although it is not necessary for the proper outcome of this method, the algorithm assigns a unique number to each accessed vertex so that vertices are now renumbered. This will prove useful in later applications of this algorithm.

```
DFS(v)
    num(v)= i++;
    for all vertices u adjacent to v
        if num(u) is 0
            attach edge(uv) to edges;
            DFS(u);

depthFirstSearch()
    for all vertices v
        num(v) = 0;
    edges = null;
    i = 1;
    while there is a vertex v such that num(v) is 0
        DFS(v);
    output edges;
```

Figure 8.3 contains an example with the numbers *num*(*v*) assigned to each vertex *v* shown in parentheses. Having made all necessary initializations, depthFirst-Search() calls DFS(a). DFS() is first invoked for vertex *a; num*(*a*) is assigned number 1. *a* has four adjacent vertices, and vertex *e* is chosen for the next invocation, DFS(e), which assigns number 2 to this vertex, that is, *num*(*e*) = 2, and puts the *edge*(*ae*) in edges. Vertex *e* has two unvisited adjacent vertices, and DFS() is called for the first of them, the vertex *f*. The call DFS(f) leads to the assignment *num*(*f*) = 3 and puts the *edge*(*ef*) in edges. Vertex *f* has only one unvisited adjacent vertex, *i*; thus, the fourth call, DFS(i), leads to the assignment *num*(*i*) = 4 and to the attaching of *edge*(*fi*) to edges. Vertex *i* has only visited adjacent vertices; hence, we return to call DFS(f) and then to DFS(e) in which vertex *i* is accessed only to learn that *num*(*i*) is not 0, whereby the *edge*(*ei*) is not included in edges. The rest of the execution can be seen easily in Figure 8.3b. Solid lines indicate edges included in the set edges.

Note that this algorithm guarantees generating a tree (or a forest, a set of trees) which includes or spans over all vertices of the original graph. A tree that meets this condition is called a *spanning tree*. The fact that a tree is generated is ascertained by the fact that the algorithm does not include in the resulting tree any edge which leads from the currently analyzed vertex to a vertex already analyzed. An edge is added to edges only if the condition in "if *num*(u) *is* 0" is true, that is, if vertex *u* reachable from vertex *v* has not been processed. As a result, certain edges in the original graph do not appear in the resulting tree. The edges included in this tree are called *forward edges* (or *tree edges*), and the edges not included in this tree are called *back edges* and are shown as dashed lines.

Figure 8.4 illustrates the execution of this algorithm for a digraph. Notice that the original graph results in three spanning trees, although we started with only two isolated subgraphs.

FIGURE **8.3**   An example of application of `depthFirstSearch()` algorithm to a graph.

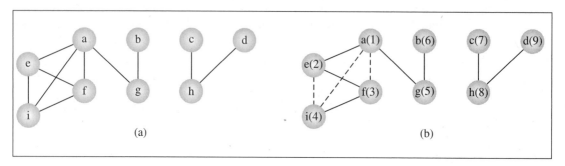

FIGURE **8.4**   `depthFirstSearch()` algorithm applied to a digraph.

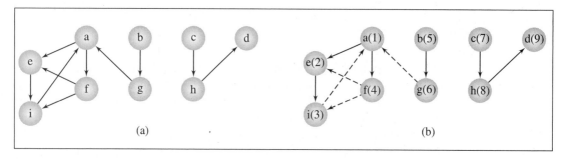

The complexity of `depthFirstSearch()` is $O(|V| + |E|)$ because (a) initializing $num(v)$ for each vertex v requires $|V|$ steps; (b) `DFS(v)` is called $deg(v)$ times for each v, that is, once for each edge of v (to spawn into more calls or to finish the chain of recursive calls), hence, the total number of calls is $2|E|$; (c) searching for vertices as required by the statement

> `while` *there is a vertex* `v` *such that num(*`v`*) is* 0

can be assumed to require $|V|$ steps. For a graph with no isolated parts, the loop makes only one iteration, and an initial vertex can be found in one step, although it may take $|V|$ steps. For a graph with all isolated vertices, the loop iterates $|V|$ times and each time a vertex can also be chosen in one step, although in an unfavorable implementation, the *i*th iteration may require *i* steps, whereby the loop would require $O(|V|^2)$ steps in total. For example, if an adjacency list is used, then for each *v*, the condition in the loop,

> `for` *all vertices* `u` *adjacent to* `v`

FIGURE **8.5**   An example of application of `breadthFirstSearch()` algorithm to a graph.

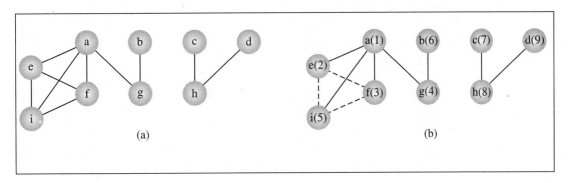

(a)   (b)

is checked *deg*(v) times. However, if an adjacency matrix is used, then the same condition is used |V| times, whereby the algorithm's complexity becomes $O(|V|^2)$.

As we shall see, many different algorithms are based on `DFS()`; however, some algorithms are more efficient if the underlying graph traversal is not depth first but breadth first. We have already encountered these two types of traversals in Chapter 6; recall that the depth-first algorithms rely on the use of a stack (explicitly, or implicitly, in recursion), and breadth-first traversal uses a queue as the basic data structure. Not surprisingly, this idea can also be extended to graphs, as shown in the following pseudocode:

```
breadthFirstSearch()
    for all vertices u
        num(u) = 0;
    edges = null;
    i = 1;
    while there is a vertex v such that num(v) == 0
        num(v)=i++;
        enqueue(v);
        while queue is not empty
            v = dequeue();
            for all vertices u adjacent to v
                if num(u) is 0
                    num(u) = i++;
                    enqueue(u);
                    attach edge(vu) to edges;
    output edges;
```

Examples of processing a simple graph and a digraph are shown in Figures 8.5 and 8.6. `breadthFirstSearch()` first tries to mark all neighbors of a vertex *v* before proceeding to other vertices, whereas `DFS()` picks one neighbor of a *v* and then proceeds to a neighbor of this neighbor before processing any other neighbors of *v*.

FIGURE **8.6**   `breadthFirstSearch()` algorithm applied to a digraph.

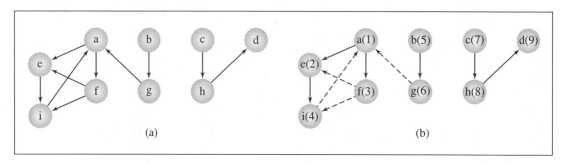

(a)   (b)

🔲 8.3 SHORTEST PATHS

Finding the shortest path is a classical problem in graph theory, and a large number of different solutions have been proposed. Edges are assigned certain weights representing, for example, distances between cities, times separating the execution of certain tasks, costs of transmitting information between locations, amounts of some substance transported from one place to another, etc. When determining the shortest path from vertex v to vertex u, information about distances between intermediate vertices w has to be recorded. This information can be recorded as a label associated with these vertices, where the label is only the distance from v to w or the distance along with the predecessor of w in this path. The methods of finding the shortest path rely on these labels. Depending on how many times these labels are updated, the methods solving the shortest path problem are divided in two classes: label-setting methods and label-correcting methods.

For *label-setting methods,* in each pass through the vertices still to be processed, one vertex is set to a value which remains unchanged to the end of the execution. This, however, limits such methods to processing graphs with only positive weights. The second category includes *label-correcting methods* which allow for the changing of *any* label during application of the method. These two methods can be applied to graphs with negative weights and with no *negative cycle*—a cycle composed of edges with weights adding up to a negative number—but they guarantee that, for all vertices, the current distances indicate the shortest path only after the processing of the graph is finished. Most of the label-setting and label-correcting methods, however, can be subsumed to the same form which allows finding the shortest paths from one vertex to all other vertices (Gallo and Pallottino 1986):

```
genericShortestPathAlgorithm(weighted simple digraph, vertex first)
    for all vertices v
        currDist(v) = ∞;
    currDist(first) = 0;
    initialize toBeChecked;
```

```
while toBeChecked is not empty
    v = a vertex in toBeChecked;
    remove v from toBeChecked;
    for all vertices u adjacent to v
        if currDist(u) > currDist(v) + weight(edge(vu))
            currDist(u) = currDist(v) + weight(edge(vu));
            predecessor(u) = v;
            add u to toBeChecked if it is not there;
```

In this generic algorithm, a label consists of two elements:

$$label(v) = (currDist(v), predecessor(v))$$

This algorithm leaves two things open: the organization of the set toBeChecked and the order of assigning new values to v in the assignment statement

v = *a vertex in* toBeChecked;

It should be clear that the organization of toBeChecked can determine the order of choosing new values for v, but it also determines the efficiency of the algorithm.

What distinguishes label-setting methods from label-correcting methods is the method of choosing the value for v, which is always a vertex in toBeChecked with the smallest current distance. One of the first label-setting algorithms was developed by Dijkstra.

In Dijkstra's algorithm, a number of paths $p_1, \ldots, p_n$ from a vertex v are tried, and each time, the shortest path is chosen among them, which may mean that the same path p_i can be continued by adding one more edge to it. But if p_i turns out to be longer than any other path that can be tried, p_i is abandoned and this other path is tried by resuming from where it was left and by adding one more edge to it. Since paths can lead to vertices with more than one outgoing edge, new paths for possible exploration are added for each outgoing edge. Each vertex is tried once, all paths leading from it are opened, and the vertex itself is put away and not used anymore. After all vertices are visited, the algorithm is finished. Dijkstra's algorithm is as follows:

```
DijkstraAlgorithm(weighted simple digraph, vertex first)
    for all vertices v
        currDist(v) = ∞;
    currDist(first) = 0;
    toBeChecked = all vertices;
    while toBeChecked is not empty
        v = a vertex in toBeChecked with minimal currDist(v);
        remove v from toBeChecked;
        for all vertices u adjacent to v and in toBeChecked
            if currDist(u) > currDist(v)+ weight(edge(vu))
                currDist(u) = currDist(v)+ weight(edge(vu));
                predecessor(u) = v;
```

Dijkstra's algorithm is obtained from the generic method by being more specific about which vertex is to be taken from toBeChecked so that the line

FIGURE **8.7**   An execution of `DijkstraAlgorithm()`.

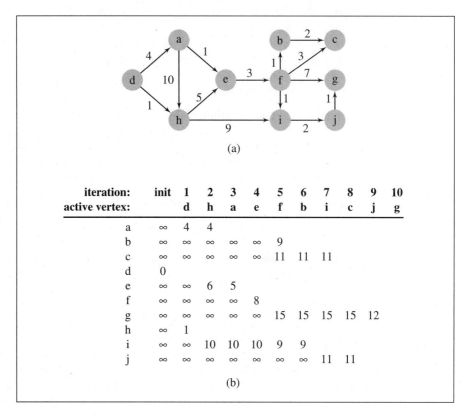

(a)

iteration:	init	1	2	3	4	5	6	7	8	9	10
active vertex:		**d**	**h**	**a**	**e**	**f**	**b**	**i**	**c**	**j**	**g**
a	∞	4	4								
b	∞	∞	∞	∞	∞	9					
c	∞	∞	∞	∞	∞	11	11	11			
d	0										
e	∞	∞	6	5							
f	∞	∞	∞	∞	8						
g	∞	∞	∞	∞	∞	15	15	15	15	12	
h	∞	1									
i	∞	∞	10	10	10	9	9				
j	∞	∞	∞	∞	∞	∞	∞	11	11		

(b)

> v = *a vertex in* `toBeChecked`;

is replaced by the line

> v = *a vertex in* `toBeChecked` *with minimal currDist(*v*)*;

and by extending the condition in the `if` statement whereby the current distance of vertices eliminated from `toBeChecked` is set permanently.[1] Note that the structure of `toBeChecked` is not specified, and the efficiency of the algorithms depends on the data type of `toBeChecked`, which determines how quickly a vertex with minimal distance can be retrieved.

Figure 8.7 contains an example. The table in this figure shows all iterations of the `while` loop. There are ten iterations because there are ten vertices. The table indicates the current distances determined up until the current iteration.

The list `toBeChecked` is initialized to {*a b . . . j*}, the current distances of all vertices are initialized to a very large value, marked here as ∞, and in the first iteration,

---

[1]Dijkstra used six sets to ascertain this condition, three for vertices and three for edges.

the current distances of *d*'s neighbors are set to numbers equal to the weights of the edges from *d*. Now, there are two candidates for the next try, *a* and *h*, since *d* was excluded from `toBeChecked`. In the second iteration, *h* is chosen, since its current distance is minimal, and then the two vertices accessible from *h*, namely, *e* and *i*, acquire the current distances 6 and 10. Now, there are three candidates in `toBeChecked` for the next try, *a*, *e*, and *i*. Since *a* has the smallest current distance, it is chosen in the third iteration. Eventually, in the tenth iteration, `toBeChecked` becomes empty and the execution of the algorithm completes.

The complexity of Dijkstra's algorithm is $O(|V|^2)$. The first `for` loop and the `while` loop are executed $|V|$ times. For each iteration of the `while` loop, (a) a vertex *v* in `toBeChecked` with minimal current distance has to be found, which requires $O(|V|)$ steps, and (b) the `for` loop iterates *deg*(*v*) times, which is also $O(|V|)$. The efficiency can be improved by using a heap to store and order vertices and adjacency lists (Johnson 1977). Using a heap turns the complexity of this algorithm into $O((|E| + |V|) \lg |V|)$; each time through the `while` loop, the cost of restoring the heap after removing a vertex is proportional to $O(\lg|V|)$. Also, in each iteration, only adjacent vertices are updated on an adjacency list so that the total updates for all vertices considered in all iterations are proportional to $|E|$, and each list update corresponds to the cost of $\lg|V|$ of the heap update.

Dijkstra's algorithm is not general enough in that it fails when negative weights are used in graphs. To see why, change the weight of *edge*(*ah*) from 10 to –10. Note that the path *d, a, h, e* is now –1, whereas the path *d, a, e* as determined by the algorithm is 5. The reason for overlooking this less costly path is that the vertices with the current distance set from ∞ to a value are not checked anymore: First, successors of vertex *d* are scrutinized and *d* is removed from `toBeChecked`, then the vertex *h* is removed from `toBeChecked`, and only afterward is the vertex *a* considered as a candidate to be included in the path from *d* to other vertices. But now, the *edge*(*ah*) is not taken into consideration because the condition in the `for` loop prevents the algorithm from doing this. To overcome this limitation, a label-correcting method is needed.

One of the first label-correcting algorithms was devised by Lester Ford. Like Dijkstra's algorithm, it uses the same method of setting current distances, but Ford's method does not permanently determine the shortest distance for any vertex until it processes the entire graph. It is more powerful than Dijkstra's method in that it can process graphs with negative weights (but not graphs with negative cycles).

As required by the original form of the algorithm, all edges are monitored to find a possibility for an improvement of the current distance of vertices so that the algorithm can be presented in this pseudocode:

```
FordAlgorithm(weighted simple digraph, vertex first)
    for all vertices v
        currDist(v) = ∞;
    currDist(first) = 0;
    while there is an edge(vu) such that currDist(u) > currDist(v) + weight(edge(vu))
        currDist(u) = currDist(v) + weight(edge(vu));
```

To impose a certain order on monitoring the edges, an alphabetically ordered sequence of edges can be used so that the algorithm can repeatedly go through the entire

FIGURE **8.8**   `FordAlgorithm()` applied to a digraph with negative weights.

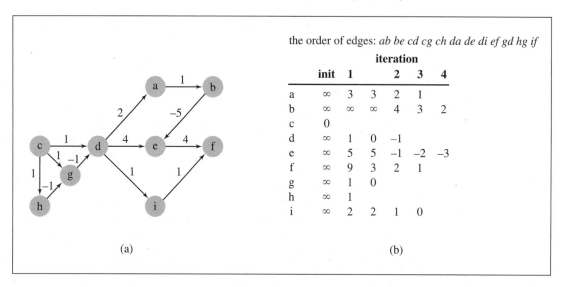

the order of edges: *ab be cd cg ch da de di ef gd hg if*

			iteration			
	init	1		2	3	4
a	∞	3	3	2	1	
b	∞	∞	∞	4	3	2
c	0					
d	∞	1	0	−1		
e	∞	5	5	−1	−2	−3
f	∞	9	3	2	1	
g	∞	1	0			
h	∞	1				
i	∞	2	2	1	0	

(a)   (b)

sequence and adjust the current distance of any vertex if needed. Figure 8.8 contains an example. The graph includes edges with negative weights. The table indicates iterations of the while loop and current distances updated in each iteration, where one iteration is defined as one pass through the edges. Note that a vertex can change its current distance during the same iteration. However, at the end, each vertex of the graph can be reached through the shortest path from the starting vertex (vertex *c* in the example in Figure 8.8).

The computational complexity of this algorithm is $O(|V||E|)$. There will be at most $|V| - 1$ passes through the sequence of $|E|$ edges, since $|V| - 1$ is the largest number of edges in any path. In the first pass, at least all one-edge paths are determined, in the second pass, all two-edge paths are determined, and so on. However, for graphs with irrational weights, this complexity is $O(2^{|V|})$ (Gallo and Pallottino 1986).

We have seen in the case of Dijkstra's algorithm that the efficiency of an algorithm can be improved by scanning edges and vertices in a certain order, which in turn depends on the data structure used to store them. The same holds true for label-correcting methods. In particular, `FordAlgorithm()` does not specify the order of checking edges. In the example illustrated in Figure 8.8, a simple solution is used in that all adjacency lists of all vertices were visited in each iteration. However, in this approach, all the edges are checked every time, which is not necessary, and more judicious organization of the list of vertices can limit the number of visits per vertex. Such an improvement is based on the `genericShortestPathAlgorithm()` by explicitly referring to the `toBeChecked` list which in `FordAlgorithm()` is used only implicitly: It simply is the set of all vertices *V* and remains such for the entire run of the algorithm. This leads us to a general form of a label-correcting algorithm as expressed in this pseudocode:

```
labelCorrectingAlgorithm(weighted simple digraph, vertex first)
    for all vertices v
        currDist(v) = ∞;
    currDist(first) = 0;
    toBeChecked = {first};
    while toBeChecked is not empty
        v = a vertex in toBeChecked;
        remove v from toBeChecked;
        for all vertices u adjacent to v
            if currDist(u) > currDist(v) + weight(edge(vu))
                currDist(u) = currDist(v) + weight(edge(vu));
                predecessor(u) = v;
                add u to toBeChecked if it is not there;
```

The efficiency of particular instantiations of this algorithm hinges on the data structure used for the toBeChecked list and on operations for extracting elements from this list and including them into it.

One possible organization of this list is a queue: Vertex v is dequeued from toBeChecked and if the current distance of any of its neighbors, u, is updated, u is enqueued onto toBeChecked. It seems like a natural choice, and in fact, it was one of the earliest, used in 1968 by C. Witzgall (Deo and Pang 1984). However, it is not without flaws, as it sometimes reevaluates the same labels more times than necessary. Figure 8.9 contains an example of an excessive reevaluation. The table in this figure shows all changes on toBeChecked implemented as a queue when labelCorrectingAlgorithm() is applied to the graph in Figure 8.8a. The vertex d is updated three times. These updates cause three changes to its successors, a and i, and two changes to another successor, e. The change of a translates into two changes to b and these into two more changes to e. To avoid such repetitious updates, a doubly ended queue, or deque, can be used.

The choice of a deque as a solution to this problem is attributed to D. D'Esopo (Pollack and Wiebenson 1960) and was implemented by Pape. In this method, the vertices included in toBeChecked for the first time are put at the end of the list; otherwise, they are added at the front. The rationale for this procedure is that if a vertex v is included for the first time, then there is a good chance that the vertices accessible from v have not been processed yet, so they will be processed after processing v. On the other hand, if v has been processed at least once, then it is likely that the vertices reachable from v are still on the list waiting for processing; by putting v at the end of the list, these vertices may very likely be reprocessed due to the update of $currDist(v)$. Therefore, it is better to put v in front of their successors to avoid an unnecessary round of updates. Figure 8.10 shows changes in the deque during the execution of labelCorrectingAlgorithm() applied to the graph in Figure 8.8a. This time, the number of iterations is dramatically reduced. Although d is again evaluated three times, these evaluations are performed before processing its successors so that a and i are processed once and e twice. However, this algorithm has a problem of its own

FIGURE **8.9**   An execution of `labelCorrectingAlgorithm()`, which uses a queue.

		active vertex																					
		c	d	g	h	a	e	i	d	g	b	f	a	e	i	d	b	f	a	i	e	b	f	e
queue		d	g	h	a	e	i	d	g	b	f	a	e	i	d	b	f	a	i	e	b	f	e
		g	h	a	e	i	d	g	b	f	a	e	i	d	b	f	a	i	e	b	f	e
		h	a	e	i	d	g	b	f	a	e	i	d	b	f	a	i	e	b	f
		e	i	d	g	b	f	a	e	i	d	b		i	e
		i	d	g	b	f		e	i	d
			i	d

a	∞	∞	3	3	3	3	3	3	2	2	2	2	2	2	2	1
b	∞	∞	∞	∞	∞	4	4	4	4	4	4	4	3	3	3	3	3	3	2
c	0
d	∞	1	1	0	0	0	0	0	0	−1
e	∞	∞	5	5	5	5	5	5	4	4	−1	−1	−1	−1	−1	−1	−2	−2	−2	−2	−2	−3
f	∞	∞	∞	∞	∞	∞	9	3	3	3	3	3	3	3	2	2	2	2	2	1
h	∞	1
i	∞	∞	2	2	2	2	2	2	1	1	1	1	1	1	1	0

FIGURE **8.10**   An execution of `labelCorrectingAlgorithm()`, which applies a deque.

		active vertex											
		c	d	g	d	h	g	d	a	e	i	b	e	f
deque		d	g	d	h	g	d	a	e	i	b	e	f
		g	h	h	a	a	a	e	i	b	f	f
		h	a	a	e	e	e	i	b	f
		e	e	i	i	i
		i	i

a	∞	∞	3	3	2	2	2	1
b	∞	∞	∞	∞	∞	∞	∞	∞	2
c	0
d	∞	1	2	0	0	0	−1
e	∞	∞	5	5	4	4	4	3	3	3	3	−3
f	∞	∞	∞	∞	∞	∞	∞	∞	7	1
h	∞	1
i	∞	∞	2	2	1	1	1	0

because in the worst case its performance is an exponential function of the number of vertices. (See Exercise 13 at the end of this chapter.) But in the average case, as Pape's experimental runs indicate, this implementation fares at least 60% better than the previous queue solution.

Instead of using a deque, which combines two queues, the two queues can be used separately. In this version of the algorithm, vertices stored for the first time are enqueued on $queue_1$ and on $queue_2$ otherwise. Vertices are dequeued from $queue_1$ if it is not empty and from $queue_2$ otherwise (Gallo and Pallottino 1988).

Another version of the label-correcting method is the *threshold algorithm,* which also uses two lists. Vertices are taken for processing from $list_1$. A vertex is added to the end of $list_1$ if its label is below the current threshold level and to $list_2$ otherwise. If $list_1$ is empty, then the threshold level is changed to a value greater than a minimum label among the labels of the vertices in $list_2$, and then the vertices with the label values below the threshold are moved to $list_1$ (Glover, Glover, and Klingman 1984).

Still another algorithm is a *small label first* method. In this method, a vertex is included at the front of a deque if its label is smaller than the label at the top of the deque; otherwise, it is put at the end of the deque (Bertsekas 1993). To some extent, this method includes the main criterion of label-setting methods. The latter methods always retrieve the minimal element from the list; the small label first method puts a vertex with the label smaller than the label of the front vertex at the top. The approach can be carried to its logical conclusion by requiring each vertex to be included in the list according to its rank so that the deque turns into a priority queue and the resulting method becomes a label-correcting version of Dijkstra's algorithm.

8.3.1 All-to-All Shortest Path Problem

Although the task of finding all shortest paths from any vertex to any other vertex seems to be more complicated than the task of dealing with one source only, a method designed by Stephen Warshall and implemented by Robert W. Floyd and P. Z. Ingerman does it in a surprisingly simple way provided an adjacency matrix is given that indicates all the edge weights of the graph (or digraph). The graph can include negative weights. The algorithm is as follows:

```
WFIalgorithm(matrix weight)
    for i = 1 to |V|
        for j = 1 to |V|
            for k = 1 to |V|
                if weight[j][k] > weight[j][i] + weight[i][k]
                    weight[j][k] = weight[j][i] + weight[i][k];
```

The outermost loop refers to vertices which may be on a path between the vertex with index j and the vertex with index k. For example, in the first iteration, when $i = 1$, all paths $v_j \ldots v_1 \ldots v_k$ are considered, and if there is currently no path from v_j to v_k and v_k is reachable from v_j, the path is established, with its weight equal to $p = weight(path(v_j v_1)) + weight(path(v_1 v_k))$, or the current weight of this path, $weight(path(v_j v_k))$, is changed to p if p is less than $weight(path(v_j v_k))$. As an example, consider the graph and the corresponding adjacency matrix in Figure 8.11. This figure also contains tables that show changes in the matrix for each value of i and the changes in paths as established by the algorithm. After the first iteration, the matrix and the graph remain the same, since a has no incoming edges (Figure 8.11a). They also remain the same in the last iteration, when $i = 5$; no change is introduced to the matrix because vertex e has no outgoing edges. A better path, one with a lower combined weight, is always chosen, if possible. For example, the direct one-edge path from b to e in Figure 8.11c is abandoned after a two-edge path from b to e is found with a lower weight, as in Figure 8.11d.

This algorithm also allows us to detect cycles if the diagonal is initialized to ∞ and not to zero. If any of the diagonal values are changed, then the graph contains a cycle. Also, if an initial value of ∞ between two vertices in the matrix is not changed to a finite value, it is an indication that one vertex cannot be reached from another.

The simplicity of the algorithm is reflected in the ease with which its complexity can be computed: Since all three `for` loops are executed $|V|$ times, its complexity is $|V|^3$. This is a good efficiency for dense, nearly complete graphs, but in sparse graphs, there is no need to check for all possible connections between vertices. For sparse graphs, it may be more beneficial to use a one-to-all method $|V|$ times, that is, apply it to each vertex separately. This should be a label-setting algorithm, which as a rule has better complexity than a label-correcting algorithm. However, a label-setting algorithm cannot work with graphs with negative weights. To solve this problem, we have to modify the graph so that it does not have negative weights and it guarantees to have the same shortest paths as the original graph. Fortunately, such a modification is possible (Edmonds and Karp 1972).

Observe first that, for any vertex v, the length of the shortest path to v is never greater than the length of the shortest path to any of its predecessors w plus the length of edge from w to v, or

$$dist(v) \leq dist(w) + weight(edge(wv))$$

for any vertices v and w. This inequality is equivalent to the inequality

$$0 \leq weight'(edge(wv)) = weight(edge(vw)) + dist(w) - dist(v)$$

Hence, changing $weight(e)$ to $weight'(e)$ for all edges e renders a graph with nonnegative edge weights. Now note that the shortest path $v_1, v_2, \ldots, v_k$ is

$$\sum_{i=1}^{k-1} weight'\left(edge\left(v_i v_{i+1}\right)\right) = \left(\sum_{i=1}^{k-1} weight\left(edge\left(v_i v_{i+1}\right)\right)\right) + dist\left(v_1\right) - dist\left(v_k\right)$$

Therefore, if the length L' of the path from v_1 to v_k is found in terms of nonnegative weights, then the length L of the same path in the same graph using the original weights, some possibly negative, is $L = L' - dist(v_1) + dist(v_k)$.

But because the shortest paths have to be known to make such a transformation, the graph has to be preprocessed by one application of a label-correcting method. Only afterward are the weights modified, and then a label-setting method is applied $|V|$ times.

FIGURE **8.11**   An execution of `WFIalgorithm()`.

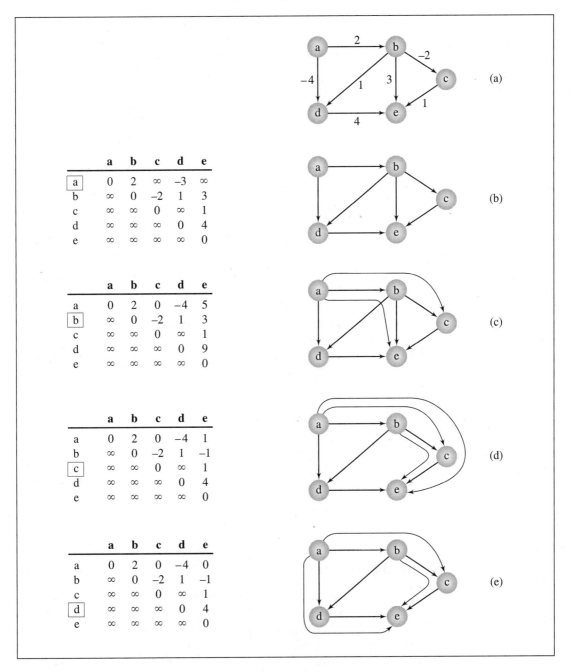

8.4 CYCLE DETECTION

Many algorithms rely on detecting cycles in graphs. We have just seen that, as a side effect, WFIalgorithm() allows for detecting cycles in graphs. However, it is a cubic algorithm, which in many situations is too inefficient. Therefore, other cycle detection methods have to be explored.

One such algorithm is obtained directly from depthFirstSearch(). For undirected graphs, it is enough to add only one line in DFS(v) to detect cycles, which is an else statement as in

```
cycleDetectionDFS(v)
    num(v) = i++;
    for all vertices u adjacent to v
        if num(u) is 0
            attach edge(uv) to edges;
            cycleDetectionDFS(u);
        else cycle detected;
```

For digraphs, the situation is a bit more complicated, since there may be edges between different spanning subtrees, called *side edges* (see *edge(ga)* in Figure 8.4b). An edge (a back edge) indicates a cycle if it joins two vertices already included in the same spanning subtree. To consider only this case, a number higher than any number generated in subsequent searches is assigned to a vertex being currently visited after all its descendants have also been visited. In this way, if a vertex is about to be joined by an edge with a vertex having a lower number, we declare a cycle detection. The algorithm is now

```
digraphCycleDetectionDFS(v)
    num(v) = i++:
    for all vertices u adjacent to v
        if num(u) is 0
            attach edge(uv) to edges;
            digraphCycleDetectionDFS(u);
        else if num (u) is not ∞
            cycle detected;
    num(v) = ∞;
```

8.4.1 Union-Find Problem

Let us recall from a preceding section that depth-first search guaranteed generating a spanning tree in which no element of edges used by depthFirstSearch() led to a cycle with other elements of edges. This was due to the fact that if vertices v and u belonged to edges, then the *edge(vu)* was disregarded by depthFirstSearch(). A problem arises when depthFirstSearch() is modified so that it can detect whether a specific *edge(vu)* is part of a cycle (see Exercise 20). Should such a modified depth-first search be applied to each edge separately, then the total run would be

FIGURE **8.12**   Concatenating two circular linked lists.

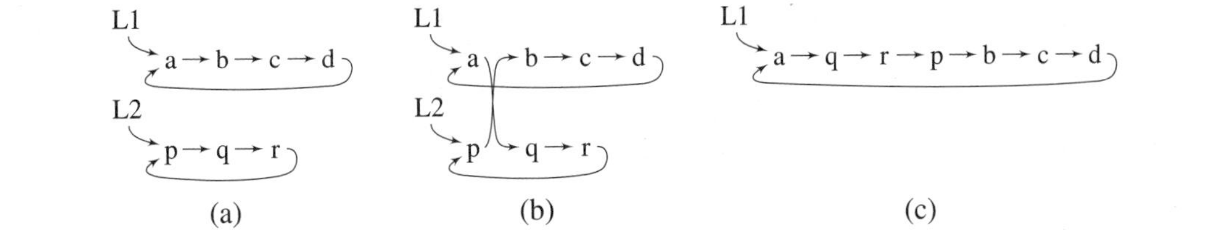

(a)   (b)   (c)

$O(|E|(|E| + |V|))$, which could turn into $O(|V|^4)$ for dense graphs. Hence, a better method needs to be found.

The task is to determine if two vertices are in the same set. Two operations are needed to implement this task: finding the set to which a vertex v belongs and uniting two sets into one if vertex v belongs to one of them and w to another. This is known as the *union-find problem.*

The sets used to solve the union-find problem are implemented with circular linked lists; each list is identified by a vertex that is the root of the three to which the vertices in the list belong. But first, all vertices are numbered with integers $0, \ldots, |V| -$ 1, which are used as indexes in three arrays: root[ ] to store a vertex index identifying a set of vertices, next[ ] to indicate the next vertex on a list, and length[ ] to indicate the number of vertices in a list.

We use circular lists to be able to combine two lists right away, as illustrated in Figure 8.12. Lists L1 and L2 (Figure 8.12a) are merged into one by interchanging next references in both lists (Figure 8.12b or, the same list, Figure 8.12c). However, the vertices in L2 have to " know" to which list they belong; therefore, their root indicators have to be changed to the new root. Since it has to be done for all vertices of list L2, then L2 should be the shorter of the two lists. To determine the length of lists, the third array is used, length[ ], but only lengths for the identifying nodes (roots) have to be updated. Therefore, the lengths indicated for other vertices that were roots (and at the beginning each of them was) are disregarded.

The union operation performs all the necessary tasks, so the find operation becomes trivial. By constantly updating the array root[ ], the set, to which a vertex j belongs, can be immediately identified, since it is a set whose identifying vertex is root[j]. Now, after the necessary initializations,

```
initialize()
    for i = 0 to |V| − 1
        root[i] = next[i] = i;
        length[i] = 1;
```

union() can be defined as follows:

FIGURE **8.13**   An example of application of union() to merge lists.

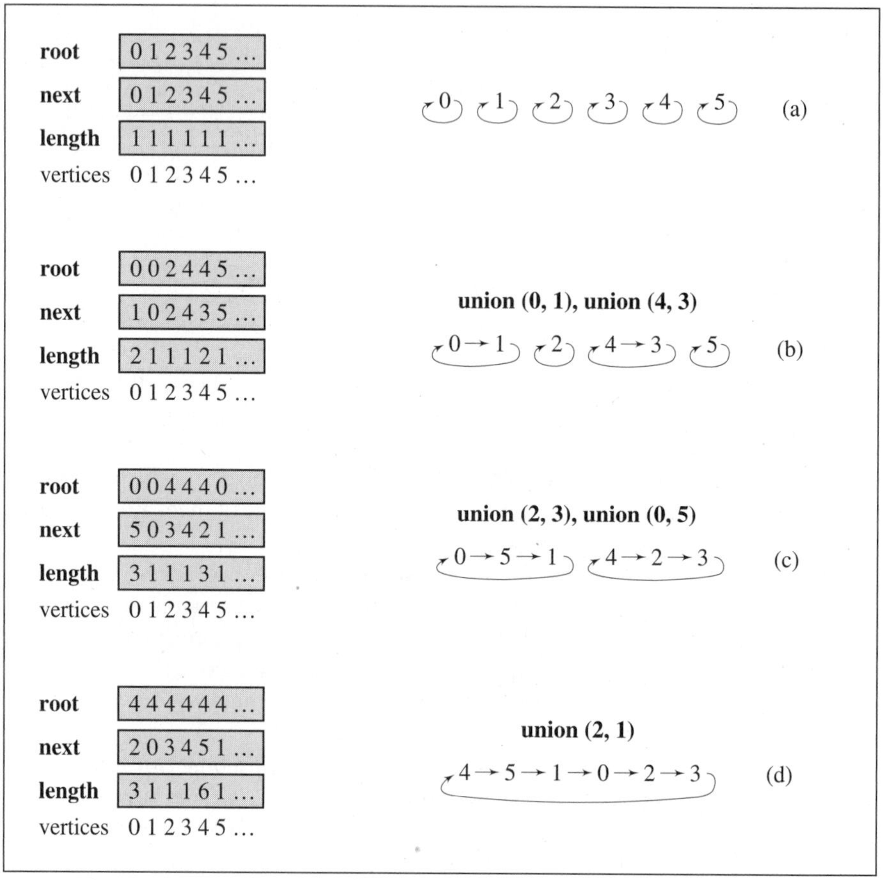

```
union(edge(vu))
   if (root[u] == root[v])                         // disregard this edge,
      return;                                       // since v and u are in
   else if (length[root[v]] < length[root[u]])     // the same set; combine
      rt = root[v];                                 // two sets into one;
      length[root[u]] += length[rt];
      root[rt] = root[u];                           // update root of root and
      for (j = next[rt]; j != rt; j = next[j])      // then other vertices
         root[j] = root[u];                         // in circular list;
      swap(next[rt],next[root[u]]);                 // merge two lists;
      add edge(vu) to spanningTree;
   else  // if length[root[v]] >= length[root[u]]
         // proceed as before, with v and u reversed;
```

FIGURE **8.14**   A graph representing (a) the airline connections between seven cities and (b–d) three possible sets of connections.

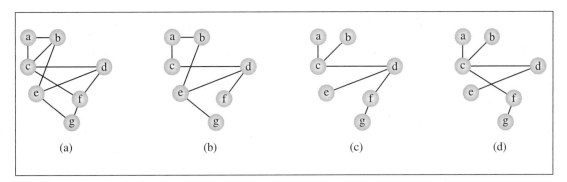

(a)   (b)   (c)   (d)

An example of the application of union() to merge lists is shown in Figure 8.13. After initialization, there are $|V|$ unary sets or one-node linked lists, as in Figure 8.13a. After executing union() several times, smaller linked lists are merged into larger ones, and each time, the new situation is reflected in the three arrays, as shown in Figures 8.13b–c.

The complexity of union() depends on the number of vertices that have to be updated when merging two lists, specifically, on the number of vertices on the shorter list, since this number determines how many times the for loop in union() iterates. Since this number can be between 1 and $|V|/2$, the complexity of union() is given by $O(|V|)$.

⌂ 8.5 Spanning Trees

Consider the graph representing the airline's connections between seven cities (Figure 8.14a). If the economic situation forces this airline to shut down as many connections as possible, which of them should be retained to make sure that it is still possible to reach any city from any other city, if only indirectly? One possibility is the graph in Figure 8.14b. City *a* can be reached from city *d* using the path *d, c, a*, but it is also possible to use the path *d, e, b, a*. Since the number of retained connections is the issue, there is still the possibility we can reduce this number. It should be clear that the minimum number of such connections form a tree because alternate paths arise as a result of cycles in the graph. Hence, to create the minimum number of connections, a spanning tree should be created, and such a spanning tree is the byproduct of depthFirstSearch(). Clearly, we can create different spanning trees (Figures 8.14c–d), that is, decide to retain different sets of connections, but all these trees have six edges and we cannot do any better than that.

The solution to this problem is not optimal in that the distances between cities have not been taken into account. Since there are alternative six-edge connections between cities, the airline uses the cost of these connections to choose the best, guaranteeing the optimum cost. This can be achieved by having maximally short distances for the six connections. This problem can now be phrased as finding a *minimum spanning tree,* which is a spanning tree in which the sum of the weights of its edges is minimal. The previous problem of finding a spanning tree in a simple graph is a case of the minimum spanning tree problem in that the weights for each edge are assumed to equal one. Therefore, each spanning tree is a minimum tree in a simple graph.

The minimum spanning tree problem has many solutions and only a handful of them are presented here. (For a review of these methods, see Graham and Hell 1985.) These algorithms can be divided in the following categories:

1. Creating and expanding at the same time many trees to be merged into larger trees (Borůvka's algorithm).

2. Expanding a set of trees to form one spanning tree (Kruskal's algorithm).

3. Creating and expanding only one tree by adding new branches to it (Jarník-Prim's algorithm).

4. Creating and expanding only one tree by adding new branches to it and possibly removing branches from it (Dijkstra's method).

8.5.1 Borůvka's Algorithm

Probably the first algorithm for finding the minimum spanning tree was devised in 1926 by Otakar Borůvka (pronounced: boh-roof-ka). In this method, we start with $|V|$ one-vertex trees, and for each vertex v, we look for an *edge(vw)* of minimum weight among all edges outgoing from v and create small trees by including these edges. Then, we look for edges of minimal weight that can connect the resulting trees to larger trees. The process is finished when one tree is created. Here is a pseudocode for this algorithm:

```
BorůvkaAlgorithnm(weighted connected undirected graph)
    make each vertex the root of a one-node tree;
    while there is more than one tree
        for each tree t
            e = minimum weight edge (vu) where v is included in t and u is not;
            create a tree by combining t and the tree that includes u
                if such a tree does not exist yet;
```

For example, for the graph in Figure 8.15a, out of seven one-vertex trees, two trees are created because, for vertices *a* and *c*, *edge(ac)* is chosen, for vertex *b*, *edge(ab)* is chosen, for vertex *d*, *edge(df)* is chosen, for vertex *e*, *edge(eg)* is chosen, and for vertices *f* and *g*, *edge(fg)* is chosen (Figure 8.15b). Afterward, for the tree(*abc*) and the tree(*defg*), *edge(cf)* is selected, since it is the shortest edge that connects these two trees, resulting in one spanning tree.

How many iterations are required? In each iteration of the `while` loop, each of the existing *r* trees is joined with an edge to at least one tree. In the worst case, *r*/2 trees are generated; in the best case, one tree is generated. In the subsequent iteration, there are *r*/4 trees and so on. In the worst case, lg $|V|$ iterations are needed, where $|V|$ is the initial number of one-vertex trees.

Borůvka's method lends itself very nicely to parallel processing, since for each tree, a minimal edge has to be found independently.

8.5.2 Kruskal's Algorithm

One popular algorithm was devised by Joseph Kruskal. In this method, all edges are ordered by weight, and then each edge in this ordered sequence is checked to see whether it can be considered part of the tree under construction. It is added to the tree if no cycle arises after its inclusion. This simple algorithm can be summarized as follows:

```
KruskalAlgorithm(weighted connected undirected graph)
    tree = null;
    edges = sequence of all edges of graph sorted by weight;
    for (i = 1; i ≤ |E| and |tree| < |V| − 1; i++)
        if e_i from edges does not form a cycle with edges in tree
            add e_i to tree;
```

Figures 8.15ca–cf contain a step-by-step example of Kruskal's algorithm.

The complexity of this algorithm is determined by the complexity of the sorting method applied, which for an efficient sorting is $O(|E| \lg |E|)$. It also depends on the complexity of the method used for cycle detection. If we use union() to implement Kruskal's algorithm, then the for loop of KruskalAlgorithm() becomes

```
for (i = 1; i ≤ |E| and |tree| < |V| − 1; i++)
    union(e_i = edge(vu));
```

Although union() can be called up to $|E|$ times, it is exited after one (the first) test if a cycle is detected and it performs a union, which is of complexity $O(|V|)$, only for $|V| − 1$ edges added to tree. Hence, the complexity of KruskalAlgorithm()'s for loop is $O(|E| + (|V| − 1)|V|)$, which is $O(|V|^2)$. Therefore, the complexity of KruskalAlgorithm() is determined by the complexity of a sorting algorithm which is $O(|E|\lg|E|)$, that is, $O(|E|\lg|V|)$.

8.5.3 Jarník-Prim's Algorithm

Another algorithm was discovered by Vojtech Jarník (pronounced: yar-neek) in 1936 and later rediscovered by Robert Prim. In this method, all of the edges are also initially ordered, but a candidate for inclusion in the spanning tree is an edge which not only does not lead to cycles in the tree, but also is incident to a vertex already in the tree:

```
JarnikPrimAlgorithm(weighted connected undirected graph)
    tree = null;
    edges = sequence of all edges of graph sorted by weight;
    for i = 1 to |V| − 1
        for j = 1 to |edges|
            if e_j from edges does not form a cycle with edges in tree and
                is incident to a vertex in tree
                    add e_j to tree;
                    break;
```

FIGURE **8.15**   A spanning tree of graph (a) found (ba–bb) with Borůvka's algorithm, (ca–cf) with Kruskal's algorithm, (da–df) with Jarník-Prim's algorithm, (ea–el) and with Dijkstra's method.

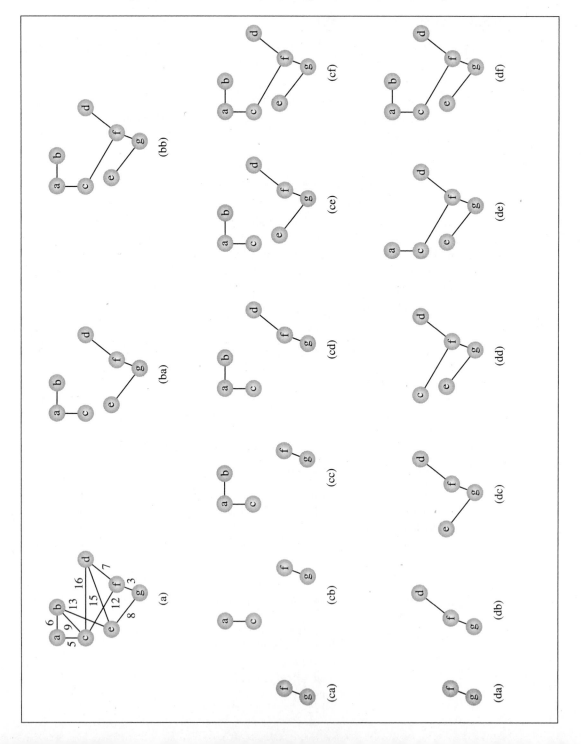

FIGURE **8.15**   *(continued)*

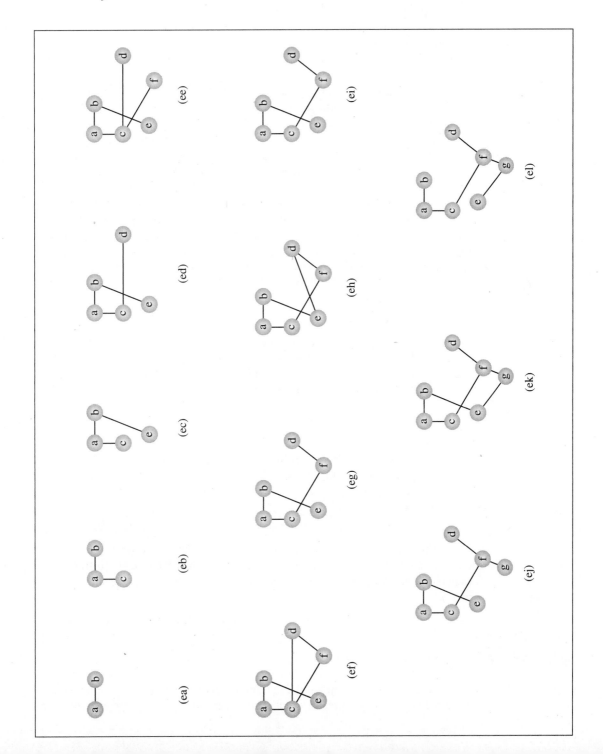

Figures 8.15da–df contain a step-by-step example of Jarník-Prim's algorithm. The spanning tree resulting from this algorithm is the same as that given by the Kruskal algorithm; however, the order in which edges have been added to the tree is different. The inner loop of `JarnikPrimAlgorithm()` can be $O(E)$ in the worst case, and since the outer loop iterates $|V| - 1$ times, the inner loop may iterate $O(|V||E|)$ times in total. However, this complexity can be substantially improved by a careful implementation of `edges`.

The difference between the Kruskal algorithm and the Jarník-Prim algorithm is that the latter always keeps the tree being constructed in one piece so that it is a tree at all stages of application of this algorithm. The Kruskal algorithm is more concerned about the outcome, so it considers it irrelevant that in the middle of its execution the spanning tree may not be a tree at all, but at best a collection of trees. Nevertheless, the Kruskal algorithm guarantees that, at the end, there is only one spanning tree. Therefore, the Jarník-Prim algorithm may be considered more elegant, as we see a tree being expanded at all times. The price for this elegance is that the only edges that can be added to the tree are the ones which are not isolated from the tree built so far, so that certain edges may need to be reconsidered several times. In the Kruskal algorithm, each edge needs to be considered only once, since if it leads to a cycle at one stage, it all the more would lead to a cycle at a later stage, and hence, it does not have to be reconsidered anymore. Thus, the Kruskal algorithm is faster.

8.5.4 Dijkstra's Method

Kruskal's and Jarník-Prim's algorithms require that all the edges be ordered before beginning to build the spanning tree. This, however, is not necessary; it is possible to build a spanning tree by using any order of edges. A method was proposed by Dijkstra (1960) and independently by Robert Kalaba, and because no particular order of edges is required here, their method is more general than the other two.

```
DijkstraMethod(weighted connected undirected graph)
    tree = null;
    edges = an unsorted sequence of all edges of graph;
    for j = 1 to |E|
        add eⱼ to tree;
        if there is a cycle in tree
            remove an edge with maximum weight from this only cycle;
```

In this algorithm, the tree is being expanded by adding to it edges one by one, and if a cycle is detected, then an edge in this cycle with maximum weight is discarded. An example of building the minimum spanning tree with this method is shown in Figures 8.15ea–el.

☐ 8.6 Connectivity

In many problems, we are interested in finding a path in the graph from one vertex to any other vertex. For undirected graphs, this means that there are no separate pieces, or subgraphs, of the graph; for a digraph, it means that there are some places in the graph to which we can get from some directions but are not necessarily able to return to the starting points.

8.6.1 Connectivity in Undirected Graphs

An undirected graph is called *connected* when there is a path between any two vertices of the graph. The depth-first search algorithm can be used for recognizing whether a graph is connected provided that the loop heading

> `while` *there is a vertex* `v` *such that num(*`v`*)* `== 0`

is removed. Then, after the algorithm is finished, we have to check whether the list `edges` includes all vertices of the graph or simply check if `i` is equal to the number of vertices.

Connectivity comes in degrees: A graph can be more or less connected, and it depends on the number of different paths between its vertices. A graph is called *n-connected* if there are at least n different paths between any two vertices; that is, there are n paths between any two vertices that have no vertices in common. A special type of graph is a *2-connected,* or *biconnected,* graph for which there are at least two different paths between any two vertices. A graph is not biconnected if a vertex can be found which always has to be included in the path between at least two vertices a and $b.$ In other words, if this vertex is removed from the graph (along with incident edges), then there is no way to find a path from a to b, which means that the graph is split into two separate subgraphs. Such vertices are called *articulation points,* or *cut vertices,* and vertices a and b in Figure 8.1d are examples of articulation points. If an edge causes a graph to be split into two subgraphs, it is called a *bridge,* as for example, the *edge(bc)* in Figure 8.1d. The subgraphs that result from removing an articulation point or a bridge are called *blocks,* or *biconnected components.* It is important to know how to decompose a graph into biconnected components.

Articulation points can be detected by extending the depth-first search algorithm. This algorithm creates a tree with forward edges (the graph edges included in the tree) and back edges (the edges not included). A vertex v in this tree is an articulation point if it has at least one subtree unconnected with any of its predecessors by a back edge; because it is a tree, certainly none of v's predecessors is reachable from any of its successors by a forward link. For example, the graph in Figure 8.16a is transformed into a depth-first search tree (Figure 8.16c), and this tree has four articulation points, $b, d, h,$ and $i,$ since there is no back edge from any node below d to any node above it in the tree and no back edge from any vertex in the right subtree of h to any vertex above $h.$ But vertex g cannot be an articulation point because its successor h is connected to a vertex above it. The four vertices divide the graph into the five blocks indicated in Figure 8.16c by dotted lines.

A special case for an articulation point is when a vertex is a root with more than one descendant. In Figure 8.16a, the vertex chosen for the root, $a,$ has three incident edges, but only one of them becomes a forward edge in Figures 8.16b and 8.16c, since the other two are processed by depth-first search. Therefore, if this algorithm again recursively reaches $a,$ there is no untried edge. If a were an articulation point, there

Figure **8.16** Finding blocks and articulation points using `blockDFS()` algorithm.

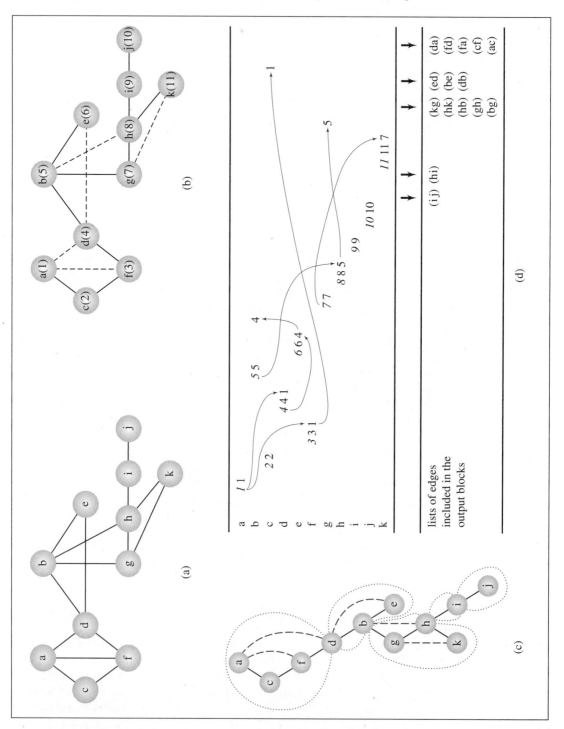

would be at least one such untried edge, and this indicates that a is a cut vertex. So a is not an articulation point. To sum up, we say that a vertex v is an articulation point

1. if v is the root of the depth-first search tree and v has more than one descendant in this tree or

2. if at least one of v's subtrees includes no vertex connected by a back edge with any of v's predecessors

To find articulation points, a parameter $pred(v)$ is used, defined as $min(num(v)$, $num(u_1), \ldots, num(u_k))$, where $u_1, \ldots, u_k$ are vertices connected by a back edge with a descendant of v or with v itself. Because the higher a predecessor of v is, the lower its number is, choosing a minimum number means choosing the highest predecessor. For the tree in Figure 8.16c, $pred(c) = pred(d) = 1$, $pred(b) = 4$, and $pred(k) = 7$.

The algorithm uses a stack to store all currently processed edges. After an articulation point is identified, the edges corresponding to a block of the graph are output. The algorithm is given as follows:

```
blockDFS(v)
    pred(v) = num(v) = i++;
    for all vertices u adjacent to v
        if edge(uv) is not on stack
            push(edge(uv));
        if num(u) is 0
            blockDFS(u);
            if pred(u) ≥ num(v)              // if there is no edge from u to a
                e = pop();                    // vertex above v, output a block
                while e != edge(vu)           // by popping all edges off the
                    output e;                 // stack until edge(vu) is
                    e = pop();                // popped off;
                output e;                     // e == edge(vu);
            else pred(v) = min(pred(v);pred(u)); // take a predecessor higher up in
        else if u is not the parent of v      // tree;
            pred(v) = min(pred(v),num(u));    // update when back edge from v is
                                              // found;
blockSearch()
    for all vertices v
        num(v) = 0;
    i = 1;
    while there is a vertex v such that num(v) == 0
        blockDFS(v);
```

An example of the execution of this algorithm is shown in Figure 8.16d as applied to the graph in Figure 8.16a. The table lists all changes in $pred(v)$ for vertices v processed by the algorithm, and the arrows show the source of the new values of $pred(v)$. For each vertex v, blockDFS(v) first assigns two numbers: $num(v)$, shown in italics, and $pred(v)$, which may change during the execution of blockDFS(v). For example, a is processed first with $num(a)$ and $pred(a)$ set to 1. The $edge(ac)$ is pushed onto the stack, and since $num(c)$ is 0, the algorithm is invoked for c. At this point, $num(c)$ and $pred(c)$

are set to 2. Next, the algorithm is invoked for f, a descendant of c, so that $num(f)$ and $pred(f)$ are set to 3, and then it is invoked for a, a descendant of f. Since $num(a)$ is not 0 and a is not f's parent, $pred(f)$ is set to $1 = \min(pred(f), num(a)) = \min(3, 1)$.

This algorithm also outputs the edges in detected blocks, and these edges are shown in Figure 8.16d at the moment they were output after popping them off the stack.

8.6.2 Connectivity in Directed Graphs

For directed graphs, connectedness can be defined in two ways depending on whether or not the direction of the edges is taken into account. A directed graph is *weakly connected* if the undirected graph with the same vertices and the same edges is connected. A directed graph is *strongly connected* if for each pair of vertices there is a path between them in both directions. The entire digraph is not always strongly connected, but it may be composed of *strongly connected components* (SCC), which are defined as subsets of vertices of the graph such that each of these subsets induces a strongly connected digraph.

To determine SCCs, we also refer to depth-first search. Let vertex v be the first vertex of an SCC for which depth-first search is applied. Such a vertex is called the *root of the SCC*. Since each vertex u in this SCC is reachable from v, $num(v) < num(u)$, and only after all such vertices u have been visited, the depth-first search backtracks to v. In this case, which is recognized by the fact that $pred(v) = num(v)$, the SCC accessible from the root can be output.

The problem now is how to find all such roots of the digraph, which is analogous to finding articulation points in an undirected graph. To that end, the parameter $pred(v)$ is also used, where $pred(v)$ is the lower number chosen out of $num(v)$ and $pred(u)$, where u is a vertex reachable from v and belonging to the same SCC as v. How can we determine whether two vertices belong to the same SCC before SCC has been determined? The apparent circularity is solved by using a stack that stores all vertices belonging to the SCCs under construction. The topmost vertices on the stack belong to the currently analyzed SCC. Although construction is not finished, we at least know which vertices are already included in the SCC. The algorithm attributed to Tarjan is as follows:

```
strongDFS(v)
  pred(v) = num(v) = i++;
  push(v);
  for all vertices u adjacent to v
    if num(u) is 0
      strongDFS(u);
      pred(v) = min(pred(v),pred(u));        // take a predecessor higher up in
    else if num(u) < num(v) and u is on stack // tree; update if back edge found
      pred(v) = min(pred(v),num(u));          // to vertex u is in the same SCC;
  if pred(v) == num(v)                         // if the root of a SCC is found,
    w = pop();                                 // output this SCC, i.e.,
    while w != v                               // pop all vertices off the stack
      output w;                                // until v is popped off;
      w = pop();
    output w;                                  // w == v;
```

FIGURE **8.17**   Finding strongly connected components with `strongDFS()` algorithm.

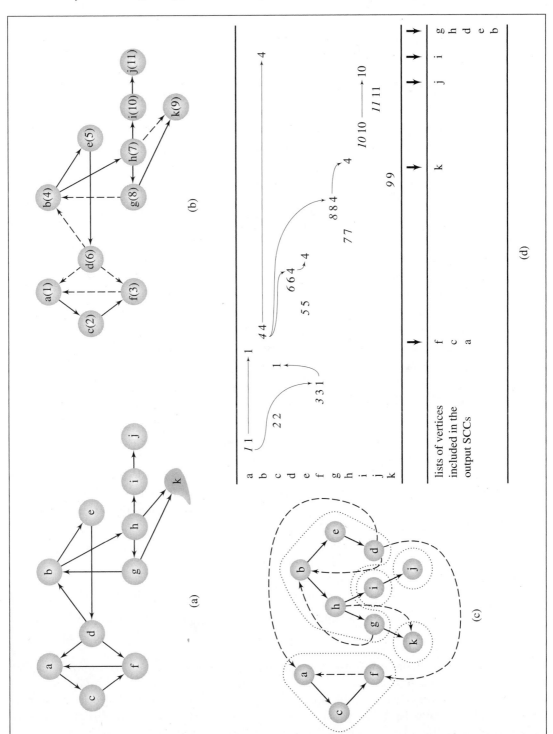

```
stronglyConnectedComponentSearch()
    for all vertices v
        num(v) = 0;
    i = 1;
    while there is a vertex v such that num(v) == 0
        strongDFS(v);
```

Figure 8.17 contains a sample execution of Tarjan's algorithm. The digraph in Figure 8.17a is processed by a series of calls to strongDFS(), which assigns to vertices a though k the numbers shown in parentheses in Figure 8.17b. During this process, five SCCs are detected: $\{a,c,f\},\{b,d,e,g,h\},\{i\},\{j\}$, and $\{k\}$. Figure 8.17c contains the depth-first search tree created by this process. Note that two trees are created so that the number of trees does not have to correspond to the number of SCCs, as the number of trees did not correspond to the number of blocks in the case for undirected graphs. Figure 8.17d indicates, in italics, numbers assigned to $num(v)$ and all changes of parameter $pred(v)$ for all vertices v in the graph. It also shows the SCCs output during the processing of the graph.

⬚ 8.7 TOPOLOGICAL SORT

In many situations, there is a set of tasks to be performed. For some pairs of tasks, it matters which task is performed first, whereas for other pairs, the order of execution is unimportant. For example, students need to take into consideration which courses are prerequisites or corequisites for other courses when making a schedule for the upcoming semester so that Computer Programming II cannot be taken before Computer Programming I, but the former can be taken along with, say, Ethics or Introduction to Sociology.

The dependencies between tasks can be shown in the form of a digraph. A *topological sort* linearizes a digraph; that is, it labels all its vertices with numbers $1, \ldots, |V|$ so that $i < j$ only if there is a path from vertex v_i to vertex v_j. The digraph must not include a cycle; otherwise, a topological sort is impossible.

The algorithm for a topological sort is rather simple. We have to find a vertex v with no outgoing edges, called a *sink* or a *minimal vertex*, and then disregard all edges leading from any vertex to v. The summary of the topological sort algorithm is as follows:

```
topologicalSort(digraph)
    for i = 1 to |V|
        find a minimal vertex v;
        num(v) = i;
        remove from digraph vertex v and all edges incident with v;
```

Figure 8.18 contains an example of an application of this algorithm. The graph in Figure 8.18a undergoes a sequence of deletions (Figures 8.18b–f) and results in the sequence g, e, b, f, d, c, a.

Actually, it is not necessary to remove the vertices and edges from the digraph while it is processed if it can be ascertained that all successors of the vertex being processed have already been processed, so they can be considered as deleted. And once again, depth-first search comes to the rescue. By the nature of this method, if the

FIGURE **8.18**   Executing topological sort.

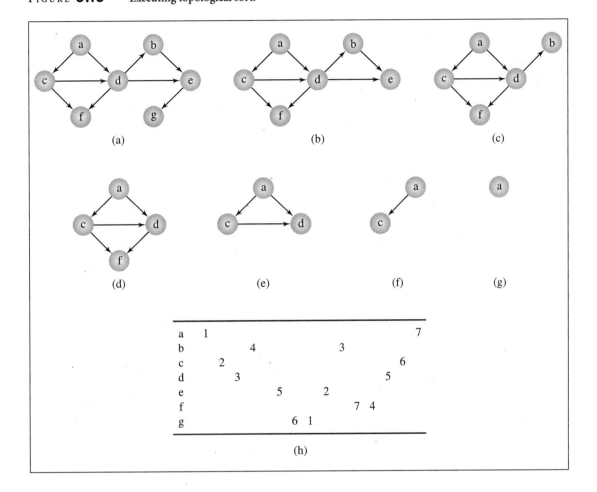

a	1						7
b			4			3	
c		2					6
d			3				5
e				5	2		
f						7	4
g				6	1		

(h)

search backtracks to a vertex *v*, then all successors of *v* can be assumed to have already been searched (that is, output and deleted from the digraph). Here is how depth-first search can be adapted to topological sort:

```
TS(v)
    num(v) = i++;
    for all vertices u adjacent to v
        if num(u) == 0
            TS(u);
        else if TSNum(u) == 0
            error;              // a cycle detected;
    TSNum(v) = j++;             // after processing all successors of v,
                               // assign to v a number larger than
                               // assigned to any of its successors;
```

```
topologicalSorting(digraph)
    for all vertices v
        num(v) = TSNum(v) = 0;
    i = j = 1;
    while there is a vertex v such that num(v) == 0
        TS(v);
    output vertices according to their TSNum's;
```

The table in Figure 8.18h indicates the order in which this algorithm assigns *num*(*v*), the first number in each row, and *TSNum*(*v*), the second number, for each vertex *v* of the graph in Figure 8.18a.

⌐ 8.8 NETWORKS

8.8.1 Maximum Flows

An important type of graph is a network. A network can be exemplified by a network of pipelines used to deliver water from one source to one destination. However, water is not simply pumped through one pipe, but through many pipes with many pumping stations in between. The pipes are of different diameter and the stations are of different power so that the amount of water that can be pumped may differ from one pipeline to another. For example, the network in Figure 8.19 has eight pipes and six pumping stations. The numbers shown in this figure are the maximum capacities of each pipeline. For example, the pipe going northeast from the source *s*, the pipe *sa*, has a capacity of 5 units (say, 5000 gallons per hour). The problem is to maximize the capacity of the entire network so that it can transfer the maximum amount of water. It may not be obvious how to accomplish this goal. Notice that the pipe *sa* coming from the source goes to a station which has only one outgoing pipe, *ab*, of capacity 4. This means that we cannot put 5 units through pipe *sa*, since pipe *ab* cannot transfer it. Also, the amount of water coming to station *b* has to be controlled as well because if both incoming pipes, *ab* and *cb*, are used to full capacity, then the outgoing pipe, *bt*, cannot process it either. It is far from obvious, especially for large networks, what the amounts of water put through each pipe should be to utilize the network maximally. Computational analysis of this particular network problem was initiated by Lester R. Ford and D. Ray Fulkerson. Since their work, scores of algorithms have been published to solve this problem.

Before the problem is stated more formally, we would like to give some definitions. A *network* is a digraph with one vertex *s*, called the *source*, with no incoming edges, and one vertex *t*, called the *sink*, with no outgoing edges. (These definitions are chosen for their intuitiveness; however, in a more general case, both source and sink can be any two vertices.) With each edge *e* we associate a number *cap*(*e*) called the *capacity* of the edge. A *flow* is a real function $f: E \rightarrow R$ that assigns a number to each edge of the network and meets these two conditions:

1. The flow through an edge *e* cannot be greater than its capacity, or $0 \leq f(e) \leq cap(e)$ (capacity constraint).

FIGURE **8.19**   A pipeline with eight pipes and six pumping stations.

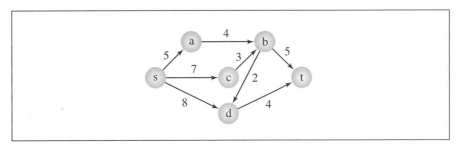

2. The total flow coming to a vertex v is the same as the total flow coming from it, or $\sum_u f(edge(uv)) = \sum_w f(edge(vw))$, where v is neither the source nor the sink (flow conservation).

The problem now is to maximize the flow f so that the sum $\sum_u f(edge(ut))$ has a maximum value for any possible function f. This is called a *maximum-flow* (or *max-flow*) *problem*.

An important concept used in the Ford-Fulkerson algorithm is the concept of cut. A *cut separating s and t* is a set of edges between vertices of set X and vertices of set $\bar{X}$; any vertex of the graph belongs to one of these sets, and source s is in X and sink t is in $\bar{X}$. For example, in Figure 8.19, if $X = \{s,a\}$, then $\bar{X} = \{b,c,d,t\}$, and the cut is the set of edges $\{(a,b),(s,c),(s,d)\}$. This means that if all edges belonging to this set are cut, then there is no way to get from s to t. Let us define the capacity of the cut as the sum of capacities of all its edges leading from a vertex in X to a vertex in $\bar{X}$; thus, $cap\{(a,b),(s,c),(s,d)\} = cap(a,b) + cap(s,c) + cap(s,d) = 19$. Now, it should be clear that the flow through the network cannot be greater than the capacity of any cut. This observation leads to the *max-flow min-cut theorem* (Ford and Fulkerson 1956):

Theorem. In any network, the maximal flow from s to t is equal to the minimal capacity of any cut.

This theorem states what is expressed in the simile of a chain being as strong as its weakest link. Although there may be cuts with great capacity, the cut with the smallest capacity determines the flow of the network. For example, although the capacity $cap\{(a,b),(s,c),(s,d)\} = 19$, two edges coming to t cannot transfer more than 9 units. Now we have to find a cut which has the smallest capacity among all possible cuts and transfer through each edge of this cut as many units as the capacity allows. To that end, a new concept is used.

A *flow-augmenting path* from s to t is a sequence of edges from s to t such that, for each edge in this path, the flow $f(e) < cap(e)$ on forward edges and $f(e) > 0$ on backward edges. It means that such a path is not optimally used yet, and it can transfer more units than it is currently transferring. If the flow for at least one edge of the path reaches its capacity, then obviously the flow cannot be augmented. Note that the path does not have to consist only of forward edges so that examples of paths in Figure 8.19 are s, a, b, t, and s, d, b, t. Backward edges are what they are, backward; they push back some units of flow, decreasing the flow of the network. If they can be eliminated, then the overall flow in the network can be increased. Hence, the process of augmenting flows of paths is not finished until the flow for such edges is zero. Our task now is to find an augmenting path if it exists. Since there may be a very large number of paths from s to t, finding an augmenting path is a nontrivial problem, and Ford and Fulkerson (1957) devised the first algorithm to accomplish it in a systematic manner.

The *labeling* phase of the algorithm consists of assigning to each vertex v a label which is the pair

$$label(v) = (parent(v), slack(v))$$

where $parent(v)$ is the vertex from which v is being accessed and $slack(v)$ is the amount of flow that can be transferred from s to v. The forward and backward edges are treated differently. If a vertex u is accessed from v through a forward edge, then

$$label(u) = (v^+, \min(slack(v), slack(edge(vu))))$$

where

$$slack(edge(vu)) = cap(edge(vu)) - f(edge(vu))$$

which is the difference between the capacity of $edge(vu)$ and the amount of flow currently carried by this edge. If the edge from v to u is backward (i.e., forward from u to v), then

$$label(u) = (v^-, \min(slack(v), f(edge(uv))))$$

After a vertex is labeled, it is stored for later processing. In this process, only this $edge(vu)$ is labeled, which allows for some more flow to be added. For forward edges, this is possible when $slack(edge(vu)) > 0$, and for backward edges when $f(edge(uv)) > 0$. However, finding one such path may not finish the entire process. The process is finished if we are stuck in the middle of the network unable to label any more edges. If we reach the sink t, the flows of the edges on the augmenting path that was just found are updated by increasing flows of forward edges and decreasing flows of backward edges, and the process restarts in the quest for another augmenting path. Here is a summary of the algorithm.

```
augmentPath(network with source s and sink t)
    for each edge e in the path from s to t
        if forward(e)
            f(e) += slack(t);
        else f(e) -= slack(t);


FordFulkersonAlgorithm(network with source s and sink t)
    set flow of all edges and vertices to 0;
    label(s) = (null,∞);
    labeled = {s};
    while labeled is not empty // while not stuck;
        detach a vertex v from labeled;
        for all unlabeled vertices u adjacent to v
            if forward(edge(vu)) and slack(edge(vu)) > 0
                label(u) = (v⁺, min(slack(v), slack(edge(vu))))
            else if backward(edge(vu)) and f(edge(uv)) > 0
```

FIGURE **8.20**   An execution of FordFulkersonAlgorithm() using depth-first search.

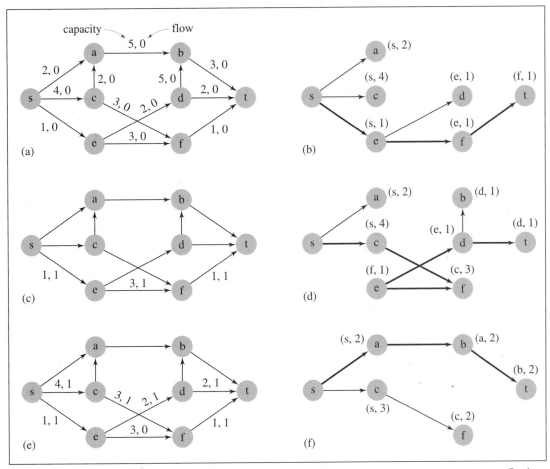

(a)   (b)   (c)   (d)   (e)   (f)

Continues

```
        label(u) = (v⁻,min(slack(v),f(edge(uv))));
    if u got labeled
        if u == t
            augmentPath(network);
            labeled = {s};    // look for another path;
        else include u in labeled;
```

Notice that this algorithm is noncommittal with respect to the way the network should be scanned. In exactly what order should vertices be included in labeled and detached from it? This question is left open and we choose push and pop as implementations of these two operations, thereby processing the network in a depth-first fashion.

Figure 8.20 illustrates an example. Each edge has two numbers associated with it, the capacity and the current flow, and initially the flow is set to zero for each edge (8.20a). We begin by putting the vertex *s* in labeled. In the first iteration of the

FIGURE **8.20**   *(continued)*

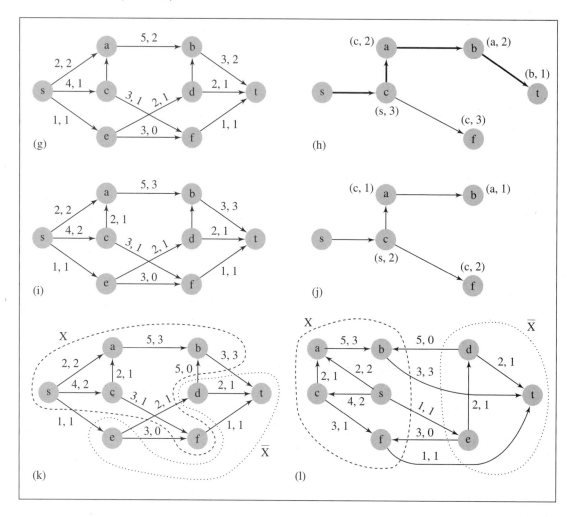

while loop, *s* is detached from `labeled`, and in the `for` loop, label (*s*,2) is assigned to the first adjacent vertex, *a*, label (*s*,4) to vertex *c*, and label (*s*,1) to vertex *e* (Figure 8.20b), and all three vertices are pushed onto `labeled`. The `for` loop is exited, and since `labeled` is not empty, the `while` loop begins its second iteration. In this iteration, a vertex is popped off from `labeled`, which is *e*, and both unlabeled vertices incident to *e*, vertices *d* and *f*, are labeled and pushed onto `labeled`. Now, the third iteration of the `while` loop begins by popping *f* from `labeled` and labeling its only unlabeled neighbor, vertex *t*. Because *t* is the sink, the flows of all edges on the augmenting path *s, e, f, t* are updated in the inner `for` loop (Figure 8.20c), `labeled` is reinitialized to {*s*}, and the next round begins to find another augmenting path.

The next round starts with the fourth iteration of the `while` loop. In its eighth iteration, the sink is reached (Figure 8.20d) and flows of edges on the new augment-

FIGURE **8.21**   An example of an inefficiency of `FordFulkersonAlgorithm( )`.

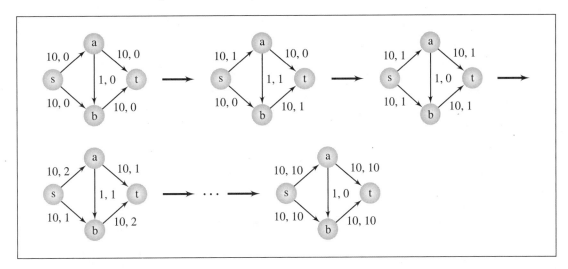

ing path are updated (Figure 8.20e). Note that this time one edge, *edge(fe)*, is a backward edge. Therefore, its flow is decremented, not incremented as is the case for forward edges. Afterward, two more augmenting paths are found and corresponding edges are updated. In the last round, we are unable to reach the sink (Figure 8.20j), which means that all augmenting edges have been found and the maximum flow has been determined.

If after finishing execution of the algorithm all vertices labeled in the last round, including the source, are put in the set X and the unlabeled vertices in the set $\overline{X}$, then we have a min-cut (Figure 8.20k). For clarity, both sets are also shown in Figure 8.20l. Note that all the edges from X to $\overline{X}$ are used in full capacity, and all the edges from $\overline{X}$ to X do not transfer any flow at all.

The complexity of this implementation of the algorithm is not necessarily a function of the number of vertices and edges in the network. Consider the network in Figure 8.21. Using a depth-first implementation, we could choose the augmenting path *s, a, b, t* with flows of all three edges set to 1. The next augmenting path could be *s, b, a, t* with flows of two forward edges set to 1 and the flow of one backward *edge(ba)* reset to 0. Next time, the augmenting path could be the same as the first, with flows of two edges set to 2 and with the vertical edge set to 1. It is clear that an augmenting path could be chosen $2 \cdot 10$ times, although there are only four vertices in the network.

The problem with `FordFulkersonAlgorithm( )` is that it uses the depth-first approach when searching for an augmenting path. But as already mentioned, this choice does not stem from the nature of this algorithm. The depth-first approach attempts to reach the sink as soon as possible. However, trying to find the shortest augmenting path gives better results. This leads to a breadth-first approach (Edmonds and Karp 1972). The breadth-first processing uses the same procedure as `FordFulkersonAlgorithm( )` except that this time `labeled` is a queue. Figure 8.22 illustrates an example.

FIGURE **8.22**   An execution of `FordFulkersonAlgorithm()` using breadth-first search.

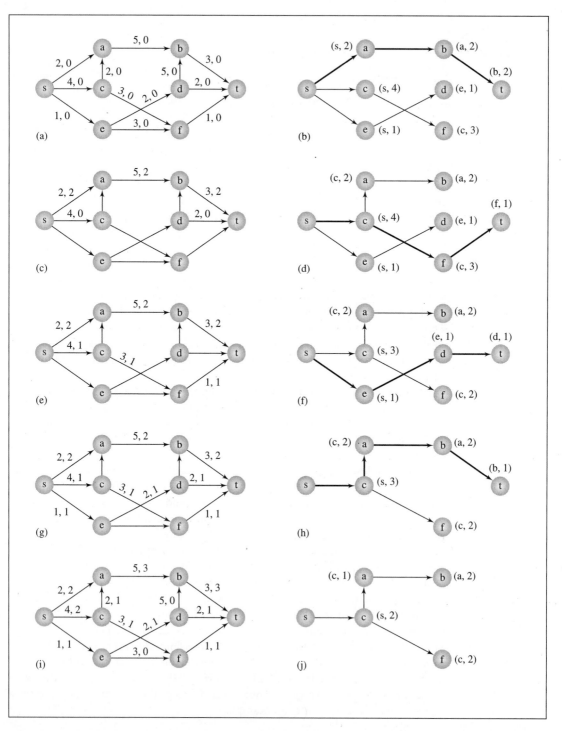

To determine one single augmenting path, the algorithm requires at most $2|E|$, or $O(|E|)$ steps, to check both sides of each edge. The shortest augmenting path in the network can have only one edge, and the longest path can have at most $|V| - 1$ edges. Therefore, there can be augmenting paths of lengths $1, 2, \ldots, |V| - 1$. The number of augmenting paths of a certain length is at most $|E|$. Therefore, to find all augmenting paths of all possible lengths, the algorithm needs to perform $O(|V||E|)$ steps. And since finding one such path is of order $O(|E|)$, the algorithm is of order $O(|V||E|^2)$.

Although the pure breadth-first search approach is better than the pure depth-first search implementation, it still is far from ideal. We will not fall into a loop of tiny increments of augmenting steps anymore, but there still seems to be a great deal of wasted effort. In breadth-first search, a large number of vertices are labeled to find the shortest path (shortest in a given iteration). Then all these labels are discarded to re-create them when looking for another augmenting path (*edge(sc)*, *edge(se)*, and *edge(cf)* in Figure 8.22b–d). Therefore, it is desirable to reduce this redundancy. Also, there is some merit to using the depth-first approach in that it attempts to aim at the goal, the sink, without expanding a number of paths at the same time and finally choosing only one and discarding the rest. Hence, the Solomonic solution appears to use both approaches, depth-first and breadth-first. Breadth-first search prepares the ground to prevent loops of small increments from happening (as in Figure 8.21) and to guarantee that depth-first search takes the shortest route. Only afterward, the depth-first search is launched to find the sink by aiming right at it. An algorithm based upon this principle was devised first by Efim A. Dinic (pronounced: dee-neetz).

In Dinic's algorithm, up to $|V| - 1$ passes (or phases) through the network are performed, and in each pass, all augmenting paths of the same length from the source to the sink are determined. Then, only some or all of these paths are augmented.

All augmenting paths form a *layered network* (also called a *level network*). Extracting layered networks from the underlying network starts from the lowest values. First, a layered network of a path of length one is found, if such a network exists. After the network is processed, a layered network of paths of length two is determined, if it exists, and so on. For example, the layered network with the shortest paths corresponding with the network in Figure 8.23a is shown in Figure 8.23b. In this network, all augmenting paths are of length three. A layered network with a single path of length one and layered networks with paths of length two do not exist. The layered network is created using breadth-first processing, and only forward edges that can carry more flow and backward edges that already carry some flow are included. Otherwise, even if an edge may lay on a short path from the source to the sink, it is not included. Note that the layered network is determined by breadth-first search that begins in the sink and ends in the source.

Now, since all the paths in a layered network are of the same length, it is possible to avoid redundant tests of edges that are part of augmenting paths. If in a current layered network there is no way to go from a vertex v to any of its neighbors, then in later tests in the same layered network there will be the same situation; hence, checking again all neighbors of v is not needed. Therefore, if such a dead end vertex v is detected, all edges incident with v are marked as blocked so that there is no possibility to get to v from any direction. Also, all saturated edges are considered blocked. All blocked edges are shown in dashed lines in Figure 8.23.

FIGURE **8.23** An execution of `DinicAlgorithm()`.

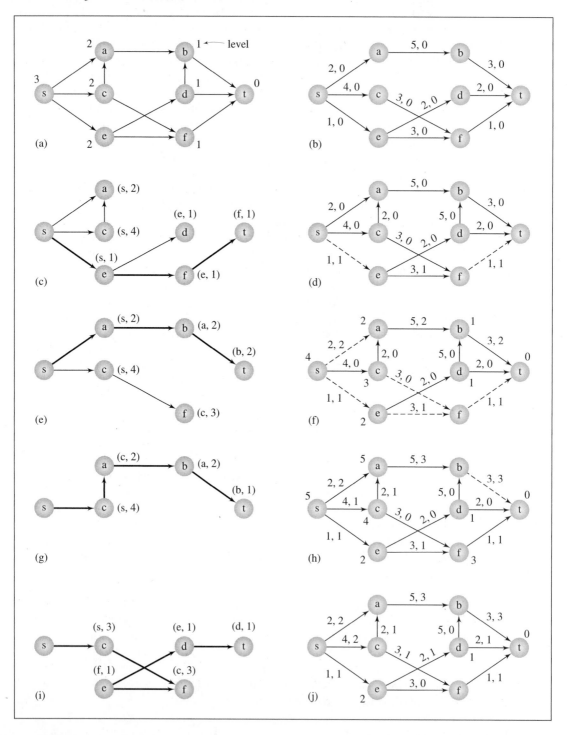

After a layered network is determined, the depth-first process finds as many augmenting paths as possible. Since all paths are of the same length, depth-first search does not go to the sink through some longer sequence of edges. After one such path is found, it is augmented and another augmenting path of the same length is looked for. For each such path, at least one edge becomes saturated so that eventually no augmenting path can be found. For example, in the layered network in Figure 8.23b that includes only augmenting paths three edges long, path *s, e, f, t* is found (Figure 8.23c), and all its edges are augmented (Figure 8.23d). Then only one more three-edge path is found, the path *s, a, b, t* (8.23e), since, for example, previous augmentation saturated *edge(ft)* so that the partial path *s, c, f* ends with a dead end. In addition, because no other vertex can be reached from *f*, all edges incident with *f* are blocked (Figure 8.23f) so that an attempt to find the third three-edge augmenting path only tests vertex *c*, but not vertex *f*, since *edge(cf)* is blocked.

If no more augmenting paths can be found, a higher level layered network is found, and augmenting paths for this network are searched for. The process stops when no layered network can be formed. For example, out of the network in Figure 8.23f, the layered network in Figure 8.23g is formed, which has only one four-edge path. To be sure, this is the only augmenting path for this network. After augmenting this path, the situation in the network is as in Figure 8.23h, and the last layered network is formed, which also has only one path, this time a path of five edges. The path is augmented (Figure 8.23j) and then no other layered network can be found. This algorithm can be summarized in the following pseudocode:

```
layerNetwork(network with source s and sink t)
    for all vertices u
        level(t) = -1;
    level(t) = 0;
    enqueue(t);
    while queue is not empty
        v = dequeue();
        for all vertices u adjacent to v such that level(u) == -1
            if forward(edge(uv)) and slack(edge(uv)) > 0 or
                backward(edge(uv)) and f(edge(vu)) > 0
                    level(u) = level(v)+1;
                    enqueue(u);
            if u == s
                return success;
    return failure;


processAugmentingPaths(network with source s and sink t)
    unblock all edges;
    labeled = {s};
    while labeled is not empty // while not stuck;
        pop v from labeled;
        for all unlabeled vertices u adjacent to v such that
            edge(vu) is not blocked and level(v) == level(u) -1
            if forward(edge(vu)) and slack(edge(vu)) > 0
```

$$label(u) = (v^+, min(slack(v), slack(edge(vu))))$$

```
       else if backward(edge(vu)) and f(edge(uv)) > 0
```

$$label(u) = (v^-, min(slack(v), f(edge(uv)))));$$

```
    if u got labeled
       if u == t
          augmentPath();
          block saturated edges;
          labeled = {s};    // look for another path;
       else push u onto labeled;
  if no neighbor of v has been labeled
     block all edges incident with v;


DinicAlgorithm(network with source s sink t)
    set flows of all edges and vertices to 0;
    label(s) = (null, ∞);
    while layerNetwork(network) is successful
       processAugmentingPaths(network);
```

What is the complexity of this algorithm? There are maximum $|V| - 1$ layerings (phases) and up to $O(|E|)$ steps to layer the network. Hence, finding all the layered networks requires $O(|V||E|)$ steps. Moreover, there are $O(|E|)$ paths per phase (per one layered network) and, due to blocking, $O(|V|)$ steps to find one path, and since there are $O(|V|)$ layered networks, in the worst case, $O(|V|^2|E|)$ steps are required to find the augmenting paths. This estimation determines the efficiency of the algorithm, which is better than $O(|V||E|^2)$ for breadth-first `FordFulkersonAlgorithm()`. The improvement is in the number of steps to find one augmenting path, which is now $O(|V|)$, not $O(|E|)$, as before. The price for this improvement is the need to prepare the network by creating layered networks, which, as established, require additional $O(|V||E|)$ steps.

The difference in pseudocode for `FordFulkersonAlgorithm()` and `processAugmentingPaths()` is not large. The most important difference is in the amplified condition for expanding a path from a certain vertex *v*: Only the edges to adjacent vertices *u* that do not extend augmenting paths beyond the length of paths in the layered network are considered.

8.8.2 Maximum Flows of Minimum Cost

In the previous discussion, edges had two parameters, capacity and flow: how much flow they can carry and how much flow they are actually carrying. But although many different maximum flows through the network are possible, we choose the one dictated by the algorithm currently in use. For example, Figure 8.24 illustrates two possible maximum flows for the same network. Note that in the first case, the *edge(ab)* is not used at all; only in the second case are all the edges transferring some flow. The breadth-first algorithm leads to the first maximum flow and finishes our quest for maximum flow after identifying it. However, in many situations, this is not a good decision. If there are many possible maximum flows, it does not mean that any one of them is equally good.

FIGURE **8.24**   Two possible maximum flows for the same network.

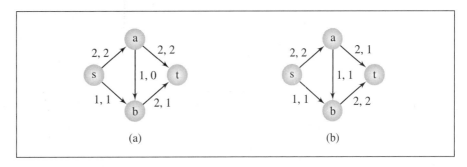

(a)   (b)

Consider the following example. If edges are roads between some locations, then it is not enough to know that a road has one or two lanes to choose a proper route. If the *distance*(*a,t*) is very long and *distance*(*a,b*) and *distance*(*b,t*) are relatively short, then it is better to consider the second maximum flow (Figure 8.24b) as a viable option rather than the first (Figure 8.24a). However, this may not be enough. The shorter way can have no pavement: It can be muddy, hilly, close to the avalanche areas, sometimes blocked by boulders, among other disadvantages. Hence, using the distance as the sole criterion for choosing a road is insufficient. Taking the roundabout way may bring us to the destination faster and cheaper (to mention only time and gasoline burned).

We clearly need a third parameter for an edge: the *cost* of transferring one unit of flow through this edge. The problem now is how to find a maximum flow at minimum cost. More formally, if for each edge *e*, the *cost*(*e*) of sending one unit of flow is determined so that it costs $n \cdot cost(e)$ to transmit n units of flow over edge *e*, then we need to find a maximum flow *f* of minimum cost, or a flow such that

$$cost(f) = \min\{\textstyle\sum_{e \in E} f(e) \cdot cost(e) : f \text{ is a maximum flow}\}$$

Finding all possible maximum flows and comparing their costs is not a feasible solution because the amount of work to find all such flows can be prohibitive. Algorithms are needed that find not only a maximum flow but the maximum flow at minimum cost.

One strategy is based on the following theorem, proven first by W. S. Jewell, R. G. Busacker, and P. J. Gowen, and implicitly used by M. Iri (Ford and Fulkerson 1962):

Theorem. If *f* is a minimal-cost flow with the flow value *v* and *p* is the minimum cost augmenting path sending a flow of value 1 from the source to the sink, then the flow *f* + *p* is minimal and its flow value is *v* + 1.

The theorem should be intuitively clear. If we determined the cheapest way to send *v* units of flow through the network and afterward found a path for sending 1 unit of flow from the source to the sink, then we found the cheapest way to send *v* + 1 units using the route which is a combination of the route already determined and the path just found. If this augmenting path allows for sending 1 unit for minimum cost, then it also allows for sending 2 units at minimum cost, and also 3 units, up to n units, where n is the maximum amount of units that can be sent through this path; that is,

$$n = \min\{capacity(e) - f(e) : e \text{ is an edge in minimum cost augmenting path}\}$$

This also suggests how we can proceed systematically to find the cheapest maximum route. We start with all flows set to zero. In the first pass, we find the cheapest way to send 1 unit and then send as many units through this path as possible. After the second iteration, we find a path to send 1 unit at least cost, and we send through this path as many units as this path can hold and so on until no further dispatch from the source can be made or the sink cannot accept any more flow.

Note that the problem of finding maximum flow of minimum cost bears some resemblance to the problem of finding the shortest path, since the shortest path can be understood as the path with minimum cost. Hence, a procedure is needed to find the shortest path in the network so that as much flow as possible can be sent through this path. Therefore, a reference to an algorithm which solves the shortest path problem should not be surprising. We modify Dijkstra's algorithm used for solving the one-to-one shortest path problem (see Exercise 7 at the end of this chapter). Here is the algorithm:

```
modifiedDijkstraAlgorithm(network, s, t)
    for all vertices u
        f(u) = 0;
        cost(u) = ∞;
    set flows of all edges to 0;
    label(s) = (null,∞,0);
    labeled = null;
    while (true)
        v = a vertex not in labeled with minimal cost(v);
        if v == t
            if cost(t) == ∞ // no path from s to t can be found;
                return failure;
            else return success;
        add v to labeled;
        for all vertices u not in labeled and adjacent to v
            if forward(edge(vu)) and slack(edge(vu)) > 0 and cost(v)+ cost(vu) < cost(u)
                label(u) = (v⁺, min(slack(v),slack(edge(vu)), cost(v)+ cost(vu))
            else if backward(edge(vu)) and f(edge(uv)) > 0 and cost(v)− cost(uv) < cost(u)
                label(u) = (v⁻, min(slack(v),f(edge(uv)), cost(v) − cost(uv));

maxFlowMinCostAlgorithm(network with source s and sink t)
    while modifiedDijkstraAlgorithm(network,s,t) is successful
        augmentPath(network,s,t);
```

modifiedDijkstraAlgorithm() keeps track of three things at a time so that the label for each vertex is the triple

$$label(u) = (parent(u), flow(u), cost(u))$$

First, for each vertex u, it records the predecessor v, the vertex through which u is accessible from the source s. Second, it records the maximum amount of flow that can be pushed through the path from s to u and eventually to t. Third, it stores the cost of passing all the edges from the source to u. For forward $edge(vu)$, $cost(u)$ is the sum of the costs already accumulated in v plus the cost of pushing one unit of flow through $edge(vu)$. For backward $edge(vu)$, the unit cost of passing through this edge is subtracted from the $cost(v)$ and stored in $cost(u)$. Also, flows of edges included in augmented paths are updated; this task is performed by augmentPath() (see p. 406).

Figure 8.25 illustrates an example. In the first iteration of the while loop, labeled becomes $\{s\}$ and the three vertices adjacent to s are labeled, $label(a) = (s,2,6)$, $label(c) = (s,4,2)$, and $label(e) = (s,1,1)$. Then the vertex with the smallest cost is chosen, namely, vertex e. Now, labeled $= \{s,e\}$ and two vertices acquire new labels, $label(d) = (e,1,3)$ and $label(f) = (e,1,2)$. In the third iteration, vertex c is chosen, since its cost, 2, is minimal. Vertex a receives a new label, $(c,2,3)$, because the cost of accessing it from s through c is smaller than accessing it directly from s. Vertex f, which is adjacent to c, does not get a new label, since the cost of sending one unit of flow from s to f through c, 5, exceeds the cost of sending this unit through e, which is 2. In the fourth iteration, f is chosen, labeled becomes $\{s,e,c,f\}$, and $label(t) = (f,1,5)$. After the seventh iteration, the situation in the graph is as pictured in Figure 8.25b. The eighth iteration is exited right after the sink t is chosen, after which the path s, e, f, t is augmented (Figure 8.25c). The execution continues, modifiedDijkstraAlgorithm() is invoked four more times and in the last invocation no other path can be found from s to t. Note that the same paths were found here as in Figure 8.20, although in a different order, which was due to the cost of these paths: 5 is the cost of the first detected path (Figure 8.25b), 6 is the cost of the second path (Figure 8.25d), 8 is the cost of the third (Figure 8.25f), and 9 is the cost of the fourth (Figure 8.25h). But the distribution of flows for particular edges allowing for the maximum flow is slightly different. In Figure 8.20k, $edge(sa)$ transmits 2 units of flow, $edge(sc)$ transmits 2 units, and $edge(ca)$ transmits 1 unit. In Figure 8.25i, the same three edges transmit 1, 3, and 2 units, respectively.

8.9 MATCHING

Suppose that there are five job openings a, b, c, d, and e and five applicants p, q, r, s, and t with qualifications shown in this table:

Applicants:	p	q	r	s	t
Jobs:	$a\,b\,c$	$b\,d$	$a\,e$	e	$c\,d\,e$

The problem is how to find a worker for each job; that is, how to match jobs with workers. There are many problems of this type. The job matching problem can be modeled with a bipartite graph. A *bipartite graph* is one in which the set of vertices V can be divided into two subsets V_1 and V_2 such that, for each $edge(vw)$, if vertex v is in one of the two sets V_1 or V_2, then w is in the other set. In this example, one set of vertices, V_1, represents applicants, the other set, V_2, represents jobs, and edges represent jobs for which applicants are qualified (Figure 8.26). The task is to find a match between job and applicants so that one applicant is matched with one job. In a general

FIGURE **8.25**   Finding a maximum flow of minimum cost.

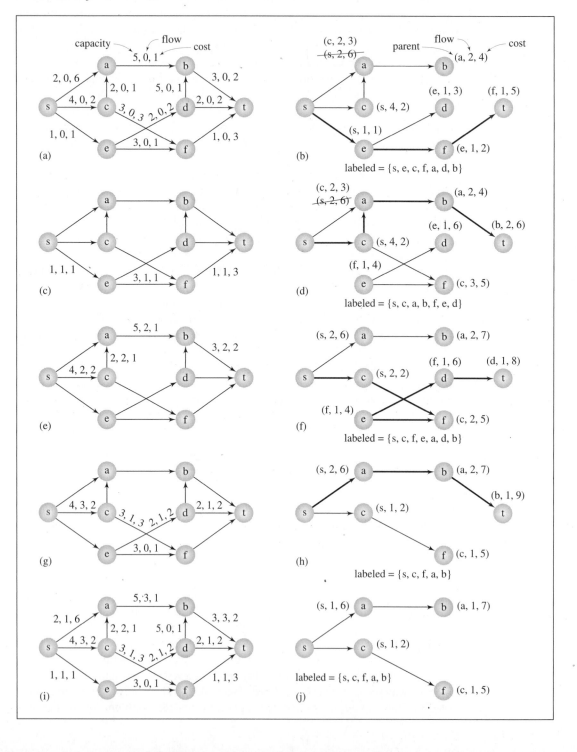

FIGURE **8.26**   Matching five applicants with five jobs.

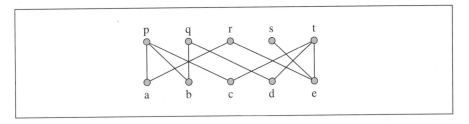

FIGURE **8.27**   A graph with matchings $M_1 = \{edge(ab), edge(ef)\}$ and $M_2 = \{edge(ab), edge(de), edge(fh)\}$.

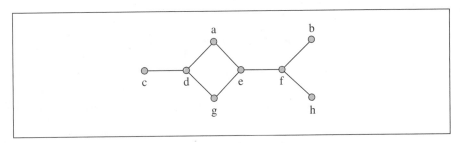

case, there may not be enough applicants, or there may be no way to assign an applicant for each opening, even if the number of applicants exceeds the number of openings. Hence, the task now is to assign applicants to as many jobs as possible.

A *matching M* in a graph $G = (V,E)$ is a subset of edges, $M \subseteq E$, such that no two edges share the same vertex; that is, no two edges are adjacent. A *maximum matching* is a matching that contains a maximum number of edges so that the number of unmatched vertices (that is, vertices not incident with edges in M) is minimal. For example, in the graph in Figure 8.27, the sets $M_1 = \{edge(cd), edge(ef)\}$ and $M_2 = \{edge(cd), edge(ge), edge(fh)\}$ are matchings, but M_2 is a maximum matching, whereas M_1 is not. A *perfect matching* is a matching that pairs all the vertices of graph G. A matching $M = \{edge(pc), edge(qb), edge(ra), edge(se), edge(td)\}$ in Figure 8.26 is a perfect matching, but there is no perfect matching for the graph in Figure 8.27. A *matching problem* consists in finding a maximum matching for a certain graph G. The problem of finding a perfect matching is also called the *marriage problem*.

An *alternating path for M* is a sequence of edges $edge(v_1v_2), edge(v_2v_3), \ldots,$ $edge(v_{k-1}v_k)$ that alternately belongs to M and to $E - M =$ set of edges that are not in M. An *augmenting path for M* is an alternating path whose both end vertices are not incident with any edge in matching M. Thus, an augmenting path has an odd number of edges, $2k + 1$, k of them belonging to M and $k + 1$ not in M. If edges in M are replaced by edges not in M, then there is one more edge in M than before the interchange. Thus, the cardinality of the matching M is augmented by one.

FIGURE **8.28**   (a) Two matchings M and N in a graph $G = (V,E)$ and (b) the graph $G' = (V, M \oplus N)$.

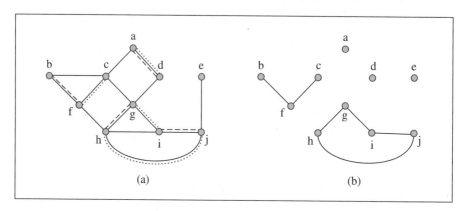

(a)   (b)

A *symmetric difference* between two sets, $X \oplus Y$, is the set

$$X \oplus Y = (X - Y) \cup (Y - X) = (X \cup Y) - (X \cap Y)$$

In other words, a symmetric difference $X \oplus Y$ includes all elements from X and Y combined except for the elements that belong at the same time to X and Y.

Lemma 1. If for two matchings M and N in a graph $G = (V,E)$ we define a set of edges $M \oplus N \subseteq E$, then each connected component of the subgraph $G' = (V, M \oplus N)$ is either (a) a single vertex, (b) a cycle with an even number of edges alternately in M and N, or (c) a path whose edges are alternately in M and N and such that each end vertex of the path is matched only by one of the two matchings M and N (i.e., the whole path should be considered, not just part, to cover the entire connected component).

Proof. For each vertex v of G', $deg(v) \le 2$, at most one edge of each matching can be incident with v; hence, each component of G' is either a single vertex, a path, or a cycle. If it is a cycle or a path, the edges must alternate between both matchings; otherwise, the definition of matching is violated. Thus, if it is a cycle, the number of edges must be even. If it is a path, then the degree of both end vertices is one so that they can be matched with only one of the matchings, not both.   ◻

Figure 8.28 contains an example. A symmetric difference between matching $M = \{edge(ad), edge(bf), edge(gh), edge(ij)\}$ marked with dashed lines and matching $N = \{edge(ad), edge(cf), edge(gi), edge(hj)\}$ shown in dotted lines is the set $M \oplus N = \{edge(bf), edge(cf), edge(gh), edge(gi), edge(hj), edge(ij)\}$, which contains one path and a cycle (Figure 8.28b). The vertices of graph G that are not incident with any of the edges in $M \oplus N$ are isolated in the graph $G' = (V, M \oplus N)$.

Lemma 2. If M is a matching and P is an augmenting path for M, then $M \oplus P$ is a matching of cardinality $|M| + 1$.

Proof. By definition of symmetric difference, $M \oplus P = (M - P) \cup (P - M)$. Except for the end vertices, all other vertices incident with edges in P are matched by edges in P. Hence, no edge in $M - P$ contains any vertex in P. Thus, edges in $M - P$ share no ver-

FIGURE **8.29** (a) Augmenting path P and a matching M and (b) the matching $M \oplus P$.

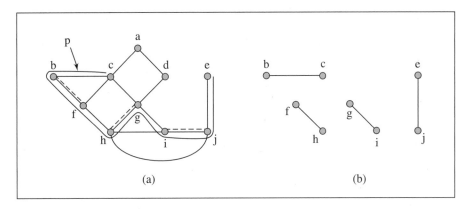

(a)   (b)

tices with edges in $P - M$. Moreover, since P is a path with every other edge in $P - M$, then $P - M$ has no edges that share vertices. Hence, $(M - P) \cup (P - M)$ is a union of two nonoverlapping matchings and thus a matching. If $|P| = 2k + 1$, then $|M - P| = |M| - k$ because all edges in $M \cup P$ are excluded, and the number of edges in P but not in M, $|P - M| = k + 1$. Because $(M - P)$ and $(P - M)$ are not overlapping, $|(M - P) \cup (P - M)| = |M - P| + |P - M| = (|M| - k) + k + 1 = |M| + 1$. ❏

Figure 8.29 illustrates this lemma. For matching $M = \{edge(bf), edge(gh), edge(ij)\}$ shown with dashed lines, and augmenting path P for M, the path c, b, f, h, g, i, j, e, the resulting matching is $\{edge(bc), edge(ej), edge(fh), edge(gi)\}$, which includes all the edges from the path P that were originally excluded from M. So in effect the lemma finds a larger matching if in an augmenting path the roles of matched and unmatched edges are reversed.

Theorem (Berge). A matching M in a graph G is maximum if there is no augmenting path connecting two unmatched vertices in G.

Proof. $\Rightarrow$ By lemma 2, if there were an augmenting path, then a larger matching could be generated; hence, M would not be a maximum matching.

$\Leftarrow$ Suppose M is not maximum and a matching N is maximum. Let $G' = (V, M \oplus N)$. By lemma 1, connected components of G' are either cycles of even length or paths (isolated vertices are not included here). If it is a cycle, then half of its edges are in N and half are in M because the edges are alternating between M and N. If it is an even path, then it also has the same number of edges from M and N. However if it is an odd path, it has more edges from N than from M, since $|N| > |M|$, and both end vertices are incident with edges from N. Hence, it is an augmenting path, which leads to contradiction with the assumption that there is no augmenting path. ❏

This theorem suggests that a maximum matching can be found by beginning with an initial matching, possibly empty, and then by repeatedly finding new augmenting paths and increasing the cardinality of matching until no such path can be found. This requires an algorithm to determine alternate paths. It is much easier to develop such an algorithm for bipartite graphs than for any graphs; therefore, we start with a discussion of this simpler case.

To find an augmenting path, breadth-first search is modified to allow for always finding the shortest path. The procedure builds a tree, called a *Hungarian tree,* with an unmatched vertex in the root consisting of alternating paths, and a success is pronounced as soon as it finds another unmatched vertex than the one in the root (that is, as soon as it finds an augmenting path). The augmenting path allows for increasing the size of matching. After no such path can be found, the procedure is finished. The algorithm is as follows:

```
findMaximumMatching(bipartite graph)
    for  all unmatched vertices v
        set level of all vertices to 0;
        set parent of all vertices to null;
        level(v) = 1;
        last = null;
        clear queue;
        enqueue(v);
        while queue is not empty and last is null
            v = dequeue();
            if  level(v) is an odd number
                for  all vertices u  adjacent to v  such that level(u)  is 0
                    if u  is unmatched          // the end of an augmenting
                        parent(u) = v;          // path is found;
                        last = u;               // this also allows to exit the while loop;
                        break;                  // exit the for loop;
                    else if u  is matched but not with v
                        parent(u) = v;
                        level(u) = level(v) + 1;
                        enqueue(u);
            else // if level(v)  is an even number
                enqueue(vertex u  matched with v);
                parent(u) = v;
                level(u) = level(v) + 1;
        if last is not null // augment matching by updating the augmenting path;
            for (u = last; u is not null; u = parent(parent(u)))
                matchedWith(u) = parent(u);
                matchedWith(parent(u)) = u;
```

An example is shown in Figure 8.30. For the current matching $M = \{(u_1, v_4), (u_2, v_2), (u_3, v_3), (u_5, v_5)\}$ (Figure 8.30a), we start from vertex u_4. First, three vertices adjacent to u_4 (namely, v_3, v_4, and v_5) are enqueued, all of them connected to u_4 with edges not in M. Then v_3 is dequeued, and since it is on an even level of the tree (Figure 8.30b), there is at most one successor to be considered, which is the vertex u_3 because $edge(u_3v_3)$ is in M and u_3 is enqueued. Then successors of v_4 and v_5 are found, that is, u_1 and u_5, respectively, after which the vertex u_3 is considered. This vertex is on an odd level; hence, all vertices directly accessible from it through edges not in M are checked. There are three

FIGURE **8.30**   Application of the findMaximumMatching() algorithm. Matched vertices are connected with solid lines.

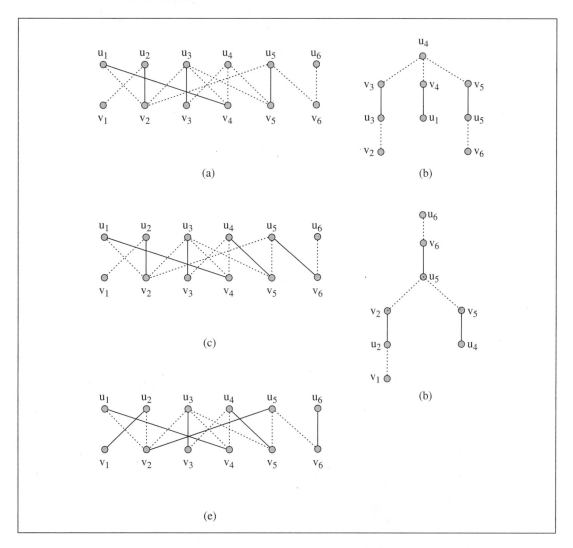

(a)

(b)

(c)

(b)

(e)

such vertices, v_2, v_4, and v_5, but only the first is not yet in the tree, so it is included now. Next, successors of u_1 are tested, but the only candidate, v_2, does not qualify since it is already in the tree. Finally, u_5 is checked, from which we arrive at an unmatched vertex v_6. This marks the end of an augmenting path; hence, the while loop is exited and then matching M is modified by including in M the edges in the newly found path that are not in M and excluding from M the edges of the path that are there. Since the path has one more edge in M than not in M, after such modification the number of edges in M is increased by one. The new matching is shown in Figure 8.30c.

After finding and modifying an augmenting path, a search for another augmenting path begins. Because there are still two unmatched vertices, there still exists a possibility that a larger matching can be found. In the second iteration of the outer `for` loop, we begin with the vertex u_6, which eventually leads to the tree as in Figure 8.30d that includes an augmenting path, which in turn gives a matching as in Figure 8.30e. There are no unmatched vertices left; thus, the maximum matching just found is also a perfect matching.

Complexity of the algorithm is found as follows. Each alternating path increases the cardinality of matching by one, and since the maximum number of edges in matching M is $|V|/2$, the number of iterations of the outer `for` loop is at most $|V|/2$. Moreover, finding one augmenting path requires $O(|E|)$ steps so that the total cost of finding a maximum matching is $O(|V||E|)$.

8.9.1 Assignment Problem

The problem of finding a suitable matching becomes more complicated in a weighted graph. In such a graph, we are interested in finding a matching with the maximum total weight. The problem is called an *assignment problem.* The assignment problem for complete bipartite graphs with two sets of vertices of the same size is called an *optimal assignment problem.*

An $O(|V|)^3$ algorithm is due to Kuhn and Munkres (Bondy and Murty 1976; Thulasiraman and Swamy 1992). For a bipartite graph $G = (V,E)$, $V = U \cup W$, we define a labeling function $f: U \cup W \rightarrow R$ such that a label $f(v)$ is a number assigned to each vertex v such that for all vertices $v, u, f(u) + f(v) \geq weight(edge(uv))$. Create a set $H = \{edge(uv) \in E: f(u) + f(v) = weight(edge(uv))\}$ and then an *equality subgraph* $G_f = (V, H)$. The Kuhn-Munkres algorithm is based on the theorem stating that if for a labeling function f and an equality subgraph G_f, graph G contains a perfect matching, then this matching is optimal. This is the algorithm:

```
optimalAssignment()
   Gf = equality subgraph for some vertex labeling f;
   M = matching in Gf;
   S = {some unmatched vertex u};  // beginning of an augmenting path P;
   T = null;
   while M is not a perfect matching
       Γ(S) = {w: ∃u∈ S: edge(uw)∈Gf} ;// vertices adjacent in Gf to the vertices in S;
       if Γ(S) == T
           d = min{(f(u) + f(w) − weight(edge(uw)): u∈S, w∉T};
           if v ∈ S
               f(v) = f(v) − d;
           else if v ∈ T
               f(v) = f(v) + d;
           construct new equality subgraph Gf and new matching M;
       else // if T ⊂ Γ(S)
           w = a vertex from Γ(S) − T;
           if w is unmatched // the end of the augmenting path P;
               P = augmenting path just found;
```

FIGURE **8.31**   An example of application of the `optimalAssignment()` algorithm.

	w_1	w_2	w_3	w_4
v_1	2	2	4	1
v_2	3	4	4	2
v_3	2	2	3	3
v_4	1	2	1	2

(a)   (b)   (c)

```
    M = M ⊕ P;
    S = {some unmatched vertex u};
    T = null;
else S = S ∪ {neighbor of w in M};
    T = T ∪ {w};
```

For an example, see Figure 8.31. A complete bipartite graph $G = (\{u_1, \ldots, u_4\} \cup \{w_1, \ldots, w_4\}, E)$ has weights defined by the matrix in Figure 8.31a.

0. For an initial labeling, we choose the function f such that $f(u) = \max(weight(edge(uw)))$, that is, the maximum weight in the weight matrix in the row for vertex u, and $f(w) = 0$, so that for the graph G, the initial labeling is as in Figure 8.31b. We choose a matching as in Figure 8.31b and set the set S to $\{u_4\}$ and set T to null.

1. In the first iteration of the `while` loop, $\Gamma(S) = \{w_2, w_4\}$, because both w_2 and w_4 are neighbors of u_4, which is the only element of S. Because $T \subset \Gamma(S)$, that is, $\varnothing \subset \{w_2, w_4\}$, the outer `else` clause is executed, whereby $w = w_2$ (we simply choose the first element if $\Gamma(S)$ not in T), and because w_2 is not matched, the inner `else` clause is executed, in which we extend S to $\{u_2, u_4\}$, because u_2 is both matched and adjacent to w_2, and extend T to $\{w_2\}$.

All the iterations are summarized in the following table.

Iteration	$\Gamma(S)$	S	w	T
0	$\varnothing$	$\{u_4\}$		$\varnothing$
1	$\{w_2, w_4\}$	$\{u_2, u_4\}$	w_2	$\{w_2\}$
2	$\{w_2, w_3, w_4\}$	$\{u_1, u_2, u_4\}$	w_3	$\{w_2, w_3\}$
3	$\{w_2, w_3, w_4\}$	$\{u_1, u_2, u_3, u_4\}$	w_4	$\{w_2, w_3, w_4\}$
4	$\{w_2, w_3, w_4\}$			

In the fourth iteration, the condition of the outer `if` statement becomes true because sets T and $\Gamma(S)$ are now equal, so the distance $d = \min\{(f(u) + f(w) - weight(edge(uw)): u \in S, w \notin T\}$ is computed. Because w_1 is the only vertex not in $T = \{w_2, w_3, w_4\}$, $d = \min\{(f(u) + f(w_1) - weight(edge(uw_1)): u \in S = \{u_1, u_2, u_3, u_4\}\} =$

min$\{(4 + 0 - 2), (4 + 0 - 2), (3 + 0 - 4), (2 + 0 - 1)\} = 1$. With this distance, the labels of vertices in graph G are updated to become labels in Figure 8.31c. The labels of all four vertices in S are decremented by d = 1, and all three vertices in T are incremented by the same value. Next, an equality subgraph is created that includes all the edges, as in Figure 8.31c, and then the matching is found that includes edges drawn with solid lines. This is a perfect matching, and hence, an optimal assignment, which concludes the execution of the algorithm.

8.9.2 Matching in Nonbipartite Graphs

The algorithm findMaximumMatching() is not general enough to properly process nonbipartite graphs. Consider the graph in Figure 8.32a. If we start building a tree using breadth-first search to determine an augmenting path from vertex c, then vertex d is on an even level, vertex e is on an odd level, and vertices a and f are on an even level. If after processing a the vertex f is processed, then only $edge(fg)$ is included in the tree because e is on an odd level; that is, the $edge(ef)$ is not in matching. But in this way, the $edge(fh)$ is not included in the tree, whereby an augmenting path c, d, e, a, b, g, f, h cannot be detected since vertex g has been labeled and hence blocks access to f and consequently to vertex h. The path c, d, e, a, b, g, f, h could be found if we used a depth-first search and expanded the path leading through a before expanding a path leading through f, since the search would first determine the path c, d, e, a, b, g, f, and then it would access h from f. However, if h was not in the graph, then the very same depth-first search would miss the path c, d, e, f, g, i because first the path c, d, e, a, b, g, f with vertices g and f would be expanded so that the detection of path c, d, e, f, g, i is ruled out.

A source of the problem is the presence of cycles with an odd number of edges. But it is not just the odd number of edges in a cycle that causes the problem. Consider the graph in Figure 8.32b. The cycle $e, a, b, p, q, r, s, g, f, e$ has nine edges, but findMaximumMatching() is successful here as the reader can easily determine (both depth-first search and breadth-first search first find path c, d, e, a, b, p and then path h, f, g, i). The problem arises in a special type of cycle with an odd number of edges, which are called blossoms. The technique of determining augmenting paths for graphs with blossoms is due to Jack Edmonds. But first some definitions.

A *blossom* is an alternating cycle $v_1, v_2, \ldots, v_{2k-1}v_1$ such that $edge(v_1v_2)$ and $edge(v_{2k-1}v_1)$ are not in matching. In such a cycle, the vertex v_1 is called the *base* of the blossom. An even length alternating path is called a *stem;* a path of length zero that has only one vertex is also a stem. A blossom with a stem whose edge in matching is incident with the base of the blossom is called a *flower*. For example, in Figure 8.32a, path c, d, e and path e are stems, and cycle e, a, b, g, f, e is a blossom with the base e.

The problems with blossoms arise if a prospective augmenting path leads to a blossom through the base. Depending on which edge is chosen to continue the path, we may or may not obtain an augmenting path. However, if the blossom is entered through any other vertex v than the base, the problem does not arise because we can choose only one of the two edges of v. Hence, an idea is to prevent a blossom from possibly harmful effects by detecting the fact that a blossom is being entered through its base. The next step is to temporarily remove the blossom from the graph

FIGURE **8.32**   Application of the findMaximumMatching() algorithm to a non-bipartite graph.

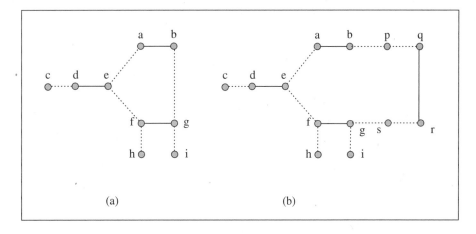

(a)   (b)

by putting in place of its base a vertex that represents such a blossom and to attach to this vertex all edges connected to the blossom. The search for an augmenting path continues, and if an augmenting path which includes a vertex representing a blossom is found, the blossom is expanded and the path through it is determined by going backward from the edge that leads to the blossom to one of the edges incident with the base.

The first problem is how to recognize that a blossom has been entered through the base. Consider the Hungarian tree in Figure 8.33a, which is generated using breadth-first search in the graph in Figure 8.31a. Now, if we try to find neighbors of *b*, then only *g* qualifies since *edge(ab)* is in matching, and thus only edges not in matching can be included starting from *b*. Such edges would lead to vertices on an even level of the tree. But *g* has already been labeled and it is located on an odd level. This marks a blossom detection. If a labeled vertex is reached through different paths, one of them requiring this vertex to be on an even level and another on a odd level, then we know that we are in the middle of a blossom entered through its base. Now we trace the paths from *g* and *b* back in the tree until a common root is found. This common root, vertex *e* in our example, is the base of the detected blossom. The blossom is now replaced by a vertex *A*, which leads to a transformed graph as in Figure 8.33b. The search for an augmenting path restarts from vertex *A* and continues until such a path is found, namely, path *c, d, A, h*. Now we expand the blossom represented by *A* and trace the augmenting path through the blossom. We do that by starting from *edge(hA)*, which is now *edge(hf)*. Since it is an edge not in matching, then from *f* only *edge(fg)* can be chosen so that the augmenting path can be alternating. Moving through vertices *f, g, b, a, e*, we determine the part of the augmenting path, *c, d, A, h*, which corresponds to *A* (Figure 8.33c) so that the full augmenting path is *c, d, e, a, b, g, f, h*. After the path is processed, we obtain a new matching as in Figure 8.33d.

FIGURE **8.33**   Processing a graph with a blossom.

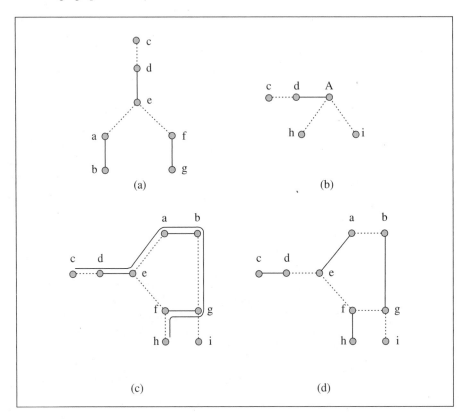

(a)

(b)

(c)

(d)

◻ 8.10 EULERIAN AND HAMILTONIAN GRAPHS

8.10.1 Eulerian Graphs

An *Eulerian trail* in a graph is a path that includes all edges of the graph only once. An *Eulerian cycle* is a cycle that is also an Eulerian trail. A graph that has an Eulerian cycle is called an *Eulerian graph*. A theorem proven by Euler says that a graph is Eulerian if every vertex of the graph is incident to an even number of edges. Also, a graph contains an Eulerian trail if it has exactly two vertices incident with an odd number of edges.

Fleury is attributed with the oldest algorithm that allows us to find an Eulerian cycle if this is possible. The algorithm takes great care in not traversing a bridge, that is, an edge whose removal would disconnect the graphs G_1 and G_2, since if traversal of G_1 is not completed before traversing such an edge to pass to G_2, it would not be possible to return to G_1. Only after the entire subgraph G_1 has been traversed can the path lead through such an edge. Fleury's algorithm is as follows:

FIGURE **8.34**   Finding an Eulerian cycle.

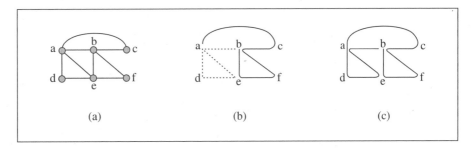

(a)   (b)   (c)

```
FleuryAlgorithm(undirected graph)
    v = a starting vertex;      // any vertex;
    path = v;
    untraversed = graph;
    while v has untraversed edges
        if edge(vu) is the only one untraversed edge
            e = edge(vu);
            remove v from untraversed;
        else e = edge(vu) in v which is not a bridge in untraversed;
        path = path + u;
        remove e from untraversed;
        v = u;
    if untraversed has no edges
        success;
    else failure;
```

Note that for cases when a vertex has more than one untraversed edge, a connectivity checking algorithm should be applied.

An example of finding an Eulerian cycle is shown in Figure 8.34. It is critical that before an edge is chosen, a test is made to determine whether the edge is a bridge in the untraversed subgraph or not. For example, if in the graph in Figure 8.34a the traversal begins in vertex b to reach vertex a through vertices e, f, and b, thereby using the path b, e, f, b, a, then we need to be careful which untraversed edge is chosen in a: edge(ab), edge(ad), or edge(ae) (Figure 8.34b). If we choose edge(ab), then the remaining three untraversed edges are unreachable, because in the yet untraversed subgraph untraversed = ({a,b,d,e}, {edge(ab), edge(ad), edge(ae), edge(de)}), edge(ab) is a bridge because it disconnects two subgraphs of untraversed, ({a,d,e}, {edge(ad), edge(ae), edge(de)} and ({b}, Ø).

8.10.2 Hamiltonian Graphs

A *Hamiltonian cycle* in a graph is a cycle that passes through all the vertices of the graph. A graph is called a *Hamiltonian graph* if it includes at least one Hamiltonian

FIGURE **8.35**   Crossover edges.

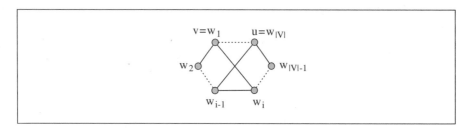

cycle. There is no formula characterizing a Hamiltonian graph. However, it is clear that all complete graphs are Hamiltonian.

Theorem (Ore 1960; Bondy and Chvátal 1976). If $edge(vu) \notin E$, graph $G^* = (V, E \cup \{edge(vu)\})$ is Hamiltonian, and $deg(v) + deg(u) \geq |V|$, then graph $G = (V, E)$ is also Hamiltonian.

Proof. Consider a Hamiltonian cycle in G^* that includes $edge(vu) \notin E$. This implies that G has a Hamiltonian path $v = w_1, w_2, \ldots, w_{|V|-1}, w_{|V|} = u$. Now we want to find two crossover edges, $edge(vw_{i+1})$ and $edge(w_iu)$, such that $w_1, w_{i+1}, w_{i+2}, \ldots, w_{|V|}, w_i, \ldots, w_2, w_1$ is a Hamiltonian cycle in G (see Figure 8.35). To see that this is possible, consider a set of S of subscripts of neighbors of v, $S = \{j: edge(vw_{j+1})\}$, and a set of T of subscripts of neighbors of u, $T = \{j: edge(w_ju)\}$. Because $S \cup T \subseteq \{1, 2, \ldots, |V| - 1\}$, $|S| = deg(v)$, $|T| = deg(u)$, and $deg(v) + deg(v) \geq |V|$, then S and T must have a common subscript so that the two crossover edges, $edge(vw_{i+1})$ and $edge(w_iu)$, exist. ❑

The theorem, in essence, says that some Hamiltonian graphs allow us to create Hamiltonian graphs by eliminating some of their edges. This leads to an algorithm that first expands a graph to a graph with more edges in which finding a Hamiltonian cycle is easy and then manipulates this cycle by adding some edges and removing other edges so that eventually a Hamiltonian cycle is formed that includes the edges that belong to the original graph. An algorithm for finding Hamiltonian cycles based on the preceding theorem is as follows (Chvátal 1985):

```
HamiltonianCycle(graph G = (V, E))
    set label of all edges to 0;
    k = 1;
    H = E;
    G_H = G;
    while G_H contains nonadjacent vertices v, u such that deg_H(v) + deg_H(u) ≥ |V|
        H = H ∪ {edge(vu)};
        G_H = (V, H);
        label(edge(vu)) = k++;
    if there exists a Hamiltonian cycle C
        while (k = max{label(edge(pq)): edge(pq)∈C}) > 0
            C = a cycle due to a crossover with each edge labeled by a number < k;
```

FIGURE **8.36** Finding a Hamiltonian cycle.

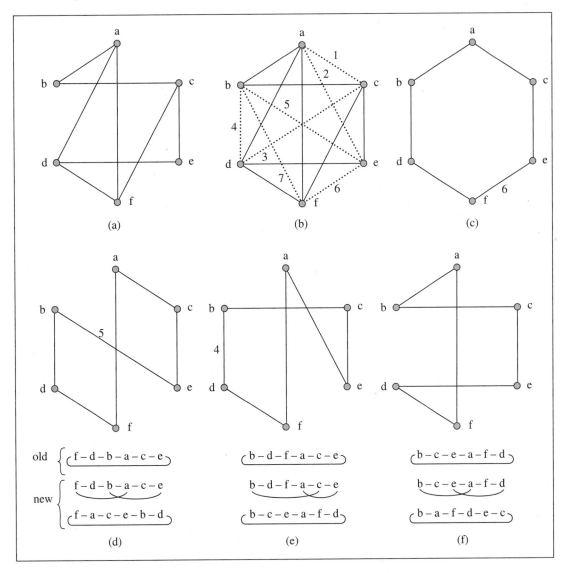

Figure 8.36 contains an example. In the first phase, the `while` loop is executed to create graph G_H based on graph G in Figure 8.36a. In each iteration, two nonadjacent vertices are connected with an edge if the total number of their neighbors is not less than the number of all vertices in the graph. We first look at all the vertices not adjacent to a. For vertex c, $deg_H(a) + deg_H(c) = 6 \geq |v| = 6$, the *edge(ac)* labeled with number 1 is included in H. Next, vertex e is considered, and because the degree of a just increased by acquiring a new neighbor, b, $deg_H(a) + deg_H(e) = 6$, so the *edge(ae)* labeled with 2 is

included in H. The next vertex, for which we try to establish new neighbors, is b of degree 2, for which there are three nonadjacent vertices, d, e, and f with degrees 2, 2, and 3, respectively; therefore, the sum of b's degree and a degree of any of the three vertices does not reach 6, and no edge is now included in H. In the next iterations of the while loop, all possible neighbors of vertices c, d, e, and f are tested, which results in graph H as in Figure 8.36b with new edges shown as dashed lines with their labels.

In the second phase of HamiltonianCycle(), a Hamiltonian cycle in H is found, a, c, e, f, d, b, a. In this cycle, an edge with the highest label is found, $edge(ef)$ (Figure 8.36c). The vertices in the cycle are so ordered that the vertices in this edge are on the extreme ends. Then by moving left to right in this sequence of vertices, we try to find crossover edges by checking edges from two neighbor vertices to the vertices at the ends of the sequence so that the edges cross each other. The first possibility is vertices d and b with $edge(bf)$ and $edge(de)$, but this pair is rejected because the label of $edge(bf)$ is greater than the largest label of the current cycle, 6. After this, the vertices b and a and the edges connecting them to the ends of the sequence $edge(af)$ and $edge(be)$ are checked; the edges are acceptable (their labels are 0 and 5), so the old cycle f, d, b, a, c, e, f is transformed into a new cycle f, a, c, e, b, d, f. This is shown beneath the diagram in Figure 8.36d with two new edges crossing each other and also in a sequence and in the diagram in Figure 8.36d.

In the new cycle, $edge(be)$ has a highest label, 5, so the cycle is presented with the vertices of this edge, b and e, shown as the extremes of the sequence b, d, f, a, c, e (Figure 8.36d). To find crossover edges, we first investigate the pair of crossover edges, $edge(bf)$ and $edge(de)$, but the label of $edge(bf)$, 7, is greater than the largest label of the current Hamiltonian cycle, 5, so the pair is discarded. Next, we try the pair $edge(ab)$ and $edge(ef)$, but because of the magnitude of label of $edge(ef)$, 6, the pair is not acceptable. The next possibility is the pair $edge(bc)$ and $edge(ae)$, which is acceptable, so a new cycle is formed, b, c, e, a, f, d, b (Figure 8.36d–e). In this cycle, a pair of crossover edges is found, $edge(ab)$ and $edge(de)$, and a new cycle is formed, b, a f, d, e, c (Figures 8.36e–f), which includes edges only with labels equal to 0, (that is, only edges from graph G), which marks the end of execution of the algorithm with the last cycle being Hamiltonian and built only from edges in G.

⬚ 8.11 CASE STUDY: DISTINCT REPRESENTATIVES

Let there be a set of committees, $C = \{C_1, \ldots, C_n\}$, each committee having at least one person. The problem is to determine, if possible, representatives from each committee so that the committee is represented by one person and each person can represent only one committee. For example, if there are three committees, $C_1 = \{M_5, M_1\}$, $C_2 = \{M_2, M_4, M_3\}$, and $C_3 = \{M_3, M_5\}$, then one possible representation is: member M_1 represents committee C_1, M_2 represents C_2, and M_5 represents C_3. However, if we have these three committees, $C_4 = C_5 = \{M_6, M_7\}$, and $C_6 = \{M_7\}$, then no distinct representation can be created, since there are only two members in all three committees combined. The latter observation has been proven by P. Hall in the *system of distinct representatives* theorem which can be phrased in the following way:

FIGURE **8.37**   (a) A network representing membership of three committees, C_1, C_2, and C_3 and (b) the first augmenting path found in this network.

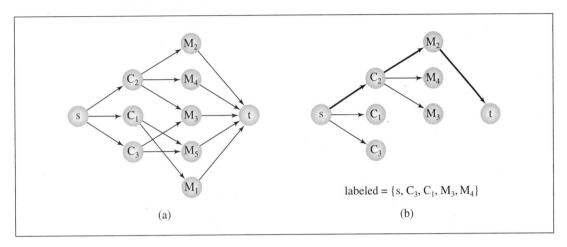

(a)   (b)

labeled = {s, C_3, C_1, M_3, M_4}

Theorem. A nonempty collection of finite nonempty sets $C_1, \ldots, C_n$ has a system of distinct representatives if for any $i \leq n$, the union $C_{k_1} \cup \ldots \cup C_{k_i}$ has at least i elements.

The problem can be solved by creating a network and trying to find a maximum flow in this network. For example, the network in Figure 8.37a can represent the membership of the three committees C_1, C_2, and C_3. There is a dummy source vertex connected to nodes representing committees, the committee vertices are connected to vertices representing their members, and the member vertices are all connected to a dummy sink vertex. We assume that each edge e's capacity $cap(e) = 1$. A system of distinct representatives is found if the maximum flow in the network equals the number of committees. The paths determined by a particular maximum flow algorithm determine the representatives. For example, member M_1 would represent the committee C_1 if a path s, C_1, M_1, t is determined.

The implementation has two main stages. First, a network is created using a set of committees and members stored in a file. Then, the network is processed to find augmenting paths corresponding to members representing committees. The first stage is specific to the system of distinct representatives. The second stage can be used for finding the maximum flow of any network since it assumes that the network has been created before it begins.

When reading committees and members from a file, we assume that the name of a committee is always followed by a colon and then by a list of members separated by commas and ended with a semicolon. An example is the following file `committees`, which includes information corresponding to the network in Figure 8.37a:

```
C2: M2, M4, M3;
C1: M5, M1;
C3: M3, M5;
```

The network is represented by the vector `vertices` storing objects of type `Vertex`. Each vertex `i` includes information necessary for proper processing of the vertex `i`: the name of the vertex, vertex slack, labeled/nonlabeled flag, adjacency list, parent in the current augmenting path, and a reference to a node `i` in the parent's adjacency list.

An adjacency list of a vertex in position `i` represents edges incident with this vertex. Each node on the list is identified by its `idNum`, which is the position in `vertices` of the same vertex. Information in each node of such a list also includes capacity of the edge, its flow, forward/backward flag, and a reference to the twin. If there is an edge from vertex `i` to `j`, then `i`'s adjacency list includes a node representing a forward edge from `i` to `j`, and `j`'s adjacency list has a node corresponding to a backward edge from `j` to `i`. Hence, each edge is represented twice in the network. If a path is augmented, then augmenting an edge means updating two nodes on two adjacency lists. To make it possible, each node on such a list points to its twin, or rather a node representing the same edge taken in the opposite direction.

In the first phase of the process, the method `readCommittees()` builds both the vector `vertices` and the adjacency list for each vertex in the vector when reading the data from the file `committees`. Both the vector and the lists include unique elements. The method also builds a separate adjacency list for the source vertex.

In the second phase, the program looks for augmenting paths. In the algorithm used here, the source node is always processed first because it is always pushed first onto stack `labeledS`. Because the algorithm requires processing only unlabeled vertices, there is no need to include the source vertex in any adjacency list, since the edge from any vertex to the source has no chance to be included in any augmenting path. In addition, after the sink is reached, the process of finding an augmenting path is discontinued, whereby no edge incident with the sink is processed, so there is no need to keep an adjacency list for the sink.

The structure created by `readCommittees()` using the file `committees` is shown in Figure 8.38; this structure represents the network shown in Figure 8.37a. The numbers in the nodes and vector elements are put by `FordFulkerson-MaxFlow()` right after finding the first augmenting path, 0, 2, 3, 1, that is, the path *source, C_2, M_2, sink* (Figure 8.37b). Nodes in the adjacency list of a vertex `i` do not include the names of vertices accessible from `i`, only their `idNum`; therefore, these names are shown above each node. The dashed lines show twin edges. In order not to clutter Figure 8.38 with too many links, only the links for two pairs of twin nodes are shown.

The output generated by the program

```
Augmenting paths:
    source => C2 => M2 => sink (augmented by 1);
    source => C1 => M5 => sink (augmented by 1);
    source => C3 => M3 => sink (augmented by 1);
```

determines the following representation: Member M_2 represents committee C_2, M_5 represents C_1, and M_3 represents C_3.

Figure 8.39 contains the code for this program.

FIGURE **8.38**   The network representation created by `FordFulkersonMaxFlow()`.

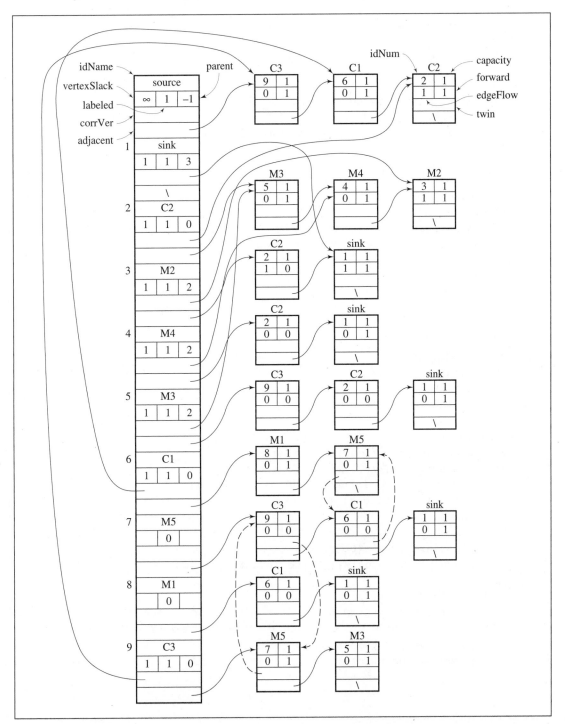

FIGURE **8.39**   An implementation of the distinct representatives problem.

```java
import java.io.*;
import java.util.*;

class Vertex {
    int idNum, capacity, edgeFlow;
    boolean forward; // direction;
    Vertex twin;      // edge in opposite direction;
    Vertex() {
    }
    Vertex(int id, int c, int ef, boolean f) {
        idNum = id; capacity = c; edgeFlow = ef; forward = f; twin = null;
    }
    public boolean equals(Object v) {
        return idNum == ((Vertex)v).idNum;
    }
    public String toString() {
        return (idNum + " " + capacity + " " + edgeFlow + " " + forward);
    }
}

class VertexInVector {
    String idName;
    int vertexSlack;
    boolean labeled = false;
    int parent;
    LinkedList adjacent = new LinkedList();
    Vertex corrVer;   // corresponding vertex: vertex on parent's
    VertexInVector() { // list of adjacent vertices with the same
    }                  // idNum as the cell's index;
    VertexInVector(String s) {
        idName = s;
    }
    public boolean equals(Object v) {
        return idName.equals(((VertexInVector)v).idName);
    }
    public void display() {
        System.out.print(idName + ' ' + vertexSlack + ' '
            + labeled + ' ' + parent + ' ' + corrVer + "-> ");
        System.out.print(adjacent);
        System.out.println();
    }
}
```

FIGURE **8.39** *(continued)*

```java
class Network {
    public Network() {
        vertices.insertElementAt(new VertexInVector(), source);
        vertices.insertElementAt(new VertexInVector(), sink);
        ((VertexInVector)vertices.elementAt(source)).idName = "source";
        ((VertexInVector)vertices.elementAt(sink)).idName  = "sink";
        ((VertexInVector)vertices.elementAt(source)).parent = none;
    }
    protected final int sink = 1, source = 0, none = -1;
    protected Vector vertices = new Vector();
    protected int edgeSlack(Vertex u) {
        return u.capacity - u.edgeFlow;
    }
    protected boolean labeled(Vertex p) {
        return ((VertexInVector)vertices.elementAt(p.idNum)).labeled;
    }
    public void display() {
        for (int i = 0; i < vertices.size(); i++) {
            System.out.print(i + ": " );
            ((VertexInVector)vertices.elementAt(i)).display();
        }
    }
    public void readCommittees(String fileName, InputStream fIn) {
        int ch = 1, pos, commPos;
        String s;
        boolean lastMember;
        Vertex memberVer, commVer;
        VertexInVector committee, member;
        try {
            while (ch > -1) {
                while (true)
                    if (ch > -1 && !Character.isLetter((char)ch)) // skip
                        ch = fIn.read();                           // nonletters;
                    else break;
                if (ch == -1)
                    break;
                s = "";
                while (ch > -1 && ch != ':') {
                    s += (char)ch;
                    ch = fIn.read();
```

Continues

FIGURE **8.39**   *(continued)*

```
        }
        committee = new VertexInVector(s.trim());
        commPos = vertices.size();
        commVer = new Vertex(commPos,1,0,false);
        vertices.addElement(committee);
        for (lastMember = false; !lastMember; ) {
            while (true)
                if (ch > -1 && !Character.isLetter((char)ch))
                    // skip
                    ch = fIn.read();
                        // nonletters;
                else break;
            if (ch == -1)
                break;
            s = "";
            while (ch > -1 && ch != ',' && ch != ';') {
                s += (char)ch;
                ch = fIn.read();
            }
            if (ch == ';')
                lastMember = true;
            member = new VertexInVector(s.trim());
            memberVer = new Vertex(0,1,0,true);
            if ((pos = vertices.indexOf(member)) == -1) {
                memberVer.idNum = vertices.size();
                member.adjacent.addFirst(new
                            Vertex(sink,1,0,true));
                member.adjacent.addFirst(commVer);
                vertices.addElement(member);
            }
            else {
                memberVer.idNum = pos;
                ((VertexInVector)vertices.elementAt(pos)).
                        adjacent.addFirst(commVer);
            }
            committee.adjacent.addFirst(memberVer);
            memberVer.twin = commVer;
            commVer.twin = memberVer;
        }
        commVer = new Vertex(commPos,1,0,true);
        ((VertexInVector)vertices.elementAt(source)).adjacent.
                            addFirst(commVer);
```

FIGURE **8.39** *(continued)*

```
            }
        } catch (IOException io) {
        }
        display();
    }
    private void label(Vertex u, int v) {
        VertexInVector uu = (VertexInVector)
                                vertices.elementAt(u.idNum);
        VertexInVector vv = (VertexInVector) vertices.elementAt(v);
        uu.labeled = true;
        if (u.forward)
            uu.vertexSlack = Math.min(vv.vertexSlack,edgeSlack(u));
        else uu.vertexSlack = Math.min(vv.vertexSlack,u.edgeFlow);
        uu.parent  = v;
        uu.corrVer = u;
    }
    private void augmentPath() {
        int sinkSlack =
                ((VertexInVector)vertices.elementAt(sink)).vertexSlack;
        Vertex u;
        VertexInVector vv;
        Stack path = new Stack();
        for (int i = sink; i != source;
             i = ((VertexInVector)vertices.elementAt(i)).parent) {
            vv = (VertexInVector) vertices.elementAt(i);
            path.push(vv.idName);
            if (vv.corrVer.forward)
                vv.corrVer.edgeFlow += sinkSlack;
            else vv.corrVer.edgeFlow -= sinkSlack;
            if (vv.parent != source && i != sink)
                vv.corrVer.twin.edgeFlow = vv.corrVer.edgeFlow;
        }
        for (int i = 0; i < vertices.size(); i++)
            ((VertexInVector)vertices.elementAt(i)).labeled = false;
        System.out.print(" source");
        while (!path.isEmpty())
            System.out.print(" => " + path.pop());
        System.out.print(" (augmented by " + sinkSlack + ");\n");
    }
    public void FordFulkersonMaxFlow() {
        int i, v;
```

Continues

FIGURE **8.39**   *(continued)*

```
            Vertex u;
            Iterator it;
            Stack labeledS = new Stack();
            for (i = 0; i < vertices.size(); i++)
                ((VertexInVector) vertices.elementAt(i)).labeled = false;
            ((VertexInVector)vertices.elementAt(source)).vertexSlack =
                Integer.MAX_VALUE;
            labeledS.push(new Integer(source));
            System.out.println("Augmenting paths:");
            while (!labeledS.isEmpty()) {    // while not stuck;
                v = ((Integer) labeledS.pop()).intValue();
                for (it = ((VertexInVector)vertices.elementAt(v)).
                        adjacent.iterator();
                     it.hasNext(); ) {
                    u = (Vertex) it.next();
                    if (!labeled(u)) {
                        if (u.forward && edgeSlack(u) > 0 ||
                            !u.forward && u.edgeFlow > 0)
                            label(u,v);
                        if (labeled(u))
                            if (u.idNum == sink) {
                                augmentPath();
                                labeledS.clear(); // look for another path;
                                labeledS.push(new Integer(source));
                                break;
                            }
                            else {
                                labeledS.push(new Integer(u.idNum));
                                ((VertexInVector)vertices.
                                        elementAt(u.idNum)).labeled = true;
                            }
                    }
                }
            }
        }
    }

class DistinctRepresentatives {
    static public void main(String args[]) {
        String fileName = "";
        Network net = new Network();
        InputStream fIn;
```

FIGURE **8.39**   *(continued)*

```
        InputStreamReader isr = new InputStreamReader(System.in);
        BufferedReader buffer = new BufferedReader(isr);
        try {
            if (args.length == 0) {
                System.out.print("Enter a file name: ");
                fileName = buffer.readLine();
                fIn = new FileInputStream(fileName);
            }
            else {
                fIn = new FileInputStream(args[0]);
                fileName = args[0];
            }
            net.readCommittees(fileName,fIn);
            fIn.close();
        } catch(IOException io) {
            System.err.println("Cannot open " + fileName);
        }
        net.FordFulkersonMaxFlow();
        net.display();
    }
}
```

◨ 8.12 Exercises

1. Look carefully at the definition of a graph. In one respect, graphs are more specific than trees. What is it?

2. What is the relationship between the sum of the degrees of all vertices and the number of edges of graph $G = (V, E)$?

3. What is the complexity of `breadthFirstSearch()`?

4. Show that a simple graph is connected if it has a spanning tree.

5. Show that a tree with n vertices has $n - 1$ edges.

6. How can `DijkstraAlgorithm()` be applied to undirected graphs?

7. How can `DijkstraAlgorithm()` be modified to become an algorithm for finding the shortest path from vertex a to b?

8. The last clause from `genericShortestPathAlgorithm()`

   add u *to* `toBeChecked` *if it is not there;*

   is not included in `DijkstraAlgorithm()`. Can this omission cause any trouble?

9. Modify `FordAlgorithm()` so that it does not fall into an infinite loop if applied to a graph with negative cycles.

10. For what digraph does the `while` loop of `FordAlgorithm()` iterate only one time? Two times?

11. Can `FordAlgorithm()` be applied to undirected graphs?

12. Make necessary changes in `FordAlgorithm()` to adapt it to solving the all-to-one shortest path problem and apply the new algorithm to vertex *f* in the graph in Figure 8.8. Using the same order of edges, produce a table similar to the table shown in this figure.

13. The D'Esopo-Pape algorithm is exponential in the worst case. Consider the following method to construct pathological graphs of *n* vertices (Kershenbaum 1981), each vertex identified by a number $1, \ldots, n$:

    ```
    KershenbaumAlgorithm()
        construct a two-vertex graph with vertices 1 and 2, and edge(1,2) = 1;
        for (k = 3; k <=n; k++)
            add vertex k;
            for (i = 2; i < k; i++)
                add edge(k,i) with weight(edge(k,i)) = weight(edge(1,i));
                weight(edge(1,i)) = weight(1,i) + 2^{k-3} + 1;
            add edge(1,k) with weight(edge(1,k)) = 1;
    ```

    The vertices adjacent to vertex 1 are put in ascending order and the remaining adjacency lists are in descending order. Using this algorithm, construct a five-vertex graph and execute the D'Esopo-Pape algorithm showing all changes in the deque and all edge updates. What generalization can you make about applying Pape's method to such graphs?

14. What do you need to change in `genericShortestPathAlgorithm()` in order to convert it to Dijkstra's one-to-all algorithm?

15. Enhance `WFIalgorithm()` to indicate the shortest paths, in addition to their lengths.

16. `WFIalgorithm()` finishes execution gracefully even in the presence of a negative cycle. How do we know that the graph contains such a cycle?

17. The original implementation of `WFIalgorithm()` given by Floyd is as follows:

```
WFIalgorithm2(matrix weight)
    for i = 1 to |V|
        for j = 1 to |V|
            if weight[j,i] < ∞
```

```
for k = 1 to |V|
   if weight[i,k] < ∞
      if (weight[j][k] > weight[j][i] + weight[i][k])
         weight[j][k] = weight[j][i] + weight[i][k];
```

Is there any advantage to this longer implementation?

18. One method of finding shortest paths from all vertices to all other vertices requires us to transform the graph so that it does not include negative weights. We may be tempted to do it by simply finding the smallest negative weight k and adding $-k$ to the weights of all edges. Why is this method inapplicable?

19. For which edges does ≤ in the inequality

$$dist(v) \leq dist(w) + weight(edge(wv)) \text{ for any vertex } w$$

become <?

20. Modify `cycleDetectionDFS()` so that it could determine whether a particular edge is part of a cycle in an undirected graph.

21. When would `KruskalAlgorithm()` require $|E|$ iterations?

22. Our implementation of `union()` requires three arrays. Is it possible to use only two of them and still have the same information concerning roots, next vertices, and lengths? Consider using negative numbers.

23. How can the second minimum spanning tree be found?

24. Is the minimum spanning tree unique?

25. How can the algorithms for finding the minimum spanning tree be used to find the maximum spanning tree?

26. The algorithm `blockSearch()`, when used for undirected graphs, relies on the following observation: In a depth-first search tree created for an undirected graph, each back edge connects a successor to a predecessor (and not, for instance, a sibling to a sibling). Show the validity of this observation.

27. What is the complexity of `blockSearch()`?

28. Blocks in undirected graphs are defined in terms of edges, and the algorithm `blockDFS()` stores edges on the stack to output blocks. On the other hand, SCCs in digraphs are defined in terms of vertices, and the algorithm `strongDFS()` stores vertices on the stack to output SCC. Why?

29. Consider a possible implementation of `topologicalSort()` by using in it the following routine:

```
minimalVertex(digraph)
   v = a vertex of digraph;
   while v has a successor
      v = successor(v);
   return v;
```

What is the disadvantage of using this implementation?

30. A *tournament* is a digraph in which there is exactly one edge between every two vertices.

   a. How many edges does a tournament have?

   b. How many different tournaments of *n* edges can be created?

   c. Can each tournament be topologically sorted?

   d. How many minimal vertices can a tournament have?

   e. A *transitive tournament* is a tournament which has *edge*(*vw*) if it has *edge*(*vu*) and *edge*(*uw*). Can such a tournament have a cycle?

31. Does considering loops and parallel edges complicate the analysis of networks? How about multiple sources and sinks?

32. FordFulkersonAlgorithm() assumes that it terminates. Do you think such an assumption is safe?

33. FordFulkersonAlgorithm() executed in a depth-first fashion has some redundancy. First, all outgoing edges are pushed onto the stack and then the last is popped off to be followed by the algorithm. For example, in the network in Figure 8.20a, first, all three edges coming out of vertex *s* are pushed, and only afterward is the last of them, *edge*(*se*), followed. Modify FordFulkersonAlgorithm() so that the first edge coming out of a certain vertex is immediately followed, and the second is followed only if the first does not lead to the sink. Consider using recursion.

34. Find the capacity of the cut determined by the set *X* = {*s,d*} in the graph in Figure 8.19.

35. What is the complexity of DinicAlgorithm() in a network where all edges have a capacity of one?

36. Why does DinicAlgorithm() start from the sink to determine a layered network?

37. The method readCommittees() in the case study uses two trees, committeeTree and memberTree, to generate adjacency lists and then initialize the vector vertices. However, one tree would be sufficient. What do you think is the reason for using two trees, not one?

38. What would be the output of the program in the case study if linked lists in Figure 8.38 were in the reverse order?

◻ 8.13 Programming Assignments

1. All algorithms discussed in this chapter for determining the minimum spanning tree have one thing in common: They start building the tree from the beginning and they add new edges to the structure which eventually becomes such a tree. However, we can go in the opposite direction and build this tree by successively removing edges to

break cycles in the graph until no circuit is left. In this way, the graph turns into the tree. The edges chosen for removal should be the edges of maximum weight among those which can break any cycle in the tree (for example, Dijkstra's method). This algorithm somewhat resembles the Kruskal method, but since it works in the opposite direction, it can be called a Kruskal method *à rebours*. Use this approach to find the minimum spanning tree for the graph of distances between at least a dozen cities.

2. Write a graphics demonstration program to show the difference between Kruskal's method and Jarník-Prim's algorithm. Randomly generate 50 vertices and display them in the left half of the screen. Then, randomly generate 200 edges and display them. Make sure that the graph is connected. After the graph is ready, create the minimum spanning tree using Kruskal's method and display each edge included in the tree. (Use a different color than the one used during graph generation.) Then, display the same graph in the right half of the screen, create the minimum spanning tree using Jarník-Prim's algorithm, and display all edges being included in the tree.

3. An important problem in database management is preventing deadlocks between transactions. A transaction is a sequence of operations on records in the database. In large databases, many transactions can be executed at the same time. This can lead to inconsistencies if the order of executing operations is not monitored. However, this monitoring may cause transactions to block each other, thereby causing a deadlock. To detect a deadlock, a wait-for graph is constructed to show which transaction waits for which. Use a binary locking mechanism to implement a wait-for graph. In this mechanism, if a record R is accessed by a transaction T, then T puts a lock on R and this record cannot be processed by any other transaction before T is finished. Release all locks put on by a transaction T when T finishes. The input is composed of the following commands: *read*(T,A), *write*(T,A), *end*(T). For example, if input is

$$read(T_1,A_1), read(T_2,A_2), read(T_1,A_2), write(T_1,A_2), end(T_1) \dots$$

then T_1 is suspended when attempting to execute the step *read*(T_1,A_2), and *edge*(T_1,T_2) is created, since T_1 waits for T_2 to finish. If T_1 does not have to wait, resume its execution. After each graph update, check for a cycle in the graph. If a cycle is detected, interrupt execution of the youngest transaction T and put its steps at the end of the input.

Note that some records might have been modified by such a transaction, so they should be restored to their state before T started. But such a modification could have been used by another transaction which should also be interrupted. In this program, do not address the problem of restoring the values of records (the problem of rolling back transactions and of cascading this rolling back). Concentrate on updating and monitoring the wait-for graph. Note that if a transaction is finished, its vertex should be removed from the graph, which may be what other transactions are waiting for.

4. Write a rudimentary spreadsheet program. Display a grid of cells with columns A through H and rows 1 through 20. Accept input in the first row of the screen. The commands are of the form *column row entry*, where *entry* is either a number, or a cell address preceded by a plus (e.g., +A5), or a string, or a function preceded by an at sign, @. The functions are: *max, min, avg,* and *sum*. During execution of your pro-

gram, build and modify the graph reflecting the situation in the spreadsheet. Show the proper values in proper cells. If a value in a cell is updated, then the values in all cells depending on it should also be modified. For example, after the following sequence of entries:

```
A1 10
B1 20
A2 30
D1 +A1
C1 @sum(A1..B2)
D1 +C1
```

both cells C1 and D1 should display the number 60.

Consider using a modification of the interpreter from Chapter 5 as an enhancement of this spreadsheet so that arithmetic expressions could also be used to enter values, such as

```
C3 2*A1
C4 @max(A1..B2) - (A2 + B2)
```

Bibliography

Ahuja, Ravindra K., Magnanti, Thomas L., and Orlin, James B., *Network Flows; Theory, Algorithms, and Applications,* Englewood Cliffs, NJ: Prentice Hall, 1993.

Bertsekas, Dimitri P., "A Simple and Fast Label Correcting Algorithm for Shortest Paths," *Networks* 23 (1993), 703–709.

Bondy, J. A. and Chvátal, V., "A Method in Graph Theory," *Discrete Mathematics* 15 (1976), 111–135.

Bondy, John A. and Murty, U. S. R., *Graph Theory with Applications,* New York: Elsevier, 1976.

Chvátal, V., "Hamiltonian Cycles," in Lawler, E. L., Lenstra, J. K., Rinnoy, Kan, A. H. G., and Shmoys, D. B. (eds.), *The Traveling Salesman Problem,* New York: Wiley, 1985, 403–429.

Deo, Narsingh and Pang, Chi-yin, "Shortest Path Algorithms: Taxonomy and Annotation," *Networks* 14 (1984), 275–323.

Dijkstra, E. W., "A Note on Two Problems in Connection with Graphs," *Numerische Mathematik* 1 (1959), 269–271.

Dijkstra, E. W., "Some Theorems on Spanning Subtrees of a Graph," *Indagationes Mathematicae* 28 (1960), 196–199.

Dinic, Efim A., "Algorithm for Solution of a Problem of Maximum Flow in a Network with Power Estimation" [Mistranslation of: with Polynomial Bound], *Soviet Mathematics Doklady* 11 (1970), 1277–1280.

Edmonds, Jack, "Paths, Trees, and Flowers," *Canadian Journal of Mathematics* 17 (1963), 449–467.

Edmonds, Jack and Johnson, Elias L., "Matching, Euler Tours and the Chinese Postman," *Mathematical Programming* 5 (1973), 88–124.

Edmonds, Jack and Karp, Richard M., "Theoretical Improvement in Algorithmic Efficiency for Network Flow Problems," *Journal of the ACM* 19 (1972), 248–264.

Floyd, Robert W., "Algorithm 97: Shortest Path," *Communications of the ACM* 5 (1962), 345.

Ford, Lester R. and Fulkerson, D. R., "Maximal Flow Through a Network," *Canadian Journal of Mathematics* 8 (1956), 399–404.

Ford, Lester R. and Fulkerson, D. R., "A Simple Algorithm for Finding Maximal Network Flows and an Application to the Hitchcock Problem," *Canadian Journal of Mathematics* 9 (1957), 210–218.

Ford, Lester R. and Fulkerson, D. R., *Flows in Networks,* Princeton, NJ: Princeton University Press, 1962.

Gallo, Giorgio and Pallottino, Stefano, "Shortest Path Methods: A Unified Approach," *Mathematical Programming Study* 26 (1986), 38–64.

Gallo, Giorgio and Pallottino, Stefano, "Shortest Path Methods," *Annals of Operations Research* 7 (1988), 3–79.

Gibbons, Alan, *Algorithmic Graph Theory,* New York: Cambridge University Press, 1985.

Glover, Fred, Glover, Randy, and Klingman, Darwin, "Computational Study of an Improved Shortest Path Algorithm," *Networks* 14 (1984), 25–36.

Gould, Ronald, *Graph Theory,* Menlo Park, CA: Benjamin/Cummings, 1988.

Graham, R. L. and Hell, Pavol, "On the History of the Minimum Spanning Tree Problem," *Annals of the History of Computing* 7 (1985), 43–57.

Hall, Philip, "On Representatives of Subsets," *Journal of the London Mathematical Society* 10 (1935), 26–30.

Ingerman, P. Z., "Algorithm 141: Path Matrix," *Communications of the ACM* 5 (1962), 556.

Johnson, Donald B., "Efficient Algorithms for Shortest Paths in Sparse Networks," *Journal of the ACM* 24 (1977), 1–13.

Kalaba, Robert, "On Some Communication Network Problems," *Combinatorial Analysis,* Providence, RI: American Mathematical Society 1960, 261–280.

Kershenbaum, Aaron, "A Note on Finding Shortest Path Trees," *Networks* 11 (1981), 399–400.

Kruskal, Joseph B., "On the Shortest Spanning Tree of a Graph and the Traveling Salesman Problem," *Proceedings of the American Mathematical Society* 7 (1956), 48–50.

Kuhn, H. W., "The Hungarian Method for the Assignment Problem," *Naval Research Logistics Quarterly* 2 (1955), 83–97.

Munkres, James, "Algorithms for the Assignment Problem and Transportation Problems," *Journal of the Society of Industrial and Applied Mathematics* 5 (1957), 32–38.

Ore, Oystein, "Note on Hamilton Circuits," *American Mathematical Monthly* 67 (1960), 55.

Papadimitriou, Christos H. and Steiglitz, Kenneth, *Combinatorial Optimization: Algorithms and Complexity,* Englewood Cliffs, NJ: Prentice Hall, 1982.

Pape, U., "Implementation and Efficiency of Moore-Algorithms for the Shortest Route Problem," *Mathematical Programming* 7 (1974), 212–222.

Pollack, Maurice and Wiebenson, Walter, "Solutions of the Shortest-Route Problem—A Review," *Operations Research* 8 (1960), 224–230.

Prim, Robert C., "Shortest Connection Networks and Some Generalizations," *Bell System Technical Journal* 36 (1957), 1389–1401.

Tarjan, Robert E., *Data Structures and Network Algorithms,* Philadelphia: Society for Industrial and Applied Mathematics, 1983.

Thulasiraman, K. and Swamy, M. N. S., *Graphs: Theory and Algorithms,* New York: Wiley, 1992.

Warshall, Stephen, "A Theorem on Boolean Matrices," *Journal of the ACM* 9 (1962), 11–12.

Sorting

The efficiency of data handling can often be substantially increased if the data are sorted according to some criteria of order. For example, it would be practically impossible to find a name in the telephone directory if the names were not alphabetically ordered. The same can be said about dictionaries, book indexes, payrolls, bank accounts, student lists, and other alphabetically organized materials. The convenience of using sorted data is unquestionable and must be addressed in computer science as well. Although a computer can grapple with an unordered telephone book more easily and quickly than a human, it is extremely inefficient to have the computer process such an unordered data set. It is often necessary to sort data before processing.

The first step is to choose the criteria which will be used to order data. This choice will vary from application to application and must be defined by the user. Very often, the sorting criteria are natural, as in the case of numbers. A set of numbers can be sorted in ascending or descending order. The set of five positive integers (5, 8, 1, 2, 20) can be sorted in ascending order resulting in the set (1, 2, 5, 8, 20) or in descending order resulting in the set (20, 8, 5, 2, 1). Names in the phone book are ordered alphabetically by last name, which is the natural order. For alphabetic and nonalphabetic characters, the ASCII code is commonly used, although other choices such as EBCDIC are possible. Once a criterion is selected, the second step is how to put a set of data in order using that criterion.

The final ordering of data can be obtained in a variety of ways, and only some of them can be considered meaningful and efficient. To decide which method is best, certain criteria of efficiency have to be established and a method for quantitatively comparing different algorithms must be chosen.

To make the comparison machine-independent, certain critical properties of sorting algorithms should be defined when comparing alternative methods. Two such properties are the number of comparisons and the number of data movements. The choice of these two properties should not be surprising. To sort a set of data, the data have to be compared and moved as necessary; the efficiency of these two operations depends on the size of the data set.

Since determining the precise number of comparisons is not always necessary or possible, an approximate value can be computed. For this reason, the number of comparisons and movements is approximated with big-O notation by giving the order of magnitude of these numbers. But the order of magnitude can vary depending on the initial ordering of data. How much time, for example, does the machine spend on data ordering if the data are already ordered? Does it recognize this initial ordering immediately or is it completely unaware of that fact? Hence, the efficiency measure also indicates the "intelligence" of the algorithm. For this reason, the number of comparisons and movements is computed (if possible) for the following three cases: best case (often, data already in order), worst case (usually, data in reverse order), and average case (data in random order). Some sorting methods perform the same operations regardless of the initial ordering of data. It is easy to measure the performance of such algorithms, but the performance itself is usually not very good. Many other methods are more flexible and their performance measures for all three cases differ.

The number of comparisons and the number of movements do not have to coincide. An algorithm can be very efficient on the former and perform poorly on the latter, or vice versa. Therefore, practical reasons must aid in the choice of which algorithm to use. For example, if only simple keys are compared, such as integers or characters, then the comparisons are relatively fast and inexpensive. If strings or arrays of numbers are compared, then the cost of comparisons goes up substantially, and the weight of the comparison measure becomes more important. If, on the other hand, the data items moved are large, such as structures, then the movement measure may stand out as the determining factor in efficiency considerations. All theoretically established measures have to be used with discretion, and theoretical considerations should be balanced with practical applications. After all, the practical applications serve as a rubber stamp for theory decisions.

Sorting algorithms, whose number can be counted in the dozens, are of different levels of complexity. A simple method can be only 20% less efficient than a more elaborate one. If sorting is used in the program once in a while and only for small sets of data, then using a sophisticated and slightly more efficient algorithm may not be desirable; the same operation can be performed using a simpler method and simpler code. But if thousands of items are to be sorted, then a gain of 20% must not be neglected. Simple algorithms often perform better with a small amount of data than their more complex counterparts whose effectiveness may only become obvious when data samples become very large.

☐ 9.1 ELEMENTARY SORTING ALGORITHMS

9.1.1 Insertion Sort

An *insertion sort* starts by considering the two first elements of the array data, which are data[0] and data[1]. If they are out of order, an interchange takes place. Then, the third element, data[2], is considered and inserted into its proper place. If

FIGURE **9.1**   The array [5 2 3 8 1] sorted by insertion sort.

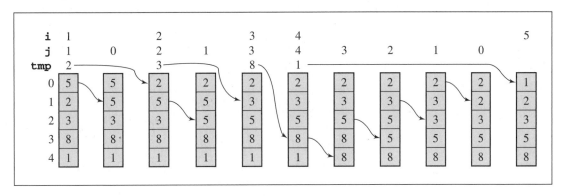

data[2] is less than data[0] and data[1], these two elements are shifted by one position; data[0] is placed at position 1, data[1] at position 2, and data[2] at position 0. If data[2] is less than data[1] and not less than data[0], then only data[1] is moved to position 2 and its place is taken by data[2]. If, finally, data[2] is not less than both its predecessors, it stays in its current position. Each element data[i] is inserted into its proper location j such that $0 \leq j \leq i$, and all elements greater than data[i] are moved by one position.

An outline of the insertion sort algorithm is as follows:

```
insertionsort(data[]) {
    for (i = 1; i < data.length; i++)
        tmp = data[i];
        move all elements data[j] greater than tmp by one position;
        place tmp in its proper position;
```

In this method, sorting is restricted only to a fraction of the array in each iteration, and only in the last pass is the whole array considered. Figure 9.1 shows what changes are made to the integer array [5 2 3 8 1] when insertionsort() executes. Since an array having only one element is already ordered, the algorithm starts sorting from the second position, position 1. Then for each element tmp = data[i], all elements greater than tmp are copied to the next position, and tmp is put in its proper place.

An implementation of insertion sort is

```
public void insertionsort(Object[] data) {
    Comparable tmp;
    int i, j;
    for (i = 1; i < data.length; i++) {
        tmp = (Comparable)data[i];
        for (j = i; j > 0 && tmp.compareTo(data[j-1]) < 0; j--)
            data[j] = data[j-1];
        data[j] = tmp;
    }
}
```

This is a generic implementation, as are implementations of the sorting algorithms that follow. For arrays of the basic type, separate implementations are needed to avoid using wrapper classes. For example, for arrays of integers, the following implementation should be used:

```
public void insertionsort(int[] data) {
    int tmp;
    int i, j;
    for (i = 1; i < data.length; i++) {
        tmp = data[i];
        for (j = i; j > 0 && tmp < data[j-1]; j--)
            data[j] = data[j-1];
        data[j] = tmp;

    }

}
```

Another version is needed for characters, for float numbers, and so on. This chapter focuses on the mechanics of the algorithms; therefore, only one generic implementation is used. However, for each sorting algorithm (except for radix sort), the number of implementations should match the number of implementations provided by Java, as discussed in Section 9.4.

An advantage of using insertion sort is that it sorts the array only when it is really necessary. If the array is already in order, no substantial moves are performed; only the variable `tmp` is initialized, and the value stored in it is moved back to the same position. The algorithm recognizes that part of the array is already sorted and stops execution accordingly. But it recognizes only this, and the fact that elements may already be in their proper positions is overlooked. Therefore, they can be moved from these positions and then later moved back. This happens to numbers 2 and 3 in the example in Figure 9.1. Another disadvantage is that if an item is being inserted, all elements greater than the one being inserted have to be moved. Insertion is not localized and may require moving a significant number of elements. Considering that an element can be moved from its final position only to be placed there again later, the number of redundant moves can slow down execution substantially.

To find the number of movements and comparisons performed by `insertionsort()`, observe first that the outer `for` loop always performs $n - 1$ iterations, where $n =$ `data.lenth`. However, the number of elements greater than `data[i]` to be moved by one position is not always the same.

The best case is when the data are already in order. Only one comparison is made for each position i, so there are $n - 1$ comparisons, which is $O(n)$, and $2(n - 1)$ moves, all of them redundant.

The worst case is when the data are in reverse order. In this case, for each i, the item `data[i]` is less than every item `data[0]`,..., `data[i-1]`, and each of them is moved by one position. For each iteration i of the outer `for` loop, there are i comparisons and, the total number of comparisons for all iterations of this loop is

$$\sum_{i=1}^{n-1} i = 1 + 2 + \cdots + (n - 1) = \frac{n(n-1)}{2} = O(n^2)$$

The number of times the assignment in the inner `for` loop is executed can be computed using the same formula. The number of times `tmp` is loaded and unloaded in the outer `for` loop is added to that, resulting in the total number of moves:

$$\frac{n(n-1)}{2} + 2(n-1) = \frac{n^2 + 3n - 4}{2} = O(n^2)$$

Only extreme cases have been taken into consideration. What happens if the data are in random order? Is the sorting time closer to the time of the best case, $O(n)$, or to the worst case, $O(n^2)$? Or is it somewhere in between? The answer is not immediately evident and requires certain introductory computations.

For every iteration i of the outer `for` loop, the number of comparisons depends on how far away the item `data[i]` is from its proper position in the currently sorted subarray `data[0 . . . i]`. If it is already in this position, only one test is performed that compares `data[i]` and `data[i-1]`. If it is one position away from its proper place, two comparisons are performed: `data[i]` is compared with `data[i-1]` and then with `data[i-2]`. Generally, if it is j positions away from its proper location, `data[i]` is compared with $j + 1$ other elements. This means that, in iteration i of the outer `for` loop, there are either $1, 2, \ldots$ or i comparisons.

Under the assumption of equal probability of occupying array cells, the average number of comparisons of `data[i]` with other elements during the iteration i of the outer `for` loop can be computed by adding all the possible numbers of times such tests are performed and dividing the sum by the number of such possibilities. The result is

$$\frac{1 + 2 + \ldots + i}{i} = \frac{\frac{1}{2}i(i+1)}{i} = \frac{i+1}{2}$$

To obtain the average number of all comparisons, the computed figure has to be added for all i's (for all iterations of the outer `for` loop) from 1 to $n - 1$. The result is

$$\sum_{i=1}^{n-1} \frac{i+1}{2} = \frac{1}{2}\sum_{i=1}^{n-1} i + \sum_{i=1}^{n-1} \frac{1}{2} = \frac{\frac{1}{2}n(n-1)}{2} + \frac{1}{2}(n-1) = \frac{n^2 + n - 2}{4}$$

which is $O(n^2)$ and approximately one-half of the number of comparisons in the worst case.

By similar reasoning, we can establish that, in iteration i of the outer `for` loop, `data[i]` can be moved either $0, 1, \ldots,$ or $i - 1$ times; that is

$$\frac{0 + 1 + \ldots + (i-1)}{i} = \frac{\frac{1}{2}i(i-1)}{i} = \frac{i-1}{2}$$

times plus two unconditional movements (to `tmp` and from `tmp`). Hence, in all the iterations of the outer `for` loop we have, on the average,

$$\sum_{i=1}^{n-1} \left(\frac{i-1}{2} + 2 \right) = \frac{1}{2}\sum_{i=1}^{n-1} i + \sum_{i=1}^{n-1} \frac{3}{2} = \frac{\frac{1}{2}n(n-1)}{2} + \frac{3}{2}(n-1) = \frac{n^2 + 5n - 6}{4}$$

movements, which is also $O(n^2)$.

This answers the question: Is the number of movements and comparisons for a randomly ordered array closer to the best or to the worst case? Unfortunately, it is closer to the latter, which means that, on the average, when the size of an array is doubled, the sorting effort quadruples.

9.1.2 Selection Sort

Selection sort is an attempt to localize the exchanges of array elements by finding a misplaced element first and putting it in its final place. The element with the lowest value is selected and exchanged with the element in the first position. Then, for n = data.length, the smallest value among the remaining elements data[1], ... , data[n-1] is found and put in the second position. This selection and placement by finding, in each pass i, the lowest value among the elements data[i],...,data[n-1] and swapping it with data[i] are continued until all elements are in their proper positions. The following pseudocode reflects the simplicity of the algorithm:

```
selectionsort(data[])
    for(i = 0; i < data.length-1; i++)
        select the smallest element among data[i],...,data[data.length-1];
        swap it with data[i];
```

It is rather obvious that n-2 should be the last value for i, since if all elements but the last have been already considered and placed in their proper position, then the *n*th element (occupying position n-1) has to be the largest. Here is a Java implementation of selection sort:

```
public void selectionsort(Object[] data) {
    int i,j,least;
    for (i = 0; i < data.length-1; i++) {
        for (j = i+1, least = i; j < data.length; j++)
            if (((Comparable)data[j]).compareTo(data[least]) < 0)
                least = j;
        swap(data,least,i);
    }
}
```

where the method swap() exchanges elements data[least] and data[i]:

```
void swap(Object[] a, int e1, int e2) {
    Object tmp = a[e1]; a[e1] = a[e2]; a[e2] = tmp;
}
```

Note that least is not the smallest element but its position.

Figure 9.2 illustrates how the array [5 2 3 8 1] is sorted by selection sort.

The analysis of the performance of the method selectionsort() is simplified by the presence of two for loops with lower and upper bounds. The outer loop executes $n - 1$ times, and for each i between 0 and n − 2, the inner loop iterates $j = (n - 1) - i$ times. Because comparisons of keys are done in the inner loop, there are

$$\sum_{i=0}^{n-2}(n-1-i) = (n-1) + \cdots + 1 = \frac{n(n-1)}{2} = O(n^2)$$

FIGURE **9.2**   The array [5 2 3 8 1] sorted by selection sort.

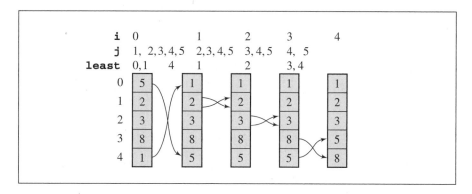

comparisons. This number stays the same for all cases. There can be some savings only in the number of swaps.

In the best case, when an ordered array is sorted, no array elements are swapped. In the worst case, when the largest element is in the first position and the remaining elements are ordered, the swapping method is called as many times as the outer loop iterates, which is $n - 1$; that is, in the worst case, the array elements are moved $3(n - 1)$ times, which is $O(n)$, a very good result.

9.1.3 Bubble Sort

A bubble sort can be best understood if the array to be sorted is envisaged as a vertical column whose smallest elements are at the top and whose largest elements are at the bottom. The array is scanned from the bottom up, and two adjacent elements are interchanged if they are found to be out of order with respect to each other. First, items `data[n-1]` and `data[n-2]` are compared and swapped if they are out of order. Next, `data[n-2]` and `data[n-3]` are compared, and their order is changed if necessary and so on up to `data[1]` and `data[0]`. In this way, the smallest element is bubbled up to the top of the array.

However, this is only the first pass through the array. The array is scanned again comparing consecutive items and interchanging them when needed, but this time, the last comparison is done for `data[2]` and `data[1]` because the smallest element is already in its proper position, namely, position 0. The second pass bubbles the second smallest element of the array up to the second position, position 1. The procedure continues until the last pass when only one comparison, `data[n-1]` with `data[n-2]`, and possibly one interchange are performed.

A pseudocode of the algorithm is as follows:

```
bubblesort(data[])
    for (i = 0; i < data.length-1; i++)
        for (j = data.length-1; j > i; --j)
            swap elements in position j and j-1 if they are out of order;
```

Figure 9.3 illustrates the changes performed in the integer array [5 2 3 8 1] during the execution of `bubblesort()`. Here is an implementation of bubble sort:

```
public void bubblesort(Object[] data) {
    int i,j;
    for (i = 0; i < data.length-1; i++)
        for (j = data.length-1; j > i; --j)
            if (((Comparable)data[j]).compareTo(data[j-1]) < 0)
                swap(data,j,j-1);
}
```

The number of comparisons is the same in each case (best, average, and worst) and equals the total number of iterations of the inner `for` loop:

$$\sum_{i=0}^{n-2} (n-1-i) = \frac{n(n-1)}{2} = O(n^2)$$

This formula also computes the number of swaps in the worst case when the array is in reverse order. In this case, $3\frac{n(n-1)}{2}$ moves have to be made.

The best case, when all elements are already ordered, requires no swaps. To find the number of moves in the average case, note if an i-cell array is in random order. Then the number of swaps can be any number between zero and $i-1$; that is, there can be either no swap at all (all items are in ascending order), one swap, two swaps, . . . or $i-1$ swaps. The array processed by the inner `for` loop is `data[i]`, . . . , `data[n-1]`, and the number of swaps in this subarray—if its elements are randomly ordered—is either zero, one, two, . . . or $n-1-i$. After averaging the sum of all these possible numbers of swaps by the number of these possibilities, the average number of swaps is obtained, which is

$$\frac{0+1+2+\cdots+(n-1-i)}{n-i} = \frac{n-i-1}{2}$$

If all these averages for all the subarrays processed by `bubblesort()` are added (that is, if such figures are summed over all iterations i of the outer `for` loop), the result is

$$\sum_{i=0}^{n-2} \frac{n-i-1}{2} = \frac{1}{2}\sum_{i=0}^{n-2}(n-1) - \frac{1}{2}\sum_{i=0}^{n-2}i$$

$$= \frac{(n-1)^2}{2} - \frac{(n-1)(n-2)}{4} = \frac{n(n-1)}{4}$$

swaps, which is equal to $\frac{3}{4}n(n-1)$ moves.

The main disadvantage of bubble sort is that it still painstakingly bubbles items step by step up toward the top of the array. It looks at two adjacent array elements at a time and swaps them if they are not in order. If an element has to be moved from the bottom to the top, it is exchanged with every element in the array. It does not skip them as selection sort did. In addition, the algorithm concentrates only on the item that is being bubbled up. Therefore, all elements that distort the order are moved, even those that are already in their final positions (see numbers 2 and 3 in Figure 9.3, the situation analogous to that in insertion sort).

Figure **9.3**   The array [5 2 3 8 1] sorted by bubble sort.

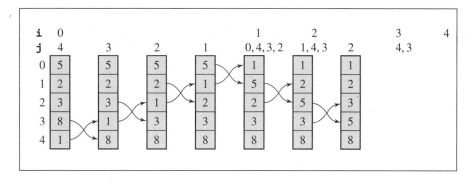

What is bubble sort's performance in comparison to insertion and selection sort? In the average case, bubble sort makes approximately twice as many comparisons and the same number of moves as insertion sort, as many comparisons as selection sort, and *n* times more moves than selection sort.

It could be said that insertion sort is twice as fast as bubble sort. In fact it is, but this fact does not immediately follow from the performance estimates. The point is that when determining a formula for the number of comparisons, only comparisons of data items have been included. The actual implementation for each algorithm involves more than just that. In bubblesort( ), for example, there are two loops, both of which compare indexes: i and data.length-1 in the first loop, j and i in the second. All in all, there are $\frac{n(n-1)}{2}$ such comparisons, and this number should not be treated too lightly. It becomes negligible if the data items are large structures. But if data consists of integers, then comparing the data takes a similar amount of time as comparing indexes. A more thorough treatment of the problem of efficiency should focus on more than just data comparison and exchange. It should also include the overhead necessary for implementation of the algorithm.

⌷ 9.2 DECISION TREES

The three sorting methods analyzed in previous sections were not very efficient. This leads to several questions: Can any better level of efficiency for a sorting algorithm be expected? Can algorithms, at least theoretically, be more efficient by executing faster? If so, when can we be satisfied with an algorithm and be sure that the sorting speed is unlikely to be increased? We need a quantitative measurement to estimate a *lower bound* of sorting speed.

This section focuses on the comparisons of two elements and not the element interchange. The questions are: On the average, how many comparisons have to be made to sort *n* elements? Or what is the best estimate of the number of item comparisons if an array is assumed to be ordered randomly?

FIGURE **9.4**   Decision trees for (a) insertion sort and (b) bubble sort as applied to the array [a b c].

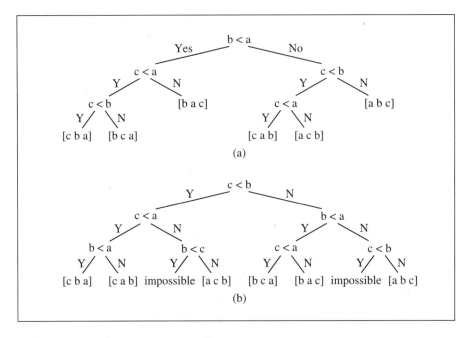

Every sorting algorithm can be expressed in terms of a binary tree in which the arcs carry the labels Y(es) or N(o). Nonterminal nodes of the tree contain conditions or queries for labels, and the leaves have all possible orderings of the array to which the algorithm is applied. This type of tree is called a *decision tree*. Since the initial ordering cannot be predicted, all possibilities have to be listed in the tree in order for the sorting procedure to grapple with any array and any possible initial order of data. This initial order determines which path is taken by the algorithm and what sequence of comparisons is actually chosen. Note that different trees have to be drawn for arrays of different length.

Figure 9.4 illustrates decision trees for insertion sort and bubble sort for an array [a b c]. The tree for insertion sort has six leaves, and the tree for bubble sort has eight leaves. How many leaves does a tree for an n-element array have? Such an array can be ordered in $n!$ different ways, as many ways as the possible permutations of the array elements, and all of these orderings have to be stored in the leaves of the decision tree. Thus, the tree for insertion sort has six leaves because $n = 3$, and $3! = 6$.

But as the example of the decision tree for bubble sort indicates, the number of leaves does not have to equal $n!$. In fact, it is never less than $n!$, which means that it can be greater than $n!$. This is a consequence of the fact that a decision tree can have leaves corresponding to failures, not only to possible orderings. The failure nodes are reached by an inconsistent sequence of operations. Also, the total number of leaves can be greater than $n!$ because some orderings (permutations) can occur in more than one leaf, since the comparisons may be repeated.

One of the interesting properties of decision trees is the average number of arcs traversed from the root to reach a leaf. Because one arc represents one comparison, the average number of arcs reflects the average number of key comparisons when executing a sorting algorithm.

As already established in Chapter 6, an i-level complete decision tree has 2^{i-1} leaves, $2^{i-1} - 1$ nonterminal nodes (for $i \geq 1$) and $2^i - 1$ total nodes. Because all noncomplete trees with the same number of i levels have fewer nodes than that, $k + m \leq 2^i - 1$, where m is the number of leaves and k the number of nonleaves. Also, $k \leq 2^{i-1} - 1$ and $m \leq 2^{i-1}$ (Section 6.1 and Figure 6.5). The latter inequality is used as an approximation for m. Hence, in an i-level decision tree, there are at most 2^{i-1} leaves.

Now, a question arises: What is a relationship between the number of leaves of a decision tree and the number of all possible orderings of an n-element array? There are $n!$ possible orderings, and each one of them is represented by a leaf in a decision tree. But the tree may also have some extra nodes due to repetitions and failures. Therefore, $n! \leq m \leq 2^{i-1}$, or $2^{i-1} \geq n!$. This inequality answers the following question: How many comparisons are performed when using a certain sorting algorithm for an n-element array in the worst case? Or rather, what is the lowest or the best figure expected in the worst case? Note that this analysis pertains to the worst case. We assume that i is a level of a tree regardless of whether or not it is complete; i always refers to the longest path leading from the root of the tree to the lowest tree level, which is also the largest number of comparisons needed to reach an ordered configuration of array stored in the root. First, the inequality $2^{i-1} \geq n!$ is transformed into $i - 1 \geq \lg(n!)$ which means that the path length in a decision tree with at least $n!$ leaves must be at least $\lg(n!)$, or rather, it must be $\lceil \lg(n!) \rceil$, where $\lceil x \rceil$ is an integer not less than x. See the example in Figure 9.5.

It can be proven that, for a randomly chosen leaf of an m-leaf decision tree, the length of the path from the root to the leaf is not less than $\lg m$ and that, both in the average case and the worst case, the required number of comparisons, $\lg(n!)$, is big-O of $n \lg n$ (see Section A.2 in Appendix A). That is, $O(n \lg n)$ is also the best that can be expected in average cases.

It is interesting to compare this approximation to some of the numbers computed for sorting methods, especially for the average and worst cases. For example, insertion sort requires only $n - 1$ comparisons in the best case, but in the average and the worst cases, this sort turns into an n^2 algorithm since the functions relating the number of comparisons to the number of elements are, for these cases, the big-Os of n^2. This is much greater than $n \lg n$, especially for large numbers. Consequently, insertion sort is not an ideal algorithm. The quest for better methods can be continued with at least the expectation that the number of comparisons should be approximated by $n \lg n$ rather than by n^2.

The difference between these two functions is best seen in Figure 9.6 if the performance of the algorithms analyzed so far is compared with the expected performance $n \lg n$ in the average case. The numbers in the table in Figure 9.6 show that if 100 items are sorted, the desired algorithm is four times faster than insertion sort and eight times faster than selection sort and bubble sort. For 1000 items, it is 25 and 50 times faster. For 10,000, the difference in performance differs by factors of 188 and 376, respectively. This can only serve to encourage the search for an algorithm embodying the performance of the function $n \lg n$.

FIGURE **9.5**   Examples of decision trees for an array of three elements.

These are some possible decision trees for an array of three elements. These trees must have at least 3! = 6 leaves. For the sake of the example, it is assumed that each tree has one extra leaf (a repetition or a failure). In the worst and average cases, the number of comparisons is $i - 1 \geq \lceil \lg(n!) \rceil$. In this example, $n = 3$, so $i - 1 \geq \lceil \lg 3! \rceil = \lceil \lg 6 \rceil \approx \lceil 2.59 \rceil = 3$. And, in fact, only for the best balanced tree (a), the nonrounded length of the average path is less than three.

Level

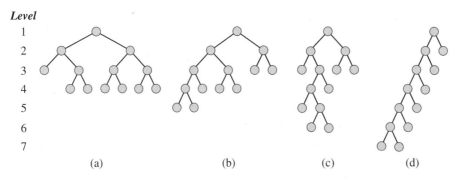

These are the sums of the lengths of the paths from the root to all leaves in trees (a) – (d) and the average path lengths:

(a) $2 + 3 + 3 + 3 + 3 + 3 + 3 = 20$; average $= \dfrac{20}{7} \approx 2.86$

(b) $4 + 4 + 3 + 3 + 3 + 2 + 2 = 21$; average $= \dfrac{21}{7} = 3$

(c) $2 + 4 + 5 + 5 + 3 + 2 + 2 = 23$; average $= \dfrac{23}{7} \approx 3.29$

(d) $6 + 6 + 5 + 4 + 3 + 2 + 1 = 27$; average $= \dfrac{27}{7} \approx 3.86$

FIGURE **9.6**   Number of comparisons performed by the simple sorting method and by an algorithm whose efficiency is estimated by the function $n \lg n$.

sort type	n	100	1,000	10,000
insertion	$\dfrac{n(n-1)}{4}$	2,475	249,750	24,997,500
selection, bubble	$\dfrac{n(n-1)}{2}$	4,950	499,500	49,995,000
expected	$n \lg n$	664	9,966	132,877

◪ 9.3 EFFICIENT SORTING ALGORITHMS

9.3.1 Shell Sort

The $O(n^2)$ limit for a sorting method is much too large and must be broken to improve efficiency and decrease run time. How can this be done? The problem is that the time required for ordering an array by the three sorting algorithms usually grows faster than the size of the array. In fact, it is customarily a quadratic function of that size. It may turn out to be more efficient to sort parts of the original array first and then, if they are at least partially ordered, to sort the entire array. If the subarrays are already sorted, we are that much closer to the best case of an ordered array than initially. A general outline of such a procedure is as follows:

> *divide* data *into* h *subarrays;*
> for (i = 1; i <= h; i++)
>   *sort subarray* data$_i$;
> *sort array* data;

If h is too small, then the subarrays data$_i$ of array data could be too large, and sorting algorithms might prove inefficient as well. On the other hand, if h is too large, then too many small subarrays are created, and although they are sorted, it does not substantially change the overall order of data. Lastly, if only one such partition of data is done, the gain on the execution time may be rather modest. To solve that problem, several different subdivisions are used, and for every subdivision, the same procedure is applied separately, as in:

> *determine numbers* h$_t$ ... h$_1$ *of ways of dividing array* data *into subarrays;*
> for (h=h$_t$; t > 1; t--, h=h$_t$)
>   *divide* data *into* h *subarrays;*
>   for (i = 1; i <= h; i++)
>   *sort subarray* data$_i$;
> *sort array* data;

This idea is the basis of the *diminishing increment sort,* also known as *Shell sort* and named after Donald L. Shell who designed this technique. Note that this pseudocode does not identify a specific sorting method for ordering the subarrays; it can be any simple method. Usually, however, Shell sort uses insertion sort.

The heart of Shell sort is an ingenious division of the array data into several subarrays. The trick is that elements spaced further apart are compared first, then the elements closer to each other are compared, and so on, until adjacent elements are compared on the last pass. The original array is logically subdivided into subarrays by picking every h_tth element as part of one subarray. Therefore, there are h_t subarrays, and for every $h = 1, \ldots, h_p$,

$$\text{data}_{h_t h}[i] = \text{data}[h_t \cdot i + (h-1)]$$

For example, if $h_t = 3$, the array data is subdivided into three subarrays $\text{data}_1, \text{data}_2$, and data_3 so that

```
data31[0] = data[0],data31[1] = data[3],...,data31[i] = data[3*i],...
data32[0] = data[1],data32[1] = data[4],...,data32[i] = data[3*i+1],...
data33[0] = data[2],data33[1] = data[5],...,data33[i] = data[3*i+2],...
```

and these subarrays are sorted separately. After that, new subarrays are created with an $h_{t-1} < h_p$ and insertion sort is applied to them. The process is repeated until no subdivisions can be made. If $h_t = 5$, the process of extracting subarrays and sorting them is called a 5-sort.

Figure 9.7 shows the elements of the array data that are five positions apart and are logically inserted into a separate array, "logically" since physically they still occupy the same positions in data. For each value of increment h_p, there are h_t subarrays, and each of them is sorted separately. As the value of the increment decreases, the number of subarrays decreases accordingly, and their sizes grow. Since much of data's disorder has been removed in the earlier iterations, on the last pass, the array is much closer to its final form than before all the intermediate h-sorts.

There is still one problem that has to be addressed, namely, choosing the optimal value of the increment. In the example in Figure 9.7, the value of 5 is chosen to begin with, then 3, and 1 is used for the final sort. But why these values? Unfortunately, no convincing answer can be given. In fact, any decreasing sequence of increments can be used as long as the last one, h_1, is equal to 1. Donald Knuth has shown that even if there are only two increments, $(\frac{16n}{\pi})^{\frac{1}{3}}$ and 1, Shell sort is more efficient than insertion sort because it takes $O(n^{\frac{5}{3}})$ time instead of $O(n^2)$. But the efficiency of Shell sort can be improved by using a larger number of increments. It is imprudent, however, to use sequences of increments such as 1, 2, 4, 8, . . . or 1, 3, 6, 9, . . . since the mixing effect of data is lost.

For example, when using 4-sort and 2-sort, a subarray, $\text{data}_{2,i}$, for $i = 1, 2$, consists of elements of two arrays, $\text{data}_{4,i}$ and $\text{data}_{4,j}$, where $j = i + 2$, and only those. It is much better if elements of $\text{data}_{4,i}$ do not meet together again in the same array since a faster reduction in the number of exchange inversions is achieved if they are sent to different arrays when performing the 2-sort. Using only powers of 2 for the increments, as in Shell's original algorithm, the items in the even and odd positions of the array do not interact until the last pass, when the increment equals 1. This is where the mixing effect (or lack thereof) comes into play. But there is no formal proof indicating which sequence of increments is optimal. Extensive empirical studies along with some theoretical considerations suggest that it is a good idea to choose increments satisfying the conditions

$$h_1 = 1$$

$$h_{i+1} = 3h_i + 1$$

and stop with h_t for which $h_{t+2} \geq n$. For $n = 10,000$, this gives the sequence

$$1, 4, 13, 40, 121, 364, 1093, 3280$$

Experimental data have been approximated by the exponential function, the estimate, $1.21n^{\frac{5}{4}}$, and the logarithmic function $.39n \ln^2 n - 2.33n \ln n = O(n \ln^2 n)$. The first

FIGURE **9.7**   The array [10 8 6 20 4 3 22 1 0 15 16] sorted by Shell sort.

data before 5-sort	10	8	6	20	4	3	22	1	0	15	16
Five subarrays before sorting	10	—	—	—	—	3	—	—	—	—	16
		8	—	—	—	—	22	—	—	—	
			6	—	—	—	—	1			
				20	—	—	—	—	0		
					4	—	—	—	—	15	
Five subarrays after sorting	3	—	—	—	—	10	—	—	—	—	16
		8	—	—	—	—	22	—	—	—	
			1	—	—	—	—	6			
				0	—	—	—	—	20		
					4	—	—	—	—	15	
data after 5-sort and before 3-sort	3	8	1	0	4	10	22	6	20	15	16
Three subarrays before sorting	3	—	—	0	—	—	22	—	—	15	
		8	—	—	4	—	—	6	—	—	16
			1	—	—	10	—	—	20		
Three subarrays after sorting	0	—	—	3	—	—	15	—	—	22	
		4	—	—	6	—	—	8	—	—	16
			1	—	—	10	—	—	20		
data after 3-sort and before 1-sort	0	4	1	3	6	10	15	8	20	22	16
data after 1-sort	0	1	3	4	6	8	10	15	16	20	22

form fits the results of the tests better. $1.21n^{1.25} = O(n^{1.25})$ is much better than $O(n^2)$ for insertion sort, but it is still much greater than the expected $O(n \lg n)$ performance.

Figure 9.8 contains a function to sort the array `data` using Shell sort. Note that before sorting starts, increments are computed and stored in the array `increments`.

The core of Shell sort is to divide an array into subarrays by taking elements h positions apart. There are three features of this algorithm that vary from one implementation to another:

1. The sequence of increments
2. A simple sorting algorithm applied in all passes except the last
3. A simple sorting algorithm applied only in the last pass, for 1-sort

In our implementation as in Shell's, insertion sort is applied in all h-sorts, but other sorting algorithms can be used. For example, Dobosiewicz uses bubble sort for the last pass and insertion sort for other passes. Incerpi and Sedgewick use two

FIGURE **9.8**   Implementation of Shell sort.

```
void Shellsort (Object[] data) {
    int i, j, k, h, hCnt, increments[] = new int[20];
    Comparable tmp;
//  create an appropriate number of increments h
    for (h = 1, i = 0; h < data.length; i++) {
        increments[i] = h;
        h = 3*h + 1;
    }
 // loop on the number of different increments h
    for (i--; i >= 0; i--) {
        h = increments[i];
      // loop on the number of subarrays h-sorted in ith pass
        for (hCnt = h; hCnt < 2*h; hCnt++) {
        // insertion sort for subarray containing every hth element
        // of array data
            for (j = hCnt; j < data.length; ) {
                tmp = (Comparable)data[j];
                k = j;
                while (k-h >= 0 && tmp.compareTo(data[k-h]) < 0) {
                    data[k] = data[k-h];
                    k -= h;
                }
                data[k] = tmp;
                j += h;
            }
        }
    }
}
```

iterations of cocktail shaker sort, a version of bubble sort in each *h*-sort, and finish with insertion sort obtaining what they call a *shakersort*. All these versions perform better than simple sorting methods, although there are some differences in performance among versions. Analytical results concerning the complexity of these sorts are not available. All results regarding complexity are of an empirical nature.

9.3.2 Heap Sort

Selection sort makes $O(n^2)$ comparisons and is very inefficient, especially for large *n*. But it performs relatively few moves. If the comparison part of the algorithm is improved, the end results can be promising.

Heap sort was invented by John Williams and uses the approach inherent to se-lection sort. Selection sort finds among the n elements the one that precedes all other $n - 1$ elements, then the least element among those $n - 1$ items, and so forth, until the array is sorted. To have the array sorted in ascending order, heap sort puts the largest element at the end of the array, then the second largest in front of it, and so on. Heap sort starts from the end of the array by finding the largest elements, whereas selection sort starts from the beginning using the smallest elements. The final order in both cases is indeed the same.

Heap sort uses a heap as described in Section 6.9. A heap is a binary tree with the following two properties:

1. The value of each node is not less than the values stored in each of its children.

2. The tree is perfectly balanced and the leaves in the last level are all in the leftmost positions.

A tree has the heap property if it satisfies condition 1. Both conditions are useful for sorting, although this is not immediately apparent for the second condition. The goal is to use only the array being sorted without using additional storage for the array elements; by condition 2, all elements are located in consecutive positions in the array starting from position 0, with no unused position inside the array. In other words, condition 2 reflects the packing of an array with no gaps.

Elements in a heap are not perfectly ordered. It is only known that the largest ele-ment is in the root node and that, for each other node, all its descendants are not greater than the element in this node. Heap sort thus starts from the heap, puts the largest element at the end of the array, and restores the heap that now has one less ele-ment. From the new heap, the largest element is removed and put in its final position, and then the heap property is restored for the remaining elements. Thus, in each round, one element of the array ends up in its final position, and the heap becomes smaller by this one element. The process ends with exhausting all elements from the heap and is summarized in the following pseudocode:

```
heapsort(data[])
    transform data into a heap;
    for (i = data.length-1; i > 1; i--)
        swap the root with the element in position i;
        restore the heap property for the tree data[0],...,data[i-1];
```

In the first phase of heap sort, an array is transformed into a heap. In this process, we use a bottom-up method devised by Floyd and described in Section 6.9.2. All steps leading to the transformation of the array [2 8 6 1 10 15 3 12 11] into a heap are illus-trated in Figure 9.9 (cf. Figure 6.58).

The second phase begins after the heap has been built (Figures 9.9g and 9.10a). At that point, the largest element, number 15, is moved to the end of the array. Its place is taken by 8, thus violating the heap property. The property has to be restored, but this time it is done for the tree without the largest element, 15. Because it is al-ready in its proper position, it does not need to be considered anymore and is re-moved (pruned) from the tree (indicated by the dashed lines in Figure 9.10). Now, the largest element among data[0],...,data[n-2] is looked for. To that end, the

FIGURE **9.9**   Transforming the array [2 8 6 1 10 15 3 12 11] into a heap.

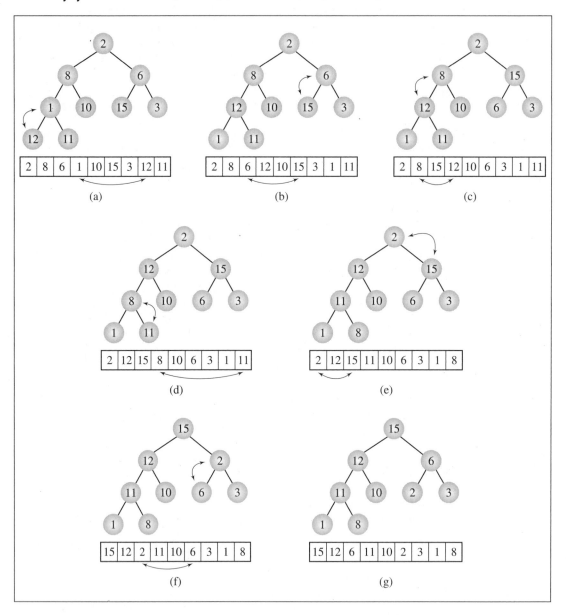

method moveDown() from Section 6.9 (Figure 6.56) is called to construct a heap out
of all the elements of data except the last, data[n−1], which results in the heap in
Figure 9.10c. Number 12 is sifted up and then swapped with 1, giving the tree in Figure 9.10d. The method moveDown() is called again to select 11 (Figure 9.10e), and
the element is swapped with the last element of the current subarray, which is 3

FIGURE **9.10**   Execution of heap sort on the array [15 12 6 11 10 2 3 1 8], which is the heap constructed in Figure 9.9.

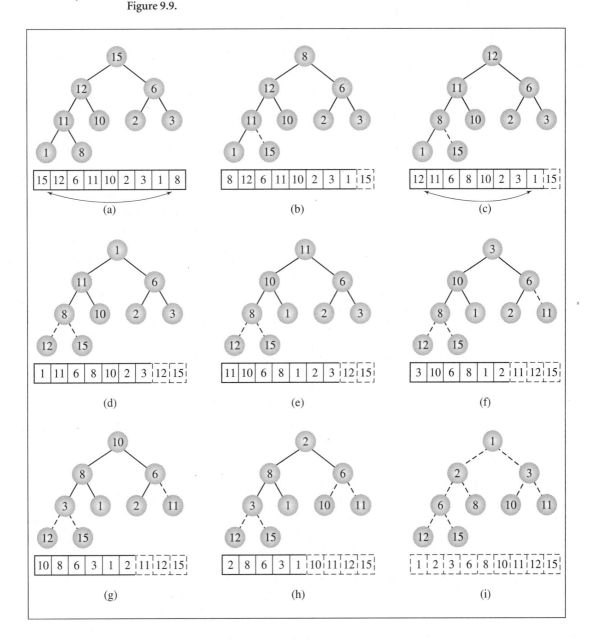

(Figure 9.10f). Now 10 is selected (Figure 9.10g) and exchanged with 2 (Figure 9.10h). The reader can easily construct trees and heaps for the next passes through the loop of `heapsort()`. After the last pass, the array is in ascending order and the tree is ordered accordingly. An implementation of `heapsort()` is as follows:

```
void heapsort(Object[] data) {
    for (int i = data.length/2 - 1; i >= 0; --i)
        moveDown(data,i,data.length-1);
    for (int i = data.length-1; i >= 1; --i) {
        swap(data,0,i);
        moveDown(data,0,i-1);
    }
}
```

Heap sort might be considered inefficient because the movement of data seems to be very extensive. First, all effort is applied to moving the largest element to the left-most side of the array in order to move it to the furthest right. But therein lies its efficiency. In the first phase, to create the heap, `heapsort()` uses `moveDown()`, which performs $O(n)$ steps (see Section 6.9.2).

In the second phase, `heapsort()` exchanges $n-1$ times the root with the element in position i and also restores the heap $n-1$ times which in the worst case causes `moveDown()` to iterate $\lg i$ times to bring the root down to the level of the leaves. Thus, the total number of moves in all executions of `moveDown()` in the second phase of `heapsort()` is $\sum_{i=1}^{n-1} \lg i$, which is $O(n \lg n)$. In the worst case, `heapsort()` requires $O(n)$ steps in the first phase, and in the second phase, $n-1$ swaps and $O(n \lg n)$ operations to restore the heap property. This gives $O(n) + O(n \lg n) + (n-1) = O(n \lg n)$ exchanges for the whole process in the worst case.

For the best case, when the array contains identical elements, `moveDown()` is called $\frac{n}{2}$ times in the first phase, but no moves are performed. In the second phase, `heapsort()` makes one swap to move the root element to the end of the array, resulting in only $n-1$ moves. Also, in the best case, n comparisons are made in the first phase and $2(n-1)$ in the second. Hence, the total number of comparisons in the best case is $O(n)$. However, if the array has distinct elements, then in the best case the number of comparisons equals $n \lg n - O(n)$ (Ding and Weiss 1991).

9.3.3 Quicksort

Shell sort approached the problem of sorting by dividing the original array into subarrays, sorting them separately, and then dividing them again to sort the new subarrays until the whole array is sorted. The goal was to reduce the original problem to subproblems that can be solved more easily and quickly. The same reasoning was a guiding principle for C. A. R. Hoare, who invented an algorithm appropriately called *quicksort*.

The original array is divided into two subarrays, the first of which contains elements less than or equal to a chosen key called the *bound* or *pivot*. The second array includes elements equal to or greater than the bound. The two subarrays can be sorted separately, but before this is done, the partition process is repeated for both subarrays. As a result, two new bounds are chosen, one for each subarray. The four subarrays are created because each subarray obtained in the first phase is now divided into two segments. This process of partitioning is carried down until there are only one-cell arrays that do not need to be sorted at all. By dividing the task of sorting a large array into two simpler tasks and then dividing those tasks into even simpler tasks, it turns out that in the process of getting prepared to sort, the data have already been sorted. Since the sorting has been somewhat dissipated in the preparation process, this process is the core of quicksort.

Quicksort is recursive in nature because it is applied to both subarrays of an array at each level of partitioning. This technique is summarized in the following pseudocode:

```
quicksort(array[])
    if array length > 1
        choose bound; // partition array into subarray₁ and subarray₂
        while there are elements left in array
            if element < bound
                include element either in subarray₁ = {el: el ≤ bound};
                or in subarray₂ = {el: el ≥ bound};
        quicksort(subarray₁);
        quicksort(subarray₂);
```

To partition an array, two operations have to be performed: A bound has to be found and the array has to be scanned to place the elements in the proper subarrays. However, choosing a good bound is not a trivial task. The problem is that the subarrays should be approximately the same length. If an array contains the numbers 1 through 100 (in any order) and 2 is chosen as a bound, then an imbalance results: The first subarray contains only one number after partitioning, whereas the second has 99 numbers.

A number of different strategies for selecting a bound have been developed. One of the simplest consists of choosing the first element of an array. That approach can suffice for some applications. However, since many arrays to be sorted already have many elements in their proper positions, a more cautious approach is to choose the element located in the middle of the array. This approach is incorporated in the implementation in Figure 9.11.

Another task is scanning the array and dividing the elements between its two subarrays. The pseudocode is vague about how this can be accomplished. In particular, it does not decide where to place an element equal to the bound. It only says that elements are placed in the first subarray if they are less than or the same as the bound and in the second if they are greater than or the same as the bound. The reason is that the difference between the lengths of the two subarrays should be minimal. Therefore, elements equal to the bound should be so divided between the two subarrays to make this difference in size minimal. The details of handling this depend on a particular implementation, and one such implementation is given in Figure 9.11. In this implementation, `quicksort(data[])` preprocesses the array to be sorted by locating the largest element in the array and exchanging it with the last element of the array. Having the largest element at the end of the array prevents the index `lower` from running off the end of the array. This could happen in the first inner `while` loop if the bound were the largest element in the array. The index `lower` would be constantly incremented eventually causing an abnormal program termination by raising the `ArrayIndexOutOfBoundsException`. Without this preprocessing, the first inner `while` loop would have to be

```
while (lower < last && data[lower].lessThan(bound)
```

FIGURE **9.11**   Implementation of quicksort.

```
void quicksort(Object[] data, int first, int last) {
    int lower = first + 1, upper = last;
    swap(data,first,(first+last)/2);
    Comparable bound = (Comparable)data[first];
    while (lower <= upper) {
        while (((Comparable)data[lower]).compareTo(bound) < 0)
            lower++;
        while (bound.compareTo(data[upper]) < 0)
            upper--;
        if (lower < upper)
            swap(data,lower++,upper--);
        else lower++;
    }
    swap(data,upper,first);
    if (first < upper-1)
        quicksort(data,first,upper-1);
    if (upper+1 < last)
        quicksort(data,upper+1,last);
}
void quicksort(Object[] data) {
    if (data.length < 2)
        return;
    int max = 0;
    // find the largest element and put it at the end of data;
    for (int i = 1; i < data.length; i++)
        if (((Comparable)data[max]).compareTo(data[i]) < 0)
            max = i;
    swap(data,data.length-1,max);    // largest el is now in its
    quicksort(data,0,data.length-2); // final position;
}
```

The first test, however, would be necessary only in extreme cases, but it would be executed in each iteration of this while loop.

In this implementation, the main property of the bound is used, namely, that it is a boundary item. Hence, as befits the boundary item, it is placed on the borderline between the two subarrays obtained as a result of one call to quicksort(). In this way, the bound is located in its final position and can be excluded from further processing. To ensure that the bound is not moved around, it is stashed in the first position, and after partitioning is done, it is moved to its proper position, which is the rightmost position of the first subarray.

Figure 9.12 contains an example of partitioning the array [8 5 4 7 6 1 6 3 8 12 10]. In the first partitioning, the largest element in the array is located and exchanged with

FIGURE **9.12** Partitioning the array [8 5 4 7 6 1 6 3 8 12 10] with `quicksort()`.

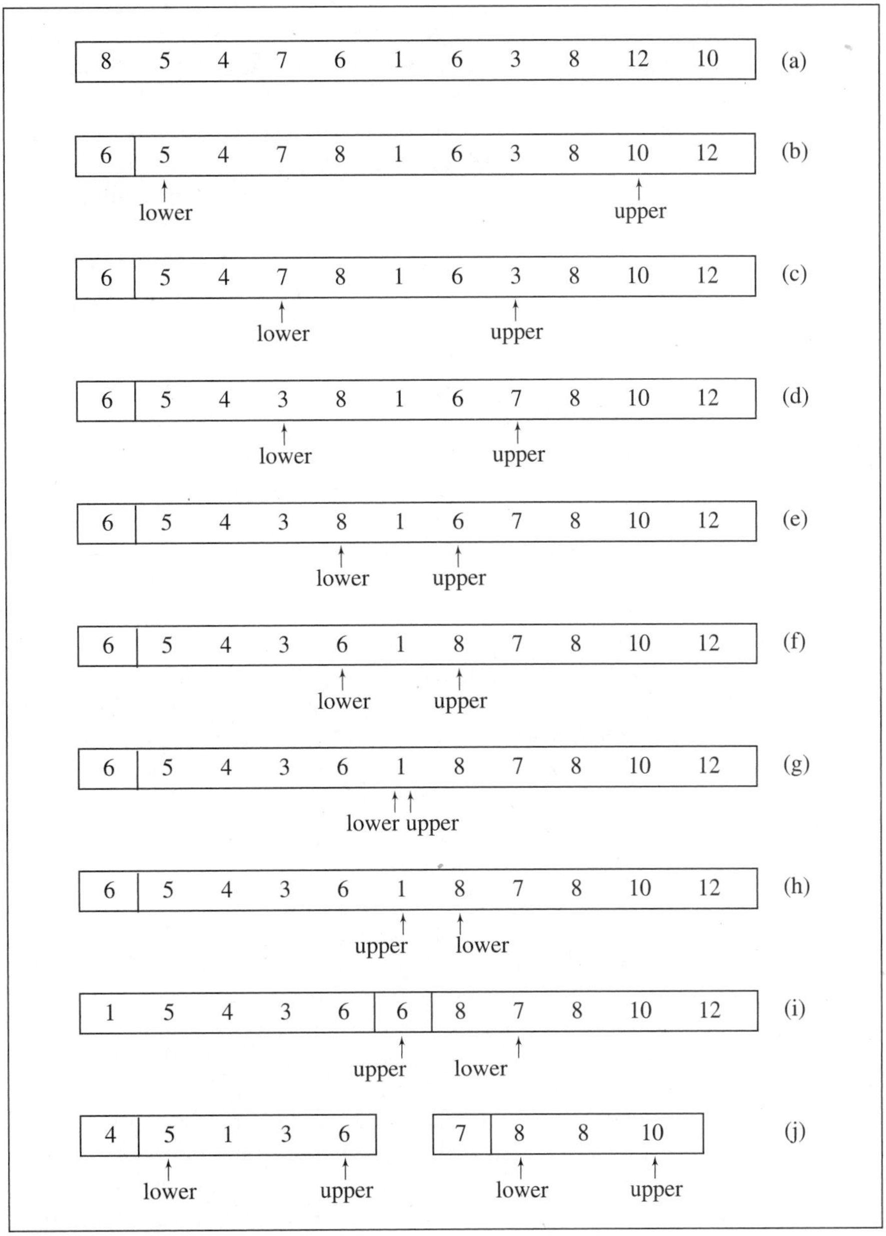

the last element resulting in the array [8 5 4 7 6 1 6 3 8 10 12]. Because the last element is already in its final position, it does not have to be processed anymore. Therefore, in the first partitioning, `lower` = 1, `upper` = 9, and the first element of the array, 8, is exchanged with the bound, 6 in position 4, so that the array is [6 5 4 7 8 1 6 3 8 10 12] (Figure 9.12b). In the first iteration of the outer `while` loop, the inner `while` loop moves `lower` to position 3 with 7, which is greater than the bound. The second inner `while` loop moves `upper` to position 7 with 3, which is less than the bound (Figure 9.12c). Next the elements in these two cells are exchanged, giving the array [6 5 4 3 8 1 6 7 8 10 12] (Figure 9.12d). Then `lower` is incremented to 4 and `upper` is decremented to 6 (Figure 9.12e). This concludes the first iteration of the outer `while` loop.

In its second iteration, neither of the two inner `while` loops modifies any of the two indexes because `lower` indicates a position occupied by 8, which is greater than the bound, and `upper` indicates a position occupied by 6, which is equal to the bound. The two numbers are exchanged (Figure 9.12f), and then both indexes are updated to 5 (Figure 9.12g).

In the third iteration of the outer `while` loop, `lower` is moved to the next position containing 8, which is greater than the bound, and `upper` stays in the same position because 1 in this position is less than the bound (Figure 9.12h). But at that point, `lower` and `upper` cross each other, so no swapping takes place, and after a redundant increment of `lower` to 7, the outer `while` loop is exited. At that point, `upper` is the index of the rightmost element of the first subarray (with the element not exceeding the bound), so the element in this position is exchanged with the bound (Figure 9.12i). In this way, the bound is placed in its final position and can be excluded from subsequent processing. Therefore, the two subarrays that are processed next are the left subarray, with elements to the left of the bound, and the right subarray, with elements to its right (Figure 9.12j). Then partitioning is performed for these two subarrays separately, and then for subarrays of these subarrays, until subarrays have less than two elements. The entire process is summarized in Figure 9.13, in which all the changes in all current arrays are indicated.

The worst case occurs if in each invocation of `quicksort()`, the smallest (or largest) element of the array is chosen for the bound. This is the case if we try to sort the array [5 3 1 2 4 6 8]. The first bound is 1, and the array is broken into an empty array and the array [3 5 2 4 6] (the largest number, 8, does not participate in partitioning). The new bound is 2, and again only one nonempty array, [5 3 4 6], is obtained as the result of partitioning. The next bound and array returned by partition are 3 and [5 4 6], then 4 and [5 6], and finally 5 and [6]. The algorithm thus operates on arrays of size $n - 1, n - 2, \ldots, 2$. The partitions require $n - 2 + n - 3 + \cdots + 1$ comparisons, and for each partition, only the bound is placed in the proper position. This results in a run time equal to $O(n^2)$, which is hardly a desirable result, especially for large arrays or files.

The best case is when the bound divides an array into two subarrays of approximately length $\frac{n}{2}$. If the bounds for both subarrays are well chosen, the partitions produce four new subarrays, each of them with approximately $\frac{n}{4}$ cells. If, again, the bounds for all four subarrays divide them evenly, the partitions give eight subarrays, each with approximately $\frac{n}{8}$ elements. Therefore, the number of comparisons performed for all partitions is approximately equal to

$$n + 2\frac{n}{2} + 4\frac{n}{4} + 8\frac{n}{8} + \ldots + n\frac{n}{n} = n(\lg n + 1)$$

FIGURE **9.13**   Sorting the array [8 5 4 7 6 1 6 3 8 12 10] with `quicksort()`.

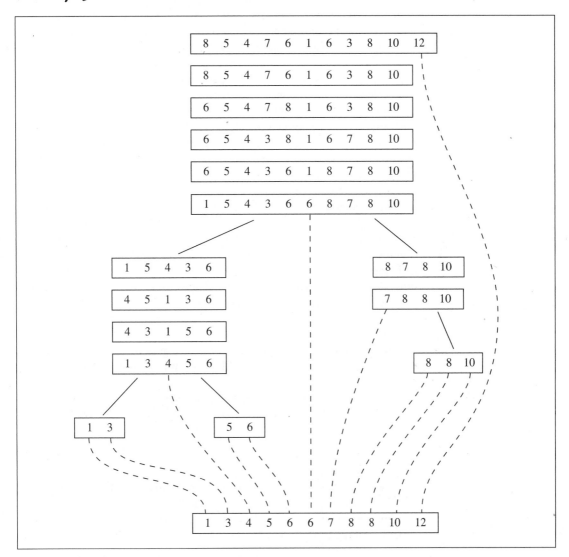

which is $O(n \lg n)$. This is due to the fact that parameters in the terms of this sum (and also the denominators) form a geometric sequence so that $n = 2^k$ for $k = \lg n$ (assuming that n is a power of 2).

To answer the question asked before: Is the average case, when the array is ordered randomly, closer to the best case, $n \lg n$, or to the worst, $O(n^2)$? Some calculations show that the average case requires only $O(n \lg n)$ comparisons (see Appendix A3), which is the desired result. The validity of this figure can be strengthened by referring to the tree obtained after disregarding the bottom rectangle in Figure 9.13.

This tree indicates how important it is to keep the tree balanced, for the smaller the number of levels, the quicker the sorting process. In the extreme case, the tree can be turned into a linked list in which every nonleaf node has only one child. That rather rare phenomenon is possible and prevents us from calling quicksort the ideal sort. But quicksort seems to be closest to such an ideal because, as analytic studies indicate, it outperforms other efficient sorting methods by at least a factor of 2.

How can the worst case be avoided? The partition procedure should produce arrays of approximately the same size, which can be achieved if a good bound is chosen. This is the crux of the matter: How can the best bound be found? Only two methods will be mentioned. The first method randomly generates a number between first and last. This number is used as an index of the bound, which is then interchanged with the first element of the array. In this method, the partition process proceeds as before. Good random number generators may slow down the execution time as they themselves often use sophisticated and time-consuming techniques. Thus, this method is not highly recommended.

The second method chooses a median of three elements: the first, middle, and last. For the array [1 5 4 7 8 6 6 3 8 12 10], 6 is chosen from the set [1 6 10], and for the first generated subarray, the bound 4 is chosen from the set [1 4 6]. Obviously, there is the possibility that all three elements are always the smallest (or the largest) in the array, but it does not seem very likely.

Is quicksort the best sorting algorithm? It certainly is—usually. It is not bulletproof, however, and some problems have already been addressed in this section. First, everything hinges on which element of the file or array is chosen for the bound. Ideally, it should be the median element of the array. An algorithm to choose a bound should be flexible enough to handle all possible orderings of the data to be sorted. Because some cases always slip by these algorithms, from time to time quicksort can be expected to be anything but quick.

Second, it is inappropriate to use quicksort for small arrays. For arrays with fewer than thirty items, insertion sort is more efficient than quicksort (Cook and Kim 1980). In this case the initial pseudocode can be changed to

```
quicksort2 (array[])
    if array.length > 30
        partition array into subarray₁ and subarray₂;
        quicksort2(subarray₁);
        quicksort2(subarray₂);
    else insertionsort(array);
```

and the implementations changed accordingly. However, the table in Figure 9.18 indicates that `quicksort2()` does appreciably improve the efficiency of `quicksort()`, particularly for arrays that are nearly sorted.

9.3.4 Mergesort

The problem with quicksort is that its complexity in the worst case is $O(n^2)$ because it is difficult to control the partitioning process. Different methods of choosing a bound attempt to make the behavior of this process fairly regular. However, there is no guarantee that partitioning results in arrays of approximately the same size. Another strategy is to make partitioning as simple as possible and concentrate on merging the two sorted arrays. This strategy is characteristic of *mergesort*. It was one of the first sorting algorithms used on a computer and was developed by John von Neumann.

The key process in mergesort is merging sorted halves of an array into one sorted array. However, these halves have to be sorted first, which is accomplished by merging the already sorted halves of these halves. This process of dividing arrays into two halves stops when the array has fewer than two elements. The algorithm is recursive in nature and can be summarized in the following pseudocode:

```
mergesort(data)
    if data  have at least two elements
        mergesort(left half of data);
        mergesort(right half of data);
        merge(both halves into a sorted list);
```

Merging two subarrays into one is a relatively simple task, as indicated in this pseudocode:

```
merge(array1, array2, array3)
    i1, i2, i3  are properly initialized;
    while both array2 and array3  contain elements
        if array2[i2] < array3[i3]
            array1[i1++] = array2[i2++];
        else array1[i1++] = array3[i3++];
    load into array1  the remaining elements of either array2 or array3;
```

For example, if array2 = [1 4 6 8 10] and array3 = [2 3 5 22], then the resulting array1 = [1 2 3 4 5 6 8 10 22].

The pseudocode for merge() suggests that array1, array2, and array3 are physically separate entities. However, for the proper execution of mergesort(), array1 is a concatenation of array2 and array3 so that array1 before the execution of merge() is [1 4 6 8 10 2 3 5 22]. In this situation, merge() leads to erroneous results, since after the second iteration of the while loop, array2 is [1 2 6 8 10] and array1 is [1 2 6 8 10 2 3 5 22]. Therefore, a temporary array has to be used during the merging process. At the end of the merging process, the contents of this temporary array are transferred to array1. Because array2 and array3 are subarrays of array1, they do not need to be passed as parameters to merge(). Instead, indexes for the beginning and the end of array1 are passed, since array1 can be a part of another array. The new pseudocode is

```
merge (array1, first, last)
    mid = (first + last) / 2;
    i1 = 0;
    i2 = first;
    i3 = mid + 1;
    while both left and right subarrays of array1  contain elements
        if array1[i2] < array1[i3]
            temp[i1++] = array1[i2++];
        else temp[i1++] = array1[i3++];
    load into temp  the remaining elements of  array1;
    load to array1  the content of temp;
```

Since the entire `array1` is copied to `temp` and then `temp` is copied back to `array1`, the number of movements in each execution of `merge()` is always the same and is equal to $2 \cdot (\texttt{last} - \texttt{first} + 1)$. The number of comparisons depends on the ordering in `array1`. If `array1` is in order or if the elements in the right half precede the elements in the left half, the number of comparisons is $(\texttt{first} + \texttt{last})/2$. The worst case is when the last element of one half precedes only the last element of the other half, as in [1 6 10 12] and [5 9 11 13]. In this case, the number of comparisons is $\texttt{last} - \texttt{first}$. For an n-element array, the number of comparisons is $n - 1$.

The pseudocode for `mergesort()` is now

```
mergesort (data, first, last)
   if first < last
       mid = (first + last) / 2;
       mergesort(data, first, mid);
       mergesort(data, mid+1, last);
       merge(data, first, last);
```

Figure 9.14 illustrates an example using this sorting algorithm. This pseudocode can be used to analyze the computing time for mergesort. For an n-element array, the number of movements is computed by the following recurrence relation:

$$M(1) = 0$$
$$M(n) = 2M\left(\frac{n}{2}\right) + 2n$$

$M(n)$ can be computed in the following way:

$$M(n) = 2\left(2M\left(\frac{n}{4}\right) + 2\left(\frac{n}{2}\right)\right) + 2n = 4M\left(\frac{n}{4}\right) + 4n$$

$$= 4\left(2M\left(\frac{n}{8}\right) + 2\left(\frac{n}{4}\right)\right) + 4n = 8M\left(\frac{n}{8}\right) + 6n$$

$$\vdots$$

$$= 2^i M\left(\frac{n}{2^i}\right) + 2in$$

Choosing $i = \lg n$ so that $n = 2^i$ allows us to infer

$$M(n) = 2^i M\left(\frac{n}{2^i}\right) + 2in = nM(1) + 2n \lg n = 2n \lg n = O(n \lg n)$$

The number of comparisons in the worst case is given by a similar relation:

$$C(1) = 0$$

$$C(n) = 2C\left(\frac{n}{2}\right) + n - 1$$

which also results in $C(n)$ being $O(n \lg n)$.

Mergesort can be made more efficient by replacing recursion with iteration (see the exercises at the end of this chapter) or by applying insertion sort to small portions of an array, a technique that was suggested for quicksort. However, mergesort has one

FIGURE **9.14**   The array [1 8 6 4 10 5 3 2 22] sorted by mergesort.

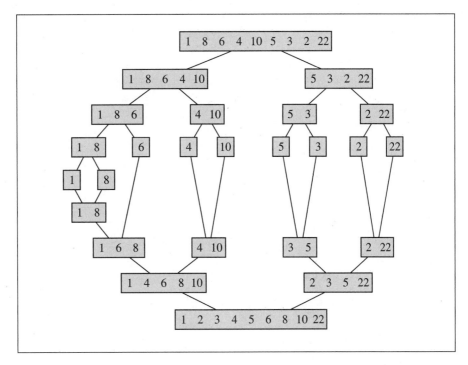

serious drawback: the need for additional storage for merging arrays, which for large amounts of data could be an insurmountable obstacle.

9.3.5 Radix Sort

Radix sort is a popular way of sorting used in everyday life. To sort library cards, we may create as many piles of cards as letters in the alphabet, each pile containing authors whose names start with the same letter. Then, each pile is sorted separately using the same method; namely, piles are created according to the second letter of the authors' names. This process continues until the number of times the piles are divided into smaller piles equals the number of letters of the longest name. This method is actually used when sorting mail in the post office, and it was used to sort 80 column cards of coding information in the early days of computers.

When sorting library cards, we proceed from left to right. This method can also be used for sorting mail since all zip codes have the same length. However, it may be inconvenient for sorting lists of integers because they may have an unequal number of digits. If applied, this method would sort the list [23 123 234 567 3] into the list [123 23 234 3 567]. To get around this problem, zeros can be added in front of each number to make them of equal length so that the list [023 123 234 567 003] is sorted

FIGURE **9.15**   Sorting the list 10, 1234, 9, 7234, 67, 9181, 733, 197, 7, 3 with radix sort.

data = [10 1234 9 7234 67 9181 733 197 7 3]

							7		
			3	7234			197		
10	9181		733	1234			67		9
piles: 0	1	2	3	4	5	6	7	8	9

pass 1

data = [10 9181 733 3 1234 7234 67 197 7 9]

9				7234					
7				1234					
3	10			733		67		9181	197
piles: 0	1	2	3	4	5	6	7	8	9

pass 2

data = [3 7 9 10 733 1234 7234 67 9181 197]

piles: 67									
10									
9									
7	197	7234					773		
3	9181	1234							
0	1	2	3	4	5	6	7	8	9

pass 3

data = [3 7 9 10 67 9181 197 1234 7234 733]

piles: 733									
197									
67									
10									
9									
7									
3	1234						7234		9181
0	1	2	3	4	5	6	7	8	9

pass 4

data = [3 7 9 10 67 197 733 1234 7234 9181]

into the list [003 023 123 234 567]. Another technique looks at each number as a string of bits so that all integers are of equal length. This approach will be discussed shortly. Still another way to sort integers is by proceeding right to left, and this method is discussed now.

When sorting integers, ten piles numbered 0 through 9 are created, and initially, integers are put in a given pile according to their rightmost digit so that 93 is put in pile 3. Then, piles are combined and the process is repeated, this time with the second rightmost digit; in this case, 93 ends up on pile 9. The process ends after the leftmost digit of the longest number is processed. The algorithm can be summarized in the following pseudocode:

```
radixsort()
    for (d = 1; d <= the position of the leftmost digit of longest number;  d++)
        distribute all numbers among piles 0 through 9 according to the  dth digit;
        put all integers on one list;
```

The key to obtaining a proper outcome is the way the ten piles are implemented and then combined. For example, if these piles are implemented as stacks, then the integers 93, 63, 64, 94 are put on piles 3 and 4 (other piles being empty):

```
pile 3:  63 93
pile 4:  94 64
```

These piles are then combined into the list 63, 93, 94, 64. When sorting them according to the second rightmost digit, the piles are as follows:

```
pile 6:  64 63
pile 9:  94 93
```

and the resulting list is 64, 63, 94, 93. The processing is finished, but the result is an improperly sorted list.

However, if piles are organized as queues, the relative order of elements on the list is retained. When integers are sorted according to the digit in position d, then within each pile, integers are sorted with regard to the part of the integer extending from digit 1 to $d-1$. For example, if after the third pass, pile 5 contains the integers 12534, 554, 3590, then this pile is ordered with respect to the two rightmost digits of each number. Figure 9.15 illustrates another example of radix sort.

An implementation of radix sort follows. The implementation is a part of class Sorts in which integer radix is assigned number 10 and integer digits is also assigned 10 (the maximum number of digits for an integer).

```
void radixsort(int[] data) {
    int d, j, k, factor;
    Queue[] queues = new Queue[radix];
    for (d = 0; d < radix; d++)
        queues[d] = new Queue();
    for (d = 1, factor = 1; d <= digits; factor *= radix, i++) {
        for (j = 0; j < data.length; j++)
            queues[(data[j] / factor) % radix].enqueue(
                                    new Integer(data[j]));
        for (j = k = 0; j < radix; j++)
            while (!queues[j].isEmpty())
                data[k++] =
                        ((Integer) queues[j].dequeue()).intValue();
    }
}
```

This algorithm does not rely on data comparison as did the previous sorting methods. For each integer from `data`, two operations are performed: division by a `factor` to disregard digits following digit *d* being processed in the current pass and division modulo `radix` (equal to 10) to disregard all digits preceding *d* for a total of $2n\text{digits} = O(n)$ operations. The operation `div` can be used which combines both / and %. In each pass, all integers are moved to piles and then back to `data` for a total of $2n\text{digits} = O(n)$ moves. The algorithm requires additional space for piles, which if implemented as linked lists, is equal to $4n$ bytes for reference fields. Our implementation uses only `for` loops with counters; therefore, it requires the same amount of passes for each case: best, average, and worst. The body of the only `while` loop is always executed *n* times to dequeue integers from all queues.

The foregoing discussion treated integers as combinations of digits. But as already mentioned, they can be regarded as combinations of bits. This time, division and division modulo are not appropriate, since for each pass, one bit for each number has to be extracted. In this case, only two queues are required.

An implementation can be given as follows:

```
void bitRadixsort(int[] data) {
    int d, j, k, factor, mask = 1;
    Queue[] queues = new Queue[2];
    queues[0] = new Queue();
    queues[1] = new Queue();
    for (d = 1; d <= bits; d++) {
        for (j = 0; j < data.length; j++)
            queues[(data[j] & mask) == 0 ? 0 : 1].enqueue(
                                new Integer(data[j]));
        mask <<= 1;
        k = 0;
        while (!queues[0].isEmpty())
            data[k++] = ((Integer)queues[0].dequeue()).intValue();
        while (!queues[1].isEmpty())
            data[k++] = ((Integer)queues[1].dequeue()).intValue();
        k = 0;
    }
}
```

Division is replaced here by the bitwise and-operation &. The variable `mask` has one bit set to 1 and the rest are set to 0. After each iteration, this 1 is shifted to the left. If `data[j]` & `mask` has a nonzero value, then `data[j]` is put in `queues[1]`; otherwise, it is put in `queues[0]`. Bitwise and is much faster than integer division, but this time 31 passes are needed; before it was only 10 (31 passes because only positive integers can be meaningfully processed with radix sort). This means $31n$ data movements as opposed to $10n$, and quicker operations cannot outweigh a larger number of moves: `bitRadixsort()` is slower, much slower, than `radixsort()`.

The problem is caused by the implementation of queues. They are implemented as linked lists, and for each item included in a particular queue, a new node has to be created and attached to the queue, and for each item copied back to the `data`, the

FIGURE **9.16**   An implementation of radix sort.

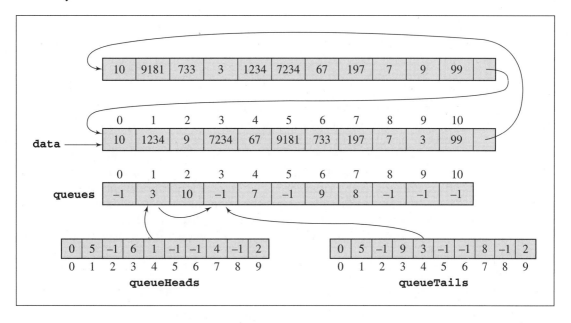

node has to be detached from the queue. Although theoretically obtained perform-ance $O(n)$ is truly impressive, it does not include operations on queues, although overall efficiency hinges upon the efficiency of queue implementation.

A better implementation is an array of size n for each queue, which requires cre-ating these queues only once. The efficiency of the algorithm depends only on the number of exchanges (copying to and from queues). However, if radix r is a large number and a large amount of data has to be sorted, then this solution requires r queues of size n and the number $(r + 1) \cdot n$ (original array included) may be unrealis-tically large.

A better solution uses one integer array `queues` of size n representing linked lists of indexes of numbers belonging to particular queues. Cell i of the array `queueHeads` contains an index of the first number in `data` which belongs to this queue, whose dth digit is i. `queueTails[]` contains a position in `data` of the last number whose dth digit is i. Figure 9.16 illustrates the situation after the first pass, for $d = 1$. `queue-Heads[4]` is 1, which means that the number in position 1 in `data`, 1234, is the first number found in `data` with 4 as the last digit. Cell `queues[1]` contains 3, which is an index of the next number in `data` with 4 as the last digit, 7234. Finally, `queues[3]` is –1 to indicate the end of the numbers meeting this condition.

The next stage orders data according to information gathered in `queues`. It copies all the data from the original array to some temporary storage and then back to this array. To avoid the second copy, two arrays can be used, constituting a two-element circular linked list. After copying, the reference to the list is moved to the next node, and the array in this node is treated as storage of numbers to be sorted. The improvement is significant since the new implementation runs at least three times faster than the implementation that uses queues (Figure 9.18).

🔲 9.4 SORTING IN `java.util`

Java provides two sets of versions of sorting methods: one for arrays and one for lists.

The first set of sorting methods is given in the utility class `Arrays`. The class `Arrays` includes methods for processing arrays, in particular, methods for searching arrays for elements with binary search, methods for filling arrays with a particular value, a method for converting an array into a list, and sorting methods. All the sorting methods in `Arrays` implement a version of the quicksort algorithm. The sorting methods are provided for arrays with elements of all elementary types except Boolean. For each type, there are two versions, one for sorting an entire array and one for sorting a subarray. For example, for integer arrays there are two sorting methods:

```
public static void sort(int[] a);
public static void sort(int[] a, int first, int last);
```

An example of sorting an integer array, integer subarray, and a character array is given in Figure 9.17. The class `Arrays` also includes four generic sorting methods:

```
public static void sort(Object[] a);
public static void sort(Object[] a, int first, int last);
public static void sort(Object[] a, Comparator c);
public static void sort(Object[] a, int first, int last, Comparator c);
```

Quicksort implemented in `Arrays`' sorting methods is based on comparison of elements. For basic data types, the comparison is obvious, but for objects, a comparison criterion must be provided by the user (except for wrapper classes). For example, if an array consists of objects of type `Person` that includes two fields, a string field and an integer field, it is not obvious what it means that one `Person` object is less than another. For this reason, the class definition should implement the `compareTo()` method whose signature is included the interface `java.lang.Comparable`. For example, class `Person` is defined as (Figure 9.17)

```
class Person implements Comparable { . . . }
```

There are two possible problems. First, there may be null objects present in an array, in which case the program crashes because `compareTo()` would be searched for in the null objects, as in

```
null.compareTo(someObject);
```

To prevent this from happening, a two-argument comparison method should be used, as in

```
compare(null,someObject);
```

FIGURE **9.17**   Demonstration of sorting functions.

```java
import java.io.*;
import java.util.*;

class Person implements Comparable {
    String name;
    int age;
    Person(String s, int i) {
        name = s; age = i;
    }
    Person() {
        this("",0);
    }
    public String toString() {
        return "(" + name + ", " + age  + ")";
    }
    public int compareTo(Object p) {
        return name.compareTo(((Person)p).name);
    }
}

class PersonComparator implements Comparator {
    public int compare(Object ob1, Object ob2) {
        if (ob1 == ob2)
            return 0;
        else if(ob1 == null)
            return -1;
        else if (ob2 == null)
            return 1;
        return ((Person)ob1).age - ((Person)ob2).age;
    }
}

class testSorts {
    public static void main(String[] ar) {
        int[] intArr1 = {4, 6, 7, 4, 2};
        int[] intArr2 = {4, 6, 7, 4, 2};
        char[] charArr = {'a', 'n', 'd', 'v', 'a'};
        Arrays.sort(intArr1); // intArr1 = [2, 4, 4, 6, 7]
        for (int i = 0; i < intArr1.length; i++)
            System.out.print(intArr1[i] + " ");
        System.out.println();
```

FIGURE **9.17**   *(continued)*

```
        Arrays.sort(intArr2,1,intArr2.length-2); // intArr2 = [4, 6, 7, 4, 2]
        Arrays.sort(charArr); // charArr = ['a', 'a', 'd', 'n', 'v']
        Person[] persons1 = {new Person("Tom",50), new Person("Lili",29),
                             new Person("Jeff",44)};
        Person[] persons2 = {new Person("Tom",50), new Person("Lili",29),
                             new Person("Jeff",44), null};
        Vector personVector = new Vector();
        LinkedList personLList1 = new LinkedList();
        LinkedList personLList2 = new LinkedList();
        ArrayList personAList = new ArrayList();
        for (int i = 0; i < persons1.length; i++) {
            personVector.add(persons1[i]);
            personLList1.add(persons1[i]);
            personLList2.add(persons1[i]);
            personAList.add(persons1[i]);
        }
        Collections.sort(personVector);
        System.out.println("personVector = " + personVector);
        // personVector = [(Jeff, 44), (Lili, 29), (Tom, 50)]
        Collections.sort(personLList1);
        // personLList1 = [(Jeff, 44), (Lili, 29), (Tom, 50)]
        Collections.sort(personLList2,new PersonComparator());
        // personLList2 = [(Lili, 29), (Jeff, 44), (Tom, 50)]
        Collections.sort(personAList);
        // personAList = [(Jeff, 44), (Lili, 29), (Tom, 50)]
        Arrays.sort(persons1);
        // persons1 = [(Jeff, 44), (Lili, 29), (Tom, 50)]
        Arrays.sort(persons2,new PersonComparator());
        // persons2 = [null, (Lili, 29), (Jeff, 44), (Tom, 50)]

        Integer[] a = {new Integer(1), new Integer(4),
                       new Integer(2), new Integer(5)};
        (new Sorts()).insertionsort(a); // a = [1, 2, 4, 5]
        Person[] persons3 = {new Person("Tom",50), new Person("Lili",29),
                             new Person("Jeff",44)};
        (new Sorts()).insertionsort(persons3);
        // persons3 = [(Lili, 29), (Jeff, 44), (Tom, 50)]
    }
}
```

Second, the user may want to apply another comparison criterion so that, for example, the `Person` objects can be ordered not by name but by age. One solution was proposed in Section 7.1.8 by defining two classes with their own versions of `compareTo()`. But this still does not solve the problem of null objects. The solution is in defining a comparator for a particular class by extending the interface `java.util.Comparator`, which includes a signature of the method `compare()`. An example of a `PersonComparator` is given in Figure 9.17. To apply a comparator, a sorting method has to be given an instance of the comparator to use the `compare()` method in sorting an array. If a comparator is not provided, the sorting method uses the `compareTo()` method.

Another set of sorting methods is included in the class `java.util.Collections` and consists of two methods:

```
public static void sort(List lst);
public static void sort(List lst, Comparator comp);
```

The two sorting methods implement mergesort and can be applied to vectors, array lists, and linked lists. Some examples are given in Figure 9.17. The figure also demonstrates an application of `insertionsort()`, discussed in Section 9.1.1, to an array of `Integer` objects and `Person` objects.

⚑ 9.5 CONCLUDING REMARKS

Figure 9.18 compares the run times for different sorting algorithms and different numbers of integers being sorted. They were all run on a Pentium 133MHz PC. At each stage, the number of integers has been doubled to see the factors by which the run times raise. These factors are included in each column except for the first three columns and are shown along with the run times. The factors are rounded to one decimal place, whereas run times (in seconds) are rounded to two decimal places. For example, heap sort requires .38 sec to sort an array of 10,000 `Integer` objects in ascending order, and .72 sec to sort 20,000 `Integer` objects also in ascending order. Doubling the amount of data is associated with the increase of run time by a factor of .72/.38 = 1.8947 ≈ 1.9 and the number 1.9 follows .72 in the fifth column.

Figure 9.18 indicates that the run time for elementary sorting methods, which are squared algorithms, grows approximately by a factor of 4 after the amount of data is doubled, whereas the same factor for nonelementary methods, whose complexity if $O(n \lg n)$ is approximately 2. This is also true for the four implementations of radix sort, whose complexity equals $2ndigits$. The table also shows that quicksort is the fastest algorithm among all sorting methods; most of the time, it runs at least twice as fast as any other algorithm.

It is important, however, that if possible, wrapper types should be avoided in sorting, and basic cases should be used instead to increase efficiency of the sorting routine. Figure 9.18 indicates times for sorting routines applied to arrays of `Integer` objects. Sorting arrays of integers is approximately 15 times faster.

FIGURE **9.18** Comparison of run times for different sorting algorithms and different numbers of integers to be sorted.

	10,000			20,000					
	Ascending	Random	Descending	Ascending		Random		Descending	
insertionSort	.05	15.82	26.92	.06	1.2	1 m 14.83	4.7	1 m 40.57	3.7
selectionSort	46.86	51.46	59.91	3 m 13.5	4.1	3 m 44.92	4.4	3 m 23.56	4.0
bubbleSort	43.06	1 m 11.24	1 m 13.05	2 m 58.51	4.1	4 m 47.81	4.0	5 m 3.90	4.2
ShellSort	.11	.22	.11	.22	2.0	.49	2.2	.33	3.0
heapSort	.38	.39	.28	.72	1.9	.88	2.3	.72	2.8
mergesort	.27	.33	.22	.50	1.8	.66	2.0	.49	2.2
quicksort	.11	.17	.11	.16	1.5	.44	2.6	.22	2.0
quicksort2	.06	.16	.11	.11	1.8	.38	2.4	.16	1.5
radixSort	1.20	1.05	1.16	2.31	1.9	1.59	1.5	2.20	1.9
bitRadixSort	2.97	1.92	2.47	6.54	2.2	4.50	2.7	5.65	2.3
radixSort2	.11	.11	.11	.21	1.9	.28	2.0	.22	2.0
bitRadixSort2	.33	.17	.27	.14	1.3	.44	2.2	.44	1.6

	40,000						80,000					
	Ascending		Random		Descending		Ascending		Random		Descending	
insertionSort	.11	18	6 m 8.93	5.0	7 m 11.82	4.3	.11	1.0	29 m 2.73	4.7	29 m 36.13	4.2
selectionSort	14 m 8.11	4.4	16 m 12.23	4.3	13 m 31.52	4.0	56 m 8.09	4.0	67 m 21.31	4.2	56 m 49.94	4.2
bubbleSort	12 m 58.95	4.4	20 m 53.62	4.4	20 m 17.92	4.0	52 m 6.90	4.0	87 m 9.62	4.2	83 m 6.68	4.1
ShellSort	.60	2.7	1.15	2.3	.72	2.2	1.32	2.2	2.75	2.4	1.59	2.2
heapSort	2.63	2.2	2.03	2.3	1.59	2.2	3.63	2.3	4.56	2.2	3.35	2.1
mergesort	1.59	2.2	1.48	2.2	.99	2.0	2.19	2.1	3.35	2.3	2.20	2.2
quicksort	.44	2.7	.93	2.1	.44	2.0	.93	2.1	2.04	2.2	.99	2.3
quicksort2	.33	3.0	.88	2.3	.33	2.0	.77	2.3	1.92	2.2	.82	2.2
radixSort	5.22	2.3	4.51	2.8	5.60	2.6	10.98	2.1	10.82	2.4	10.00	1.8
bitRadixSort	9.94	1.5	11.31	2.2	17.68	3.1	28.40	2.9	31.04	2.7	29.00	1.6
radixSort2	.55	2.6	.61	2.2	.55	2.5	1.16	2.1	1.26	2.1	1.15	2.1
bitRadixSort2	.93	2.1	1.15	1.3	.88	2.0	1.83	2.0	2.42	2.1	1.98	2.3

◰ 9.6 CASE STUDY: ADDING POLYNOMIALS

Adding polynomials is a common algebraic operation and is usually a simple calculation. It is a known rule that, to add two terms, they must contain the same variables raised to the same powers, and the resulting term retains these variables and powers, except that its coefficient is computed by simply adding coefficients of both terms. For example,

$$3x^2y^3 + 5x^2y^3 = 8x^2y^3$$

but $3x^2y^3$ and $5x^2z^3$ or $3x^2y^3$ and $5x^2y^2$ cannot be conveniently added because the first pair of terms has different variables, and the variables in the second pair are raised to different powers. We would like to write a program that computes the sum of two polynomials entered by the user. For example, if

$$3x^2y^3 + 5x^2w^3 - 8x^2w^3z^4 + 3$$

and

$$-2x^2w^3 + 9y - 4xw - x^2y^3 + 8x^2w^3z^4 - 4$$

are entered, the program should output

$$-4wx + 3w^3x^2 + 2x^2y^3 + 9y - 1$$

To be more exact, the input and output for this problem should be as follows:

```
Enter two polynomials ended with a semicolon:
3x2y3 + 5x2w3 - 8x2w3z4 + 3;
- 2x2w3 + 9y - 4xw - x2y3 + 8x2w3z4 - 4;
The result is:
 - 4wx + 3w3x2 + 2x2y3 + 9y - 1
```

It has to be observed that the order of variables in a term is irrelevant; for example, x^2y^3 and y^3x^2 represent exactly the same term. Therefore, before any addition is performed, the program should order all of the variables in each term to make the terms homogeneous and add them properly. Thus, there are two major tasks to be implemented: ordering variables in each term of both polynomials and adding the polynomials. But before we embark on the problem of implementing the algorithms, we have to decide how to represent polynomials in Java. Out of many possibilities, a linked list representation is chosen with each node on the list representing one term. A term contains information about a coefficient, variables, and exponents included in the term. Because each variable and its exponent belong together, they are also kept together in an object of type `Variable`. Also, because the number of variables can vary from one term to another, a vector of the `Variable` objects is used to store in one node information concerning variables in one term. A polynomial is simply a linked list of such nodes. For example,

$$-x^2y + y - 4x^2y^3 + 8x^2w^3z^4$$

is represented by the list in Figure 9.19a, which in Java looks like the list in Figure 9.19b.

FIGURE **9.19**   A linked list representation of the expression $-x^2y + y - 4x^2y^3 + 8x^2w^3z^4$.

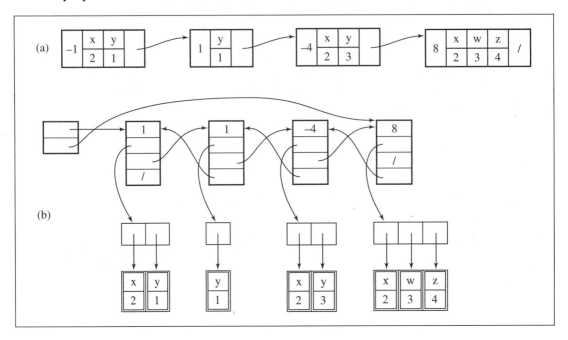

The first operation to perform on these polynomials is to order variables in their terms. After a polynomial is entered, each term is sorted separately by sorting vectors accessible from the nodes of the list.

The second task is to add the polynomials. The process begins by creating a linked list consisting of copies of nodes of the polynomials to be added. In this way, the two polynomials are not affected and can be used in other operations.

Now, addition is reduced to simplification. In the linked list, all equal terms (equal except for the coefficients) have to be collapsed together, and redundant nodes must be eliminated. For example, if the list being processed is as in Figure 9.20a, then the resulting list in Figure 9.20b results from the simplification operation.

When printing the result, remember that not everything should be printed. If the coefficient is zero, a term is omitted. If it is one or minus one, the term is printed, but the coefficient is not included (except for the sign), unless the term has just a coefficient. If an exponent is one, it is also omitted.

Another printing challenge is ordering terms in a polynomial, that is, converting a somewhat disorganized polynomial

$$-z^2 - 2w^2x^3 + 5 + 9y - 5z - 4wx - x^2y^3 + 3w^2x^3z^4 + 10yz$$

into the tidier form

$$-4wx - 2w^2x^3 + 3w^2x^3z^4 - x^2y^3 + 9y + 10yz - 5z - z^2 + 5$$

To accomplish this, the linked list representing a polynomial has to be sorted.

Figure 9.21 contains the complete code for the program to add polynomials.

FIGURE **9.20**   Transforming (a) a list representing the expression $-x^2y^3 + 3x^2y^3 + y^2z + 2x^2y^3 - 2y^2z$ into (b) a list representing a simplified version of this expression, $4x^2y^3 - y^2z$.

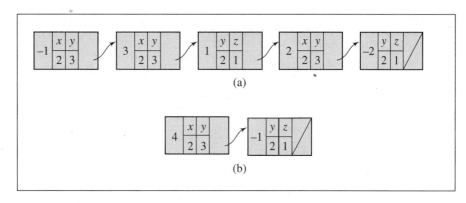

(a)

(b)

FIGURE **9.21**   Implementation of program to add polynomials.

```java
import java.io.*;
import java.util.*;

class Variable implements Comparable, Cloneable {
    char id;
    int exp;
    Variable() {
    }
    Variable(char c, int i) {
        id = c; exp = i;
    }
    public int compareTo(Object v) {
        return id - ((Variable)v).id;
    }
    public boolean equals(Object v) {
        return id == ((Variable)v).id && exp == ((Variable)v).exp;
    }
    public Object clone() {
        return new Variable(id,exp);
    }
}

class Term implements Comparable, Cloneable {
    public Term() {
    }
```

FIGURE **9.21** *(continued)*

```
    int coeff;
    Vector vars = new Vector();
    public Object clone() {
        Term t = new Term();
        t.coeff = coeff;
        t.vars = (Vector) vars.clone();
        for (int i = 0; i < vars.size(); i++)
            t.vars.setElementAt(((Variable)vars.elementAt(i)).clone(),i);
        return t;
    }
 /** two terms are equal if all variables are the same and
   * corresponding variables are raised to the same power;
   * the first cell of the node containing a term is excluded
   * from comparison, since it stores coefficient of the term;
   */
    public boolean equals(Object term) {
        int i;
        for (i = 0; i < Math.min(vars.size(),((Term)term).vars.size()) &&
                    vars.elementAt(i).equals(((Term)term).vars.elementAt(i)); i++);
        return i == vars.size() && vars.size() == ((Term)term).vars.size();
    }
    public int compareTo(Object term2) {
        if (vars.size() == 0)
            return 1;            // this is just a coefficient;
        else if (((Term)term2).vars.size() == 0)
            return -1;           // term2 is just a coefficient;
        Variable var1, var2;
        for (int i = 0; i < Math.min(vars.size(),((Term)term2).vars.size()); i++) {
            var1 = (Variable)vars.elementAt(i);
            var2 = (Variable)((Term)term2).vars.elementAt(i);
            if (var1.id < var2.id)
                return -1;       // this precedes term2;
            else if (var2.id < var1.id)
                return 1;        // term2 precedes this;
            else if (var1.exp < var2.exp)
                return -1;       // this precedes term2;
            else if (var2.exp < var1.exp)
                return 1;        // term2 precedes this;
        }
        return vars.size() - ((Term)term2).vars.size();
    }
}
```

FIGURE **9.21**   *(continued)*

```
class Polynomial {
    private LinkedList terms = new LinkedList();
    Polynomial() {
    }
    private void error(String s) {
        System.out.println(s);
        Runtime.getRuntime().exit(-1);
    }
    Polynomial add(Polynomial polyn2) {
        ListIterator p1, p2;
        Polynomial result = new Polynomial(), tmp = new Polynomial();
        Term term1, term2;
        int i;
        for (p1 = terms.listIterator(); p1.hasNext(); ) // create new polynomial
            result.terms.add(((Term)p1.next()).clone());//  out of copies
        for (p2 = polyn2.terms.listIterator(); p2.hasNext(); ) // of this
            result.terms.add(((Term)p2.next()).clone());// polynomial and polyn2;
        for (i = 0, p1 = result.terms.listIterator(); p1.hasNext();
                i++, p1 = result.terms.listIterator(i)) {
            term1 = (Term) p1.next();
            for (p2 = p1; p2.hasNext(); ) {
                term2 = (Term) p2.next();
                if (term1.equals(term2)) {
                    term2.coeff += term1.coeff;
                    result.terms.remove(term1);
                    if (term2.coeff == 0)      // remove terms with zero
                        result.terms.remove(term2); //  coefficients;
                    i = -1; // to become i = 0 after autoincrement;
                    break;
                }
            }
        }
        java.util.Collections.sort(result.terms);
        return result;
    }
    void get(InputStream fIn) {
        int ch = ' ', i, sign, exp;
        boolean coeffUsed;
        char id;
        Term term = new Term();
```

FIGURE **9.21** *(continued)*

```java
try {
    while (ch > -1) {
        coeffUsed = false;
        while (true)
            if (ch > -1 && Character.isWhitespace((char)ch)) // skip
                ch = fIn.read();                    // blanks;
            else break;
        if (!Character.isLetterOrDigit((char)ch) &&
            ch != ';' && ch != '-' && ch != '+')
            error("Wrong character entered2");
        if (ch == -1)
            break;
        sign = 1;
        while (ch == '-' || ch == '+') {   // first get sign(s) of Term
            if (ch == '-')
                sign *= -1;
            ch = fIn.read();
            while (Character.isWhitespace((char)ch))
                ch = fIn.read();
        }
        if (Character.isDigit((char)ch)) { // and then its coefficient;
            String number = "";
            while (Character.isDigit((char)ch)) {
                number += (char) ch;
                ch = fIn.read();
            }
            while (Character.isWhitespace((char)ch))
                ch = fIn.read();
            term.coeff = sign * Integer.valueOf(number).intValue();
            coeffUsed = true;
        }
        else term.coeff = sign;
        for (i = 0; Character.isLetterOrDigit((char)ch); i++) {
            id = (char) ch;        // process this term:
            ch = fIn.read();       // get a variable name
            if (Character.isDigit((char)ch)) {  // and an exponent
                String number = "";             // (if any);
                while (Character.isDigit((char)ch)) {
                    number += (char) ch;
                    ch = fIn.read();
                }
                exp = Integer.valueOf(number).intValue();
```

FIGURE **9.21**   *(continued)*

```
                      while (Character.isWhitespace((char)ch))
                          ch = fIn.read();
                  }
                  else exp = 1;
                  term.vars.addElement(new Variable(id,exp));
              }
              terms.add(term.clone());
              term.vars = new Vector();
              while (Character.isWhitespace((char)ch))
                  ch = fIn.read();
              if (ch == ';')              // finish if a semicolon is entered;
                  if (coeffUsed || i > 0)
                      break;
                  else error("Term is missing");  // e.g., 2x - ; or just ';'
              else if (ch != '-' && ch != '+')    // e.g., 2x  4y;
                  error("wrong character entered");
          }
      } catch (IOException io) {
      }
      for (Iterator p = terms.iterator(); p.hasNext(); ) {
          term = (Term) p.next();          // order alphabetically variables
          if (term.vars.size() > 1)        // in each term separately;
              Collections.sort(term.vars);
      }
  }
  void display() {
      boolean afterFirstTerm = false;
      Term term;
      for (Iterator it = terms.iterator(); it.hasNext(); ) {
          term = (Term) it.next();
          System.out.print(" ");
          if (term.coeff < 0)              // put '-' before polynomial
              System.out.print("-");       // and between terms (if needed);
          else if (afterFirstTerm)         // don't put '+' in front of
              System.out.print("+");       // polynomial;
          afterFirstTerm = true;
          System.out.print(" ");           // print a coefficient if
          if (term.vars.size() == 0 ||     // the term has only
              Math.abs(term.coeff) != 1)   // a coefficient or coefficient
              System.out.print(Math.abs(term.coeff)); // is not 1 or -1;
          for (int i = 1; i <= term.vars.size(); i++) {
```

Continues

FIGURE **9.21**   *(continued)*

```
                    Variable var = (Variable) term.vars.elementAt(i-1);
                    System.out.print(var.id);    // print a variable name
                    if (var.exp != 1)            // and an exponent, only
                        System.out.print(var.exp); // if it is not 1.
                }
            }
            System.out.println();
        }
    }

class AddPolyn {
    static public void main(String[] a) {
        Polynomial polyn1 = new Polynomial(), polyn2 = new Polynomial();
        System.out.println("Enter two polynomials, each ended with a semicolon:");
        polyn1.get(System.in);
        polyn2.get(System.in);
        System.out.println("The result is:");
        polyn1.add(polyn2).display();
    }
}
```

☐ 9.7 EXERCISES

1. Many operations can be performed faster on sorted than on unsorted data. For which of the following operations is this the case?

   a. checking whether one word is an anagram of another word, e.g., *plum* and *lump*

   b. finding an item with a minimum value

   c. computing an average of values

   d. finding the middle value (the median)

   e. finding the value which appears most frequently in the data

2. The method bubblesort() is inefficient because it continues execution after an array is sorted by performing unnecessary comparisons. Therefore, the number of comparisons in the best and worst cases is the same. The implementation can be improved by making a provision for the case when the array is already sorted. Modify bubblesort() by adding a flag to the outer for loop indicating whether or not it is necessary to make the next pass. Set the flag to true every time an interchange occurs, which indicates that there is a need to scan the array again.

3. Will `bubblesort()` work properly if the inner loop

   ```
   for (int j = n-1; j > i; --j)
   ```

   is replaced by

   ```
   for (int j = n-1; j > 0; --j)
   ```

   What is the complexity of the new version?

4. In our implementation of bubble sort, a sorted array was scanned bottom-up to bubble up the smallest element. What modifications are needed to make it work top-down to bubble down the largest element?

5. A *cocktail shaker sort* designed by Donald Knuth is a modification of bubble sort in which the direction of bubbling changes in each iteration: In one iteration, the smallest element is bubbled up; in the next, the largest is bubbled down; in the next, the second smallest is bubbled up; and so forth. Implement this new algorithm and explore its complexity.

6. Insertion sort goes sequentially through the array when making comparisons to find a proper place for an element currently processed. Consider using binary search instead and give a complexity of the resulting insertion sort.

7. Draw decision trees for all the elementary sorting algorithms as applied to the array [a b c d].

8. Which of the algorithms discussed in this chapter is easily adaptable to singly linked lists? To doubly linked lists?

9. What exactly are the smallest and largest numbers of movements and comparisons to sort four elements using `Shellsort()`, `heapsort()`, `quicksort()`, and `mergesort()`?

10. Implement and test `mergesort()`.

11. Show that for mergesort the number of comparisons $C(n) = n \lg n - 2^{\lg n} + 1$.

12. Implement and analyze the complexity of the following nonrecursive version of mergesort. First, merge subarrays of length 1 into $\frac{n}{2}$ two-cell subarrays, possibly one of them being a one-cell array. The resulting arrays are then merged into $\frac{n}{4}$ four-cell subarrays possibly, with one smaller array, having one, two, or three cells, etc., until the entire array is ordered. Note that this is a bottom-up approach to the mergesort implementation as opposed to the top-down approach discussed in this chapter.

13. `mergesort()` merges the subarrays of an array that is already in order. Another top-down version of mergesort alleviates this problem by merging only *runs*, subarrays with ordered elements. Merging is applied only after two runs are determined. For example, in the array [6 7 8 3 4 10 11 12 13 2], runs [6 7 8] and [3 4] are first merged to become [3 4 6 7 8], then runs [10 11 12 13] and [2] are merged to become [2 10 11 12 13], and finally, runs [3 4 6 7 8] and [2 10 11 12 13] are merged to become [2 3 4 6 7 8 10 11 12 13]. Implement this algorithm and investigate its complexity. A mergesort that takes advantage of a partial ordering of data (that is, uses the runs) is called a *natural sort*. A version that disregards the

runs by always dividing arrays into (almost) even sections is referred to as *straight merging*.

14. To avoid doubling the workspace needed when arrays are sorted with mergesort, it may be better to use a linked list of data instead of an array. In what situations is this approach better? Implement this technique and discuss its complexity.

15. A sorting algorithm is said to be *stable* if equal keys remain in the same relative order in the output as they are in the initial array; if a[i] equals a[j] for $i < j$ and then the *i*th element ends up in the *k*th position, and the *i*th element in the *m*th position, then $k < m$. Which sorting algorithms are stable?

16. Consider a *slow sorting* algorithm, which applies selection sort to every *i*th element of an *n*-element array, where *i* takes on values $n/2, n/3, \ldots, n/n$ (Julstrom 1992). First, selection sort is applied to two elements of the array, the first and the middle element, then to three elements, separated by the distance $n/3$, etc., and finally, to every element. Compute the complexity of this algorithm.

◻ 9.8 PROGRAMMING ASSIGNMENTS

1. At the end of the section discussing quicksort, two techniques for choosing the bound were mentioned; using a randomly chosen element from the file and using a median element of the first, middle, and last elements of the array. Implement these two versions of quicksort, apply them to large arrays, and compare their run times.

2. Implement different versions of Shell sort by mixing simple sorts used in *h*-sorts, 1-sort, and different sequences of increments. Run each version with (at least) any of the following sequences:

   a. $h_1 = 1, h_{i+1} = 3h_i + 1$ and stop with h_t for which $h_{t+2} \geq n$ (Knuth)
   b. $2^k - 1$ (Hibbard)
   c. $2^k + 1$ (Papernov and Stasevich)
   d. Fibonacci numbers
   e. $\frac{n}{2}$ is the first increment and then $h_i = .75h_{i+1}$ (Dobosiewicz)

   Run all these versions for at least five sets of data of sizes 1000, 5000, 10,000, 50,000, and 100,000. Tabulate and plot the results and try to approximate them with some formula expressing the complexity of these versions.

3. Extend the program from the case study to include polynomial multiplication.

4. Extend the program from the case study to include polynomial differentiation. For the rules, see the exercises in Chapter 5.

Bibliography

Sorting Algorithms

Flores, Ivan, *Computer Sorting,* Englewood Cliffs, NJ: Prentice Hall, 1969.

Knuth, Donald E., *The Art of Computer Programming, Vol. 3: Sorting and Searching,* Reading, MA: Addison-Wesley, 1998.

Lorin, Harold, *Sorting and Sort Systems,* Reading, MA: Addison-Welsey, 1975.

Mehlhorn, Kurt, *Data Structures and Algorithms, Vol. 1: Sorting and Searching,* Berlin: Springer, 1984.

Reynolds, Carl W., "Sorts of Sorts," *Computer Language* (March 1988), 49–62.

Rich, R., *Internal Sorting Methods Illustrated with PL/1 Programs,* Englewood Cliffs, NJ: Prentice Hall, 1972.

Shell Sort

Dobosiewicz, W., "An Efficient Variation of Bubble Sort," *Information Processing Letters* 11 (1980), 5–6.

Gale, David and Karp, Richard M., "A Phenomenon in the Theory of Sorting," *Journal of Computer and System Sciences* 6 (1972), 103–115.

Incerpi, Janet and Sedgwick, Robert, "Practical Variations of Shellsort," *Information Processing Letters* 26 (1987/88), 37–43.

Shell, Donald L., "A High-Speed Sorting Procedure," *Communications of the ACM* 2 (1959), 30–32.

Weiss, Mark A. and Sedgewick, Robert, "Tight Lower Bounds for Shellsort," *Journal of Algorithms* 11 (1990), 242–251.

Heap Sort

Carlsson, S., "Average-Case Results on Heapsort," *BIT* 27 (1987), 2–17.

Ding, Yuzheng and Weiss, Mark A., "Best Case Lower Bounds for Heapsort," *Computing* 49 (1992), 1–9.

Wegener, Ingo, "Bottom-up-Heap Sort, A New Variant of Heap Sort Beating on Average Quick Sort," in Rovan, B. (ed.), *Mathematical Foundations of Computer Science,* Berlin: Springer, 1990, 516–522.

Williams, John W. J., "Algorithm 232: Heapsort," *Communications of the ACM* 7 (1964), 347–348.

Quicksort

Cook, Curtis R. and Kim, Do Jin, "Best Sorting Algorithm for Nearly Sorted Lists," *Communications of the ACM* 23 (1980), 620–624.

Dromey, R. G., "Exploiting Partial Order with Quicksort," *Software Practice and Experience* 14 (1984), 509–518.

Frazer, William D. and McKellar, Archie C., "Samplesort: A Sampling Approach to Minimal Storage Tree Sorting," *Journal of the ACM* 17 (1970), 496–507.

Hoare, Charles A. R., "Algorithm 63: Quicksort," *Communications of the ACM* 4 (1961), 321.

Hoare, Charles A. R., "Quicksort," *Computer Journal* 2 (1962), 10–15.

Huang, B. C. and Knuth, Donald, "A One-Way, Stackless Quicksort Algorithm," *BIT* 26 (1986), 127–130.

Motzkin, Dalia, "Meansort," *Communications of the ACM* 26 (1983), 250–251.

Sedgewick, Robert, *Quicksort*, New York: Garland, 1980.

Mergesort

Dvorak, S. and Durian, B., "Unstable Linear Time $O(1)$ Space Merging," *The Computer Journal* 31 (1988), 279–283.

Huang, B. C. and Langston, M. A., "Practical In-Place Merging," *Communications of the ACM* 31 (1988), 348–352.

Knuth, Donald, "Von Neumann's First Computer Program," *Computing Surveys* 2 (1970), 247–260.

Slow Sorting

Julstrom, A., "Slow Sorting: A Whimsical Inquiry," *SIGCSE Bulletin* 24 (1992), No. 3, 11–13.

Decision Trees

Moret, B. M. E., "Decision Trees and Algorithms," *Computing Surveys* 14 (1982), 593–623.

Hashing

The main operation used by the searching methods described in the preceding chapters was comparison of keys. In a sequential search, the table that stores the elements is searched successively, and the key comparison determines whether or not an element has been found. In a binary search, the table that stores the elements is divided successively into halves to determine which cell of the table to check, and again, the key comparison determines whether or not an element has been found. Similarly, the decision to continue the search in a binary search tree in a particular direction is accomplished by comparing keys.

A different approach to searching calculates the position of the key in the table based on the value of the key. The value of the key is the only indication of the position. When the key is known, the position in the table can be accessed directly, without making any other preliminary tests, as required in a binary search or when searching a tree. This means that the search time is reduced from $O(n)$, as in a sequential search, or from $O(\lg n)$, as in a binary search, to 1 or at least $O(1)$; regardless of the number of elements being searched, the run time is always the same. But this is just an ideal, and in real applications, this ideal can only be approximated.

We need to find a function h which can transform a particular key K, be it a string, number, record, etc., into an index in the table used for storing items of the same type as K. The function h is called a *hash function*. If h transforms different keys into different numbers, it is called a *perfect hash function*. To create a perfect hash function, which is always the goal, the table has to contain at least the same number of positions as the number of elements being hashed. But the number of elements is not always known ahead of time. For example, a compiler keeps all variables used in a program in a symbol table. Real programs use only a fraction of the vast number of possible variable names, so a table size of 1000 cells is usually adequate.

But even if this table can accommodate all the variables in the program, how can we design a function h which allows the compiler to immediately access the position associated with each variable? All the letters of the variable name can be added together and the sum can be used as an index. In this case, the table needs 3782 cells (for a variable K made out of 31 letters "z," $h(K) = 31 \cdot 122 = 3782$). But even with this size, the function h does not return unique values. For example, $h(\text{"abc"}) = h(\text{"acb"})$. This problem is called *collision* and is discussed later. The worth of a hash function depends on how well it avoids collisions. Avoiding collisions can be achieved by making the function more sophisticated, but this sophistication should not go too far because the computational cost in determining $h(K)$ can be prohibitive, and less sophisticated methods may be faster.

☐ 10.1 HASH FUNCTIONS

The number of hash functions that can be used to assign positions to n items in a table of m positions (for $n \leq m$) is equal to m^n. The number of perfect hash functions is the same as the number of different placements of these items in the table and is equal to $\frac{m!}{(m-n)!}$ For example, for 50 elements and a 100-cell array, there are $100^{50} = 10^{100}$ hash functions out of which "only" 10^{94} (one in a million) are perfect. Most of these functions are too unwieldy for practical applications and cannot be represented by a concise formula. However, even among functions that can be expressed with a formula, the number of possibilities is vast. This section discusses some specific types of hash functions.

10.1.1 Division

A hash function must guarantee that the number it returns is a valid index to one of the table cells. The simplest way to accomplish this is to use division modulo *TSize* = *sizeof(table)*, as in $h(K) = K \bmod TSize$, if K is a number. It is best if *TSize* is a prime number. Otherwise, $h(K) = (K \bmod p) \bmod TSize$ for some prime $p > TSize$ can be used. However, nonprime divisors may work equally well as prime divisors provided they do not have prime factors less than 20 (Lum et al., 1971). The division method is usually the preferred choice for the hash function if very little is known about the keys.

10.1.2 Folding

In this method, the key is divided into several parts (which conveys the true meaning of the word *hash*). These parts are combined or folded together and are often transformed in a certain way to create the target address. There are two types of folding: *shift folding* and *boundary folding*.

The key is divided into several parts and these parts are then processed using a simple operation such as addition to combine them in a certain way. In shift folding, they are put underneath one another and then processed. For example, a social security number (SSN) 123–45–6789 can be divided into three parts, 123, 456, 789, and then these parts can be added. The resulting number, 1368, can be divided modulo *TSize* or, if the size of the table is 1000, the first three digits can be used for the address. To be sure, the division can be done in many different ways. Another possibility is to divide the same number 123-45-6789 into five parts (say, 12, 34, 56, 78, and 9), add them, and divide the result modulo *TSize.*

With boundary folding, the key is seen as being written on a piece of paper which is folded on the borders between different parts of the key. In this way, every other part will be put in the reverse order. Consider the same three parts of the SSN: 123, 456, and 789. The first part, 123, is taken in the same order, then the piece of paper with the second part is folded underneath it so that 123 is aligned with 654, which is the second part, 456, in reverse order. When the folding continues, 789 is aligned with the two previous parts. The result is 123+654+789=1566.

In both versions, the key is usually divided into even parts of some fixed size plus some remainder and then added. This process is simple and fast, especially when bit patterns are used instead of numerical values. A bit-oriented version of shift folding is obtained by applying the exclusive or operation, ˆ.

In the case of strings, one approach processes all characters of the string by "xor'ing" them together and using the result for the address. For example, for the string "abcd," $h($"abcd"$) = $"a"ˆ"b"ˆ"c"ˆ"d." However, this simple method results in addresses between the numbers 0 and 127. For better result, chunks of strings are "xor'ed" together rather than single characters. These chunks are composed of the number of characters equal to the number of bytes in an integer. Since an integer in Java is four bytes long, $h($"abcdefgh"$) = $"abcd" xor "efgh" (most likely divided modulo *TSize*). Such a function is used in the case study in this chapter.

10.1.3 Mid-Square Function

In the mid-square method, the key is *squared* and the middle or *mid* part of the result is used as the address. If the key is a string, it has to be preprocessed to produce a number by using, for instance, folding. In a mid-square hash function, the entire key participates in generating the address so that there is a better chance that different addresses are generated for different keys. For example, if the key is 3121, then $3121^2 = 9740641$, and for the 1000-cell table, $h(3121) = 406$, which is the middle part of 3121^2. In practice, it is more efficient to choose a power of 2 for the size of the table and extract the middle part of the bit representation of the square of a key. If we assume that the size of the table is 1024, then, in this example, the binary representation of 3121^2 is the bit string 100101000*1010000101*100001 with the middle part shown in italics. This middle part, the binary number 0101000010, is equal to 322. This part can easily be extracted by using a mask and a shift operation.

10.1.4 Extraction

In the extraction method, only a part of the key is used to compute the address. For the social security number 123–45–6789, this method might use the first four digits, 1234, the last four, 6789, the first two combined with the last two, 1289, or some other combination. Each time, only a portion of the key is used. If this portion is carefully chosen, it can be sufficient for hashing provided the omitted portion distinguishes the keys only in an insignificant way. For example, in some university settings, all international students' ID numbers start with 999. Therefore, the first three digits can be safely omitted in a hash function which uses student IDs for computing table positions. Similarly, the starting digits of the ISBN code are the same for all books published by the same publisher (e.g., 0534 for Brooks/Cole Publishing Company). Therefore, they should be excluded from the computation of addresses if a data table contains only books from one publisher.

10.1.5 Radix Transformation

Using the radix transformation, the key K is transformed into another number base; K is expressed in a numerical system using a different radix. If K is the decimal number 345, then its value in base 9 (nonal) is 423. This value is then divided modulo *TSize*, and the resulting number is used as the address of the location to which K should be hashed. Collisions, however, cannot be avoided. If *TSize* = 100, then although 345 and 245 (decimal) are not hashed to the same location, 345 and 264 are because 264 decimal is 323 in the nonal system, and both 423 and 323 return 23 when divided modulo 100.

⌐ 10.2 COLLISION RESOLUTION

Note that straightforward hashing is not without its problems, since for almost all hash functions, more than one key can be assigned to the same position. For example, if the hash function h_1 applied to names returns the ASCII value of the first letter of each name, i.e., $h_1(name) = name[0]$, then all names starting with the same letter are hashed to the same position. This problem can be solved by finding a function which distributes names more uniformly in the table. For example, the function h_2 could add the first two letters, i.e., $h_2(name) = name[0] + name[1]$, which is better than h_1. But even if all the letters are considered, i.e., $h_3(name) = name[0] + \cdots + name[\texttt{strlen}(name) - 1]$, the possibility of hashing different names to the same location still exists. The function h_3 is the best of the three because it distributes the names most uniformly for the three defined functions, but it also tacitly assumes that the size of the table has been increased. If the table had only 26 positions, which is the number of different values returned by h_1, there is no improvement using h_3 instead of h_1. Therefore, one more factor can contribute to avoiding conflicts between hashed keys, namely, the size of the table. Increasing this size may lead to better hashing, but not always! These two factors—hash function and table size—may minimize the number of collisions, but they cannot completely eliminate them. The problem of collision has to be dealt with in a way that always guarantees a solution.

There are scores of strategies that attempt to avoid hashing multiple keys to the same location. Only a handful of these methods are discussed in this chapter.

FIGURE **10.1**   Resolving collisions with the linear probing method. Subscripts indicate the home positions of the keys being hashed.

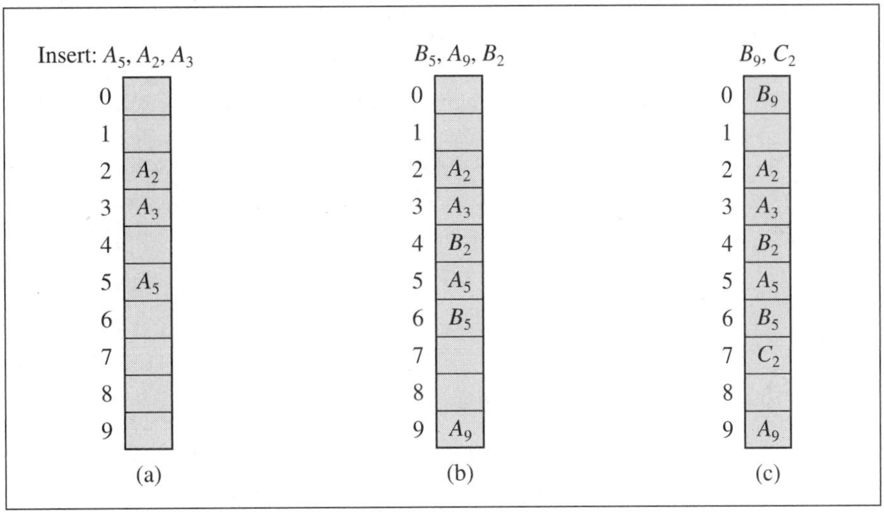

Insert: A_5, A_2, A_3

0	
1	
2	A_2
3	A_3
4	
5	A_5
6	
7	
8	
9	

(a)

B_5, A_9, B_2

0	
1	
2	A_2
3	A_3
4	B_2
5	A_5
6	B_5
7	
8	
9	A_9

(b)

B_9, C_2

0	B_9
1	
2	A_2
3	A_3
4	B_2
5	A_5
6	B_5
7	C_2
8	
9	A_9

(c)

10.2.1 Open Addressing

In the open addressing method, when a key collides with another key, the collision is resolved by finding an available table entry other than the position (address) to which the colliding key is originally hashed. If position $h(K)$ is occupied, then the positions in the probing sequence

$$norm(h(K) + p(1)), norm(h(K) + p(2)), \ldots, norm(h(K) + p(i)), \ldots$$

are tried until either an available cell is found or the same positions are tried repeatedly or the table is full. Function p is a *probing function*, i is a *probe*, and *norm* is a *normalization function*, most likely, division modulo the size of the table.

The simplest method is *linear probing*, for which $p(i) = i$, and for the ith probe, the position to be tried is $(h(K) + i)$ mod *TSize*. In linear probing, the position in which a key can be stored is found by sequentially searching all positions starting from the position calculated by the hash function until an empty cell is found. If the end of the table is reached and no empty cell has been found, the search is continued from the beginning of the table and stops—in the extreme case—in the cell preceding the one from which the search started. Linear probing, however, has a tendency to create clusters in the table. Figure 10.1 contains an example where a key K_i is hashed to the position i. In Figure 10.1a, three keys—A_5, A_2, and A_3—have been hashed to their home positions. Then B_5 arrives (Figure 10.1b), whose home position is occupied by A_5. Since the next position is available, B_5 is stored there. Next, A_9 is stored with no problem, but B_2 is stored in position 4, two positions from its home address. A large cluster has already been formed.

Next, B_9 arrives. Position 9 is not available, and since it is the last cell of the table, the search starts from the beginning of the table, whose first slot can now host B_9. The next key, C_2, ends up in position 7, five positions from its home address.

In this example, the empty cells following clusters have a much greater chance to be filled than other positions. This probability is equal to $(sizeof(cluster) + 1)/TSize$. Other empty cells have only $1/TSize$ chance of being filled. If a cluster is created, it has a tendency to grow, and the larger a cluster becomes, the larger is the likelihood that it will become even larger. This fact undermines the performance of the hash table for storing and retrieving data. The problem at hand is how to avoid cluster buildup. An answer can be found in a more careful choice of the probing function p.

One such choice is a quadratic function so that the resulting formula is

$$p(i) = h(K) + (-1)^{i-1}((i+1)/2)^2 \text{ for } i = 1, 2, \ldots, TSize - 1$$

This rather cumbersome formula can be expressed in a simpler form as a sequence of probes:

$$h(K) + i^2, h(K) - i^2 \text{ for } i = 1, 2, \ldots, (TSize - 1)/2$$

Including the first attempt to hash K, this results in the sequence:

$$h(K), h(K) + 1, h(K) - 1, h(K) + 4, h(K) - 4, \ldots, h(K) + (TSize - 1)^2/4,$$
$$h(K) - (TSize - 1)^2/4$$

all divided modulo $TSize$. The size of the table should not be an even number, since only the even positions or only the odd positions are tried depending on the value of $h(K)$. Ideally, the table size should be a prime $4j + 3$ of an integer j, which guarantees the inclusion of all positions in the probing sequence (Radke 1970). For example, if $j = 4$, then $TSize = 19$, and assuming that $h(K) = 9$ for some K, the resulting sequence of probes is[1]

$$9, 10, 8, 13, 5, 18, 0, 6, 12, 15, 3, 7, 11, 1, 17, 16, 2, 14, 4$$

The table from Figure 10.1 would have the same keys in a different configuration, as in Figure 10.2. It still takes two probes to locate B_2 in some location, but for C_2, only four probes are required, not five.

Note that the formula determining the sequence of probes chosen for quadratic probing is not $h(K) + i^2$, for $i = 1, 2, \ldots, TSize - 1$, because the first half of the sequence

$$h(K) + 1, h(K) + 4, h(K) + 9, \ldots, h(K) + (TSize - 1)^2$$

covers only half of the table, and the second half of the sequence repeats the first half in the reverse order. For example, if $TSize = 19$, and $h(K) = 9$, then the sequence is

$$9, 10, 13, 18, 6, 15, 7, 1, 16, 14, 14, 16, 1, 7, 15, 6, 18, 13, 10$$

---

[1]Special care should be taken for negative numbers. When implementing these formulas, the operator % means division modulo a modulus. However, this operator is usually implemented as the *remainder* of division. For example, −6 % 23 is equal to −6, and not to 17, as expected. Therefore, when using the operator % for the implementation of division modulo, the modulus (the right operand of %) should be added to the result when the result is negative. Therefore, (−6 % 23) + 23 returns 17.

FIGURE **10.2** Using quadratic probing for collision resolution.

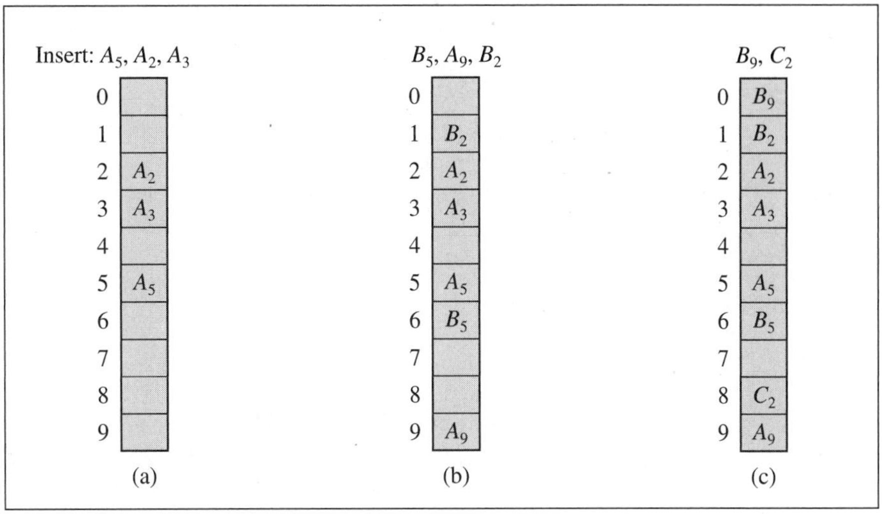

This is not an accident. The probes which render the same address are of the form

$$i = TSize/2 + 1 \text{ and } j = TSize/2 - 1$$

and they are probes for which

$$i^2 \bmod TSize = j^2 \bmod TSize$$

that is,

$$(i^2 - j^2) \bmod TSize$$

In this case,

$$(i^2 - j^2) = (TSize/2 + 1)^2 - (TSize/2 - 1)^2$$
$$= (TSize^2/4 + TSize + 1 - TSize^2/4 + TSize - 1)$$
$$= 2\,TSize$$

and to be sure, $2\,TSize \bmod TSize = 0$.

Although using quadratic search gives much better results than linear probing, the problem of cluster buildup is not avoided altogether, since for keys hashed to the same location, the same probe sequence is used. Such clusters are called *secondary clusters*. These secondary clusters, however, are less harmful than primary clusters.

Another possibility is to have p be a random number generator (Morris 1968), which eliminates the need to take special care about the table size. This approach prevents the formation of secondary clusters, but it causes a problem with repeating the same probing sequence for the same keys. If the random number generator is initialized at the first invocation, then different probing sequences are generated for the same key

K. Consequently, *K* is hashed more than once to the table and even then it might not be found when searched. Therefore, the random number generator should be initialized to the same seed for the same key before beginning the generation of the probing sequence. This can be achieved in Java by using the `setSeed()` method with a parameter that depends on the key; for example, $p(i) = $ `setSeed`$(sizeof(K)) \cdot i$ or `setSeed`$(K[0])$ $+ i$. Also, the constructor `Random()` with a parameter can be used. To avoid relying on `setSeed()`, a random number generator can be written which assures that each invocation generates a unique number between 0 and *TSize* − 1. The following algorithm was developed by Robert Morris for tables with $TSize = 2^n$ for some integer *n*:

```
int r = 1;
generateNumber()
    r = 5*r;
    r = mask out n + 2 low-order bits of r;
    return r/4;
```

The problem of secondary clustering is best addressed with *double hashing*. This method utilizes two hash functions, one for accessing the primary position of a key, *h*, and a second function, h_p, for resolving conflicts. The probing sequence becomes

$$h(K), h(K) + h_p(K), \ldots, h(K) + i \cdot h_p(K), \ldots$$

(all divided modulo *TSize*). The table size should be a prime number so that each position in the table can be included in the sequence. Experiments indicate that secondary clustering is generally eliminated because the sequence depends on the values of h_p which, in turn, depend on the key. Therefore, if the key K_1 is hashed to the position *j*, the probing sequence is

$$j, j + h_p(K_1), j + 2 \cdot h_p(K_1), \ldots$$

(all divided modulo *TSize*). If another key K_2 is hashed to $j + h_p(K_1)$, then the next position tried is $j + h_p(K_1) + h_p(K_2)$, not $j + 2 \cdot h_p(K_1)$, which avoids secondary clustering if h_p is carefully chosen. Also, even if K_1 and K_2 are hashed primarily to the same position *j*, the probing sequences can be different for each. This, however, depends on the choice of the second hash function, h_p, which may render the same sequences for both keys. This is the case for function $h_p(K) = k.\texttt{length}$ when both keys are of the same length.

Using two hash functions can be time-consuming, especially for sophisticated functions. Therefore, the second hash function can be defined in terms of the first, as in $h_p(K) = i \cdot h(K) + 1$. The probing sequence for K_1 is

$$j, 2j + 1, 3j + 1, \ldots$$

(modulo *TSize*). If K_2 is hashed to $2j + 1$, then the probing sequence for K_2 is

$$2j + 1, 4j + 3, 6j + 4, \ldots$$

which does not conflict with the former sequence. Thus, it does not lead to cluster buildup.

How efficient are all these methods? Obviously, it depends on the size of table and on the number of elements already in the table. The inefficiency of these methods is especially evident for *unsuccessful searches*, searching for elements not in the table.

FIGURE **10.3**   Formulas approximating, for different hashing methods, the average numbers of trials for successful and unsuccessful searches (Knuth 1998).

	Linear Probing	Quadratic Probin[a]	Double Hashing
successful search	$\dfrac{1}{2}\left(1+\dfrac{1}{1-LF}\right)$	$1-\ln(1-LF)-\dfrac{LF}{2}$	$\dfrac{1}{LF}\ln\dfrac{1}{1-LF}$
unsuccessful search	$\dfrac{1}{2}\left(1+\dfrac{1}{(1-LF)^2}\right)$	$\dfrac{1}{1-LF}-LF-\ln(1-LF)$	$\dfrac{1}{1-LF}$

$$\text{Load Factor} \quad LF = \frac{\text{number of elements in the table}}{\text{table size}}$$

[a] the formulas given in this column approximate any open addressing method which causes secondary clusters to arise, and quadratic probing is only one of them.

The more elements in the table, the more likely it is that clusters will form (primary or secondary) and the more likely it is that these clusters are large.

Consider the case when linear probing is used for collision resolution. If K is not in the table, then starting from the position $h(K)$, all consecutively occupied cells are checked; the longer the cluster, the longer it takes to determine that K, in fact, is not in the table. In the extreme case, when the table is full, we have to check all the cells starting from $h(K)$ and ending with $(h(K) - 1)$ mod $TSize$. Therefore, the search time increases with the number of elements in the table.

There are formulas which approximate the number of times for successful and unsuccessful searches for different hashing methods. These formulas were developed by Donald Knuth and are considered by Thomas Standish to be "among the prettiest in computer science." Figure 10.3 contains these formulas. Figure 10.4 contains a table showing the number of searches for different percentages of occupied cells. This table indicates that the formulas from Figure 10.3 provide only approximations of the number of searches. This is particularly evident for the higher percentages. For example, if 90% of the cells are occupied, then linear probing requires 50 trials to determine that the key being searched for is not in the table. However, for the full table of 10 cells, this number is 10, not 50.

For the lower percentages, the approximations computed by these formulas are closer to the real values. The table in Figure 10.4 indicates that if the table is 65% full, then linear probing requires, on average, fewer than two trials to find an element in the table. Since this number is usually an acceptable limit for a hash function, linear probing requires 35% of the spaces in the table to be unoccupied to keep performance at an acceptable level. This may be considered too wasteful, especially for very large tables or files. This percentage is lower for a quadratic search (25%) and for double hashing (20%), but it may still be considered large. Double hashing requires one cell out of five to be empty, which is a relatively high fraction. But all these problems can be solved by allowing more than one item to be stored in a given position or in an area associated with one position.

FIGURE **10.4**   The average numbers of successful searches and unsuccessful searches for different collision resolution methods.

LF	Linear Probing Successful	Unsuccessful	Quadratic Search Successful	Unsuccessful	Double Hashing Successful	Unsuccessful
0.05	1.0	1.1	1.0	1.1	1.0	1.1
0.10	1.1	1.1	1.1	1.1	1.1	1.1
0.15	1.1	1.2	1.1	1.2	1.1	1.2
0.20	1.1	1.3	1.1	1.3	1.1	1.2
0.25	1.2	1.4	1.2	1.4	1.2	1.3
0.30	1.2	1.5	1.2	1.5	1.2	1.4
0.35	1.3	1.7	1.3	1.6	1.2	1.5
0.40	1.3	1.9	1.3	1.8	1.3	1.7
0.45	1.4	2.2	1.4	2.0	1.3	1.8
0.50	1.5	2.5	1.4	2.2	1.4	2.0
0.55	1.6	3.0	1.5	2.5	1.5	2.2
0.60	1.8	3.6	1.6	2.8	1.5	2.5
0.65	1.9	4.6	1.7	3.3	1.6	2.9
0.70	2.2	6.1	1.9	3.8	1.7	3.3
0.75	2.5	8.5	2.0	4.6	1.8	4.0
0.80	3.0	13.0	2.2	5.8	2.0	5.0
0.85	3.8	22.7	2.5	7.7	2.2	6.7
0.90	5.5	50.5	2.9	11.4	2.6	10.0
0.95	10.5	200.5	3.5	22.0	3.2	20.0

10.2.2 Chaining

Keys do not have to be stored in the table itself. In *chaining*, each position of the table is associated with a linked list or *chain* of structures whose `info` fields store keys or references to keys. This method is called *separate chaining*, and a table of references (pointers) is called a *scatter table*. In this method, the table can never overflow, since the linked lists are only extended upon the arrival of new keys, as illustrated in Figure 10.5. For short linked lists, this is a very fast method, but increasing the length of

FIGURE **10.5**   In chaining, colliding keys are put on the same linked list.

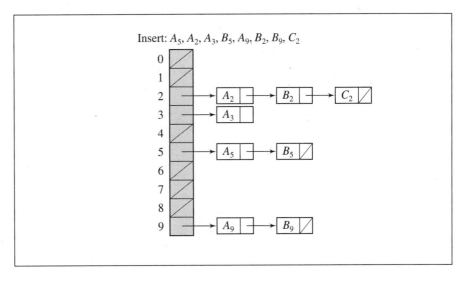

these lists can significantly degrade retrieval performance. Performance can be improved by maintaining an order on all these lists so that, for unsuccessful searches, an exhaustive search is not required in most cases or by using self-organizing linked lists (Pagli 1985).

This method requires additional space for maintaining references. The table stores only references and each node requires one reference field. Therefore, for n keys, $n + TSize$ references are needed, which for large n can be a very demanding requirement.

A version of chaining called *coalesced hashing* (or *coalesced chaining*) combines linear probing with chaining. In this method, the first available position is found for a key colliding with another key, and the index of this position is stored with the key already in the table. In this way, a sequential search down the table can be avoided by directly accessing the next element on the linked list. Each position *pos* of the table includes two fields: an `info` field for a key and `next` field with the index of the next key which is hashed to *pos*. Available positions can be marked by, say, −2 in `next`; −1 can be used to indicate the end of a chain. This method requires $TSize \cdot (sizeof(reference) + sizeof(\texttt{next}))$ more space for the table in addition to the space required for the keys. This is less than for chaining, but the table size limits the number of keys that can be hashed into the table.

An overflow area known as a *cellar* can be allocated to store keys for which there is no room in the table.

Figure 10.6 illustrates an example where coalesced hashing puts a colliding key in the last position of the table. In Figure 10.6a, no collision occurs. In Figure 10.6b, B_5 is put in the last cell of the table, which is found occupied by A_9 when it arrives. Hence,

FIGURE **10.6**   Coalesced hashing puts a colliding key in the last available position of the table.

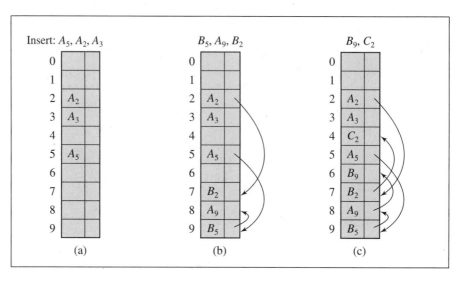

FIGURE **10.7**   Coalesced hashing which uses a cellar.

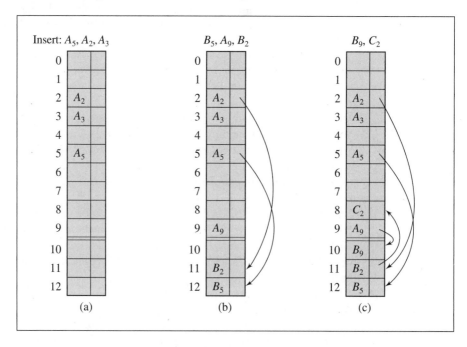

FIGURE **10.8**   Collision resolution with buckets and linear probing method.

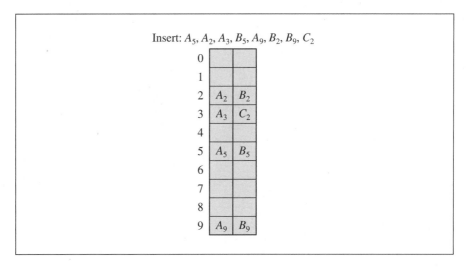

Insert: $A_5, A_2, A_3, B_5, A_9, B_2, B_9, C_2$

A_9 is attached to the list accessible from position 9. In Figure 10.6c, two new colliding keys are added to the corresponding lists.

Figure 10.7 illustrates coalesced hashing which uses a cellar. Noncolliding keys are stored in their home positions, as in Figure 10.7a. Colliding keys are put in the last available slot of the cellar and added to the list starting from their home position, as in Figure 10.7b. In Figure 10.7c, the cellar is full, so an available cell is taken from the table when C_2 arrives.

10.2.3 Bucket Addressing

Another solution to the collision problem is to store colliding elements in the same position in the table. This can be achieved by associating a *bucket* with each address. A bucket is a block of space large enough to store multiple items.

By using buckets, the problem of collisions is not totally avoided. If a bucket is already full, then an item hashed to it has to be stored somewhere else. By incorporating the open addressing approach, the colliding item can be stored in the next bucket if it has an available slot when using linear probing, as illustrated in Figure 10.8, or it can be stored in some other bucket when, say, quadratic probing is used.

The colliding items can also be stored in an overflow area. In this case, each bucket includes a field that indicates whether the search should be continued in this area or not. It can be simply a yes/no marker. In conjunction with chaining, this marker can be the number indicating the position in which the beginning of the linked list associated with this bucket can be found in the overflow area (see Figure 10.9).

FIGURE **10.9**   Collision resolution with buckets and overflow area.

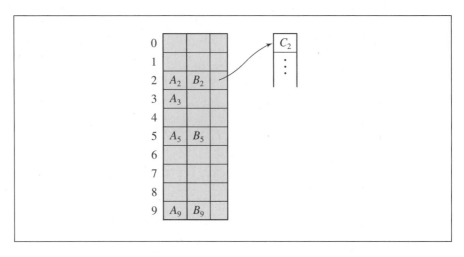

◪ 10.3 DELETION

How can we remove data from a hash table? With a chaining method, deleting an element leads to the deletion of a node from a linked list holding the element. For other methods, a deletion operation may require a more careful treatment of collision resolution, except for the rare occurrence when a perfect hash function is used.

Consider the table in Figure 10.10a in which the keys are stored using linear probing. The keys have been entered in the following order: A_1, A_4, A_2, B_4, B_1. After A_4 is deleted and position 4 is freed (Figure 10.10b), we try to find B_4 by first checking position 4. But this position is now empty, so we may conclude that B_4 is not in the table. The same result occurs after deleting A_2 and marking cell 2 as empty (Figure 10.10c). Then, the search for B_1 is unsuccessful, since if we are using linear probing, the search terminates at position 2. The situation is the same for the other open addressing methods.

If we leave deleted keys in the table with markers indicating that they are not valid elements of the table, any subsequent search for an element does not terminate prematurely. When a new key is inserted, it overwrites a key which is only a space filler. However, for a large number of deletions and a small number of additional insertions, the table becomes overloaded with deleted records, which increases the search time because the open addressing methods require testing the deleted elements. Therefore, the table should be purged after a certain number of deletions by moving undeleted elements to the cells occupied by deleted elements. Cells with deleted elements which are not overwritten by this procedure are marked as free. Figure 10.10d illustrates this situation.

FIGURE **10.10**   Linear search in the situation where both insertion and deletion of keys are permitted.

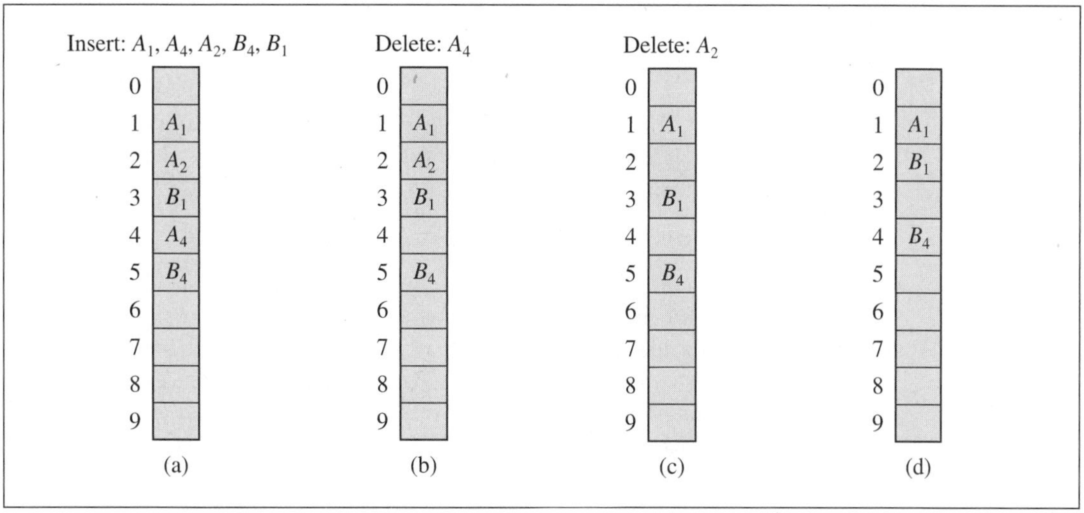

☐ 10.4 PERFECT HASH FUNCTIONS

All the cases discussed so far assume that the body of data is not precisely known. Therefore, the hash function only rarely turned out to be an ideal hash function in the sense that it immediately hashed a key to its proper position and avoided any collisions. In most cases, some collision resolution technique had to be included, since sooner or later, a key would arrive which conflicted with another key in the table. Also, the number of keys is rarely known in advance, so the table had to be large enough to accommodate all the arriving data. Moreover, the table size contributed to the number of collisions: A larger table has a smaller number of collisions (provided the hash function took table size into consideration). All this was caused by the fact that the body of data to be hashed in the table was not precisely known ahead of time. Therefore, a hash function was first devised and then the data were processed.

In many situations, however, the body of data is fixed, and a hash function can be devised after the data are known. Such a function may really be a perfect hash function if it hashes items on the first attempt. In addition, if such a function requires only as many cells in the table as the number of data so that no empty cell remains after hashing is completed, it is called a *minimal perfect hash function*. Wasting time for collision resolution and wasting space for unused table cells are avoided in a minimal perfect hash function.

Processing a fixed body of data is not an uncommon situation. Consider the following examples: a table of reserved words used by assemblers or compilers, files on unerasable optical disks, dictionaries, and lexical databases.

Algorithms for choosing a perfect hash function usually require tedious work due to the fact that perfect hash functions are rare. As already indicated for 50 elements and a 100-cell array, only one in 1 million is perfect. Other functions lead to collisions.

10.4.1 Cichelli's Method

One algorithm to construct a minimal perfect hash function was developed by Richard J. Cichelli. It is used to hash a relatively small number of reserved words. The function is of the form

$$h(word) = (length(word) + g(firstletter(word)) + g(lastletter(word))) \bmod TSize$$

where g is the function to be constructed. The function g assigns values to letters so that the resulting function h returns unique hash values for all words in a predefined set of words. The values assigned by g to particular letters do not have to be unique. The algorithm has three parts: computation of the letter occurrences, ordering the words, and searching. The last step is the heart of this algorithm and uses an auxiliary function `try()`. Cichelli's algorithm for constructing g and h is as follows:

choose a value for `max`;
compute the number of occurrences of each first and last letter in the set of all words;
order all words in accordance to the frequency of occurrence of the first and the last letters;

```
    search(wordList)
    if wordList is empty
         halt;
    word = first word from wordList;
    wordList = wordList with the first word detached;
    if the first and the last letters of word are assigned g-values
            try(word,-1,-1); // -1 signifies 'value already assigned'
            if success
                search (wordList);
            put word at the beginning of wordList and detach its hash value;
    else if neither the first nor the last letters has a g-value
        for each n,m in {0,...,Max}
            try(word,n,m);
            if success
                search (wordList);
                put word at the beginning of wordList and detach its hash value;
    else if either the first or the last letter has a g-value
        for each n in {0,...,Max}
            try(word,-1,n) or try(word,n,-1);
            if success
              search (wordList);
               put word at the beginning of wordList and detach its hash value;


try(word,firstLetterValue,lastLetterValue)
    if h(word) has not been claimed
         reserve h(word);
```

FIGURE **10.11**   Subsequent invocations of the searching procedure with *Max* = 4 in Cichelli's algorithm assign the indicated values to letters and to the list of reserved hash values. The asterisks indicate failures.

				reserved hash values
Euterpe	E = 0	h = 7		{7}
Calliope	C = 0	h = 8		{7 8}
Erato	O = 0	h = 5		{5 7 8}
Terpsichore	T = 0	h = 2		{2 5 7 8}
Melpomene	M = 0	h = 0		{0 2 5 7 8}
Thalia	A = 0	h = 6		{0 2 5 6 7 8}
Clio		h = 4		{0 2 4 5 6 7 8}
Polyhymnia	P = 0	h = 1		{0 1 2 4 5 6 7 8}
Urania	U = 0	h = 6 *		{0 1 2 4 5 6 7 8}
Urania	U = 1	h = 7 *		{0 1 2 4 5 6 7 8}
Urania	U = 2	h = 8 *		{0 1 2 4 5 6 7 8}
Urania	U = 3	h = 0 *		{0 1 2 4 5 6 7 8}
Urania	U = 4	h = 1 *		{0 1 2 4 5 6 7 8}
Polyhymnia	P = 1	h = 2 *		{0 2 4 5 6 7 8}
Polyhymnia	P = 2	h = 3		{0 2 3 4 5 6 7 8}
Urania	U = 0	h = 6 *		{0 2 3 4 5 6 7 8}
Urania	U = 1	h = 7 *		{0 2 3 4 5 6 7 8}
Urania	U = 2	h = 8 *		{0 2 3 4 5 6 7 8}
Urania	U = 3	h = 0 *		{0 2 3 4 5 6 7 8}
Urania	U = 4	h = 1		{0 1 2 3 4 5 6 7 8}

> *assign* `firstLetterValue` *and/or* `lastLetterValue` *as g-values of firstletter(*`word`*)*
> *and/or*
> *lastletter(*`word`*)*
> *if not* `-1` (*i.e., not assigned*)
> *return* *success*;
> *return* *failure*;

We can use this algorithm to build a hash function for the names of the nine Muses: Calliope, Clio, Erato, Euterpe, Melpomene, Polyhymnia, Terpsichore, Thalia, and Urania. A simple count of the letters renders the number of times a given letter occurs as a first and last letter (case sensitivity is disregarded): E (6), A (3), C (2), O (2), T (2), M (1), P (1), and U (1). According to these frequencies, the words can be put in the following order: Euterpe (E occurs six times as the first and the last letter), Calliope, Erato, Terpsichore, Melpomene, Thalia, Clio, Polyhymnia, and Urania.

Now the procedure `search()` is applied. Figure 10.11 contains a summary of its execution, in which `Max` = 4. First, the word Euterpe is tried. E is assigned the *g*-value of 0, whereby *h*(Euterpe) = 7, which is put on the list of reserved hash values. Everything goes well until Urania is tried. All five possible *g*-values for U result in an already reserved hash value. The procedure backtracks to the preceding step, when Polyhymnia was tried. Its current hash value is detached from the list, and the g-value of 1 is tried for P, which causes a failure, but 2 for P gives 3 for the hash value, so the algorithm can continue. Urania is tried again five times, then the fifth attempt is successful. All the names have been assigned unique hash values and the search process is finished. If the g-values for each letter are A = C = E = O = M = T = 0, P = 2, and U = 4, then h is the minimal perfect hash function for the nine Muses.

The searching process in Cichelli's algorithm is exponential since it uses an exhaustive search, and thus, it is inapplicable to a large number of words. Also, it does not guarantee that a perfect hash function can be found. For a small number of words, however, it usually gives good results. This program often needs to be run only once, and the resulting hash function can be incorporated into another program. Cichelli applied his method to the Pascal reserved words. The result was a hash function that reduced the run time of a Pascal cross-reference program by 10% after it replaced the binary search used previously.

There have been many successful attempts to extend Cichelli's technique and overcome its shortcomings. One technique modified the terms involved in the definition of the hash function. For example, other terms, the alphabetical positions of the second to last letter in the word, are added to the function definition (Sebesta and Taylor 1986), or the following definition is used (Haggard and Karplus 1986):

$$h(word) = length(word) + g_1(firstletter(word)) + \cdots + g_{length(word)}(lastletter(word))$$

Cichelli's method can also be modified by partitioning the body of data into separate buckets for which minimal perfect hash functions are found. The partitioning is performed by a grouping function, gr, which for each word indicates the bucket to which it belongs. Then a general hash function is generated whose form is

$$h(word) = bucket_{gr(word)} + h_{gr(word)}(word)$$

(e.g., Lewis and Cook 1986). The problem with this approach is that it is difficult to find a generally applicable grouping function tuned to finding minimal perfect hash functions.

Both these ways—modifying hash function and partitioning—are not entirely successful if the same Cichelli's algorithm is used. Although Cichelli ends his paper with the adage: "When all else fails, try brute force," the attempts to modify his approach included devising a more efficient searching algorithm to circumvent the need for brute force. One such approach is incorporated in the FHCD algorithm.

10.4.2 The FHCD Algorithm

An extension of Cichelli's approach is a method devised by Thomas Sager. The FHCD algorithm (Fox et al. 1992) is a modification of Sager's method, and it is discussed in this section. The FHCD algorithm searches for a minimal perfect hash function of the form

$$h(word) = h_0(word) + g(h_1(word)) + g(h_2(word))$$

(modulo $TSize$), where g is the function to be determined by the algorithm. To define the functions h_i, three tables—T_0, T_1, and T_2—of random numbers are defined, one for each function h_i. Each word is equal to a string of characters $c_1 c_2 \ldots c_m$ corresponding to a triple $(h_0(word), h_1(word), h_2(word))$ whose elements are calculated according to the formulas

$$h_0 = (T_0(c_1) + \cdots + T_0(c_m)) \bmod n$$
$$h_1 = (T_1(c_1) + \cdots + T_1(c_m)) \bmod r$$
$$h_2 = ((T_2(c_1) + \cdots + T_2(c_m)) \bmod r) + r$$

where n is the number of all words in the body of data, r is a parameter usually equal to $n/2$ or less, and $T_i(c_j)$ is the number generated in table T_i for c_j. The function g is found in three steps: *mapping, ordering,* and *searching.*

In the mapping step, n triples $(h_0(word), h_1(word), h_2(word))$ are created. The randomness of functions h_i usually guarantees the uniqueness of these triples; should they not be unique, new tables T_i are generated. Next, a *dependency graph* is built. It is a bipartite graph with half of its vertices corresponding to the h_1 values and labeled 0 through $r-1$ and the other half to the h_2 values and labeled r through $2r-1$. Each word corresponds to an edge of the graph between the vertices $h_1(word)$ and $h_2(word)$. The mapping step is expected to take $O(n)$ time.

As an example, we again use the set of names of the nine Muses. To generate three tables T_i, the random number generator from class Random can be used, and with these tables, a set of nine triples is computed, as shown in Figure 10.12a. Figure 10.12b contains a corresponding dependency graph with $r = 3$. Note that some vertices cannot be connected to any other vertices, and some pairs of vertices can be connected with more than one arc.

The ordering step rearranges all the vertices so that they can be partitioned into a series of levels. When a sequence $v_1, \ldots, v_t$ of vertices is established, then a level $K(v_i)$ of keys is defined as a set of all the edges which connect v_i with those v_js for which $j \le i$. The sequence is initiated with a vertex of maximum degree. Then, for each successive position i of the sequence, a vertex v_i is selected from among the vertices having at least one connection to the vertices $v_1, \ldots, v_{i-1}$ which has maximal degree. When no such vertex can be found, any vertex of maximal degree is chosen from among the un-selected vertices. Figure 10.12c contains an example.

In the last step, searching, hash values are assigned to keys level by level. The g-value for the first vertex is chosen randomly among the numbers $0, \ldots, n-1$. For the other vertices, because of their construction and ordering, we have the following relation: If $v_i < r$, then $v_i = h_1$. Thus, each word in $K(v_i)$ has the same value $g(h_1(word)) = g(v_i)$. Also, $g(h_2(word))$ has already been defined, since it is equal to some v_j which has already been processed. Analogical reasoning can be applied to the case when $v_i > r$ and then $v_i = h_2$. For each word, either $g(h_1(word))$ or $g(h_2(word))$ is known. The second g-value is found randomly for each level so that the values obtained from the formula of the minimal perfect hash function h indicate the positions in the hash table that are available. Because the first choice of a random number will not always fit all words on a given level to the hash table, both random numbers may need to be tried.

The searching step for the nine Muses starts with randomly choosing $g(v_1)$. Let $g(2) = 2$, where $v_1 = 2$. The next vertex is $v_2 = 5$ so that $K(v_2) = \{Erato\}$. According to Figure 10.12a, $h_0(Erato) = 3$, and because the edge *Erato* connects v_1 and v_2, either $h_1(Erato)$ or $h_2(Erato)$ must be equal to v_1. We can see that $h_1(Erato) = 2 = v_1$; hence,

FIGURE **10.12**   Applying the FHCD algorithm to the names of the nine Muses.

Value of:	h_0	h_1	h_2
Calliope	(0	1	5)
Clio	(7	1	4)
Erato	(3	2	5)
Euterpe	(6	2	3)
Melpomene	(3	1	5)
Polyhymnia	(8	2	4)
Terpsichore	(8	0	5)
Thalia	(8	2	3)
Urania	(0	2	4)

(a)

(b)

Level	Node	Arcs
0	2	
1	5	Erato
2	1	Calliope, Melpomene
3	4	Clio, Polyhymnia, Urania
4	3	Euterpe, Thalia
5	0	Terpsichore

(c)

Level	Vertex	g-value		
0	2	2		
1	5	6	$h(\text{Erato})$	$= (3 + 2 + 6) \ \% \ 9 = 2$
2	1	4	$h(\text{Calliope})$	$= (0 + 4 + 6) \ \% \ 9 = 1$
2	1	4	$h(\text{Melpomene})$	$= (3 + 4 + 6) \ \% \ 9 = 4$
3	4	2	$h(\text{Clio})$	$= (7 + 6 + 2) \ \% \ 9 = 6$
3	4	2	$h(\text{Polyhymnia})$	$= (8 + 6 + 2) \ \% \ 9 = 7$
3	4	2	$h(\text{Urania})$	$= (0 + 6 + 2) \ \% \ 9 = 8$
4	3	4	$h(\text{Euterpe})$	$= (6 + 2 + 4) \ \% \ 9 = 3$
4	3	4	$h(\text{Terpsichore})$	$= (8 + 2 + 4) \ \% \ 9 = 5$
4	3	4	$h(\text{Thalia})$	$= (8 + 4 + 6) \ \% \ 9 = 0$

(d)

Function g	
0	4
1	4
2	2
3	4
4	2
5	6

(e)

$g(h_1(\text{Erato})) = g(v_1) = 2$. A value for $g(v_2) = g(h_2(\text{Erato})) = 6$ is chosen randomly. From this, $h(\text{Erato}) = (h_0(\text{Erato}) + g(h_1(\text{Erato})) + g(h_2(\text{Erato}))) \bmod TSize = (3 + 2 + 6) \bmod 9 = 2$. This means that position 2 of the hash table is no longer available. The new g-value, $g(5) = 6$, is retained for later use.

Now, $v_3 = 1$ is tried, with $K(v_3) = \{\text{Calliope, Melpomene}\}$. The h_0-values for both words are retrieved from the table of triples, and the $g(h_2)$-values are equal to 6 for both words, since $h_2 = v_2$ for both of them. Now we must find a random $g(h_1)$-value such that the hash function h computed for both words renders two numbers different from 2, since position two is already occupied. Assume that this number is 4. As a result, h(Calliope) = 1 and h(Melpomene) = 4. Figure 10.12d contains a summary of all the steps. Figure 10.12e shows the values of the function g. Through these values of g, the function h becomes a minimal perfect hash function. However, since g is given in tabular form and not with a neat formula, it has to be stored as a table to be used every time function h is needed, which may not be a trivial task. The function $g : \{0, \ldots, 2r-1\} \rightarrow \{0, \ldots, n-1\}$, and the size of g's domain increases with r. The parameter r is approximately $n/2$, which for large databases means that the table storing all values for g is not of a negligible size. This table has to be kept in main memory to make computations of the hash function efficient.

♠ 10.5   Hash Functions for Extendible Files

All the methods discussed so far work on tables of fixed sizes. This is a reasonable assumption for arrays, but for files it may be too restrictive. After all, file sizes change dynamically by adding new elements or deleting old ones. Some hashing techniques can be used in this situation, such as coalesced hashing or hashing with chaining, but some of them may be inadequate. New techniques have been developed which specifically take into account the variable size of the table or file. We can distinguish two classes of such techniques: directory and directoryless.

In the directory schemes, key access is mediated by the access to a directory or an index of keys in the structure. There are several techniques and modifications to those techniques in the category of the directory schemes. We mention only a few: *expandable hashing* (Knott 1971), *dynamic hashing* (Larson 1978), and *extendible hashing* (Fagin et al. 1979). All three methods distribute keys among buckets in a similar fashion. The main difference is the structure of the index (directory). In expandable hashing and dynamic hashing, a binary tree is used as an index of buckets. On the other hand, in extendible hashing, a directory of records is kept in a table.

One directoryless technique is *virtual hashing,* defined as "any hashing which may dynamically change its hashing function" (Litwin 1978). This change of hashing function compensates for the lack of a directory. An example of this approach is linear hashing (Litwin 1980). In the following pages, one method from each category is discussed.

10.5.1   Extendible Hashing

Assume that a hashing technique is applied to a dynamically changing file composed of buckets, and each bucket can hold only a fixed number of items. Extendible hashing accesses the data stored in buckets indirectly through an index that is dynamically adjusted to reflect changes in the file. The characteristic feature of extendible hashing is the organization of the index, which is an expandable table.

A hash function applied to a certain key indicates a position in the index and not in the file (or table of keys). Values returned by such a hash function are called

FIGURE **10.13** An example of extendible hashing.

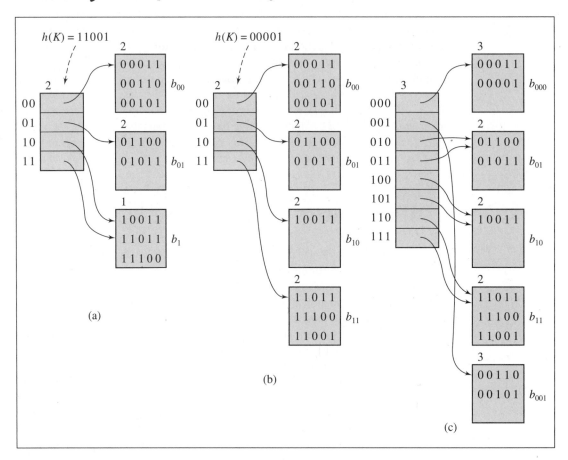

(a)

(b)

(c)

pseudokeys. In this way, the file requires no reorganization when data are added to it or deleted from it, since these changes are indicated in the index. Only one hash function *h* can be used, but depending on the size of the index, only a portion of the address $h(K)$ is utilized. A simple way to achieve this effect is by looking at the address $h(K)$ as a string of bits from which only the *i* leftmost bits can be used. The number *i* is called the *depth* of the directory. In Figure 10.13a, the depth is equal to two.

As an example, assume that the hash function *h* generates patterns of five bits. If this pattern is the string 01011 and the depth is two, then the two leftmost bits, 01, are considered to be the position in the directory containing the reference to a bucket in which the key can be found or into which it is to be inserted. In Figure 10.13, the values of *h* are shown in the buckets, but these values only represent the keys that are actually stored in these buckets.

Each bucket has a *local depth* associated with it that indicates the number of left-most bits in $h(K)$. The leftmost bits are the same for all keys in the bucket. In Figure 10.13, the local depths are shown on top of each bucket. For example, the bucket b_{00} holds all keys for which $h(K)$ starts with 00. More important, the local depth indicates whether the bucket can be accessed from only one location in the directory or from at least two. In the first case, when the local depth is equal to the depth of directory, it is necessary to change the size of the directory after the bucket is split in the case of overflow. When the local depth is smaller than the directory depth, splitting the bucket only requires changing half of the references pointing to this bucket so that they point to the newly created one. Figure 10.13b illustrates this case. After a key with h-value 11001 arrives, its two first bits (since depth = 2) direct it to the fourth position of the directory, from which it is sent to the bucket b_1, which contains keys whose h-value starts with 1. An overflow occurs, and b_1 is split into b_{10} (the new name for the old bucket) and b_{11}. The local depths of these two buckets are set to two. The reference from position 11 points now to b_{11}, and the keys from b_1 are redistributed between b_{10} and b_{11}.

The situation is more complex if overflow occurs in a bucket with a local depth equal to the depth of the directory. For example, consider the case when a key with h-value 00001 arrives at the table in Figure 10.13b and is hashed through position 00 (its first two bits) to bucket b_{00}. A split occurs, but the directory has no room for the reference to the new bucket. As a result, the directory is doubled in size so that its depth is now equal to three, b_{00} becomes b_{000} with an increased local depth, and the new bucket is b_{001}. All the keys from b_{00} are divided between the new buckets: Those whose h-value starts with 000 become elements of b_{000}; the remaining keys, those with prefix 001, are put in b_{001}, as in Figure 10.13c. Also, all the slots of the new directory have to be set to their proper values by having *newdirectory*$[2 \cdot i]$ = *olddirectory*$[i]$ and *newdirectory*$[2 \cdot i + 1]$ = *olddirectory*$[i]$ for i's ranging over positions of the *olddirectory*, except for the position referring to the bucket which just has been split.

The following algorithm inserts a record into a file using extendible hashing.

```
extendibleHashingInsert(K)
    bitPattern = h(K);
    p = directory[depth(directory) leftmost bits of bitPattern];
    if space is available in bucket b_d pointed to by p
        place K in the bucket;
    else split bucket b_d into b_d0 and b_d1;
        set local depth of b_d0 and b_d1 to depth(b_d) + 1;
        distribute records from b_d between b_d0 and b_d1;
        if depth(b_d) < depth(directory)
            update the half of the references which pointed to b_d to point to b_d1;
        else double the directory and increment its depth;
            set directory entries to proper references;
```

An important advantage of using extendible hashing is that it avoids a reorganization of the file if the directory overflows. Only the directory is affected. Because the directory in most cases is kept in main memory, the cost of expanding and updating it

FIGURE **10.14**   Splitting buckets in the linear hashing technique.

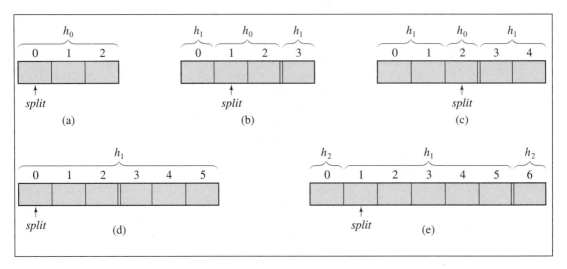

(a)   (b)   (c)

(d)   (e)

is very small. However, for large files of small buckets, the size of the directory can become so large that it may be put in virtual memory or explicitly in a file, which may slow down the process of using the directory. Also, the size of the directory does not grow uniformly, since it is doubled if a bucket with a local depth equal to the depth of the directory is split. This means that for large directories there will be many redundant entries in the directory. To rectify the problem of an overgrown directory, David Lomet proposed using extendible hashing until the directory becomes too large to fit into main memory. Afterward, the buckets are doubled instead of the directory, and the bits in the bit pattern $h(K)$ that come after the first *depth* bits are used to distinguish between different parts of the bucket. For example, if *depth* = 3 and a bucket b_{10} has been quadrupled, its parts are distinguished with bit strings 00, 01, 10, and 11. Now, if $h(K) = 10101101$, the key K is searched for in the second portion, 01, of b_{101}.

10.5.2 Linear Hashing

Extendible hashing allows the file to expand without reorganizing it, but it requires storage space for an index. In the method developed by Witold Litwin, no index is necessary because new buckets generated by splitting existing buckets are always added in the same linear way, so there is no need to retain indexes. To this end, a reference *split* indicates which bucket is to be split next. After the bucket pointed to by *split* is divided, the keys in this bucket are distributed between this bucket and the newly created bucket which is added to the end of the table. Figure 10.14 contains a sequence of initial splits in which *TSize* = 3. Initially, the reference *split* is zero. If the loading factor exceeds a certain level, a new bucket is created, keys from bucket zero are distributed between bucket zero and bucket three, and *split* is incremented. How is this distribution performed? If only one hash function is used, then it hashes keys from bucket zero to bucket zero before and after splitting. This means that one function is not sufficient.

At each level of splitting, linear hashing maintains two hash functions, h_{level} and $h_{level+1}$, such that $h_{level}(K) = K$ mod ($TSize \cdot 2^{level}$). The first hash function, h_{level}, hashes keys to buckets which have not yet been split on the current level. The second function, $h_{level+1}$ is used for hashing keys to already split buckets. The algorithm for linear hashing is as follows:

initialize: `split = 0; level = 0;`

```
linearHashingInsert(K)
    if h_level(K) < split        // bucket h_level(K) has been split
        hashAddress = h_level+1(K);
    else hashAddress = h_level(K);
```
insert `K` *in a corresponding bucket or an overflow area if possible;*
while the loading factor is high or `K` *not inserted*
    create a new bucket with index `split + TSize *` 2^{level};
    redistribute keys from bucket `split` *between buckets* `split` *and* `split + TSize *` 2^{level};
```
    split++;
    if split == TSize * 2^level  // all buckets on the current
                                 // level have been split;
        level++;                 // proceed to the next level
        split = 0;
```
try to insert `K` *if not inserted yet;*

It may still be unclear when to split a bucket. Most likely, as the algorithm assumes, a threshold value of the loading factor is used to decide whether or not to split a bucket. This threshold has to be known in advance, and its magnitude is chosen by the program designer. To illustrate, assume that keys can be hashed to buckets in a file. If a bucket is full, the overflowing keys can be put on a linked list in an overflow area. Consider the situation in Figure 10.15a. In this figure, $TSize = 3$, $h_0(K) = K$ mod $TSize$, $h_1(K) = K$ mod $2 \cdot TSize$. Let the size of the overflow area $OSize = 3$, and let the highest acceptable loading factor which equals the number of elements divided by the number of slots in the file and in the overflow area be 80%. The current loading factor in Figure 10.15a is 75%. If the key 10 arrives, it is hashed to location 1, but the loading factor increases to 83%. The first bucket is split and the keys are redistributed using function h_1, as in Figure 10.15b. Note that the first bucket had the lowest load of all three buckets, and yet it was the bucket that was split.

Assume that 21 and 36 have been hashed to the table (Figure 10.15c), and now 25 arrives. This causes the loading factor to increase to 87%, resulting in another split, this time the split of the second bucket, which results in the configuration shown in Figure 10.15d. After hashing 27 and 37, another split occurs, and Figure 10.15e illustrates the new situation. Because *split* reached the last value allowed on this level, it is assigned the value of zero, and the hash function to be used in subsequent hashing is h_1, the same as before, and a new function, h_2, is defined as K mod $4 \cdot TSize$. All of these steps are summarized in the following table:

FIGURE **10.15**   Inserting keys to buckets and overflow areas with the linear hashing technique.

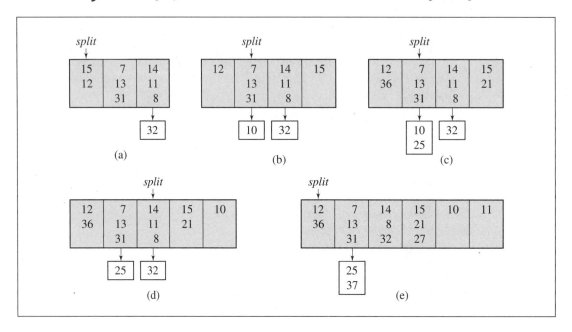

K	$h(K)$	Number of Items	Number of Cells	Loading Factor	Split	Hash Functions	
		9	9 + 3	9/12 = 75%	0	$K \bmod 3$	$K \bmod 6$
10	1	10	9 + 3	10/12 = 83%	0	$K \bmod 3$	$K \bmod 6$
		10	9 + 3	10/15 = 67%	1	$K \bmod 3$	$K \bmod 6$
21	3	11	12 + 3	11/15 = 73%	1	$K \bmod 3$	$K \bmod 6$
36	0	12	12 + 3	12/15 = 80%	1	$K \bmod 3$	$K \bmod 6$
25	1	13	12 + 3	13/15 = 87%	1	$K \bmod 3$	$K \bmod 6$
		13	12 + 3	13/18 = 72%	2	$K \bmod 3$	$K \bmod 6$
27	3	14	15 + 3	14/18 = 78%	2	$K \bmod 3$	$K \bmod 6$
37	1	15	15 + 3	15/18 = 83%	2	$K \bmod 3$	$K \bmod 6$
		15	18 + 3	15/21 = 71%	0	$K \bmod 6$	$K \bmod 12$

Note that linear hashing requires the use of some overflow area because the order of splitting is predetermined. In the case of files, this may mean more than one file access. This area can be explicit and different from buckets, but it can be introduced somewhat in the spirit of coalesced hashing by utilizing empty space in the buckets

(Mullin 1981). In a directory scheme, on the other hand, an overflow area is not necessary, although it can be used.

As in a directory scheme, linear hashing increases the address space by splitting a bucket. It also redistributes the keys of the split bucket between the buckets that result from the split. Because no indexes are maintained in linear hashing, this method is faster and requires less space than previous methods. The increase in efficiency is particularly noticeable for large files.

▲ 10.6 HASHING IN `java.util`

Java provides the class `Hashtable` with methods to operate on hash tables. Class hierarchy in `java.util` is as follows

Object ⇒ Dictionary ⇒ Hashtable

`Hashtable` is an implementation of interface `Map`. A map is a collection that holds pairs (key, value) or entries. Operation of `Hashtable` methods for integer sets is illustrated in Figure 10.16.

`Hashtable` objects are expandable hash tables that automatically adjust the capacity of the table if the load factor is surpassed. The default load factor equals .75 and the default table capacity equals 101, which is a prime number. The user can choose another load factor and capacity when creating a `Hashtable` object with one of the four constructors. The program in Figure 10.17 demonstrates the operation of some of the `Hashtable` methods. A new entry is inserted in a bucket of the hash table indicated by the `hashCode()` method of the key object that is the first parameter of the method `put()`. The value generated by `hashCode()` is then used internally by the hash table object to produce an actual hash value.

An attempt to add an entry with the same key as an existing entry results in replacing the value of the existing entry with the value of the entry being added. At any time, methods `keySet()` and `entrySet()` can be applied to generate a set of keys and a set of entries in the table. The set generated with `entrySet()` includes objects of type `Map.Entry` and thus the methods from the `Map.Entry` interface can be applied to this set (cf. Figure 7.31a). All keys of the hash table can also be included in one *enumeration* object with the method `keys()` and all entries in one *enumeration* object with `values()`.

The object `hashTable1` in Figure 10.17 is declared to have an initial capacity of 4 so that after adding the fourth object to the table, the default load factor of 75% is exceeded and thus the method `rehash()` is automatically invoked. Note that after adding new elements when the load factor is not exceeded, the new element is put in one of the existing buckets of the table. Printing the table shows that some of the old elements are slid to the right to make room for the new element. But after adding the fourth object, which is `Person("Frank",30)`, the elements of the table are reordered by applying an adjusted hash function to all the elements and hashing them to the new table of double size.

FIGURE **10.16**

Method	Operation
void clear()	remove all the objects from the hash table
Object clone()	return the copy of the hash table without cloning its elements
boolean contains(val)	return true if the hash table contains the object val; raise NullPointerException if val is null
boolean containsKey(key)	return true if the hash table contains the object key; raise NullPointerException if key is null
boolean containsValue(val)	return true if the hash table contains the object val; raise NullPointerException if val is null
Enumeration elements()	return an enumeration of the values in the hash table
Set entrySet()	return a set containing all the pairs (key, value) in the hash table
boolean equals(ht)	return true if the current hash table and object ht contain equal objects in the same order
Object get(key)	return the object associated with key
int hashCode()	return the hash code for the hash table
Hashtable()	create an empty hash table with initial capacity equal to 101 and the load factor equal to .75
Hashtable(ic)	create an empty hash table with initial capacity ic and the load factor equal to .75
Hashtable(ic, lf)	create an empty hash table with initial capacity ic and the load factor lf
Hashtable(map)	create a hash table with copies of elements from map
boolean isEmpty()	return true if the hash table contains no elements, false otherwise
Enumeration keys()	return an enumeration containing all the keys of the hash table
Set keySet()	return a set containing all the keys of the hash table
Object put(key, value)	put the pair (key, value) in the hash table; return a value associated with key if there is any in the hash table, null otherwise
void putAll(map)	add objects from map to the current hash table
rehash()	a protected method to increase the capacity of the hash table
Object remove(key)	remove the pair (key, value) from the hash table and return the value associated currently with key in the hash table, null otherwise
int size()	return the number of objects in the hash table
String toString()	return a string representation of the hash table that contains the string representation of all the objects
Collection values()	return a Collection object with all the values contained in the hash table

FIGURE **10.17**

```
import java.io.*;
import java.util.*;

class Person {
    String name;
    int age;
    Person(String s, int i) {
        name = s; age = i;
    }
    Person() {
        this("",0);
    }
    public String toString() {
        return "(" + name + "," + age  + ")";
    }
    public boolean equals(Object p) {
        return name.equals(((Person)p).name);
    }
}

class SSN {
    int value;
    SSN(int i) {
        value = i;
    }
    public boolean equals(Object ob) {
        return value == ((SSN)ob).value;
    }
    public int hashCode() {
        return (value & 0x0000ffff) + (value >>> 16);
    }
    public String toString() {
        return "" + value;
    }
}

class testHashtable {
    static void print(Iterator it) {
        if (it.hasNext()) {
            System.out.print(it.next());
            while (it.hasNext())
```

Continues

FIGURE **10.17** (*continued*)

```
                System.out.print(", " + it.next());
        }
        System.out.println();
    }
    static void print(Enumeration e) {
        if (e.hasMoreElements()) {
            System.out.print(e.nextElement());
            while (e.hasMoreElements())
                System.out.print(", " + e.nextElement());
        }
        System.out.println();
    }
    public static void main(String[] ar) {
        Hashtable hashTable1 = new Hashtable(4);
        hashTable1.put(new Integer(123456789),new Person("Larry",25));
        hashTable1.put(new Integer(111111111),new Person("Kathy",30));
        System.out.println(hashTable1);
        // {111111111=(Kathy,30), 123456789=(Larry,25)}
        hashTable1.put(new Integer(222222222),new Person("Kathy",20));
        System.out.println(hashTable1);
        // {111111111=(Kathy,30), 222222222=(Kathy,20), 123456789=(Larry,25)}
        print(hashTable1.entrySet().iterator());
        // 111111111=(Kathy,30), 222222222=(Kathy,20), 123456789=(Larry,25)
        print(hashTable1.keySet().iterator());
        // 111111111, 222222222, 123456789
        print(hashTable1.elements());
        // (Kathy,30), (Kathy,20), (Larry,25)
        print(hashTable1.keys());
        // 111111111, 222222222, 123456789
        print(hashTable1.values().iterator());
        // (Kathy,30), (Kathy,20), (Larry,25)
        Iterator it = hashTable1.values().iterator();
        ((Person)it.next()).age = 28;
        System.out.println(hashTable1);
        // {111111111=(Kathy,28), 222222222=(Kathy,20), 123456789=(Larry,25)}
        hashTable1.put(new Integer(111111111),new Person("Jerry",20));
        System.out.println(hashTable1);
        // {111111111=(Jerry,20), 222222222=(Kathy,20), 123456789=(Larry,25)}
        hashTable1.put(new Integer(111111113),new Person("Frank",30));
        System.out.println(hashTable1);
        // {111111113=(Frank,30), 123456789=(Larry,25), 222222222=(Kathy,20),
111111111=(Jerry,20)}
```

FIGURE **10.17** (*continued*)

```
        System.out.println(hashTable1.get(new Integer(111111111)));    // (Jerry,20)
        System.out.println(hashTable1.contains(new Person("Jerry",20)));      // true
        System.out.println(hashTable1.containsValue(new Person("Jerry",20))); // true
        System.out.println(hashTable1.remove(new Integer(111111111))); // (Jerry,20)
        System.out.println(hashTable1);
        // {111111113=(Frank,30), 123456789=(Larry,25), 222222222=(Kathy,20)}

        Hashtable hashTable2 = new Hashtable();
        hashTable2.put(new SSN(123456789),new Person("Larry",28));
        hashTable2.put(new SSN(111111111),new Person("Kathy",30));
        System.out.println(hashTable2);
        // {111111111=(Kathy,30), 123456789=(Larry,28)}
        hashTable2.put(new SSN(222222222),new Person("Kathy",20));
        System.out.println(hashTable2);
        // {111111111=(Kathy,30), 222222222=(Kathy,20), 123456789=(Larry,28)}
        hashTable2.put(new SSN(111111111),new Person("Jerry",25));
        System.out.println(hashTable2);
        // {111111111=(Jerry,25), 222222222=(Kathy,20), 123456789=(Larry,28)}
        hashTable2.put(new SSN(111111113),new Person("Frank",30));
        System.out.println(hashTable2);
        // {111111113=(Frank,30), 111111111=(Jerry,25), 222222222=(Kathy,20),
        // 123456789=(Larry,28)}
    }
}
```

The `hashCode()` method applied for `hashTable1` is a built-in method of the `Integer()` class which simply returns the integer for which an `Integer` object is created. The user can redefine this method, and, in fact, must redefine this method in user-defined types. If the method is not redefined, then `hashCode()` inherited from the class `Object` is applied, which returns the address of a particular object. As an example, consider the class `SSN` which, if it were possible, should be an extension of `Integer()`, but the latter is a final class, so its extension cannot be produced. `SSN()`'s `hashCode()` generates a hash code that is the sum of the first two bytes constituting an integer and the last two bytes. For example, the hash code for integer 0x12345678 equals 0x1234 + 0x5678.

⬛ 10.7 CASE STUDY: HASHING WITH BUCKETS

The most serious problem to be solved in programs which rely on a hash function to insert and retrieve items from an undetermined body of data is resolving collision. Depending on the technique, allowing deletion of items from the table can significantly increase the complexity of the program. In this case study, a program is developed that allows the user to insert and delete elements from the file `names` interactively. This file contains names and phone numbers and is initially ordered alphabetically. At the end of the session, the file is ordered with all updates included. To that end, the `outfile` is used throughout the execution of the program. `outfile` is the file of buckets initialized as empty. Elements that cannot be hashed to the corresponding bucket in this file are stored in the file `overflow`. At the end of the session both files are combined and sorted to replace the contents of the original file `names`.

The `outfile` is used here as the hash table. First, this file is prepared by filling it with `tableSize * bucketSize` empty records (one record is simply a certain number of bytes). Next, all entries of `names` are transferred to `outfile` to buckets indicated by the hash function. This transfer is performed by the method `insertion()`, which includes the hashed item in the bucket indicated by the value computed by the method `hash()` or in `overflow` if the bucket is full. In the latter case, `overflow` is searched from the beginning, and if a position occupied by a deleted record is found, the overflow item replaces it. If the end of `overflow` is reached, the item is put at the end of this file.

After initializing `outfile`, a menu is displayed and the user chooses to insert a new record, delete an old one, or exit. For insertion, the same method is used as before. No duplicates are allowed. When the user wants to delete an item, the hash function is used to access the corresponding bucket, and the linear search of positions in the bucket is performed until the item is found, in which case the deletion marker "#" is written over the first character of the item in the bucket. However, if the item is not found and the end of the bucket is reached, the search continues sequentially in `overflow` until either the item is found and marked as deleted or the end of the file is encountered.

If the user chooses to exit, the undeleted entries of `overflow` are transferred to `outfile`, and all undeleted entries of `outfile` are sorted using an external sort. To that end, quicksort is applied both to `outfile` and to an array `positions[]` which contains the addresses of entries in `outfile`. For comparison, the entries in `outfile` can be accessed, but the elements in `positions[]` are moved, not the elements of `outfile`.

After this indirect sorting is accomplished, the data in `outfile` have to be put in alphabetical order. This is accomplished by transferring entries from `outfile` to `unsorted` using the order indicated in `positions[]`, that is, by going down the array and retrieving the entry in `outfile` through the address stored in the currently accessed cell. After transferring `putfile` to `unsorted`, `names` is deleted and `unsorted` is renamed `names`.

Here is an example. If the contents of the original file are

```
Adam 123-4567          Brenda 345-5352       Brendon 983-7373
Charles 987-1122       Jeremiah 789-4563     Katherine 823-1573
Patrick 757-4532       Raymond 090-9383      Thorsten 929-6632
```

the hashing generates the outfile:

```
Katherine 823-1573    |******************||
Adam 123-4567         |Brenda 345-5352    ||
Raymond 090-9383      |Thorsten 929-6632  ||
```

and the file overflow:

```
Brendon 983-7373      |Charles 987-1122   ||
Jeremiah 789-4563     |Patrick 757-4532   ||
```

(The vertical bars are *not* included in the file; one bar divides the records in the same bucket, and two bars separate different buckets.)

After inserting Carol 654-6543 and deleting Brenda 345-5352 and Jeremiah 789-4563, the file's contents are:

```
outfile:
Katherine 823-1573    |Carol 654-6543     ||
Adam 123-4567         |#renda 345-5352    ||
Raymond 090-9383      |Thorsten 929-6632  ||
```

and overflow:

```
Brendon 983-7373      |Charles 987-1122   ||
#eremiah 789-4563     |Patrick 757-4532   ||
```

A subsequent insertion of Maggie 733-0983 and deletion of Brendon 983-7373 changes only overflow:

```
#rendon 983-7373      |Charles 987-1122   ||
Maggie 733-0983       |Patrick 757-4532   ||
```

After the user chooses to exit, undeleted records from overflow are transferred to outfile, which now includes:

```
Katherine 823-1573    |Carol 654-6543     ||
Adam 123-4567         |#renda 345-5352    ||
Raymond 090-9383      |Thorsten 929-6632  ||
Charles 987-1122      |Maggie 733-0983    ||
Patrick 757-4532      |
```

This file is sorted and the outcome is:

```
Adam 123-4567         |Carol 654-6543     ||
Charles 987-1122      |Katherine 823-1573 ||
Maggie 733-0983       |Patrick 757-4532   ||
Raymond 090-9383      |Thorsten 929-6632  ||
```

Figure 10.18 contains the code for this program.

FIGURE **10.18**   Implementation of hashing using buckets.

```java
import java.io.*;
import java.io.File;

class FileHashing {
    final int bucketSize = 2, tableSize = 3, strLen = 20;
    final int recordLen = strLen;
    final byte empty = '*', delMarker = '#';
    long[] positions;
    InputStreamReader isr = new InputStreamReader(System.in);
    BufferedReader buffer = new BufferedReader(isr);
    RandomAccessFile outfile;
    RandomAccessFile sorted;
    RandomAccessFile overflow;
    FileHashing() {
    }

    void print(byte[] s) { // print a byte array;
        for(int k = 0; k < s.length; k++)
            System.out.print((char)s[k]);
    }

    long hash(byte[] s) {
        long xor = 0, pack;
        int i, j, slength; // exclude trailing blanks:
        for (slength = s.length; s[slength-1] == ' '; slength--);
        for (i = 0; i < slength; ) {
            for (pack = j = 0; ; j++, i++) {
                pack |= (long) s[i];  // include s[i] in the rightmost
                if (j == 3 || i == slength - 1) { // byte of pack;
                    i++;
                    break;
                }
                pack <<= 8;
            }                   // xor at one time 8 bytes from s;
            xor ^= pack;  // last iteration may put less
        }                   // than 8 bytes in pack;
        return (xor % tableSize) * bucketSize * recordLen;
    }// return byte position of home bucket for s;

    byte[] getName() throws IOException {
        System.out.print("Enter a name & phone#: ");
        String s = buffer.readLine();
```

FIGURE **10.18** *(continued)*

```
        for (int i = s.length(); i < recordLen; i++)
            s += ' ';
        return s.getBytes(); // s => line
    }

    int comparesTo(byte[] s1, byte[] s2) {  // same length
        for (int i = 0; i < s1.length; i++) // of s1 and s2
            if (s1[i] != s2[i])             ]  // assumed;
                return s1[i] - s2[i];
        return 0;
    }

    void insert() throws IOException {
        insertion(getName());
    }

    void insertion(byte[] line) throws IOException {
        byte[] name = new byte[recordLen];
        boolean done = false, inserted = false;
        int counter = 0;
        long address = hash(line);
        outfile.seek(address);
        while (!done && outfile.read(name) != -1) {
            if (name[0] == empty || name[0] == delMarker) {
                outfile.seek(address+counter*recordLen);
                outfile.write(line);
                done = inserted = true;
            }
            else if (comparesTo(name,line) == 0) {
                print(line);
                System.out.println(" is already in the file");
                return;
            }
            else counter++;
            if (counter == bucketSize)
                done = true;
            else outfile.seek(address+counter*recordLen);
        }
        if (!inserted) {
            done = false;
            counter = 0;
```

Continues

FIGURE **10.18**   *(continued)*

```
            overflow.seek(0);
            while (!done && overflow.read(name) != -1) {
                if (name[0] == delMarker)
                    done = true;
                else if (comparesTo(name,line) == 0) {
                    print(line);
                    System.out.println(" is already in the file");
                    return;
                }
                else counter++;
            }
            if (done)
                overflow.seek(counter*recordLen);
            else overflow.seek(overflow.length());
            overflow.write(line);
        }
    }


    void delete() throws IOException {
        byte[] line = getName();
        long address = hash(line);
        outfile.seek(address);
        int counter = 0;
        boolean done = false, deleted = false;
        byte[] name = new byte[recordLen];
        while (!done && outfile.read(name) != -1) {
            if (comparesTo(line,name) == 0) {
                outfile.seek(address+counter*recordLen);
                outfile.write(delMarker);
                done = deleted = true;
            }
            else counter++;
            if (counter == bucketSize)
                done = true;
            else outfile.seek(address+counter*recordLen);
        }
        if (!deleted) {
            done = false;
            counter = 0;
            overflow.seek(0);
            while (!done && overflow.read(name) != -1) {
                if (comparesTo(line,name) == 0) {
```

F IGURE **10.18**   *(continued)*

```
                    overflow.seek(counter*recordLen);
                    overflow.write(delMarker);
                    done = deleted = true;
                }
                else counter++;
                overflow.seek(counter*recordLen);
            }
        }
        if (!deleted) {
            print(line);
            System.out.println(" is not in database");
        }
    }

    void swap(long[] arr, int i, int j) {
        long tmp = arr[i]; arr[i] = arr[j]; arr[j] = tmp;
    }

    int partition(int low, int high) throws IOException {
        byte[] rec = new byte[recordLen];
        byte[] pivot = new byte[recordLen];
        int i, lastSmall;
        swap(positions,low,(low+high)/2);
        outfile.seek(positions[low]*recordLen);
        outfile.read(pivot);
        for (lastSmall = low, i = low+1; i <= high; i++) {
            outfile.seek(positions[i]*recordLen);
            outfile.read(rec);
            if (comparesTo(rec,pivot) < 0) {
                lastSmall++;
                swap(positions,lastSmall,i);
            }
        }
        swap(positions,low,lastSmall);
        return lastSmall;
    }

    void sort(int low, int high) throws IOException {
        if (low < high) {
            int pivotLoc = partition(low, high);
            sort(low, pivotLoc-1);
```

Continues

FIGURE **10.18** *(continued)*

```
                sort(pivotLoc+1, high);
        }
    }

    void sortFile() throws IOException {
        byte[] rec = new byte[recordLen];
        sort(1,(int)positions[0]); // positions[0] contains the # of elements;
        for (int i = 1; i <= positions[0]; i++) { // put data from
            outfile.seek(positions[i]*recordLen);  // outfile in sorted order
            outfile.read(rec);
            sorted.write(rec);                      // in file sorted;
        }
    }


    // data from overflow file and outfile are all stored in outfile and
    // prepared for external sort by loading positions of the data to an array;

    void combineFiles() throws IOException {
        byte[] rec = new byte[recordLen];
        int counter = bucketSize*tableSize;
        outfile.seek(outfile.length());
        overflow.seek(0);
        while (overflow.read(rec) != -1) { // transfer from
            if (rec[0] != delMarker) {     // overflow to outfile only
                counter++;                 // valid (undeleted) items;
                outfile.write(rec);
            }
        }
        positions = new long[counter+1];
        outfile.seek(0);           // load to the array positions
        int arrCnt = 1;            // of valid data stored in output file;
        for (int i = 0; i < counter; i++) {
            outfile.seek(i*recordLen);
            outfile.read(rec);
            if (rec[0] != empty && rec[0] != delMarker)
                positions[arrCnt++] = i;
        }
        positions[0] = --arrCnt; // store the number of data in position 0;
    }


    void ProcessFile(String fileName) {
        char command = '1';
```

FIGURE **10.18** *(continued)*

```java
        byte[] line = new byte[recordLen];
        String commandLine;
        try {
            (new File(".\\","outfile")).delete();
            (new File(".\\","overflow")).delete();
            (new File(".\\","sorted")).delete();
            RandomAccessFile fIn = new RandomAccessFile(fileName,"rw");
            outfile = new RandomAccessFile("outfile","rw");
            sorted = new RandomAccessFile("sorted","rw");
            overflow = new RandomAccessFile("overflow","rw");
            for (int i = 1; i <= tableSize*bucketSize*recordLen; i++)
                outfile.write(empty);        // initialize outfile;
            while (fIn.read(line) != -1)    // load fIn to outfile;
                insertion(line);
            while (command != '3') {
                System.out.print("Enter your choice "
                            + "(1. insert, 2. delete, 3. exit): ");
                commandLine = buffer.readLine();
                command = commandLine.charAt(0);
                if (command == '1')
                    insert();
                else if (command == '2')
                    delete();
                else if (command != '3')
                    System.out.println("Wrong command entered, please retry.");
            }
            combineFiles();
            sortFile();
            outfile.close();
            sorted.close();
            overflow.close();
            fIn.close();
            (new File(".\\","names")).delete();
            (new File(".\\","sorted")).renameTo(new File(".\\","names"));
        } catch (IOException ioe) {
        }
    }

    static public void main(String args[]) {
        String fileName = "";
        InputStreamReader isr = new InputStreamReader(System.in);
```

Continues

FIGURE **10.18** *(continued)*

```
        BufferedReader buffer = new BufferedReader(isr);
        FileHashing fClass = new FileHashing();
        try {
            if (args.length == 0) {
                System.out.print("Enter a file name: ");
                fileName = buffer.readLine();
            }
            else fileName = args[0];
        } catch(IOException io) {
            System.err.println("Cannot open " + fileName);
        }
        fClass.ProcessFile(fileName);
    }
}
```

◻ 10.8 EXERCISES

1. What is the minimum number of keys which are hashed to their home positions using the linear probing technique? Show an example using a 5-cell array.

2. Consider the following hashing algorithm (Bell and Kaman 1970). Let Q and R be the quotient and remainder obtained by dividing K by $TSize$ and let the probing sequence be created by the following recurrence formula:

$$h_i(K) = \begin{cases} R & \text{if } i = 0 \\ (h_{i-1}(K) + Q) \bmod TSize & \text{otherwise} \end{cases}$$

What is the desirable value of $TSize$? What condition should be imposed on Q?

3. Is there any advantage to using binary search trees instead of linked lists in the separate chaining method?

4. In Cichelli's method for constructing the minimal hash function, why are all words first ordered according to the occurrence of the first and the last letters? The subsequent searching algorithm does not make any reference to this order.

5. Trace the execution of the searching algorithm used in Cichelli's technique with $Max = 3$. (See the illustration of such a trace for $Max = 4$ in Figure 10.11.)

6. In which case does Cichelli's method not guarantee to generate a minimal perfect hash function?

7. Apply the FHCD algorithm to the nine Muses with $r = n/2 = 4$ and then with $r = 2$. What is the impact of the value of r on the execution of this algorithm?

8. Strictly speaking, the hash function used in extendible hashing also dynamically changes. In what sense is this true?

9. Consider an implementation of extendible hashing that allows buckets to be pointed to by only one reference. The directory contains null references so that all references in the directory are unique except the null references. What keys are stored in the buckets? What are the advantages and disadvantages of this implementation?

10. How would the directory used in extendible hashing be updated after splitting if the last *depth* bits of $h(K)$ are considered an index to the directory, not the first *depth* bits?

11. List the similarities and differences between extendible hashing and B$^+$-trees.

12. What is the impact of the uniform distribution of keys over the buckets in extendible hashing on the frequency of splitting?

13. Apply the linear hashing method to hash numbers 12, 24, 36, 48, 60, 72, and 84 to an initially empty table with three buckets and with three cells in the overflow area. What problem can you observe? Can this problem bring the algorithm to a halt?

14. Outline an algorithm to delete a key from a table when the linear hashing method is used for inserting keys.

15. The method `hash()` applied in the case study uses the exclusive or (xor) operation to fold all the characters in a string. Would it be a good idea to replace it by bitwise-and or bitwise-or?

□ 10.9 Programming Assignments

1. As discussed in this chapter, the linear probing technique used for collision resolution has a rapidly deteriorating performance if a relatively small percentage of the cells are available. This problem can be solved using another technique for resolving collisions, and also by finding a better hash function, ideally, a perfect hash function. Write a program that evaluates the efficiency of various hashing functions combined with the linear probing method. Have your program write a table similar to the one in Figure 10.4, which gives the averages for successful and unsuccessful trials of locating items in the table. Use string methods and a large text file whose words will be hashed to the table. Here are some examples of hash functions (all values are divided modulo *TSize*):

    a. FirstLetter(s) + SecondLetter(s) + $\cdots$ + LastLetter(s)

    b. FirstLetter(s) + LastLetter(s) + length(s) (Cichelli)

    c. ```
for (i = 0, index = 0; i < s.length; i++)
        index = (26 * index + s.charAT(i) - ' '); (Ramakrishna)
```
```

2. Another way of improving the performance of hashing is to allow reorganization of the hash table during insertions. Write a program that compares the performance of linear probing with the following self-organization hashing methods:

   a. *Last-come-first-served hashing* places a new element in its home position, and in case of a collision, the element that occupies this position is inserted in another position using a regular linear probing method to make room for the arriving element (Poblete and Munro 1989).

   b. *Robin Hood hashing* checks the number of positions two colliding keys are away from their home positions and continues searching for an open position for the key closer to its home position (Celis et al. 1985).

3. Write a program that inserts records into a file and retrieves and deletes them using either extendible hashing or the linear hashing technique.

4. Extend the program presented in the case study by creating a linked list of overflowing records associated with each bucket of the intermediate file `outfile`. Note that if a bucket has no empty cells, the search continues in the overflow area. In the extreme case, it may mean that the bucket holds only deleted items and new items are inserted in the overflow area. Therefore, it may be advantageous to have a purging method that, after a certain number of deletions, is automatically invoked. This method transfers items from the overflow area to the main file which are hashed to buckets with deleted items. Write such a method.

Bibliography

Bell, James R. and Kaman, Charles H., "The Linear Quotient Hash Code," *Communications of the ACM* 13 (1970), 675–677.

Celis, P., Larson P., and Munro J. I., "Robin Hood Hashing," *Proceedings of the 26th IEEE Symposium on the Foundations of Computer Science,* Portland, OR, 1985, 281–288.

Cichelli, Richard J., "Minimal Perfect Hash Function Made Simple," *Communications of the ACM* 23 (1980), 17–19.

Czech, Zbigniew J. and Majewski, Bohdan S., "A Linear Time Algorithm for Finding Minimal Perfect Hash Functions," *Computer Journal* 36 (1993), 579–587.

Enbody, R. J. and Dy, H. C., "Dynamic Hashing Schemes," *Computing Surveys* 20 (1988), 85–113.

Fagin, Ronald, Nievergelt, Jurg, Pippenger, Nicholas, and Strong, H. Raymond, "Extendible Hashing—A Fast Access Method for Dynamic Files," *ACM Transactions on Database Systems* 4 (1979), 315–344.

Fox, Edward A., Heath, Lenwood S., Chen, Qi F., and Daoud, Amjad M., "Practical Minimal Perfect Hash Functions for Large Databases," *Communications of the ACM* 35 (1992), 105–121.

Haggard, G. and Karplus, K., "Finding Minimal Perfect Hash Functions," *SIGCSE Bulletin* 18 (1986), No. 1, 191–193.

Knott, G. D., "Expandable Open Addressing Hash Table Storage and Retrieval," *Proceedings of the ACM SIGFIDET Workshop on Data Description, Access, and Control* (1971), 186–206.

Knuth, Donald, *The Art of Computer Programming,* Vol. 3, Reading, MA: Addison-Wesley, 1998.

Larson, Per A., "Dynamic Hashing," *BIT* 18 (1978), 184–201.

Larson, Per A., "Dynamic Hash Tables," *Communications of the ACM* 31 (1988), 446–457.

Lewis, Ted G. and Cook, Curtis R., "Hashing for Dynamic and Static Internal Tables," *IEEE Computer* (October 1986), 45–56.

Litwin, Witold, "Linear Hashing: A New Tool for File and Table Addressing," *Proceedings of the Sixth Conference of Very Large Databases* (1980), 212–223.

Litwin, Witold, "Virtual Hashing: A Dynamically Changing Hashing," *Proceedings of the Fourth Conference of Very Large Databases* (1978), 517–523.

Lomet, David B., "Bounded Index Exponential Hashing," *ACM Transactions on Database Systems* 8 (1983), 136–165.

Lum, V. Y., Yuen, P. S. T., and Dood, M., "Key-to-Address Transformation Techniques: A Fundamental Performance Study on Large Existing Formatted Files," *Communications of the ACM* 14 (1971), 228–239.

Morris, Robert, "Scatter Storage Techniques," *Communications of the ACM* 11 (1968), 38–44.

Mullin, James K., "Tightly Controlled Linear Hashing Without Separate Overflow Storage," *BIT* 21 (1981), 390–400.

Pagli, L., "Self-Adjusting Hash Tables," *Information Processing Letters* 21 (1985), 23–25.

Poblete, Patricio V. and Munro, J. Ian, "Last-Come-First-Served Hashing," *Journal of Algorithms* 10 (1989), 228–248.

Radke, Charles E., "The Use of the Quadratic Search Residue," *Communications of the ACM* 13 (1970), 103–105.

Sager, Thomas J., "A Polynomial Time Generator for Minimal Perfect Hash Functions," *Communications of the ACM* 28 (1985), 523–532.

Sebesta, Robert W. and Taylor, Mark A., "Fast Identification of Ada and Modula-2 Reserved Words," *Journal of Pascal, Ada, and Modula-2* (March/April 1986), 36–39.

Tharp, Alan L., *File Organization and Processing,* New York: Wiley, 1988.

Vitter, Jeffrey S. and Chen, Wen C., *Design and Analysis of Coalesced Hashing,* New York: Oxford University Press, 1987.

Data Compression

Transfer of information is essential for the proper functioning of any structure on any level and any type of organization. The faster an exchange of information occurs, the smoother the structure functions. Improvement of the rate of transfer can be achieved by improving the medium through which data are transferred or by changing the data themselves so that the same information can be transmitted within a shorter time interval.

Information can be represented in a form which exhibits some redundancy. For example, in a database, it is enough to say about a person that he is "M" or she is "F," instead of spelling out the whole words, "male" and "female," or to use 1 and 2 to represent the same information. The number one hundred twenty-eight can be stored as 80 (hexadecimal), 128, 1000000 (binary), CXXVIII, $\rho\kappa\eta$ (the Greek language used letters as digits), or | | | . . . | (128 bars). If numbers are stored as the sequences of digits representing them, then 80 is the shortest form. Numbers are represented in binary form in computers.

11.1 CONDITIONS FOR DATA COMPRESSION

When transferring information, the choice of the data representation determines how fast the transfer is performed. A judicious choice can improve the throughput of a transmission channel without changing the channel itself. There are many different methods of *data compression* (or *compaction*) that reduce the size of the representation without affecting the information itself.

Assume that there are n different symbols used to code messages. For a binary code, $n = 2$; for morse code, $n = 3$: the dot, the dash, and the blank separating the sequences of dots and dashes that represent letters. Assume also that all symbols m_i forming a set M have been independently chosen and are known to have probabilities of occurrence $P(m_i)$, and the symbols are coded with strings of 0s and 1s. Then $P(m_1)$ $+ \cdots + P(m_n) = 1$. The information content of the set M, called the *entropy* of the source M, is defined by

$$L_{ave} = P(m_1)L(m_1) + \cdots + P(m_n)L(m_n) \tag{11.1}$$

where $L(m_i) = -\lg(P(m_i))$, which is the minimum length of a codeword for symbol m_i. Claude E. Shannon established in 1948 that Equation 11.1 gives the best possible average length of a codeword when the source symbols and the probabilities of their use are known. No data compression algorithm can be better than L_{ave}, and the closer it is to this number, the better is its compression rate.

For example, if there are three symbols m_1, m_2, and m_3 with the probabilities .25, .25, and .5, respectively, then the lengths of the codewords assigned to them are:

$$-\lg(P(m_1)) = -\lg(P(m_2)) = -\lg(.25) = \lg\left(\frac{1}{.25}\right) = \lg(4) = 2 \text{ and}$$

$$-\lg(P(m_3)) = \lg(2) = 1$$

and the average length of a codeword is

$$L_{ave} = P(m_1) \cdot 2 + P(m_2) \cdot 2 + P(m_3) \cdot 1 = 1.5$$

Various data compression techniques attempt to minimize the average codeword length by devising an optimal code (that is, an assignment of codewords to symbols) that depends on the probability P with which a symbol is being used. If a symbol is issued infrequently, it can be assigned a long codeword. For frequently issued symbols, very short encodings are more to the point.

Some restrictions need to be imposed on the prospective codes:

1. Each codeword corresponds to exactly one symbol.

2. Decoding should not require any look ahead; after reading each symbol it should be possible to determine whether the end of a string encoding a symbol of the original message has been reached. A code meeting this requirement is called a code with the *prefix property*, and it means that no codeword is a prefix of another codeword. Therefore, no special punctuation is required to separate two codewords in a coded message.

The second requirement can be illustrated by three different encodings of three symbols as given in the following table:

Symbol	Code$_1$	Code$_2$	Code$_3$
A	1	1	11
B	2	22	12
C	12	12	21

The first code does not allow us to make a distinction between AB and C, since both are coded as 12. The second code does not have this ambiguity, but it requires a look ahead, as in 1222: The first 1 can be decoded as A. The following 2 may indicate that A was improperly chosen, and 12 should have been decoded as C. It may be that

A is a proper choice if the third symbol is 2. Since 2 is found, AB is chosen as the tentatively decoded string, but the fourth symbol is another 2. Hence, the first turn was wrong, and A has been ill-chosen. The proper decoding is CB. All these problems arise because both $code_1$ and $code_2$ violate the prefix property. Only $code_3$ can be unambiguously decoded as read.

For an optimal code, two more stipulations are specified.

3. The length of the codeword for a given symbol m_i should not exceed the length of the codeword of a less probable symbol m_j; that is, if $P(m_i) \leq P(m_j)$, then $L(m_i) \geq L(m_j)$ for $1 \leq i, j \leq n$.

4. In an optimal encoding system, there should not be any unused short codewords either as stand-alone encodings or as prefixes for longer codewords, since this would mean that longer codewords were created unnecessarily. For example, the sequence of codewords $01, 000, 001, 100, 101$ for a certain set of five symbols is not optimal because the codeword 11 is not used anywhere; this encoding can be turned into an optimal sequence $01, 10, 11, 000, 001$.

In the following sections, several data compression methods are presented. To compare the efficiency of these methods when applied to the same data, the same measure is used. This measure is the *compression rate* (also called the *fraction of data reduction*), and it is defined as the ratio

$$\frac{\text{length(input)} - \text{length(output)}}{\text{length(input)}} \tag{11.2}$$

It is expressed as a percentage indicating the amount of redundancy removed from the input.

11.2 HUFFMAN CODING

The construction of an optimal code was developed by David Huffman, who utilized a tree structure in this construction: a binary tree for a binary code. The algorithm is surprisingly simple and can be summarized as follows:

```
Huffman()
    for each symbol create a tree with a single root node and order all trees
        according to the probability of symbol occurrence;
    while more than one tree is left
        take the two trees t₁, t₂ with the lowest probabilities p₁, p₂ (p₁ ≤ p₂)
            and create a tree with t₁ and t₂ as its children and with
            the probability in the new root equal to p₁ + p₂;
    associate 0 with each left branch and 1 with each right branch;
    create a unique codeword for each symbol by traversing the tree from the root
        to the leaf containing the probability corresponding to this
        symbol and by putting all encountered 0s and 1s together;
```

The resulting tree has a probability of 1 in its root.

It should be noted that the algorithm is not deterministic in the sense of producing a unique tree because, for trees with equal probabilities in the roots, the algorithm does not prescribe their positions with respect to each other either at the beginning or during execution. If t_1 with probability p_1 is in the sequence of trees and the new tree t_2 is created with $p_2 = p_1$, should t_2 be positioned to the left of t_1 or to the right? Also, if there are three trees t_1, t_2, and t_3 with the same lowest probability in the entire sequence, which two trees should be chosen to create a new tree? There are three possibilities for choosing two trees. As a result, different trees can be obtained depending on where the trees with equal probabilities are placed in the sequence with respect to each other. Regardless of the shape of the tree, the average length of the codeword remains the same.

To assess the compression efficiency of the Huffman algorithm, a definition of the *weighted path length* is used, which is the same as Equation 11.1 except that $L(m_i)$ is interpreted as the number of 0s and 1s in the codeword assigned to symbol m_i by this algorithm.

Figure 11.1 contains an example for the five letters A, B, C, D, and E with probabilities .39, .21, .19, .12, and .09, respectively. The tree in Figures 11.1a and 11.1b are different in the way in which the two nodes containing a probability of .21 have been chosen to be combined with tree .19 to create a tree of .40. Regardless of the choice, the lengths of the codewords associated with the five letters A through E are the same, namely, 2, 2, 2, 3, and 3, respectively. However, the codewords assigned to them are slightly different, as shown in Figures 11.1c and 11.1d, which present abbreviated (and more commonly used) versions of the way the trees in Figures 11.1a and 11.1b were created. The average length for the latter two trees is

$$L_{\text{Huf}} = .39 \cdot 2 + .21 \cdot 2 + .19 \cdot 2 + .12 \cdot 3 + .09 \cdot 3 = 2.21$$

which is very close to 2.09 (only 5% off), the average length computed according to Equation 11.1:

$$L_{\text{ave}} = .39 \cdot 1.238 + .21 \cdot 2.252 + .19 \cdot 2.396 + .12 \cdot 3.059 + .09 \cdot 3.474 = 2.09$$

Corresponding letters in Figures 11.1a and 11.1b have been assigned codewords of the same length. Obviously, the average length for both trees is the same. But each way of building a Huffman tree, starting from the same data, should result in the same average length, regardless of the shape of the tree. Figure 11.2 shows two Huffman trees for the letters P, Q, R, S, and T with the probabilities .1, .1, .1, .2 and .5, respectively. Depending on how the lowest probabilities are chosen, different codewords are assigned to these letters with different lengths, at least for some of them. However, the average length remains the same and is equal to 2.0.

The Huffman algorithm can be implemented in a variety of ways, at least as many as the number of ways a priority queue can be implemented. The priority queue is the natural data structure in the context of the Huffman algorithm since it requires removing the two smallest probabilities and inserting the new probability in the proper position.

One way to implement this algorithm is to use a singly linked list of references to trees, which reflects closely what Figure 11.1a illustrates. The linked list is initially ordered according to the probabilities stored in the trees, all of them consisting of just a

FIGURE **11.1**   Two Huffman trees created for five letters A, B, C, D, and E with probabilities .39, .21, .19, .12, and .09.

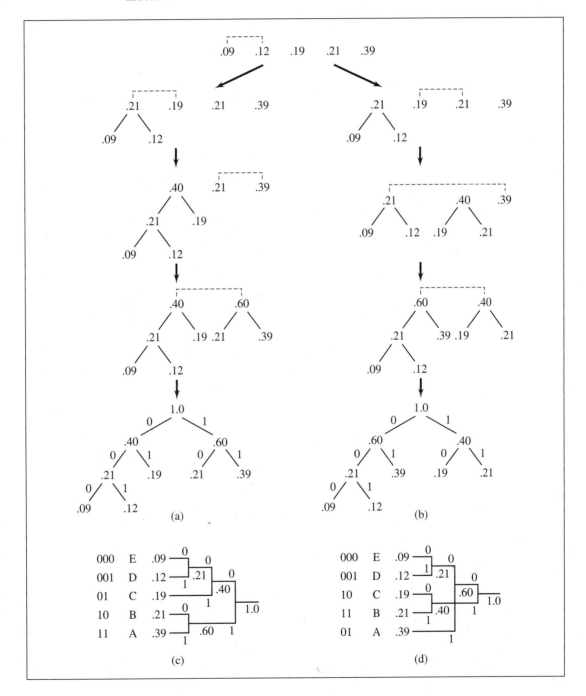

FIGURE **11.2**   Two Huffman trees generated for letters P, Q, R, S, and T with probabilities .1, .1, .1, .2, and .5.

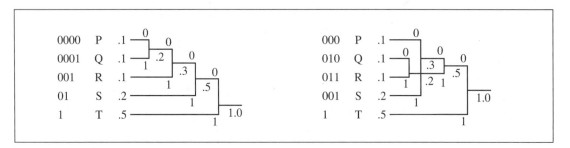

root. Then, repeatedly, the two trees with the smallest probabilities are chosen; the tree with the smaller probability is replaced by a newly created tree, and the node with the reference to the tree with the higher probability is removed from the linked list. From trees having the same probability in their roots, the first tree encountered is chosen.

In another implementation, all probability nodes are first ordered, and that order is maintained throughout the operation. From such an ordered list, the first two trees are always removed to create a new tree from them, which is inserted close to the end of the list. To that end, a doubly linked list of references to trees with immediate access to the beginning and to the end of this list can be used. Figure 11.3 contains a trace of the execution of this algorithm for the letters A, B, C, D, and E with the same probabilities as in Figure 11.1. Codewords assigned to these letters are also indicated in Figure 11.3. Note that they are different from the codewords in Figure 11.1, although their lengths are the same.

The two preceding algorithms built Huffman trees bottom-up by starting with a sequence of trees and collapsing them together to a gradually smaller number of trees and, eventually, to one tree. However, this tree can be built top-down, starting from the highest probability. But only the probabilities to be placed in the leaves are known. The highest probability, to be put in the root, is known if lower probabilities, in the root's children, have been determined; the latter are known if still lower probabilities have been computed and so on. Therefore, creating nonterminal nodes has to be deferred until the probabilities to be stored in them are found. It is very convenient to use the following recursive algorithm to implement a Huffman tree:

```
createHuffmanTree(prob)
    declare the probabilities p₁, p₂, and the Huffman tree Htree;
    if only two probabilities are left in prob
        return a tree with p₁, p₂ in the leaves and p₁ + p₂ in the root;
    else remove the two smallest probabilities from prob and assign them to p₁ and p₂;
        insert p₁ + p₂ to prob;
        Htree = createHuffmanTree(prob);
        in Htree make the leaf with p₁ + p₂ the parent of two leaves with p₁ and p₂;
        return Htree;
```

FIGURE **11.3**   Using a doubly linked list to create the Huffman tree for the letters from Figure 11.1.

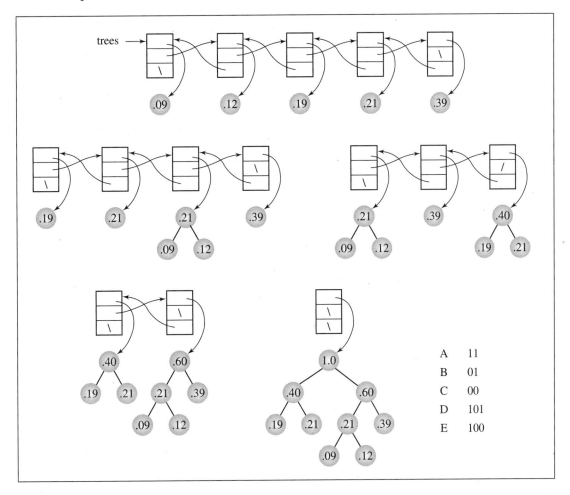

Figure 11.4 contains a summary of the trace of the execution of this algorithm for the letters A, B, C, D, and E with the probabilities as shown in Figure 11.1. Indentation indicates consecutive calls to `createHuffmanTree()`.

One implementation of a priority queue is a min heap which can also be used to implement this algorithm. In this heap, each nonterminal node has a smaller probability than the probabilities in its children, and because the smallest probability is in the root, that one is simple to remove. But after it is removed, the root is empty. Therefore, the largest element is put in the root and the heap property is restored. Then the second element can be removed from the root and replaced with a new element which represents the sum of the probability of the root and the probability previously removed.

FIGURE **11.4**   Top-down construction of a Huffman tree using recursive implementation.

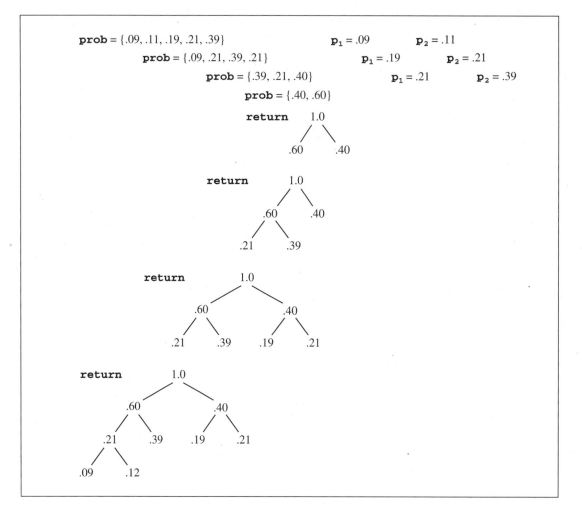

Afterward, the heap property has to be restored again. After one such sequence of operations, the heap has one less node: Two probabilities from the previous heap have been removed and a new one has been added. But it is not enough to create the Huffman tree: The new probability is a parent of the probabilities just removed, and this information must be retained. To that end, three arrays can be used: *indexes* containing the indexes of the original probabilities and the probabilities created during the process of creating the Huffman tree; *probabilities,* an array of the original and newly created probabilities; and *parents,* an array of indexes indicating the position of the parents of the elements stored in *probabilities.* A positive number in *parents* indicates the left child, and a negative number indicates the right child. Codewords are created by accumulating 0s and 1s when going from leaves to the root using the array *parents,* which functions as an array of references. It is important to note that in this particular implementation probabilities are sorted indirectly: The heap is actually made up of indexes to probabilities, and all exchanges take place in *indexes.*

Figure 11.5 illustrates an example of using a heap to implement the Huffman algorithm. The heaps in steps (a), (e), (i), and (m) in Figure 11.5 are ready for processing. First, the highest probability is put in the root, as in steps (b), (f), (j), and (n) of Figure 11.5. Next, the heap is restored, as in steps (c), (g), (k), and (o), and the root probability is set to the sum of the two smallest probabilities, as in steps (d), (h), (l), and (p). Processing is complete when there is only one node in the heap.

Using the Huffman tree, a table can be constructed which gives the equivalents for each symbol in terms of 1s and 0s encountered along the path leading to each of the leaves of the tree. For our example, the tree from Figure 11.3 will be used, and the resulting table is

A	11
B	01
C	00
D	101
E	100

The coding process transmits coded equivalents of the symbols to be sent. For example, instead of sending ABAAD, the sequence 11011111101 is dispatched with the average number of bits per one letter equal to $11/5 = 2.2$, almost the same as 2.09, the value specified by the formula for L_{ave}. To decode this message, the conversion table has to be known to the message receiver. Using this table, a Huffman tree can be constructed with the same paths as the tree used for coding, but its leaves would (for the sake of efficiency) store the symbols instead of their probabilities. In this way, upon reaching a leaf, the symbol can be retrieved directly from it. Using this tree, each symbol can be decoded uniquely. For example, if 1001101 is received, then we try to reach a leaf of the tree using the path indicated by leading 1s and 0s. In this case, 1 takes us to the right, 0 to the left, and another 0 again to the left, whereby we end up in a leaf containing E. After reaching this leaf, decoding continues by starting from the root of the tree and trying to reach a leaf using the remaining 0s and 1s. Since 100 has been processed, 1101 has to be decoded. Now, 1 takes us to the right and another 1 again to the right, which is a leaf with A. We start again from the root, and the sequence 01 is decoded as B. The entire message is now decoded as EAB.

At this point, a question can be asked: Why send 11011111101 instead of ABAAD? This is supposed to be data compression, but the coded message is twice as long as the original. Where is the advantage? Note precisely the way in which messages are sent. A, B, C, D, and E are single letters, and letters, being characters, require one byte (eight bits) to be sent, using the extended ASCII code. Therefore, the message ABAAD requires five bytes (40 bits). On the other hand, 0s and 1s in the coded version can be sent as single bits. Therefore, if 11011111101 is regarded not as a sequence of the characters "0" and "1," but as a sequence of bits, then only 11 bits are needed to send the message, about one-fourth of what is required to send the message in its original form, ABAAD.

FIGURE **11.5**   Huffman algorithm implemented with a heap.

```
        .09        0              .39        4             .12        1
        / \       / \             / \       / \            / \       / \
     .12  .19    1   2         .12  .19    1   2        .21  .19    3   2
     / \         / \           / \         / \          / \         / \
  .21  .39     3    4       .21  .09     3   0       .39  .09     4   0

indexes   [ 0  1  2  3  4 ]
probabilities [.09 .12 .19 .21 .39]              (b)                       (c)
            (a)
```

```
   .21 = .12 + .09   5        .19       2          .39       4          .21       3
        / \         / \        / \     / \          / \     / \          / \     / \
     .21  .19      3   2    .21  .21  3   5      .21  .21  3   5      .39  .21  4   5
     /            /         /         /          /         /          /         /
  .39           4       .39        4          .19        2          .19        2

indexes   [ 5  3  2  4 ]
probabilities [.09 .12 .19 .21 .39 .21]         (e)               (f)               (g)
parents   [ 5  -5 ]
            (d)
```

```
   .40 = .21 + .19   6        .21       3          .40       6          .39       4
        / \         / \        / \     / \          / \     / \          / \     / \
     .39  .21      4   3    .39  .40  4   6      .39  .21  4   3      .40  .21  6   3

indexes   [ 6  4  3 ]
probabilities [.09 .12 .19 .21 .39 .21 .40]      (i)               (j)               (k)
parents   [ 5  -5  6  -6 ]
            (h)
```

```
   .60 = .39 + .21   7        .40       6          .60       7          .60       7
        /            /         /         /          /         /          /         /
     .40            6       .60        7         .40        6         .40        6

indexes   [ 7  6 ]
probabilities [.09 .12 .19 .21 .39 .21 .40 .60]   (m)               (n)               (o)
parents   [ 5  -5  6  -6  7  -7 ]
            (l)
```

```
          1.0
indexes   [ 8 ]                                          1.0            A    10
probabilities [.09 .12 .19 .21 .39 .21 .40 .60 1.0]      / \            B    11
parents   [ 5  -5  6  -6  7  -7  8  -8 ]             .40     .60        C    00
                                                    / \     / \         D    011
            (p)                               .19  .21  .39  .21        E    010
                                                 / \
                                            .09  .12            (q)
```

This example raises one problem: Both the encoder and the decoder have to use the same coding, the same Huffman tree. Otherwise, the decoding will be unsuccessful. How can the encoder let the decoder know which particular code has been used? There are at least three possibilities:

1. Both the encoder and decoder agree beforehand on a particular Huffman tree and both use it for sending any message.

2. The encoder constructs the Huffman tree afresh every time a new message is sent and sends the conversion table along with the message. The decoder either uses the table to decode the message or reconstructs the corresponding Huffman tree and then performs the translation.

3. The decoder constructs the Huffman tree during transmission and decoding.

The second strategy is more versatile, but its advantages are visible only when large files are encoded and decoded. For our simple example, ABAAD, sending both the table of codewords and the coded message 11011111101 is hardly perceived as data compression. However, if a file contains a message of 10,000 characters using the characters A through E, then the space saved is significant. Using the probabilities indicated earlier for these letters, we project that there are approximately 3900 As, 2100 Bs, 1900 Cs, 1200 Ds, and 900 Es. Hence, the number of bits needed to code this file is

$$3900 \cdot 2 + 2100 \cdot 2 + 1900 \cdot 2 + 1200 \cdot 3 + 900 \cdot 3 = 22{,}100 \text{ bits} = 2762.5 \text{ bytes}$$

which is approximately one-fourth the 10,000 bytes required for sending the original file. Even if the conversion table is added to the file, this proportion is only minimally affected.

However, even with this approach, there may be some room for improvement. As indicated, an ideal compression algorithm should give the same average codeword length as computed from Equation 11.1. The symbols from Figure 11.1 have been assigned codewords whose average length is 2.21, approximately 5% worse than the ideal 2.09. Sometimes, however, the difference is larger. Consider, for example, three symbols X, Y, and Z with probabilities .1, .1, and .8. Figure 11.6a shows a Huffman tree for these symbols, with codewords assigned to them. The average length, according to this tree, is

$$L_{\text{Huf}} = 2 \cdot .1 + 2 \cdot .1 + 1 \cdot .8 = 1.2$$

and the best expected average, L_{ave}, is .922. Therefore, there is a possibility we can improve the Huffman coding by approximately 23.2%, ignoring the fact that, at this point, a full 23.2% improvement is not possible because the average is below 1. How is this possible? As already stated, all Huffman trees result in the same average weighted path length. Therefore, no improvement can be expected if only the symbols X, Y, and Z are used to construct this tree.

On the other hand, if all possible pairs of symbols are used for building a Huffman tree, the data rate can be reduced. Figure 11.6b illustrates this procedure. Out of three symbols X, Y, and Z, nine pairs are created whose probabilities are computed by multiplying the probability of both symbols. For example, since the probability for both X and Y is .1, the probability of pair XY is .01 = .1 · .1. The average L_{Huf} is 1.92

FIGURE **11.6** Improving the average length of the codeword by applying the Huffman algorithm (b) to pairs of letters (a) instead of single letters.

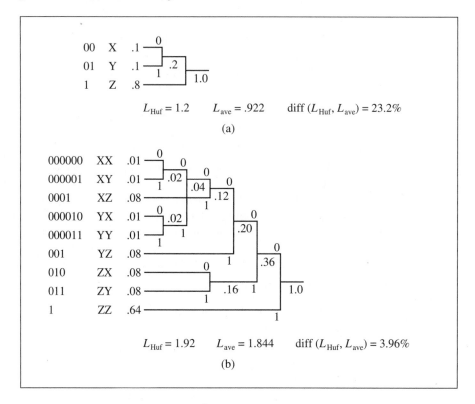

and the expected average L_{ave} is 1.84 (twice the previous L_{ave}), with the difference between these averages being 4%. This represents a 19.2% improvement at the cost of including a larger conversion table (nine entries instead of three) as part of the message to be sent. If the message is large and the number of symbols used in the message is relatively small, then the increase in the size of the table is insignificant. However, for a large number of symbols, the size of the table may be much too large to notice any improvement. For 26 English letters, the number of pairs is 676 which is considered relatively small. But if all printable characters have to be distinguished in an English text, from the blank character (ASCII code 32), to the tilde (ASCII code 126), plus the carriage return character, then there are $(126 - 32 + 1) + 1 = 96$ characters and 9216 pairs of characters. Many of these pairs are not likely to occur at all (e.g., XQ or KZ), but even if 50% of them are found, the resulting table containing these pairs along with codewords associated with them may be too large to be useful.

Using pairs of symbols is still a good idea, even if the number of symbols is large. For example, a Huffman tree can be constructed for all symbols and for all pairs of symbols that occur at least five times. The efficiency of the variations of Huffman encoding can be measured by comparing the size of compressed files. Experiments were performed on an English text, PL/1 program file, and a digitized photographic image (Rubin 1976). When only single characters were used, the compression rates were approximately 40%, 60%, and 50%, respectively. When single characters were used along with the 100 most frequent groups (not only two characters long), the compression rates were 49%, 73%, and 52%. When the 512 most frequent groups were used, the compression rates were around 55%, 71%, and 62%.

11.2.1 Adaptive Huffman Coding

The foregoing discussion assumed that the probabilities of messages are known in advance. A natural question is: How do we know them?

One solution computes the number of occurrences of each symbol expected in messages in some fairly large sample of texts of, say, 10 million characters. For messages in natural languages such as English, such samples may include some literary works, newspaper articles, and a portion of an encyclopedia. After each character's frequency has been determined, a conversion table can be constructed for use by both the sending and receiving ends of the data transfer. This eliminates the need to include such a table every time a file is transmitted.

However, this method may not be useful for sending some specialized files, even if written in English. A computer science paper includes a much higher percentage of digits and parentheses, especially if it includes extensive illustrations in LISP or Java code, than a paper on the prose of Jane Austen. In such circumstances, it is more judicious to use the text to be sent to determine the needed frequencies, which also requires enclosing the table as overhead in the file being sent. A preliminary pass through this file is required before an actual conversion table can be constructed. However, the file to be preprocessed may be very large, and preprocessing slows down the entire transmission process. Second, the file to be sent may not be known in its entirety when it is being sent, and yet compression is necessary: For example, when a text is being typed and sent line by line, then there is no way to know the contents of the whole file at the time of sending. In such a situation, adaptive compression is a viable solution.

An adaptive Huffman encoding technique was devised first by Robert G. Gallager and then improved by Donald Knuth. The algorithm is based on the following *sibling property:* If each node has a sibling (except for the root) and the breadth-first right-to-left tree traversal generates a list of nodes with nonincreasing frequency counters, it can be proven that a tree with the sibling property is a Huffman tree (Faller 1974, Gallager 1978).

In adaptive Huffman coding, the Huffman tree includes a counter for each symbol, and the counter is updated every time a corresponding input symbol is being coded. Checking whether the sibling property is retained assures that the Huffman tree under construction is still a Huffman tree. If the sibling property is violated, the tree has to be restructured to restore this property. Here is how this is accomplished.

First, it is assumed that the algorithm maintains a doubly linked list `nodes` that contains the nodes of the tree ordered by breadth-first right-to-left tree traversal. A *block*$_i$ is a part of the list where each node has frequency i, and the first node in each block is called a *leader*. For example, Figure 11.7 shows the Huffman tree and also the list nodes = (**7** 4 3 2 **2** 2 1 1 1 1 **0**) that has six blocks—*block*$_7$, *block*$_4$, *block*$_3$, *block*$_2$, *block*$_1$, and *block*$_0$—with leaders shown with counters in boldface.

FIGURE **11.7**   Doubly linked list nodes formed by breadth-first right-to-left tree traversal.

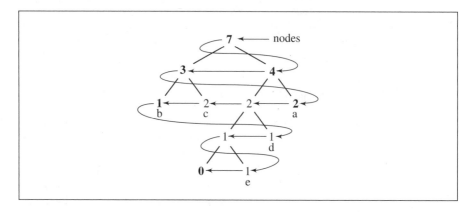

All unused symbols are kept in one node with a frequency of 0, and each symbol encountered in the input has its own node in the tree. Initially, the tree has just one 0-node that includes all symbols. If an input symbol did not yet appear in the input, the 0-node is split in two, with the new 0-node containing all symbols except the newly encountered one and the node referring to this new symbol with counter set to 1; both nodes become children of the one parent whose counter is also set to 1. If an input symbol already has a node p in the tree, its counter is incremented. However, such an increment may endanger the sibling property, so this property has to be restored by exchanging the node p with the leader of the block to which p currently belongs, except when this leader is p's parent. This node is found by going in nodes from p toward the beginning of this list. If p belongs to $block_i$ before increment, it is swapped with the leader of this block, whereby it is included in $block_{i+1}$. Then the counter increment is done for the p's possibly new parent, which may also lead to a tree transformation to restore the sibling property. This process is continued until the root is reached. In this way, the counters are updated on the *new* path from p to the root rather than on its old path. For each symbol, the codeword is issued, which is obtained by scanning the Huffman tree from the root to the node corresponding to this symbol *before* any transformation in the tree takes place.

There are two different types of codewords transmitted during this process. If a symbol being coded has already appeared, then the normal coding procedure is applied: The Huffman tree is scanned from the root to the node holding this symbol to determine its codeword. If a symbol appears in the input for the first time, it is in the 0-node, but just sending the Huffman codeword of the 0-node does not suffice. Therefore, along with the codeword allowing us to reach the 0-node, the codeword is sent which indicates the position of the encountered symbol. For the sake of simplicity, we assume that position n is coded as n 1s followed by a 0. Zero is used to separate the 1s from those belonging to the next codeword. For example, when the letter c is coded for the first time, its codeword, 001110, is a combination of the codeword for the 0-node, 00, and the codeword 1110 indicating that c can be found in the third position in the

FIGURE **11.8**   Transmitting the message "aafcccbd" using an adaptive Huffman algorithm.

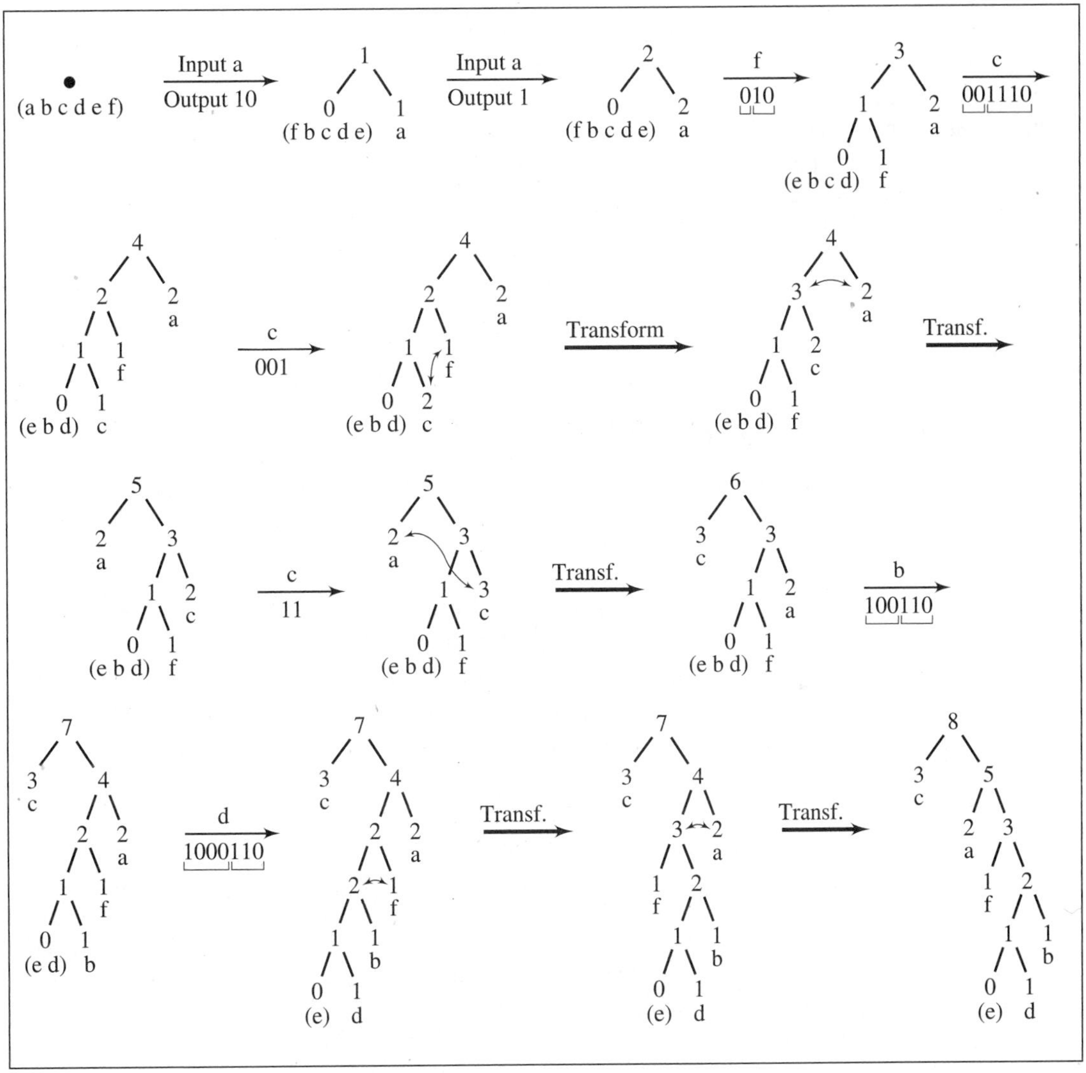

list of unused symbols associated with 0-node. These two codewords (or rather, parts of one codeword) are marked in Figure 11.8 by underlining them separately. After a symbol is removed from the list in 0-node, its place is taken by the last symbol of this list. This also indicates that the encoder and receiver have to agree on the alphabet being used and its ordering. The algorithm is shown in this pseudocode:

```
FGKDynamicHuffmanEncoding(symbol s)
    p = leaf that contains symbol s;
    c = Huffman codeword for s;
```

```
if p is the 0-node
    c = c concatenated with the number of 1s representing position of s in 0-node and with 0;
    write the last symbol in 0-node over s in this node;
    create a new node q for symbol s and set its counter to 1;
    p = new node to become the parent of both 0-node and node q;
    counter(p) = 1;
    include the two new nodes to nodes;
else increment counter(p);
while p is not the root
    if p violates the sibling property
        if the leader of the block_i that still includes p is not parent(p)
            swap p with the leader;
    p = parent(p);
    increment counter(p);
return codeword c;
```

A step-by-step example for string *aafcccbd* is shown in Figure 11.8.

1. Initially, the tree includes only the 0-node with all the source letters (*a, b, c, d, e, f*). After the first input letter, *a*, only the codeword for the position occupied by *a* in the 0-node is output. Because it is the first position, one 1 is output followed by a 0. The last letter in the 0-node is placed in the first position, and a separate node is created for the letter *a*. The node, with the frequency count set to 1, becomes a child of another new node that is also the parent of the 0-node.

2. After the second input letter, also an *a*, 1 is output, which is the Huffman codeword for the leaf that includes *a*. The frequency count of *a* is incremented to 2, which violates the sibling property, but because the leader of the block is the parent of node p (that is, of node *a*), no swap takes place; only p is updated to point to its parent, and then p's frequency count is incremented.

3. The third input letter, *f*, is a letter output for the first time; thus, the Huffman codeword for the 0-node, 0, is generated first, followed by the number of 1s corresponding to the position occupied by *f* in the 0-node, followed by 0: 10. The letter *e* is put in place of letter *f* in the 0-node, a new leaf for *f* is created, and a new node becomes the parent of the 0-node and the leaf just created. Node p, which is the parent of leaf *f*, does not violate the sibling property, so p is updated, p = *parent*(p), thereby becoming the root that is incremented.

4. The fourth input letter is *c*, which appears for the first time in the input. The Huffman codeword for the 0-node is generated followed by three 1s and a 0 because *c* is the third letter in the 0-node. After that, *d* is put in place of *c* in the 0-node, and *c* is put in a newly created leaf; p is updated twice allowing for incrementing counters of two nodes, left child of the root and the root itself.

5. The letter *c* is the next input letter; thus, first the Huffman codeword for its leaf is given, 001. Next, because the sibling property is violated, the node p (that is, the leaf *c*), is swapped with the leader *f* of $block_1$ that still includes this leaf. Then, p = *parent*(p), and the new parent p of the *c* node is incremented, which leads to another violation of the sibling property and to an exchange of node p with the leader of

block$_2$, namely, with the node *a*. Next, p = *parent*(p), node p is incremented, but because it is the root, the process of updating the tree is finished.

6. The sixth input letter is *c*, which has a leaf in the tree; so first, the Huffman codeword, 11, of the leaf is generated and the counter of node *c* is incremented. The node p, which is the node *c*, violates the sibling property, so p is swapped with the leader, node *a*, of *block$_3$*. Now, p = *parent*(p), p's counter is incremented, and because p is the root, the tree transformation is concluded for this input letter. The remaining steps can be traced in Figure 11.8.

It is left to the reader to make appropriate modifications to this pseudocode to obtain a `FGKDynamicHuffmanDecoding`(*codeword* c) algorithm.

It is possible to design a Huffman coding that does not require any initial knowledge of the set of symbols used by the encoder (Cormack and Horspool 1984). The Huffman tree is initialized to a special escape character. If a new symbol is to be sent, it is preceded by the escape character (or its current codeword in the tree) and followed by the symbol itself. The receiver can now know this symbol so that if its codeword arrives later on, it can be properly decoded. The symbol is inserted in the tree by making the leaf *L* with the lowest frequency a nonleaf so that *L* has two children, one pertaining to the symbol previously in *L* and one to the new symbol.

Adaptive Huffman coding surpasses simple Huffman coding in two respects: It requires only one pass through the input, and it adds only an alphabet to the output. Both versions are relatively fast, and more important, they can be applied to any kind of file, not only to text files. In particular, they can compress object or executable files, not only text files. The problem with executable files, however, is that they generally use larger character sets than source code files, and the distribution of these characters is more uniform than in text files. Therefore, the Huffman trees are large, the codewords are of similar length, and the output file is not much smaller than the original; it is compressed merely by 10–20%.

11.3 SHANNON-FANO CODE

Another efficient method that generates an optimal code as *n* approaches infinity was developed by C. E. Shannon and R. M. Fano. The algorithm is as follows:

> *Order the set of symbols according to the frequency of occurrence;*
> `ShannonFano` (*sequence* S)
>   `if` S *has two elements*
>   *attach* 0 *to the codeword of one element and* 1 *to the codeword of another;*
>   `else if` S *has more than one element*
>   *divide* S *into two subsequences,* S$_1$ *and* S$_2$, *with the minimal*
>   *difference between probabilities of each subsequence;*
>   *extend the codeword for each symbol in* S$_1$ *by attaching* 0, *and attaching*
>   *1 to each codeword for symbols in* S$_2$;
>   `ShannonFano` (S$_1$);
>   `ShannonFano` (S$_2$);

FIGURE **11.9** Execution of Shannon-Fano algorithm applied to five letters A, B, C, D, and E with probabilities .39, .21, .19, .12, and .09.

E	.09	000
D	.12	001
C	.19	01
B	.21	10
A	.39	11

Figure 11.9 contains the same symbols as Figure 11.1. First, the sequence $S = (A, B, C, D, E)$ is divided into subsequences $S_1 = (C, D, E)$ and $S_2 = (A, B)$ since the difference between $P(S_1) = P(C) + P(D) + P(E)$ and $P(S_2) = P(A) + P(B)$ is the smallest among all subsequences of S obtained by dividing S into two sequences. The next closest candidate is subsequences (A) and (B, C, D, E) with probabilities .39 and .61, but these subsequences are rejected since the difference, $.61 - .39$, is greater than $.6 - .4$. The codeword for each letter from S_1 starts with 0, and the codeword for S_2 starts with 1. Next, the sequence S_1 is divided into $S_{11} = (D, E)$ and $S_{12} = (C)$ with probabilities .21 and .19. The codewords for D and E are extended by attaching 0 to them, and the codeword for C by attaching 1 so that the latter becomes 01. Since the sequence S_{11} has two elements, the codeword for one of them, E, is extended by adding another 0 and the codeword for D is extended by adding 1. Sequence S_2 also has two elements and their codewords are also appropriately extended. Figure 11.9 summarizes these steps.

The average length of the codewords generated by the Shannon-Fano method for the five letters A, B, C, D, and E with probabilities .39, .21, .19, .12, and .09 is

$$L_{SF} = .39 \cdot 2 + .21 \cdot 2 + .19 \cdot 2 + .12 \cdot 3 + .09 \cdot 3 = 2.21$$

which is the same as the average codeword length generated by the Huffman algorithm. Generally, however, this is not the case. The closer the probabilities are to negative powers of 2, the more efficient the Shannon-Fano algorithm becomes; it can only give results as good as the Huffman algorithm and cannot surpass it.

Both the Huffman and Shannon-Fano algorithms are concerned with redundancy. Therefore, symbols with different probabilities are represented by variable-length codewords as they assign shorter codewords to more frequently used characters. This reduces the storage required for a coded message and reduces the time needed to transmit the message. A serious drawback of both algorithms is the requirement to know the probabilities before the coding begins, although adaptive Huffman code alleviates this problem. Also, the codes resulting from the application of both algorithms are very sensitive and require a flawless transmission of data, since the change of only one bit changes the message being transferred. An area of active research is the construction and analysis of self-correcting codes that account for possible distortion during transmission.

◻ 11.4 RUN-LENGTH ENCODING

A *run* is defined as a sequence of identical characters. For example, the string $s =$ "aaabba" has three runs: a run of three "a"s followed by runs of two "b"s and of one "a." The run-length encoding technique takes advantage of the presence of runs and represents them in an abbreviated, compressed form.

If runs are of the same characters, as in the string $s =$ "nnnn***r%%%%%%%," then instead of transmitting this string, information about runs can be transferred. Each run is coded by the pair (n, ch), where ch is a character and n is the integer representing the number of consecutive characters ch in the run. The string s is coded as 4n3*1r7%. However, a problem arises if one of the characters being transferred is a digit, as in 11111111111544444, which is represented as 1111554 (for eleven 1s, one 5, and five 4s). Therefore, for each run, instead of the number n, a character can be used whose ASCII value is n. For example, the run of 43 consecutive letters "c" is represented as +c ("+" has ASCII code 43), and the run of 49 1s is coded as 11 ("1" has ASCII code 49).

This technique is only efficient when at least two-character runs are transmitted, because for one-character runs, the codeword is twice as long as the character. Therefore, the technique should be applied only to runs of at least two characters. This requires using a marker indicating that what is being transmitted is either a run in an abbreviated form or a literal character. Three characters are needed to represent a run: a compression marker cm, a literal character ch, and a counter n, which make up a triple $\langle cm, ch, n \rangle$. The problem of choosing the compression marker is especially delicate, since it should not be confused with a literal character being transmitted. If a regular text file is transmitted, then the character '~'+1 can be chosen. If there is no restriction on the characters transmitted, then whenever the compression marker itself occurs in the input file, we transmit the compression markers twice. The decoder discards one such marker upon receiving two of them in a row and retains just one as part of the data being received. For example, %% in a `printf` statement in C indicates to print just one percent sign. Since for each literal marker two of them must be sent, an infrequently used marker should be chosen. In addition, runs of markers are not sent in compressed form.

Since compressing runs results in a sequence of three characters, this technique should be applied to runs of at least four characters. The maximum length of a run that can be represented by the triple $\langle cm, ch, n \rangle$ is 255 for 8-bit ASCII if the number n represents the number of characters in the run. But because only runs of four or more characters are encoded, n can represent the number of actual characters in the run minus 4. For example, if $n = 1$, then there are five characters in the run. In this case, the longest run representable by one triple has 259 characters.

Run-length encoding is only modestly efficient for text files in which only the blank character has a tendency to be repeated. In this case, a predecessor of this technique can be applied, *null suppression,* which compresses only runs of blanks and eliminates the need to identify the character being compressed. As a result, pairs $\langle cm, n \rangle$ are used for runs of three or more blanks. This simple technique is used in the IBM 3780 BISYNC transmission protocol where throughput gain is between 30 and 50%.

Run-length encoding is very useful when applied to files which are almost guaranteed to have many runs of at least four characters. One example is relational databases. All records in the same relational database file have to be of equal length. Records (rows, tuples) are collections of fields, which may be—and most often are— longer than the information stored in them. Therefore, they have to be padded with some character, thereby creating a large collection of runs whose only purpose is to fill up free space in each field of every record.

Another candidate for compression using run-length encoding is fax images, which are composed of combinations of black and white pixels. For low resolution, there are about 1.5 million pixels per page. Thus, transmission of one page at 28,800 bps requires about 1 minute. Clearly, some compression method is necessary.

A serious drawback of run-length encoding is that it relies entirely on the occurrences of runs. In particular, this method taken by itself is unable to recognize the high frequency of the occurrence of certain symbols which call for short codewords. For example, AAAABBBB can be compressed, since it is composed of two runs, but ABABABAB cannot, although both messages are made up of the same letters. On the other hand, ABABABAB is compressed by Huffman encoding into the same number of codewords as AAAABBBB without taking into consideration the presence of runs. Therefore, it seems appropriate to combine both methods as in this chapter's case study.

⌨ 11.5 ZIV-LEMPEL CODE

The problem with some of the methods discussed thus far is that they require some knowledge about the data before encoding takes place. A "pure form" of the Huffman encoder has to know the frequencies of symbol occurrences before codewords are assigned to the symbols. Some versions of the adaptive Huffman encoding can circumvent this limitation, not by relying on previous knowledge of the source characteristics, but by building this knowledge in the course of data transmission. Such a method is called a *universal coding scheme,* and Ziv-Lempel code is an example of a universal data compression code.

In a version of the Ziv-Lempel method called LZ77, a buffer of symbols is maintained. The first l_1 positions hold the l_1 most recently encoded symbols from the input, and the remaining l_2 positions contain the l_2 symbols about to be encoded. In each iteration, starting from one of the first l_1 positions, the buffer is searched for a substring matching a prefix of a string located in the second portion of the buffer. If such a match is found, a codeword is transmitted; the codeword is a triple composed of the position in which the match was found, the length of match, and the first mismatching symbol. Then, the entire content of the buffer is shifted to the left by the length of match plus one. Some symbols are shifted out. Some new symbols from the input are shifted in. To initiate this process, the first l_1 positions are filled up with l_1 copies of the first symbol of the input.

As an example, consider the case when $l_1 = l_2 = 4$, and the input is the string "aababacbaacbaadaaa. . . ." Positions in the buffer are indexed with the numbers 0–7. The initial situation is shown at the top of Figure 11.10. The first symbol of the input

FIGURE **11.10**   Encoding the string "aababacbaacbaadaaa..." with LZ77.

Input	Buffer	Code Transmitted
aababacbaacbaadaa...	aaaa	a
aababacbaacbaadaa...	aaaaaaba	22b
abacbaacbaadaaa...	aaababac	23c
baacbaadaaa...	abacbaac	12a
cbaadaaa...	cbaacbaa	03a
daaa...	cbaadaaa	30d
aaa...	...	

is "a," and positions 0 through 3 are filled up with "a"s. The first four symbols of the input, "aaba," are placed in the remaining positions. The longest prefix matching any substring which begins in any position between 0 and 3 is "aa." Therefore, the generated codeword is a triple $\langle 2, 2, b \rangle$, or simply 22b: The match starts in position two, it is two symbols long, and the symbol following this match is "b." Next, a left shift occurs, three "a"s are shifted out, and the string "bac" is shifted in. The longest match also starts in position two and is three symbols long, namely, "aba," with "c" following it. The issued codeword is 23c. Figure 11.10 illustrates a few more steps.

The numbers l_1 and l_2 are chosen in this example so that only two bits are needed for each. Because each symbol requires one byte (eight bits), one codeword can be stored in 12 bits. Therefore, l_1 and l_2 should be powers of 2, so that no binary number is unused. If l_1 is 5, then three bits are needed to code all possible positions 0 through 4, and the three-bit combinations corresponding to the numbers 5, 6, and 7 are not used.

A more frequently applied version of Ziv-Lempel algorithm called LZW uses a table of codewords created during data transmission. A simple algorithm for encoding can be presented as follows (Welch 1984; Miller and Wegman 1985):

```
LZWcompress()
     enter all letters to the table;
     initialize string s  to the first letter from input;
     while  any input left
          read character c;
          if s+c  is in the table
              s = s+c;
          else output codeword(s);
              enter s+c  to the table;
              s = c;
     output codeword(s);
```

String s is always at least one-character long. After reading a new character, the concatenation of string s and character c is checked in the table. A new character is read if the concatenation s+c is in the table. If it is not, the codeword for s is output, the concatenation s+c is stored in the table, and s is initialized to c. Figure 11.11 shows a trace of the execution of this procedure applied to the input "aababacbaacbaadaaa. . . ." The figure contains the generated output, the strings included in the table in full form and in abbreviated form, represented by a number and a character.

A crucial component of efficiency is the organization of the table. Clearly, for more realistic examples, hundreds and thousands of entries can be expected in this table so that an efficient searching method has to be used. A second concern is the size of the table, which grows particularly when new long strings are entered in it. The problem of size is addressed by storing in the table codewords for the prefix and the last characters of strings. For example, if "ba" is assigned the codeword 7, then "baa" can be stored in the table as a number of its prefix, "ba," and the last character, "a," that is, as 7a. In this way, all table entries have the same length. The problem of searching is addressed by using a hash function.

For decoding, the same table is created by updating it for each incoming codeword except the first. For each codeword, a corresponding prefix and a character are retrieved from the table. Since the prefix is also a codeword (except for single characters), it requires another table lookup, as the entire string is decoded. This is clearly a recursive procedure which may be implemented with an explicit stack. This is necessary since the decoding process applied to prefixes yields a string in the reverse order. The decoding procedure can be summarized as follows:

```
LZWdecompress()
    enter all letters to the table;
    read priorcodeword and output one character corresponding to it;
    while codewords are still left
        read codeword;
        if codeword is not in the table // special case: c+s+c+s+c, also if s is null;
            enter in table string(priorcodeword) + firstchar(string(priorcodeword));
            output string(priorcodeword) + firstchar(string(priorcodeword));
        else enter in table string(priorcodeword) + firstchar(string(codeword));
            output string(codeword);
        priorcodeword = codeword;
```

This relatively simple algorithm has to consider a special case, when a codeword being processed has no corresponding entry in the table. This situation arises when the string being decoded contains a substring "cScSc," where "c" is a single character, and "cS" is already in the table.

All of the discussed compression algorithms are widely used. UNIX has three compression programs: *pack* uses the Huffman algorithm, *compact* is based on the adaptive Huffman method, and *compress* uses LZW coding. According to system manuals, *pack* compresses text files by 25–40%, *compact* by 40%, and *compress* by 40–50%. The rate of compression is better for Ziv-Lempel coding. It is also faster.

encoder		index (codeword)	table full string	abbreviated string
input	output			
		1	a	a
		2	b	b
		3	c	c
a		4	d	d
a	1	5	aa	1a
b	1	6	ab	1b
ab	2	7	ba	2a
a	6	8	aba	6a
c	1	9	ac	1c
ba	3	10	cb	3b
ac	7	11	baa	7a
baa	9	12	acb	9b
d	11	13	baad	11d
aa	4	14	da	4a
a	5	15	aaa	5a
	...			

🖻 11.6 CASE STUDY: HUFFMAN METHOD WITH RUN-LENGTH ENCODING

As indicated in the discussion of run-length encoding, this method is suitable for files which are almost guaranteed to have many runs of at least four symbols; otherwise, no compression is achieved. The Huffman algorithm, on the other hand, can be applied to files with any runs, including runs of one to three symbols long. This method can be applied to single symbols, such as letters, but also to pairs of symbols, to triples, and to a collection of variable length sequences of symbols. Incorporating run-length encoding in the Huffman method works exceedingly well for files with many long runs and moderately well for files with a small number of runs and a large number of different symbols.

FIGURE **11.12**   (a) Contents of the array data after the message AAABAACCAABA has been processed. (b) Huffman tree generated from these data.

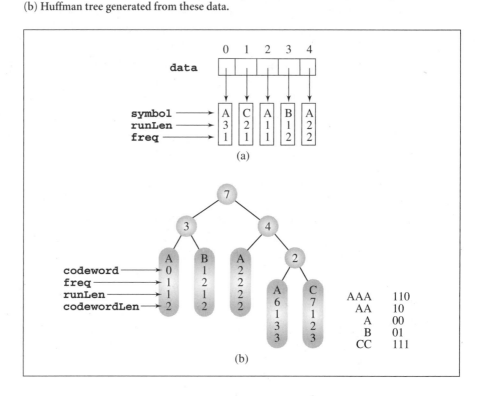

(a)

(b)

For files with no runs, this method is reduced to plain Huffman encoding. In this approach, a file to be compressed is scanned first to determine all runs, including one-, two-, and three-symbols long. Runs composed of the same symbols but of different length are treated as different "super-symbols" which are used to create a Huffman tree. For example, if the message to be compressed is AAABAACCAABA, then the super-symbols included in the Huffman tree are AAA, B, AA, CC, and A, and not symbols A, B, and C. In this way, the number of codewords to be created grows from three for the symbols to five for the super-symbols. The conversion table becomes larger, but the codewords assigned to the runs are much shorter than in straight runlength encoding. In run-length encoding, this codeword is always three bytes long (24 bits). In Huffman code, it may be even one bit long.

First, an input file is scanned and all super-symbols are collected in the vector data by the method garnerData() and sorted according to the frequency of occurrence. Figure 11.12a illustrates the positions of the data in the sorted vector. Next, the sorted data are stored in the output file to be used by the decoder to create the same Huffman tree that the encoder is about to create. createHuffmanTree() generates the tree of Huffman codewords using information collected in data. To that end, a doubly linked list of single node trees similar to the list in Figure 11.3 is created first.

Then, repeatedly, the two trees with the lowest frequencies are combined to create one tree, which eventually results in one Huffman tree, as in Figure 11.12b.

After the tree has been created, the positions of all nodes, in particular the leaves, can be determine whereby the codewords of all symbols in the leaves can be generated. Each node in this tree has seven data members, but only five of them are shown, just for leaves. The codewords are stored as numbers which represent binary sequences of 0s and 1s. For example, the codeword for CC is 7, 111 in binary. However, these numbers are always the same length, and 7 is stored as 3 bits set to 1 preceded by 29 bits set to 0, 0 . . . 0111. It is, therefore, unclear how many bits out of 32 are included in the sequence representing the codeword for a certain symbol. Is it 111, 0111, 00111, or some other sequence? The codeword field for single As is 0. Is the codeword for A 0, 00, 000, or some more 0s? To avoid ambiguity, the codewordLen field stores the number of bits included in the codeword for a given symbol. Since codewordLen for A is 2 and codeword is 0, then the codeword sequence representing A is 00.

After the Huffman tree is generated and the leaves are filled with relevant information, the process of coding information in the input file can be initiated. Because searching for particular symbols directly in the tree is too time-consuming, an array chars[] of linked lists corresponding to each ASCII symbol is created. The nodes of the linked lists are simply leaves of the tree linked through right references, and each list has as many nodes as the number of different run lengths of a given symbol in the input file. It gives immediate access to a particular linked list, but some linked lists may be long if there are many run lengths of a given symbol.

Next, the file is scanned for the second time to find each super-symbol and its corresponding codeword in the Huffman tree and to transmit it to the output file. As the sequences are retrieved from the tree, they are tightly packed into a four-byte numerical variable pack. The first encountered super-symbol in the input file is AAA with codeword 110, which is stored in pack so that pack contains the sequence 0 . . . 0110. After B is retrieved from the file, its code, 01, is attached to the end of pack. As a result, the contents of pack have to be shifted to the left by two positions to make room for 01, and then 01 is stored in it using the bitwise or operation |. Now, pack contains the string 0..011001. After pack is filled up with codewords, it is output as a sequence of four bytes to the output file.

Particular care has to be taken to put exactly 32 bytes in pack. When there are fewer available positions in pack than the number of bits in a codeword, only a portion of the codeword is put in pack. Then pack is output and the remaining portion of the codeword is put in pack before any other symbol is encoded. For example, if pack currently contains 001 . . . 10011, pack can take only two more bits. Since the codeword 1101 is four bits long, the contents of pack are shifted to the left by two positions, 1 . . . 1001100, and the first two bits of the codeword, 11, are put at the end of pack after which pack's contents are 1 . . . 1001111. Next, pack is output as four bytes (characters), and then the remaining two bits of the codeword, 01, are put into pack, which now contains 0 . . . 001.

Another problem is with the last codewords. The encoder fills the output file with bytes (in this case, with chunks of four bytes), each containing eight bits. What happens if there are no symbols left, but there is still room in pack? The decoder has to know that some bits at the end of file should not be decoded. If they are, some spurious characters will be added to the decoded file. In this implementation, the problem is solved by transmitting at the beginning of the encoded file the number of characters to be decoded. The decoder decodes only this number of codewords. Even if some bits are left in the encoded file, they are not included in the decoding process. This is a problem which arises in our example. The message AAABAACCAABA is encoded as the sequence of codewords 110,01,10,111,10,01,00, and the contents of pack are 00000000000000001100110111100100. If the encoding process is finished, the contents are shifted to the left by the number of unused bits, whereby pack becomes 11001101111001000000000000000000 and is output as a sequence of four bytes, 11001101, 1100100, 00000000, and 00000000 or, in more readable decimal notation, as 205, 228, 0, and 0. The last 16 bits do not represent any codewords, and if it is not indicated, they are decoded as eight As, whose codeword is 00. To prevent this, the output file includes the number of encoded characters, namely, 12: A, A, A, B, A, A, C, C, A, A, B, and A. The output file also includes the number of all symbols in the Huffman tree. For this example, it is the number 5, since five different super-symbols can be found in the input file and in the Huffman tree: AAA, B, AA, CC, and A. Therefore, the structure of the output file is as follows: the number of super-symbols, data.Size(), number of characters, contents of data (symbols, run lengths, and frequencies), and codewords of all super-symbols found in the input file.

Decoder is much simpler than encoder because it uses information supplied by the encoder in the header of the encoded message. Decoder recreates first the vector data[] in inputFrequencies(), then reconstructs the Huffman tree with the same createHuffmanTree() and createCodewords() decoder used, and finally, in decode(), scans the tree in the order determined by the stream of bits in the compressed file to find in its leaves the encrypted symbols.

As expected, this implementation gives particularly good results for database files, with a compression rate of 60%. The compression rate for LISP files is 50% (runs of parentheses), for text files, 40%, and for executable files, merely 13%.

Figure 11.13 contains the complete code for the encoder.

FIGURE **11.13**   Implementation of Huffman method with run-length encoding.

```
//************************  HuffmanCoding.java  *********************

import java.io.*;
import java.util.Date;

class HuffmanNode {
    byte symbol;
    int codeword;
    int freq;
    int runLen;
    int codewordLen;
```

FIGURE **11.13**   *(continued)*

```java
    HuffmanNode left = null, right = null;
    HuffmanNode() {
    }
    HuffmanNode(byte s, int f, int r) {
        this(s,f,r,null,null);
    }
    HuffmanNode(byte s, int f, int r, HuffmanNode lt, HuffmanNode rt) {
        symbol = s; freq = f; runLen = r; left = lt; right = rt;
    }
}

class ListNode {
    HuffmanNode tree;
    ListNode next = null, prev = null;
    ListNode() {
    }
    ListNode(ListNode p, ListNode n) {
        prev = p; next = n;
    }
}

class DataRec implements Comparable {
    byte symbol;
    int runLen;
    int freq;
    DataRec() {
    }
    DataRec(byte s, int r) {
        symbol = s; runLen = r; freq = 1;
    }
    public boolean equals(Object el) {
        return symbol == ((DataRec)el).symbol &&
                runLen == ((DataRec)el).runLen;
    }
    public int compareTo(Object el) {
        return freq - ((DataRec)el).freq;
    }
}

class HuffmanCoding {
    HuffmanCoding() {
```

Figure **11.13**   *(continued)*

```
    }
    final int ASCII = 256,
               intBytes = 4,  // bytes per int;
               bits = 8;       // bits per byte;
    HuffmanNode HuffmanTree;
    HuffmanNode[] chars = new HuffmanNode[ASCII + 1];
    java.util.Vector data = new java.util.Vector();
    long charCnt;

    void error(String s) {
        System.err.println(s); System.exit(-1);
    }

    void garnerData(RandomAccessFile fIn) throws IOException {
        int ch, ch2, runLen, i;
        DataRec r;
        for (ch = fIn.read(); ch != -1; ch = ch2) {
            for (runLen = 1, ch2 = fIn.read(); ch2 != -1 && ch2 == ch; runLen++)
                ch2 = fIn.read();
            r = new DataRec((byte)ch,runLen);
            if ((i = data.indexOf(r)) == -1)
                 data.addElement(r);
            else ((DataRec)data.elementAt(i)).freq++;
        }
        java.util.Collections.sort(data);
    }

    void outputFrequencies(RandomAccessFile fIn, RandomAccessFile fOut)
                            throws IOException {
        fOut.writeInt(data.size());
        fOut.writeLong(fIn.getFilePointer());
        for (int j = 0; j < data.size(); j++) {
            fOut.write(((DataRec)data.elementAt(j)).symbol);
            fOut.writeInt(((DataRec)data.elementAt(j)).runLen);
            fOut.writeInt(((DataRec)data.elementAt(j)).freq);
        }
    }

    void inputFrequencies(RandomAccessFile fIn) throws IOException {
        int dataIndex = fIn.readInt();
        charCnt = fIn.readLong();
```

FIGURE **11.13**   *(continued)*

```
    DataRec r;
    data.ensureCapacity(dataIndex);
    for (int j = 0; j < dataIndex; j++) {
        r = new DataRec();
        r.symbol = (byte) fIn.read();
        r.runLen = fIn.readInt();
        r.freq = fIn.readInt();
        data.addElement(r);
    }
}


void createHuffmanTree() {
    ListNode p, newNode, head, tail;
    int newFreq;
    DataRec r;
    head = tail = new ListNode();           // initialize list pointers;
    r = (DataRec)data.elementAt(0);
    head.tree = new HuffmanNode(r.symbol,r.freq,r.runLen);
    for (int i = 1; i < data.size(); i++) { // create the rest of the list;
        tail.next = new ListNode(tail,null);
        tail = tail.next;
        r = (DataRec)data.elementAt(i);
        tail.tree = new HuffmanNode(r.symbol,r.freq,r.runLen);
    }
    while (head != tail) {                   // create one Huffman tree;
        newFreq = head.tree.freq + head.next.tree.freq; // two lowest
                                                        // frequencies
        for (p = tail; p != null && p.tree.freq > newFreq; p = p.prev);
        newNode = new ListNode(p,p.next);
        p.next = newNode;
        if (p == tail)
            tail = newNode;
        else newNode.next.prev = newNode;
        newNode.tree =
            new HuffmanNode((byte)0,newFreq,0,head.tree,head.next.tree);
        head = head.next.next;
        head.prev = null;
    }
    HuffmanTree = head.tree;
}
```

Continues

FIGURE **11.13** *(continued)*

```
void createCodewords(HuffmanNode p, int codeword, int lvl) {
    if (p.left == null && p.right == null) {     // if p is a leaf,
        p.codeword    = codeword;                // store codeword
        p.codewordLen = lvl;                     // and its length,
    }
    else {                                        // otherwise add 0
        createCodewords(p.left,  codeword<<1,   lvl+1);// for left branch
        createCodewords(p.right,(codeword<<1)+1,lvl+1);// and 1 for right;
    }
}


void transformTreeToArrayOfLists(HuffmanNode p) {
    if (p.left == null && p.right == null) {     // if p is a leaf,
        p.right = chars[p.symbol+128];           // include it in
        chars[p.symbol+128] = p;                 // a list associated
    }                                             // with symbol found in p;
    else {                                        // add 128 to change the
        transformTreeToArrayOfLists(p.left);     // range of bytes from
        transformTreeToArrayOfLists(p.right);    // [-128, 127] to
    }                                             // [0, 255];
}


void encode(RandomAccessFile fIn, RandomAccessFile fOut) throws IOException {
    int packCnt = 0, hold, maxPack = 4 * bits, pack = 0;
    int ch, ch2, bitsLeft, runLen;
    HuffmanNode p;
    for (ch = fIn.read(); ch != -1; ) {
        for (runLen = 1, ch2 = fIn.read();  ch2 != -1 && ch2 == ch; runLen++)
            ch2 = fIn.read();
        for (p = chars[(byte)ch+128]; p != null && runLen != p.runLen;
                                p = p.right)
            ;
        if (p == null)
            error("A problem in transmitCode()");
        if (p.codewordLen < maxPack - packCnt) { // if enough room in
            pack = (pack << p.codewordLen) | p.codeword; // pack to store
            packCnt += p.codewordLen;            // new codeword, shift its
        }                                         // content to the left
                                                  // and attach new codeword;
        else {                                    // otherwise move
            bitsLeft = maxPack - packCnt;         // pack's content to
            pack <<= bitsLeft;                    // the left by the
```

FIGURE **11.13**   *(continued)*

```
                if (bitsLeft != p.codewordLen) {     // number of left
                    hold = p.codeword;               // spaces and if new
                    hold >>>= p.codewordLen - bitsLeft;// codeword is longer
                    pack |= hold;                    // than room left, transfer
                }                                    // only as many bits as
                                                     // can be fitted in pack;
                else pack |= p.codeword;             // if new codeword
                                                     // exactly fits in
                                                     // pack, transfer it;

                fOut.writeInt(pack);                 // output pack as
                                                     // four bytes;
                if (bitsLeft != p.codewordLen) {     // transfer
                    pack = p.codeword;               // unprocessed bits
                    packCnt = maxPack - (p.codewordLen - bitsLeft);// of new
                    packCnt = p.codewordLen - bitsLeft;// codeword to pack;
                }
                else packCnt = 0;
            }
            ch = ch2;
        }
        if (packCnt != 0) {
            pack <<= maxPack - packCnt; // transfer leftover codewords
            fOut.writeInt(pack);        // and some 0's;
        }
    }
    void compressFile(String inFileName, RandomAccessFile fIn) throws IOException
    {
        String outFileName = new String(inFileName+".z");
        RandomAccessFile fOut = new RandomAccessFile(outFileName,"rw");
        Date start = new Date();
        garnerData(fIn);
        outputFrequencies(fIn,fOut);
        createHuffmanTree();
        createCodewords(HuffmanTree,0,0);
        for (int i = 0; i <= ASCII; i++)
            chars[i] = null;
        transformTreeToArrayOfLists(HuffmanTree);
        fIn.seek(0);
        encode(fIn,fOut);
    }
```

FIGURE **11.13** *(continued)*

```java
    void decode(RandomAccessFile fIn, RandomAccessFile fOut) throws IOException {
        int chars, j, ch, bitCnt = 1, mask = 1;
        HuffmanNode p;
        mask <<= bits - 1;  // change 00000001 to 100000000
        for (chars = 0, ch = fIn.read(); ch != -1 && chars < charCnt; ) {
            for (p = HuffmanTree; ; ) {
                if (p.left == null && p.right == null) {
                    for (j = 0; j < p.runLen; j++)
                        fOut.write(p.symbol);
                    chars += p.runLen;
                    break;
                }
                else if ((ch & mask) == 0)
                    p = p.left;
                else p = p.right;
                if (bitCnt++ == bits) {  // read next character from FIn
                    ch = fIn.read();     // if all bits in ch are checked;
                    bitCnt = 1;
                }                        // otherwise move all bits in ch
                else ch <<= 1;           // to the left by one position;
            }
        }
    }

    void decompressFile(String inFileName, RandomAccessFile fIn)
                        throws IOException {
        String outFileName = new String(inFileName+".dec");
        RandomAccessFile fOut = new RandomAccessFile(outFileName,"rw");
        Date start = new Date();
        inputFrequencies(fIn);
        createHuffmanTree();
        createCodewords(HuffmanTree,0,0);
        for (int i = 0; i <= ASCII; i++)
            chars[i] = null;
        decode(fIn,fOut);
    }
}


//************************* HuffmanEncoder.java *********************

import java.io.*;
```

FIGURE **11.13**   *(continued)*

```
class HuffmanEncoder {
    static public void main (String args[]) {
        String fileName = "";
        HuffmanCoding Htree = new HuffmanCoding();
        RandomAccessFile fIn;
        InputStreamReader isr = new InputStreamReader(System.in);
        BufferedReader buffer = new BufferedReader(isr);
        try {
            if (args.length == 0) {
                System.out.print("Enter a file name: ");
                fileName = buffer.readLine();
                fIn = new RandomAccessFile(fileName,"r");
            }
            else {
                fIn = new RandomAccessFile(args[0],"r");
                fileName = args[0];
            }
            Htree.compressFile(fileName,fIn);
            fIn.close();
        } catch(IOException io) {
            System.err.println("Cannot open " + fileName);
        }
    }
}


//*********************** HuffmanDecoder.java ***********************

import java.io.*;

class HuffmanDecoder {
    static public void main (String args[]) {
        String fileName = "";
        HuffmanCoding Htree = new HuffmanCoding();
        RandomAccessFile fIn;
        InputStreamReader isr = new InputStreamReader(System.in);
        BufferedReader buffer = new BufferedReader(isr);
        try {
            if (args.length == 0) {
                System.out.print("Enter a file name: ");
                fileName = buffer.readLine();
                fIn = new RandomAccessFile(fileName,"r");
```

Continues

FIGURE **11.13**   *(continued)*

```
        }
        else {
            fIn = new RandomAccessFile(args[0],"r");
            fileName = args[0];
        }
        Htree.decompressFile(fileName,fIn);
        fIn.close();
    } catch(IOException io) {
        System.err.println("Cannot open " + fileName);
    }
  }
}
```

⊡ 11.7 EXERCISES

1. For which probabilities $P(m_i)$ of n symbols is the average length maximal? When is it minimal?

2. Find L_{ave} for the letters X, Y, and Z and their probabilities .05, .05, and .9 and compare it to L_{Huf} computed for single letters and pairs of letters, as in Figure 11.6. Does L_{Huf} satisfactorily approximate L_{ave}? How can we remedy the problem?

3. Assess the complexity of all the implementations of the Huffman algorithm suggested in this chapter.

4. What are the lengths of the Huffman codewords of the least probable messages with respect to each other?

5. In the adaptive Huffman algorithm, first the codeword for an encountered symbol is issued and then the conversion table is updated. Could the table be updated first and then the new codeword for this symbol be issued? Why or why not?

6. The methods `createCodewords()` and `transformTreeToArrayOfLists()` used in the case study seem to be vulnerable because the first thing they both do is access the field `left` of node p, which would be dangerous if p were null; therefore, the body of both methods should apparently be preceded by the condition `if (p != 0)`. Explain why this is not necessary.

7. What problem arises if, in run-length encoding, triples of the form $\langle cm, n, ch \rangle$ are used instead of triples of the form $\langle cm, ch, n \rangle$?

8. Explain the significance of putting all probabilities in order before starting the Shannon-Fano method.

9. In Figure 11.10, $l_1 = l_2 = 4 = 2^2$. In what respect does the choice of $l_1 = l_2 = 16 = 2^4$ simplify the implementation of LZ77?

10. In which situation does LZ77 perform best? Worst?

11. Describe the process of decoding using LZ77. What string is coded by this sequence of codewords: b,31a,23b,30c,21a,32b?

12. Using LZW with the table initialized with the letters a, b, c, decode the string coded as 1 2 4 3 1 4 9 5 8 12 2.

◪ 11.8 Programming Assignments

1. A large number of messages with very low probabilities in a long series of messages require a large number of very long codewords (Hankamer 1979). Instead, one codeword can be assigned to all these messages, and if needed, this codeword is sent along with the message. Write a program for coding and decoding this approach by adapting the Huffman algorithm.

2. Write an encoder and decoder that uses the run-length encoding technique.

3. Write an encoder and a decoder using run-length encoding to transmit voice, with the voice simulated by a certain function f. Voice is generated continuously, but it is measured at $t_0, t_1, \ldots$, where $t_i - t_{i-1} = \delta$, for some time interval δ. If $|f(t_i) - f(t_{i-1})| < \epsilon$ for some tolerance ϵ, then the numbers $f(t_i)$ and $f(t_{i-1})$ are treated as equal. Therefore, for runs of such equal values, a compressed version can be transmitted in the form of a triple $\langle cm, f(t_i), n \rangle$ with cm being a negative number. In Figure 11.14, circles represent the numbers included in a run indicated by the first preceding bullet; in this example, two runs are sent. What is a potential danger of this technique, known also as the *zero-order predictor*? How can this be solved? Try your program on the functions $\frac{\sin n}{n}$ and $\ln n$.

4. Static dictionary techniques are characterized by using a predefined dictionary of patterns encoded with unique codewords. After a dictionary is established, the problem of using it most efficiently still remains. For example, for a dictionary = {*ability, ility, pec, re, res, spect, tab*}, the word *respectability* can be broken down in two ways: *res, pec, tab, ility* and *re, spect, ability;* that is, the first division requires four codewords for this word, whereas the second requires only three. The algorithm parses the word or words and determines which one of the two choices will be made. Of course, for a large dictionary, there may be more than two possible parsings of the same word or phrase. By far the most frequently used technique is a *greedy algorithm* that finds the longest match in the dictionary. For our example, the match *res* is longer than *re;* therefore, the word *respectability* is divided into four components with the greedy strategy. An optimal parsing can be found by adapting a shortest path algorithm.

FIGURE **11.14**   A function representing voice frequency.

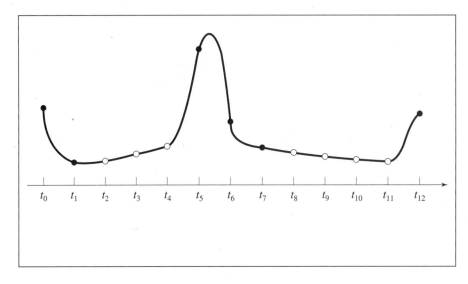

(Schuegraf and Heaps 1974; Bell, Cleary, and Witten 1990). Write a program that for a dictionary of patterns compresses a text file. For each string *s*, create a digraph with *s*.length nodes. Edges are labeled with the dictionary patterns and their codeword lengths are edges' costs. Two nodes *i* and *j* are connected with an edge if the dictionary contains a pattern *s*.charAT(*i*) . . . *s*.charAT(*j*–1). The shortest path represents the shortest sequences of codewords for patterns found in the path.

Bibliography

Data Compression Methods

Bell, Timothy C., Cleary, J. G., and Witten, Ian H., *Text Compression*, Englewood Cliffs, NJ: Prentice Hall, 1990.

Lelever, Debra A. and Hirschberg, Daniel S., "Data Compression," *ACM Computing Surveys* 19 (1987), 261–296.

Lynch, Thomas J., *Data Compression: Techniques and Applications*, New York: Van Nostrand Reinhold, 1985.

Rubin, Frank, "Experiments in Text File Compression," *Communications of the ACM* 19 (1976), 617–623.

Schuegraf, E. J. and Heaps, H. S., "A Comparison of Algorithms for Data-Base Compression by Use of Fragments as Language Elements," *Information Storage and Retrieval* 10 (1974), 309–319.

Smith, Peter D., *An Introduction to Text Processing*, Cambridge, MA: MIT Press, 1990, Ch. 4.

Huffman Coding

Cormack, Gordon V. and Horspool, R. Ingel, "Algorithms for Adaptive Huffman Codes," *Information Processing Letters* 18 (1984), 159–165.

Faller, Newton, "An Adaptive System for Data Compression," *Conference Record of the Seventh IEEE Asilomar Conference on Circuits, Systems, and Computers,* San Francisco: IEEE, 1974, 593–597.

Gallager, Robert G., "Variations on a Theme of Huffman," *IEEE Transactions on Information Theory* IT-24 (1978), 668–674.

Hankamer, M., "A Modified Huffman Procedure with Reduced Memory Requirement," *IEEE Transactions on Communication* COM-27 (1979), 930–932.

Huffman, David A., "A Method for the Construction of Minimum-Redundancy Codes," *Proceedings of the Institute of Radio Engineers* 40 (1952), 1098–1101.

Knuth, Donald E., "Dynamic Huffman Coding," *Journal of Algorithms* 6 (1985), 163–180.

Run-Length Encoding

Pountain, Dick, "Run-Length Encoding," *Byte* 12 (1987), No. 6, 317–320.

Ziv-Lempel Code

Miller, Victor S. and Wegman, Mark N., "Variations on a Theme by Ziv and Lempel," in Apostolico, A. and Galil, Z. (eds.), *Combinatorial Algorithms on Words,* Berlin: Springer, 1985, 131–140.

Welch, Terry A., "A Technique for High-Performance Data Compression," *Computer* 17 (1984), 6, 8–19.

Ziv, Jacob and Lempel, Abraham, "A Universal Algorithm for Sequential Data Compression," *IEEE Transactions on Information Theory* IT-23 (1977), 337–343.

Memory Management

The preceding chapters rarely looked behind the scenes to see how programs are actually executed and how variables of different types are stored. The reason is that this book emphasizes data structures rather than the inner workings of the computer. The latter belongs more to a book about operating systems or assembly language programming than to a discussion of data structures.

But at least in one case, such a reference was inescapable, namely, when discussing recursion in Chapter 5. Using recursion was explained in terms of the run-time stack and how a computer actually works.

The *heap* is the region of main memory from which portions of memory are dynamically allocated upon request of a program. (This heap has nothing to do with the special tree structure called a heap in Section 6.9.) In languages such as FORTRAN, COBOL, or BASIC, the compiler determines how much memory is needed to run programs. In languages that allow dynamic memory allocation, the amount of memory required cannot always be determined prior to the program run. To that end, the heap is used. If a C program requests memory by issuing `malloc()` or `calloc()` and a C++ or Java program does it by issuing a call to `new`, a certain amount of bytes is allocated from the heap, and the address to the first byte of this portion is returned. Also, in these languages, unused memory has to be specifically released by the programmer through `dispose()` in Pascal, `free()` in C, and `delete` in C++. In some languages, there is no need to explicitly release memory. Unused memory is simply abandoned and then automatically reclaimed by the operating system. Automatic storage reclamation is a luxury that is not part of every language environment. It emerged with LISP and it is part of functional languages, but logic languages and most object-oriented languages also have automatic storage reclamation, to mention only Smalltalk, Prolog, Modula-3, and Eiffel.

The maintenance of free memory blocks, assigning specific memory blocks to the user programs if necessary and cleaning memory from unneeded blocks to return them to the memory pool, is performed by a part of the operating system called a *memory manager.* The memory manager also performs other functions, such as scheduling access to shared data, moving code and data between main and secondary memory, and keeping one process away from another. This is particularly important in the multiprogramming system, where many different processes can reside in memory at the same time and the CPU serves for a brief amount of time each of the processes in turn. The processes are put in memory in free spaces and removed if either space is needed for other processes to be served or after their completed execution.

One problem which a well-designed memory manager has to solve is that of the configuration of available memory. In particular, after many allocations and deallocations, the heap is divided into small pieces of available memory sandwiched between chunks of memory in use. If a request comes to allocate *n* bytes of memory, the request may not be met if there is not enough contiguous memory in the heap, although the total of available memory may far surpass *n*. This phenomenon is called *external fragmentation.* Changing memory configuration and, in particular, putting available memory in one part of the heap and allocated memory in another solve this problem. Another problem is *internal fragmentation,* when allocated memory chunks are larger than requested. External fragmentation amounts to the presence of wasted space between allocated segments of memory; internal fragmentation amounts to the presence of unused memory inside the segments.

□ 12.1 THE SEQUENTIAL-FIT METHODS

A simple organization of memory could require a linked list of all memory blocks which is updated after a block is either requested or returned. The blocks on such linked lists can be organized in a variety of ways, according to the block sizes or the block addresses. Whenever a block is requested, a decision has to be made concerning which block to allocate and how to treat the portion of the block exceeding the requested size.

For reasons of efficiency, doubly linked lists of blocks are maintained with links residing in the blocks. Each available block of memory uses a portion of itself for two links. Also, both available and reserved blocks have two fields to indicate their status (available or reserved) and their size.

In the sequential-fit methods, all available memory blocks are linked together, and the list is searched to find a block whose size is larger than or the same as the requested size. A simple policy for handling returned blocks of memory is to coalesce them with neighboring blocks and reflect this fact by properly adjusting the links in the linked list.

The order of searching the list for such a block determines the division of these methods into several categories. The *first-fit* algorithm allocates the first block of memory large enough to meet the request. The *best-fit* algorithm allocates a block which is closest in size to the request. The *worst-fit* method finds the largest block on the list so that, after returning its portion equal to the requested size, the remaining

FIGURE **12.1**   Memory allocation using sequential-fit methods.

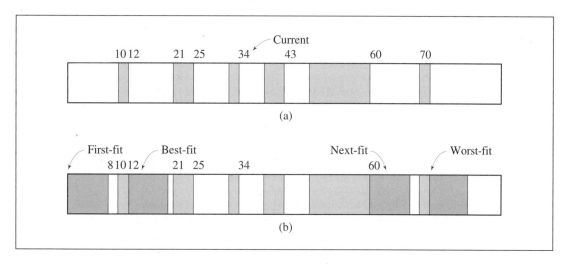

part is large enough to be used in later requests. The *next-fit* method allocates the next available block that is sufficiently large.

Figure 12.1a contains a memory configuration after several requests and returns of memory blocks. Figure 12.1b illustrates which portion of memory would be allocated by which sequential-fit method to satisfy a request for 8KB of memory.

The most efficient method is the first-fit procedure. The next-fit method is of comparable speed but causes more extensive external fragmentation because it scans the list of blocks starting from the current position and reaches the end of the list much earlier than the first-fit method. But the best-fit algorithm is even worse in that respect since it searches for the closest match with respect to size. The parts of blocks remaining after returning the required size are small and practically unusable. The worst-fit algorithm attempts to prevent this type of fragmentation by avoiding, or at least delaying, the creation of small blocks.

The way the blocks are organized on the list determines how fast the search for an available block succeeds or fails. For example, to optimize the best-fit and the worst-fit methods, the blocks should be arranged by size. For other methods, the address ordering is adequate.

□ 12.2 THE NONSEQUENTIAL-FIT METHODS

The sequential-fit methods being what they are, they may become inefficient for large memory. In the case of large memory, a nonsequential search is desirable. One strategy divides memory into an arbitrary number of lists, each list holding blocks of the same size (Ross 1967). Larger blocks are split into smaller blocks to satisfy requests and new lists may be created. Since the number of such lists can become large, they can be organized as a tree.

Another approach is based on the observation that the number of sizes requested by a program is limited, although the sizes may differ from one program to another. Therefore, the lists of blocks of different sizes can be kept short if it can be determined which sizes are the most popular. This leads to an *adaptive exact-fit* technique that dynamically creates and adjusts storage block lists which fit the requests exactly (Oldehoeft and Allan 1985).

In adaptive exact-fit, a size-list of block lists of a particular size returned to the memory pool during the last T allocations is maintained. A block b is added to a particular block list if this block list holds blocks of b's size and b has been returned by the program. When a request comes for a block of b's size, a block from its block list is detached to meet the request. Otherwise a more time-consuming search for a block in memory is triggered using one of the sequential-fit methods.

The exact-fit method disposes of entire block lists if no request comes for a block from this list in the last T allocations. In this way, lists of infrequently used block sizes are not maintained, and the list of block lists is kept small to allow a sequential search of this list. Because it is not a sequential search of the memory, the exact-fit method is not considered a sequential-fit method.

Figure 12.2 contains an example of a size-list and a heap created using the adaptive exact-fit method. The memory is fragmented, but if a request comes for a block of size 7, the allocation can be done immediately, since the size-list has an entry for size 7; thus, memory does not have to be searched. A simple algorithm for allocating blocks is as follows:

```
t = 0;
allocate (reqSize)
   t++;
   if a block list b1 with reqSize blocks is on sizeList
      lastref(b1) = t;
      b = head of blocks(b1);
      if b was the only block accessible from b1
         detach b1 from sizeList;
   else b = search-memory-for-a-block-of(reqSize);
   dispose of all block lists on sizeList for which t - lastref(b1) < T;
   return b;
```

A procedure for returning blocks is even simpler.

This algorithm highlights the problem of memory fragmentation. The algorithm must be expanded to deal with this problem successfully. One solution is to write a method to compact memory after a certain number of allocations and deallocations. A noncompacting approach may consist in liquidating the size-list and building it anew after some predetermined period. The authors of this method claim that fragmentation problems "failed to materialize," but that can be attributed to the configurations of their tests. Such problems certainly materialize in sequential-fit methods and in another nonsequential-fit strategy to be discussed in the next section.

FIGURE **12.2**   An example configuration of a size-list and heap created by the adaptive exact-fit method.

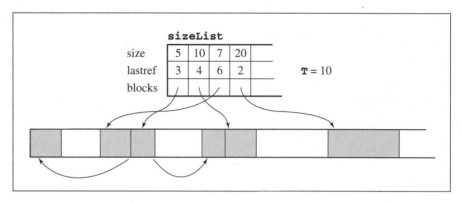

12.2.1 Buddy Systems

Nonsequential memory management methods known as *buddy systems* do not just assign memory in sequential slices, but divide it into two buddies which are merged whenever possible. In the buddy system, two buddies are never free. A block can have either a buddy used by the program or none.

The classic buddy system is the *binary buddy system* (Knowlton 1965). The binary buddy system assumes that storage consists of 2^m locations for some integer m, with addresses $0, \ldots, 2^m - 1$, and that these locations can be organized into blocks whose lengths can only be powers of 2. There is also an array `avail[]` such that, for each $i = 0, \ldots, m$, `avail[i]` is the head of a doubly linked list of blocks of the same size, 2^i.

The name of this method is derived from the fact that each block of memory (except the entire memory) is coupled with a buddy *of the same size* which participates with the block in reserving and returning chunks of memory. The buddy of a block of length 2^i is determined by complementing bit $i + 1$ in the address of this block. This is strictly related to the lengths of blocks, which can only be powers of 2. In particular, all blocks of size 2^i have 0s in the i rightmost positions and differ only in the remaining bits. For example, if memory has only eight locations, then the possible addresses of blocks of size one are $\{000, 001, 010, 011, 100, 101, 110, 111\}$, addresses of blocks of size two are $\{000, 010, 100, 110\}$, of size four $\{000, 100\}$, and of size eight $\{000\}$. Note that in the second set of addresses, the last bit is 0, and the addresses refer to blocks of size 2^1. The addresses in the third set have two ending 0s, since the size of the blocks is 2^2. Now, for the second set, there are two pairs of blocks and their buddies: $\{(000, 010), (100, 110)\}$; for the third set, there is only one pair, $(000, 100)$. Hence, the difference between the address of a block of size 2^i and the address of its buddy is only in bit $i + 1$.

If a request arrives to allocate a memory block of size s, then the buddy system returns a memory block whose size is greater than or equal to s. Since there are many candidates for such blocks, the list of such blocks is checked in `avail[]` whose size k is the smallest among all $k \geq s$. This list of blocks can be found in location `avail[k]`. If the list is empty, then the next list of blocks is checked in position $k + 1$, then in

FIGURE **12.3**　　　Block structure in the binary buddy system.

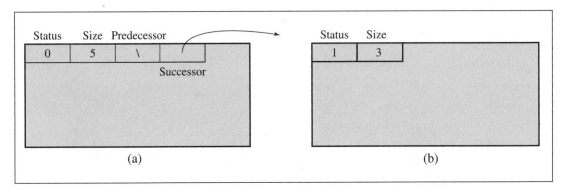

(a)　　　　　　　　　　　　　　　　　(b)

position $k + 2$, and so on. The search continues until a nonempty list is found (or the end of avail[ ] is reached), and then a block is detached from it.

The algorithm for memory allocation in binary buddy systems is as follows:

```
size of memory = 2^m for some m;
avail[i] = -1 for i = 0, ..., m-1;
avail[m] = first address in memory;
reserve(reqSize)
    roundedSize = ⌈lg(reqSize)⌉;
    availSize = min(roundedSize, ..., m) for which avail[availSize] > -1;
    if no such availSize exists
        failure;
    block = avail[availSize];
    detach block from list avail[availSize];
    while (rounded Size < availSize)    // while an available block
        availSize--;                    // is too large - split it;
        block = left half of block;
        insert buddy of block in list avail[availSize];
    return block;
```

Each free block of the buddy system should include four fields indicating its status, its size, and its two neighbors in the list. On the other hand, reserved blocks include only a status field and a size field. Figure 12.3a illustrates the structure of a free block in the buddy system. The block is marked as free with the status field set to 0. The size is specified as 2^5 locations. No predecessor is specified, so this block is pointed to by avail[5]. The size of its successor is also 2^5 locations. Figure 12.3b illustrates a reserved block whose status field is set to 1.

Figure 12.4 contains an example of reserving three blocks, assuming that the memory in use is of size $2^7 = 128$ locations. First, the entire memory is free (Figure 12.4a). Then, 18 locations are requested, so roundedSize = ⌈lg(18)⌉ = 5. But avail-Size = 7, so the memory is split into two buddies, each of size 2^6. The second buddy

Figure **12.4**   Reserving three blocks of memory using the binary buddy system.

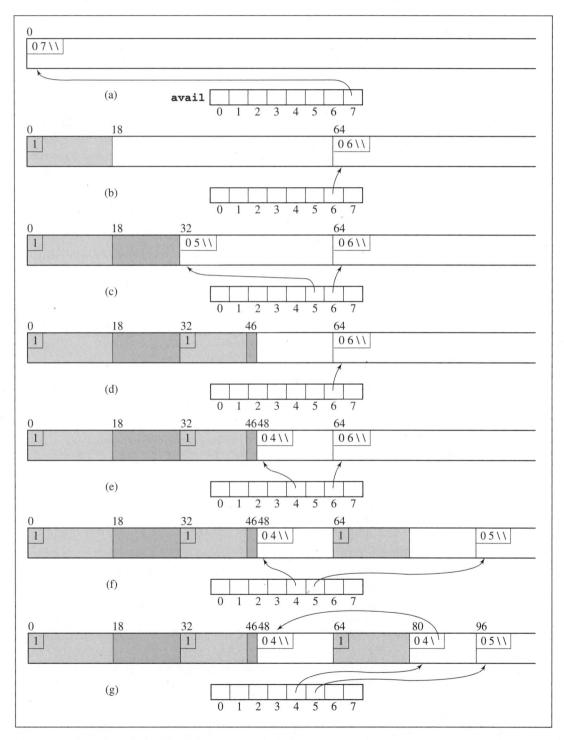

is marked as available by setting the status field and including it into the list avail[6] (Figure 12.4b). availSize is still greater than roundedSize, so another iteration of the while loop of reserve() is executed. The first block is split into two and the second buddy is included in the list avail[5] (Figure 12.4c). The first buddy is marked as reserved and returned to the caller of reserve() for use. Note that only a portion of the returned block is really needed. However, the entire block is marked as reserved.

Next, a block of 14 locations is requested; now, roundedSize = ⌈lg(14)⌉ = 4, availSize = 5, and the block pointed to by avail[5] is claimed (Figure 12.4d). This block is too large since roundedSize < availSize, so the block is divided into two buddies. The first buddy is marked as reserved and returned, and the second is included in a list (Figure 12.4e). Finally, a block of 16 locations is requested. After two iterations of the while loop of reserve(), the configuration pictured in Figure 12.4g emerges; there are two available blocks of 16 locations and both are linked up together in list avail[4].

To be sure, blocks of memory are not only claimed, but they are returned; hence, they have to be included in the pool of available blocks. Before they are included, the status of each block's buddy is checked. If the buddy is available, the block is combined with its buddy to create a block twice as large as before the combination. If the buddy of the new block is available, it is also combined with its buddy, resulting in a still larger block of memory. This process continues until the entire memory is combined into one block or a buddy is not available. This coalescing creates blocks of available memory as large as possible. The algorithm of including a block in the pool of available blocks is as follows:

```
include(block)
    blockSize = size(block);
    buddy = address(block) with bit blockSize+1 set to its complement;
    while status(buddy) is 0                    // buddy has not
            and size(buddy) == blockSize        // been claimed;
            and blockSize != lg(size of memory) // buddy exists;
        detach buddy from list avail[blockSize];
        block = block plus body;  // coalesce block and its buddy;
        set status(block) to 0;
        blockSize++;
        buddy = address(now extended block) with bit blockSize+1 set to its complement;
    include block in list avail[blockSize];
```

Figure 12.5 illustrates this process. A block previously claimed is now released (Figure 12.5a), and because the buddy of this block is free, it is combined with the block resulting in double-sized block, which is included in the list avail[5] (Figure 12.5b). Releasing another block allows the memory manager to combine this block with its buddy and the resulting block with its buddy (Figure 12.5c). Note that the free portion of the leftmost block (marked with the darker screen) did not participate in this coalescing process and is still considered occupied. Also, the two rightmost blocks in Figure 12.5c, although adjacent, were not combined because they are not buddies. Buddies in the binary buddy method have to be of the same size.

FIGURE **12.5**   (a) Returning a block to the pool of blocks, (b) resulting in coalescing one block with its buddy. (c) Returning another block leads to two coalescings.

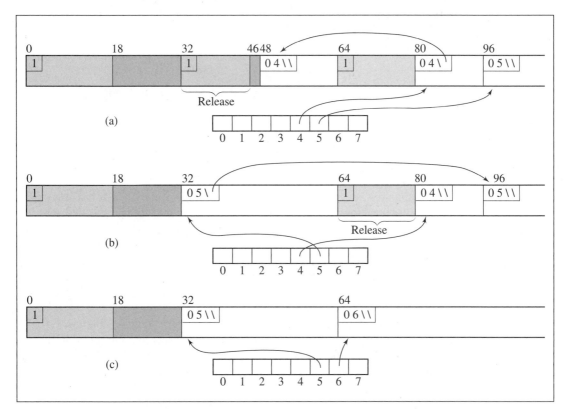

The binary buddy system, although relatively efficient in terms of speed, may be inefficient in terms of space. Figure 12.4d shows that the two leftmost blocks amount to a size of 48 locations, but only 32 of them are in use, since the user really needs 18 + 14 locations. This means that one-third of these two blocks is wasted. This can get even worse if the number of locations requested is always slightly more than a power of 2. In this case, approximately 50% of memory is not in actual use. This is a problem with internal fragmentation that results from the need to round all requests to the nearest larger power of 2.

Also, there may be a problem with external fragmentation; a request may be re- fused although the amount of available space is sufficient to meet it. For example, for the configuration of memory in Figure 12.4g, a request for 50 locations is refused be- cause there is no block available with a size of 64 locations or more. A request for 33 locations is treated similarly and for the same reason, although there are 33 available consecutive locations. But one of these locations belongs to another block which puts it out of reach.

These problems are brought about by the fact that the binary buddy system uses a simple division of blocks into two even parts, which results in the division of memory not sufficiently tuned to incoming requests. The sequence of block sizes possible in this system is $1, 2, 4, 8, 16, \ldots, 2^m$. An improvement of the binary buddy system can be obtained if this sequence is rendered by the recurrence equation

$$s_i = \begin{cases} 1 & \text{if } i = 0 \\ s_{i-1} + s_{i-1} & \text{otherwise} \end{cases}$$

which can be considered a particular case of a more general equation:

$$s_i = \begin{cases} c_1 & \text{if } i = 0, \\ \vdots & \vdots \\ c_k & \text{if } i = k-1 \\ s_{i-1} + s_{i-2} & \text{otherwise} \end{cases}$$

If $k = 1$, then this equation renders the equation for the binary buddy system. If $k = 2$, then the obtained formula is a very familiar equation for a Fibonacci sequence:

$$s_i = \begin{cases} 1 & \text{if } i = 0,1 \\ s_{i-1} + s_{i-1} & \text{otherwise} \end{cases}$$

This leads to the *Fibonacci buddy system* developed by Daniel S. Hirschberg. He chose 3 and 5 as the values for s_0 and s_1. If $k > 2$, then we enter the realm of the *generalized Fibonacci systems* (Hinds 1975).

The problem with the Fibonacci buddy system is that finding a buddy of a block is not always simple. In the binary buddy system, the information stored in the size field of the block is sufficient to compute the address of the buddy. If the size holds the number k, then the address of the buddy is found by complementing the bit $k + 1$ in the address of the block. This works regardless of whether the block has a right buddy or a left buddy. The reason for this simplicity is that only powers of 2 for the sizes of all blocks are used, and each block and its buddy are of the same size.

In the Fibonacci system, this approach is inapplicable, yet it is necessary to know whether a returned block has a right or a left buddy in order to combine the two. Not surprisingly, finding the buddy of a block may be rather demanding in terms of time or space. To this end, Hirschberg used a table which could have nearly 1000 entries if buffers of up to 17,717 locations are allowed. His method can be simplified if a proper flag is included in each block, but a binary Left/Right flag may be insufficient. If block b_1 marked as Left is coalesced with its buddy, block b_2, then the question is: How do you find the buddy of the resulting block, b_3? An elegant solution uses two binary flags instead of one: a buddy-bit and a memory-bit (Cranston and Thomas 1975). If a block b_1 is split into blocks b_{left} and b_{right}, then buddy-bit(b_{left}) = 0, buddy-bit(b_{right}) = 1, memory-bit(b_{left}) = buddy-bit(b_1), and finally, memory-bit(b_{right}) = memory-bit(b_1) (see Figure 12.6a). The last two assignments preserve some information about predecessors: Memory-bit(b_{left}) indicates whether its parent is a left or right buddy, and memory-bit(b_{right}) is a bit of information to indicate the same status for one of the predecessors of its parent. Note that the coalescing process is an exact reversal of splitting (see Figure 12.6b).

FIGURE **12.6**   (a) Splitting a block of size *Fib(k)* into two buddies using the buddy-bit and the memory-bit.
(b) Coalescing two buddies utilizing information stored in buddy- and memory-bits.

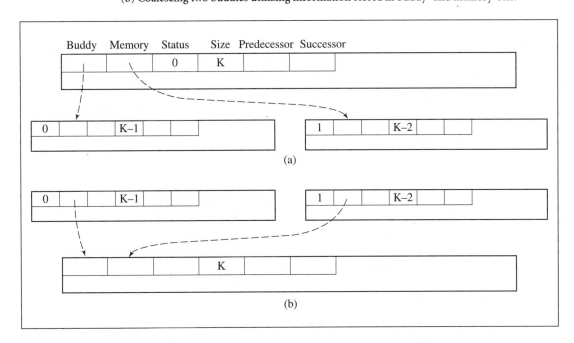

(a)

(b)

The algorithms for reserving blocks and for returning them are in many respects
similar to the algorithms used for the binary buddy system. An algorithm for reserving blocks is as follows:

```
avail[i] = -1 for i = 0, ..., m-1;
avail[m] = first address in memory;
```

```
reserveFib(reqSize)
    availSize = the position of the first Fibonacci number greater than reqSize
                for which avail[availSize] > -1;
    if no such availSize exists
        failure;
    block = avail[availSize];
    detach block from list avail[availSize];
    while Fib(availSize-1) > reqSize // while an available block is
                                     // too large - split it; choose
        if reqSize ≤ Fib(availSize-2) // smaller of the buddies if it's
            insert block's larger part in avail[availSize-1]; // large enough;
            block = block's smaller part;
```

```
    else insert block's smaller part in avail[availSize-2];
        block = block's larger part;
    availSize = size(block);
    set flags(block);
    set flags(block's buddy);
return block;
```

Another extension of the binary buddy system in a *weighted buddy system* (Shen and Peterson 1974). Its goal, as in the case of Fibonacci systems, is to decrease the amount of internal fragmentation by allowing more block sizes than in the binary system. Block sizes in the weighted buddy system in memory of 2^m unary blocks are 2^k for $0 \le k \le m$, and $3 \cdot 2^k$, for $0 \le k \le m - 2$; the sizes are 1, 2, 3, 4, 6, 8, 12, 16, 24, 32, ..., which is nearly twice as many different sizes than in the binary method. If necessary, blocks of size 2^k are split into blocks $3 \cdot 2^{k-2}$ and 2^{k-2}, and the blocks of size $3 \cdot 2^k$ are split into blocks 2^{k+1} and 2^k. Note that the buddy of a 2^k block cannot be uniquely determined because it can have a right buddy either of size 2^{k+1} or $3 \cdot 2^k$, or it can have a left buddy of size 2^{k-1}. To distinguish between these three cases, a two-bit flag *type* is added to each block. However, simulations indicate that the weighted buddy system is three times slower and generates larger external fragmentation than the binary buddy system. As mentioned, the weighted buddy system requires two additional bits per block, and the algorithm is more complex than in the binary buddy system, since it requires considering more cases when coalescing blocks.

A buddy system that takes a middle course between the binary system and the weighted system is a *dual buddy system* (Page and Hagins 1986). This method maintains two separate memory areas, one with block sizes 1, 2, 4, 8, 16, ..., 2^i, ... and another with block sizes 3, 6, 9, 18, 36, ..., $3 \cdot 2^j$, ... In this way, the binary buddy method is applied in two areas. Internal fragmentation of the dual method is more or less halfway between that of the binary and weighted methods. External fragmentation in the dual buddy system is almost the same as that of the binary buddy system.

To conclude this discussion, observe that internal fragmentation is often inversely proportional to external fragmentation because internal fragmentation is avoided if allocated blocks are as close in size to the requested blocks as possible. But this means that some small splinter blocks are generated which are of little use. These small blocks can be compacted together to form a large block with sequential-fit methods, but compaction does not square very well with the buddy system approach. In fact, the variant buddy system, which is an elaboration of the weighted buddy method, attempts to compact memory, but the complexity of the algorithm undermines its usefulness (Bromley 1980).

♠ 12.3 GARBAGE COLLECTION

As mentioned at the beginning of this chapter, some languages have automatic storage reclamation in their environment so that no explicit return on unused memory cells must be done by any program. The program can allocate memory through the function new, but there is no need to return back to the operating system the allocated memory block if the block is not needed any longer. The block is simply abandoned, and it will be reclaimed by a method called a *garbage collector* that is automatically invoked to collect unused memory cells when the program is idle or when memory resources are exhausted.

The garbage collector views the heap as a collection of memory cells, or nodes, each cell composed of several fields. Depending on the garbage collector, the fields can be different. For example, in LISP, a cell has two pointers, *head* and *tail* (or in LISP terminology, *car* and *cdr*), to other cells, except for atomic cells that have no pointers. The cells include headers with such elements as an atom/nonatom flag and a marked/unmarked flag. Data that are included may be stored in yet another field of a cell or in the portion of atomic cells used for pointers in nonatomic cells. Moreover, if variable sized cells are used, the header includes the number of bytes in the data field. Using more than two pointer fields is also possible. References to all linked structures currently utilized by the program are stored in a *root set* which contains all *root pointers*. The garbage collector's task is to determine those parts of memory which are accessible from any of these pointers and parts which are not currently in use and can be returned to the free memory pool.

Garbage collection methods usually include two phases, which may be implemented as distinct passes or can be integrated:

1. The *marking* phase—to identify all currently used cells.

2. The *reclamation* phase—when all unmarked cells are returned to the memory pool; this phase can also include heap compaction.

12.3.1 Mark-and-Sweep

A classical method of collecting garbage is the *mark-and-sweep* technique, which clearly distinguishes the two phases. First, memory cells currently in use are marked by traversing each linked structure, and then the memory is swept to glean unused (garbage) cells and put them together in a memory pool.

Marking

A simple marking procedure looks very much like preorder tree traversal. If a node is not marked, then it is marked, and if it is not an atomic node, marking continues for its *head* and for its *tail*:

```
marking (node)
   if node is not marked
      mark node;
      if node is not an atom
         marking(head(node));
         marking(tail(node));
```

This procedure is called for each element of the root set. The problem with this succinct and elegant algorithm is that it may cause the run-time stack to overflow, which is a very real prospect considering the fact that the list being marked can be very long. Therefore, an explicit stack can be used so that there is no need to store on the run-time stack the data necessary to properly resume execution after returning from recursive calls. Here is an example of an algorithm that uses an explicit stack:

```
markingWithStack (node)
   push(node);
   while stack is not empty
      node = pop();
      while node is an unmarked nonatom
         mark node;
         push(tail(node));
         node = head(node);
      if node is an unmarked atom
         mark node;
```

The problem of an overflow is not avoided altogether. If the stack is implemented as an array, the array may turn out to be too small. If it is implemented as a linked list, it may be impossible to use, since the stack requires memory resources which have just been used up and in the restoration of which the stack was supposed to participate. There are two ways to avoid this predicament: by using a stack of limited size and invoking some operations in case of stack overflow or by trying not to use any stack at all.

A useful algorithm that requires no explicit stack was developed by Schorr and Waite. The basic idea is to, in a sense, incorporate the stack in the list being processed. This technique belongs in the same category as the stackless tree traversal techniques discussed in Section 6.4.3. In the Schorr and Waite marking method, some links are temporarily reversed when traversing the list to "remember" the path back, and their original setting is restored after marking all cells accessible from a position in which the reversal has been performed. When a marked node or an atom is encountered, the algorithm returns to the preceding node. However, it can return to a node through the *head* field or through the *tail* field. In the former case, the *tail* path has to be explored, and the algorithm has to use a marker to indicate whether both *head* and *tail* paths have been checked or only the *head* path has been checked. To that end, the algorithm uses one additional bit called a *tag* bit. If the *head* of a cell is accessed, then the tag bit remains zero so that, upon return to this cell, the path accessible from *tail* will be followed, in which case the tag bit is set to one and reset to zero upon return. The summary of the algorithms is as follows:

```
invertLink (p1, p2, p3)
   tmp = p3;
   p3 = p1;
   p1 = p2;
   p2 = tmp;

SWmarking (curr)
   prev = null;
   while (1)
      mark curr;
      if head(curr) is marked or atom
```

```
        if head(curr) is an unmarked atom
            mark head(curr);
    while tail(curr) is marked or atom
        if tail(curr) is an unmarked atom
            mark tail(curr);
        while prev is not null and tag(prev) is 1// go back
            tag(prev) = 0;
            invertLink(curr,prev,tail(prev));
        if prev is not null
            invertLink(curr,prev,head(prev));
        else finished;
    tag(curr) = 1;
    invertLink(prev,curr,tail(curr));
else invertLink(prev,curr,head(curr));
```

Figure 12.7 illustrates an example. Each part of this figure shows changes in the list after the indicated operations have been performed. Note that atom nodes do not require a tag bit. Figure 12.7a contains the list before marking. Each nonatomic node has four parts: a marking bit, a tag bit, and *head* and *tail* fields. The marking and tag bits are initialized to 0. There is one more bit not shown in this figure, an atom/nonatom flag.

Here is a description of each iteration of the `while` loop and the figure number which contains the structure of the list after that iteration.

Iteration 1: Execute `invertLink(prev,curr,`*head*`(curr))` (Figure 12.7b).

Iteration 2: Execute another `invertLink(prev,curr,`*head*`(curr))` (Figure 12.7c).

Iteration 3: Execute still another `invertLink(prev,curr,`*head*`(curr))` (Figure 12.7d).

Iteration 4: Mark *tail*(curr) and execute `invertLink(curr,prev,`*head*`(prev))` (Figure 12.7e), execute another `invertLink(curr,prev,`*head*`(prev))` (Figure 12.7f), set *tag*(curr) to 1, and execute `invertLink(prev,curr,`*tail*`(curr))` (Figure 12.7g).

Iteration 5: Mark *tail*(curr) to 1, set *tag*(prev) to 0, and execute `invertLink(curr,prev,`*tail*`(prev))` (Figure 12.7h). Execute `invertLink(curr,prev,`*head*`(prev))` (Figure 12.7i), set *tag*(curr) to 1, and execute `invertLink(prev,curr,`*tail*`(curr))` (Figure 12.7j).

Iteration 6: Set *tag*(prev) to 0 and execute `invertLink(curr,prev,`*tail*`(prev))` (Figure 12.7k). The algorithm completes and `prev` becomes *null.*

Note that the algorithm has no problem with cycles in lists. `SWmarking()` is slower than `markingWithStack()`, since it requires two visits per cell, reference maintenance, and an additional bit. Hence, disposing of a stack does not seem to be the best solution. Other approaches attempt to combine a stack with some form of overflow handling. Schorr and Waite proposed such a solution by resorting to their link inversion technique if a fixed-length stack becomes full. Other techniques are more discriminating about what information should be stored on the stack. For example, `markingWithStack()` unnecessarily pushes onto the stack the nodes which have empty *tail* fields, nodes whose processing is finished after the *head* path is finished.

FIGURE **12.7**   An example of execution of the Schorr and Waite algorithm for marking used memory cells.

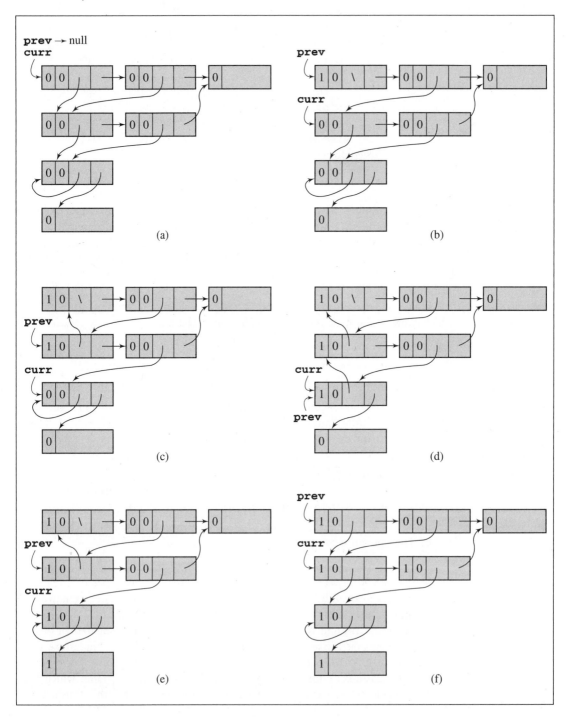

FIGURE **12.7**   *(continued)*

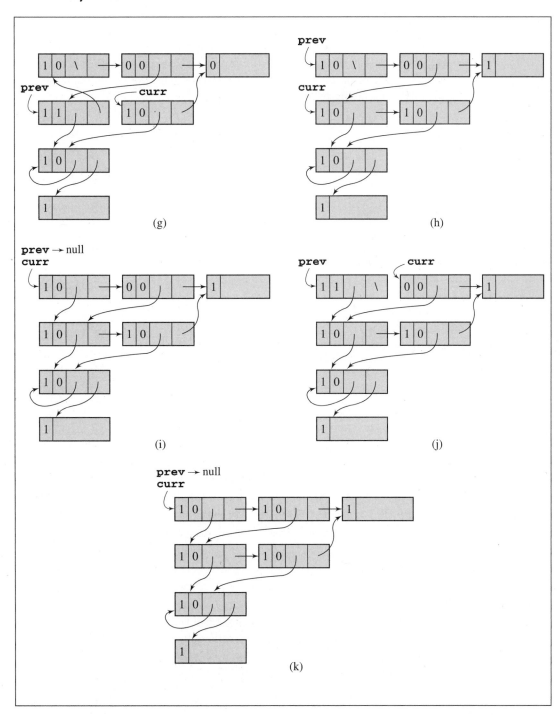

The method devised by Wegbreit requires no tag bit and uses a bit stack instead of a reference stack to store one bit for each node on the trace path whose *head* and *tail* fields both reference nonatoms. The trace path is the path from the current node to the root pointer. But as in the Schorr and Waite algorithm, link inversion is still in use. An improvement of this method is the fastmark algorithm (Kurokawa 1981). As in Wegbreit's method, the fastmark algorithm retains information about nodes which refer to nonatoms on the stack. But the stack stores references to nodes, not bits, so link inversion is not necessary.

```
fastmark(node)
    if node is not an atom
        mark node;
        while (true)
            if both head(node) and tail(node) are marked or atoms
                if stack is empty
                    finished;
                else node = pop();
            else if only tail(node) is not marked nor is it atom
                mark tail(node);
                node = tail(node);
            else if only head(node) is not marked nor is it atom
                mark head(node);
                node = head(node);
            else if both head(node) and tail(node) are not marked nor are they atoms
                mark both head(node) and tail(node);
                push(tail(node));
                node = head(node);
```

The reader is encouraged to apply this algorithm to the list in Figure 12.7a. However, the vexing problem of stack overflow is still not completely resolved. Although the fastmark algorithm claims to require approximately 30 locations in most situations, some degenerate cases may occur which require thousands of locations in the stack. Therefore, fastmark has to be extended to be robust. The basic idea of the resulting *stacked-node-checking algorithm* is to delete from the stack nodes that are already marked or nodes whose *head* or *tail* path has already been traced. However, even this improved algorithm runs out of space occasionally, in which situation "it gives up and advises a fatal stack overflow error" (Kurokawa 1981). Hence, the Schorr and Waite approach with its two techniques, stacking and list reversal, is more reliable although slower.

Space Reclamation

After all the cells currently in use have been marked, the reclamation process returns all unmarked locations in memory to the heap pool by going sequentially through the heap, cell by cell, starting from the highest address and inserting all unmarked locations in the *avail-list*. Upon completion of this process, all locations on the *avail-list* are in ascending order. During this process, all mark bits are reset to 0 so that at the end the mark bits of all used and unused locations are 0. This simple algorithm is as follows:

```
sweep()
    for each location from the last to the first
        if mark(location) is 0
            insert location in front of availList;
        else set mark(location) to 0;
```

The `sweep()` algorithm makes a pass through the entire memory. If we add a pass required for marking and the subsequent maintenance of the `availList` containing locations sparsely scattered throughout the heap, this rather undesirable situation calls for improvement.

Compaction

After the reclamation process is complete, the available locations are interspersed with the cells being used by the program. This requires *compaction*. If all available cells are in contiguous order, then there is no need to maintain the `availList`. Also, if garbage collection is used for reclaiming cells of variable cells, then having all available cells in sequence is highly desirable. Compaction is also necessary when garbage collection processes virtual memory. In this way, responses to memory requests can be performed with a minimal number of accesses. Another situation in which compacting is beneficial is when the run-time stack and a heap are used at the same time. The heap and the stack are in opposite sides of memory and they grow toward one another. If occupied memory cells on the heap can be kept away from the stack, then the stack has more room for expansion.

A simple *two-pointer algorithm* for heap compaction uses an approach similar to the one utilized in partitioning in quicksort: Two references scan the heap starting from opposite sides of memory. After the first reference finds an unmarked cell and the second finds a marked cell, the contents of the marked cell are moved to the unmarked cell and its new location is recorded in the old location. This process continues after the references cross. Then, the compacted part is scanned to readjust the *head* and *tail* references. If the references of the copied cells refer to locations beyond the compacted area, the old locations are accessed to retrieve the new address. Here is the algorithm:

```
compact()
    lo = the bottom of heap;
    hi = the top of heap;
    while lo < hi   // scan the entire heap;
        while cell(lo) is marked
            lo++;
        while cell(hi) is not marked
            hi++;
        unmark cell(hi);
        move cell(hi) to position *lo;
        tail cell(hi--) = lo++; // leave forwarding address;
    lo = the bottom of heap;
    while lo <= hi        // scan only the compacted area;
```

FIGURE **12.8**   An example of heap compaction.

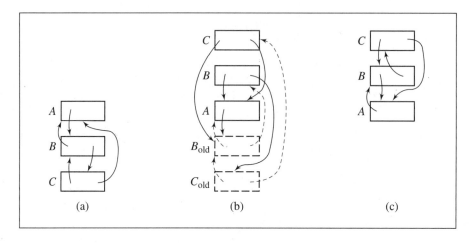

```
if  cell(lo)  is not atom and head(cell(lo)) > hi
    headcell(lo)) =  tail( head(cell(lo)));
if  cell(lo)  is not atom and tail(cell(lo)) > hi
    tail(cell(lo)) =  tail( tail(cell(lo)));
lo++;
```

Figure 12.8 illustrates this process in the case of two available spots in front of cell *A* to which cells *B* and *C* can be moved. Figure 12.8a illustrates the situation in the heap before compaction. In Figure 12.8b, cells B and C have been moved into these spots with the *tail* fields of the old cells indicating the new positions. Figure 12.8c illustrates the compacted part of the heap after checking the *head* and *tail* fields of all cells and updating them in case they referred to positions beyond the compacted area.

This simple algorithm is inefficient in that it requires one pass through the heap to mark cells, one pass to move marked cells into contiguous locations, and one pass through the compacted area to update references; two and a half heap passes are required. One way to reduce the number of passes is to integrate marking and sweeping, which opens up a new category of methods.

12.3.2 Copying Methods

Copying algorithms are cleaner than the previous methods in that they do not touch garbage. They process only the cells accessible from the root pointers and put them together; the unprocessed cells are available. An example of a copying method is the *stop-and-copy algorithm* which divides the heap in two *semispaces,* one of which is only used for allocating memory (Fenichel and Yochelson 1969). After the allocation reference reaches the end of the semispace, all the cells being used are copied to the second semispace, which becomes an active space, and the program resumes execution (see Figure 12.9).

FIGURE **12.9**   (a) A situation in the heap before copying the contents of cells in use from semispace$_1$ to semispace$_2$ and (b) the situation right after copying. All used cells are packed contiguously.

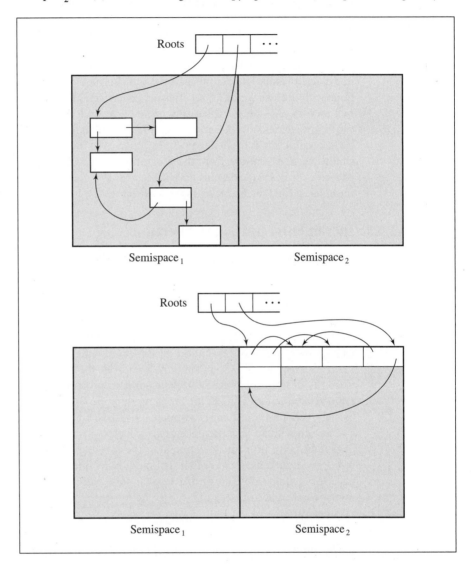

Lists can be copied using breadth-first traversal (Cheney 1970). If lists were just binary trees with no cross references, the algorithm would be the same as the breadth-first tree traversal discussed in Section 6.4.1. However, lists can have cycles, and cells on one list can point to cells on another. In the latter case, this algorithm would produce multiple copies of the same cell. In the former case it would fall into an infinite loop. The problem can be easily solved, as in compact(), by retaining a forward address in the cell being copied. This allows the copying procedure to refer to a cell after it has already been copied. This algorithm requires no marking phase and no stack. The breadth-first traversal also allows it to combine two tasks: copying lists and updating references. The algorithm deals with garbage only indirectly because it does not really access unneeded cells. The more garbage that is in memory, the faster the algorithm.

Note that the cost of garbage collection decreases with the increase in the size of the heap (semispaces). Actually, not only does the number of collections drop with the increase of the heap, but the time per one collection decreases, which is a more unexpected result. For example, a program run in 4MB memory requires 34 collections with the average of 6.8 seconds per collection. The same program run in 16MB memory requires only 3 collections with 2.7 seconds per collection—a very significant improvement. To be sure, if memory is really large (64MB in this example), no garbage collection is needed (Appel 1987). This also indicates that shifting the responsibility for free locations from the programmer (as in C++ or Pascal) to the garbage collector (as in Java) does not have to lead to slower programs. All this is true under the assumption that a large memory is available.

12.3.3 Incremental Garbage Collection

Garbage collectors are invoked automatically when the available memory resources become scanty. If this happens during the execution of a program, the garbage collector suspends program execution until the garbage collector finishes its task. Garbage collection may take several seconds, which may turn into minutes in time-sharing systems. This situation may not be acceptable in real-time systems in which the fast response of a program is vital. Therefore, it is often desirable to create *incremental garbage collectors* whose execution is interleaved with the execution of the program. Program execution is suspended only for a brief moment, allowing the collector to clean the heap to some extent, leaving some unprocessed portion of the heap to be cleaned later. But therein lies the problem. After the collector partially processes some lists, the program can change or mutate those lists. For this reason, a program used in connection with an incremental garbage collection is called a *mutator*. Such changes have to be taken into consideration after the collector resumes execution, possibly to reprocess some cells or entire lists. This additional burden indicates that incremental collectors require more effort than regular collectors. In fact, it has been shown that incremental collectors require twice the processing power of regular collectors (Wadler 1976).

Copying Methods in Incremental Garbage Collection

An incremental algorithm based on the stop-and-copy technique has been devised by Henry Baker (1978). As in stop-and-copy, the Baker algorithm also uses two semispaces, called *fromspace* and *tospace*, which are both active to ensure proper cooperation between the mutator and the collector. The basic idea is to allocate cells in tospace starting from its top and always copy the same number, k, of cells from fromspace to tospace upon request. In this way, the collector can perform its task without incurring any undue interruption of the mutator's work. After all reachable cells have been copied to tospace, the roles of the semispaces are interchanged.

The collector maintains two references. The first reference is *scan*, which points to a cell whose *head* and *tail* lists should be copied to tospace if they still are in fromspace. Since these lists may be larger than *k*, they may not be processed at one time. Up to *k* cells accessible by breadth-first traversal are copied from fromspace, and the copies are put at the end of the queue. This queue is simply accessible by the second reference, *bottom*, which points to the beginning of the free space in tospace. The collector can process *tail* of the current cell during the same time slice, but it may wait until the next turn. Figure 12.10 contains an example. If a request comes to allocate a cell whose *head* points to *P* and *tail* to *Q* (as in LISP's *cons*(*P, Q*)), with both *P* and *Q* residing in tospace, then a new cell is allocated in the upper part of tospace with both its reference fields properly initialized. Assuming that *k* = 2, two cells are copied from the *head* list of the cell pointed to by *scan*, and the *tail* is processed when the next request comes. As in stop-and-copy, Baker's algorithm retains a forwarding address in the original cell in fromspace to its copy in tospace just in case later allocations refer to this original.

Special care must be taken when the *head* and/or *tail* of a cell being allocated refer to a cell in fromspace that is either already copied or still in fromspace. Because the cells at the top of tospace are not processed by the collector, retaining a reference in any of them to fromspace cells leads to fatal consequences after fromspace becomes tospace because the latter cells are now considered available and filled with new contents. The mutator could at one point use the reference to the original, and at a later point could use a copy, leading to inconsistencies. Hence, the mutator is preceded by a *read barrier* which precludes utilizing references to cells in fromspace. In the case of a reference to fromspace, we have to check whether this cell has a forwarding address, an address in its *tail* to a location in tospace. If the answer is yes, the forwarding address is used in the allocation. Otherwise, the cell referred to in the current allocation has to be copied *before* the actual allocation takes place. For example, if the *head* of a cell to be allocated is to point to *P*, a cell in fromspace which has already been copied, as illustrated in Figure 12.11a, *P*'s new address is stored in *head* (see Figure 12.11b). If the *tail* of the new cell is to point to *Q*, which is still untouched in fromspace, *Q* is copied to tospace (along with one descendant, since *k* = 2) and only afterward is the *tail* of the new cell initialized to the copy of *Q*.

Baker's algorithm lends itself to various modifications and improvements. For example, to avoid constant condition tests when allocating new cells, an indirection field is included in every cell. If a cell is in tospace, the indirection field points to itself; otherwise, it points to its copy in tospace (Brooks 1984). Tests are avoided, but indirection references have to be maintained for every cell instead. Another way to solve this problem is by utilizing hardware facilities if available. For example, memory protection facilities can prevent the mutator's access to cells not processed by the collector: All pages of the heap with unprocessed cells are read-protected (Ellis, Li, and Appel 1988). If the mutator attempts to access such a page, the access is trapped and an exception raised, forcing the collector to process this page so that the mutator can resume execution. But this method can undermine the incremental collection, since after the semispaces change roles, traps are invoked frequently, and each trap requires that an entire page of the heap be processed. Some additional provisions may be needed such as not requiring a scan of the entire page in case of a trap. On the other hand, if the heap is not accessed too frequently, this is not a problem.

FIGURE **12.10**   A situation in memory (a) before and (b) after allocating a cell with *head* and *tail* references referring to cells *P* and *Q* in tospace according to the Baker algorithm.

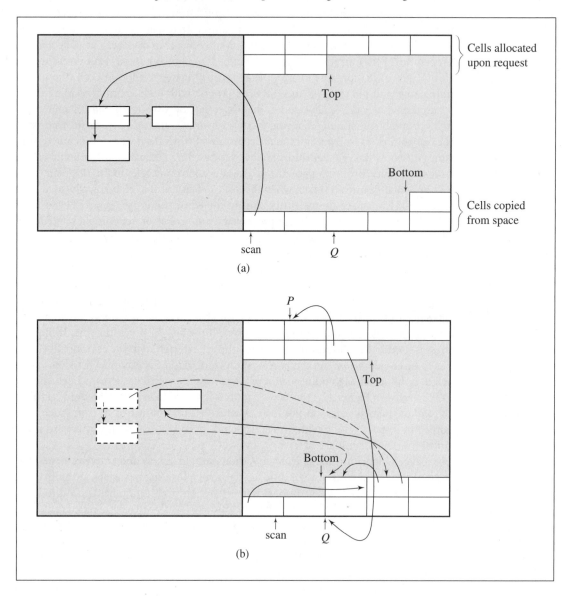

An interesting modification to Baker's algorithm is a technique based on the observation that most allocated cells are needed for a very short time; only some of them are used for longer timespans. This leads to a *generational garbage collection* technique which divides all allocated cells into at least two generations and focuses its attention on the youngest generation which generates most of the garbage. Such cells do not

FIGURE **12.11**   Changes performed by the Baker algorithm when addresses *P* and *Q* refer to cells in from-space, *P* to an already copied cell, *Q* to a cell still in fromspace.

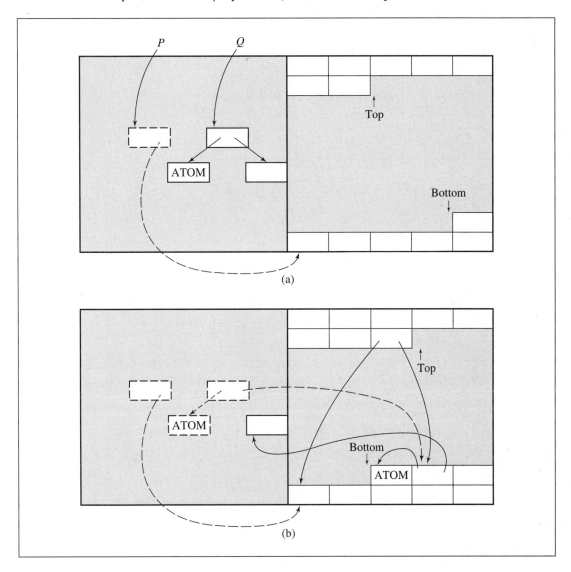

need to be copied, saving the garbage collector some work. Moreover, the constant checking and copying of long-lived cells is unnecessarily wasteful, so testing garbage production among such cells is performed only infrequently.

In a classic version of a generational garbage collector, the address space is divided into several regions, $r_1 \ldots, r_n$, not just into tospace and fromspace; each of these regions holds cells of the same generation (Lieberman and Hewitt 1983). Most references

FIGURE **12.12**　A situation in three regions (a) before and (b) after copying reachable cells from region r_i to region r'_i in the Lieberman-Hewitt technique of generational garbage collection.

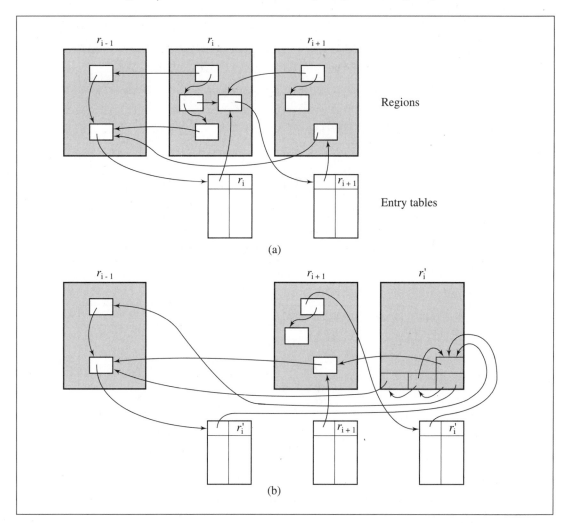

point to cells of an older generation. Some of them, however, can point forward in time (e.g., when LISP's *rplaca* is used). In this method, such forward references are made indirectly through an *entry table* associated with each region. A reference from a region r_i does not point to a cell c in a region r_{i+j} but to a cell c' in the entry table associated with r_{i+j}; c' contains a reference to c. If a region r_i becomes full, all reachable cells are copied to another region r'_i, and all regions with generations younger than r_i are visited to update references referring to cells which just have been transferred to the new region. Regions with generations older than r_i do not have to be visited. Presumably only a few references in the entry table of r_i are updated (see Figure 12.12).

The problem of cleaning the entry tables can be solved by storing in each table, along with each reference, a unique identifier for a region to which the reference refers. The identifier is updated along with the reference. Some references may be abandoned, as the reference in the entry table for region r_{i+1} in Figure 12.12b, and they are ready to be cleaned up after the region itself is abandoned.

Noncopying Methods

In incremental methods based on copying, the problem is not so much with the content of the original cells and its copy, but with their positions or addresses in memory, which by necessity have to be different. The mutator must not treat these addresses on a par; otherwise, the program crashes. Therefore, some mechanisms are needed to maintain the integrity of addressing, and the read barrier serves this purpose. But we may need to avoid copying altogether; after all, the first garbage collection method, mark-and-sweep, did not use copies. However, because of the exhaustive and uninterrupted passes, the mark-and-sweep method was too costly, and in real-time systems, it is simply unacceptable. Yet, the simplicity of this method is very appealing, and an attempt was made by Taiichi Yuasa to adapt it to real-time constraints, with satisfactory results.

Yuasa's algorithm also has two phases; one for marking reachable (used) cells and one for sweeping the heap by including in *avail-list* all unused (unmarked) cells. The marking phase is similar to that used in the mark-and-sweep method except that it is incremental; each time the marking procedure is invoked, it marks only k_1 cells for some small constant k_1. After k_1 cells have been marked, the mutator resumes execution. The constant k_2 is used during the sweeping phase to decide how many cells have to be processed before execution is turned over to the mutator. The garbage collector remembers whether it is in the middle of marking or sweeping. The procedure for marking or sweeping is always invoked after one cell is requested from the heap by a procedure which creates one new root pointer and initializes its *head* and *tail* fields, as in the following pseudocode:

```
createRootPtr(p,q,r)  // Lisp's cons
    if  collector is in the marking phase
        mark up to k₁ cells;
    else if  collector is in the sweeping phase
        sweep up to k₂ cells;
    else if  the number of cells on availList is low
        push all root pointers onto collector's stack st;
    p = first cell on availList;
    head(p) = q;
    tail(p) = r;
    mark p  if it is in the unswept portion of heap;
```

Remember that the mutator can scramble some graphs accessible from root pointers, which is particularly important if it happens during the marking phase, since it may cause certain cells to remain unmarked even though they are accessible. Figure 12.13 contains an example. After all of the roots have been pushed onto stack st (Figure 12.13a), and roots r_3 and r_2 have been processed and root r_1 is being

FIGURE **12.13**   An inconsistency that results if, in Yuasa's noncopying incremental garbage collector, a stack is not used to record cells possibly unprocessed during the marking phase.

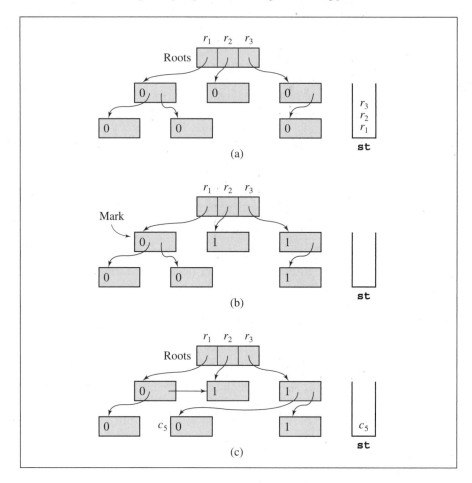

processed (Figure 12.13b), the mutator executes two assignments: $head(r_3)$ is changed to $tail(r_1)$, and $tail(r_1)$ is assigned r_2 (Figure 12.13c). If the marking process is now restarted, it has no chance to mark $head(r_3) = c_5$, since the entire graph r_3 is assumed to have been processed. This leads to including the cell $head(r_3)$ in the *avail-list* during the sweeping phase. To prevent that, the method which updates either *head* or *tail* of any cell pushes the old value of the field being updated onto the stack used by the garbage collector. For example,

```
updateTail(p,q)  // Lisp's rplacd
    if collector is in the marking phase
        mark tail(p);
        st.push(tail(p));
    tail(p) = q;
```

FIGURE **12.14**   Memory changes during the sweeping phase using Yuasa's method.

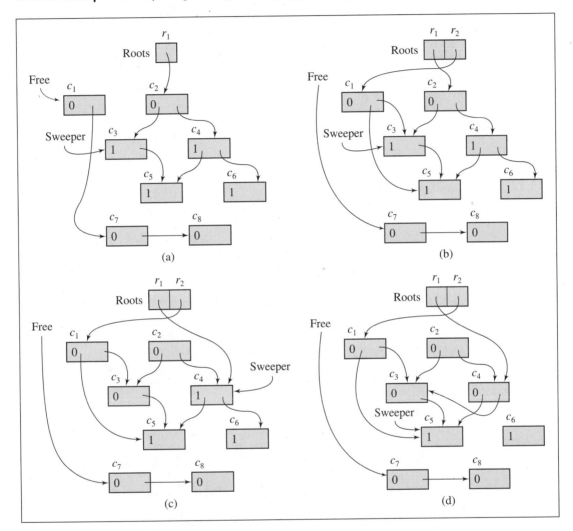

In the marking phase, the stack st is popped up k_1 times, and for each reference p popped off, its *head* and *tail* are marked.

The sweeping phase incrementally goes through the heap, includes in *avail-list* all unmarked cells, and unmarks all marked cells. For the sake of consistency, if a new cell is allocated, it remains unmarked if a certain part of the heap has been already swept. Otherwise, the next round of marking could lead to distorted results. Figure 12.14 illustrates an example. The reference *sweeper* has already reached cell c_3, and now the mutator requests a new cell by executing `createRootPtr`(r_2, c_5, c_3), whereby the first cell is detached from *avail-list* and made a new root (Figure 12.14b). But the newly allocated cell is not marked because it precedes *sweeper* in the heap.

If some cell is released in the swept area, it becomes garbage, but it is not swept up until sweeping restarts from the beginning of memory. For example, after assigning $tail(r_1)$ to r_1, cell c_2 becomes unreachable, and yet it is not reclaimed now by adding it to *avail-list* (Figure 12.14c). The same thing happens to cells having higher addresses than the current value of *sweeper*, as is the case with cell c_6 after assigning $tail(r_2)$ to $tail(r_1)$ (Figure 12.14d). This is called *floating garbage;* floating garbage is collected in the next cycle.

⌐ 12.4 Concluding Remarks

When assessing the efficiency of memory management algorithms, and especially garbage collectors, we have to be careful to avoid Paul Wilson's castigation that standard textbooks overstress the asymptotic complexity of algorithms missing the key point: "the constant factors associated with various costs" (Wilson 1992). This is especially apparent in the case of nonincremental algorithms whose cost is usually proportional either to the size n of the heap (mark-and-sweep) or to the number m of reachable cells (stop-and-copy). This is an immediate indication of the superiority of the latter techniques, especially when the number of surviving cells is small compared to the heap size. However, when we take into consideration that the cost of sweeping is minuscule compared to the cost of copying, the difference in efficiency is not so obvious. In fact, as has been shown, real-time performances of the mark-and-sweep and stop-and-copy techniques are very similar (Zorn 1990).

This example indicates that there are two main sources affecting the efficiency of algorithms: the behavior of the program and the characteristics of the underlying hardware. If a program allocates memory for a long time, then m approaches n; scanning only reachable cells is close to scanning the entire heap (or its region). This is especially important for generational garbage collectors, whose efficiency relies on the assumption that most allocated cells are used for a very brief interval. On the other hand, if sweeping a cell is not much faster than copying it, then copying techniques have an edge.

Asymptotic complexity is too imprecise, and the published research on memory management indicates little preoccupation with computing this characteristic of algorithms. "The constant factors associated with various costs" are much more relevant. Also, fine-grained measures of efficiency are proposed but not all of them are easy to measure, such as the amount of work per memory cell reclaimed, rate of object creation, average lifetime of objects, or the density of accessible objects (Lieberman and Hewitt 1983).

Memory management algorithms are usually closely tied to the hardware which may determine which algorithm is chosen. For example, garbage collection can be substantially sped up if some dedicated hardware is used. In LISP machines, the read barrier is implemented in hardware and microcode, which points to those incremental garbage collectors that rely on this barrier. Without hardware support, processing time in such collectors takes approximately 50% of program run time. If this hardware support is lacking, noncopying algorithms are a better choice. In real-time systems, where the responsiveness of the computer is the issue, additional overhead of the garbage collector is added. It may be less noticeable than in the case of nonincremental collectors, since at no time does a program have to wait in a visible way for the collector to finish its task. However, the tuning of incremental methods should be proportional to real-time constraints.

♙ 12.5 CASE STUDY: AN IN-PLACE GARBAGE COLLECTOR

Copying algorithms for garbage collectors are efficient in that they do not require processing unused cells. Cells that are not processed are considered garbage at the end of collection. However, these algorithms are inefficient in copying reachable cells from one semispace to another. An in-place garbage collector attempts to retain the advantages of copying algorithms without producing copies of the reachable cells (Baker 1992).

The in-place algorithm constantly maintains two doubly linked lists: `freeCells` and `nonFreeCells`. The list `freeCells` initially contains all cells of `heap[]`, and a cell is moved from `freeCells` to the other list if a request comes to construct a list or construct a new atom. After `freeCells` becomes empty, the method `collect()` is invoked. This method first transfers all root pointers from `nonFreeCells` to an intermediate list `markDescendants` and sets their `marked` field to true. Then, `collect()` detaches from `markDescendants` cell by cell to transfer each cell to another temporary list, `markedCells`. For each nonatom cell, `collect()` attaches to `markDescendants` unmarked `head` and `tail` references to be processed later. In the case study, they are attached to the beginning of `markDescendants`, thereby leading to depth-first traversal of list structures. For breadth-first traversal (as in Cheney's algorithm), they have to be attached to the end of `markDescendants`, which requires another reference to the end of the list. Note that, although a cell is transferred to `markedCells`, it is also marked to prevent infinite loops in case of cyclic structures and redundant processing in case of interconnected noncycling structures.

After the list `markDescendants` becomes empty, all reachable cells of `heap[]` have been processed and `collect()` is almost done. Before returning from `collect()`, all cells left in `nonFreeCells` become members of `freeCells`, and all marked cells are put on `nonFreeCells` after setting their `marked` fields to false. The user `program()` can now resume.

To be sure, the garbage collector is part of the program's environment and is executed in the background almost unbeknown to the user. To exemplify the workings of a garbage collector, some elements of the program background are simulated in the case study, in particular the heap and the symbol table.

The heap is implemented as an array of objects with two flag fields, atom/nonatom and marked/nonmarked, and two reference fields which are really integer fields indicating positions in `heap[]` of the previous and next cells (if any). In accordance with this implementation, both permanent lists, `freeCells` and `nonFreeCells`, and both temporary lists, `markDescendants` and `markedCells`, are simply integers indicating the index in heap[ ] of the first cell on a given list (if any).

The symbol table is implemented as an integer array roots[ ] of root pointers. No explicit variable names are used, only indexes to heap[ ] cells. For example, if roots is [3 2 4 0], then only four variables are currently in use by program( ), roots[0] through roots[3], and these variables are pointing to cells 3, 2, 4, and 0 in heap[ ]. The numbers 0–3 can be seen as subscripts to more palpable variable names, such as var_0, var_1, var_2 and var_3.

The user program( ) is just a coarse simulator which does nothing but require allocations and reallocations on heap[ ]. These requirements are generated randomly and classified by the type of requirement: 20% are atom (re)allocations, 20% are list (re)allocations, 20% are head updates, 20% are tail updates, and the remaining 20% are deallocations. Deallocations are simulated by the method deallocate( ), which decides whether an existing root variable should be assigned empty (which represents the null reference) or a local block is exited upon which all local variables are removed, which in turn means that memory assigned to them is free. The percentages can be assigned differently, and the distribution of assignments can be tuned to the number of assignments already made. This is just a matter of introducing changes in program( ). Also, the size of heap[ ] and the size of roots[ ] can be modified.

The user program( ) randomly generates a number rn between 0 and 99 to indicate the operation to be performed. Then, variables are randomly chosen from roots[ ]. For example, if rn is 11, roots[ ] is [3 2 4 0], and p is 2, then the cell roots[p] = 4 of heap[ ] indicated by variable 2 becomes an atom by storing the value of val in its value field and the atom field is set to true. If p is 4, this indicates that a new variable (variable 4, or var_4) has to be created in position 4 of roots[ ], and position roots[4] is assigned the first value from freeCells.

To see that this program does something, a simple printList( ) method is supplied, which prints elements on a given list, and a printHeap( ) method outputs the contents of heap[ ] and of roots[ ]. Here is an example of an output generated by printHeap( ) and by printList( ) called twice from printHeap( ) for a heap of six cells:

```
roots: 1 5 3
(0: -1 2 false false 0 0) (1: 5 4 false false 1 4)
(2: 0 -1 false false 2 2) (3: 4 -1 true false 130)
(4: 1 3 true false 129) (5: -1 1 false false 5 1)
freeCells: (0 0 0)(2 2 2)
nonFreeCells: (5 5 1)(1 1 4)(4 129)(3 130)
```

This output represents the situation illustrated in Figure 12.15. Figure 12.15a shows the contents of heap with links prev and next used by lists freeCells and nonFreeCells and info field. For nonatom cells, this field references an object with two fields, head and tail, for atom cells, info field references an object that stores some value. Because of the number of crisscrossing links, the same situation is presented in Figure 12.15b, where the cells are organized by their connections rather than the positions in heap.

Figure 12.16 contains the listing of the program.

FIGURE **12.15** An example of a situation on the heap.

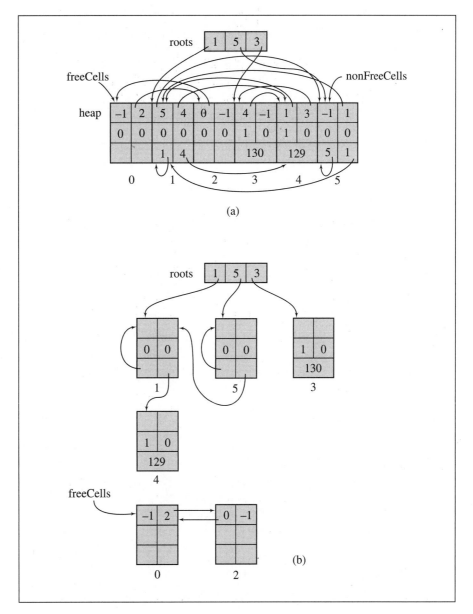

FIGURE **12.16**   Implementation of an in-place garbage collector.

```java
//*************************  Heap.java  *************************
import java.util.Random;

class Value {
    int value;
    Value(int v) {
        value = v;
    }
}

class Links {
    int head = -1, tail = -1;
    Links(int h, int t) {
        head = h; tail = t;
    }
}

class Cell {
    boolean atom;
    boolean marked = false;
    int prev = -1, next = -1;
    Object info = null; // either Value or Links;
}

class Heap {
    final int maxHeap = 6, maxRoot = 50, empty   = -1;
    int rootCnt = 0;
    boolean OK = true;
    Cell[] heap = new Cell[maxHeap];
    int[] roots = new int[maxRoot];
    int freeCells = empty, nonFreeCells = empty;
    Random rd = new Random(10);
    Heap() {
        for (int i = maxHeap-1; i >= 0; i--) {
            heap[i] = new Cell();
            freeCells = insert(i,freeCells);
        }
        for (int i = maxRoot-1; i >= 0; i--)
            roots[i] = empty;
    }
    void updateHead(int p, int q) {        // Lisp's rplaca;
```

F I G U R E   **12.16**   *(Continued)*

```
        if (roots[p] != empty && !heap[roots[p]].atom)
            ((Links)heap[roots[p]].info).head = roots[q];
    }
    void updateTail(int p, int q) {        // Lisp's rplacd;
        if (roots[p] != empty && !heap[roots[p]].atom)
            ((Links)heap[roots[p]].info).tail = roots[q];
    }
    int detach(int cell, int list) {
        if (heap[cell].next != empty)
            heap[heap[cell].next].prev = heap[cell].prev;
        if (heap[cell].prev != empty)
            heap[heap[cell].prev].next = heap[cell].next;
        if (cell == list)                  // head of the list;
            return heap[cell].next;
        else return list;
    }
    int insert(int cell, int list) {
        heap[cell].prev = empty;
        if (cell == list)   // don't create a circular list;
            heap[cell].next = empty;
        else heap[cell].next = list;
        if (list != empty)
            heap[list].prev = cell;
        return cell;
    }
    void collect() {
        int p, markDescendants = empty, markedCells  = empty;
        for (p = 0; p < rootCnt; p++) {
            if (roots[p] != empty) {
                nonFreeCells    = detach(roots[p],nonFreeCells);
                markDescendants = insert(roots[p],markDescendants);
                heap[roots[p]].marked = true;
            }
        }
        printList(markDescendants,"markDescendants C1 "+p);
        for (p = markDescendants; p != empty; p = markDescendants) {
            markDescendants = detach(p,markDescendants);
            markedCells     = insert(p,markedCells);
            if (!heap[p].atom) {
                if (!heap[((Links)heap[p].info).head].marked) {
```

FIGURE **12.16** *(continued)*

```
                        nonFreeCells    = detach(((Links)heap[p].info).head,
                                    nonFreeCells);
                        markDescendants = insert(((Links)heap[p].info).head,
                                    markDescendants);
                        heap[((Links)heap[p].info).head].marked = true;
                    }
                    if (!heap[((Links)heap[p].info).tail].marked) {
                        nonFreeCells    = detach(((Links)heap[p].info).tail,
                                    nonFreeCells);
                        markDescendants = insert(((Links)heap[p].info).tail,
                                    markDescendants);
                        heap[((Links)heap[p].info).tail].marked = true;
                    }
                }
            }
        }
        printList(markedCells,"MarkedCells");
        for (p = markedCells; p != empty; p = heap[p].next)
            heap[p].marked = false;
        freeCells    = nonFreeCells;
        nonFreeCells = markedCells;
    }
    boolean allocateAux(int p) {
        if (p == maxRoot) {
            System.out.println("No room for new roots");
            return !OK;
        }
        if (freeCells == empty)
            collect();
        if (freeCells == empty) {
            System.out.println("No room in heap for new cells");
            return !OK;
        }
        if (p == rootCnt)
            rootCnt++;
        roots[p] = freeCells;
        freeCells    = detach(roots[p],freeCells);
        nonFreeCells = insert(roots[p],nonFreeCells);
        return OK;
    }
    void allocateAtom (int p, int val) {        // an instance of Lisp's setf;
```

FIGURE **12.16**   *(continued)*

```java
        if (allocateAux(p) == OK) {
            heap[roots[p]].atom = true;
            heap[roots[p]].info = new Value(val);
        }
    }
    void allocateNonAtom(int p, int q, int r) { // Lisp's cons;
        if (allocateAux(p) == OK) {
            heap[roots[p]].atom = false;
            heap[roots[p]].info = new Links(roots[q],roots[r]);
        }
    }
    void deallocate(int p) {
        if (rootCnt > 0)
            if (Math.abs(rd.nextInt()) % 2 == 0)
                roots[p] = roots[--rootCnt]; // remove variable when exiting a
                                             // block;
            else roots[p] = empty; // set variable to null;
    }
    void printList(int list, String name) {
        System.out.print(name + ": ");
        int i;
        for (i = list; i != empty; i = heap[i].next) {
            System.out.print("(" + i + " ");
            if (heap[i].atom)
                System.out.print(((Value)heap[i].info).value);
            else if (heap[i].info != null)
                System.out.print(((Links)heap[i].info).head + " " +
                                 ((Links)heap[i].info).tail);
            System.out.print(") ");
        }
        System.out.println();
    }
    void printHeap() {
        System.out.print("roots: ");
        for (int i = 0; i < rootCnt; i++)
            System.out.print(roots[i] + " ");
        System.out.println();
        for (int i = 0; i < maxHeap; i++) {
            System.out.print("(" + i + ": " + heap[i].prev + " "
                 + heap[i].next + " "+ heap[i].atom + " " + heap[i].marked + " ");
```

Continues

FIGURE **12.16** *(continued)*

```java
            if (heap[i].atom)
                System.out.print(((Value)heap[i].info).value);
            else if (heap[i].info != null)
                System.out.print(((Links)heap[i].info).head + " " +
                                  ((Links)heap[i].info).tail);
            System.out.print(") ");
        }
        System.out.println();
        printList(freeCells,"FreeCells");
        printList(nonFreeCells,"NonFreeCells");
    }
}


//************************* Collector.java ***********************

import java.util.Random;

class Collector {
    static Heap heap = new Heap();
    static Random rd = new Random(10);
    static int val = 123;
    static void program() {
        int rn, p, q = 1, r = 1;
        if (heap.rootCnt == 0) { // call heap.allocateAtom(0,val++);
            p = 0;
            rn = 1;
        }
        else {
            rn = Math.abs(rd.nextInt()) % 100 + 1;
            p  = Math.abs(rd.nextInt()) % (heap.rootCnt+1); // possibly
            q  = Math.abs(rd.nextInt()) % heap.rootCnt;     // new root;
            r  = Math.abs(rd.nextInt()) % heap.rootCnt;
        }
        if (rn <= 20)
            heap.allocateAtom(p,val++);
        else if (rn <= 40)
            heap.allocateNonAtom(p,q,r);
        else if (rn <= 60)
            heap.updateHead(q,r);
        else if (rn <= 80)
            heap.updateTail(q,r);
        else heap.deallocate(p);
```

FIGURE **12.16**   *(continued)*

```
        heap.printHeap();
    }
    static public void main(String a[]) {
        for (int i = 0; i < 50; i++)
            program();
    }
}
```

🔲 12.6 EXERCISES

1. What happens to the first-fit method if it is applied to a list ordered by block sizes?

2. How does the effort leading to coalescing blocks in sequential-fit methods depend on the order of blocks on the list? How can possible problems caused by these orders be solved?

3. The *optimal-fit* method determines which block to allocate after examining a sample of blocks to find the closest match to the request and then finds the first block exceeding this match (Campbell 1971). What does the efficiency of this method depend on? How does this algorithm compare to the efficiency of other sequential-fit methods?

4. In what circumstances can the size-list in the adaptive exact-fit method be empty (except at the beginning)? What is its maximal size and when can it be this size?

5. Why in the buddy system are doubly linked, not singly linked, lists of blocks used?

6. Give an algorithm for returning blocks to the memory pool using the Fibonacci buddy system.

7. Apply `markingWithStack()` to the left degenerate and right degenerate list structures in Figure 12.17. How many calls to `pop()` and `push()` are executed for each case? Are all of them necessary? How would you optimize the code to avoid unnecessary operations?

8. In a *reference count method* of garbage collection, each cell *c* has a counter field whose value indicates how many other cells refer (point) to it. The counter is incremented every time another cell refers to *c* and decremented if a reference is deleted. The garbage collector uses this counter when sweeping the heap: If a cell's count is zero, the cell can be reclaimed since it is not pointed to by any other cell. Discuss the advantages and disadvantages of this garbage collection method.

FIGURE **12.17**   (a) Left degenerate and (b) right degenerate list structures.

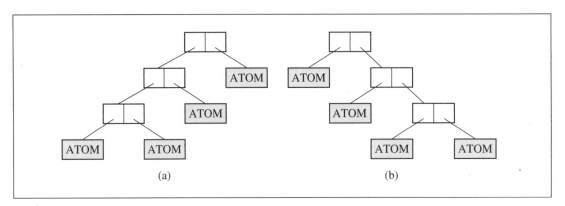

9. In Baker's algorithm, the scanning performed by the collector should be finished before *bottom* reaches *top* in tospace to flip spaces. What should the value of *k* be to ensure this? Assume that *n* is the maximum number of cells required by a program, and 2*m* is the number of cells in fromspace and in tospace. What is the impact of doubling the value of *k* when it is an integer and when it is a fraction (for example, if it is .5, then one copy is made per two requests)?

10. In a modification of Baker's algorithm which requires updating heap pages in the case when the mutator's access is trapped (Ellis, Li, and Appel 1988), there is a problem with objects that may cross the page boundary. Suggest a solution to this problem.

♠ 12.7 PROGRAMMING ASSIGNMENTS

1. Implement the following memory allocation method developed by W. A. Wulf, C. B. Weinstock, and C. B. Johnsson (Standish 1980) called the *quick-fit* method. For an experimentally found number *n* of the most frequently requested sizes of blocks, this method uses an array *avail* of *n* + 1 cells, each cell *i* pointing to a linked list of blocks of size *i*. The last cell (*n* + 1) refers to a block of other less frequently needed sizes. It may also be a reference to a linked list, but because of possibly a large number of such blocks, another organization is recommended, such as a binary search tree. Write methods to allocate and deallocate blocks. If a block is returned, coalesce it with its neighbors. To test your program, randomly generate sizes of blocks to be allocated from memory simulated by an array whose size is a power of 2.

2. In the dual buddy system, two parts of memory are managed by the binary buddy method. But the number of such areas can be larger (Page and Hagins 1986). Write a program to operate on three such areas with block sizes of the form 2^i, $3 \cdot 2^j$, and $5 \cdot 2^k$. For a requested block size *s*, round *s* to the nearest block size which can be generated by

FIGURE **12.18** A heap with two regions for Appel's generational garbage collection.

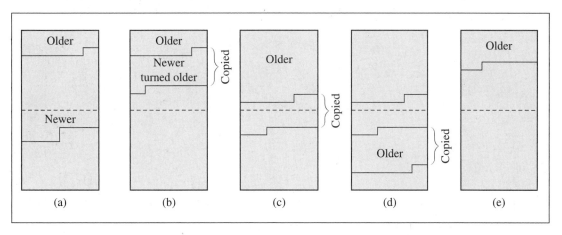

this method. For example, size 11 is rounded up to 12, which is the number from the second area. If this request cannot be accommodated in this area, 12 is rounded up to the next possibly available number, which is 15, a number from the third area. If there is no available block of this or greater size in this area either, the first area is tried. In case of failure, keep requests on a list and process them as soon as a block of sufficient size is coalesced. Run your program changing three parameters: the intervals for which blocks are reserved, the number of incoming requests, and the overall size of memory.

3. Implement a simple version of a generational garbage collector which uses only two regions (Appel 1989). The heap is divided into two even parts. The upper part holds cells which have been copied from the lower part as cells reachable from the root pointers. The lower part is used for memory allocation and holds only newer cells (see Figure 12.18a). After this part becomes full, the garbage collector cleans it by copying all reachable cells to the upper part (Figure 12.18b), after which allocations are made starting from the beginning of the lower part. After several turns, the upper part becomes full too, and the cells being copied from the lower part are in reality copied to the lower part (Figure 12.18c). In this case, the cleanup process of the upper part is begun by copying all reachable cells from the upper part to the lower part (Figure 12.18d), and then all reachable cells are copied to the beginning of the upper part (Figure 12.18e).

4. The case study presents an in-place nonincremental garbage collector. Modify and extend it to become an incremental collector. In this case, `program()` becomes `mutator()`, which allows the method `collect()` to process k cells for some value of k. To prevent `mutator()` from introducing inconsistencies in structures possibly not completely processed by `collect()`, `mutator()` should transfer any unmarked cells from `freeCells` to `markDescendants`.

Another very elegant modification is obtained by grouping all four lists in a circular list, creating what Henry Baker (1992) called a *treadmill* (Figure 12.19a). Reference

FIGURE **12.19**   Baker's treadmill.

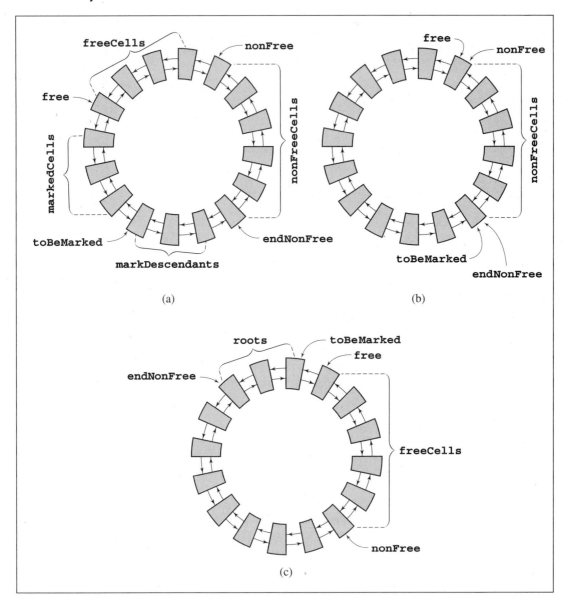

free is moved in a clockwise direction if a new cell is requested; reference toBe-
Marked is moved k times when allowed by the mutator. For each nonatom cell currently scanned by toBeMarked, its *head* and *tail* are transferred in front of
toBeMarked if they are not marked. After toBeMarked meets endNonFree, there
are no cells to be marked, and after free meets nonFree, there are no free cells on the

list of free cells (Figure 12.19b). In this case, what remains between `nonFree` and `endNonFree` (former `nonFreeCells`) is garbage, and hence, it can be utilized by the mutator. Therefore, the roles of `nonFree` and `endNonFree` are exchanged; it is as though `nonFreeCells` became `freeCells` (Figure 12.19c). All root pointers are transferred to a part of the treadmill between `toBeMarked` and `endFree` (to create a seed of the former `markDescendants`, and the mutator can resume execution.

Bibliography

Memory Management

Smith, Harry F., *Data Structures: Form and Function,* San Diego, CA: Harcourt-Brace-Jovanovich, 1987, Ch. 11.

Standish, Thomas A., *Data Structure Techniques,* Reading, MA: Addison-Wesley, 1980, Chs. 5 and 6.

Sequential-Fit Methods

Campbell, J.A., "A Note on an Optimal-Fit Method for Dynamic Allocation of Storage," *Computer Journal* 14 (1971), 7–9.

Nonsequential-Fit Methods

Oldehoeft, Rodney R. and Allan, Stephen J., "Adaptive Exact-Fit Storage Management," *Communications of the ACM* 28 (1985), 506–511.

Ross, Douglas T., "The AED Free Storage Package," *Communications of the ACM* 10 (1967), 481–492.

Buddy Systems

Bromley, Allan G., "Memory Fragmentation in Buddy Methods for Dynamic Storage Allocation," *Acta Informatica* 14 (1980), 107–117.

Cranston, Ben and Thomas, Rick, "A Simplified Recombination Scheme for the Fibonacci Buddy System," *Communications of the ACM* 18 (1975), 331–332.

Hinds, James A., "An Algorithm for Locating Adjacent Storage Blocks in the Buddy System," *Communications of the ACM* 18 (1975), 221–222.

Hirschberg, Daniel S., "A Class of Dynamic Memory Allocation Algorithms," *Communications of the ACM* 16 (1973), 615–618.

Knowlton, Kenneth C., "A Fast Storage Allocator," *Communications of the ACM* 8 (1965), 623–625.

Page, Ivor P. and Hagins, Jeff, "Improving Performance of Buddy Systems," *IEEE Transactions on Computers* C-35 (1986), 441–447.

Shen, Kenneth K. and Peterson, James L., "A Weighted Buddy Method for Dynamic Storage Allocation," *Communications of the ACM* 17 (1974), 558–562.

Garbage Collection

Appel, Andrew W., "Garbage Collection Can Be Faster Than Stack Allocation," *Information Processing Letters* 25 (1987), 275–279.

Appel, Andrew W., "Simple Generational Garbage Collection and Fast Allocation," *Software—Practice and Experience* 19 (1989), 171–183.

Baker, Henry G., "List Processing in Real Time on a Serial Computer," *Communications of the ACM* 21 (1978), 280–294.

Baker, Henry G., "The Treadmill: Real-Time Garbage Collection Without Motion Sickness," *ACM SIGPLAN Notices* 27 (1992), No. 3, 66–70.

Brooks, Rodney A., "Trading Data Space for Reduced Time and Code Space in Real-Time Collection on Stock Hardware," *Conference Record of the 1984 ACM Symposium on Lisp and Functional Programming,* Austin, TX, 1984, 108–113.

Cheney, C. J., "A Nonrecursive List Compacting Algorithm," *Communications of the ACM* 13 (1970), 677–678.

Cohen, Jacques, "Garbage Collection of Linked Data Structures," *Computing Surveys* 13 (1981), 341–367.

Ellis, John R., Li, Kai, and Appel, Andrew W., "Real-Time Concurrent Collection on Stock Multiprocessors," *SIGPLAN Notices* 23 (1988), No. 7, 11–20.

Fenichel, Robert R. and Yochelson, Jerome C., "A Lisp Garbage-Collector for Virtual-Memory Computer Systems," *Communications of the ACM* 12 (1969), 611–612.

Jones, Richard and Lins, Rafael, *Garbage Collection: Algorithms for Automatic Dynamic Memory Management,* Chichester: Wiley, 1996.

Kurokawa, Toshiaki, "A New Fast and Safe Marking Algorithm," *Software—Practice and Experience* 11 (1981), 671–682.

Layer, D. Kevin and Richardson, Chris, "Lisp Systems in the 1990s," *Communications of the ACM* 34 (1991), No. 9, 49–57.

Lieberman, Henry and Hewitt, Carl, "A Real-Time Garbage Collector Based on the Lifetimes of Objects," *Communications of the ACM* 26 (1983), 419–429.

Schorr, H. and Waite, W. M., "An Efficient Machine-Independent Procedure for Garbage Collection in Various List Structures," *Communications of the ACM* 10 (1967), 501–506.

Wadler, Philip L., "Analysis of Algorithm for Real-Time Garbage Collection," *Communications of the ACM* 19 (1976), 491–500, 20 (1977), 120.

Wegbreit, Ben, "A Space-Efficient List Structure Tracing Algorithm," *IEEE Transactions on Computers* C-21 (1972), 1009–1010.

Wilson, Paul R., "Uniprocessor Garbage Collection Techniques," in Bekkers, Yves and Cohen, Jacques (eds.), *Memory Management,* Berlin: Springer, 1992, 1–42.

Yuasa, Taiichi, "Real-Time Garbage Collection on General-Purpose Machine," *Journal of Systems and Software* 11 (1990), 181–198.

Zorn, Benjamin, "Comparing Mark-and-Sweep and Stop-and-Copy Garbage Collection," *Proceedings of the 1990 ACM Conference on Lisp and Functional Programming,* Nice, 1990, 87–98

Computing Big-O

A.1 HARMONIC SERIES

In some computations in this book, the convention H_n is used for harmonic numbers. The *harmonic numbers* H_n are defined as the sums of the *harmonic series*, a series of the form $\sum_{i=1}^{n} \frac{1}{i}$. This is a very important series for the analysis of searching and sorting algorithms. It is proved that

$$H_n = \ln n + \gamma + \frac{1}{2n} - \frac{1}{12n^2} + \frac{1}{120n^4} - \epsilon$$

where $n \geq 1$, $0 < \epsilon < \frac{1}{256n^6}$, and *Euler's constant* $\gamma \approx 0.5772$. This approximation, however, is very unwieldy and, in the context of our analyses, not necessary in this form. H_n's largest term is almost always $\ln n$, the only increasing term in H_n. Thus, H_n can be referred to as $O(\ln n)$.

A.2 APPROXIMATION OF THE FUNCTION LG($N!$)

The roughest approximation of $\lg(n!)$ can be obtained by observing that each number in the product $n! = 1 \cdot 2 \cdot \cdots \cdot (n-1) \cdot n$ is less than or equal to n. Thus, $n! \leq n^n$ (only for $n = 1$, $n = n^n$), which implies that $\lg(n!) < \lg(n^n) = n \lg n$—that is, $n \lg n$ is an upper bound of $\lg(n!)$—and that $\lg(n!)$ is $O(n \lg n)$.

Let us also find a lower bound for $\lg(n!)$. If the elements of the product $n!$ are grouped appropriately, as in

$$P_{n!} = (1 \cdot n)(2 \cdot (n-1))(3 \cdot (n-2)) \cdots (i \cdot (n-i+1)) \ldots, \text{for } 1 \leq i \leq \frac{n}{2}$$

then it can be noted that there are $\frac{n}{2}$ such terms and $n! = P_{n!}$ for even ns or $\frac{n+1}{2}$ terms and $n! = P_{n!}\frac{n+1}{2}$ for odd ns. We claim that each term of $P_{n!}$ is not less than n, or

$$1 \le i \le \frac{n}{2} \Rightarrow i(n - i + 1) \ge n$$

In fact, this holds because

$$\frac{n}{2} \ge i = \frac{i(i-1)}{i-1} \Rightarrow i(n - 2i + 2) \ge n$$

and, as can easily be checked,

$$i \ge 1 \Rightarrow (n - 2i + 2) \le (n - i + 1)$$

We have shown that $n! = P_{n!} \ge n^{\frac{n}{2}}$, which means that $\lg(n!) \ge \frac{n}{2} \lg n$. This assumes that n is even. If n is odd, it has to be raised to the power of $\frac{n+1}{2}$, which introduces no substantial change.

The number $\lg(n!)$ has been estimated using the lower and upper bounds of this function, and the result is $\frac{n}{2} \lg n \le \lg(n!) \le n \lg n$. To approximate $\lg(n!)$, lower and upper bounds have been used that both grow at the rate of $n \lg n$. This implies that $\lg(n!)$ grows at the same rate as $n \lg n$ or that $\lg(n!)$ is not only $O(n \lg n)$ but also $\Theta(n \lg n)$. In other words, any sorting algorithm using comparisons on an array of size n must make at least $O(n \lg n)$ comparisons in the worst case. Thus, the function $n \lg n$ approximates the optimal number of comparisons in the worst case.

However, this result seems unsatisfactory because it refers only to the worst case, and such a case occurs only occasionally. Most of the time, average cases with random orderings of data occur. Is the number of comparisons really better in such cases and is it a reasonable assumption that the number of comparisons in the average case can be better than $O(n \lg n)$? Unfortunately, this conjecture has to be rejected, and the following computations prove it false.

Our conjecture is that, in any binary tree with m leaves and two children for each nonterminal node, the average number of arcs leading from the root to a leaf is greater than or equal to $\lg m$.

For $m = 2$, $\lg m = 1$, if there is just a root with two leaves, then there is only one arc to every one of them. Assume that the proposition holds for a certain $m \ge 2$ and that

$$\text{Ave}_m = \frac{p_1 + \cdots + p_m}{m} \ge \lg m$$

where each p_i is a path (the number of arcs) from the root to node i. Now consider a randomly chosen leaf with two children about to be attached. This leaf converted to a nonterminal node has an index m (this index is chosen to simplify the notation) and a path from the root to the node m is p_m. After adding two new leaves, the total number of leaves is incremented by one and the path for both these appended leaves is $p_{m+1} = p_m + 1$. Is it now true that

$$\text{Ave}_{m+1} = \frac{p_1 + \cdots + p_{m-1} + 2p_m + 2}{m + 1} \ge \lg(m + 1)$$

From the definition of Ave_m and Ave_{m+1} and from the fact that $p_m = \text{Ave}_m$ (since leaf m was chosen randomly),

$$(m + 1)\text{Ave}_{m+1} = m\text{Ave}_m + p_m + 2 = (m + 1)\text{Ave}_m + 2$$

Is it now true that

$$(m + 1)\text{Ave}_{m+1} \geq (m + 1) \lg(m + 1)$$

or

$$(m + 1)\text{Ave}_{m+1} = (m + 1)\text{Ave}_m + 2 \geq (m + 1) \lg m + 2 \geq (m + 1) \lg(m + 1)$$

This is transformed into

$$2 \geq \lg\left(\frac{m + 1}{m}\right)^{m+1} = \lg\left(1 + \frac{1}{m}\right) + \lg\left(1 + \frac{1}{m}\right)^m \rightarrow \lg 1 + \lg e = \lg e \approx 1.44$$

which is true for any $m \geq 1$. This completes the proof of the conjecture.

This proves that for a randomly chosen leaf of an m-leaf decision tree, the reasonable expectation is that the path from the root to the leaf is not less than $\lg m$. The number of leaves in such a tree is not less than $n!$, which is the number of all possible orderings of an n-element array. If $m \geq n!$, then $\lg m \geq \lg(n!)$. That is the unfortunate result indicating that an average case also requires, like the worst case, $\lg(n!)$ comparisons (length of path = number of comparisons), and as already estimated, $\lg(n!)$ is $O(n \lg n)$. This is also the best that can be expected in average cases.

⊿ A.3 BIG-O FOR AVERAGE CASE OF QUICKSORT

Let $C(n)$ be the number of comparisons required to sort an array of n cells. Because the arrays of size 1 and 0 are not partitioned, $C(0) = C(1) = 0$. Assuming a random ordering of an n-element array, any element can be chosen as the bound; the probability that any element will become the bound is the same for all elements. With $C(i - 1)$ and $C(n - i)$ denoting the numbers of the comparisons required to sort the two subarrays, there are

$$C(n) = n - 1 + \frac{1}{n} \sum_{i=1}^{n} (C(i - 1) + C(n - i)), \text{ for } n \geq 2$$

comparisons, where $n - 1$ is the number of comparisons in the partition of the array of size n. First, some simplification can be done:

$$C(n) = n - 1 + \frac{1}{n}\left(\sum_{i=1}^{n} C(i - 1) + \sum_{i=1}^{n} C(n - i)\right)$$

$$= n - 1 + \frac{1}{n}\left(\sum_{i=1}^{n} C(i - 1) + \sum_{j=1}^{n} C(j - 1)\right)$$

$$= n - 1 + \frac{2}{n} \sum_{i=0}^{n-1} C(i)$$

or

$$nC(n) = n(n - 1) = 2 \sum_{i=0}^{n-1} C(i)$$

To solve the equation, the summation operator is removed first. To that end, the last equation is subtracted from an equation obtained from it,

$$(n+1)C(n+1) = (n+1)n + 2\sum_{i=0}^{n} C(i)$$

resulting in

$$(n+1)C(n+1) - nC(n) = (n+1)n - n(n-1) + 2\left(\sum_{i=0}^{n} C(i) - \sum_{i=0}^{n-1} C(i)\right) = 2C(n) + 2n$$

from which

$$\frac{C(n+1)}{n+2} = \frac{C(n)}{n+1} + \frac{2n}{(n+1)(n+2)} = \frac{C(n)}{n+1} + \frac{4}{n+2} - \frac{2}{n+1}$$

This equation can be expanded, which gives

$$\frac{C(2)}{3} = \frac{C(1)}{2} + \frac{4}{3} - \frac{2}{2} = \frac{4}{3} - \frac{2}{2}$$

$$\frac{C(3)}{4} = \frac{C(2)}{3} + \frac{4}{4} - \frac{2}{3}$$

$$\frac{C(4)}{5} = \frac{C(3)}{4} + \frac{4}{5} - \frac{2}{4}$$

$$\vdots$$

$$\frac{C(n)}{n+1} = \frac{C(n-1)}{n} + \frac{4}{n+1} - \frac{2}{n}$$

$$\frac{C(n+1)}{n+2} = \frac{C(n)}{n+1} + \frac{4}{n+2} - \frac{2}{n+1}$$

from which

$$\frac{C(n+1)}{n+2} = \left(\frac{4}{3} - \frac{2}{2}\right) + \left(\frac{4}{4} - \frac{2}{3}\right) + \left(\frac{4}{5} - \frac{2}{4}\right) + \cdots + \left(\frac{4}{n+1} - \frac{2}{n}\right)$$

$$+ \left(\frac{4}{n+2} - \frac{2}{n+1}\right)$$

$$= -\frac{2}{2} + \frac{2}{3} + \frac{2}{4} + \frac{2}{5} + \cdots + \frac{2}{n} + \frac{2}{n+1} + \frac{4}{n+2}$$

$$= -4 + 2H_{n+2} + \frac{2}{n+2}$$

Note that H_{n+2} is a harmonic number. Using an approximation for this number (cf. Section A.1)

$$C(n) = (n+1)\left(-4 + 2H_{n+1} + \frac{2}{n+1}\right)$$

$$= (n+1)\left(-4 + 2O(\ln n) + \frac{2}{n+1}\right)$$

$$= O(n \lg n)$$

◨ A.4 AVERAGE PATH LENGTH IN A RANDOM BINARY TREE

In Chapter 6, an approximation is used for the average path length in a randomly created binary search tree. Assuming that

$$P_n(i) = \frac{(i-1)(P_{i-1}+1) + (n-i)(P_{n-i}+1)}{n}$$

this approximation is given by this recurrence relation

$$P_1 = 0$$

$$P_n = \frac{1}{n}\sum_{i=1}^{n} P_n(i) = \frac{1}{n^2}\sum_{i=1}^{n}((i-1)(P_{i-1}+1) + (n-i)(P_{n-i}+1))$$

$$P_n = \frac{2}{n^2}\sum_{i=1}^{n-1} i(P_i + 1) \tag{1}$$

From this, we also have

$$P_{n-1} = \frac{2}{(n-1)^2}\sum_{i=1}^{n-2} i(P_i + 1) \tag{2}$$

After multiplying this equation by $\frac{(n-1)^2}{n^2}$ and subtracting the resulting equation from (1), we have

$$P_n = P_{n-1}\frac{(n-1)^2}{n^2} + \frac{2(n-1)(P_{n-1}+1)}{n^2} = \frac{(n-1)}{n^2}((n+1)P_{n-1}+2)$$

After successive applications of this formula to each P_{n-i}, we have

$$P_n = \frac{n-1}{n^2}\left((n+1)\frac{(n-2)}{(n-1)^2}\left(n\frac{(n-3)}{(n-2)^2}\left((n-1)\frac{(n-4)}{(n-3)^2}\left(\cdots\frac{1}{2^2}(3P_1+2)\cdots\right)+2\right)+2\right)+2\right)$$

$$P_n = 2\left(\frac{n-1}{n^2} + \frac{(n+1)(n-2)}{(n-1)n^2} + \frac{(n+1)(n-3)}{n(n-1)(n-2)} + \frac{(n+1)(n-4)}{n(n-2)(n-3)} + \cdots + \frac{n+1}{2\cdot 3n}\right)$$

$$P_n = 2\left(\frac{n+1}{n}\right)\sum_{i=1}^{n-1}\frac{n-i}{(n-i+1)(n-i+2)} = 2\left(\frac{n+1}{n}\right)\sum_{i=1}^{n-1}\left(\frac{2}{n-i+2} - \frac{1}{n-i+1}\right)$$

$$P_n = 2\left(\frac{n+1}{n}\right)\frac{2}{n+1} + 2\left(\frac{n+1}{n}\right)\left(\sum_{i=1}^{n}\frac{1}{i} - 2\right) = 2\left(\frac{n+1}{n}\right)H_n - 4$$

So, P_n is $O(2 \ln n)$.

Name Index

Subject Index